U.S. Department of Justice
Office of Justice Programs
National Institute of Justice

The FINGERPRINT SOURCEBOOK

U.S. Department of Justice
Office of Justice Programs
810 Seventh Street N.W.
Washington, DC 20531

Eric H. Holder, Jr.
Attorney General

Laurie O. Robinson
Assistant Attorney General

John H. Laub
Director, National Institute of Justice

This and other publications and products of the National Institute of Justice can be found at:

National Institute of Justice
www.nij.gov

Office of Justice Programs
Innovation • Partnerships • Safer Neighborhoods
www.ojp.usdoj.gov

CONTENTS

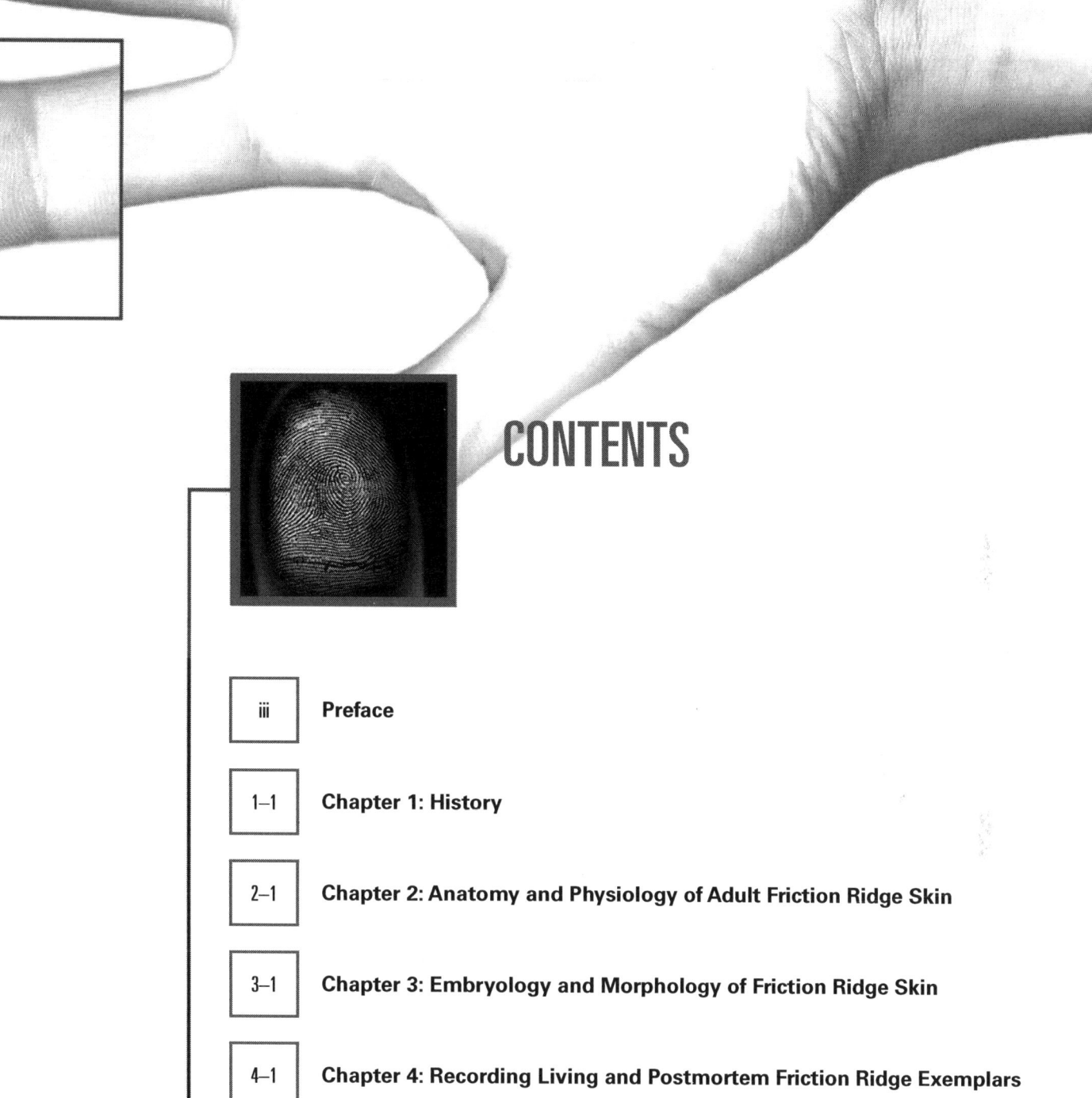

iii	**Preface**
1–1	**Chapter 1: History**
2–1	**Chapter 2: Anatomy and Physiology of Adult Friction Ridge Skin**
3–1	**Chapter 3: Embryology and Morphology of Friction Ridge Skin**
4–1	**Chapter 4: Recording Living and Postmortem Friction Ridge Exemplars**
5–1	**Chapter 5: Systems of Friction Ridge Classification**
6–1	**Chapter 6: Automated Fingerprint Identification System (AFIS)**
7–1	**Chapter 7: Latent Print Development**

CONTENTS

8–1   **Chapter 8: The Preservation of Friction Ridges**

9–1   **Chapter 9: Examination Process**

10-1   **Chapter 10: Documentation of Friction Ridge Impressions: From the Scene to the Conclusion**

11-1   **Chapter 11: Equipment**

12-1   **Chapter 12: Quality Assurance**

13-1   **Chapter 13: Fingerprints and the Law**

14–1   **Chapter 14: Scientific Research Supporting the Foundations of Friction Ridge Examinations**

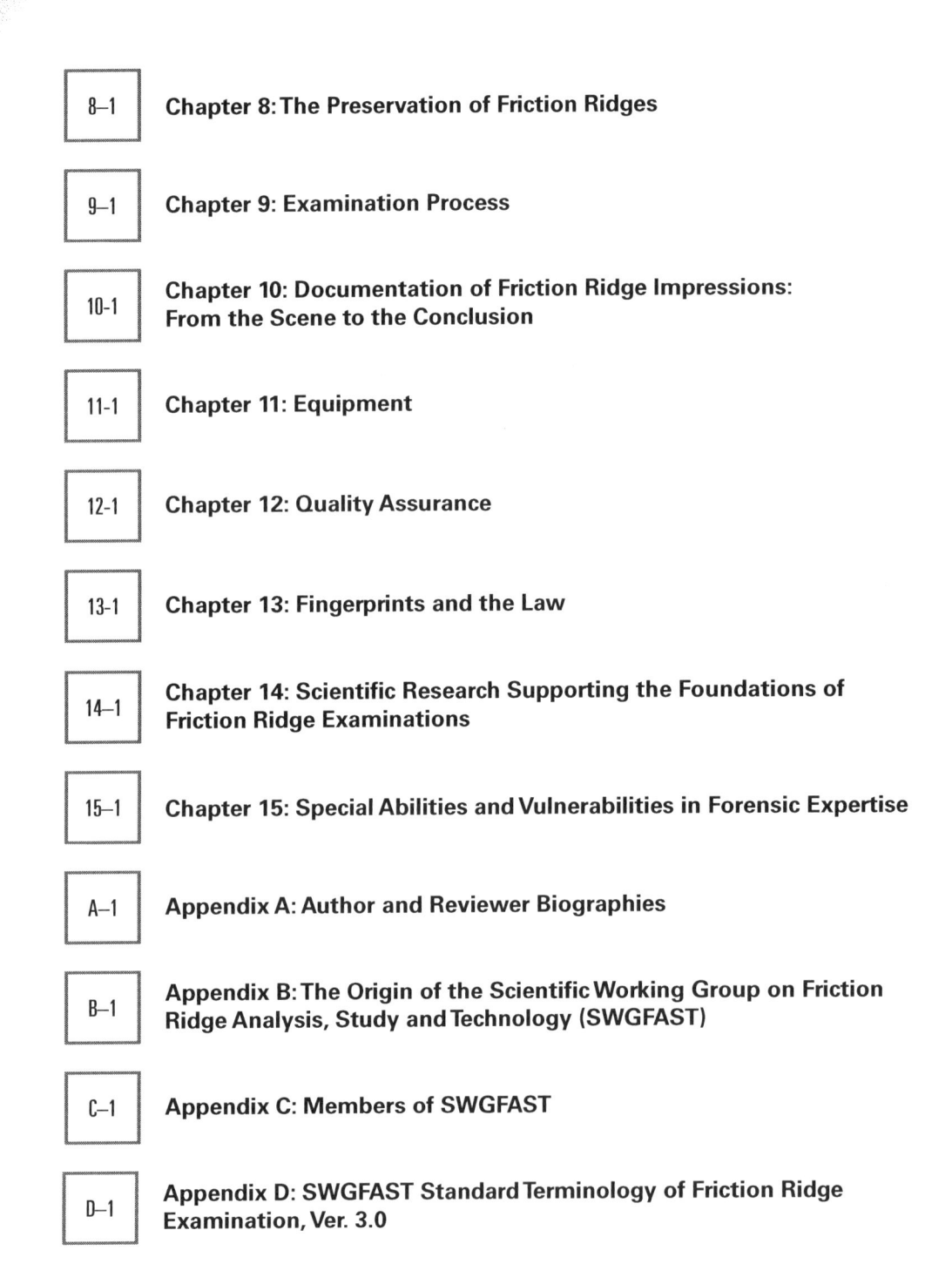

15–1   **Chapter 15: Special Abilities and Vulnerabilities in Forensic Expertise**

A–1   **Appendix A: Author and Reviewer Biographies**

B–1   **Appendix B: The Origin of the Scientific Working Group on Friction Ridge Analysis, Study and Technology (SWGFAST)**

C–1   **Appendix C: Members of SWGFAST**

D–1   **Appendix D: SWGFAST Standard Terminology of Friction Ridge Examination, Ver. 3.0**

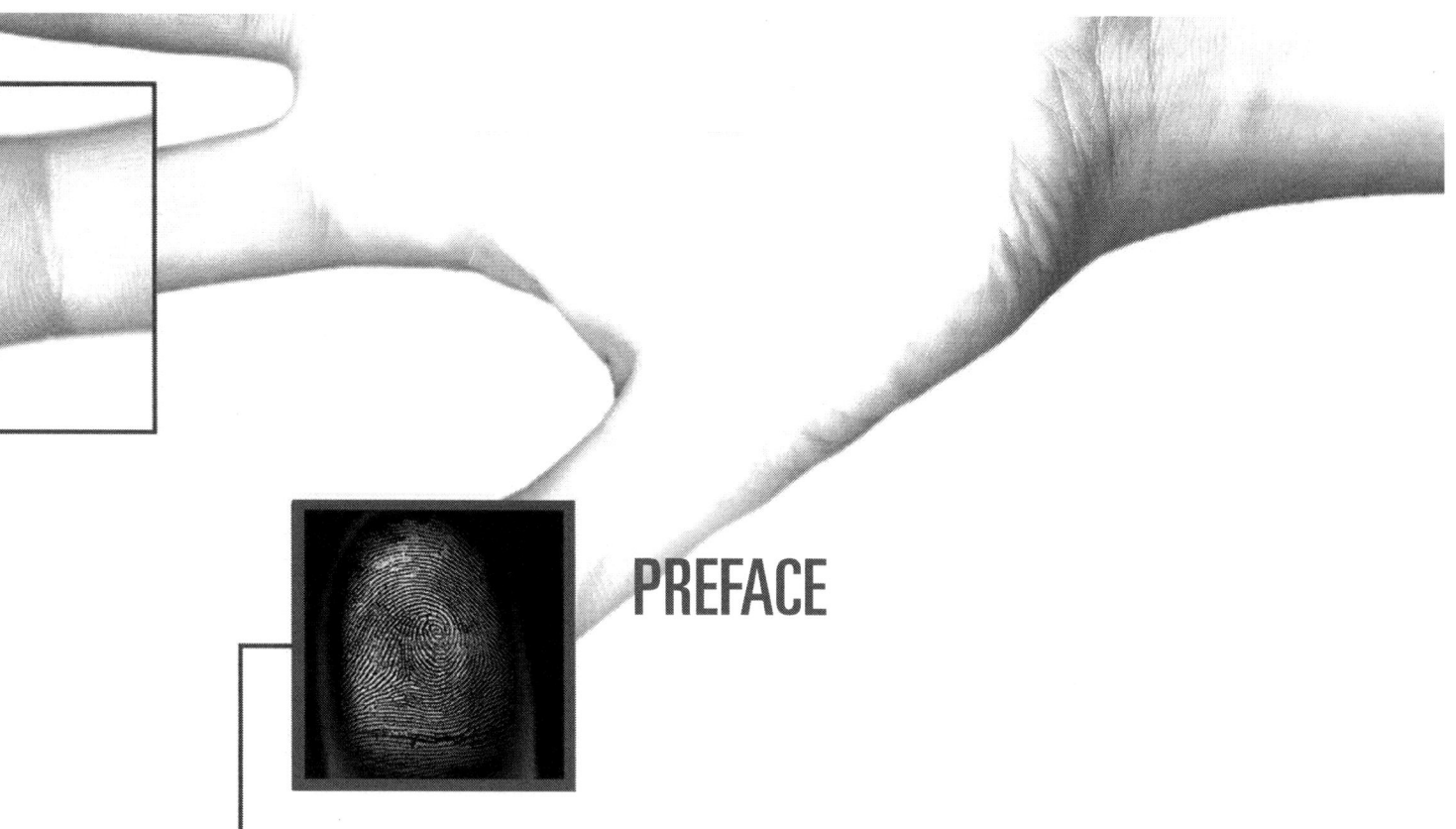

PREFACE

The idea of *The Fingerprint Sourcebook* originated during a meeting in April 2002. Individuals representing the fingerprint, academic, and scientific communities met in Chicago, Illinois, for a day and a half to discuss the state of fingerprint identification with a view toward the challenges raised by *Daubert* issues. The meeting was a joint project between the International Association for Identification (IAI) and West Virginia University (WVU). One recommendation that came out of that meeting was a suggestion to create a sourcebook for friction ridge examiners, that is, a single source of researched information regarding the subject. This sourcebook would provide educational, training, and research information for the international scientific community.

The Scientific Working Group on Friction Ridge Analysis, Study and Technology (SWGFAST) prepared an outline of the subjects that should be included in the sourcebook. Charles Illsley, a SWGFAST member, prepared a grant proposal for submission to the National Institute of Justice (NIJ) for funding of the project, with Frank Fitzpatrick as the project director and Alan and Debbie McRoberts as the sourcebook editors. Although many participants in the project were, and some remain, active members of SWGFAST, participation in the project was not restricted to SWGFAST members.

NIJ provided grant funding to the WVU Forensic Science Initiative to support the project and a call for authors and reviewers was extended throughout the forensic community. The prospective authors were asked to prepare a detailed outline and an introduction (approximately 250 to 750 words) for each chapter that they hoped to write. They were also asked to provide a curriculum vitae. Two or more individuals volunteered for most chapters and some chapters had as many as seven volunteers. Reviewers critiqued the introductions and outlines for the various chapters, and Frank Fitzpatrick and I made the final selection of chapter authors. Multiple reviewers for each chapter participated and are listed at the end of each chapter. The curricula vitae for all of the authors and most reviewers are included in the appendix.

After the selection of authors was made and the chapters were assigned to the various authors and coauthors, the chapters were written and multiple rounds of author revisions and review were completed. The chapters were then edited and reviewed again. The chapters were then submitted to

PREFACE

NIJ, where additional review and editing occurred. During the NIJ edit and review process, Chapter 15 (Special Abilities and Vulnerabilities in Forensic Expertise) was added to the project because of contemporary importance placed on that research. Those NIJ employees—and contractors, in particular Danielle Weiss and David Fialkoff—who participated in reviewing, editing, and finalizing this book should be congratulated for their efforts in bringing this project to completion.

For those of us who have worked in the field of fingerprint identification during the last 50 years, the influence of the Federal Bureau of Investigation's (FBI's) leadership in providing fingerprint training is well known. However, with the creation of SWGFAST in 1995, the FBI showed great leadership in providing a mechanism to promote consensus standards within our diverse forensic community. A brief sketch about the origin of SWGFAST and a list of the past and current members of SWGFAST are included in the appendix.

In the history of fingerprints, no previous effort of this magnitude has been made to assemble as much reviewed information into a single source. I would like to extend my appreciation and the appreciation of future readers to all those authors and reviewers who contributed so much time and effort to make this book a reality.

Alan McRoberts,
Editor

CHAPTER 1

HISTORY

Jeffery G. Barnes

CONTENTS

- **3**   1.1 Introduction
- **3**   1.2 Ancient History
- **4**   1.3 221 B.C. to A.D. 1637
- **5**   1.4 17th and 18th Centuries
- **6**   1.5 19th Century
- **11**   1.6 20th Century
- **17**   1.7 Conclusion
- **17**   1.8 Reviewers
- **17**   1.9 References
- **18**   1.10 Additional Information

CHAPTER 1

HISTORY

Jeffery G. Barnes

1.1 Introduction

The long story of that inescapable mark of identity has been told and retold for many years and in many ways. On the palm side of each person's hands and on the soles of each person's feet are prominent skin features that single him or her out from everyone else in the world. These features are present in friction ridge skin which leaves behind impressions of its shapes when it comes into contact with an object. The impressions from the last finger joints are known as fingerprints. Using fingerprints to identify individuals has become commonplace, and that identification role is an invaluable tool worldwide.

What some people do not know is that the use of friction ridge skin impressions as a means of identification has been around for thousands of years and has been used in several cultures. **Friction ridge skin impressions were used as proof of a person's identity in China perhaps as early as 300 B.C., in Japan as early as A.D. 702, and in the United States since 1902.**

1.2 Ancient History

Earthenware estimated to be 6000 years old was discovered at an archaeological site in northwest China and found to bear clearly discernible friction ridge impressions. **These prints are considered the oldest friction ridge skin impressions found to date;** however, it is unknown whether they were deposited by accident or with specific intent, such as to create decorative patterns or symbols (Xiang-Xin and Chun-Ge, 1988, p 277). In this same Neolithic period, friction ridges were being left in other ancient materials by builders (Ashbaugh, 1999, pp 12–13). Just as someone today might leave impressions in cement, early builders left impressions in the clay used to make bricks (Berry and Stoney, 2001, pp 8–9).

Other ancient artifacts have been found that have ridge patterns on them that were clearly carved rather than left as accidental impressions. Examples of ancient artifacts displaying what might be considered friction ridge designs include megalithic artworks in the tomb of Gavr'inis on an island just off the west coast of France and in the tomb at Newgrange on the coast of Ireland (Figure 1–1).

1.3 221 B.C. to A.D. 1637

The Chinese were the first culture known to have used friction ridge impressions as a means of identification. The earliest example comes from a Chinese document entitled "The Volume of Crime Scene Investigation—Burglary", from the Qin Dynasty (221 to 206 B.C.). The document contains a description of how handprints were used as a type of evidence (Xiang-Xin and Chun-Ge, 1988, p 283).

During the Qin through Eastern Han dynasties (221 B.C. to 220 A.D.), the most prevalent example of individualization using friction ridges was the clay seal. Documents consisting of bamboo slips or pages were rolled with string bindings, and the strings were sealed with clay (Xiang-Xin and Chun-Ge, 1988, pp 277–278). On one side of the seal would be impressed the name of the author, usually in the form of a stamp, and on the other side would be impressed the fingerprint of the author. The seal was used to show authorship and to prevent tampering prior to the document reaching the intended reader. It is generally recognized that it was both the fingerprint and the name that gave the document authenticity.

The fingerprint impressed into the clay seal is a definite example of intentional friction ridge skin reproduction as a means of individualization. It is clear that the Chinese understood the value of friction ridge skin prior to the Christian era (Laufer, 1912, p 649).

After the invention of paper by the Chinese in A.D. 105, it became common to sign documents using friction ridge skin. It was standard practice in China to place an impression—either palmprints, phalangeal (lower finger joint) marks, or fingerprints—on all contract-type documents (Xiang-Xin and Chun-Ge, 1988, pp 282–284). In A.D. 650, the Chinese historian Kia Kung-Yen described a previously used means of identification, writing, "Wooden tablets were inscribed with the terms of the contract and notches were cut into the sides at the identical places so that the tablets could later be matched, thus proving them genuine; the significance of the notches was the same as that of the fingerprints of the present time" (Ashbaugh, 1999, p 17).

FIGURE 1–1

One of the stones of Newgrange (Courtesy of http://www.ancient-wisdom.co.uk.)

This statement tends to confirm that fingerprints were used for individualization in China.

The use of friction ridge skin impressions in China continued into the Tang Dynasty (A.D. 617–907), as seen on land contracts, wills, and army rosters. It can be postulated that with the Chinese using friction ridge skin for individualization and trading with other nations in Asia, these other nations might have adopted the practice. For example, in Japan, a "Domestic Law" enacted in A.D. 702 required the following: "In case a husband cannot write, let him hire another man to write the document and after the husband's name, sign with his own index finger" (Ashbaugh, 1999, p 17–18; Lambourne, 1984, p 24). This shows at least the possibility that the Japanese had some understanding of the value of friction ridge skin for individualization.

Additionally, in India, there are references to the nobility using friction ridge skin as signatures:

> In A.D. 1637, the joint forces of Shah Jahan and Adil Khan, under the command of Khan Zaman Bahadur, invaded the camp of Shahuji Bhosle, the ruler of Pona (in the present day Maharashtra). The joint army defeated Shahuji, who was compelled to accept the terms of peace:
>
>> Since the garrison (of Shahuji) was now reduced to great extremities ....[,] Shahuji wrote frequently to Khan Bahadur in the most humble strain, promising to pay allegiance to the crown. He at the same time solicited a written treaty ... stamped with the impression of his hand. (Sodhi and Kaur, 2003a, pp 126–136)

The above text is an example of the nobility's use of palmprints in India to demonstrate authenticity of authorship when writing an important document. **It is believed that the use of prints on important documents was adopted from the Chinese, where it was used generally, but in India it was mainly reserved for royalty** (Sodhi and Kaur, 2003a, pp 129–131). The use of friction ridge skin as a signature in China, Japan, India, and possibly other nations prior to European discovery is thus well documented.

FIGURE 1–2

Dr. Nehemiah Grew (1641–1712). (Courtesy of Smithsonian Institution Libraries.)

FIGURE 1–3

Dr. Marcello Malpighi (1628–1694). (Reprinted from Locy (1908). Image captured from Google Books.)

1.4 17th and 18th Centuries

In the late 17th century, European scientists began publishing their observations of human skin. **Friction ridge skin was first described in detail by Dr. Nehemiah Grew** (Figure 1–2) in the 1684 paper *Philosophical Transactions of the Royal Society of London*. Dr. Grew's description marked the beginning in the Western Hemisphere of friction ridge skin observations and characterizations (Ashbaugh, 1999, p 38; Lambourne, 1984, p 25). In 1685, Govard Bidloo, a Dutch anatomist, published *Anatomy of the Human Body*, which included details of the skin and the papillary ridges of the thumb but failed to address individualization or permanence (Ashbaugh, 1999, p 39; Felsher, 1962, pp 6–12). In 1687, the Italian physiologist Marcello Malpighi (Figure 1–3) published *Concerning the External Tactile Organs*, in which the function, form, and structure of friction ridge skin was discussed. **Malpighi is credited with being the first to use the newly invented microscope for medical studies.** In his treatise, Malpighi noted that ridged skin increases friction between an object and the skin's surface; friction ridge skin thus enhances traction for walking and

1–9

grasping (New Scotland Yard, 1990; Ashbaugh, 1999, p 40). In recognition of Malpighi's work, a layer of skin (stratum Malpighi) was named after him.

Although friction ridge skin had been studied for a number of years, it would be 1788 before the uniqueness of this skin was recognized in Europe. J. C. A. Mayer, a German doctor and anatomist, wrote a book entitled *Anatomical Copper-plates with Appropriate Explanations*, which contained detailed drawings of friction ridge skin patterns. Mayer wrote, "Although the arrangement of skin ridges is never duplicated in two persons, nevertheless the similarities are closer among some individuals. In others the differences are marked, yet in spite of their peculiarities of arrangement all have a certain likeness" (Cummins and Midlo, 1943, pp 12–13). **Mayer was the first to write that friction ridge skin is unique.**

1.5 19th Century

English wood engraver and ornithologist Thomas Bewick (1753–1828) published many books with wood engravings of birds and other animals. Three woodcuts (made in 1809, 1818, and 1826) included a fingermark, and the latter two had the legend "Thomas Bewick, his mark" (Herschel, 1916, 32–33). The woodcuts (Figure 1–4) were very detailed, but it is unknown whether Bewick understood the value of friction ridge skin for individualization (Galton, 1892, p 26; Lambourne, 1984, p 26).

In his 1823 thesis titled "Commentary on the Physiological Examination of the Organs of Vision and the Cutaneous System", Dr. Johannes E. Purkinje (1787–1869), professor at the University of Breslau in Germany, classified fingerprint patterns into nine categories and gave each a name (Figure 1–5) (Lambourne, 1984, p 26; Galton, 1892, pp 85–88). **Although Dr. Purkinje went no further than naming the patterns, his contribution is significant because his nine pattern types were the precursor to the Henry classification system** (Herschel, 1916, pp 34–35; Galton, 1892, pp 67, 119). (For more on Purkinje, see Chapter 5. For more on the Henry system, see p 10.)

German anthropologist Hermann Welcker (1822–1898) of the University of Halle led the way in the study of friction ridge skin permanence. **Welcker began by printing his own right hand in 1856 and then again in 1897, thus gaining credit as the first person to start a permanence study.** However, in the paper Welcker published in

FIGURE 1–4

Bewick's published fingermarks. (Courtesy of the Natural History Society of Northumbria, Hancock Museum.)

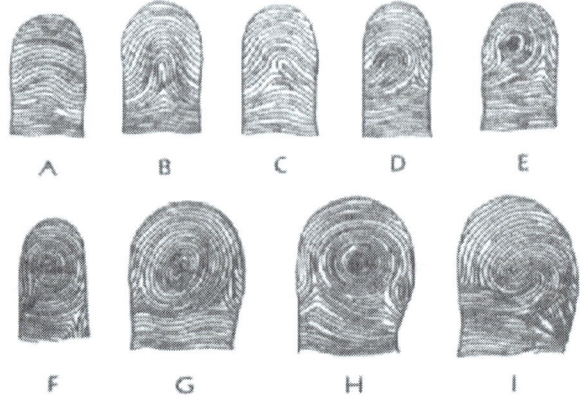

FIGURE 1–5

Purkinje's nine types of finger patterns. (A: Transverse curves, B: Central longitudinal stria, C: Oblique stria, D: Oblique sinus, E: Almond, F: Spiral, G: Ellipse or elliptical whorl, H: Circle or circular whorl, and I: Double whorl). (Reprinted with permission from Cumming and Midlo (1943). Copyright 1943 Dover Publications Inc.)

1898, he sought no credit, but rather seemed only to offer assistance to prior claims of permanence in reference to friction ridge skin (Wilder and Wentworth, 1918, pp 339–340). Welcker is not cited often. **Generally, the credit for being the first person to study the persistence of friction ridge skin goes to Sir William James Herschel.**

Herschel (Figure 1–6) was born in England and moved in 1853, at age 20, to Bengal, India, to serve as a British Administrator for the East India Company. In 1858, he experimented with the idea of using a handprint as a signature by having a man named Rajyadhar Konai put a stamp of his right hand on the back of a contract for road binding materials. The contract was received and accepted as valid. **This spontaneous printing of Konai's hand thus led to the first official use of friction ridge skin by a European.** The success of this experiment led Herschel to begin a long exploration of friction ridge skin, and over the next year he went on to collect multiple fingerprints from family, friends, colleagues, and even himself. In 1860, he was promoted to magistrate and given charge of Nuddea, a rural subdivision in Bengal. While there, he recognized more identification possibilities for the use of friction ridge skin, especially in fighting and preventing fraud.

Upon his appointment as Magistrate and Collector at Hooghly, near Calcutta, in 1877, Herschel was able to institute the recording of friction ridge skin as a method of individualization on a widespread basis. Herschel was in charge of the criminal courts, the prisons, the registration of deeds, and the payment of government pensions, all of which he controlled with fingerprint identification. On August 15, 1877, Herschel wrote what is referred to as the "Hooghly Letter" to Bengal's Inspector of Jails and the Registrar General, describing his ideas and suggesting that the fingerprint system be expanded to other geographical areas. While proposing even further uses of this means of individualization, the Hooghly Letter also explained both the permanence and uniqueness of friction ridge skin (Herschel, 1916, pp 22–23).

Herschel continued his study of the permanence of friction ridge skin throughout his lifetime. He published prints of himself taken in 1859, 1877, and 1916 to demonstrate this permanence (Herschel, 1916, pp 22–31).

In 1877, Thomas Taylor (1820–1910), a microscopist for the U.S. Department of Agriculture, gave a lecture concerning prints and their possible applications concerning crime. Taylor proposed the idea of using bloody prints found at crime

FIGURE 1–6

Sir William James Herschel (1833–1917). (Reprinted from private collection (1913). Courtesy of West Virginia University Libraries.)

FIGURE 1–7

Henry Faulds (1843–1930). (Reprinted from Faulds (1922). Courtesy of West Virginia University Libraries.)

scenes as a means to identify suspects. The lecture was published in the July 1877 issue of *The American Journal of Microscopy and Popular Science* (Ashbaugh, 1999, p 26).

Henry Faulds (Figure 1–7) became interested in friction ridge skin after seeing ridge detail on pottery found on a Japanese beach (Faulds, 1880). He was born at Beith, in Ayrshire, in 1843, and entered Anderson's College in Glasgow, graduating as a Licentiate of the Royal Faculty of Physicians and Surgeons in 1871. Faulds, as a medical missionary, opened a hospital in Tsukiji, Japan, working there from 1873 until 1885 (Lambourne, 1984, p 33). During that time, Faulds conducted independent research by collecting prints of both monkeys and people. In a letter dated February 16, 1880, to the famed naturalist Charles Darwin, Faulds wrote that friction ridges were unique and classifiable, and alluded to their permanence (Lambourne, 1984, pp 34–35). In October 1880, Faulds submitted an article for publication to the journal *Nature* in order to inform other researchers of his findings (Faulds, 1880, p 605). In that article, Faulds proposed using friction ridge individualization at crime scenes and gave two practical examples.

In one example, a greasy print on a drinking glass revealed who had been drinking some distilled spirits. In the other, sooty fingermarks on a white wall exonerated an accused individual (Faulds, 1880, p 605). **Faulds was the first person to publish in a journal the value of friction ridge skin for individualization, especially its use as evidence.** (For more on Faulds, see Chapter 5.)

While Herschel and Faulds were studying friction ridge skin, another scientist was devising an alternate identification method. Alphonse Bertillon (Figure 1–8) was a clerk in the Prefecture of Police in Paris, France. In 1879, Bertillon began studying the body measurements of various individuals and devised anthropometry, which was first put to use in 1882. Anthropometry is the study of body measurements for identification purposes. Bertillon's anthropometric method measured height, reach (middle finger to middle finger of outstretched arms), trunk, length of head, width of head, length of right ear, width of right ear, length of left foot, length of left middle finger, length of left little finger, and length of left forearm. With the success of anthropometry, Bertillon was made the Chief of the Department of Judicial Identity in 1888 (Rhodes, 1956, p 103). (For more on Bertillon, see Chapter 5.)

Anthropometry is a scientific and biometric way to individualize and was used on criminals throughout most of the world from its inception in 1882 until 1914. As friction ridge skin identification became more prevalent after experimentation proved its usefulness, fingerprints were added to anthropometric records. Thus, a complete anthropometric record would include the 11 body measurements, 2 photographs (front face and right side), and a set of all 10 fingerprints. Even though not officially adopted as a sole means of identification in France or elsewhere in Europe, the concept of using friction ridge skin for individualization was gaining momentum.

In the United States, geologist Gilbert Thompson guarded his checks against forgery by signing across an impression of his finger. Thompson did this while working on a project in New Mexico in 1882 (Galton, 1892, p 27).

In 1883, another American, Samuel Langhorne Clemens (1835–1910), better known as Mark Twain, wrote the story of his life in the book *Life on the Mississippi* and included a passage about the permanence and uniqueness of the print of the ball of the thumb (Twain, 1883, pp 160–161). In 1884, Clemens wrote the novel *The Tragedy of Pudd'nhead Wilson*. In it, he tells the story of a lawyer who spends his time collecting prints from the local townsfolk and then uses them to solve a murder. Not only does Clemens explain the permanence and uniqueness of friction ridge skin, the book also features several courtroom demonstrations: the first shows how each person's prints are different on each finger, the second shows that even identical twins have different prints from one another, the third shows how the prints made from the fingers can be individualized, and the last catches the murderer. The story is told using critical knowledge of friction ridge skin (Twain, 1884, pp 128–137). Although anthropometry was the current method of identification in the early 1880s, Clemens's writings illustrate that the value of friction ridge skin to uniquely identify an individual was becoming increasingly well known.

A publication in 1883 by Dr. Arthur Kollmann of Hamburg, Germany, *The Tactile Apparatus of the Hand of the Human Races and Apes in Its Development and Structure*, added to the research being conducted on friction ridge skin. Kollmann studied the embryological development of friction ridge skin, proposing that ridges are formed by lateral pressure between nascent ridges and that ridges are discernible in the fourth month of fetal life and are fully formed in the sixth (Galton, 1892, p 58). **Kollman was the first to identify the presence and locations of the volar pads on the hands and feet** (Hale, 1952, p 162; Ashbaugh, 1999, p 41). (For an explanation of volar pads, see chapter 3.) The studies of Kollmann were followed in

FIGURE 1–8

Alphonse Bertillon (1853–1913). (Reprinted from McClaughry (1922). Courtesy of West Virginia University Libraries.)

1888 with the publication in Germany of *On the Morphology of the Tactile Pads of Mammals* by Hermann Klaatsch. Klaatsch studied the walking surfaces of mammals other than humans, which led to his theory that the orderly arrangement of sweat glands into rows was an evolutionary change (Galton, 1892, p 60).

The scientific study of friction ridge skin was also taken up by a prominent scientist of the time, Sir Francis Galton (Figure 1–9). Galton was born February 16, 1822, in Sparkbrook, England, and was a cousin of Charles Darwin. Most of Galton's research focused on hereditary matters, which led him to the study of anthropometry and, later, fingerprints. Galton was looking to understand the hereditary nature of the physical body and what, if anything, it could tell about an individual (Caplan and Torpey, 2001, p 274). Visitors to his anthropometric laboratory were voluntarily measured seventeen different ways. These measurements were recorded on a card that was copied and given to the visitors as a souvenir (ca. 1885). From this data, he realized that forearm length correlated with height and derived the first example of what statisticians now call a correlation coefficient (a numerical value identifying the strength of the relationship between variables). Galton continued to take anthropometric measurements, and he added the printing of the thumbs and then the printing of all 10 fingers. **As the author of the first book on fingerprints (*Finger Prints*, 1892), Galton established that friction ridge skin was unique and persistent.** He also concluded that there was no link between friction ridge skin and the character of the individual with that skin. Because Galton was the first to define and name specific print minutiae, the minutiae became known as Galton details (Figure 1–10). Galton's details consist of a uniting or dividing ridge (bifurcation), the end or beginning of a ridge (ending ridges), a short island (short ridge), and an enclosure (two bifurcations facing each other) (Galton, 1892, p 54). (For more on Galton, see Chapter 5.)

While Galton conducted research that would further advance the science of fingerprints, fingerprints were being used practically as well. In 1886, I. W. Taber, a photographer in San Francisco, proposed using thumbprints to identify Chinese immigrants (Lambourne, 1984, pp 46–47). In 1889, the Director-General of the Post Offices in India was collecting thumbprints from employees to prevent individuals who had been fired from being rehired. Using thumbprints for identity worked well to prevent fraudulent practices (Henry, 1934, pp 8–9). The French medical/legal scientist René Forgeot published a thesis in 1891 in which he

FIGURE 1–9

Sir Francis Galton (1822–1911). (Reprinted from Pearson (1914). Courtesy of West Virginia University Libraries.)

FIGURE 1–10

Minutiae diagram. (a and b: Bifurcations, c: Enclosure, d and e: Ending ridges, and f: Island). (Reprinted from Galton (1892).)

proposed using powders and chemicals to develop latent prints at crime scenes in order to individualize the person who had touched an object (Galton, 1892, p 46).

Another leading fingerprint researcher of this time period was Juan Vucetich. Vucetich was employed as a statistician with the Central Police Department in La Plata, Argentina, until his promotion to the head of the bureau of Anthropometric Identification. Vucetich, having studied Galton's research, began to experiment with fingerprints in 1891. He started recording the fingerprints of criminals and devised his own classification system (Lambourne, 1984, pp 58–59). **Vucetich's classification system and individualization of prisoners through the use of fingerprints were the first practical uses of the fingerprint science by law enforcement personnel.** Other countries soon looked into using a fingerprint system to identify prisoners. (For more on Vucetich, see Chapter 5.)

In 1892, in Buenos Aires, Argentina, a murder was solved using thumbprint evidence found at the crime scene. The two children of Francisca Rojas were found murdered. Rojas herself had a throat wound. She accused a man named Velasquez of the murder, stating that he was jealous because she refused to marry him since she was in love with another man. The local authorities brutally beat Velasquez hoping for a confession. When Velasquez did not confess, Inspector Eduardo Alvarez was brought in from La Plata to

CHAPTER 1 | History

conduct a thorough investigation. Inspector Alvarez began by examining the scene of the crime and found a bloody thumbprint on the door. Having been trained by Juan Vucetich to compare fingerprints, Alvarez removed the section of the door with the print and compared the bloody thumbprint with the thumbprints of Francisca Rojas. When confronted and shown that her own thumbprint matched the thumbprint on the door, she confessed to the murders (New Scotland Yard, 1990, pp 8–9; Beavan, 2001, pp 114–116). **The Rojas murder case is considered to be the first homicide solved by fingerprint evidence, and Argentina became the first country to rely solely on fingerprints as a method of individualization** (Lambourne, 1984, pp 58–59).

The Troup Committee, named for its chairman, Charles Edward Troup, was formed in 1893 to investigate current and possible future methods of identifying habitual criminals in England. After extensive research into previous methods of identification (such as photographs and the memories of police officers) as well as the new methods of anthropometry and fingermarks, the Troup Committee came to a compromise. The committee, like Sir Francis Galton, recognized weaknesses inherent in the filing and retrieving of fingermarks. Anthropometry and fingerprints were both considered to be effective methods of identification, but at the time, fingerprints did not have an adequate classification system. The committee thus felt compelled to use both systems and recommended that five major anthropometric measurements be taken and used for primary classification and that fingermarks be attached as an additional component of the classification system. The committee's recommendations were followed in England and in Bengal. By 1894, all newly arrested criminals were measured and fingerprinted in those two jurisdictions (Lambourne, 1984, pp 46–51).

In 1894, Sir Edward Richard Henry (Figure 1–11), Inspector General of Police for the Lower Provinces, Bengal, collaborated with Galton on a method of classification for fingerprints. With the help of Indian police officers Khan Bahadur Azizul Haque and Rai Bahaden Hem Chandra Bose, the Henry classification system was developed. Once the classification system was developed and proved to be effective, Henry wrote to the government of India asking for a comparative review of anthropometry and fingerprints. Charles Strahan, Surveyor General of India, and Alexander Pedler, a chemist, were sent to Bengal to meet with Henry to investigate the two methods of identification. Toward the end of March 1897, they sent a report to the government of India that stated, "In conclusion, we are of opinion that the method of identification by means of finger prints, as worked on the system of recording impressions and of classification used in Bengal, may be safely adopted as being superior to the anthropometrics method—(1) in simplicity of working; (2) in the cost of apparatus; (3) in the fact that all skilled work is transferred to a central or classification office; (4) in the rapidity with which the process can be worked; and (5) in the certainty of the results." (Henry, 1934, p 79) Thus in 1897, the government of India sanctioned the sole use of fingerprints as a means of identification for prisoners. (For more on Henry, see Chapter 5.)

Just as the use of friction ridge skin for individualization was becoming more prevalent, research to better understand its evolution and purpose was also proceeding. **David Hepburn of the University of Edinburgh, Scotland, is credited with being the first to recognize that friction ridges assist with grasping** by increasing the level of friction between the ridges and the grasped object. Hepburn's paper, "The Papillary Ridges on the Hands and Feet of Monkeys and Men", published in 1895 (Hepburn, 1895, pp 525–537), dealt with the evolution of the volar pads and named two of the volar pads found in the palm: the hypothenar and thenar. As research into the form and function of friction ridge skin increased, so did the study on how to use fingerprints effectively as a means of individualization.

Harris Hawthorne Wilder, Professor of Zoology at Smith College, was studying primates when he was struck by the resemblance of their volar friction ridges to those of humans. Wilder published his first paper in 1897, entitled "On

FIGURE 1–11

Sir Edward Richard Henry (1850–1931). (Reprinted from Finger Print Publishing Association (1919). Courtesy of West Virginia University Libraries.)

1–14

the Disposition of the Epidermic Folds Upon the Palms and Soles of Primates". During the next three decades, Wilder continued research in morphology (the biological study of the form and structure of living organisms), the methodology of plantar and palmar dermatoglyphics (the study of friction ridges) (Cummins and Midlo, 1943, p 22), genetics, and racial differences. **Wilder was the first to suggest that the centers of disturbance of primate friction ridge formations actually represented the locations of the volar pads.** He also developed the hypothesis of a relationship between primate friction ridge patterns and volar pads.

A criminal case in Bengal in 1898 is considered to be the first case in which fingerprint evidence was used to secure a conviction (Sodhi and Kaur, 2003b, pp 1–3):

> The manager of a tea garden situated in the district of Julpaiguri on the Bhutan frontier was found lying on his bed with his throat cut, his despatch box and safe having been rifled and several hundred rupees carried away. It was suggested that one of the coolies employed on the garden had committed the deed, as the deceased had the reputation of being a hard taskmaster, or that his cook, upon whose clothes were some blood spots, might be the culprit. There was suspicion also against the relatives of a woman with whom the murdered man had a liaison, also against a wandering gang of Kabulis of criminal propensities who had lately encamped in the neighbourhood. A representation was also made that the deceased had an enemy in an ex-servant whom he had caused to be imprisoned for theft. Inquiry, however, satisfied the police that there was no evidence to incriminate the coolies or the relatives of the woman or the Kabulis, and it was ascertained that the ex-servant had been released from jail some weeks before, and no one could say that he had since been seen in the district. The cook's statement that the marks on his clothes were stains from a pigeon's blood which he killed for his master's dinner was supported by the Chemical Analyst's report. Fortunately amongst the papers in the despatch box was found a calendar in book form, printed in the Bengali character, with an outside cover of light-blue paper on which were noticed two faint brown smudges. Under a magnifying glass one smudge was decipherable as a portion of the impression of one of the digits of some person's right hand. In the Central Office of the Bengal Police, the finger impressions of all persons convicted of certain offences are classified and registered, and the impression on the calendar when compared there was found to correspond exactly with the right thumb impression of Kangali Charan, the ex-servant above referred to. He, in consequence, was arrested in Birbhum, a district some hundreds of miles away, and brought to Calcutta, where his right thumb impression was again taken, and the police in the meantime set about collecting corroborative evidence. The Chemical Examiner to Government certified that the brown marks on the calendar were mammalian blood, the inference being that the actual murderer or some associate had knocked his blood-stained thumb against the calendar when rummaging amongst the papers in the despatch box for the key of the safe. The accused was committed to stand his trial before a judge and assessors, charged with murder and theft, and finally was convicted of having stolen the missing property of the deceased, the assessors holding that it would be unsafe to convict him of murder as no one had seen the deed committed, but recording their opinion that the charge of theft had been conclusively established against him. This conviction was upheld by the judges of the Supreme Court, to which the case was taken on appeal (Henry, 1934, pp 57–60).

In December 1900, the Belper Committee in England, chaired by Lord Belper, recommended that all criminal identification records be classified by the fingerprint system (Lambourne, 1984, p 64). **With this recommendation, the Henry Classification System and the individualization of criminals by means of fingerprints became standard practice in England and would eventually be adopted in most English-speaking countries.** During this transition, other events taking place would also demonstrate the advantage of recording friction ridge skin.

1.6 20th Century

The first trial in England that relied on fingerprint evidence involved Inspector Charles Stockley Collins of Scotland Yard. Collins testified to an individualization made in a burglary case. **That 1902 trial and subsequent conviction marked the beginning of fingerprint evidence in the courts of England** (Lambourne, 1984, pp 67–68).

In October 1902, Alphonse Bertillon, made an individualization in Paris, France, with fingerprints:

> On October 17, 1902, he [Bertillon] was called to aid the investigation of the murder of Joseph Reibel. A glass panel from a nearby cabinet had been broken, and

some bloody fingerprints were discovered on one of the broken pieces. These were dutifully photographed and preserved. After determining that they did not match the victim's prints, Bertillon began a search of his anthropometric cards, upon which, by that late date, he had added fingerprint impressions as a routine matter in addition to his measurements. Eventually he found a card which contained fingerprint impressions that showed areas that matched the prints taken from the crime scene. The report of the case describes the isolation of three points of resemblance in the thumb-print, four in the index and middle finger, and six in the print from the ring finger. The murderer, Henri Leon Scheffer, was apprehended and brought to justice. (Kingston and Kirk, 1965, p 62)

As a result of the above case, Bertillon is given credit for solving the first murder in Europe with the use of only fingerprint evidence.

The first systematic use of fingerprints in the United States was in 1902 by Dr. Henry P. de Forest of the New York Civil Service Commission. De Forest established the practice of fingerprinting civil service applicants in order to prevent imposters from taking tests for otherwise unqualified people. Applicants were fingerprinted when they submitted their applications, when they turned in each test, and when they officially reported to duty (de Forest, 1938, pp 16–20).

In 1903, after several months of fingerprinting criminals upon their release, Captain James H. Parke of New York state developed the American Classification System. **The use of the American Classification System and subsequent fingerprinting of all criminals in the state of New York was the first systematic use of fingerprinting for criminal record purposes in the United States** (McGinnis, 1963, pp 4–5). Although the American Classification System did not gain widespread acceptance throughout the United States, it did not take long before the science of fingerprints spread nationwide.

Within fingerprint history, there is a famous story about an incident that signaled the downfall of the use of anthropometric measurements in favor of fingerprinting. A man was arrested in 1903 and brought to the Leavenworth prison in Kansas. The man claimed that his name was Will West and that he had never been previously arrested. Prison personnel took the man's Bertillon measurements and his photograph to facilitate a prison records check. The records showed that a man named William West, with very similar anthropometric measurements and a striking resemblance to the new inmate, was already incarcerated in Leavenworth prison. Guards sent to check William West's cell may have suspected they were dealing with an escapee; instead, they found William West asleep in his bed. After comparing records of both men, prison personnel seemed unable to tell the men apart. Upon taking and comparing the fingerprints of both prisoners, it was clear that the fingerprint method of identification could distinguish between the two men. (Cole, 2001, pp 140–146; Chapel, 1941, pp 11–13).

The William and Will West story is somewhat sensationalized and omits prison record information, uncovered by later researchers, indicating that William and Will West both corresponded with the same family members and thus were probably related. Prison records also cite that Leavenworth inmate George Bean reported that he knew William and Will West in their home territory before prison, and that they were twin brothers (Nickell, 1980, pp 3–9). Their exact relationship is still unknown. What is factual is that the two West men were not unusual; many people have similar anthropometric measurements. It is generally accepted that identical twins will have the same or almost the same anthropometric measurements, yet easily differentiated fingerprints. The superiority of fingerprints over anthropometry is thus clear.

At the 1904 World's Fair in Saint Louis, there were three booths demonstrating identification methods. One booth displayed the anthropometric method and was run by Emerson E. Davis from New York. Captain James J. Parke, from New York, and Inspector John Kenneth Ferrier, of New Scotland Yard, each set up a booth displaying the fingerprint method of identification. Inspector Ferrier discussed the fingerprint method with many individuals at the fair, several of whom were in charge of their own police departments throughout the United States. He also showed visitors an instance where the anthropometric measurements of two men varied by only a millimeter and how the fingerprints were different (Myers, 1938, p 19). After the fair, Ferrier remained in the United States to teach fingerprinting, including how to use powder to develop latent prints (Myers, 1938, pp 19–21). Ferrier's students went on to teach fingerprinting to law enforcement and military communities throughout the rest of America.

On October 19, 1904, Inspector Ferrier and Major M. W. McClaughry began fingerprinting all inmates at the Leavenworth, KS, federal prison. **These fingerprint**

records became the beginning of the U.S. Government's fingerprint collection (Myers 1938, pp 19–20).

In 1904, Inez Whipple published the paper, "The Ventral Surface of the Mammalian Chiridium". Whipple's survey into mammalian palm and sole configurations formed an important part of the modern scientific knowledge on the subject and is considered a landmark in the fields of genetics and ridgeology (Ashbaugh, 1999, p 43). Her treatise was on the evolution of friction ridge skin and its development as mankind evolved. Whipple theorized that mammals lost hair from scales on volar surfaces; volar scales fused into rows; and ridges evolved according to the need for friction to facilitate locomotion and grasping. She gave locations of the volar pads and explained possible forces that affect ridge growth. (Whipple, 1904, pp 261–368). Whipple, who became Inez Wilder after marriage, was undoubtedly influenced by her coworker and husband, Harris Hawthorne Wilder (see p 16).

In 1905, Inspector Charles S. Collins of Scotland Yard testified to the individualization of a suspect's fingerprint on a cash box. The case involved the murder of a man and his wife. Two brothers, Alfred and Albert Stratton, were the defendants. Collins explained to the jury the classification of fingerprints and how to effect an individualization. Then, he demonstrated the characteristics he had marked on a chart as matching Alfred Stratton's right thumb. Collins claimed that in all his years of experience, he had never found two prints to have more than three characteristics in common. In this case, there were 11 characteristics in common. Supplementing eyewitness statements, the individualization of Alfred Stratton's right thumb impression was the strongest piece of evidence in the case. Both brothers were found guilty of the murders and sentenced to death. This case is referred to as the Deptford Murder Trial, in reference to the address of the crime, and **it was the first murder trial in England in which fingerprints were used as evidence.**

Also in 1905, in the case of *Emperor* v *Abdul Hamid*, a court in India decided that no expert was required to testify to the individualization of prints, and an appellate court agreed. They believed that participants in the court could just as easily make a comparison as anyone else and that an expert was not necessary (Cole, 2001, p 170). Other courts would later disagree with the position that no expertise is required to individualize fingerprints.

Murder suspect Thomas Jennings was convicted in 1910 after testimony by four experts who individualized Jennings' fingerprints from a porch railing at the crime scene. The experts were Michael P. Evans, head of the Bureau of Identification of the Chicago Police Department; William M. Evans, previously of the Bureau of Identification of the Chicago Police Department; Edward Foster, an inspector with Dominion Police in Ottawa, Canada; and **Mary Holland, a trainer of Navy* personnel and the first American female instructor of fingerprinting.** All four witnesses testified that the fingerprints on the railing were made by Jennings. Other evidence also incriminated the defendant, such as Jennings's proximity to the murder scene 13 minutes after the murder while carrying a recently fired pistol containing cartridges similar to ones found at the murder scene.

The defense appealed the case, claiming the fingerprint evidence was improperly admitted and that it was not necessary to use a fingerprint examiner as an expert witness. The opinion delivered by the Illinois appellate court confirming the conviction including the following:

> We are disposed to hold from the evidence of the four witnesses who testified and from the writings we have referred to on this subject, that there is a scientific basis for the system of finger-print identification and that the courts are justified in admitting this class of evidence; that this method of identification is in such general and common use that the courts cannot refuse to take judicial cognizance of it.

> From the evidence in this record we are disposed to hold that the classification of finger-print impressions and their method of identification is a science requiring study. While some of the reasons which guide an expert to his conclusions are such as may be weighed by any intelligent person with good eyesight from such exhibits as we have here in the record, after being pointed out to him by one versed in the study of finger prints, the evidence in question does not come within the common experience of all men of common education in the ordinary walks of life, and therefore the court and jury were properly aided by witnesses of peculiar and special experience on this subject. [*People* v *Jennings* 1911, pp 9–10]

After being upheld on appeal, ***People* v *Jennings* became a landmark legal case because it was the first American**

---

*In 1907, the Navy adopted the practice of fingerprinting of applicants (Myers, 1938, p 15).

appellate case regarding the admissibility of fingerprint expert testimony. The appellate court concluded that fingerprint identification is a science and that expert testimony was appropriate to aid members of the court in understanding fingerprint evidence.

In 1911, Lieutenant Joseph Faurot, a New York Police Department fingerprint expert presented testimony in a burglary case. He individualized defendant Charles Crispi's fingerprint on a pane of glass removed from a door at the crime scene point of entry. In a dramatic courtroom demonstration, Faurot took the inked prints of the 12 jurors and other court personnel and then left the room. Faurot's assistant had a jury member place a print on a pane of glass to simulate the conditions of the burglary. Faurot returned to the courtroom, developed the print left on the glass, and identified the developed print to the proper juror. Next, Faurot gave each juror a set of charts showing marked characteristics in common between the known prints of Crispi and the print left on the piece of glass at the burglary scene. Each juror was then able to compare the prints along with Faurot. The demonstrations were so impressive that the defendant changed his plea to guilty. ***People v Crispi* (1911) is considered to be the first conviction obtained with fingerprint evidence alone in the United States** (despite the defendant's courtroom plea

A TIMELINE OF FINGERPRINT FIRSTS

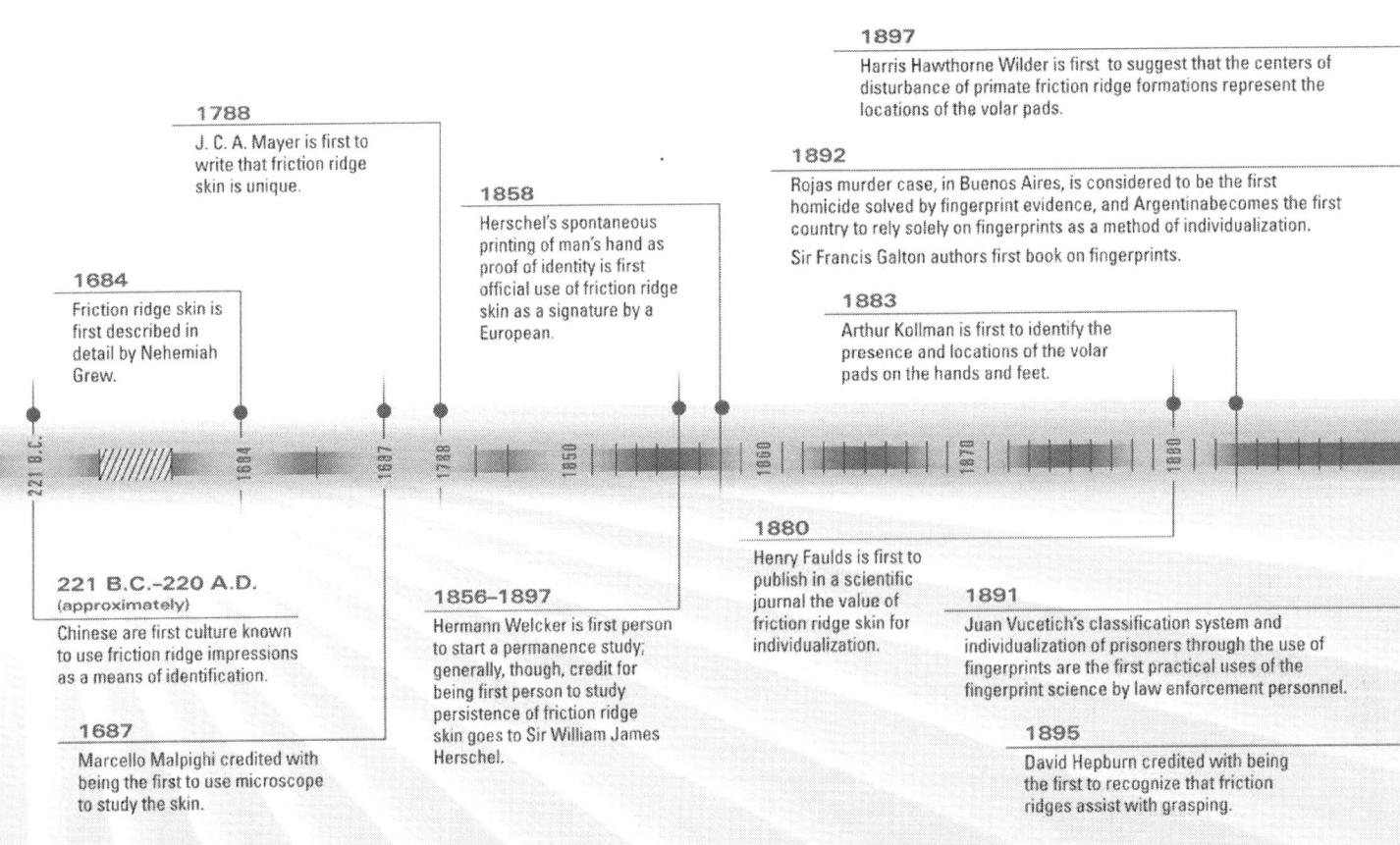

change) (Cole, 2001, pp 181–185; Wilder and Wentworth, 1918, pp 283–284).

In 1914, Dr. Edmond Locard published "The Legal Evidence by the Fingerprints". Locard was Director of the Laboratory of Police at Lyons, France, and was a student of Alphonse Bertillon. Locard's 1914 article, and others published soon afterwards, explained the theory of poroscopy and how the use of pores could supplement a fingerprint comparison by lending supporting data. Dr. Locard's study into the sweat pores of friction ridge skin is one more example of law enforcement personnel conducting research into fingerprint science (Locard, 1914, p 321).

In 1918, Harris Hawthorne Wilder and Bert Wentworth (Police Commissioner of Dover, NH) collaborated to publish *Personal Identification: Methods for the Identification of Individuals, Living or Dead*, exemplifying how, through joint effort, the fields of science and law enforcement could function together.

In their book, Wilder and Wentworth state, "The patterns of the friction skin are individual, and, taken together, impossible to duplicate in another individual. The separate ridges, too, show numerous details, which are also so individual that a small area of friction skin, taken even in the most featureless portion, cannot be matched by any other piece"

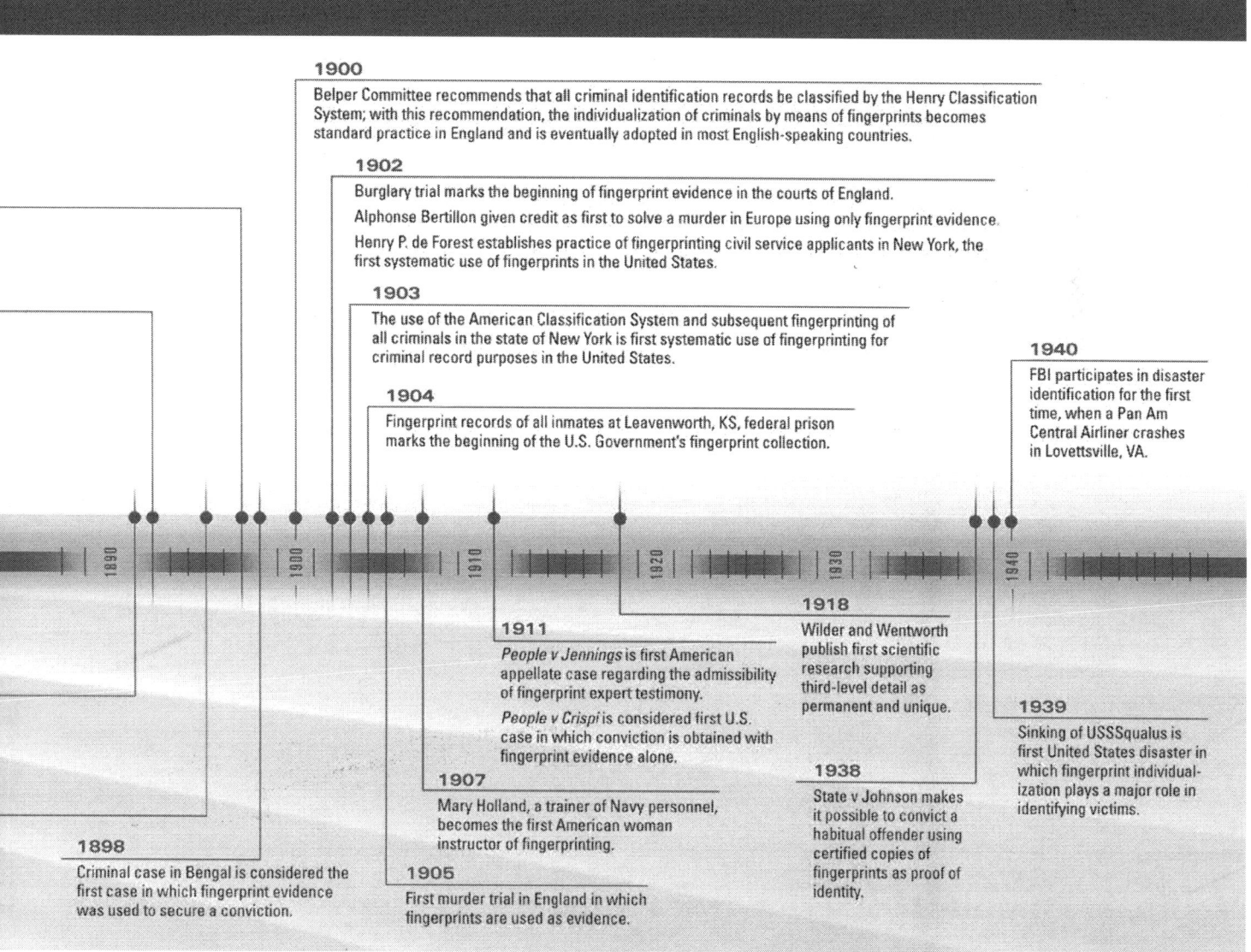

(Wilder and Wentworth, 1918, p 134). **This was the first scientific research supporting third level detail as permanent and unique.**

Because of the use of friction ridge skin as a means of identification, prisons throughout the United States acquired large fingerprint collections. The collections from Leavenworth and the files of the National Police Bureau of Criminal Identification were combined (810,188 records) on July 1, 1924, establishing the Identification Division in the U.S. Justice Department's Bureau of Investigation. The Identification Division was placed under the charge of a young assistant director of the Bureau named John Edgar Hoover (Cole, 2001, pp 238, 245; Myers, 1938, p 8). Eventually the Bureau of Investigation would become the Federal Bureau of Investigation (FBI), led by J. Edgar Hoover for many years.

In April 1939, the Supreme Court of Washington State upheld the decision of the Superior Court of King County on the conviction of a habitual offender. **This was a major step, because the case decision (*State* v *Johnson*, 1938) made it possible to convict a habitual offender using certified copies of fingerprints as proof of identity as opposed to requiring officials from other locations to testify to prior convictions to establish the individual as a habitual offender** (Myers, 1942, p 16).

Fingerprint individualization has also been used in noncriminal matters, such as the identification of disaster victims. **The first United States disaster in which fingerprint individualization played a major role was when the *USS Squalus* sank on May 23, 1939.** The submarine sank stern-first to the bottom of the ocean in 240 feet of water. James Herbert Taylor, Superintendent of the Identification Division, United States Navy, conducted the identification operation. All the bodies were identified through the use of fingerprints (Myers, 1942, p 18).

In 1940, a court in Hamilton, TX, declared the fingerprint method of identification to be valid. Newton Grice was convicted of burglary based on his fingerprint on a pane of glass removed from a door. Grice appealed the conviction on the grounds that the fingerprint evidence was insufficient to prove that he had been at the location and handled the item in question. The appellate judge, Thomas Beauchamp, proclaimed that since thousands of prints had been taken, classified, and filed in the United States, with none being the same as any other, there was more than enough proof that fingerprints are unique. The judge ruled that defense attorneys need to take the time to actually find prints that are in common in two different individuals rather than simply make the argument that it is possible. Judge Beauchamp upheld the conviction and stated that he felt that fingerprints are unique, and he placed the burden of proof on the defense to prove that fingerprints are not unique (Myers, 1942, pp 22–23).

Also in 1940, the FBI participated in disaster identification for the first time, when a Pan Am Central Airliner crashed in Lovettsville, VA, with an FBI agent and an FBI stenographer on board. The members of the FBI Identification Division's Single Fingerprint Section were dispatched to identify the bodies of the FBI employees. FBI fingerprint specialists helped identify the bodies of all 25 victims from the crash. This was the beginning of the FBI Disaster Squad, which still responds to disasters today.

Several years later, Dr. Harold Cummins (1893–1976) of Tulane University in New Orleans, LA, conducted a great deal of research on friction ridge skin. By examining fetuses in various stages of growth and health, Cummins made many contributions to the modern understanding of friction ridge skin. Cummins's book *Fingerprints, Palms, and Soles—An Introduction to Dermatoglyphics* (published in 1943 with his coauthor Charles Midlo) describes the formation and development of volar pads on the human fetus. Cummins notes that volar pad regression takes place almost concurrently with the beginning of friction ridge development; that the size, location, growth, and configuration of the volar pad affects the friction ridge patterns; and that disease or birth defects have an effect on the growth of volar pads (Cummins and Midlo, 1943, pp 178–186).

In 1952, Dr. Alfred R. Hale, also of Tulane University, published a thesis titled "Morphogenesis of the Volar Skin in the Human Fetus". By studying cross sections of fetal skin, Hale was able to describe the formation of friction ridges during fetal development and the differential growth of friction ridges, which is the major premise of friction ridge identification (Ashbaugh, 1999, p 53).

Salil Kumar Chatterjee (1905–1988) of Calcutta, India, published the book *Finger, Palm, and Sole Prints* in 1953, but Chatterjee is best known for his 1962 article "Edgeoscopy" (Chatterjee, 1962, pp 3–13), in which he described his theory of using specific ridge-edge shapes to supplement fingerprint individualization. He defined ridge shapes including straight, convex, peak, table, pocket, concave, and angle. Chatterjee believed that these edge shapes could be used to assist in making individualizations (Ashbaugh, 1999, p 160). (For more on Chatterjee, see Chapter 5.)

In 1976, Dr. Michio Okajima of Japan published the paper "Dermal and Epidermal Structures of the Volar Skin". The main contribution from his work is the study of incipient ridges, which appear as smaller ridges in friction ridge impressions (Ashbaugh, 1999, p 58).

In 1984, Brigitte Lacroix, Marie-Josephe Wolff-Quenot, and Katy Haffen of Strasbourg, France, published "Early Human Hand Morphology: An Estimation of Fetal Age". The paper discussed the three phases of the development of the hand (Ashbaugh, 1999, pp 58–59).

Dr. William Babler of Marquette University in Milwaukee, WI, published "Embryological Development of Epidermal Ridges and Their Configurations" in 1991. That paper reviewed prior work by other scientists and the research Babler performed relative to the "prenatal relationship between epidermal ridge dimension and bone dimension of the hand" (Babler, 1991, p 106).

1.7 Conclusion

Study, research, and experimentation have led to and supported fingerprints as a means of individualization and a forensic tool of incalculable value. The research and practical knowledge accumulated over the course of many centuries well supports the science.

As time moves forward and people continue to study any science, that science grows and becomes better understood. No one has said it better than Johann Wolfgang von Goethe: "The history of a science is the science itself" (Kline, 1980, p 7).

1.8 Reviewers

The reviewers critiquing this chapter were Debbie Benningfield, Mike Campbell, Christine L. Craig, Laura A. Hutchins, Ginger A. Kobliska, William F. Leo, Bridget Lewis, Charles Richardson, Michelle L. Snyder, and Juliet H. Wood.

1.9 References

Ashbaugh, D. R. *Quantitative-Qualitative Friction Ridge Analysis: An Introduction to Basic and Advanced Ridgeology;* CRC Press: Boca Raton, FL, 1999.

Babler, W. J. Embryologic Development of Epidermal Ridges and Their Configurations. In *Dermatoglyphics: Science in Transition;* Plato, C., Garruto, R. M., Schaumann, B. A., Eds.; Birth Defects: Original Article Series; March of Dimes: New York, 1991; pp 95–112.

Beavan, C. *Fingerprints: The Origins of Crime Detection and the Murder Case That Launched Forensic Science;* Hyperion: New York, 2001.

Berry, J.; Stoney, D. A. History and Development of Fingerprinting. In *Advances in Fingerprint Technology,* 2nd ed.; Lee, H. C., Gaensslen, R. E., Eds.; CRC Press: Boca Raton, FL, 2001; pp 1–40.

Caplan, J., Torpey, J. Eds. *Documenting Individual Identity: The Development of State Practices in the Modern World;* Princeton University Press: Princeton, NJ, 2001.

Chapel, C. E. *Fingerprinting: A Manual of Identification;* Coward McCann: New York, 1941.

Chatterjee, S. K. Edgeoscopy. *Finger Print and Ident. Mag.* 1962, *44* (3), 3–13.

Cole, S. A. *Suspect Identities: A History of Fingerprinting and Criminal Identification;* Harvard University Press: Cambridge, MA, 2001.

Cummins, H.; Midlo, C. *Finger Prints, Palms and Soles: An Introduction to Dermatoglyphics;* Dover: New York, 1943.

de Forest, H. P. The First Finger-Print File in the United States. *Finger Print and Ident. Mag.* 1938, 19, 16–20.

Faulds, H. On the Skin—Furrows of the Hand. *Nature* 1880, 22, 605.

Faulds, H. A Manual of Practical Dactylography. London: The "Police Review" Publishing Co., Ltd., 1922.

Felsher, I. M. A Quick Look at Dermatoglyphics. *Ident. News* 1962, *12* (7), 6–12.

Finger Print Publishing Association. *Finger Print Magazine* 1919, 1 (1), cover photo.

Galton, F. *Finger Prints;* MacMillan: New York, 1892.

Hale, A. Morphogenesis of Volar Skin in the Human Fetus. *Am. J. Anat.* 1952, *91* (1), 147–173.

Henry, E. R. *Classification and Uses of Fingerprints*, 7th ed.; H. M. Stationery Office: London, 1934.

Hepburn, D. The Papillary Ridges on the Hands and Feet of Monkeys and Men. *Scientific Transactions of the Royal Dublin Society* 1895, *5* (2), 525–537.

Herschel, W. J. *The Origin of Finger-Printing;* Oxford University Press: London, 1916.

Kingston, C. R.; Kirk, P. L. Historical Development and Evaluation of the "12 Point Rule" in Fingerprint Identification. *Int. Crim. Police Rev.* 1965, *20* (186), 62–69.

Kline, M. *Mathematics: The Loss of Certainty;* Oxford University Press: New York, 1980.

Lambourne, G. *The Fingerprint Story;* Harrap: London, 1984.

Laufer, B. *History of the Finger-Print System;* Smithsonian Institution: Washington, DC, 1912.

Locard, E. La Preuve Judiciaire par les Empreintes Digitales (The Legal Evidence by the Fingerprints). *De Médecine Légale et de Psychologie Normale et Pathologique (Of Forensic Medicine and of Normal and Pathological Psychology)* 1914, *29*, 321.

Locy, W. A. *Biology and its Makers;* Henry Holt and Co.: New York, 1908; p 204.

McClaughry, M. W. History of the Introduction of the Bertillon System Into the United States. *Finger Print Magazine* 1922, *3* (10), 4.

McGinnis, P. D. *American System of Fingerprint Classification;* New York State Department of Correction, Division of Identification: New York, 1963.

Myers, H. J. II. The First Complete and Authentic History of Identification in the United States. *Finger Print and Ident. Mag.* 1938, *20* (4), 3–31.

Myers, H. J. II. Supplemental History of Identification in the United States. *Finger Print and Ident. Mag.* 1942, *25* (6), 3–28.

New Scotland Yard. *Fingerprint History: A Synopsis of the Development of the System of Fingerprint Identification with Particular Reference to New Scotland Yard;* Metropolitan Police, New Scotland Yard: London, 1990.

Nickell, J. The Two Will Wests—A New Verdict. *J. Police Sci. and Admin.* 1980, *8* (4), 406–413.

Pearson, K. *The Life, Letters and Labours of Francis Galton, Volume I: Birth 1822 to Marriage 1853.* London: Cambridge University Press, 1914.

People v *Jennings* (*State of Illinois* v *Jennings*), 252 Ill. 534, 96 N.E. 1077 (1911).

Rhodes, H. *Alphonse Bertillon: Father of Scientific Detection;* Abelard-Schuman: London, 1956.

Sodhi, G. S.; Kaur, J. Indian Civilization and the Science of Fingerprinting. *Indian J. of Traditional Knowledge* 2003a, *2* (2), 126–136.

Sodhi, G. S.; Kaur, J. World's First Conviction on Fingerprint Identification. *National Crime Records Bureau Gazette* 2003b, *15* (2), 1–3.

State v *Johnson* (*State of Washington* v *Johnson*), 194 Wash. 438, 78 P. 2d 561 (1938).

Twain, M. *Life on the Mississippi;* James R. Osgood & Co.: Boston, 1883. (U.S. edition).

Twain, M. *The Tragedy of Pudd'nhead Wilson;* C.L. Webster: New York, 1884.

Whipple, I. L. The Ventral Surface of the Mammalian Chiridium. *Zeitschrift für Morphologie und Anthropologie (Journal of Morphology and Anthropology)* 1904, *7*, 261–368.

Wilder, H. H.; Wentworth, B. *Personal Identification;* The Gorham Press: Boston, 1918.

Xiang-Xin, Z.; Chun-Ge, L. The Historical Application of Hand Prints in Chinese Litigation. *J. Forensic Ident.* 1988, *38* (6), 277–284.

1.10 Additional Information

Åström, P.; Eriksson, S. A. Fingerprints and Archaeology. In *Studies in Mediterranean Archaeology;* Paul Åströms förlag: Göteborg, Sweden, 1980.

Cole, S. A. Grandfathering Evidence: Fingerprint Admissibility Rulings from Jennings to Llera Plaza and Back Again. *Am. Crim. L. Rev.* 2004, *41* (3), 1189–1276.

Kevles, D. J. *In the Name of Eugenics, Genetics and the Uses of Human Heredity;* Knopf: New York, 1985.

CHAPTER 2

ANATOMY AND PHYSIOLOGY OF ADULT FRICTION RIDGE SKIN

Alice V. Maceo

CONTENTS

- 3 2.1 Introduction
- 3 2.2 Anatomy
- 14 2.3 Physiology
- 16 2.4 Persistence of the Friction Ridge Skin
- 24 2.5 Conclusion
- 25 2.6 Reviewers
- 25 2.7 References

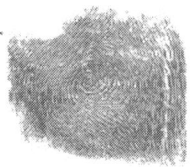

CHAPTER 2

ANATOMY AND PHYSIOLOGY OF ADULT FRICTION RIDGE SKIN

Alice V. Maceo

2.1 Introduction

The anatomy and physiology of the friction ridge skin form the basis for several critical elements that underlie the examination process. The anatomy and physiology explain how the features of the skin persist, how the features of the skin age, how the skin responds to injury, and why scars that form are unique. Another element explained by the structure of the skin is the mechanics of touch. Understanding how the friction ridge skin reacts when it contacts a surface can provide valuable assistance during the examination of friction ridge impressions.

2.2 Anatomy

2.2.1 Outer Morphology of Friction Ridge Skin

The outer morphology of the friction ridge skin is a direct reflection of its function. The ridges and sweat pores allow the hands and feet to grasp surfaces firmly, and the creases allow the skin to flex. Ridges, creases, and mature scars of the friction ridge skin are durable morphological features.

Warts, wrinkles, blisters, cuts, and calluses may also appear on the friction ridge skin and are frequently transient morphological features. The anatomy and physiology of a feature determine whether the feature is durable or transient in nature. Figure 2–1 is an image of a left palm displaying the normal morphology of friction ridge skin.

2.2.2 General Anatomy of Skin

The skin is an organ composed of three anatomical layers: epidermis, dermis, and hypodermis. These anatomical layers together function to provide the body with a protective barrier, body temperature regulation, sensation, excretion,

CHAPTER 2 | Anatomy and Physiology of Adult Friction Ridge Skin

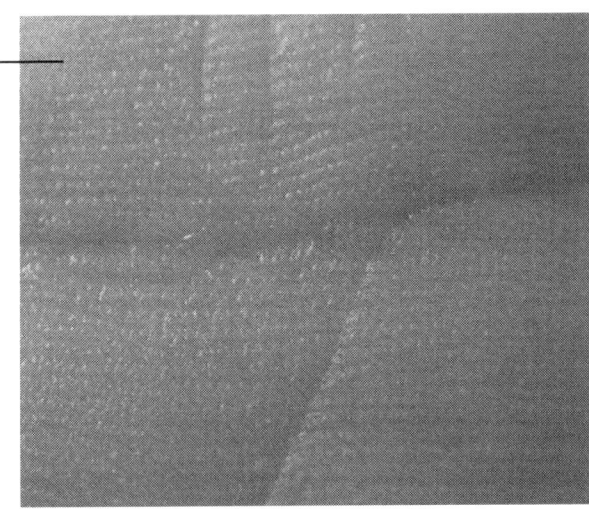

FIGURE 2–1

Friction ridge skin of the left palm.

immunity, a blood reservoir, and synthesis of vitamin D (Tortora and Grabowski, 1993, p 127).

The outer layer of skin is the epidermis. The epidermis prevents water loss through evaporation, acts as a receptor organ, and provides a protective barrier for the underlying tissues. Melanocytes, the pigment-producing cells of the epidermis, play a key role in the protective barrier. The pigmentation produced by the melanocytes shields the DNA of the keratinocytes (primary cell type of the epidermis) from the sun's harmful rays. Additionally, the melanocytes are responsible for the synthesis of vitamin D (Freinkel and Woodley, 2001, p 120).

The dermis is a layer of connective tissue that supports the epidermis. It is a network of cells, fibers, blood vessels, and gelatinous material that provides structural support and nourishment for the epidermis. The dermis serves as a blood reserve and participates in sensory reception and temperature regulation.

The hypodermis lies under the dermis and is a loose connective tissue that contains a pad of adipose cells (fat) that contour the body and serve as an energy reserve. Fibers link the epidermis to the dermis and the dermis to the hypodermis.

The only skin appendage of the friction ridge skin is the eccrine sweat gland. Although sweat glands are distributed over almost the entire skin surface, the friction ridge skin has the highest concentration of eccrine glands, 2500–3000/2.5 cm^2 (Freinkel and Woodley, 2001, p 49). The sweat glands of the friction ridge skin are also the largest on the body. Eccrine sweat glands participate in temperature regulation by secreting sweat and assist in the excretion of metabolic waste (e.g., urea) (Junqueira and Carneiro, 2003, p 369).

2.2.3 Structure of Friction Ridge Skin

The ridges and furrows on the surface of the friction ridge skin are firmly rooted in the dermis by primary ridges (under-the-surface ridges) and secondary ridges (under the valleys). Figure 2–2 illustrates the structure of friction ridge skin. The primary and secondary ridges are interlocked with the dermis to provide support and strength to the friction ridge skin. Additionally, sweat glands extend from the primary ridges and are anchored in the dermis or hypodermis.

2.2.4 Epidermis

The epidermis is described as a "stratified, continually renewing epithelium that exhibits progressive differentiation (keratinization, cornification) in a basal to superficial direction" (Freinkel and Woodley, 2001, p 19). In other words, the epidermis is a layered tissue that must constantly replace the cells leaving the surface. New cells are generated in the basal layer and pushed toward the surface. As the cells move toward the surface, they undergo sequential changes in chemical composition.

The epidermis is composed of several different types of cells: keratinocytes, melanocytes, Langerhans cells, and Merkel cells. The keratinocytes are the cells that undergo differentiation and are lost at the surface. The epidermis is the protective barrier; it is imperative that the skin balance the number of new keratinocytes created with the number of keratinocytes leaving the surface. This balance is achieved by communication and adhesion.

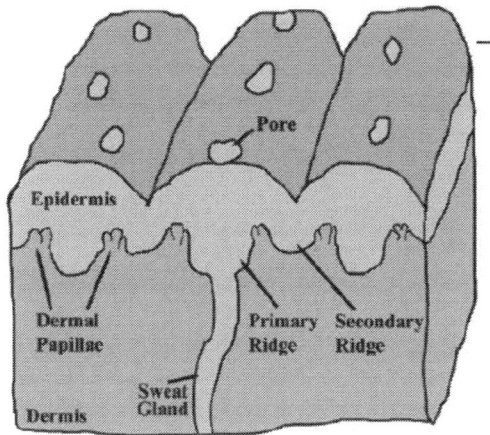

FIGURE 2–2

Structure of friction ridge skin.

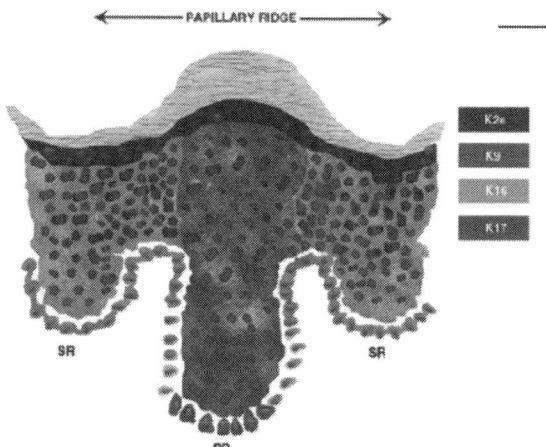

FIGURE 2–3

Distribution of keratin in the primary (PR) and secondary (SR) ridges. Keratin K9 is predominantly expressed in the suprabasal layer and stratum spinosum of the primary ridges. Keratin K17 is expressed in clusters in the basal layer of the primary ridges. Keratin K16 is expressed in the secondary ridges. (Artwork by Brandon Smithson, re-drawn from Swensson et al. (1998), p 773.)

2.2.5 Keratinocytes

The primary cell of the epidermis is the keratinocyte. Keratinocytes account for 90–95% of the epidermal cells (Freinkel and Woodley, 2001, p 19). Even though keratinocytes change in chemical composition as they reach the surface, all keratinocytes are distinguishable by the presence of keratin intermediate filaments.

Keratin is a durable protein organized into bundles (filaments) that extend throughout the cell and provide structural support. Keratin reinforces the skin cells so that they do not break when subjected to physical stress. There are about 20 varieties of keratin distributed throughout the epidermis, designated K1 through K20 (Freinkel and Woodley, 2001, p 20). The keratinocytes of the friction ridge skin express keratins not expressed elsewhere on the body, specifically K9, K6, and K16 (Swennson et al., 1998, p 770).

Keratinocytes of the friction ridge skin also express a more complex pattern of keratin distribution than the rest of the skin. K9 is found only in the keratinocytes above the basal layer of the primary ridges (Swennson et al., 1998, p 770). The basal keratinocytes in the deepest part of the primary ridges express K17 (Swennson et al., 1998, p 771). The basal keratinocytes along the vertical segments of the primary ridges express K6 (Swennson et al., 1998, p 770). K16 is found only in the keratinocytes of the secondary ridges and in the keratinocytes above the dermal papillae (Swennson et al., 1998, p 771). Figure 2–3 illustrates the keratin distribution in the friction ridge skin.

The differences in the keratin produced and distributed across the friction ridge skin are attributed to the greater amount of mechanical stress on the friction ridge skin (Swennson et al., 1998, p 767). The keratin produced in the

CHAPTER 2 | Anatomy and Physiology of Adult Friction Ridge Skin

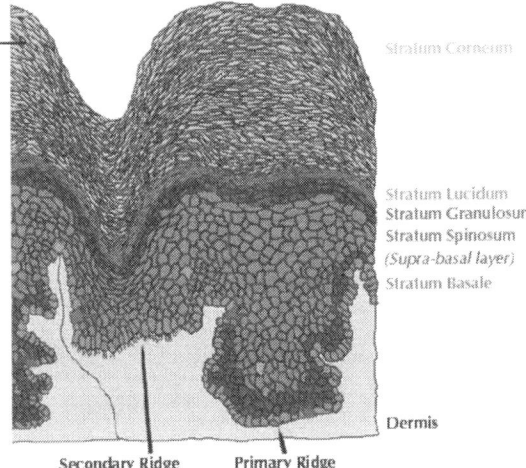

FIGURE 2–4

Layers of the epidermis.

cells of the primary ridges (K9) is more durable than the keratin produced in the secondary ridges (K16). From a mechanical standpoint, the surface ridges withstand most of the compression when the friction ridge skin touches a surface, thereby necessitating enhanced durability. The more pliable keratin produced in the secondary ridges allows the furrows to act as a hinge between the stiffer surface ridges (Swennson et al., 1998, p 772).

2.2.6 Layers of the Epidermis

Figure 2–4 is a color-coded illustration of the five layers of keratinocytes in the friction ridge skin epidermis: stratum basale, stratum spinosum, stratum granulosum, stratum lucidum, and stratum corneum. There is an informal layer, the suprabasal layer, between the stratum basale and the stratum spinosum in the primary ridges.

Nearly all the cells illustrated in Figure 2–4 are keratinocytes. The only exceptions are the occasional brown, grey, and green cells that represent the melanocytes, Langerhans cells, and Merkel cells, respectively.

The layers of the epidermis are named on the basis of microscopic appearance of the keratinocytes in slide preparations. The keratinocytes change in appearance and composition as they are pushed toward the surface and undergo differentiation. During the stages of differentiation, the cells become keratinized (filled with keratin).

2.2.6.1 Stratum Basale. The stratum basale is the innermost layer of the epidermis and consists of a single layer of keratinocytes with occasional melanocytes and Merkel cells.

The keratinocytes in the basal layer continually divide and are the wellspring of all the keratinocytes in the upper layers.

Figure 2–5 is an image of two adjacent basal keratinocytes. Each keratinocyte contains a large nucleus. The nucleus consists of a lighter-stained chromatin and a darker-stained nucleolus. Chromatin is the active DNA specific for that particular cell type (keratinocyte in this instance). The nucleolus is compacted DNA responsible for synthesizing ribosomes. Ribosomes are structures in the cell that help build proteins. The basal cells are connected to the basement membrane zone by hemidesmosomes. The hemidesmosomes link the basal cells to the dermis via the basal lamina. The basal lamina is broken down into two regions: lamina lucida and lamina densa. Desmosomes and focal tight junctions attach the basal keratinocytes to each other. There are small spaces between the cells. These intercellular spaces allow nutrients and signals that have passed from the dermis via the basement membrane zone to diffuse throughout the keratinocytes of the basal layer.

Basal Cell Mitosis. When a basal keratinocyte divides, it undergoes mitosis. Mitosis is the mechanism by which a cell replicates its DNA, the two copies of the DNA migrate to different sides of the cell, and the cell physically separates into two. Each cell contains a complete copy of the DNA. When a basal keratinocyte divides in the epidermis, the original cell remains in the basal layer (cell A in Figure 2–6) and the newly generated cell sits on top of it (cell B in Figure 2–6). When the basal keratinocytes divide again, the first generated cell (B) is displaced into the stratum spinosum by the newly generated cell (cell C in Figure

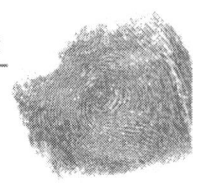

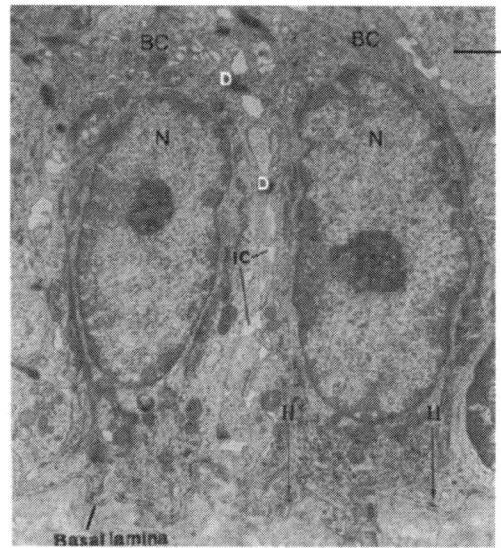

FIGURE 2–5

Two adjacent basal cells (BC), each containing a large nucleus (N). The basal lamina (lamina lucida and lamina densa) lies just below the plasma membrane of the basal keratinocytes. Hemidesmosomes (H) occur regularly along the plasma membrane. Intercellular spaces (IC) are spaces between cells where the cells are not attached by desmosomes (D). Magnification = 2680 X. (Reprinted with permission from Montagna and Parakkal (1974), p 28.)

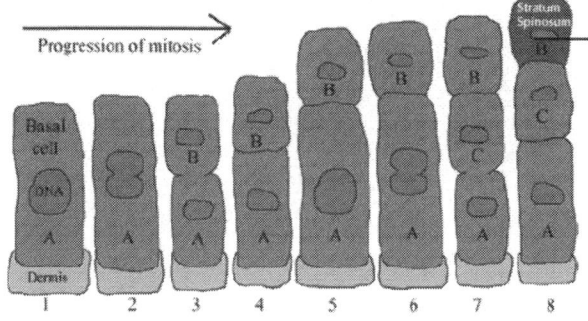

FIGURE 2–6

Sequence of mitosis of basal keratinocytes: (1) cell A replicates its DNA; (2) the DNA is pulled to opposing ends of the cell; (3) cell A divides; (4) cell B is created; (5) cell A replicates its DNA again; (6) the DNA is pulled to opposing ends of cell A; (7) cell A divides to create cell C; (8) cell C pushes previously generated cell B upward, where it begins to differentiate and becomes part of the stratum spinosum.

2–6). The cycle continues, each new cell pushing the older cells toward the surface of the epidermis.

Basement Membrane Zone. The keratinocytes of the stratum basale are associated with the dermis via the basement membrane zone. The basement membrane zone contains elements of both the epidermis and dermis. In addition to providing structural support to the skin, the basement membrane zone is the filter through which nutrients pass from the dermal blood vessels to the basal keratinocytes (Freinkel and Woodley, 2001, p 133).

The basement membrane zone includes the portion of the plasma membrane of the basal keratinocytes that sits on the dermal–epidermal junction. As shown in Figure 2–7, the basal keratinocytes have specialized attachment plaques, termed hemidesmosomes, that project anchoring filaments down toward the dermis (Freinkel and Woodley, 2001, p 134). The area just below the basal cells containing these anchoring filaments is called the lamina lucida.

The dermis contributes the lamina densa and sublamina densa fibrillar zone to the basement membrane zone. The lamina densa contains protein (e.g., collagen fibers). The filaments of the hemidesmosomes in the lamina lucida are interwoven with the fibers of the lamina densa (Freinkel and Woodley, 2001, p 136). The sublamina densa fibrillar zone is the uppermost portion of the dermis and contains elastic fibers, additional collagen fibers, and anchoring plaques (Freinkel and Woodley, 2001, p 145). The fibers and anchoring plaques of the sublamina densa fibrillar zone are interwoven with the fibers of the lamina densa.

The hemidesmosomes of the basal keratinocytes and the interlocking fibers throughout the basement membrane zone prevent the basal cells from migrating. The basal keratinocytes are locked down to their position in the epidermis.

Anchoring Cell Junctions: Desmosomes and Focal Tight Junctions. The keratinocytes of the basal layer, and throughout the layers of the epidermis, are tightly

FIGURE 2–7

Basement membrane zone.

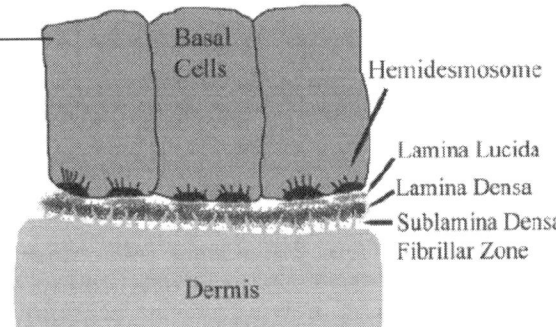

FIGURE 2–8

SEM and schematic of a desmosome linking adjacent skin cells of a salamander. Magnification = 5500 X. (Reprinted with permission from Wolfe (1993), p 257.)

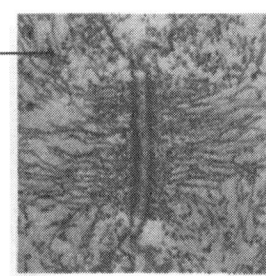 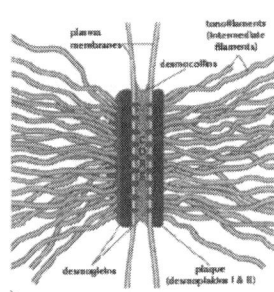

bound to one another via desmosomes (Junqueira and Carneiro, 2003, p 370) and focal tight junctions (Tortora and Grabowski, 1993, p 97). Desmosomes are round plaques that bind together the plasma membranes of adjacent cells. Figure 2–8 shows (a) a scanning electron microscope (SEM) image and (b) a schematic of a desmosome. Keratin fibers extend from the desmosome plaque to the interior of each cell, creating an interior scaffold that supports the cell (Wan et al., 2003, p 378).

Desmosomes exist between cells throughout the entire epidermis (friction ridge skin and nonfriction ridge skin). There is, however, variation. Desmosomes vary in size, depending on the body location of the skin. The desmosomes between the keratinocytes of the friction ridge skin are larger than those of nonfriction ridge skin (Wan et al., 2003, p 384). Along with larger desmosomes, the keratinocytes of the friction ridge skin also have a greater density of keratin (Wan et al., 2003, p 379). The increase in the size of the desmosomes and density of keratin indicates that desmosomes are site specific, depending on the amount of physical stress the particular area of skin must endure (Wan et al., 2003, p 386).

Desmosomes also show variation within the layers of the epidermis. Desmosomes undergo modifications as the cells progress outward from the basal layer of the epidermis. In the friction ridge skin, the desmosomes increase in size as the cells enter the stratum spinosum (Wan et al., 2003, p 385). Desmosomes are continually reinforced as the cells are pushed toward the surface. Upon reaching the outer portion of the stratum corneum, the desmosomes are broken down to release the cells from the surface (Freinkel and Woodley, 2001, p 25).

Focal tight junctions (Figure 2–9) are small "spot welds" of the cells' surfaces (Flaxman and Nelson, 1974, p 329). The cell membranes of adjacent cells are fused together, eliminating intercellular space. Focal tight junctions provide additional anchoring between cells and provide a low-resistance electrical pathway for communication between cells (Cavoto and Flaxman, 1972, p 373).

Basal Cell Heterogeneity. The basal keratinocytes of the primary ridges are structurally different from the basal cells of the secondary ridges. The basal keratinocytes of the primary ridges contain less keratin than the basal cells of the secondary ridges. The junction of the basal cells of the

Anatomy and Physiology of Adult Friction Ridge Skin | CHAPTER 2

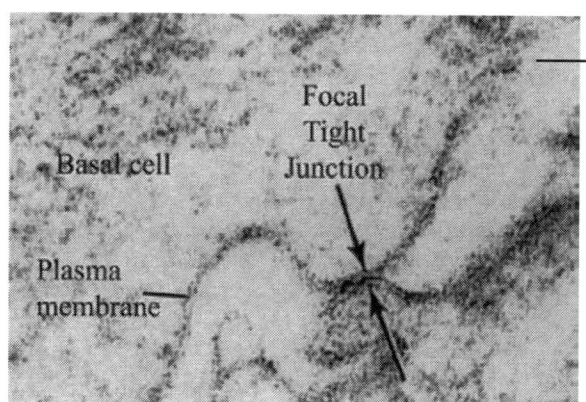

FIGURE 2–9

Electron micrograph of a focal tight junction between adjacent keratinocytes.

Magnification = 12500 X. (Reprinted with permission from Cavoto and Flaxman (1972), p 372.)

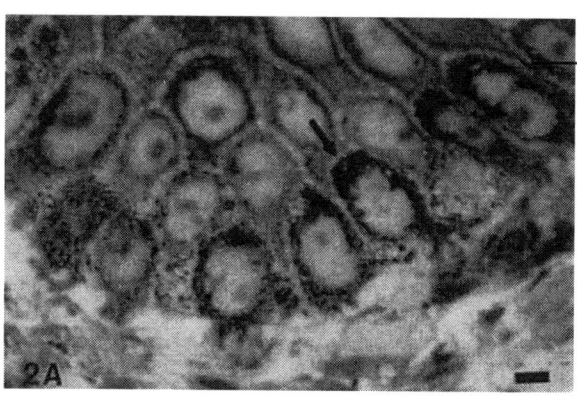

FIGURE 2–10

Basal cells of the primary ridges. Scale bar is 10 µm. (Reprinted with permission from Lavker and Sun (1983), p 123.)

primary ridges with the basement membrane is slightly undulated (Figure 2–10), whereas basal cells of the secondary ridges contain long projections that extend deep into the dermis (Figure 2–11) (Lavker and Sun, 1982, p 1240).

The differences in the structure of the basal cells in the primary and secondary ridges explain their differences in function. The basal cells of secondary ridges, with long projections into the dermis, serve an anchoring function (Lavker and Sun, 1982, p 1239). The basal cells of the primary ridges have a morphology similar to stem cells and can be induced to multiply by tissue demand or injury (Lavker and Sun, 1982, p 1239). The basal cells also differ in the rate at which they multiply. The basal cells of the secondary ridges divide more frequently than the primary ridges because the basal cells of the primary ridges give rise to cells that divide in the suprabasal layer.

Suprabasal Layer. The basal keratinocytes of the secondary ridges continuously divide—each basal cell dividing to push one cell at a time into the stratum spinosum. The basal cells of the primary ridges behave a little differently.

The basal keratinocyte of the primary ridge divides to create a new cell. This new cell does not immediately enter the stratum spinosum and commit to differentiation. The newly generated cell, termed a transient amplifying cell, undergoes a couple of cell divisions while it sits in the suprabasal layer (Lavker and Sun, 1983, p 121). After cell divisions are complete, the transient amplifying cells are pushed upward into the stratum spinosum and begin differentiation. More cells are produced in the primary ridges than in the secondary ridges because of the transient amplifying cells. The cells of the primary ridges maintain the surface ridges, where more cells are needed because of greater abrasion.

2.2.6.2 Stratum Spinosum. As the keratinocytes are pushed toward the surface, they begin to undergo differentiation. The cells become polyhedral in shape and desmosomes (cell junctions) are reinforced. Keratin production is increased, and the keratin filaments are organized concentrically around the nucleus and extend into the desmosomes (Freinkel and Woodley, 2001, p 23). New

CHAPTER 2 Anatomy and Physiology of Adult Friction Ridge Skin

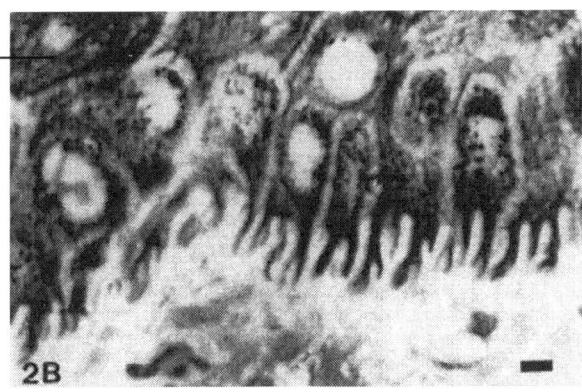

FIGURE 2–11

Basal cells of the secondary ridges. Scale bar is 10 μm. (Reprinted with permission from Lavker and Sun (1983), p 123.)

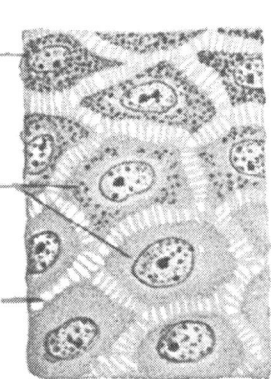

FIGURE 2–12

Cells of the stratum spinosum and stratum granulosum (with keratohyalin granules). Magnification = 1400 X. (Reprinted with permission from Eroschenko (1993), p 127.)

structures, lamellar granules, appear in the cells as the cells are pushed toward the limit of the stratum spinosum. Lamellar granules are pockets of lipids that first appear in the stratum spinosum but do not become active until the cells reach the stratum granulosum (Freinkel and Woodley, 2001, p 24). Figure 2–12 is a microscope slide preparation of the keratinocytes of the stratum spinosum and stratum granulosum. The stratum spinosum is so named because of the spiny appearance of the cells in microscope slide preparations. During the process of making the slide, the cells dehydrate, causing them to shrink away from one another. The spines are where the desmosomes are still holding the cells together.

2.2.6.3 Stratum Granulosum. As the cells are pushed toward the surface, they continue structural and chemical modification. Keratinocytes entering the stratum granulosum contain characteristic keratohyalin granules (Figure 2-12). The keratinocytes are programmed to fill with keratin; the keratohyalin granules contain proteins (profilaggrin, keratin, and loricrin) that facilitate the process (Freinkel and Woodley, 2001, p 23). The lamellar granules become active as the cells reach the upper portion of the stratum granulosum. The lamellar granules release their lipid content

into the space between the cells. The lipids coat the cells, providing the skin with a hydrophobic barrier (Freinkel and Woodley, 2001, p 24).

2.2.6.4 Stratum Lucidum. The keratinocytes undergo an abrupt transition to the stratum lucidum. The cells are keratinized and have completed their programmed cell death (Freinkel and Woodley, 2001, p 24). Although the cells are no longer living, chemical activity continues inside the cells as the final modifications are made to the keratin.

2.2.6.5 Stratum Corneum. With layer upon layer of nonviable, terminally differentiated keratinocytes, the stratum corneum is the significant epidermal layer that allows skin to act as a major barrier. The arrangement of keratinocytes is described as a "brick-and-mortar model". The keratin-filled cells (bricks) are surrounded by the lipids (mortar) secreted while the cells were in the stratum granulosum (Freinkel and Woodley, 2001, p 25). Although they are dead, the cells of the stratum corneum continue to undergo modification as they are pushed from the deeper portion of the stratum corneum to the surface of the skin. The cells in the deeper portion of the stratum corneum are thicker and have more densely packed keratin, a weaker cell

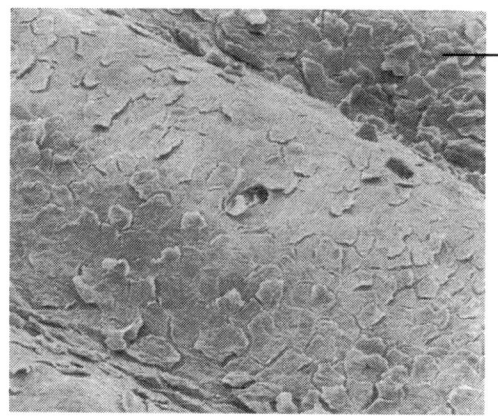

FIGURE 2–13

Surface of the friction ridges showing the cells shedding from the surface. (Reprinted with permission from Montagna and Parakkal (1974), p 25.)

membrane, and more cell-to-cell attachments (Freinkel and Woodley, 2001, p 25). As the cells are pushed toward the surface, the cell membrane becomes more rigid and the desmosomes are degraded. These changes allow the cells to shed when they reach the surface (Figure 2–13).

2.2.7 Nonkeratinocytes

Communication of the keratinocytes with the melanocytes, Langerhans cells, and Merkel cells is necessary for the skin to function properly.

Melanocytes produce the pigments that are deposited into the keratinocytes. This pigment, melanin, protects the genetic material of the keratinocytes from ultraviolet damage (Junqueira and Carneiro, 2003, p 371). Melanocytes reside in the basal layer of the epidermis and, in addition to providing the surrounding keratinocytes with melanin, produce vitamin D.

The Langerhans cells are an extension of the body's immune system. Upon exposure to invading bacteria, Langerhans cells initiate an alert that causes the body to recruit more aggressive immune cells (T cells) to attack the invaders (Freinkel and Woodley, 2001, p 30).

The Merkel cells are an extension of the nervous system and participate in the transmission of the sensation of touch: "shape, size, and texture of objects and two-point discrimination" (Dillion et al., 2001, p 577). Merkel cells occur sporadically in the basal layer of the epidermis and are associated with free nerve endings from the dermis.

2.2.8 Dermis

2.2.8.1 Papillary Dermis. The dermis is the connective tissue that supports the epidermis and binds it to the hypodermis. The dermis is composed of two layers: the papillary layer and the reticular layer. The outer papillary layer is a loose connective tissue containing anchoring fibrils and numerous dermal cells. The anchoring fibrils secure the dermis to the epidermis via the basement membrane zone. The papillary layer of the dermis forms the dermal papillae.

2.2.8.2 Dermal Papillae. Dermal papillae are malleable, peglike projections of the papillary dermis between the primary and secondary ridges. The malleable nature of the dermal papillae is important because the epidermal–dermal junction remodels with age and in response to sheering stress on the surface of the skin (Misumi and Akiyoshi, 1984, p 53; Chacko and Vaidya, 1968, p 107). During the remodeling, the epidermis forms sheets of tissue that cross-link adjacent primary and secondary ridges. These sheets of tissue are called anastomoses. As the epidermal anastamoses form, the dermal papillae are molded into increasingly more complex structures (Hale, 1952, p 153). The detail of Figure 2–14 illustrates the dermal papillae and anastomoses. The formation of dermal papillae and epidermal anastomoses increases the surface area of attachment between the epidermis and dermis, thereby increasing the bond between the epidermis and dermis.

2.2.8.3 Reticular Dermis. The reticular dermis is a compact connective tissue containing large bundles of collagen and elastic fibers. The organization of these fibers provides the dermis with strength and resilience (Freinkel and Woodley, 2001, p 38). The reticular dermis is connected to the hypodermis by a network of fibers.

2.2.8.4 Circulatory System of the Dermis. There are two plexuses of arterial blood vessels in the dermis. One plexus lies between the papillary and reticular dermis and the other between the reticular dermis and the hypodermis

FIGURE 2–14

Cross section of friction ridge skin with detail of the epidermis separated from the dermis to display the dermal papillae and complementary epidermal anastomoses.

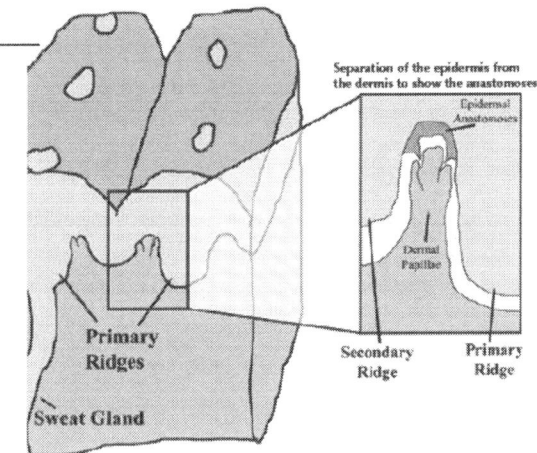

FIGURE 2–15

Circulation system of the skin. (Adapted with permission from Freinkel and Woodley (2001), p 177.)

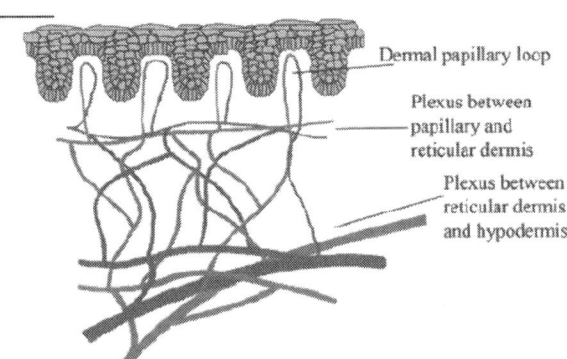

(Junqueira and Carneiro, 2003, p 376). Capillaries extend from the arterial plexus and into the dermal papillae to form the dermal papillary loop (Figure 2–15) (Freinkel and Woodley, 2001, p 38).

Blood passes from the arterial capillaries in the dermal papillae to the venous capillaries. Veins are organized into three plexuses: one associated with each arterial plexus and a third plexus in the middle of the reticular dermis (Junqueira and Carneiro, 2003, p 376).

2.2.8.5 Nervous System of the Dermis. A vast network of sensory and autonomic nerve branches innervates the dermis. The autonomic nerve network is responsible for controlling blood flow and glandular secretions (sweat). The sensory system contains receptors for sensations: touch, temperature, pain, and itch (Freinkel and Woodley, 2001, p 153). The dermis participates in sensory perception via free nerve endings, Meissner corpuscles, Ruffini corpuscles, and Pacinian corpuscles. Free nerve endings and Meissner corpuscles are found in the dermal papillae. Free nerve endings are found in each dermal papilla and provide a rapid response to stimuli (Freinkel and Woodley, 2001, p 157). Meissner corpuscles (Figure 2-16) are found in about every fourth papilla and function as touch receptors (Freinkel and Woodley, 2001, p 160). Pacinian and Ruffini corpuscles are located throughout the dermis and also function in the transmission of pressure (Freinkel and Woodley, 2001, p 158).

2.2.9 Sweat Glands

Although the skin produces several appendages (e.g., hair, nails, sebaceous glands), the eccrine sweat gland is the only appendage of the friction ridge skin. Eccrine sweat glands are found all over the body surface and function primarily in thermoregulation. The sweat glands do not function individually but rather as groups or simultaneously

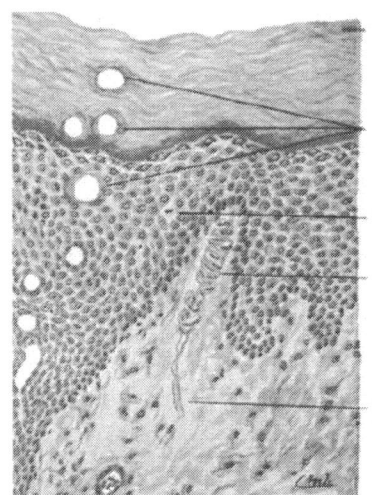

FIGURE 2–16

Section of palm skin showing Meissner's corpuscle in a dermal papilla. Magnification = 100 X. (Reprinted with permission from Eroschenko (1993), p 127.)

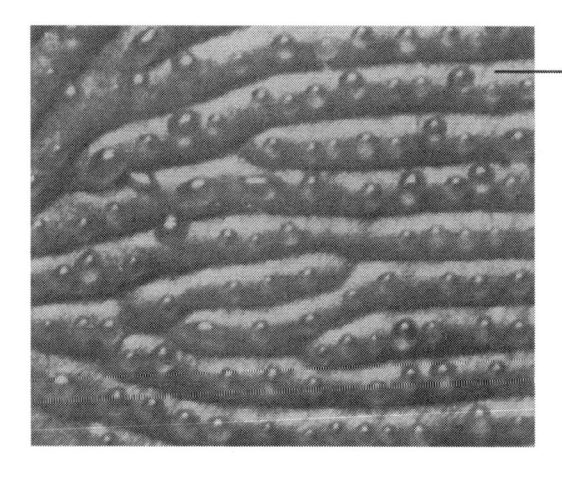

FIGURE 2–17

Sweat emitting from the pores on the friction ridge skin. (Reprinted with permission from Montagna and Parakkal (1974), p 381.)

over the entire surface of the body (Freinkel and Woodley, 2001, p 47). The sweat glands of the palms and soles are larger, more active, and denser than in any other area of skin. Figure 2–17 is an image of the friction ridge skin sweating.

Eccrine sweat glands are classified as simple tubular glands whose ducts open at the skin surface (Junqueira and Carneiro, 2003, p 380). As shown in Figure 2–18, the coiled secretory portion of the gland is embedded in the dermis or hypodermis, and the duct extends through the epidermis. The fluid secreted by the eccrine sweat glands is predominantly water (99.0–99.5%) (Freinkel and Woodley, 2001, p 71). The remaining constituents of sweat include sodium chloride, potassium, ammonia, urea, lactate, uric acid, creatinine and creatine, amino acids, sugars, immunoglobulin A, epidermal growth factor, and select hormones, enzymes, and vitamins (Freinkel and Woodley, 2001, p 71).

2.2.10 Hypodermis

Beneath the fibrous reticular dermis there is an abrupt transition to the adipose tissue of the hypodermis. Adipose (fat) tissue serves as an energy reserve, cushions the skin, contours the body, and allows for mobility of the skin over underlying structures (Freinkel and Woodley, 2001, p 39). The dermis and hypodermis are physically connected through interlocking fibers and share blood vessel and nerve networks (Freinkel and Woodley, 2001, p 39). The primary cell of the hypodermis is the adipocyte. Adipocytes are organized in lobules by fibrous connective tissue and store the subcutaneous fat.

FIGURE 2–18

Sweat gland. (Reprinted with permission from Eroschenko (1993), p 129.)

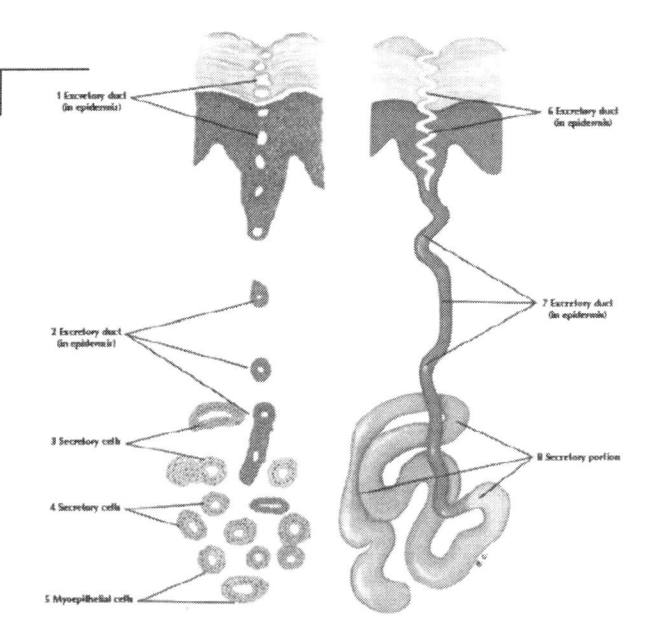

2.3 Physiology

The epidermis exists in a dynamic, steady state. Cells lost at the surface must be replaced (dynamic) in order for the skin to maintain (steady) its protective barrier (state). The concept of keeping things the same despite constant input and output of materials and energy is referred to as homeostasis. Homeostasis is defined as "the condition in which the body's internal environment remains relatively constant, within physiological limits" (Tortora and Grabowski, 1993, p 9). Homeostasis is critical to the functioning of all organisms. Homeostasis of the skin is achieved through physical attachments and the careful regulation of cell production in the stratum basale via cell communication.

2.3.1 Physical Attachments

There are structural features of the overall skin and of the skin cells that maintain the structure of the epidermis (even though skin cells are always sloughing at the surface). There are three levels of attachment in the friction ridge skin: the primary/secondary ridge attachment with anastomoses, the basement membrane zone, and cell-to-cell attachments.

2.3.1.1 Primary and Secondary Ridges. The first level of attachment is the topography at the junction of the epidermis and dermis. The alternating system of primary and secondary ridges on the bottom of the epidermis provides general structural support for the surface ridges and furrows. The sweat glands of the primary ridges are firmly attached in the dermis or hypodermis. Additional reinforcement of this system is provided by dermal papillae and epidermal anastomoses.

2.3.1.2 Basement Membrane Zone. The second level of attachment is the basement membrane. The basement membrane is a fibrous sheet that attaches the basal keratinocytes of the epidermis to the underlying dermis. The basement membrane is generated by the basal keratinocytes of the epidermis and the fibroblasts of the dermis. The basal cells of the epidermis have specialized attachment plaques, termed hemidesmosomes, which project fibers down toward the dermis. The dermis projects anchoring fibers back up toward the epidermis. These fibers originating from the epidermal basal cells and from the dermis are interwoven to create the fibrous sheet that locks the epidermis to the dermis. The hemidesmosomes and interlocking fibers prevent the basal cells from migrating. The basal keratinocytes are locked down to their position in the epidermis.

2.3.1.3 Cell-to-Cell Attachments. The third level of attachment consists of the cell-to-cell attachments of the keratinocytes throughout the layers of the epidermis. Desmosomes and focal tight junctions attach the keratinocytes to one another. Desmosomes are reinforced as the cells move from the basal layer to the surface. Upon reaching the outer portion of the stratum corneum, the desmosomes and focal tight junctions are broken down to release the cells from the surface.

FIGURE 2–19

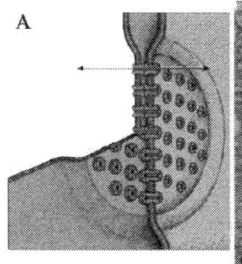

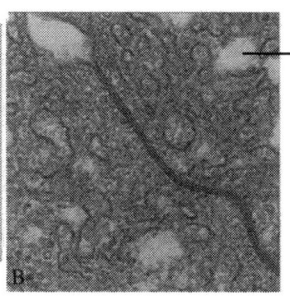

(A) Model of a gap junction demonstrating the channels that connect the cells; (B) SEM of gap junction between two rat liver cells. Magnification = 59,000 X. (Reprinted with permission from Junqueira and Carneiro (2003), p 74.)

2.3.2 Cell Communication

Skin must maintain the protective barrier while existing in a dynamic steady state (i.e., cells leaving the surface must be replaced). The rate at which basal cells divide in the basal layer must coincide with the rate at which cells are leaving at the surface. There must be a mechanism in place to control the rate of cell division of the basal keratinocytes and to monitor the thickness of the skin. This mechanism is cell communication. The keratinocytes are in constant communication with one another and with the melanocytes, Langerhans cells, and Merkel cells. The keratinocytes are also in communication with the rest of the body via the dermis.

2.3.2.1 Gap Junctions. Rapid communication between cells is achieved via gap junctions. Gap junctions are connections between the cell membranes of adjacent cells that permit the direct exchange of small molecules, ions, and hormones. Figure 2–19 contains a diagram and an electron micrograph of a gap junction between cells. Rapid communication via gap junctions results in the keratinocytes acting in a coordinated manner rather than as independent units (Junqueira and Carneiro, 2003, p 72).

2.3.2.2 Cell Surface Receptors. In addition to the direct cell-to-cell communication through gap junctions, cells also have modified proteins embedded in the outer membrane that can respond to signals sent through the blood or from other cells in the epidermis. When a signal molecule binds to the outer surface of the membrane protein, it causes a cascade of reactions inside the cell to elicit the appropriate response.

2.3.3 Regulation of Keratinocyte Proliferation

2.3.3.1 Cell Cycle. Cell communication is necessary for monitoring and adjusting the rate at which the basal cells divide. The cell cycle describes the stages of DNA replication and cell division. The five phases of the cell cycle are represented as G0, G1, S, G2, and M. G1 is the time gap that occurs after the cell has divided and before the cell begins replication of its DNA for the next division. G1 is the resting period between mitoses. The duration of G1 is the most variable phase of the cell cycle, and modifications to its duration greatly influence the number of basal cells produced (Freinkel and Woodley, 2001, p 202). During G1, the cell reaches a critical restriction point and monitors conditions to determine whether it will enter the next phase of the cell cycle, the S phase, synthesis. During the S phase, the cell replicates its DNA, a process that takes about 8–12 hours (Freinkel and Woodley, 2001, p 202).

Once replication of the DNA is complete, the cell enters a second gap phase, G2, for approximately 8 hours. During the G2 phase, the cell reaches a second critical restriction point and evaluates the results of DNA replication before entering mitosis (Freinkel and Woodley, 2001, p 203). The M phase, mitotic phase, is the physical division of the cell into two, each containing a complete copy of the DNA.

Upon completion of mitosis, the basal cells may enter into G1 and continue the cell cycle or they may enter G0. Basal cells entering G0 are no longer cycling but may re-enter the cell cycle upon receipt of the appropriate signal (Freinkel and Woodley, 2001, p 203). The new cells created by the basal cells will either withdraw from the cell cycle and begin differentiation or cycle a few more times (transient amplifying cells) before differentiating. The cells that have started to differentiate are the cells entering the stratum spinosum.

2.3.3.2 Regulation of Cell Cycle. There are many opportunities throughout the cell cycle to regulate the rate at which the basal cells undergo mitosis. Signals that stimulate proliferation are received via cell surface receptors. These signals include hormones, proteins, ions (particularly calcium), and vitamins A and D. Once received, the signal triggers the production of two types of partnered proteins inside the cell: cyclins and cyclin-dependent kinases (Freinkel and Woodley,

2001, p 205). The kinases are responsible for advancing the cells through the G1 and G2 phases of the cell cycle. The kinases must bind the appropriate cyclins to accomplish this task. Cyclins are short-lived, unstable proteins. By controlling the availability of cyclins, the ability of the kinases to progress the cells through mitosis is also controlled.

Calcium is also important for a cell's progression through the cell cycle. Calcium binds to a small protein, calmodulin. The calcium–calmodulin complex is a necessary component of the spindle apparatus that separates the two copies of the DNA produced during the S phase of the cell cycle. Calmodulin also makes structural changes inside the cell to induce replication of the DNA during the S phase (Freinkel and Woodley, 2001, p 204).

2.3.3.3 Inhibitors of Mitosis. If the basal cells are responsible for balancing the number of cells produced with the number of cells leaving the surface, there must be some mechanism for them to "know" how many cells are in the outer layers so they can shut down production as needed. This process, common to all living organisms, is called a feedback mechanism.

As the keratinocytes are pushed toward the surface, they undergo radical changes in their internal and external biochemistry. When the cells reach the stratum granulosum, they release the contents of the lamellar granules to provide the "mortar" between the cells. Molecules released by the differentiating cells, referred to as chalones, diffuse through the intercellular spaces and eventually reach the basal cells (Freinkel and Woodley, 2001, p 205). The basal cells, via cell surface receptors, monitor the concentration of chalones. The more cells that differentiate, the higher the concentration of chalones. If the concentration becomes too high, the chalones signal the basal cells to halt the cell cycle. In this manner, the chalones provide feedback to the basal cells regarding the number of differentiating cells in the outer layers.

2.3.3.4 Genetics of Cell Cycle Regulation. Stimulatory signals and inhibitory signals act on oncogenes and tumor suppressor genes, respectively. Oncogenes are the genes that, when translated, generate the proteins necessary for a cell to undergo mitosis. Tumor suppressor genes are genes whose protein products inhibit mitosis. An example of the cell cycle genetic regulation in the epidermis would be as follows: (1) the basal cells bind a stimulatory hormone on a cell surface receptor; (2) a cascade of reactions takes place inside the cell that results in the genes for cyclins being translated; (3) the production of cyclins activates the kinases, pushing the cells through mitosis; (4) the concentration of chalones rises as the newly generated cells differentiate; (5) chalones diffuse to the basal cells and bind to the appropriate cell surface receptor; (6) a cascade of reactions inside the cells results in the translation of a tumor suppressant gene; and (7) the resultant suppressor protein binds to and inactivates the kinases, thereby halting the cell cycle.

2.4 Persistence of the Friction Ridge Skin

The friction ridge skin persists because of the physical attachments throughout the skin and the regulation of keratinocyte production and differentiation. The three-dimensional morphology of the surface ridge is maintained by the combination of increased cell production in the suprabasal layer of the primary ridges (under-the-surface ridges) and the enhanced anchorage of the basal cells in the secondary ridges (under-the-surface furrows). The basal layer of keratinocytes provides the template for the surface ridges and furrows. Cell communication ensures that basal cell proliferation is stimulated and inhibited in a coordinated manner. As the basal keratinocytes divide, the cell-to-cell attachments ensure that the cells move toward the surface in concert.

2.4.1 Aging of Friction Ridge Skin

Aging is defined by Dr. Barbara Gilchrest as "an irreversible process which begins or accelerates at maturity and which results in an increasing number and/or range of deviations from the ideal state and/or decreasing rate of return to the ideal state" (Gilchrest, 1984, p 5). The friction ridge skin, although durable, undergoes subtle changes as a person ages. The arrangement of the friction ridges does not change; the ridges and furrows maintain their position in the skin. Advancing age has two effects on the friction ridge skin: (1) the surface ridges tend to flatten, making them appear "less sharp" (Okajima, 1979, p 193), and (2) loss of elasticity in the dermis causes the skin to become flaccid and to wrinkle.

2.4.1.1 Flattened Ridges. The friction ridges tend to flatten because of a combination of atrophy of the epidermis and remodeling of the dermal papillae. The remodeling of the dermal papillae is the most striking change in the friction ridge skin. Dermal remodeling continues throughout an

Anatomy and Physiology of Adult Friction Ridge Skin | **CHAPTER 2**

FIGURE 2–20

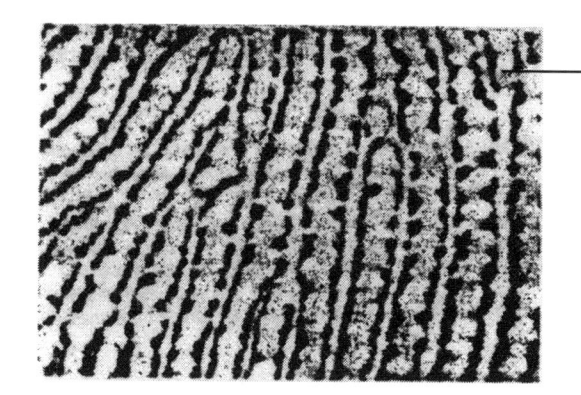

Dermal surface interdigital area of palm of 30-week-old fetus. (Reprinted with permission from Okajima (1975), p 249.)

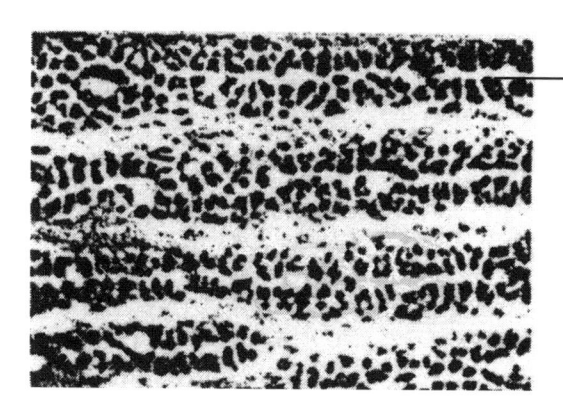

FIGURE 2–21

Dermal surface finger apex of an adult. (Reprinted with permission from Okajima (1975), p 249.)

individual's lifetime and varies across the surface of the palm and sole, depending on how much sheering stress has occurred in that particular area. Chacko and Vaidya (1968, p 105) describe three categories of dermal papillae (DRI, DRII, and DRIII) based on the increasing complexity and branching of the papillae. All three types of dermal papillae are found across the palm and sole but show greater variation on the palm (Chacko and Vaidya, 1968, p 107). The greater variation on the palm is attributed to the wider range of uses of the hand compared to the foot.

In Figures 2–20 and 2–21, the epidermis has been removed and the dermal papillae stained with toluidine blue (Okajima, 1975, p 244). The dark-stained areas of Figures 2–20 and 2–21 are the tips of the dermal papillae. Figure 2–20 is the dermal surface of a 30-week-old fetus. Typical of fetal skin, the dermal papillae are arranged in a very orderly double row under each surface ridge.

As the skin ages and is exposed to sheering stress, the existing dermal papillae branch out, and new small papillae form to increase the adhesion of the epidermis to the dermis (Misumi and Akiyoshi, 1984, p 49). Figure 2–21 is the dermal surface of an adult finger. The number of dermal papillae tends to increase with age, and the papillae become more crowded.

Occasionally, new dermal papillae will also form underneath the furrows of the surface ridges (below the secondary ridges). Dermal papillae that form underneath the surface furrows can range from short and "pebble-like" to the same size as the dermal papillae under the surface ridges (Okajima, 1979, p 193). As the dermal papillae under the furrows become larger, the surface ridges become flatter. Flattening of the surface ridges usually occurs with age (Okajima, 1979, p 193).

The increase in the complexity and number of dermal papillae as a person ages is not reflected in the configuration of the surface ridges and furrows (Misumi and Akiyoshi, 1984, p 53). The epidermis responds to the dermal papillae by forming complementary anastomoses to attach to the branching papillae. The dermal papillae/epidermal anastomoses formation does not affect the basal layer of keratinocytes. That layer is buffered from the dermal changes by the basement membrane and continues to reproduce the surface ridges.

The effects of age on the epidermis also contribute to the flattening of the surface ridges; however, that impact is significantly less compared to the changes in the dermis. The epidermis maintains the thickness of the stratum corneum throughout an individual's lifetime (Lavker et al., 1987, p 46). This is necessary, considering the role of the epidermis as the outer protective barrier. The capacity of the basal keratinocytes to proliferate, however, decreases by 30–50% from the age of 30 to the age of 80 (Gilchrest, 1984, p 21). The slower rate of proliferation results in a thinning of the living layers of the epidermis (stratum basale, stratum spinosum, and stratum granulosum) (Lavker, 1979, p 60).

The remodeling of the dermal papillae, particularly when the dermal papillae form under-the-surface furrows, and the overall thinning of the epidermis contribute to the flattening of the surface ridges that occurs naturally with age. The flattening of the ridges does not affect the sequence and lengths of the surface's ridges and furrows. However, as the ridges flatten, it may be increasingly difficult to follow the ridges and furrows in an impression of the friction ridge skin. Flattening may also diminish the visibility of the edges and contours of the ridges in an impression of the friction ridge skin. It should be noted that the friction ridge skin is quite durable and that the flattening of the ridges occurs slowly, over the course of several decades.

2.4.1.2 Wrinkles. Wrinkles are the result of mechanical changes that take place in the skin as it ages (Kligman et al., 1985, p 41). In other words, there are no special structures formed by the epidermis or dermis at the site of a wrinkle (Kligman et al., 1985, p 40). The overall changes that take place in the skin, particularly in the dermis, as a person ages alter the mechanical properties of the skin. The dermis thins as the network of collagen and elastin fibers becomes compacted. Additionally, the collagen starts to unravel, and the elastin fibers lose their elasticity. The compaction and degradation of the fiber networks in the dermis causes the skin to be "less stretchable, less resilient, more lax, and prone to wrinkling" (Lavker et al., 1989, p 65). The skin becomes loose and simply folds in on itself, creating a wrinkle.

2.4.2 Wound Healing

The friction ridge skin persists throughout an individual's lifetime. The morphology of the friction ridges can be altered only if the basal keratinocyte template is altered. Figures 2–22 through 2–30 are diagrams of a skin model that demonstrate the cellular response of the keratinocytes to a wound. Figure 2–22 shows the intact skin, and Figure 2–23 illustrates the skin after injury. Upon assault, keratinocytes have been removed and damaged, and the dermis has been injured.

Injury causes the basal keratinocytes to undergo remarkable changes in their structure and physiology to repair the wound. The scar formed by the process of repair results in a new, unique, and persistent feature of the friction ridge skin. The process of wound healing is broken down into three phases, although there is considerable overlap: inflammation, proliferation and tissue formation, and tissue remodeling.

2.4.2.1 Phase I: Inflammation. Inflammation begins immediately after the injury. The disruption of the blood vessels in the dermis causes blood to spill into the surrounding tissue. The platelets from the blood direct the clotting of the blood and send out signals to recruit cells from the immune system and the cells of the dermis (Freinkel and Woodley, 2001, p 282). The immune cells kill bacteria and scavenge damaged cells. The dermal cells (fibroblasts) are concentrated in the wound area to repair the dermis. Additionally, endothelial cells (cells from the blood vessels) begin to repair the damaged blood vessels. It should be noted that the repair of the dermis and epidermis occurs underneath the formed blood clot, although the blood clot is not shown in the following diagrams.

2.4.2.2 Phase II: Proliferation and Tissue Formation. As the fibroblasts and endothelial cells continue to repair the dermis, the basal keratinocytes on the edge of the wound take control of the healing process to start Phase II. As a result of the injury, the basal keratinocytes are suddenly exposed to the dermis by disruption of the basement membrane. Contact with the dermis causes the basal keratinocytes to undergo dramatic changes: The desmosomes and hemidesmosomes dissolve, actin filaments form inside the periphery of the cell, and pseudopodia (footlike projections) are extended from the cell (Rovee and Maibach, 2004, p 61).

The dissolution of the desmosomes and hemidesmosomes releases the basal keratinocytes from their firm attachments. The actin filaments, which act like miniature cell muscles, and the pseudopodia allow the skin cells to crawl across the wound. As the basal keratinocytes at the edge of the wound crawl, the basal keratinocytes behind them divide to create additional cells to help cover the wound (Rovee and Maibach, 2004, p 61).

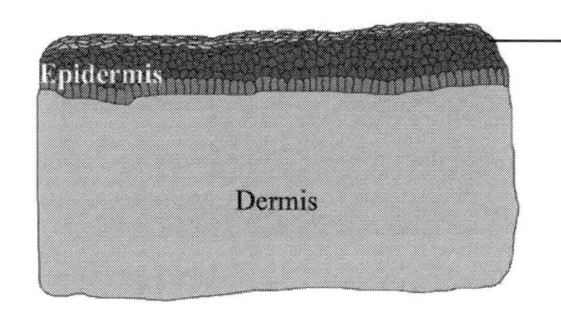

Anatomy and Physiology of Adult Friction Ridge Skin | **CHAPTER 2**

FIGURE 2–22

Intact keratinocyte layers.

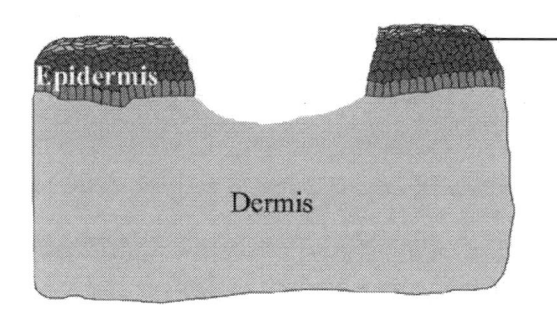

FIGURE 2–23

Injured skin.

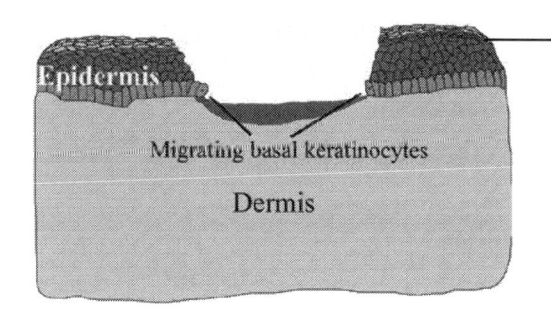

FIGURE 2–24

Repair of the dermis and start of migration of basal keratinocytes at the edge of the wound.

As the opposing sheets of basal keratinocytes move toward one another, the dermis contracts the wound bed to shorten the distance keratinocytes have to migrate to cover the wound (Darby and Hewitson, 2007, p 145). In the friction ridge skin, this contraction creates the classic puckering of the ridges at the scar site. Figure 2–24 demonstrates the repair of the dermis and the beginning of the basal keratinocyte migration. Figure 2–25 demonstrates the puckering of the skin surface as the keratinocytes migrate and the dermis contracts to close the wound. Figure 2–25 also demonstrates the proliferation of the basal keratinocytes behind the migrating cells.

When the leading cells of migrating basal keratinocytes contact each other, they form gap junctions (Flaxman and Nelson, 1974, p 327). These gap junctions reestablish communication. The keratinocytes stop migrating and begin reconstituting the basement membrane (including hemidesmosomes) and the desmosomes and tight junctions between the keratinocytes. Once the basal layer is reestablished, the basal keratinocytes begin dividing, and the upward migration of cells occurs until the appropriate skin thickness is attained (Rovee and Maibach, 2004, p 64). Figures 2–26 through 2–30 illustrate the basal keratinocytes reforming the layers of the epidermis.

FIGURE 2–25

Continued migration of basal keratinocytes and production of new keratinocytes.

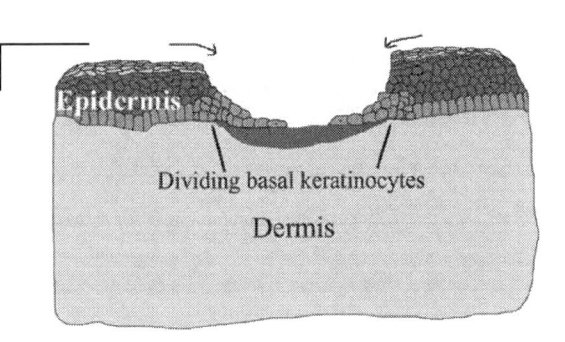

FIGURE 2–26

Migrating basal keratinocytes meet in the middle of the wound and reconstitute the basement membrane.

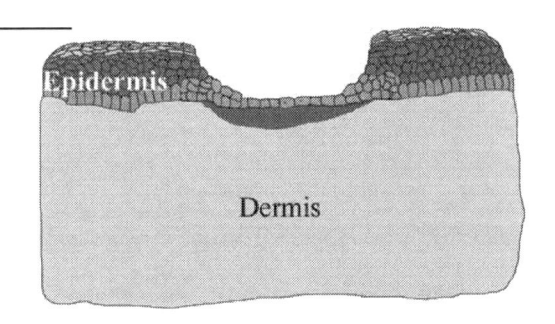

FIGURE 2–27

Newly formed basal layer begins dividing to reconstitute the upper layers.

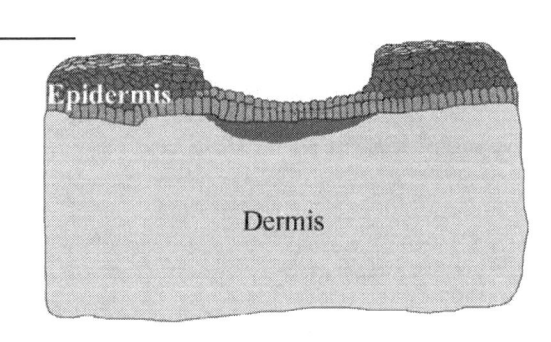

Once the appropriate barrier has been formed, the scab formed by the blood clot during Phase I is released, and the skin returns to its normal physiological state. The friction ridges are not reconstituted. The new basal layer of keratinocytes covering the wound forms the new template for the epidermis at that site. No primary or secondary ridges are formed; consequently, the epidermis does not regenerate the surface ridges and furrows. Additionally, sweat glands are not re-formed. When the sweat glands are damaged as a result of the injury, the cells of the gland also migrate to cover the wound, and the glands are lost (Freinkel and Woodley, 2001, p 284).

2.4.2.3 Phase III: Tissue Remodeling. Once the epidermis has resurfaced, Phase III begins in the dermis. The dermis continues to remodel and reinforce the scar tissue for weeks or months after the injury (Freinkel and Woodley, 2001, p 292).

2.4.2.4 Friction Ridge Skin Wound Healing Model. Figures 2–31 through 2–40 are diagrams created to illustrate wound healing in friction ridge skin. The skin undergoes the same series of events described above, but this model will focus on the layers, rather than the cells, as the skin heals. The layers of the epidermis are color-coded the same as Figure 2–4 (stratum corneum—yellow, stratum lucidum

FIGURE 2–28

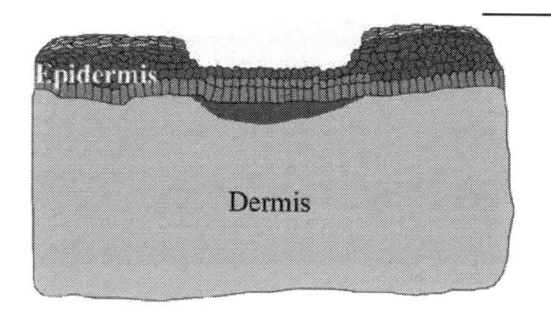

Keratinocytes undergo differentiation as they are pushed toward the surface.

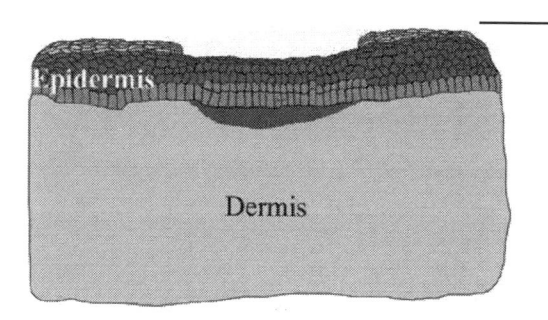

FIGURE 2–29

Continued differentiation of the keratinocytes.

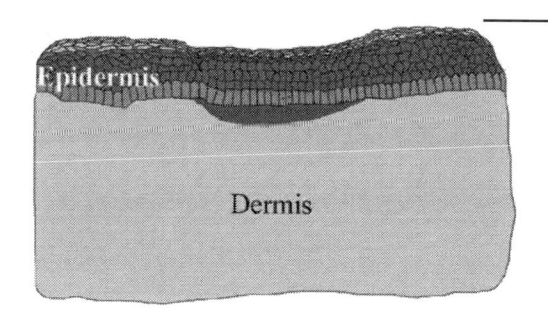

FIGURE 2–30

New epidermis is completely formed

—orange, stratum granulosum—red, stratum spinosum—dark pink, stratum basale—blue, dermis—light pink), and the friction ridge skin is viewed from three-dimensional and aerial perspectives.

2.4.2.5 The Outer Surface of Scars and the Resultant Impressions. The formation of the scars explains what is seen on the skin and subsequently on the impressions left by the skin. Scars may appear as a void, or may contain partial voids, in an impression because all or part of the newly formed epidermis sits below the level of the surface ridges. Like friction ridges, scars are three-dimensional structures with surface contours and edges. Also like the friction ridges, the features of the scars will have some variability in appearance, depending on deposition pressure and movement. Figure 2–41 (p 2–24) is an image of a finger bearing a mature scar and an inked impression of the same finger.

2.4.2.6 Uniqueness of Scars. Scars are unique for the very same reason the friction skin is unique: developmental noise (i.e., chance events that occur during development). Richard Lewontin, research professor at Harvard University, describes developmental noise in the following manner: "Wherever cell growth and division are involved, we can expect such noise to contribute its effects. The

CHAPTER 2 Anatomy and Physiology of Adult Friction Ridge Skin

FIGURE 2–31
Intact friction ridge skin.

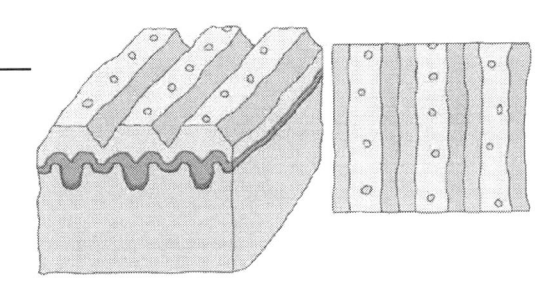

FIGURE 2–32
Injured friction ridge skin.

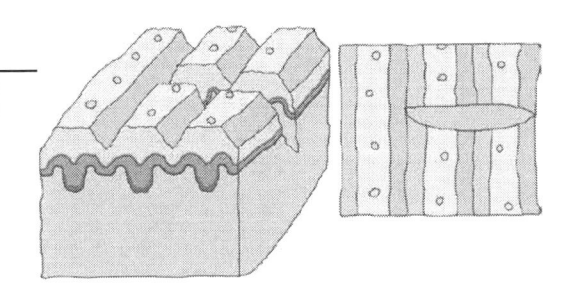

FIGURE 2–33
Repair of the dermis.

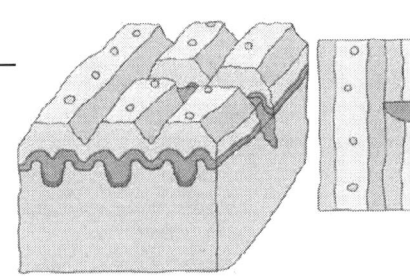

FIGURE 2–34
Initial migration of basal keratinocytes.

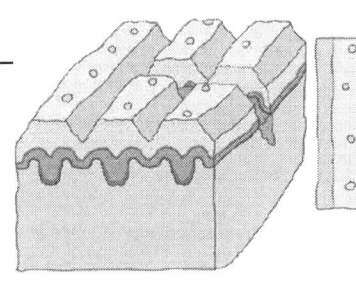

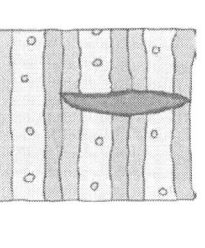

FIGURE 2–35
Continued migration of basal keratinocytes and pinching of upper layers of skin.

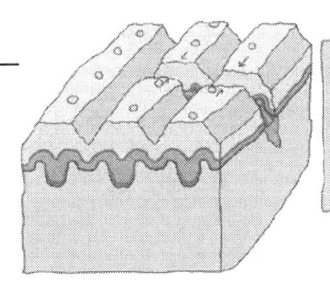

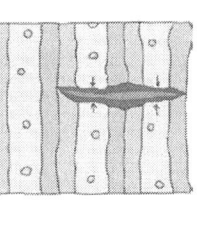

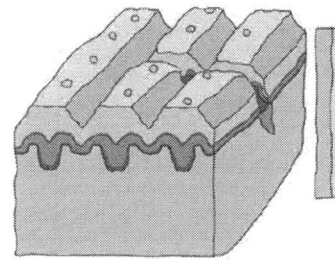

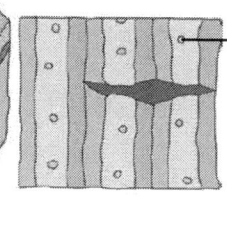

Anatomy and Physiology of Adult Friction Ridge Skin | **CHAPTER 2**

FIGURE 2–36

Final migration of basal keratinocytes and reconstitution of the basement membrane.

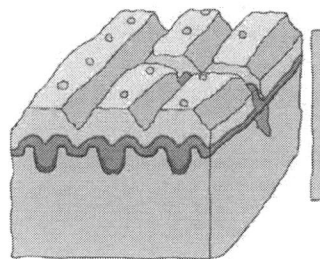

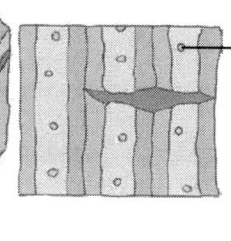

FIGURE 2–37

Basal keratinocytes begin dividing and new cells differentiate to form the stratum spinosum.

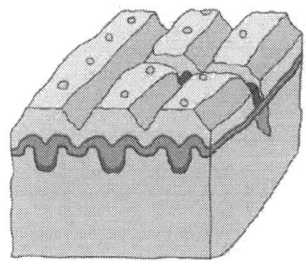

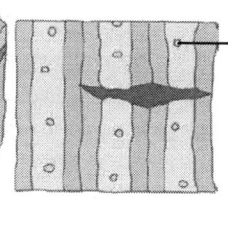

FIGURE 2–38

Basal keratinocytes continue to divide and the cells continue to differentiate, forming the stratum granulosum.

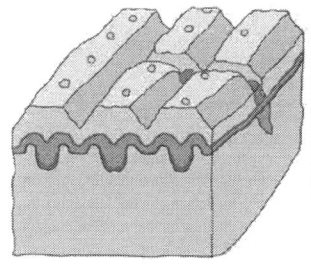

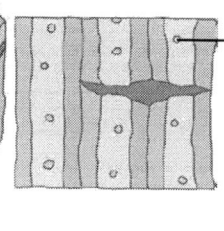

FIGURE 2–39

Formation of the stratum lucidum.

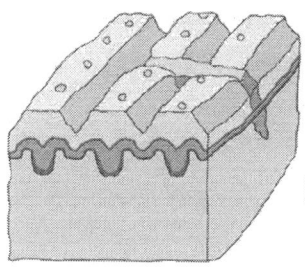

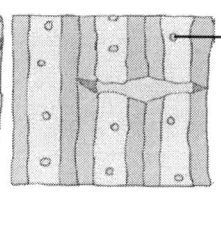

FIGURE 2–40

Complete repair of the epidermis, forming a nonridged scar.

2–23

FIGURE 2–41

Mature scar on the friction ridge skin and the resulting impression with ink (position reversed).

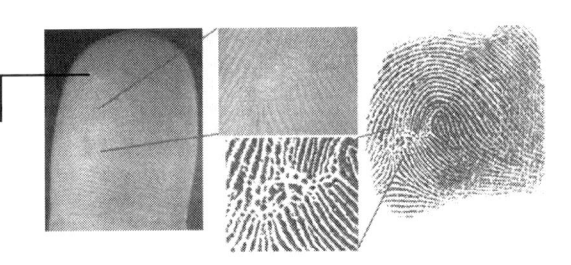

FIGURE 2–42

Known prints of a subject taken in July 1990 and September 2004.

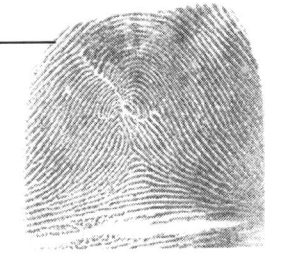

exact placement of hair follicles on our heads, the distribution of small moles on our bodies, a hundred such small details of our morphology, are largely under the influence of such random events in development" (Lewontin, 1995, p 26).

When the friction ridges are forming on the fetus and when the basal keratinocytes are activated by an injury, they are under the influence of developmental noise. The cells are rapidly proliferating and are tasked with forming the fetal skin or reconstituting injured skin. These cells are guided but not given specific instructions on their position in the epidermis. In the case of an injury, the cells rapidly proliferate and migrate. The reconstitution of the stratum basale (the new template for the surface) and the effects on the surrounding epidermis (pinching) are the result of this guided, yet random, process. Two injuries cannot duplicate the same scar (Maceo, 2005, p 160).

2.4.2.7 Persistence of Scars. Scars persist for the same reason that the friction ridges persist: attachment sites and regulation of keratinocyte mitosis. The basal keratinocytes regenerate the basement membrane, reestablishing the attachment of the epidermis to the dermis. The keratinocytes also reestablish the cell-to-cell attachments: desmosomes and tight junctions. The keratinocytes resume communication with each other; with the melanocytes, Langerhans, and Merkel cells; and with the dermis.

Communication allows for homeostatic regulation of cell division in the basal layer, ensuring that the epidermis retains its appropriate thickness. As the cells divide, they move outward in concert and maintain the surface features of the scar (Maceo, 2005, p 160). The impressions in Figure 2–42 were taken more than 14 years apart and demonstrate the persistent nature of scars.

2.4.2.8 Comparison of Impressions Bearing Scars. The use of scars in the comparison of friction ridge impressions has the same basis, and follows the same application, as the use of friction ridges. Once formed, scars are unique and persistent. When an impression of the skin is made, the features of the scar will be reproduced at varying levels of clarity. The clarity of the detail in the impression may reveal the overall configuration of the scar, the position (path) of the scar in the skin, and detailed edge shapes of the scar. This detail makes the scar itself useful in the examination of friction ridge impressions.

2.5 Conclusion

The persistence of the friction ridge skin is explained by the physical attachments of the skin and by the regulated replacement of cells lost at the surface of the skin. The persistent nature of the friction ridge skin makes it an ideal anthropological feature to use as a means of identifying individuals. The structure of the skin also provides a mechanism through which to describe distortion. Variation in the appearance of friction ridge impressions is due to the flexibility of the skin. Understanding that the skin distributes pressure into the more flexible furrows offers valuable insight during the analysis of friction ridge impressions.

Despite its durability, the friction ridge skin is subject to injury and aging. Understanding the aging process provides a basis for variation in appearance of impressions from the same source taken many years apart. Aging processes are particularly critical when explaining the loss of the minute details along the edges of the ridges and the existence of wrinkles. The response of the skin to an injury and the later maintenance of the newly formed skin (scar) provide a basis for the unique features and persistence of scars. The unique and persistent nature of scars allows for their use during the examination of friction ridge impressions. The manner in which skin injuries heal provides an explanation for the variation in appearance of impressions of the skin before and after the injury.

To rely upon the friction ridge skin as a means to identify people, it is necessary to understand why the impressions of the friction ridge skin can be used and what the physical limitations of the friction ridge skin are. If the variation in appearance between two impressions of the friction ridge skin goes beyond the physical limitations of the skin, the impressions cannot be from the same source.

2.6 Reviewers

The reviewers critiquing this chapter were Jeffrey G. Barnes, Patti Blume, Mary Ann Brandon, Brent T. Cutro, Sr., Lynne D. Herold, Andre A. Moenssens, Michelle L. Snyder, John R. Vanderkolk, and Kasey Wertheim.

2.7 References

Cavoto, F. V.; Flaxman, B. A. Communication Between Normal Human Epidermal Cells in Vitro. *J. Invest. Dermatol.* 1972, *59* (5), 370–374.

Chacko, L. W.; Vaidya, M. C. The Dermal Papillae and Ridge Patterns in Human Volar Skin. *ACTA Anatomica (Basel)* 1968, *70* (1), 99–108.

Darby, I. A.; Hewitson, T. D. Fibroblast Differentiation in Wound Healing and Fibrosis. *Int. Rev. of Cytol.* 2007, *257*, 143–179.

Dillion, Y.; Haynes, J.; Henneberg, M. The Relationship of the Number of Meissner's Corpuscles to Dermatoglyphic Characters and Finger Size. *J. Anatomy* 2001, *199* (5), 577–584.

Eroschenko, V. *di Fiore's Atlas of Histology With Functional Correlations,* 7th ed.; Lea & Febiger: Philadelphia, 1993.

Flaxman, B. A.; Nelson, B. K. Ultrastructural Studies of the Early Junctional Zone Formed by Keratinocytes Showing Contact Inhibition of Movement in Vitro. *J. Invest. Dermatol.* 1974, *63* (4), 326–330.

Freinkel, R. K.; Woodley, D. T. *The Biology of Skin;* The Parthenon: New York, 2001.

Gilchrest, B. *Skin and Aging Processes;* CRC Press, Inc.: Boca Raton, FL, 1984.

Hale, A. Morphogenesis of Volar Skin in the Human Fetus. *American J. Anatomy* 1952, *91* (1), 147–173.

Junqueira, L. C.; Carneiro, *Journal of Basic Histology,* 10th ed.; Lange Medical Books: New York, 2003.

Kligman, A.; Zheng, P.; Lavker, R. M. The Anatomy and Pathogenesis of Wrinkles. *British J. Dermatol.* 1985, *113* (1), 37–42.

Lavker, R. M. Structural Alterations in Exposed and Unexposed Aged Skin. *J. Invest. Dermatol.* 1979, *73* (1), 59–66.

Lavker, R. M.; Sun, T. T. Heterogeneity in Epidermal Basal Keratinocytes and Functional Correlations. *Science* 1982, *215* (4537), 1239–1241.

Lavker, R. M.; Sun, T. T. Epidermal Stem Cells. *J. Invest. Dermatol.* 1983, *81* (1) (Suppl.), 121–127.

Lavker, R. M.; Zheng, P.; Dong, G. Aged Skin: A Study by Light, Transmission Electron, and Scanning Electron Microscopy. *J. Invest. Dermatol.* 1987, *88* (3) (Suppl.), 44–51.

Lavker, R. M.; Zheng, P.; Dong, G. Morphology of Aged Skin. *J. Geriatric Dermatol.* 1989, *5* (1), 53–67.

Lewontin, R. *Human Diversity;* Scientific American Library: New York, 1995.

Maceo, A. The Basis for the Uniqueness and Persistence of Scars in the Friction Ridge Skin. *Fingerprint Whorld* 2005, *31* (121), 147–161.

Misumi, Y.; Akiyoshi, T. Scanning Electron Microscopic Structure of the Finger Print as Related to the Dermal Surface. *The Anatomical Record* 1984, *208* (1), 49–55.

Montagna, W.; Parakkal, P. *The Structure and Function of Skin,* 3rd ed.; Academic Press: New York, 1974.

Okajima, M. Development of Dermal Ridges in the Fetus. *J. Med. Genet.* 1975, *12* (3), 243–250.

Okajima, M. Dermal and Epidermal Structures of the Volar Skin. In *Dermatoglyphics—Fifty Years Later;* Birth Defects Original Article Series; March of Dimes: Washington, DC, 1979; pp 179–198.

Rovee, D. T.; Maibach, H. I. *The Epidermis in Wound Healing;* CRC Press: New York, 2004.

Swensson, O.; Langbein, L.; McMillan, J. R.; Stevens, H. P.; Leigh, I. M.; McClean, W. H. I.; Lane, E. B.; Jeady, R. A. Specialized Keratin Expression Pattern in Human Ridged Skin as an Adaptation to High Physical Stress. *British J. Dermatol.* 1998, *139* (5), 767–775.

Tortora, G.; Grabowski, S. R. *Principles of Anatomy and Physiology,* 7th ed.; Harper Collins: New York, 1993.

Wan, H.; Dopping-Hepenstal, P.; Gratian, M.; Stone, M.; McGrath, J.; Eady, R. Desmosomes Exhibit Site-Specific Features in Human Palm Skin. *Experimental Dermatol.* 2003, *12* (4), 378–388.

Wolfe, S. *Molecular and Cellular Biology;* Wadsworth: Belmont, CA, 1993.

CHAPTER 3

EMBRYOLOGY AND MORPHOLOGY OF FRICTION RIDGE SKIN

Kasey Wertheim

CONTENTS

- 3 3.1 Introduction
- 4 3.2 Embryology: Establishing Uniqueness and Pattern Formation in the Friction Ridge Skin
- 5 3.3 Limb Development
- 7 3.4 Differentiation of the Friction Ridge Skin
- 8 3.5 Primary Ridge Formation
- 11 3.6 Secondary Ridge Formation
- 12 3.7 Pattern Formation
- 18 3.8 Genetics
- 21 3.9 Uniqueness: Developmental Noise
- 22 3.10 Summary: Keys to Uniqueness and Pattern Formation
- 22 3.11 Reviewers
- 24 3.12 References

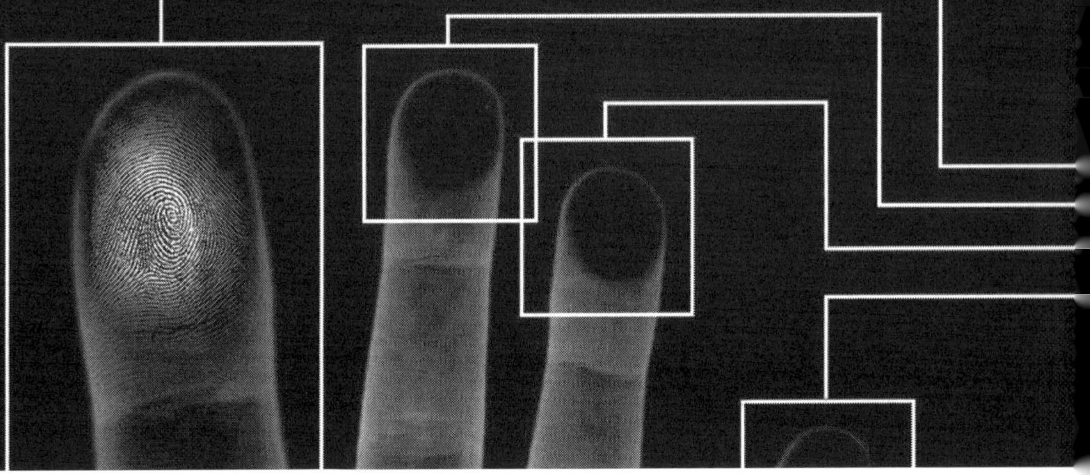

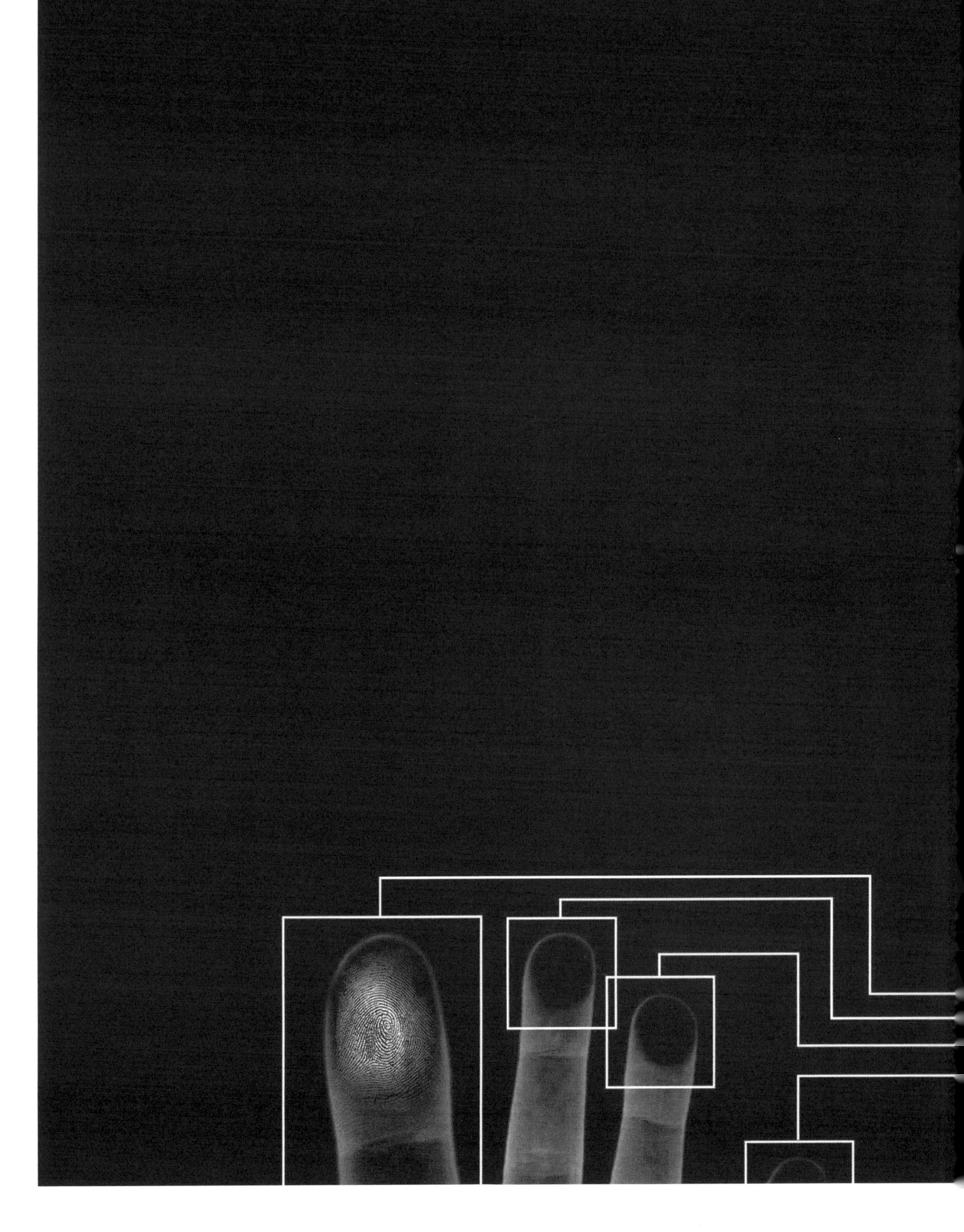

CHAPTER 3

EMBRYOLOGY AND MORPHOLOGY OF FRICTION RIDGE SKIN

Kasey Wertheim

3.1 Introduction

Friction ridge skin has unique features that persist from before birth until decomposition after death. Upon contact with a surface, the unique features of friction ridge skin may leave an impression of corresponding unique details. Two impressions can be analyzed, compared, and evaluated, and if sufficient quality and quantity of detail is present (or lacking) in a corresponding area of both impressions, a competent examiner can effect an individualization or exclusion (identify or exclude an individual). The analysis, comparison, evaluation, and verification (ACE-V) methodology, combined with the philosophy of quantitative–qualitative examinations, provide the framework for practical application of the friction ridge examination discipline. But at the heart of the discipline is the fundamental principle that allows for conclusive determinations: the source of the impression, friction ridge skin, is unique and persistent.

Empirical data collected in the medical and forensic communities continues to validate the premises of uniqueness and persistence. One hundred years of observations and statistical studies have provided critical supporting documentation of these premises. Detailed explanations of the reasons behind uniqueness and persistence are found in specific references that address very small facets of the underlying biology of friction ridge skin. This chapter brings together these references under one umbrella for the latent print examiner to use as a reference in understanding why friction ridge skin is unique and persistent.

The basis of persistence is found in morphology and physiology; the epidermis faithfully reproduces the three-dimensional ridges due to physical attachments and constant regulation of cell proliferation and differentiation. But, the basis of uniqueness lies in embryology; the unique features of the skin are established between approximately 10.5 and 16 weeks estimated gestational age (EGA) due to developmental noise.

3.2 Embryology: Establishing Uniqueness and Pattern Formation in the Friction Ridge Skin

3.2.1 Introduction to Embryology

The uniqueness of friction ridge skin falls under the larger umbrella of biological uniqueness. No two portions of any living organism are exactly alike. The intrinsic and extrinsic factors that affect the development of any individual organ, such as human skin, are impossible to duplicate, even in very small areas. The uniqueness of skin can be traced back to the late embryological and early fetal development periods.

3.2.2 Early Embryological Development: 0–2 Weeks EGA (Raven and Johnson, 1992, pp 1158–1159)

The process of embryological development begins with fertilization of the egg and continues through a period of rapid cell division called "cleavage". In mammalian eggs, an inner cell mass is concentrated at one pole, causing patterned alterations during cleavage. Although egg cells contain many different substances that act as genetic signals during early embryological development, these substances are not distributed uniformly. Instead, different substances tend to be clustered at specific sites within the growing embryo. During growth, signal substances are partitioned into different daughter cells, endowing them with distinct developmental instructions. In this manner, the embryo is prepatterned to continue developing with unique cell orientation.

3.2.3 Late Embryological Development: 3–8 Weeks EGA (Raven and Johnson, 1992, pp 1160–1164)

The first visible results of prepatterning can be seen immediately after completion of the cleavage divisions as different genes are activated. Certain groups of cells move inward toward the center of the sphere in a carefully orchestrated migration called "gastrulation". This process forms the primary tissue distinctions between ectoderm, endoderm, and mesoderm. The ectoderm will go on to form epidermis, including friction ridge skin; the mesoderm will form the connective tissue of the dermis, as well as muscle and elements of the vascular system; and the endoderm goes on to form the organs.

Once specialized, the three primary cell types begin their development into tissue and organs. The process of tissue differentiation begins with neurulation, or the formation of the notochord (the precursor to the spinal cord and brain) as well as the neural crest (the precursor to much of the embryo's nervous system). Segmented blocks of tissue that become muscles, vertebrae, and connective tissue form on either side of the notochord. The remainder of the mesoderm moves out and around the inner endoderm, forming a hollow chamber that will ultimately become the lining of the stomach and intestines.

During late embryological development, the embryo undergoes "morphogenesis", or the formation of shape. Limbs rapidly develop from about 4 weeks EGA, and the arms, legs, knees, elbows, fingers, and toes can all be seen in the second month. During this time, the hand changes from a paddlelike form to an adult form, including the formation of the fingers and rotation of the thumb. Also during this time, swellings of mesenchyme called "volar pads" appear on the palms of the hands and soles of the feet. Within the body cavity, the major organs such as the liver, pancreas, and gall bladder become visible. By the end of week 8, the embryo has grown to about 25 millimeters in length and weighs about 1 gram.

3.2.4 Fetal Growth: 9–12 Weeks EGA

During the third month, the embryo's nervous system and sense organs develop, and the arms and legs begin to move. Primitive reflexes such as sucking are noticed, and early facial expressions can be visualized. Friction ridges begin to form at about 10.5 weeks EGA and continue to mature in depth as the embryo passes into the second trimester. From this point on, the development of the embryo is essentially complete, and further maturation is referred to as fetal growth rather than embryonic development.

3.2.5 Second Trimester

The second trimester is marked by significant growth to 175 millimeters and about 225 grams. Bone growth is very active, and the body becomes covered with fine hair called lanugo, which will be lost later in development. As the placenta reaches full development, it secretes numerous hormones essential to support fetal bone growth and energy. Volar pads regress and friction ridges grow until about 16 weeks EGA, when the minutiae become set.

FIGURE 3–1

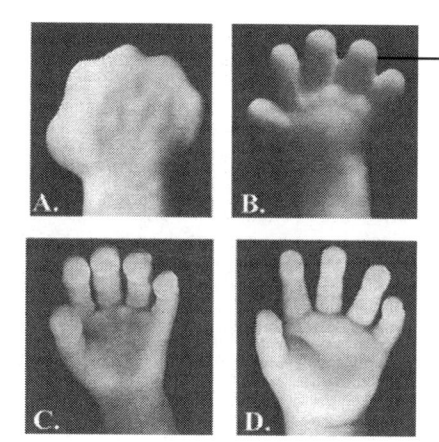

Growth of the hand progresses from (A) a paddle-like form (magnification = 19.5 X), (B) continues as the fingers separate (magnification = 17.3 X) and (C) the volar pads become prominent (magnification = 7.7 X), and (D) achieves infantlike appearance by 8 weeks EGA (magnification = 4.2 X). (Reprinted with permission from Cummins (1929).)

Sweat glands mature, and the epidermal–dermal ridge system continues to mature and grow in size. By the end of the second trimester, sweat ducts and pores appear along epidermal ridges, and the fetus begins to undergo even more rapid growth.

3.2.6 Third Trimester

In the third trimester, the fetus doubles in weight several times. Fueled by the mother's bloodstream, new brain cells and nerve tracts actively form. Neurological growth continues long after birth, but most of the essential development has already taken place in the first and second trimesters. The third trimester is mainly a period for protected growth.

3.3 Limb Development

3.3.1 Hand Development

During the initial phases of formation, the hand undergoes significant changes in topography. Until approximately 5–6 weeks EGA, the hand appears as a flat, paddlelike structure with small protrusions of tissue that will become fingers. From 6 to 7 weeks EGA, these finger protrusions in the hand plate begin to form muscle and cartilage that will become bone at later stages of hand growth (Figure 3–1).

From 7 to 8 weeks EGA, the fingers begin to separate and the bone begins to "ossify" or harden. By 8 weeks EGA, the joints begin to form between the bones of the hand, and the external hand morphology appears similar in proportion to that of an infant.

3.3.2 Volar Pad Development

Volar pads (Figure 3–2) are transient swellings of tissue called mesenchyme under the epidermis on the palmar surface of the hands and soles of the feet of the human fetus (Figure 3–3).

The interdigital pads appear first, around 6 weeks EGA, followed closely in time by the thenar and hypothenar pads. At approximately 7–8 weeks EGA, the volar pads begin to develop on the fingertips, starting with the thumb and progressing toward the little finger in the same radio-ulnar gradient that ridge formation will follow. Also at about 8 weeks EGA, the thenar crease begins to form in the palm, followed by the flexion creases in the fingers at around 9 weeks EGA (Kimura, 1991).

3.3.3 Volar Pad "Regression"

The pads remain well rounded during their rapid growth around 9–10 weeks EGA, after which they begin to demonstrate some individual variation in both shape and position (Babler, 1987; Burdi et al., 1979; Cummins, 1926, 1929). During the period from 8 to 10 weeks EGA, thumb rotation is achieved (Lacroix et al., 1984, p 131). Also at about 10 weeks EGA, the flexion creases of the toes begin formation, followed at about 11 weeks EGA by the distal transverse flexion crease in the palm, and at about 13 weeks EGA by the proximal transverse flexion crease in the palm (Kimura, 1991).

As a result of the volar pads' slowing growth, their contour becomes progressively less distinct on the more rapidly growing surface (Figure 3–4). This process has been defined as "regression" (Lacroix et al., 1984, pp 131–133),

CHAPTER 3   Embryology and Morphology of Friction Ridge Skin

FIGURE 3–2

A low-power scanning electron microscope view of a fetal hand displaying prominent digital and palmar volar pads. (Reprinted with permission from Carlson (1999), p 152.)

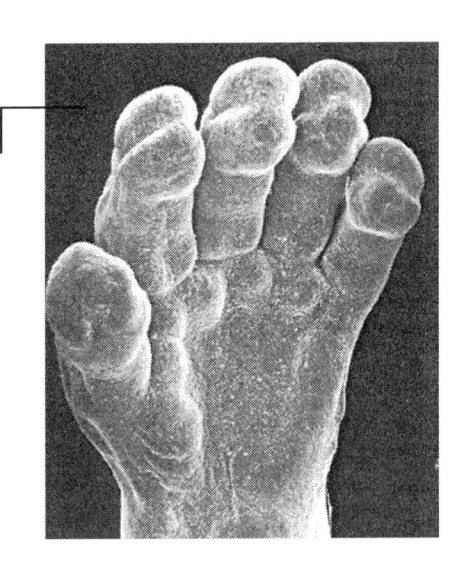

FIGURE 3–3

Normally, 11 volar pads develop and regress on each limb (one on each digit and six on the larger surface of the palm or sole). The hypothenar pad of the palm is divided into distal (Hd) and proximal (Hp) portions. The first (I) interdigital volar pad is also divided into two portions, making a total of 13 potential elevations on each surface. On plantar surfaces, the proximal portions of the hypothenar pad (Hp) and the thenar pad (Thp) are absent, leaving 11 distinct plantar elevations. (Reprinted with permission from Cummins (1929), p 114.)

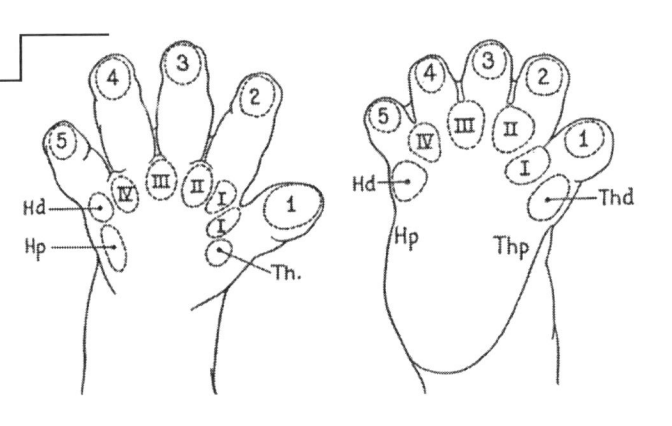

FIGURE 3–4

Drawings that represent a volar pad from initial formation until complete regression, excluding growth of the size of the finger. Actual EGA values are highly variable and are included only as approximations in this figure. (Reprinted with permission from Wertheim and Maceo (2002), p 61.)

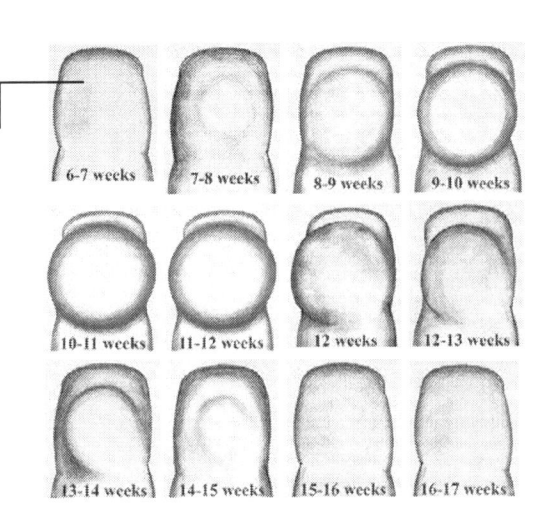

3–6

FIGURE 3–5

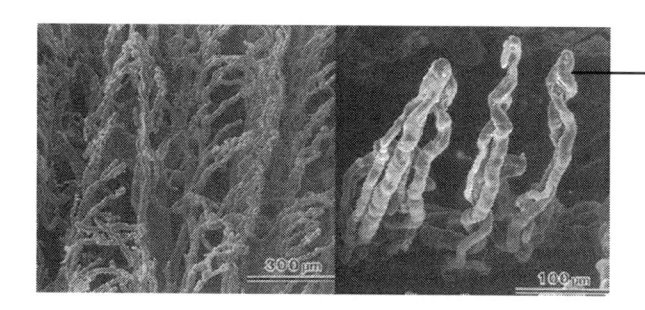

Scanning electron micrograph of a resin cast of the fine vascularature of the finger of an 85-year-old man shows a complex pattern of capillary loops in dermal ridges. Approximate magnification = 150 X (left) and 700 X (right). (Reprinted with permission from Montagna et al. (1992).)

but it is important to understand that the pad is not actually shrinking; rather, the volar pads are overtaken by the faster growth of the larger surrounding surface. The volar pads of the palm begin to regress as early as 11 weeks EGA, followed closely by the volar pads of the fingers. By 16 weeks EGA, volar pads have completely merged with the contours of the fingers, palms, and soles of the feet (Cummins, 1929, p 117).

3.4 Differentiation of the Friction Ridge Skin

3.4.1 Development of the Epidermis

The primitive epidermis is established at approximately 1 week EGA, when ectoderm and endoderm are separately defined. A second layer of epidermis forms at about 4–5 weeks EGA. The outermost of the three layers is the periderm. The middle layer, which is the actual epidermis, is composed of basal keratinocytes (named because of the keratins these cells manufacture). At about 8 weeks EGA, the basal cells between the epidermis and the dermis begin to consistently divide and give rise to daughter cells that move vertically to form the first of the intermediate cell layers (Holbrook, 1991b, p 64). At this point, the embryonic epidermis is three to four cell layers thick, but it is still smooth on its outer and inner surfaces. Keratinocytes are tightly bound to each other by desmosomes, and the cells of the basal layer are attached to the basement membrane by hemidesmosomes (Holbrook, 1991a, p 5).

3.4.2 Development of the Dermis

The first dermal components to originate from the mesoderm are fibroblasts. These irregular branching cells secrete proteins into the matrix between cells. Fibroblasts synthesize the structural (collagen and elastic) components that form the connective tissue matrix of the dermis. During the period 4–8 weeks EGA, many of the dermal structures begin formation. Elastic fibers first appear around 5 weeks EGA at the ultrastructural level in small bundles of 20 or fewer fibrils (Holbrook, 1991b, pp 64–101). Nerve development occurs in different stages from 6 weeks EGA onwards. Neurovascular bundles and axons with growth cones are seen in the developing dermis as early as 6 weeks EGA (Moore and Munger, 1989, pp 128–130). In fact, axons can be traced to the superficial levels of the dermis, and in some cases they almost abut the basal lamina of the epidermis. By 9 weeks EGA, innervation (the appearance of nerve endings) of the epidermis has begun to occur, although there are some Merkel cells in the epidermis that are not yet associated with axons. In embryos older than 10 weeks EGA, Merkel cells are predominant in the developing epidermis, and their related axons and neurofilaments are present in the dermis (Moore and Munger, 1989, p 127; Smith and Holbrook, 1986).

The dermis becomes distinguishable from deeper subcutaneous tissue due largely to a horizontal network of developing blood vessels. From 8 to 12 weeks EGA, vessels organize from dermal mesenchyme and bring much-needed oxygen and hormones to the underside of the developing epidermis. Unlike other epidermal structures, blood vessels continue to alter with aging, as some capillary loops are lost and new ones arise from the interpapillary network. This continues into late adulthood (Figure 3–5) (Smith and Holbrook, 1986).

A second vascular network forms deep in the reticular dermis by about 12 weeks EGA. Unlike the developing primary ridges, the vascular network is not a permanent structure. There is significant reorganization of capillary beds during the period 8–20 weeks EGA to keep pace with skin growth; even after birth, microcirculation continues to form and remodel (Holbrook, 1991b, p 100; Smith and Holbrook, 1986).

FIGURE 3–6

A reconstruction of the first three-dimensional undulations that occur on the underside of the fetal volar epidermis at the epidermal–dermal junction. (Artwork by Brandon Smithson. Re-drawn from Hale (1952), p 152.)

FIGURE 3–7

A histological cross section of 10.5-week EGA fetal volar skin at the onset of rapid localized cellular proliferation. (Image provided by William Babler.)

3.5 Primary Ridge Formation

3.5.1 Initiation of Primary Ridge Formation

At around 10–10.5 weeks EGA, basal cells of the epidermis begin to divide rapidly (Babler, 1991, p 98; Holbrook and Odland, 1975, p 17). As volar epidermal cells divide, shallow "ledges" (Hale, 1952) can be seen on the bottom of the epidermis. These ledges delineate the overall patterns that will become permanently established on the volar surfaces several weeks later (Babler, 1991, p 101; Evatt, 1906). Primary ridges are the first visual evidence of interaction between the dermis and epidermis and are first seen forming as continuous ridges (Figure 3–6).

The prevailing theory of events before the visualization of primary ridge structure involves centers of active cell proliferation (Figure 3–7), which will become the centers of sweat gland development (Babler, 1991, p 98).

According to this theory, the "units" of rapidly multiplying cells increase in diameter, somewhat randomly, growing into one another (Figure 3–8) along lines of relief perpendicular to the direction of compression.

Furthermore, according to this theory, as the series of localized proliferations "fuse" together, the resulting linear ridges of rapidly dividing epidermal cells fold into the dermis, creating the first visible ridge structure at the epidermal–dermal junction (Ashbaugh, 1999, p 79). Another plausible theory is that developing nerves may interact with epidermal cells to stimulate clustered interactions that blend together in the early stages of ridge development.

At the time of embryonic friction ridge formation, the central nervous and cardiovascular systems are undergoing a critical period of development (Hirsch, 1964). Researchers have reported innervation at the sites of ridge formation immediately preceding the appearance of friction ridges and suggest that innervation could be the trigger mechanism for the onset of proliferation (Bonnevie, 1924; Dell and Munger, 1986; Moore and Munger, 1989). Several researchers even postulate that the patterning of the capillary–nerve pairs at the junction of the epidermis and the dermis is the direct cause of primary ridge alignment (Dell and Munger, 1986; Hirsch and Schweichel, 1973; Moore and Munger, 1989; Morohunfola et al., 1992).

Early research on pattern distribution established "developmental fields", or groupings of fingers on which patterns had a greater tendency to be similar (Meier, 1981; Roberts, 1982; Siervogel et al., 1978). Later discoveries confirmed the neurological relation of spinal cord sections C–6, C–7, and C–8 to innervation of the fingers (Heimer, 1995). Specifically, Kahn and colleagues (2001) reported that a

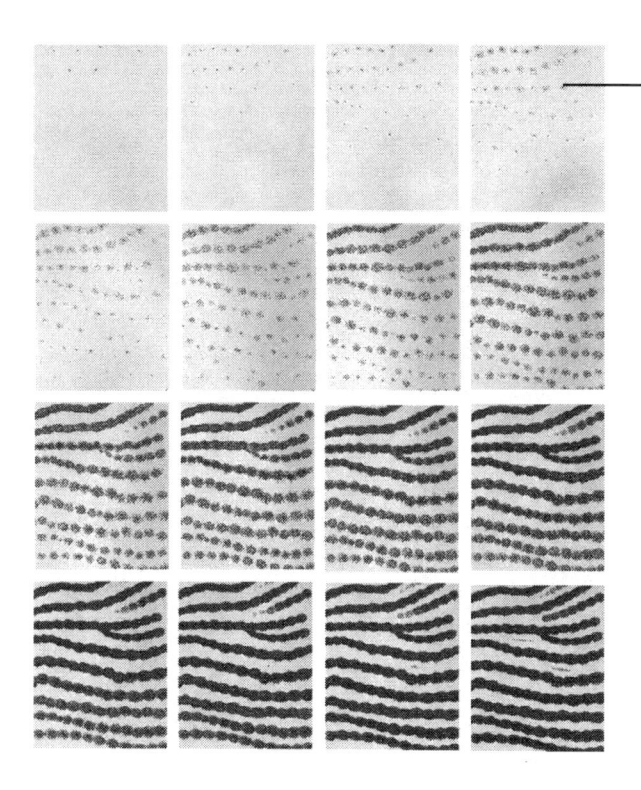

FIGURE 3–8
These drawings represent the theory that just before ridge formation, localized cellular proliferations grow together into what will appear as ridges at around 10.5 weeks EGA. (Reprinted with permission from Wertheim and Maceo (2002), p 49.)

large ridge-count difference between C–8-controlled fingers 4 and 5 may predict a larger waist-to-thigh ratio and, therefore, an increased risk of some major chronic diseases such as heart disease, cancer, and diabetes. Other interesting hypotheses have been published regarding the connection between innervation and friction ridge patterning, but the main consideration for the purposes of friction ridge formation is that specific parts of the nervous system are undergoing development at the same time that ridges begin to appear on the surface of the hands.

The presence of nerves and capillaries in the dermis before friction ridge formation may be necessary for friction ridge proliferation. It would seem that complex simultaneous productions such as friction ridge formation would benefit from being in communication with the central nervous system or the endocrine and exocrine (hormone) systems (Smith and Holbrook, 1986). However, it is doubtful that nerves or capillaries independently establish a map that directly determines the flow of the developing friction ridges. It seems more likely that the alignment of the nerves and capillaries is directed by the same stresses and strains on the developing hand that establish ridge alignment (Babler, 1999; Smith and Holbrook, 1986). It is well recognized in cell biology that physical pressure on a cellular system can trigger electrochemical changes within

that system. Merkel cells occupy the epidermis just prior to innervation along those pathways (Holbrook, 1991a), suggesting that even before ridge formation, the stresses created by the different growth rates of the dermis and epidermis are causing differential cell growth along invisible lines that already delineate pattern characteristics (Loesch, 1973). Regardless of the trigger mechanism controlling the onset of the first primary ridge proliferations, the propagation of primary ridges rapidly continues.

3.5.2 Propagation of Primary Ridge Formation

Primary ridges mature and extend deeper into the dermis (Figure 3–9) for a period of approximately 5.5 weeks, from their inception at 10.5 weeks EGA until about 16 weeks EGA. The cell growth during this phase of development is along the primary ridge, in what has been labeled the "proliferative compartment". The proliferative compartment encompasses basal and some suprabasal cells, ultimately governed by stem cells, and is responsible for new skin cell production of the basal layer of skin (Lavker and Sun, 1983).

3.5.3 Minutiae Formation

Although the exact mechanisms for formation of minutiae are unclear, the separate accounts of many researchers

CHAPTER 3   Embryology and Morphology of Friction Ridge Skin

FIGURE 3–9

Histological cross section of fetal volar skin between 10.5 and 16 weeks EGA. During this time, primary ridges (as marked by the arrow) increase in depth and breadth. (Image provided by William Babler.)

FIGURE 3–10

Drawings that illustrate the theoretical formation of minutiae arising from expansion of the volar surface during the critical stage (frames 1–10) and continuing to increase in size after secondary ridge formation (frames 11–16). (Reprinted with permission from Wertheim and Maceo (2002), p 51.)

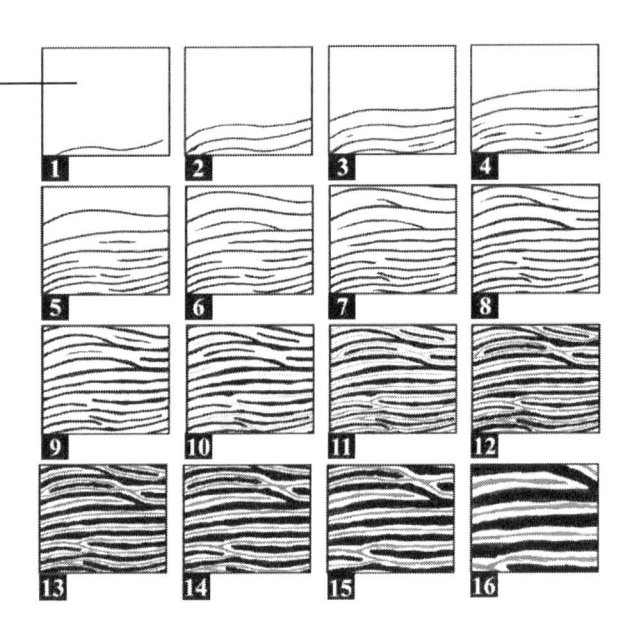

who have examined fetal tissue allow for a fairly accurate reconstruction of the morphogenesis of friction ridges in successive stages of the development process. Figure 3–10 illustrates the process of minutiae formation as hypothesized by a general consensus of the literature.

Many events happen during this rapid period of primary ridge growth. The finger rapidly expands, new primary ridges form across the finger, and the existing primary ridges begin to separate because of growth of the digit. As existing ridges separate, the tendency of the surface to be continually ridged creates a demand for new ridges. Hale reports that new ridges pull away from existing primary ridges to fill in these gaps, creating bifurcations by mechanical separation. Ending ridges form when a developing ridge becomes sandwiched between two established ridges. According to this theory, "fusion between adjacent ridges [which have already formed] seems improbable, although there is no evidence for or against this process" (Hale, 1952, p 167).

Other models explain ridge detail in nature as a chemical reaction–suppression scheme in which morphogens react and diffuse through cells, causing spatial patterns (Murray, 1988, p 80). According to these models, hormones circulate first through newly formed capillaries just before ridge formation in the epidermis, offering another potential factor in the genesis of ridge formation (Smith and Holbrook, 1986).

FIGURE 3–11

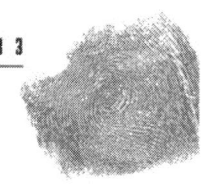

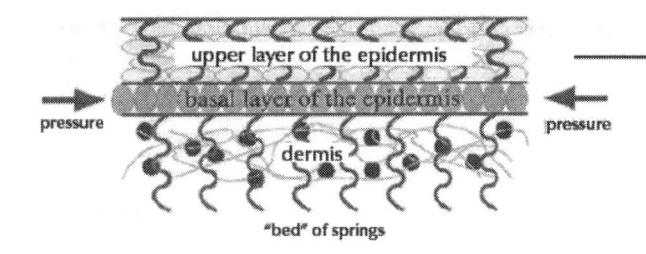

A drawing that represents the state of the epidermal–dermal boundary just before ridge formation. (Reprinted with permission from Kücken and Newell (2005), p 74.)

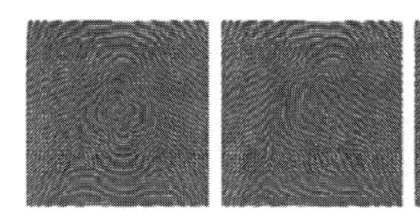

FIGURE 3–12

Computer simulations demonstrating that bounded stress fields across a three-dimensional spherical surface produce fingerprintlike patterns. (Reprinted with permission from Kücken and Newell (2005), p. 79.)

A recent model of the process of friction ridge morphogenesis has been likened to mechanical instability (Kücken and Newell, 2005). Building on the folding hypothesis of Kollmann (1883) and Bonnevie (1924), Kücken and Newell (2005) consider the basal layer as "an overdamped elastic sheet trapped between the neighboring tissues of the intermediate epidermis layer and the dermis", which they mathematically model as "beds of weakly nonlinear springs" (Figure 3–11).

Their computer program models the results of forcing enough compressive stress to cause a buckling instability on a virtual three-dimensional elastic sheet constrained by fixed boundaries on two sides. The resulting ridge patterns are similar to all three major fingerprint pattern types oriented by the upper fixed boundary of the nailbed and the lower fixed boundary of the distal interphalangeal flexion crease (Figure 3–12).

Regardless of the exact mechanism of minutiae formation (mechanical or static; fusion or chemical), the exact location of any particular bifurcation or ridge ending within the developing ridge field is governed by a random series of infinitely interdependent forces acting across that particular area of skin at that critical moment. Slight differences in the mechanical stress, physiological environment, or variation in the timing of development could significantly affect the location of minutiae in that area of skin.

3.6 Secondary Ridge Formation

3.6.1 Initiation of Secondary Ridge Formation

By 15 weeks EGA, the primary ridges are experiencing growth in two directions: the downward penetration of the sweat glands and the upward push of new cell growth. Generally, the entire volar surface is ridged by 15 weeks EGA. Okajima (1982) shows a fully ridged palm of a 14-week-old fetus (Figure 3–13).

Between 15 and 17 weeks EGA, secondary ridges appear between the primary ridges on the underside of the epidermis (Babler, 1991, p 98). Secondary ridges are also cell proliferations resulting in downfolds of the basal epidermis. At this time in fetal development, the randomly located minutiae within the friction ridge pattern become permanently set (Hale, 1952, pp 159–160), marking the end of new primary ridge formation (Figure 3–14) (Babler, 1990, p 54).

3.6.2 Propagation of Secondary Ridge Formation

As the secondary ridges form downward and increase the surface area of attachment to the dermis, the primary ridges are pushing cells toward the surface to keep pace with the growing hand. These two forces, in addition to cell adhesion, cause infolding of the epidermal layers above the attachment site of the secondary ridges (Hale, 1952). As

FIGURE 3–13

Image of a 14-week EGA fetal palm stained with toluidine blue. (Reprinted with permission from Okajima (1982), p 185 (no magnification given).)

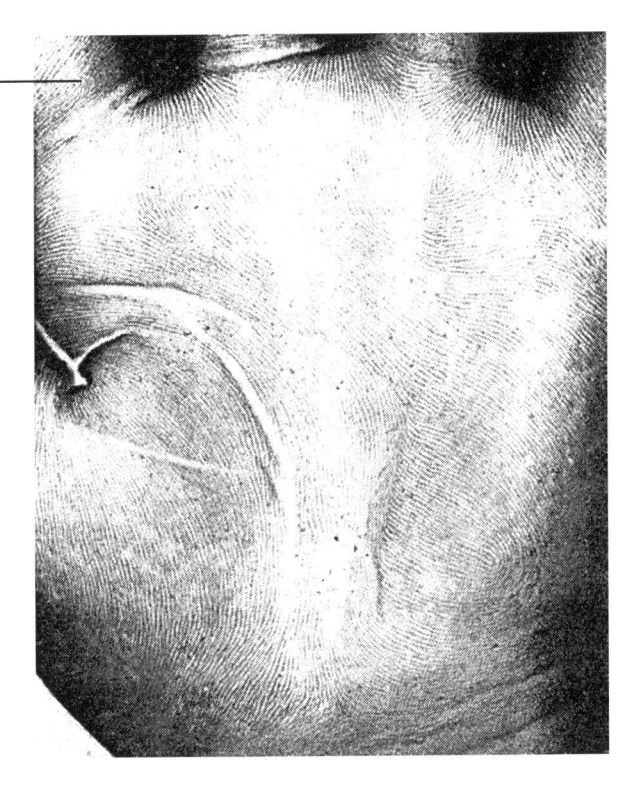

FIGURE 3–14

A histological cross section of fetal volar skin representing the onset of secondary ridge formation between maturing primary ridges (as marked by the arrows) at about 16 weeks EGA. (Image provided by William Babler.)

secondary ridges continue to mature from 16 to 24 weeks EGA, this structure is progressively mirrored on the surface of friction ridge skin as the furrows (Burdi et al., 1979, pp 25–38) (Figure 3–15).

3.6.3 Formation of Dermal Papillae

Dermal papillae are the remnants of dermis left projecting upward into the epidermis when anastomoses bridge primary and secondary ridges (Figures 3–16 and 3–17). They begin to form at approximately 23 weeks EGA (Okajima, 1975) and continue to become more complex throughout fetal formation and even into adulthood (Chacko and Vaidya, 1968; Misumi and Akiyoshi, 1984).

3.7 Pattern Formation

3.7.1 Shape of the Volar Pad

It is observed throughout the physical world that ridges tend to align perpendicularly to physical compression across a surface (Figure 3–18).

Embryology and Morphology of Friction Ridge Skin | **CHAPTER 3**

FIGURE 3–15

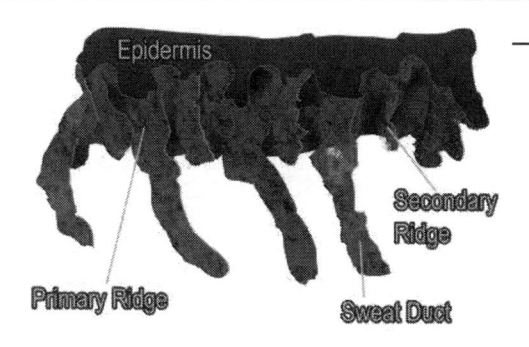

A reconstruction of the secondary ridges continuing to form on the underside of the fetal volar epidermis between existing primary ridges with sweat ducts. (Artwork by Brandon Smithson. Re-drawn from Hale (1952), p 153.)

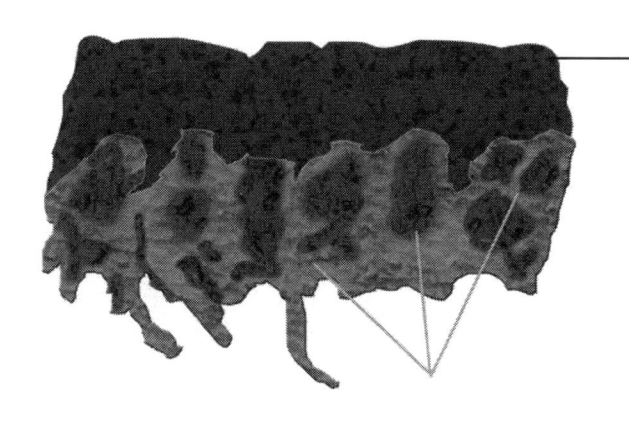

FIGURE 3–16

A reconstruction of the underside of the epidermis of fetal volar skin that represents anastomoses bridging primary and secondary ridges and cordoning off sections of dermis that remain protruding upward as "dermal papillae" or "papillae pegs". (Artwork by Brandon Smithson. Re-drawn from Hale (1952), p 154.)

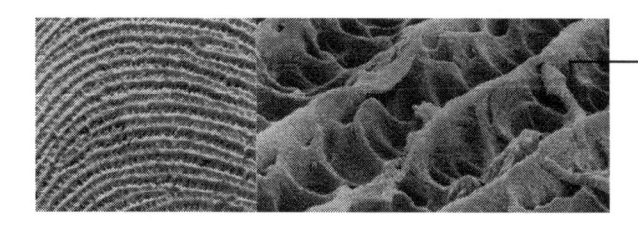

FIGURE 3–17

A scanning electron microscope view of the complex understructure of human epidermis as the dermis has been removed (inverted). Magnification (approximate) = 8 X (left) and 80 X (right). (Reprinted with permission from Montagna and Parakkal (1974), pp 34–35.)

Ridges also form transversely to the lines of growth stress in friction skin. The predominant growth of the hand is longitudinal (lengthwise) and ridges typically cover the volar surface transversely (side to side). This phenomenon is seen in the ridge flow across the phalanges.

Bonnevie first hypothesized in 1924 that volar pad height affects friction ridge patterns (Bonnevie, 1924, p 4). Disruptions in the shape of the volar surfaces of the hands and feet create stresses in directions other than longitudinal. The ridges flow in a complex manner across these three-dimensional structures.

The distinction between the size, height, and shape of the volar pad, and the effects of differences in each of these elements on a friction ridge pattern, is a difficult topic to study (Chakraborty, 1991; Jamison, 1990; Mavalwala et al., 1991). However, almost all research points to the conclusion that the shape of the volar pad influences the stress across the skin that directs ridge alignment. One contrary viewpoint to this conclusion exists. In 1980, Andre G. de Wilde proposed a theory that pattern formation is directed much earlier in fetal life, before volar pads form, while the hand is still in a paddlelike shape (De Wilde, 1980). He

3–13

FIGURE 3–18

When tension is applied across the top of a semiflexible membrane, forces of compression occur on the bottom. The natural relief of compression forces creates ridges forming transversely to the stress. (Reprinted with permission from Wertheim and Maceo (2002), p 57.)

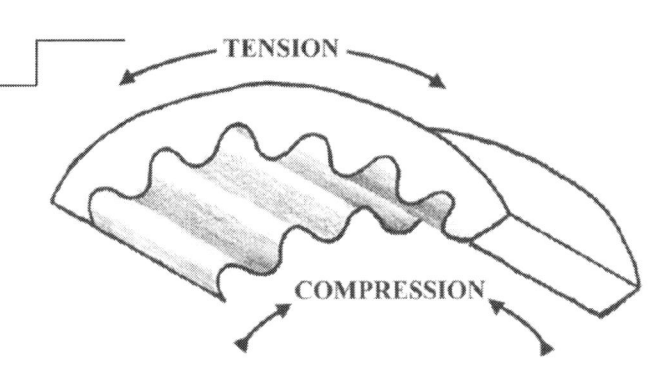

FIGURE 3–19

The loxodrome results when an elastic film is stretched evenly over a hemisphere. Ridges form concentrically around the apex of the membrane disruption. The mathematical formula for this pattern can be found in tensor calculus, a field that offers much promise in predicting ridge formation across volar surfaces. (Reprinted with permission from Wertheim and Maceo (2002), p 62.)

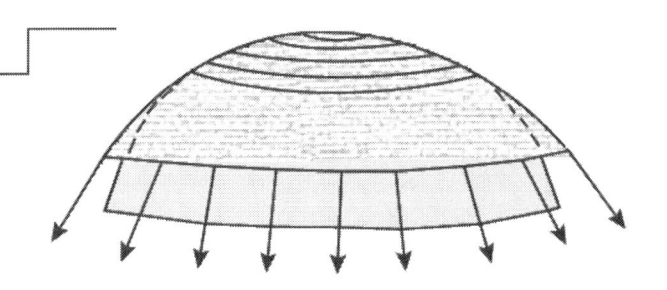

hypothesized that ridges direct the size and shape of the volar pads. However, no other theoretical or empirical support for this theory could be found. All other research indicates that friction ridges align according to volar pad shape and symmetry at approximately 10.5 weeks EGA.

3.7.1.1 Symmetrical Volar Pad. The growth and regression of the volar pads produce variable physical stresses across the volar surface that affect the alignment of the ridges as the ridges first begin to form. Whether ridge flow will conform to a whorl or a loop pattern appears highly correlated with the symmetry of the stress across the surface of the finger. If the volar pad and other elements of finger growth are symmetrical during the onset of primary ridge formation, then a symmetrical pattern (a whorl or an arch) will result. Ridges will form concentrically around the apex of a volar pad that is high and round when the generating layer of friction ridge skin first begins to rapidly produce skin cells. The ridge flow from a symmetrical volar pad conforms to the navigational pattern of the loxodrome (Figure 3–19) (Mulvihill and Smith, 1969; Elie, 1987). Research in both the medical and mathematical fields suggests that this same physical model applies across the entire volar surface of the hands and feet (Cummins, 1926, 1929; Loesch, 1973; Penrose and O'Hara, 1973).

3.7.1.2 Asymmetrical Volar Pad. The degree of asymmetry of the finger volar pad when ridges first begin to form determines the asymmetry of the pattern type. Many researchers have reported that asymmetrical "leaning" pads form looping patterns and that low or absent volar pads form arch patterns (Cummins, 1926, p 138). Babler perhaps conducted the most scientific validation of the correlation between pad symmetry and pattern type through extensive examination of fetal abortuses (Babler, 1978).

Cummins published an extensive analysis of malformed hands to demonstrate the effect of the growth and topology of the hand on ridge direction (Cummins, 1926). Cummins also concluded that ridge direction is established by the contours of the hands and feet at the time of ridge formation. Penrose examined friction ridge pattern formation from a mathematical perspective, arriving at the same conclusion (Loesch, 1973; Penrose and Plomley, 1969). More recently, Kücken and Newell (2005) modeled stress fields across bounded three-dimensional, spherical virtual surfaces, creating relatively accurate-appearing ridge patterns (Figure 3–20).

If the volar pad and other growth factors of the finger are asymmetrical during the critical stage, then that same

FIGURE 3–20

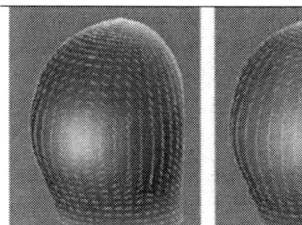

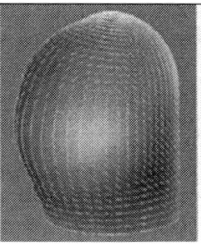

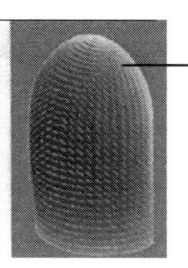

Computer models demonstrating directional field points (tic marks) stretched in the direction of stress. The white spot illustrates the degree of compressive stress and the location where ridge formation takes place first (center of the white portion represents the apex of the pad). (Reprinted with permission from Kücken and Newell (2005), p 79.)

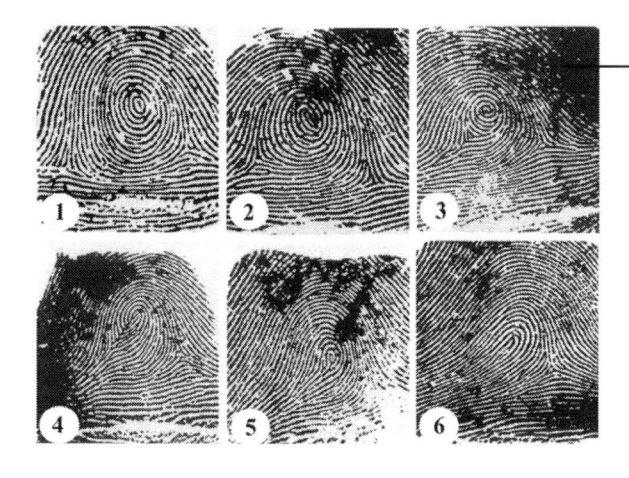

FIGURE 3–21

Six different fingerprint patterns from different individuals, representing the continuum of volar pad symmetry at the onset of friction ridge proliferation, ranging from (1) nearly symmetrical to (6) very displaced. (Reprinted with permission from Wertheim and Maceo (2002), p 69.)

degree of asymmetry will be reflected in the ridge flow of the resulting pattern. This biological process cannot be thought of as limited to the extremes of volar pad regression, occurring either completely symmetrically or asymmetrically (leaning all the way to one side). In fact, there is a continuum involved from whorl patterns to loop patterns. Figure 3–21 illustrates several patterns from different individuals whose volar pads were theoretically the same approximate size at the critical stage (i.e., the volar pads had similar ridge counts), but differed in the degree of their symmetry.

Subtle variations in the symmetry of a volar pad could affect the formation of a whorl pattern versus a central pocket loop whorl pattern, or a central pocket loop whorl pattern versus a loop pattern. Any one of the numerous genetic or environmental factors present during the critical stage could cause a slight deviation in the normal developmental symmetry of the volar pad and, therefore, affect the resulting pattern type.

3.7.2 Size of the Volar Pad

3.7.2.1 Pattern Size. The size, particularly the height, of the volar pad during primary ridge formation affects the ridge count from the core to the delta of normal friction ridge patterns (Bonnevie, 1924; Mulvihill and Smith, 1969; Siervogel et al., 1978). Researchers have observed that ridges that form on high, pronounced volar pads conform to the surface as high-count whorl patterns. Conversely, ridges that form on a finger with a low or absent volar pad create low-count or arch-type patterns (Babler, 1987, pp 300–301). Holt (1968) reported that the total finger ridge count (TFRC) of all 10 fingers, taken by adding the ridge counts from the core to the delta in loops, or the core toward the radial delta in whorls, is the most inheritable feature in dermatoglyphics. This combined information points directly to the conclusion that timing events related to volar pad and friction ridge formation affect friction ridge patterns.

3.7.2.2 Timing Events. The ridge count of a friction ridge pattern is related to two different events: the timing of the onset of volar pad regression and the timing of the onset of primary ridge formation. Differences in the timing of either event will affect the ridge count of that particular pattern. For example, early onset of volar pad regression would lead to a volar pad that was in a more regressed state at the time of the onset of primary ridge formation, and a relatively low-ridge-count pattern (or arch) would likely result. Conversely, overall late onset of volar pad regression would mean that the pad was still relatively large

FIGURE 3–22

Chart A illustrates the effects of two independent timing events on the resulting ridge count of a friction ridge pattern. Chart B illustrates their combined effects on pattern ridge count. (Reprinted with permission from Wertheim and Maceo (2002), p 65.)

when primary ridges began forming, and a high-ridge-count pattern would more likely result (Figure 3–22). This theory is supported by a study that found that "late maturers" had higher-than-average ridge counts, and "early maturers" had lower-than-average ridge counts (Meier et al., 1987).

If the onset of volar pad regression occurred at the normal time, then earlier-than-average onset of primary ridge formation would occur on a larger-than-average volar pad, leading to a higher-than-average ridge count. Likewise, later-than-average onset of primary ridge formation would occur on a smaller-than-average volar pad, leading to a lower-than-average ridge count (Figure 3–22A). When both early and late timing of both factors are taken into account, the results become even more complex (Figure 3–22B).

To make matters even more complex, the size of the volar pad with respect to the finger is also affected by many factors. Diet and chemical intake of the mother (Holbrook, 1991b), hormone levels (Jamison, 1990), radiation levels (Bhasin, 1980), and any other factors that affect the growth rate of the fetus during the critical stage could all indirectly affect the ridge counts of the developing friction ridges on the finger. It is important to remember that anything that affects the tension across the surface of the finger could affect the resulting ridge alignment and pattern type. However, Holt's findings seem to indicate that timing events, rather than environmental factors, play the dominant role in determining TFRC (Holt, 1968).

3.7.2.3 Delta Placement. The onset of cellular proliferation, which begins primary ridge formation, occurs first in three distinct areas: (1) the apex of the volar pad (which corresponds to the core of the fingerprint pattern); (2) the distal periphery, or tip of the finger (near the nailbed); and (3) the distal interphalangeal flexion crease area (below the delta(s) in a fingerprint) (Figure 3–23).

As ridge formation continues, new proliferation occurs on the edges of the existing ridge fields in areas that do not yet display primary ridge formation. These three "fields" of ridges converge as they form, meeting in the delta area of the finger. This wavelike process of three converging fields allows for the visualization of how deltas most likely form (Figure 3–24).

The concept of "converging ridge fields" also offers a way to visualize the difference between the formation of high- versus low-ridge-count patterns. If ridges begin forming on the apex (center) of the pad first and proceed outward before formation begins on the tip and joint areas, then by the time the fields meet, a relatively large distance will have been traversed by the field on the apex of the pad; in that instance, a high-count pattern will be formed (Figure 3–25). However, if the ridges form first on the two outermost portions and proceed inward, and formation begins at the last instant on the apex of the pad, then only a few ridges may be formed by the time the fields meet; in that instance, a very low-count pattern is observed (Figure 3–26). The combined observations of different researchers examining friction ridges on the finger during the critical stage of development further support the validity of this model (Babler, 1991, 1999; Dell and Munger, 1986; Hirsch and Schweichel, 1973).

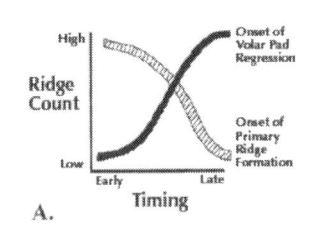

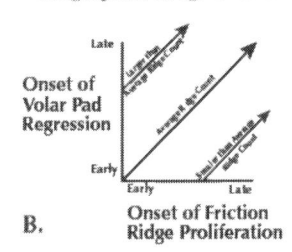

3.7.3 Combined Effect of Timing and Symmetry on Ridge Formation

When it is understood that timing and symmetry control two very different elements of ridge flow, it becomes easy

Embryology and Morphology of Friction Ridge Skin | CHAPTER 3

FIGURE 3–23

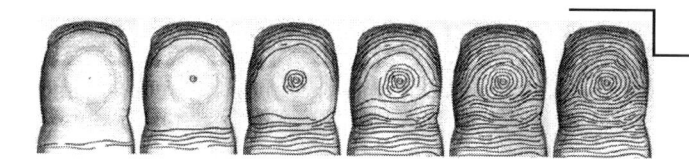

A drawing depicting the normal starting locations of ridge formation and subsequent coverage across the surface of a finger. (Reprinted with permission from Wertheim and Maceo (2002), p 66.)

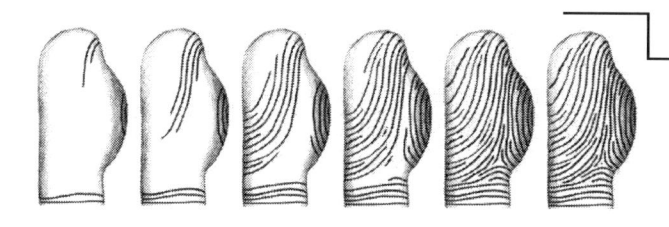

FIGURE 3–24

A drawing that depicts an easy way to visualize how deltas form from three converging ridge fields. (Reprinted with permission from Wertheim and Maceo (2002), p 66.)

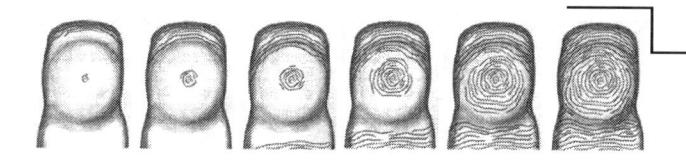

FIGURE 3–25

A drawing that depicts the likely progression of ridges on a high-ridge-count pattern. (Reprinted with permission from Wertheim and Maceo (2002), p 67.)

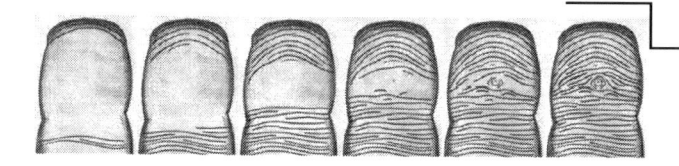

FIGURE 3–26

A drawing that depicts the likely progression of ridges on a low-ridge-count pattern. (Reprinted with permission from Wertheim and Maceo (2002), p 67.)

to see how both small and large loop and whorl patterns form. A finger pad that regresses symmetrically will form a whorl pattern, regardless of early or late timing of friction ridge formation with respect to volar pad regression. If the timing of the onset of primary ridge formation in this situation is early in fetal life, then the volar pad will still be high on the finger, and the whorl pattern will have a high ridge count. If timing is later in fetal life, after the pad has almost completely been absorbed into the contours of the finger, then a low-count whorl pattern will result. With further regression, an arch pattern will form (Figure 3–27).

Likewise, asymmetrical finger pads will form loop patterns and will also be affected by timing. If ridges begin forming early with respect to volar pad regression on an asymmetrical pad, then the pad will be large, and a high-count loop will result. Later timing leads to a low-count loop or arch-type pattern (Figure 3–28). Again, volar pad placement is not simply symmetrical or asymmetrical; a continuum of volar pad symmetry occurs and accounts for the variety of pattern types observed.

A regression scheme seems to exist whereby the volar pad is symmetrical at the onset and becomes progressively more asymmetrical as it regresses. This is supported by general fingerprint pattern statistics that show that more than one-half of all fingerprint patterns are ulnar loops. More specifically, this scheme is supported by fetal research that has determined that early timing of primary ridge formation leads to a higher percentage (95 percent) of whorls (Babler, 1978, p 25). Also, low- and high-ridge-count patterns occur less frequently than average-count patterns (Cowger, 1983). All research tends to indicate that volar pads regress from an early symmetrical position to an asymmetrical position later in fetal life. Although this is the norm, it is certainly not without exception, because whorl patterns with extremely

FIGURE 3–27

These different fingerprint patterns (bottom) were formed on completely different, but symmetrical, volar pads (top). The drawings on the top illustrate the likely fetal condition of the symmetrical volar pad that produced the resulting print below it. From left to right, the images show the results of the combined timing of the onset of friction ridge proliferation versus volar pad regression. (Reprinted with permission from Wertheim and Maceo (2002), p 71.)

FIGURE 3–28

These different fingerprint patterns (bottom) were formed on different, asymmetrical volar pads (top). The drawings on the top illustrate the likely fetal condition of the asymmetrical volar pad that produced the resulting print below it. From left to right, the images show the results of the combined timing of the onset of friction ridge proliferation versus volar pad regression. (Reprinted with permission from Wertheim and Maceo (2002), p 71.)

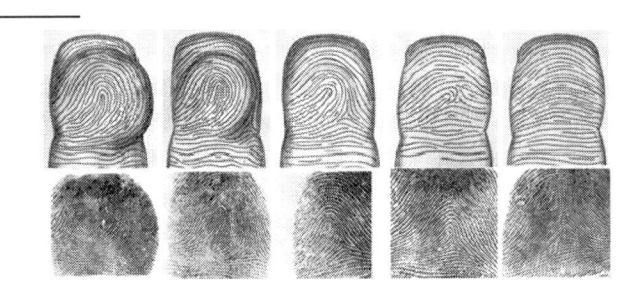

low ridge counts and loop patterns with extremely high ridge counts can both be found with relative ease in even small collections of recorded fingerprints.

3.8 Genetics

3.8.1 Introduction to Genetic Diversity and Friction Ridge Skin

In 1904, Inez Whipple presented research that provided a detailed theory of evolutionary progression of the volar surface (Whipple, 1904). Ashbaugh succinctly summarizes Whipple's proposition of the evolutionary genesis of friction ridges:

> Early mammals were covered with a scale-like skin surface. Each scale had one hair protruding from it and an accompanying oil or sebaceous gland. On volar areas, which are the bottoms of the hands and feet, hairs slowly disappeared due to surface use. The pore that was related to the hair changed from a sebaceous gland to a sweat gland. Its purpose, to keep the surface skin damp which enhanced the grip of the volar surface.

Starting in all likelihood as a mutation, scales started to line up in rows and fuse together. This further assisted the grip of the skin surface by increasing friction. Through natural selection, this mutation became prevalent. Scales slowly evolved into wart-like units with pore openings near the centre. The fusing of these wart formations into rows is the predecessor to the friction ridge, the individual wart being the equivalent of a ridge dot (Ashbaugh, 1991, p 27).

Fourteen years after Whipple's phylogenetic (evolutionary history) theory was presented, researchers diverged from her theory and presented an ontogenetic (individual developmental or embryonic history) model, suggesting that fusion of warts into ridges occurs during embryonic development (Wilder and Wentworth, 1918). In 1926, Cummins refuted the ontogenetic scheme (Cummins, 1926, p 134). However, Hale later included the ontogenetic model in his conclusions (Hale, 1952). Literature since that time has been mixed. Multiple researchers have demonstrated that the first visual evidence of interaction between the dermis and the epidermis is ridges, not a series of units, protruding into the dermis (Figure 3–6, p 3-8). Perhaps with advances in technology, the theory that localized cell proliferations grow together into linear ridges before the appearance of the ridge as a structure will be demonstrated. Until then, fusion of units into ridges remains a possible model of development that could provide individuality before the appearance of the first ridge structures. The term "ridge unit" might be limited to a description of an adult sweat pore and surrounding ridge (Ashbaugh, 1999, pp 25, 35), with the term "localized proliferation" being used to describe theoretical events of fetal formation (Babler, 1987, p 298).

3.8.2 The Role of Genetics

Every aspect of the growth and development of a single cell into a fully formed human is initiated by a genetic blueprint. The capacity to form friction ridges is inherent within the developing embryo. The patterns that these ridges form, however, are limited by nature and are defined by the fingerprint community as whorls, loops, arches, combinations and transitions of these basic patterns, or lack of a pattern (Hirsch, 1964). Although genetics may direct when and where ridges will form by providing the blueprint for proteins, nature provides the boundaries for patterning through physical mechanisms (Ball, 1999).

Proteins direct cellular activity by facilitating biochemical processes within the cell. These processes depend not only on the protein derived from the gene but also on the many other nonprotein components of the cell such as sugars, lipids, hormones, inorganic elements (e.g., oxygen), inorganic compounds (e.g., nitric oxide), and minerals. Additionally, the physical environment around and within cells, including surface tension, electrical charge, and viscosity, contributes to the way the cell functions (Ball, 1999).

Genetic information directs cellular function, serves as a link between generations, and influences an individual's appearance. Some aspects of appearance are similar for each individual of that species (i.e., those characteristics that define the species). However, within the species, for each aspect of an individual's appearance, many genes and external factors affect the final outcome of physical appearance. The genes involved with a specific attribute (e.g., skin color) produce the appropriate proteins, which in turn react with each other and with the many nongenetic components of the cell in complex biochemical pathways during the growth and development of the fetus (Ball, 1999). These biochemical pathways proceed under the omnipresent influence of external factors.

Although DNA is crucial for providing the blueprint for the development of a particular model, there are so many steps between the genesis of the DNA-encoded protein and the final product that even two individuals who originated from the same DNA would produce two completely unique models.

Perhaps Jamison best describes the interplay between genes and the environment in friction ridge skin:

> Since dermatoglyphic formation cannot be derived solely from either genetic or environmental factors, it must result from an interaction of the two types of factors. This interaction is probably far from being simple and it most likely involves a multiple step reciprocal positive feedback relationship (Maruyama, 1963) in which either a genetically or an environmentally-based factor causes a change in the uterine environment, leading to a genetic response (perhaps in the form of a "switch mechanism", as in Roberts (1986)), which then leads to an increasingly complex series of genetic-environmental interactive responses (Jamison, 1990, p 103).

The ultimate example of the role of the environment in friction ridge formation is monozygotic twins, who share identical genetic information and very similar intrauterine environments, but on many occasions have very different patterns. The role of genetics is currently understood by the indication that several main genes, in conjunction with a number of modifying genes, may be responsible for volar patterning, but it is well established that friction ridge patterning is also affected by the environment (Chakraborty, 1991; Hirsch, 1964; Loesch, 1982, 1983; Slatis et al., 1976; Weninger et al., 1976).

Like many traits, genetics influences pattern formation indirectly by contributing to the timing of the onset of friction ridge skin, the timing of the onset of volar pad regression, the growth rate of the fetus, and other factors. Stresses across small areas of skin are not inherited, but rather they represent one of many environmental factors that influence pattern formation.

Until recently (Chakraborty, 1991; Mavalwala et al., 1991), most researchers in the field of genetics and physical anthropology have traditionally viewed TFRC as evidence of direct genetic control of fingerprint pattern formation (Bonnevie, 1924; Holt, 1968). The research of Sara Holt (1968) regarding the inheritability of TFRC is a significant finding that supports the two-tiered development scheme suggested by this and other literary reviews of fingerprint pattern formation. Logic also supports this scheme. Genetically controlled timed events would be less susceptible to environmental variations, and, therefore, TFRC would be more inheritable than pattern type. Additionally, the wide range of patterns found on the palms (Malhotra, 1982) demonstrates the complex nature of factors that affect ridge alignment. Patterning and ridge counts are indirectly inherited and are not affected by only one developmental factor. However, ridge flow and ridge count are both affected by tension across the surface of growing fetal skin.

3.8.3 Familial Studies

3.8.3.1 Ethnic Variation. Thousands of anthropological studies have been conducted on distinct populations to identify trends in fingerprint pattern formation. Perhaps one of the most comprehensive reviews of this tremendous body of research was conducted by Jamshed Mavalwala, resulting in a 300-page bibliography of dermatoglyphic references (Mavalwala, 1977). The major result from this body of work was the demonstration that intratribal variations in friction ridge pattern frequencies were greater than intertribal variations. Likewise, intraspecies variations in primates were greater than interspecies variations. The body of literature on ethnic variation suggests that multiple genes affect pattern formation and that those genes interact with respect to final pattern characteristics.

3.8.3.2 Abnormalities. The medical community has been, and continues to be, interested in dermatoglyphics (Durham et al., 2000; Kahn et al., 2001; Schaumann and Opitz, 1991) and creases (Kimura, 1991) as indicators of abnormal fetal development during the critical stage. Although there is evidence that interest has waned in recent decades (Reed, 1991), it was reported in 1991 that significantly more than 3,500 articles in the international literature dealt with different aspects of dermatoglyphics (Mavalwala, 1977). Although many articles relate certain medical conditions to statistically significant occurrences of abnormal ridge pattern combinations, many researchers still heed the warning that "dermatoglyphics may be of uncertain, if any, diagnostic value due to the lack of a specific dermatoglyphic stereotype in individual patients" (Schaumann, 1982, pp 33–34).

Harold Cummins was perhaps one of the most prominent researchers on the specific reasons behind abnormal friction ridge pattern development (Cummins, 1923, 1926).

From dozens of developmental-defect case studies, he concluded that "whatever the nature of the defect, the [ridge] configurations occur as systems partly or wholly unlike the normal, but obviously conforming to the irregularities of the part" (Cummins, 1926, p 132). Later in his career, Cummins established that the absence of dermal ridges can be caused by chromosomal abnormalities (Figure 3–29) (Cummins, 1965). Other research (Schaumann and Alter, 1976) has attributed a more pronounced condition, dysplasia, to localized deviation in normal nerve branching during fetal development (Figure 3–30).

A third and much more extreme (and rare) condition involves the complete lack of ridge features on the fingers and palms of the hands as well as the toes and soles of the feet. Cummins hypothesizes that in epidermolysis, or the death and dissolution of the epidermis, the disintegrated epidermis sloughs, and the denuded surface is gradually covered by a growth of skin cells arising from the dermis after the capacity has gone for the epidermal–dermal junction to produce ridges (Cummins, 1965). Other researchers indicate that this condition, also known as aplasia, appears to stem from a chromosomal abnormality linked to the complete lack of nerve development in the epidermis at the time ridges are supposed to form. In a 1965 article, Cummins postulates that epidermolysis can be inherited, citing three generations of a family, 13 of whom lacked ridges over fingers, palms, toes, and soles (Cummins, 1965). Schaumann and Alter (1976) reproduce a family tree showing 16 of 28 family members from four generations having congenital ridge aplasia, and go on to reference other evidence of the inheritance of ridge anomalies (Figure 3–31).

Goradia and colleagues (1979) make a convincing argument that there is a continuum between normal epidermal ridges, disassociated ridges, and aplasia. They cite cases of overlap in the same person between normal and disassociated ridges as well as overlap between disassociated ridges and areas with no discernible pattern. Additionally, the authors bring to light that certain chromosomal abnormalities have been found to be associated with both disassociation and aplasia.

Although not a typical abnormality, incipient ridges, also described as "rudimentary", "interstitial", or "nascent" ridges, are not present in the majority of friction ridge impressions. When they are present on an individual, studies have shown them to be hereditary (Penrose and Plomley, 1969). In 1979, Okajima examined incipient ridges and affirmed earlier research indicating that these structures are

FIGURE 3–29

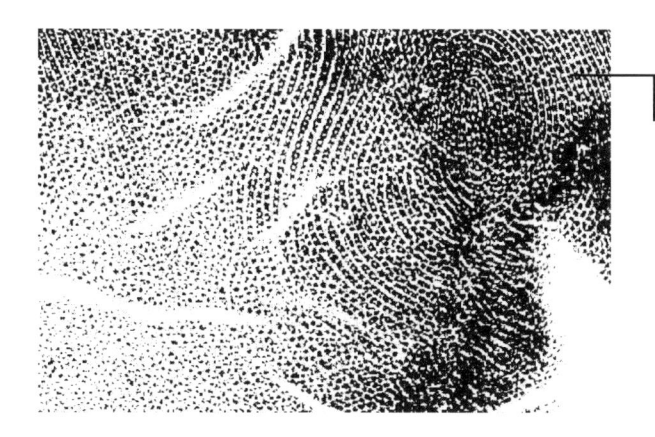

An impression showing normal ridges (top right), mildly disassociated ridges (middle), and severely disassociated ridges (bottom left) in a patient with a chromosomal abnormality. (Reprinted with permission from Schaumann and Alter (1976), p 98.)

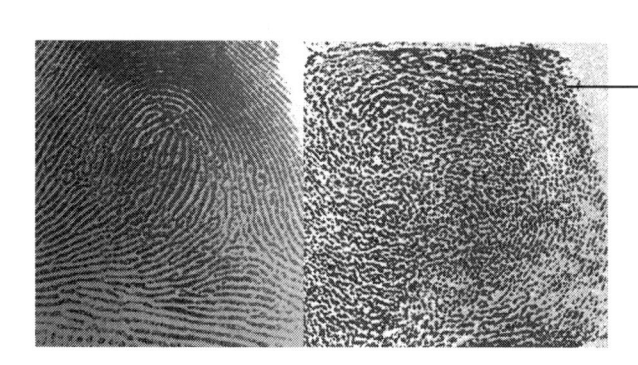

FIGURE 3–30

Impressions of epidermis displaying mild (left) and severe (right) dysplasia. (Reprinted with permission from Schaumann and Alter (1976), pp 94–96.)

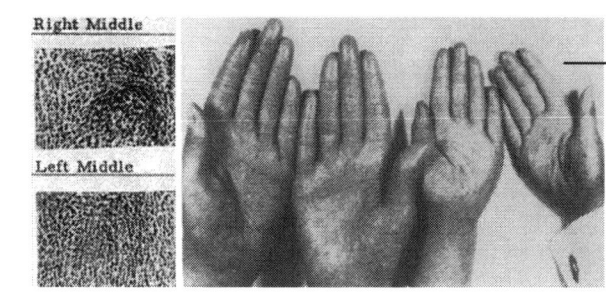

FIGURE 3–31

Impressions (left) of fragmented or absent ridges from a subject with aplasia (Reprinted with permission of the March of Dimes from Goradia et al., 1979). Overall image (right) of the hands of a mother and daughter with aplasia. (Reprinted with permission from Schaumann and Alter (1976), p 91.)

permanent, although they carry no sweat glands (Okajima, 1979) (Figure 3–32).

3.9 Uniqueness: Developmental Noise

3.9.1 Ridge Path

The uniqueness of friction skin is imparted from the permanent base structure through a myriad of random forces, which, themselves, are affected by a seemingly infinite number of factors. The fetal volar pads play a major role in affecting the tensions that directly influence pattern formation (volar pad symmetry) and ridge count (volar pad size), but minutiae formation occurs on a much smaller level. Localized stresses (tensions and compressions), resulting from growth of the tissue layers of the digit and interactions with existing ridge fields, create the foundations for second-level uniqueness.

3.9.2 Ridge Morphology

Ridge morphology (third-level detail) is the surface manifestation of a unique heterogeneous cellular community

FIGURE 3–32

A photograph (magnification = 13 X) of incipient ridges (left) and the dermal surface under the ridges (right) showing double-row arrangement of dermal papillae, marking them as permanent features of friction ridge skin. (Reprinted with permission of the March of Dimes from Okajima (1979), p 191.)

along the basement membrane, which constantly feeds the epidermis a three-dimensional portrait of its uniqueness. It is completely inconceivable that the physical stresses and cellular distributions that create that community could be exactly duplicated, on any level, in two different areas of developing fetal tissue. Each individual section of every ridge is unique. Therefore, any ridge arrangement, regardless of quantity, cannot be replicated. Wide variations in the amount of detail that is recorded from the three-dimensional skin to the two-dimensional impression during any given contact may result in the impossibility of individualization of some latent impressions, but the arrangement of features on the skin and the resulting details in the impression on a surface are still unique.

3.9.3 Maturation of the Skin

After maturation of the primary and secondary ridges at 24 weeks EGA, anastomoses begin to cross through the dermis (Hale, 1952), linking primary and secondary ridges and molding the upper portion of the dermis into papillae pegs. Papillae continue to change form even into late adulthood and become complex (Misumi and Akiyoshi, 1984). Although the shape of the epidermal–dermal boundary may change over time, the rate of skin cell production in the basal layer of skin does not become spatially incongruent. It is for this reason that changes in the shape of the basal layer "sheet" do not produce features that appear significantly different on the surface (Figure 3–33). The consistent rate of basal skin cell proliferation in neighboring areas of skin provides consistent unique detail to the surface of skin. The pattern increases many times over in size, but the sequence of ridges never changes throughout fetal and adult life, barring injury or disease that affects the basal layer of skin.

3.10 Summary: Keys to Uniqueness and Pattern Formation

3.10.1 Uniqueness

As the skin progresses through the entire process of ridge formation (Figure 3–34), many factors contribute to the end result: complete structural uniqueness, from ridge path to ridge shape. Although genetics has been shown to play a role in pattern formation, it does not determine the arrangement of minutiae or ridge shapes within the pattern. The morphogenesis of these finer details is a product of the unique developmental noise that occurs in that area of skin during the critical period of friction ridge formation.

3.10.2 Pattern Formation

The fetal volar pads play a major role in influencing pattern formation (volar pad symmetry) and ridge count (volar pad size), but the volar pads do not directly cause ridge alignment. Instead, the volar pads affect the topology of the surface and the overall tension and compression across the developing epidermal–dermal junction, which in turn directly affects friction ridge alignment during the critical stage of ridge development. Any stress or strain on the developing finger during the critical stage (Figure 3–35) of friction ridge formation could affect ridge alignment.

3.11 Reviewers

The reviewers critiquing this chapter were Jeffrey G. Barnes, Patti Blume, Mary Ann Brandon, Brent T. Cutro, Sr., Lynne D. Herold, Michelle L. Snyder, and John R. Vanderkolk.

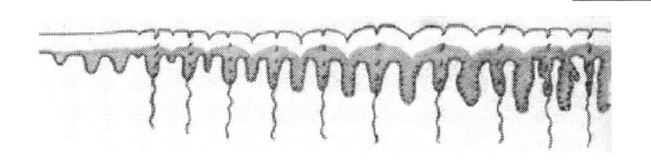

Embryology and Morphology of Friction Ridge Skin | **CHAPTER 3**

FIGURE 3–33

An illustration of the progression of the structure of volar skin from fetal life (left) through late adulthood (right). (Reprinted with permission from Wertheim and Maceo (2002), p 39.)

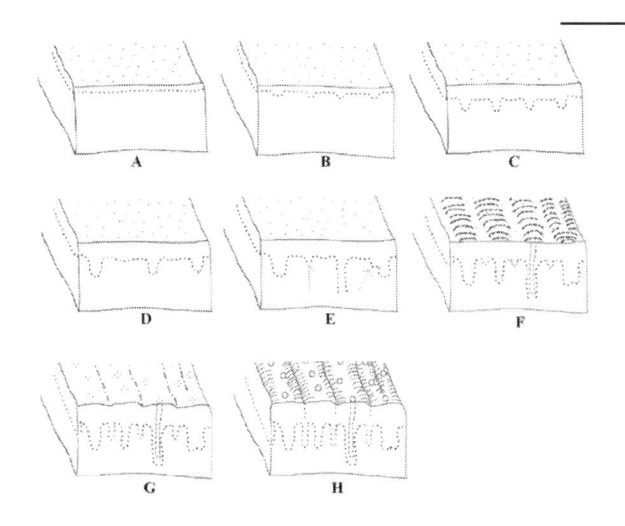

FIGURE 3–34

Drawings representing volar skin before (A), during (B–E), and after (F–H) the critical stage of friction ridge formation: (A) undifferentiated friction ridge skin; (B) initiation of primary ridge formation at the epidermal–dermal border; (C) primary ridges increasing in depth; (D) skin growth separating existing primary ridges; (E) new primary ridge growth between existing primary ridges (sweat ducts are forming); (F) initiation of secondary ridge growth between primary ridges; (G) secondary ridge maturation combined with surface ridge appearance; (H) entire system begins maturation process (approximately 24 weeks EGA). (Reprinted with permission from Wertheim and Maceo (2002), p 56.)

FIGURE 3–35

A chart showing the consensus of the literature regarding estimated time frames for the onset (becoming larger) and regression (becoming smaller) of the volar pads, as well as the onset and growth of the primary and secondary ridges.

3.12 References

Ashbaugh, D. R. Ridgeology. *J. Forensic Ident.* 1991, *41* (1), 16–64.

Ashbaugh, D. R. *Quantitative–Qualitative Friction Ridge Analysis: An Introduction to Basic and Advanced Ridgeology;* CRC Press: Boca Raton, FL, 1999.

Babler, W. J. Prenatal Selection and Dermatoglyphic Patterns. *Am. J. Physical Anthropol.* 1978, *48* (1), 21–28.

Babler, W. J. Prenatal Development of Dermatoglyphic Patterns: Associations with Epidermal Ridge, Volar Pad, and Bone Morphology. *Collegium Anthropologicum* 1987, *11* (2), 297–303.

Babler, W. J. Prenatal Communalities in Epidermal Ridge Development. In *Trends in Dermatoglyphic Research;* Durham, N., Plato, C., Eds.; Kluwer Academic Press: Dordrecht, Netherlands, 1990; pp 54–68.

Babler, W. J. Embryologic Development of Epidermal Ridges and Their Configurations. In *Dermatoglyphics: Science in Transition;* Plato, C., Garruto, R., Schaumann, B., Eds.; Birth Defects Original Article Series; March of Dimes: New York, 1991; pp 95–112.

Babler, W. J. Marquette University, Milwaukee, WI. Personal communication, 1999.

Ball, P. *The Self-Made Tapestry: Pattern Formation in Nature;* Oxford University Press: New York, 1999.

Bhasin, M. Effect of Natural Background Radiation on Dermatoglyphic Traits. *Acta Anthropogenetica* 1980, *4* (1–2), 1–27.

Bonnevie, K. Studies on Papillary Patterns on Human Fingers. *J. Genetics* 1924, *15,* 1–112.

Burdi, A.R., Babler, W. J., Garn, S.M. Monitoring Patterns of Prenatal Skeletal Development. In *Dermatoglyphics—Fifty Years Later;* Birth Defects Original Article Series 15(6); March of Dimes: Washington, DC, 1979; pp 25–38.

Carlson, B. *Human Embryology and Development Biology;* Mosby: New York, 1999.

Chacko, S; Vaidya, M. The Dermal Papillae and Ridge Patterns in Human Volar Skin. *Acta Anatomica (Basel)* 1968, *70* (1), 99–108.

Chakraborty, R. The Role of Heredity and Environment on Dermatoglyphic Traits. In *Dermatoglyphics: Science in Transition;* March of Dimes: Washington, DC, 1991; pp 151–191.

Cowger, J. F. *Friction Ridge Skin: Comparison and Identification of Fingerprints;* Elsevier Science: New York, 1983.

Cummins, H. The Configurations of Epidermal Ridges in a Human Acephalic Monster. *Anatomical Record* 1923, *26* (1), 1–13.

Cummins, H. Epidermal Ridge Configurations in Developmental Defects, with Particular References to the Ontogenetic Factors Which Condition Ridge Direction. *Am. J. Anatomy* 1926, *38* (1), 89–151.

Cummins, H. The Topographic History of the Volar Pads (Walking Pads; Tastballen) in the Human Embryo. *Contributions to Embryol.* 1929, *20,* 105–126.

Cummins, H. Loss of Ridged Skin Before Birth. *Finger Print Ident. Mag.* 1965, *46,* 3–7, 23.

Dell, D.; Munger, B. The Early Embryogenesis of Papillary (Sweat Duct) Ridges in Primate Glabrous Skin: The Dermatotopic Map of Cutaneous Mechanoreceptors and Dermatoglyphics. *J. Comp. Neurol.* 1986, *244* (4), 511–532.

De Wilde, A. G. A Theory Concerning Ridge Pattern Development. *Bull. Int. Dermatoglyphics Assoc.* 1980, *8* (1), 2–18.

Durham, N., Fox, K., Plato, C., Eds. *The State of Dermatoglyphics: The Science of Finger and Palm Prints;* Edwin Mellen Press: New York, 2000.

Elie, J. A New Methodological Approach to Dermatoglyphic Variability. *Can. Rev. Physical Anthropol.* 1987, *6* (1), 54–63.

Evatt, E. J. The Development and Evolution of the Papillary Ridges and Patterns of the Volar Surfaces of the Hand. *J. Anatomy* 1906, *41,* 66–70.

Goradia, R.; Davis, B.; DeLeon, R. Familial Ridge Dissociation-Aplasia and X-Chromosome Aneuploidy. In *Dermatoglyphics—Fifty Years Later;* Birth Defects Original Article Series; March of Dimes: Washington, DC, 1979; pp 591–607.

Hale, A. Morphogenesis of Volar Skin in the Human Fetus. *Am. J. Anatomy* 1952, *91* (1), 147–173.

Heimer, L. *The Human Brain and Spinal Cord: Functional Neuroanatomy and Dissection Guide,* 2nd ed.; Springer-Verlag: New York, 1995.

Hirsch, W. Biological Aspects of Finger Prints, Palms, and Soles. *Fingerprint and Ident. Mag.* 1964, 3–17.

Hirsch, W.; Schweichel, J. U. Morphological Evidence Concerning the Problem of Skin Ridge Formation. *J. Mental Deficiency Res.* 1973, *17* (1), 58–72.

Holbrook, K. A. Structure and Development of the Skin. In *Pathophysiology of Dermatologic Diseases,* 2nd ed.; Soter, M., Baden, H., Eds.; McGraw-Hill: New York, 1991a; pp 3–43.

Holbrook, K. A. Structure and Function of the Developing Human Skin. In *Biochemistry and Physiology of the Skin;* Goldsmith, L., Ed.; Oxford University Press: New York, 1991b; pp 64–101.

Holbrook, K. A.; Odland, G. F. The Fine Structure of Developing Human Epidermis: Light Scanning, and Transmission Electron Microscopy of the Periderm. *J. Invest. Dermatol.* 1975, *65* (1), 16–38.

Holt, S. B. *The Genetics of Dermal Ridges;* Charles C. Thomas: Springfield, IL, 1968.

Jamison, C. Dermatoglyphics and the Geschwind Hypothesis I: Theoretical Background and Palmar Results of Dyslexia II. Digital Results of Dyslexia and Developmental Implications. In *Trends in Dermatoglyphic Research;* Durham, N., Plato, C., Eds.; Kluwer Academic Press: Dordrecht, Netherlands, 1990; pp 99–135.

Kahn, H.; Ravindranath, R.; Valdez, R.; Venkat Narayan, K. M. Fingerprint Ridge-Count Difference between Adjacent Fingertips (dR45) Predicts Upper-Body Distribution: Evidence for Early Gestational Programming. *Am. J. Epidemiol.* 2001, *153* (4), 338–344.

Kimura, S. Embryological Development of Flexion Creases. In *Dermatoglyphics Science in Transition;* March of Dimes: Washington, DC, 1991; pp 113–129.

Kollmann, A. *Der Tastapparat der Hand der menschlichen Rassen und der Affen in seiner Entwickelung und Gliederung (The Tactile Apparatus of the Hand of the Human Races and Apes in Its Development and Structure);* Voss Verlag: Hamburg, Germany, 1883.

Kücken, M.; Newell, A. Fingerprint Formation. *J. Theoretical Biol.* 2005, *235* (1), 71–83.

Lacroix, B.; Wolff-Wuenot, M.; Haffen, K. Early Human Hand Morphology: An Estimation of Fetal Age. *Early Human Development* 1984, *9* (2), 127–136.

Lavker, R. M.; Sun, T. T. Epidermal Stem Cells. *J. Invest. Dermatol.* 1983, *81* (1) (Suppl.), 121s–127s.

Loesch, D. The Contributions of L.S. Penrose to Dermatoglyphics. *J. Mental Deficiency Res.* 1973, *17* (1), 1–17.

Loesch, D. Genetic Studies of Dermatoglyphics—Advances and Limitations. *Progress in Dermatoglyphic Res.* 1982, *84,* 45–77.

Loesch, D. *Quantitative Dermatoglyphics: Classification, Genetics, and Pathology;* Oxford University Press: New York, 1983.

Malhotra, K. Progress in Genetics of Palmar Pattern Ridge Counts in Man. *Progress in Dermatoglyphic Res.* 1982, *84,* 111–128.

Maruyama, M. The Second Cybernetics: Deviation-Amplifying Mutual Causal Processes. *Am. Scientist* 1963, *5* (2), 164–179.

Mavalwala, J. *Dermatoglyphics: An International Bibliography;* Mouton: Chicago, 1977.

Mavalwala, J.; Mavalwala, P.; Kamali, S. Issues of Sampling and of Methodologies in Dermatoglyphics. In *Dermatoglyphics: Science in Transition;* March of Dimes: Washington, DC, 1991; pp 291–303.

Meier, R. J. Sequential Developmental Components of Digital Dermatoglyphics. *Human Biol.* 1981, *53* (4), 557–573.

Meier, R. J.; Goodson, C. S.; Roche, E. Dermatoglyphic Development and Timing of Maturation. *Human Biol.* 1987, *59* (2), 357–373.

Misumi, Y.; Akiyoshi, T. Scanning Electron Microscopic Structure of the Finger Print as Related to the Dermal Surface. *The Anatomical Record* 1984, *208* (1), 49–55.

Montagna, W.; Parakkal, P. *The Structure and Function of Skin,* 3rd ed.; Academic Press: New York, 1974.

Montagna, W.; Kligman, A.; Carlisle, K. *Atlas of Normal Human Skin;* Springer-Verlag: New York, 1992.

Moore, S. J.; Munger, B. The Early Ontogeny of the Afferent Nerves and Papillary Ridges in Human Digital Glabrous Skin. *Dev. Brain Res.* 1989, *48* (1), 119–141.

Morohunfola, K.; Munger, B.; Jones, T. The Differentiation of the Skin and its Appendages. I. Normal Development of Papillary Ridges. *The Anatomical Record* 1992, *232* (4), 587–598.

Mulvihill, J. J.; Smith, D. W. The Genesis of Dermatoglyphics. *J. Pediatr.* 1969, *75* (4), 579–589.

Murray, J. D. How the Leopard Gets Its Spots. *Scientific American* 1988, 80.

Okajima, M. Development of Dermal Ridges in the Fetus. *J. Med. Genet.* 1975, *12* (3), 243–250.

Okajima, M. Dermal and Epidermal Structures of the Volar Skin. In *Dermatoglyphics—Fifty Years Later;* Birth Defects Original Article Series; March of Dimes: Washington, DC, 1979; pp 179–188.

Okajima, M. A Methodological Approach to the Development of Epidermal Ridges Viewed on the Dermal Surface of Fetuses. In *Progress in Dermatoglyphic Research;* Alan R. Liss, Inc.: New York, 1982; pp 175–188.

Penrose, L.; O'Hara, P. The Development of Epidermal Ridges. *J. Med. Genet.* 1973, *10* (3), 201–208.

Penrose, L.; Plomley, N. Structure of Interstitial Epidermal Ridges. *Zeitschrift für Morphologie und Anthropologie* 1969, *61* (1), 81–84.

Raven, P.; Johnson, G. *Biology,* 3rd ed.; Mosby Year Book: St. Louis, MO, 1992.

Reed, T. Impact of Changes in Medical Genetics on Teaching and Disseminating Information on Dermatoglyphics. In *Dermatoglyphics: Science in Transition;* March of Dimes: Washington, DC, 1991; pp 305–319.

Roberts, D. Population Variation in Dermatoglyphics: Field Theory. *Progress in Dermatoglyphic Res.* 1982, *84,* 79–91.

Roberts, D. The Genetics of Human Fetal Growth. In *Human Growth, A Comprehensive Treatise;* Falkner, F.; Tanner, J., Eds.; Plenum Press: New York, 1986; vol. 3, pp 113–143.

Schaumann, B. Medical Applications of Dermatoglyphics. *Progress in Dermatoglyphic Res.* 1982, *84,* 33–34.

Schaumann, B.; Alter, M. *Dermatoglyphics in Medical Disorders;* Springer-Verlag: New York, 1976.

Schaumann, B.; Opitz, J. Clinical Aspects of Dermatoglyphics. In *Dermatoglyphics: Science in Transition;* March of Dimes: Washington, DC, 1991; pp 193–228.

Siervogel, R. M.; Roche, A.; Roche, E. Developmental Fields for Dermatoglyphic Traits as Revealed by Multivariate Analysis. *Human Biol.* 1978, *50* (4), 541–556.

Slatis, H.; Katznelson, M.; Bonne-Tamir, B. The Inheritance of Fingerprint Patterns. *Am. J. Hum. Genet.* 1976, *28* (3), 280–289.

Smith, L. T.; Holbrook, K. A. Embryogenesis of the Dermis in Human Skin. *Pediatr. Dermatol.* 1986, *3* (4), 271–280.

Weninger, M.; Aue-Hauser, G.; Scheiber, V. Total Finger Ridge-Count and the Polygenic Hypothesis: A Critique. *Human Biol.* 1976, *48* (4), 713–725.

Wertheim, K.; Maceo, A. The Critical Stage of Friction Ridge Pattern Formation. *J. Forensic Ident.* 2002, *52* (1), 35–85.

Whipple, I., The Ventral Surface of the Mammalian Chiridium, With Special Reference to the Conditions Found in Man. *Zeitschrift für Morphologie und Anthropologie* 1904, *7,* 261–368.

Wilder, H. H.; Wentworth, B. *Personal Identification;* The Gorham Press: Boston, 1918.

# CHAPTER 4

RECORDING LIVING AND POSTMORTEM FRICTION RIDGE EXEMPLARS

BRENT T. CUTRO, SR.

CONTENTS

- 3   4.1 Introduction
- 3   4.2 Equipment
- 5   4.3 Recording Fingerprints, Palmprints, and Footprints of Living Subjects
- 10   4.4 Recording Postmortem Friction Ridge Detail
- 17   4.5 Summary
- 18   4.6 Reviewers
- 18   4.7 References

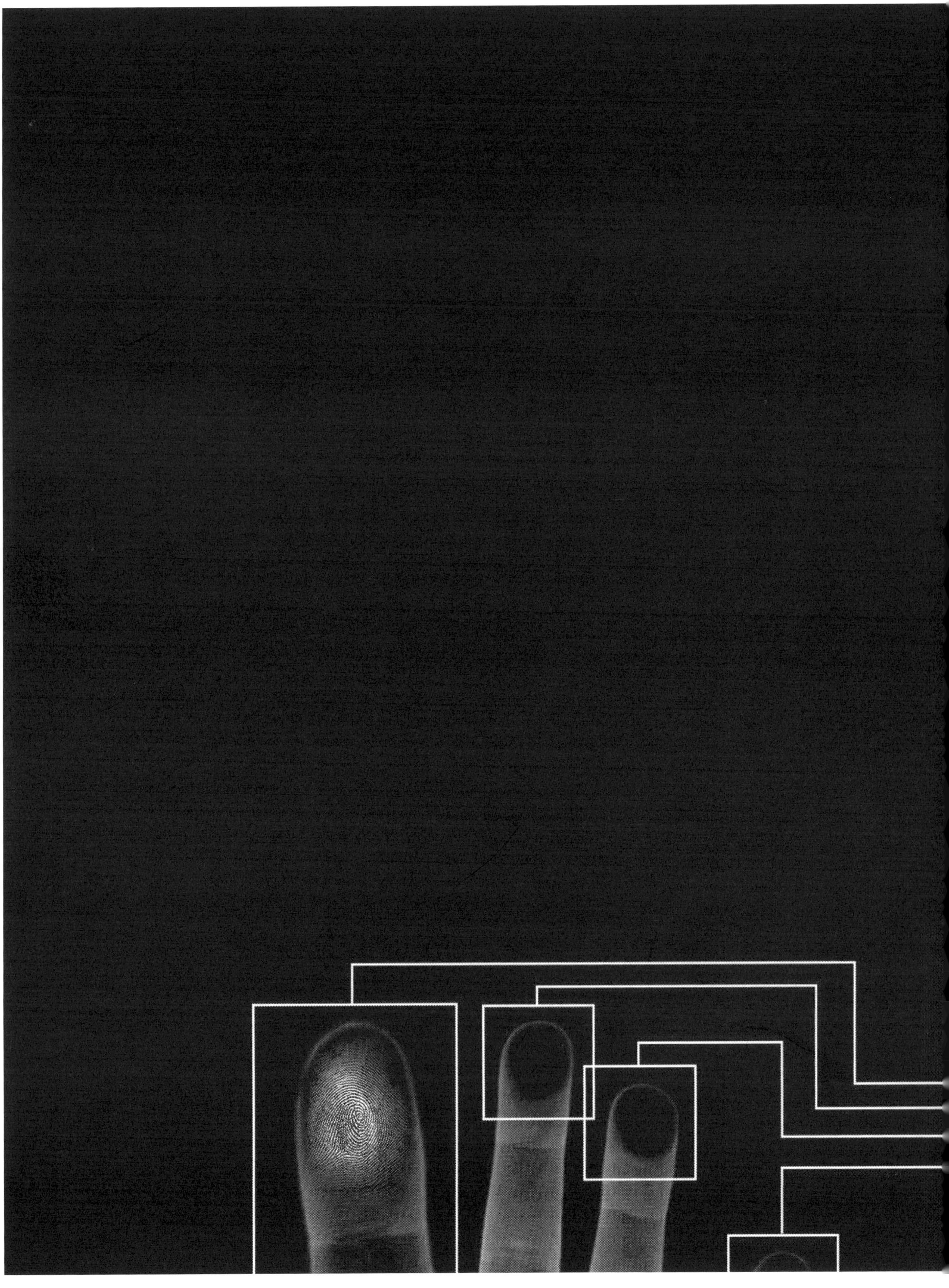

RECORDING LIVING AND POSTMORTEM FRICTION RIDGE EXEMPLARS

BRENT T. CUTRO, SR.

4.1 Introduction

The skin is both the largest organ and the first line of protection in the human body. Completely covering the body from head to toe, the skin is primarily consistent in nature everywhere except for the areas covering the palmar surfaces of the fingers and hands and the plantar surfaces of the toes and feet. The skin on these areas is referred to as *friction ridge skin*. Obtaining legible recordings of these areas of skin is crucial for subsequent comparisons to latent impressions recovered from crime scenes, for comparison against previous records, or for input into automated fingerprint identification systems (AFIS).

Inked prints, record prints, standards, and *exemplars* are all terms that are used to describe the recording of these unique details.

4.2 Equipment

Various types of equipment, inks, scanning devices, and techniques are used to record friction ridge detail. Although the concept of recording friction ridge detail seems basic, care and determination should always be exercised in order to obtain the best quality recordings because complete and legible recordings are a necessity in latent print examinations.

The equipment that is needed to record friction ridge detail includes an ink roller, an inking plate (constructed of glass or a smooth metal, such as stainless steel), fingerprint or palmprint cards for recording the prints, and a quality black ink formulated for this purpose (Figure 4–1). These items can be obtained from various forensic or printing supply companies. Only inks formulated for forensic purposes should be used, because other types of inks (printer's ink, writing ink, or rubber stamp ink) are too light, too thin,

CHAPTER 4 Recording Living and Postmortem Friction Ridge Exemplars

or do not dry quickly enough on the recording cards; this retained moisture could cause subsequent smearing of the prints. An alternative to the ink-and-roller method is the use of micro-reticulated thermoplastic resin pads or ceramic inking pads, both of which are impregnated with special permanent and nonfading inks. These products contain enough ink to record up to 50,000 fingerprints and should last approximately two years without replenishing. Cleanup is easy, and the ink dries quickly on recording cards (Olsen, 1978, pp 90–91). Advances in ink technology have improved certain characteristics of some of these inks, resulting in more user-friendly products.

A fingerprint stand is also useful. The fingerprint stand can be placed at a height that is necessary to comfortably record friction ridge detail while conveniently holding within its built-in storage bins all of the equipment needed for this purpose.

The standard cards that are used to record prints are 8" x 8". This size has space for two rows of five rolled fingerprints and space for plain or flat prints of the fingers under the rows of rolled prints. These cards are white and are usually lightweight cardboard or heavy paper stock. Fingerprint cards are handled countless times and may be stored in files for many years. For these reasons, the texture and strength of the card must be such that it will withstand frequent handling (Olsen, 1978, pp 59–60).

Figure 4–2 shows two rows of fingerprints (*rolled impressions*) in the center of the card. The blocks begin with the thumb of the right hand as #1, the right index finger as #2, and so on through the right little finger, #5. The left hand then begins with the thumb, designated #6, the left index finger is #7, and so on through the left little finger, #10. Another set of impressions would appear below these. They are referred to as *plain*, *flat*, or *simultaneous* impressions

FIGURE 4–1

Equipment and ink used to record friction ridge exemplars.

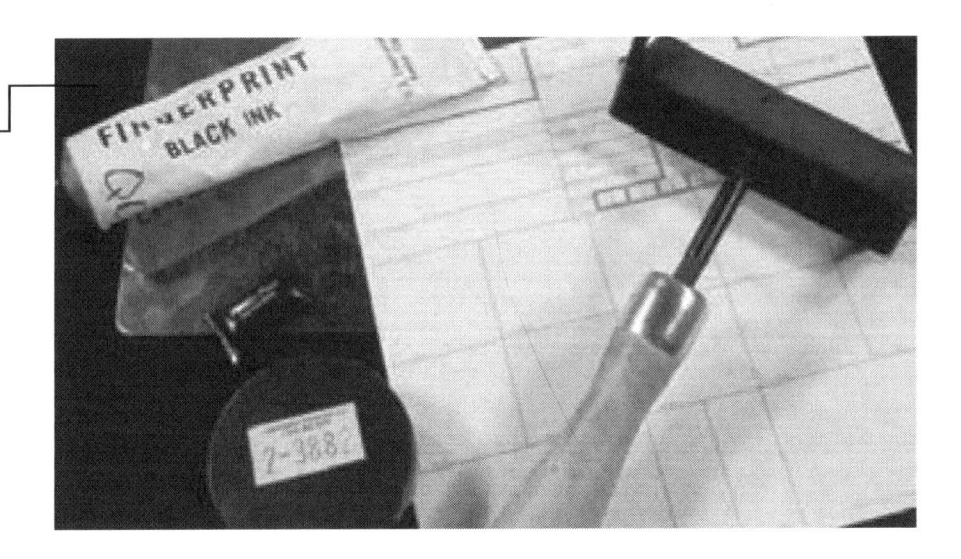

FIGURE 4–2

Two rows of rolled impressions in center of fingerprint card.

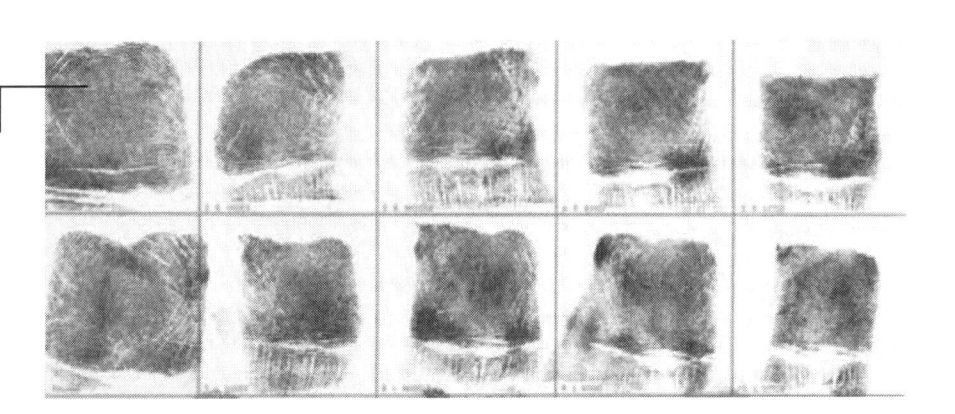

4–4

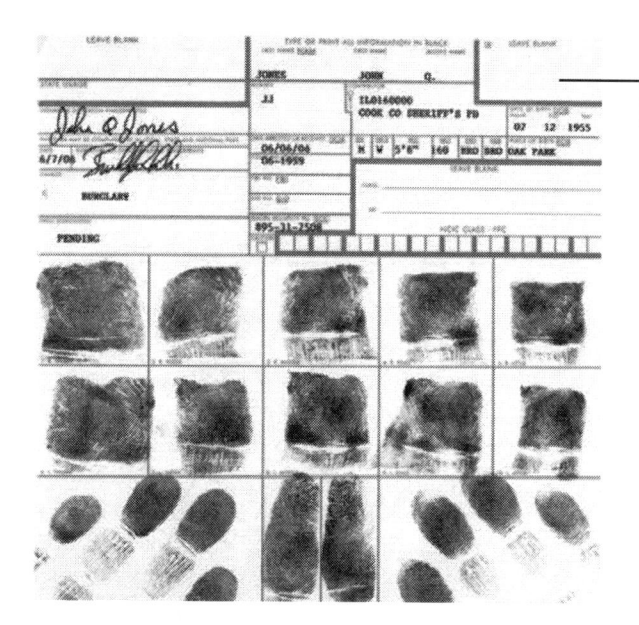

FIGURE 4–3

Completely recorded fingerprint card.

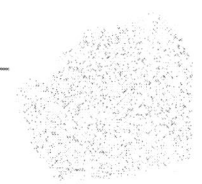

and serve as a verification of the finger sequence of the rolled impressions (Olsen, 1978, pp 60–62). See Figure 4–3.

In addition to the spaces for the fingerprint impressions, there is room on the card to record information about the person being printed (e.g., name, date of birth), information about the agency, and space for the date and signatures of the subject and technician.

Livescan technology replaces the process of using ink to record friction ridge detail. The friction ridge surfaces to be recorded are placed on a scanner that records the detail in a matter of seconds. High-resolution scanners can produce images that rival the quality of ink recordings, and the digital images are easily reproduced and distributed electronically. The process of rolling the finger impressions (and plain impressions) on the scanner platen is the same as for the actual recording of inked impressions on a card, but without the ink.

4.3 Recording Fingerprints, Palmprints, and Footprints of Living Subjects

Legible and completely recorded fingerprint cards, such as the one in Figure 4–3, are adequate for classification or comparison purposes and for scanning into AFIS.

4.3.1 Recording Fingerprints

The basic method of recording friction ridge detail on the hands or feet can be accomplished by applying a thin coat of black ink directly to the skin's surface using a roller or by coating an inking plate with the ink and rolling the fingers onto the plate. Next, the inked skin is pressed on a surface of contrasting color, such as a white piece of paper or a fingerprint card. The difference in elevation between the ridges and the furrows of the friction ridge skin leaves a print that is a recording of the unique detail of the friction ridge skin (Cowger, 1983, p 10).

To begin this process, if using the ink-and-roller method, a small amount of ink is deposited at the edge, center, and opposite edge of a thoroughly cleaned inking plate. The ink is then rolled and smoothed out. The ink should look black, not gray. A gray color means that there is not enough ink on the plate. The ink should not look wet. If the ink looks wet, too much ink has been placed on the plate, and this could result in a smearing of the print. After the proper amount of ink has been rolled onto the plate, the next step is to ink the fingers (Cowger, 1983, p 10).

Before any ink is applied to the fingers, the fingers must be inspected to ensure that they are clean and dry, because contaminants can interfere with proper recording. If the subject's fingers are too dry, a moisturizing hand lotion may be applied sparingly to soften the fingers. If the subject's fingers are too moist, they must be dried individually or, in case of excess moisture, wiped with an alcohol wipe and then dried. Regardless of what method of recording is used (ink and roller, Porelon Pad, or scanning device), the fingers should be rolled away from the body, and the thumbs should be rolled toward the body (thumbs in, fingers out). This procedure allows the fingers and thumbs to be rolled from an awkward position to a more relaxed position and is less likely to produce smeared recordings. To completely roll each finger, with the subject standing in front of and facing the cardholder, the hand should be firmly grasped in such a manner that the finger is extended and the other fingers are out of the way. The inking plate and the cardholder should be side by side, with the cardholder nearest the operator (Olsen, 1978, p 66). The hand is then rotated so that the side of the finger can be placed on the inking plate. While one of the operator's hands grasps the hand of the subject, the operator's other hand holds the end of the finger or thumb being printed to keep it from slipping, to apply light pressure, and to guide the roll (Figure 4–4). Two key factors to remember are control and pressure (Cowger, 1983, p 11). For best results, the subject should not help with the process and should be asked to remain in a relaxed posture. The finger or thumb is then rotated 180° (i.e., nail edge to nail edge) and is immediately lifted from the plate and rolled in the same manner in the appropriate box on the fingerprint card that has been previously placed in the cardholder.

The fingers and thumbs should be rolled on the card or scanning device in the same sequence in which the spaces appear on the card, starting with the right thumb and ending with the left little finger (Olsen, 1978, p 66). The plain (i.e., flat or simultaneous) impressions are recorded by grouping the fingers from each hand and pressing them on the inking plate. The grouped fingers, numbers 2–5 and 7–10, are then pressed on the fingerprint card or scanning device in the appropriate boxes, taking care not to superimpose these impressions over the rolled impressions. The thumbs are inked and recorded separately in the same manner. The fingers and thumbs that are recorded in these boxes should not be rolled from side to side. As the fingers and thumbs are lifted from the card or scanning device, they should be rolled toward the tips of the fingers by keeping pressure on the fingers and lifting the subject's wrists so as to record as much friction ridge detail as possible toward the top of the pattern area.

4.3.2 Recording Palmprints

Palmprints are recorded in much the same manner as fingerprints; however, a cylindrical device is often used to facilitate the process to ensure complete recording of all friction ridge detail. The palms are not pressed on an inking plate. Rather, the roller is loaded with ink from the inking plate and the ink roller is used to apply a thin coat

FIGURE 4–4

Position of operator's hands.

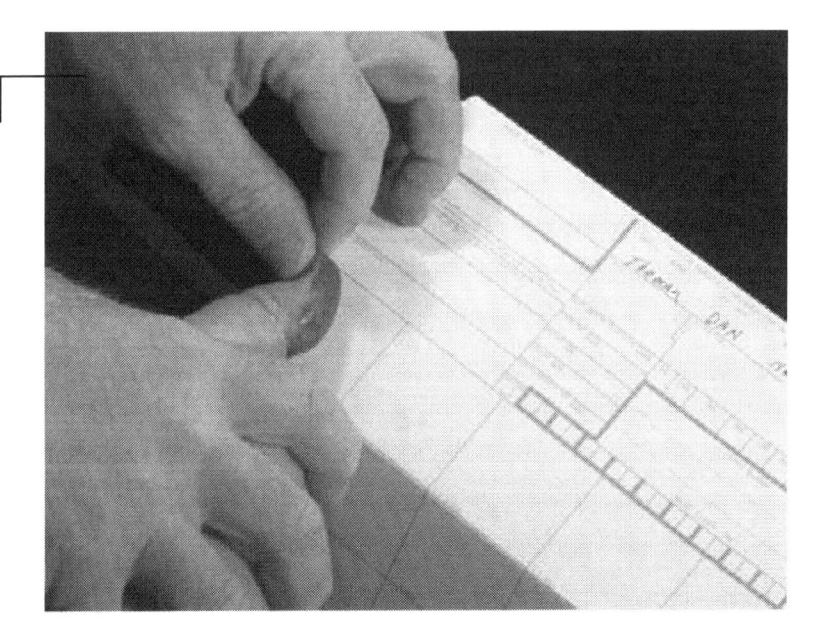

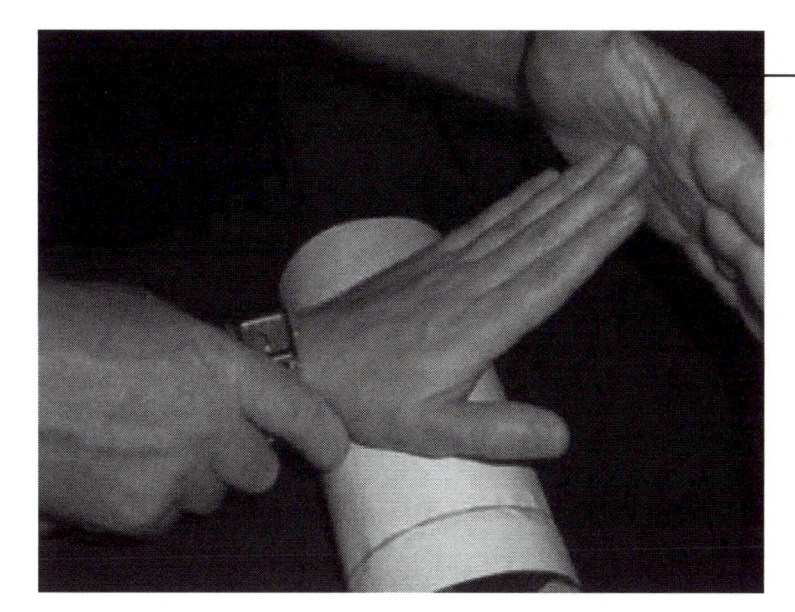

Recording Living and Postmortem Friction Ridge Exemplars **CHAPTER 4**

FIGURE 4–5

Recording palmprint exemplars using a cylinder.

of ink directly to the hands from the base and edges of the palms to the tips of the fingers. Care must be exercised to ensure complete coverage of ink to all areas containing friction ridge detail.

To record palmprints, a standard 8" x 8" card or heavy plain white bond paper is attached to a cylinder approximately 3" in diameter. Removable adhesive tape or rubber bands may be used to attach the paper to the cylinder. (Some technicians prefer to let the paper "ride" across the cylinder without attaching it, taking care to prevent slippage.) The inked palm is then rolled either from the base of the palm toward the fingers or from the fingers to the base of the palm. Either way is acceptable and is generally left to the discretion of the technician. Most technicians prefer beginning at the base of the palm and rolling toward the fingers because this gives the technician more control over the subject and position of the print on the card (Olsen, 1978, p 74). The hand can simply be pulled rather than pushed across the surface, which also tends to help prevent lateral movement of the subject's hand. The palm must be recorded in one smooth, unceasing motion to prevent smudging or distortion (Figure 4–5). Light pressure should also be applied while rolling in order to maintain completeness and to adequately record the centers of the palms. (Extending the thumb to the side will also help eliminate voids in the center of the recorded palm.) The thumbs are recorded separately because of their position on the hand. The extreme side of the palm, opposite of the thumb, referred to as the "writer's palm" (i.e., the edge of the hypothenar area), is also recorded separately on the palmprint card. The card is removed from the cylinder and placed on a hard flat surface. This area of the palm is then pressed on the palmprint card, with the little finger extended, to the right of the previously recorded palmprint for the right hand and to the left of the previously recorded palmprint for the left hand, if space allows. The thumb area of the palm (thenar area) is then recorded in the same manner and placed to the left side of the previously recorded right palmprint and to the right side of the previously recorded left palmprint, again, if space allows. If adequate space does not allow for the thenar and hypothenar areas to be recorded on the same card, separate cards should be used for these recordings.

An easy alternative method for recording palmprints is with the use of a white adhesive lifting material, such as Handiprint® (Kinderprint Co.), and black fingerprint powder. The fingerprint powder is lightly applied with a soft fingerprint brush to the entire surface of the palm. The adhesive material is separated from the backing and pressed onto the palm while smoothing from the center to the sides. The flexible adhesive conforms to the creases and crevices of the palm with minimal slippage, which aids in producing a high-contrast, completely recorded palmprint. The adhesive lifter is then peeled from the palm and placed onto a clear acetate cover, thus preserving the impression for subsequent comparisons.

4–7

4.3.3 Recording Major Case Prints

Major case prints* (also referred to as *major criminal prints*) are a recording of all the friction ridge detail covering the hands. If necessary, this may also include a recording of all the friction ridge detail on the feet. In addition to legible and completely recorded fingerprints and palmprints, major case prints include a legible and completely recorded set of the tips of the fingers, from just below the nail to the center of the fingers, rolled from one side of the nail to the other, as well as completely recorded lower joints of the fingers, including the extreme sides. Major case prints are often required for comparison to unknown impressions that have been collected from crime scenes, and these impressions may include areas of friction ridge detail that are not routinely recorded.

To begin, a complete set of the subject's fingerprints should be recorded as previously described. Next, all of the remaining friction ridge detail on the phalangeal areas of the thumbs and fingers is recorded using 8" x 8" cards or white bond paper firmly attached to the edge of a table. Beginning with the right thumb, a thin coat of ink is applied to all of the friction ridge detail with an ink roller, from the base of the thumb to the tip, including the extreme sides of the finger. Usually beginning at the lower left corner of the paper, the extreme left side of the thumb is firmly pressed on the paper. The thumb is removed by lifting from the base of the thumb to the tip. This will record the extreme left side of the thumb and tip. Next to this impression, the center of the thumb is placed on the paper and is removed in the same manner, thus completely recording the friction ridge detail from the base of the thumb to the tip. The extreme right side of the thumb is then placed to the right of the center portion, thus recording the extreme right side of the thumb and tip. Lastly, above the three recorded areas of the thumb, the extreme left side of the tip of the thumb is placed on the paper and rolled to the extreme right side with one continuous motion. This group of recorded friction ridge details of the thumb should be labeled "#1", or "right thumb", above the rolled tip (Figure 4–6). This process should be repeated with the remaining four fingers of the right hand, moving counterclockwise around the paper.

Another method that is preferred by some latent print examiners is to roll the entire finger with one continuous motion from extreme side to extreme side, including the lower phalanges, to ensure continuity of the impression.

*The Scientific Working Group on Friction Ridge Analysis, Study and Technology (SWGFAST) has proposed a change in terminology from "major case prints" to "complete friction ridge exemplars" [SWGFAST, 2006, pp 619–627].

FIGURE 4–6

Friction ridge detail of right thumb from a set of major case prints.

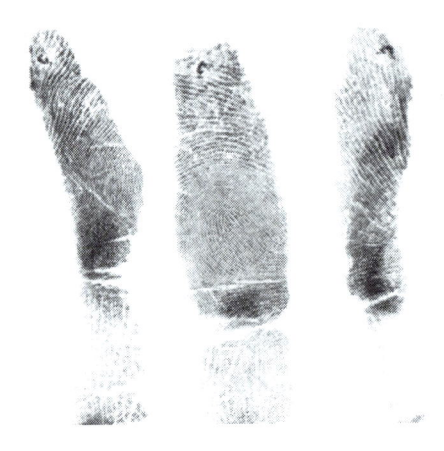

The tip areas are also positioned and recorded above these impressions in the same manner.

This procedure is then repeated for the left hand. To complete the major case print process, a legible and completely recorded set of palmprints is then recorded in the previously described manner.

4.3.4 Recording Footprints

On occasion it may become necessary to record a subject's footprints. The same basic procedures as with recording palmprints are used; however, because of the large size of an adult foot, a larger cylinder and paper must be used.

The cylinder used for this process should be approximately 5" in diameter and should hold an 8.5" x 14" (legal size) sheet of heavy white bond paper attached to the cylinder, as previously described. The foot should be rolled across the paper in the same manner as the palmprints, in one smooth, continuous motion from the heel of the foot toward the toe, with the toes passing completely over the cylinder. Recordings of the feet may also be obtained by applying ink to the bottoms of the subject's feet with a roller and instructing the subject to walk across paper that has been laid out on the floor. This, however, requires cooperation from the subject and may not produce satisfactory recordings, because excessive pressure and movement of the feet may blur or smear the impressions. Another method (Olsen, 1978, p 75) is to mount a card or paper on a flat board. With the subject in a sitting position and with the leg elevated and supported, the paper is pressed against the subject's inked foot.

4.3.5 Unusual Circumstances

Problems ranging from temporary disabilities (e.g., wounds and blisters) to permanent disabilities (e.g., amputated fingers, extra fingers, webbed fingers, arthritis, or palsy) may be present when obtaining known standards. The occupation of the subject (e.g., brick layer) may also affect the ability to obtain legible recordings. In these cases, the friction ridge detail may be affected or worn to the point that a legible recording may be difficult. However, with patience, skill, and some ingenuity, it is possible to obtain satisfactory recordings.

Obtaining legible recordings from injured fingers or palms can be difficult, so a notation of any temporary disabilities (e.g., fresh cuts, wounds, bandaged fingers, or large blisters) should be made in the corresponding block on the fingerprint or palmprint card. If classification or input into an AFIS database is necessary, however, it is advisable to defer recording the fingerprints of the subject, if possible, until after the temporary injury has healed.

Certain occupations can also pose problems to friction ridge skin, because people who consistently work with their hands tend to have worn, rough, dry, or damaged friction ridges on their fingers and palms, to the point that it is difficult to obtain legible recordings of their friction ridge detail. This problem may be overcome by applying skin-softening lotion to the hands and fingers prior to recording. In addition, applying a very small amount of ink to the inking plate (so as not to get ink into the furrows and to ensure that only the tops of the ridges will be covered) may improve the fine detail (FBI, 1979, p 127).

These same techniques are also useful when obtaining known standards from elderly individuals or small children with very fine ridge detail. The use of ice held against the friction ridge skin may also facilitate the recording of the fine detail (Olsen, 1978, p 83). On occasion, a subject's friction ridges may be so fine that the ink completely covers the ridges and furrows. In these cases, instead of using ink, using a brush to lightly dust the friction ridge skin with black fingerprint powder may be necessary to record the very fine friction ridge detail. White opaque lifting material (e.g., Handiprint®) with a transparent cover is then used to record the impressions directly from the fingers (Olsen, 1978, p 84). The finger numbers should be marked on the transparent covers to prevent any confusion and to ensure the correct orientation of the impressions. The lifts are then cut to fit inside the appropriate blocks on the fingerprint card and are secured with clear tape.

A notation of any permanent disabilities should be recorded in the appropriate block on the fingerprint card (e.g., "missing at birth" if the subject was born without certain fingers). In cases of amputation, a notation should be made in the appropriate block on the fingerprint card. If only a portion of the first joint of the finger is affected, it should be recorded as completely as possible and a notation should be made.

In cases of bent or disfigured fingers, the tools (e.g., special ink rollers or spatulas and a curved strip holder) that are used for obtaining prints from deceased individuals can be used to record the friction ridge detail.

If a subject has more than 10 fingers (polydactyly), the thumb and the 4 fingers next to the thumb should be recorded on the fingerprint card in the usual manner. Any remaining fingers should be recorded on the other side of the card, and a notation should be made. Webbed fingers (syndactyly) should be recorded as completely as possible, also with a notation on the card concerning this congenital abnormality (FBI, 1979, p 128).

4.4 Recording Postmortem Friction Ridge Detail

One of the most challenging, and also rewarding, aspects of latent print examination is the determination of the identity of deceased individuals. Various methods and techniques may be used to facilitate the successful recording and preservation of postmortem friction ridge detail. In circumstances involving unknown deceased infants, it is often necessary to obtain postmortem footprints, because hospital personnel usually record only footprint standards of newborn babies.

When decomposition, desiccation (dryness), or maceration (separation and softening of skin by soaking in liquid) of the friction ridge skin precludes satisfactory recordings with traditional methods, the hands, fingers, or feet of the deceased may be surgically removed by a medical examiner and submitted to a laboratory, where advanced procedures may be conducted.

Many techniques have been developed to effectively process postmortem friction ridge skin. It is important to realize that successful development, recording, and individualization of an often small area of available friction ridge skin could be the most valuable lead in solving a homicide case or in providing closure to a grieving family. Therefore, the latent print examiner must have experience and knowledge in this area. The condition of the friction ridge skin will dictate the various methods and techniques that should be used to successfully record valuable friction ridge detail.

Recording the friction ridge detail from deceased individuals can, at times, present quite a challenge. Satisfactory recordings of recently deceased individuals can most often be performed much like recording the prints of live individuals, utilizing some specific tools to facilitate this process. Obtaining recordings of friction ridge detail from skin that is decomposed, mummified, charred, or macerated, however, may be much more difficult.

4.4.1 General Recording of Recently Deceased Subjects

If the hands are in reasonably good condition, obtaining satisfactory recordings of the friction ridge detail from the fingers is usually accomplished by straightening the fingers and flattening the palm. To facilitate this process, the deceased should be positioned with the face and palms down on a table (prone position) (FBI, 1979, p 136). The fingers and palms should be clean and dry. If rigor mortis (stiffening of the muscles) has set in, it is possible to break the rigor by forcibly straightening the digits, which can then be recorded by using equipment intended for this purpose (e.g., a spoon-shaped tool, as seen in Figure 4–7). As always, prior to handling any type of biohazardous material,

FIGURE 4–7

A spoon-shaped tool with fingerprint card used for postmortem friction ridge recording.

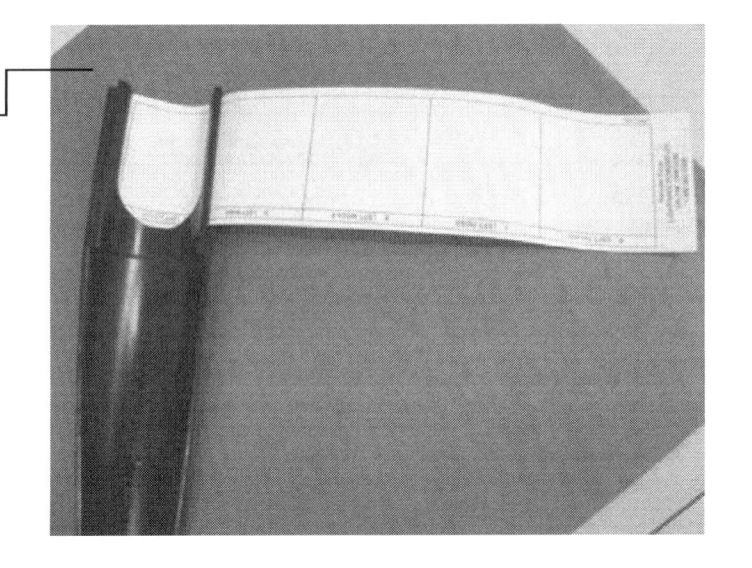

care should be taken to ensure that personal protective equipment (e.g., gloves, face mask, and eye protection) is worn at all times.

If only the fingers are of concern, it is possible to print them by pressing on the finger just above the knuckle. This will straighten the finger and separate it from the others, facilitating proper recording. The palm can be recorded by bending it forward at the wrist. It may be possible to obtain adequate recordings by recording various areas of the palm separately (Cowger, 1983, p 29). If rigor mortis is present, "It is better to take advantage of this condition than to try to overcome it, by bending the wrist still further toward the inner forearm and pressing the fingers one at a time toward the palm or wrist. In this position, they separate and straighten out in such a way that each finger can be printed without interference" (Olsen, 1978, p 85). "If breaking rigor is difficult or ineffective, or if the hand is so curled that the fingers or palm will not straighten sufficiently when pressed inward, it may be necessary to cut the tendons which cause the curling to occur" (Cowger, 1983, p 29). (It is advisable that only legally designated persons perform this activity, because there are restrictions in some jurisdictions concerning the dissection of human remains.)

There are many satisfactory methods of applying ink to the fingers of a deceased individual. One method is to use a spatula that contains a thin coat of ink that has been applied by an ink roller. The ink is then transferred to the fingers by manually rolling it around the fingers. A standard fingerprint card may then be cut into two strips of five blocks or into single blocks. A strip holder or spoon is used to hold the strip. The strip or block is then placed in the spoon with the top of the strip toward the handle of the spoon. The inked fingers are then rolled in their corresponding blocks from nail edge to nail edge, as previously described. This procedure is repeated on different strips until legible impressions are obtained. If individual cards are used, it is advisable to have more than 10 squares cut and ready in case some of them are ruined or the pattern area is not completely recorded (Olsen, 1978, p 86). Another method for extremely difficult cases is to use black fingerprint powder and white adhesive lifting material such as Handiprint®.

4.4.2 Recording Decomposed Friction Ridge Skin

Putrefied skin (skin that is in a state of decomposition or rotting) is fragile. Such putrefaction is usually a result of various biological factors such as bacteria, fungi, or fermentation. Parasites may have also infiltrated this necrotic tissue. Extreme care should be exercised when examining and handling this fragile friction ridge skin.

If, upon examination, friction ridge skin is present, discernible, and not badly damaged, it may be possible, using extreme care, to simply ink and record the friction ridge skin. However, if the friction ridge skin is rubbery and is separating from the underlying tissues or is too fragile for the technician to apply ink in the usual manner, the friction ridge skin may be removed from the underlying tissue. The skin must then be cleaned and dried and may be recorded by placing each finger, or friction ridge skin, over the technician's gloved finger or palm to ink and record as if the friction ridge skin were the technician's. As always, care in documenting which fingers are recorded is important. It is also recommended to photograph the visible ridge detail prior to any technique that may cause further deterioration of the friction skin.

A 10–15% soaking solution of formaldehyde may be used in extreme cases to firm up the skin to facilitate this process. Formaldehyde, however, can cause the skin to become very firm and brittle, causing the skin to split. The skin should soak for an hour or so until sufficiently firm. Once hardened, the friction ridge skin should be removed, patted dry, and recorded (FBI, 1979, pp 143–144). Another similar method suggests soaking the fingers or friction skin in 10% formaldehyde solution for several hours. The skin is then rinsed gently with running water, rinsed in laboratory-quality isopropanol to remove any excess moisture, patted dry, and recorded as previously described (Miller, 1995, p 603).

In many cases, especially if the decomposition is advanced, discernible friction ridge detail may not be present because the top layers of friction ridge skin may be completely decomposed or destroyed. In these instances, the bottom layers or underside of the friction ridge skin, as well as the dermis, may reveal discernible friction ridge detail and can be recorded successfully.

One method that is used to record the underside of friction ridge skin is lightly coating the underside of the epidermal layer of the friction ridge skin with fingerprint powder before applying ink. The underside of the friction ridge skin is then rolled on a section of the adhesive side of fingerprint lift tape (Rice, 1988a, p 100).

To proceed, the friction ridge skin must be completely dried by placing the skin between paper towels. With the underside of the epidermal layer of the skin exposed, it is lightly dusted with black fingerprint powder and positioned over the technician's own gloved finger. The skin is then coated using an ink roller in the usual manner or rolled on an inking slab that has been coated with ink to apply a thin, even coat of fingerprint ink. The fingerprint powder is necessary to facilitate removal of the skin from the tape. The skin is then rolled across the adhesive side of a section of transparent or frosted fingerprint tape. It is important to note that the impression resulting from this method on the adhesive side of the tape will be in the correct orientation for comparison when placed adhesive-side down in the appropriate block on the fingerprint card, or, if recording palms, on the palmprint card. The impressions will be tonally reversed (white ridges) because the furrows (valleys), as opposed to the ridges, will be inked and recorded. If necessary, tonal reversal can be corrected photographically (Rice, 1988a, pp 98–100).

If the friction ridge skin is too brittle to attempt the previously described methods, the underside of the friction ridge skin may be photographed. To accomplish this, "it may be advisable to trim the skin, flatten it out between two pieces of glass, and photograph it in that position" (FBI, 1979, p 144).

The skin is trimmed by carefully and meticulously removing the excess flesh by scraping, cutting, and trimming until only the friction ridge skin remains and can be flattened satisfactorily between two pieces of glass. Another method to further enhance friction ridge detail is to use transmitted lighting. This is accomplished by shining a light through the skin toward the lens of the camera when photographing. If the skin is still not transparent enough, soaking the skin in xylene for approximately five minutes before photographing or keeping the skin immersed in xylene while photographing is recommended. Once a suitable photograph is obtained, the negative may be printed as necessary to provide correct orientation of the impression for subsequent comparison to known standards (FBI, 1979, pp 145–147).

4.4.3 Recording Macerated Friction Ridge Skin

Maceration occurs when friction ridge skin is immersed, usually in water, for an extended period of time. The epidermal layer absorbs water, often swells, and can loosen from the dermis within a few hours after immersion (FBI, 1979, p 151).

If the friction ridge skin is not too badly damaged, the skin should be carefully cleaned, wiped with alcohol, and recorded as previously described for recently deceased subjects. If the skin has separated from the dermal layer and is wrinkled, it may be possible to pull the skin from the back of the finger to smooth out the pattern area by pinching the skin tightly. This will facilitate inking and recording (FBI, 1979, p 151). Stretching of the friction ridge skin in this manner may also facilitate the recording of palmprints and footprints.

It is important to note that this type of process may enlarge the pattern area of the fingers, which may be significant when conducting an AFIS search with some systems. The epidermis from a "de-gloved" hand can be as much as 33% larger than the dermis. For this reason, if an AFIS search does not reveal an individualization using the original recording, the print should be searched again at 70% of its original size (Leas, 2006).

In such instances when the skin is wrinkled but not pliable, thus not allowing the skin to be stretched smoothly across the pattern area, tissue builder or glycerin may be injected into the bulb of the finger to round out the pattern area. A string tied just above the injection site will help prevent the fluid from escaping. Often, the skin may be loose and somewhat damaged yet have most of the pattern area still intact. If this is the case, the friction ridge skin should be carefully removed, cleaned, and placed in alcohol for about one minute. The skin is then carefully placed over the technician's gloved finger to facilitate inking and recording (FBI, 1979, p 151).

As always, friction ridge detail may also be photographed on the finger or cut and prepared, as previously described for decomposed friction ridge skin, to be placed between two pieces of glass and photographed with reflected or transmitted light. If no discernible friction ridge detail is present on the outer layers of the epidermis, it is possible

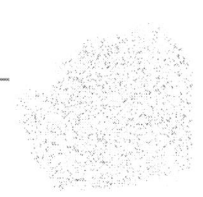

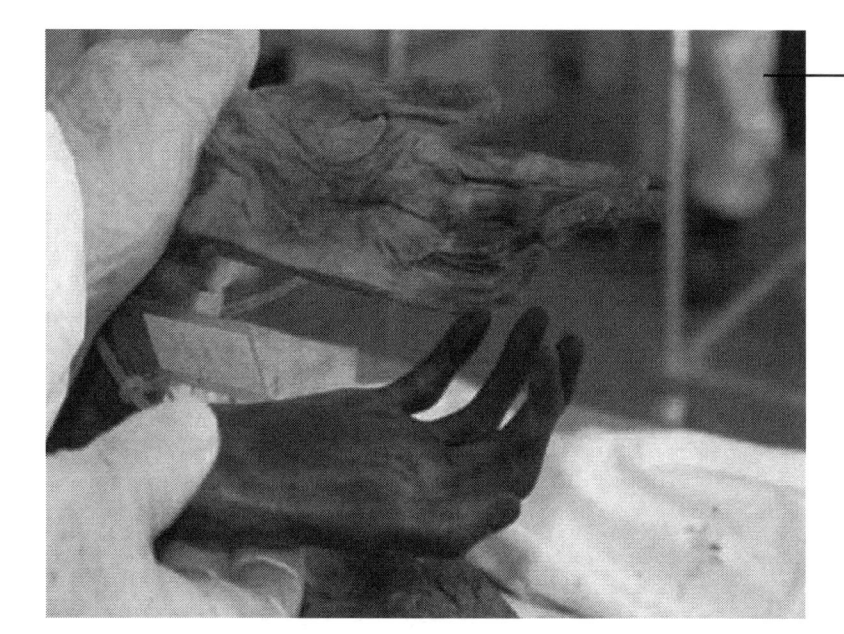

Recording Living and Postmortem Friction Ridge Exemplars | CHAPTER 4

FIGURE 4–8

Photographs of macerated hand before (top hand) and after (bottom hand) "boiling" treatment.

(Photo courtesy of the FBI Disaster Squad.)

that the underside of the epidermis or the top of the dermis may be recorded or photographed, as described previously for decomposed friction ridge skin.

For situations in which the epidermis is missing or has been totally destroyed because of prolonged immersion in a liquid, a method known as osmotic rehydration (the boiling method) can produce very satisfactory results. This method produces the best results when used on hands or feet that are soft and pliable, with no epidermis present, and with the ridges of the dermis appearing flat. The hot water plumps the dermis, thus facilitating the recording of the ridges. To proceed, water is heated in a pot to just below boiling point (~200 °F) and maintained at this temperature. The friction ridge skin being processed is immersed in the heated water for 10 seconds. A shorter time is recommended for fine ridge detail (e.g., as children have) or where advanced decomposition is present. A longer time, up to 30 seconds, may be necessary at the examiner's discretion. The raised friction ridge detail should be carefully cleaned, if necessary, with a soft-bristled toothbrush and water in the direction of the ridge flow, wiped with alcohol, and lightly dusted with black fingerprint powder. A white adhesive lifting material is then used to record and preserve the friction ridge detail (Leas, 2006) (Figure 4–8).

4.4.4 Recording Desiccated Friction Ridge Skin

Traditional methods to obtain recordings of friction ridge detail from desiccated skin usually involve removing the hands or feet and subjecting the skin to many hours of potentially destructive chemical rehydration soaking and softening techniques. Although these methods work well to rehydrate the friction ridge skin, and will be discussed in further detail, a much less destructive and time-consuming method is available. This method involves the use of a silicone product (Mikrosil) to successfully record friction ridge detail that has been subjected to various types of destructive conditions such as desiccation, hardening, or wrinkling. Removal of the hands or feet is not always necessary, and this procedure may be accomplished at the mortuary or morgue.

To begin, the friction ridge skin must be cleaned and dried. The fingers should be separated to keep the silicone casts from sticking together. A light coat of black fingerprint powder is applied with a soft fingerprint brush to the friction ridges. The casting material is then mixed according to the included instructions and applied to each finger or other areas of friction ridge skin. After approximately 15 minutes, the casts are peeled off one at a time and marked accordingly, thus revealing a "high contrast, highly detailed, three-dimensional mold" (Tomboc and Schrader, 2005, p 473) (Figure 4–9). These silicone casts may then be photographed and preserved. When the casts are examined, the friction ridge details will be black and will be in the same orientation as if they had been recorded on a fingerprint or palmprint card. On severely damaged or decomposed friction ridge skin, Greenwop powder, which fluoresces under ultraviolet light, and black casting material may also be used. The resulting casts are then photographed using ulraviolet

CHAPTER 4 Recording Living and Postmortem Friction Ridge Exemplars

FIGURE 4–9

Cast being removed from finger. (Reprinted from Tomboc and Schrader, 2005, p 478.)

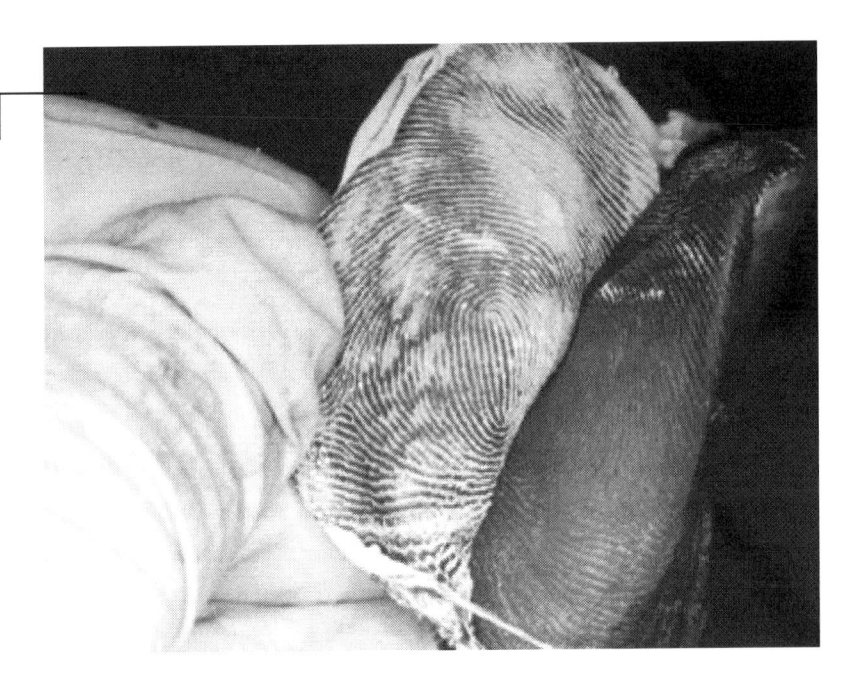

light (Tomboc and Schrader, 2005, p 474). If this method should fail to produce discernible friction ridge detail, the traditional methods of rehydration and softening must be implemented. Once the skin is rehydrated and softened, the Mikrosil method may be used subsequent to the traditional methods to facilitate satisfactory recordings of any restored friction ridge detail.

4.4.5 Traditional Rehydration Method

This method is used primarily when extreme drying and dehydration of the friction ridge skin has caused excessive shriveling and wrinkling of the tissues, thus precluding sufficient recordings using less destructive methods. Individual fingers or toes should be placed in separate 75 mL capped bottles, nail-side down. The bottles should be labeled with the subject's name, case number, and the finger or toe number. Photographs should be taken of any friction ridge detail prior to the rehydration process, because this procedure is potentially destructive to the tissues.

It is advisable to start with one finger before processing the remaining fingers, in order to determine the degree of destruction caused by the process. The 75 mL capped bottles are filled with enough 1% to 3% sodium or potassium hydroxide (FBI, 1979, pp 147–148) solution to cover the friction ridge detail. The capped bottles are refrigerated for approximately 24 to 48 hours (Rice, 1988b, p 153). Each bottle should be checked every 4 to 6 hours for excessive destruction. The friction ridge detail is checked periodically until the inner layers of skin are pliable such that the skin will give slightly under pressure. As previously mentioned, sodium and potassium hydroxide solutions are destructive to the tissues and will cause shedding of some of the outer layers of friction ridge skin. The outer layers of the friction ridge skin may be removed by gently brushing the skin (in the direction of the ridge flow) under warm running water with a soft-bristled toothbrush containing powdered hand cleaner. If the ridge detail is prominent, and the friction ridge skin is soft and pliable, the skin is then ready to be recorded. At this point, the epidermis should be white and soft. If, however, the friction ridge skin appears flat and stiff, it may then be soaked in a solution of dishwashing liquid and water in the same manner as with the hydroxide solution. (If this step is needed, one tablespoon of the dishwashing liquid should be placed in the 75 mL jar with enough warm water added to cover the friction ridge detail.) The friction ridge skin should soak at room temperature for approximately 24 to 48 hours, again being checked every 4 to 6 hours. This process may also cause further shedding of the tissues, which should be removed using a soft-bristled toothbrush, as described previously.

Once the friction ridge skin is soft and pliable with prominent and discernible friction ridge detail, the friction ridge skin is ready to be recorded. The length of time the skin should soak in these solutions depends on the extent of desiccation. However, if left too long, the friction ridge skin could potentially be destroyed (Rice, 1988b, pp 152–155).

Recording Living and Postmortem Friction Ridge Exemplars | **CHAPTER 4**

FIGURE 4–10

Lifting sheet is placed on top of duct seal. (Photo courtesy of the FBI Latent Print Unit.)

4.4.6 Recording Rehydrated Friction Ridge Skin

Although the rehydration process should cause the friction ridge skin to become soft and pliable, the loose and wrinkled friction ridge skin may make recording difficult with some methods. As always, to avoid confusion, the fingers should be recorded one at a time. The previously described method of recording rehydrated friction skin (Tomboc and Schrader, 2005, pp 471–479) has been found to be successful after rehydrating with traditional methods. However, another procedure (Rice, 1988b, pp 152–155) involves the use of tissue builder or glycerin to "fill out" the friction ridge skin by carefully injecting the material into the tip of the finger, from the nail side toward the center of the finger, after the skin has been rehydrated.

To begin, the fingers should be tied with string around the distal phalangeal joint (first joint) to prevent the material to be injected from escaping. Enough material is injected into the finger to round out the friction ridge skin, enabling successful recording. A locking hemostat is then clamped to the finger as an extension of the finger to facilitate the recording process. The finger must now be completely dry for proper adhesion of the fingerprint ink. To accomplish this, the finger should be gently dried with paper towels and lightly dusted with fingerprint powder. Excess moisture and powder may be removed by rolling the finger on paper towels until the fingers are sufficiently dry. The friction ridge skin is then coated with a thin layer of fingerprint ink, either by rolling on an inked plate or by rolling ink on the friction ridge skin with an ink roller. The finger is then recorded in the usual manner by applying light pressure to the nail side of the finger while rolling it on an index card or other suitable recording card. This process should be repeated until satisfactory results are obtained. The recorded prints are then placed in the appropriate blocks on a standard fingerprint card.

If satisfactory results cannot be obtained using this ink-and-roll method, it is possible to obtain satisfactory recordings using powder and lifting tape (Rice, 1988b, p 155). A light dusting of black fingerprint powder is applied to the friction ridge detail. A piece of lifting tape is then placed on the friction ridge detail at one side and lightly pressed over the friction ridge detail to the other side while smoothing. The tape is then removed and placed on a piece of clear Mylar-type plastic. One might also use white opaque lifting sheets with a transparent cover (Olsen, 1978, p 98).

Putty can serve as a cushion on which to roll the finger. Putty (i.e., duct seal) is moldable and nondrying. (It is used in plumbing and electrical work and is available in hardware stores.) A ball of duct seal is placed on the working surface and flattened. A piece of a lifting sheet is placed on top of the duct seal and the powdered finger is rolled onto the lifting sheet (Figures 4–10 and 4–11). The duct seal allows the lifting sheet to mold into the extreme wrinkles of the finger, creating a fingerprint impression of the entire area of the finger (Figure 4–12).

4–15

CHAPTER 4 Recording Living and Postmortem Friction Ridge Exemplars

FIGURE 4–11

The powdered finger is rolled onto the lifting sheet. (Photo courtesy of the FBI Latent Print Unit.)

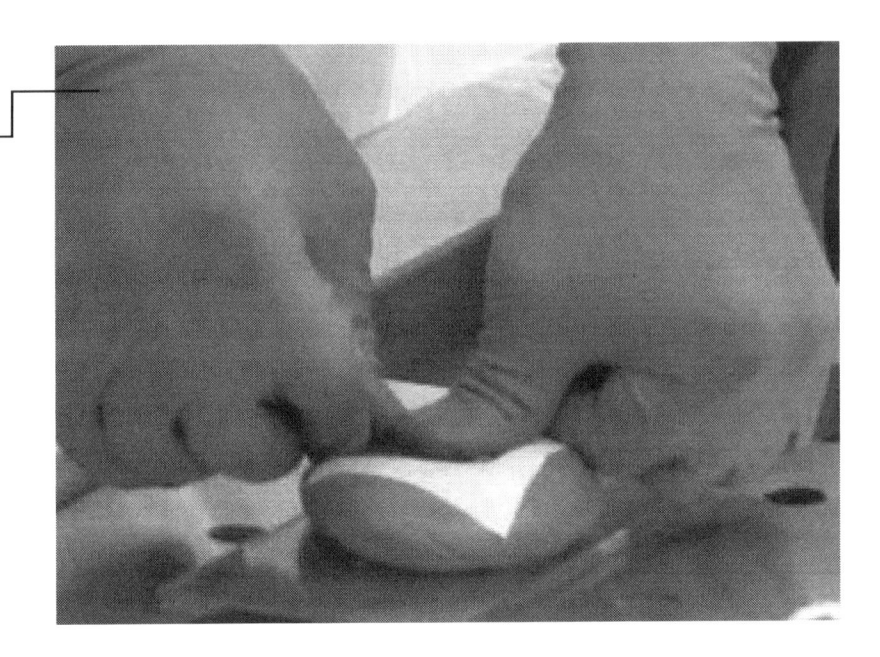

FIGURE 4–12

Postmortem fingerprint on lifting sheet. (Photo courtesy of the FBI Latent Print Unit.)

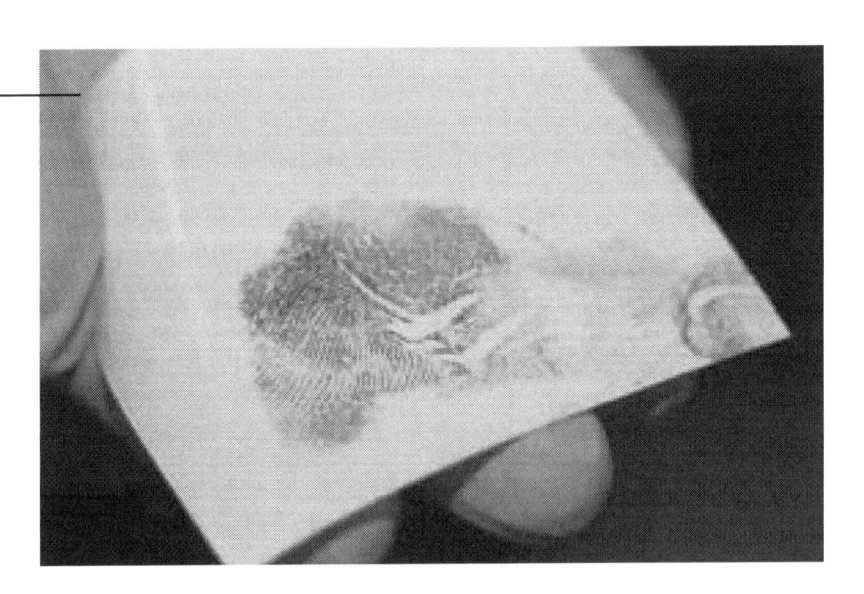

Regardless of the tape that is used, the recorded impression is now placed in the appropriate block (adhesive-side up) on the fingerprint card with the correct orientation. (When using transparent fingerprint tape, if the recorded impression were to be placed adhesive-side down on the fingerprint card, the fingerprint impression would be reversed.) The clear lift should then be marked directly on the lift with the correct orientation, finger number, and all other appropriate markings.

4.4.7 Recording Charred Friction Ridge Skin

On occasion, it may be necessary to obtain recordings of friction ridge detail that has been subjected to intense fire. Charring of the skin can occur, producing very brittle, often easily destroyed skin. Care must be exercised not to destroy the epidermal layer of friction ridge skin should removal of the hands or feet become necessary. As a worst-case scenario for severely charred skin, photography of any discernible friction ridge detail using oblique (side-to-side) lighting may be the only method that will produce satisfactory results (FBI, 1979, p 150).

The correct procedure to record friction ridge detail that has been subjected to desiccation and charring will be determined by the level of destruction to the friction ridge skin. Fortunately, in some cases, the friction ridge skin on the fingers and palms is somewhat protected by the tightening of the flexor muscles, ligaments, and tendons in the hands and arms which, as a result of intense heat, draw the fingers into a tightly clenched fist (pugilistic attitude). Intense heat also tends to cause a separation of the epidermal layer from the dermal layer of the friction ridge skin.

One method involves completing the separation of the epidermal layer from the dermal layer of the skin through refrigeration (Rice, 1992, pp 18–25). To facilitate inking and recording, an ink roller is used to deposit a thin coat of ink onto the pattern (ridge side) of the skin. The skin is then flipped over and rolled on the backside, recording the friction ridge detail on a standard card.

To begin this procedure, the hands (or feet) are removed by a medical examiner or pathologist and placed into separate containers labeled with appropriate markings. The containers are then refrigerated for approximately 5 to 7 days, checking each day for skin separation. When the skin separates, it is milky-white and looks "like a wrinkled latex glove that is one size too large for the wearer" (Rice, 1992, p 19). Subsequent to the removal of the skin, any loose, charred flesh or foreign material should be carefully removed by lightly brushing with a soft-bristled toothbrush to expose as much discernible friction ridge detail as possible. In addition, examinations should be conducted separately to prevent any mix-up of friction ridge skin. The friction ridge skin is then removed from the palms by carefully cutting along the outer edges with curved-tip scissors. Incisions are also made at the base of the palms, the base of the fingers, and at the base of the thumbs. Friction ridge skin from the feet is removed by making incisions along the outer edges of the feet, at the base of the heels, and at the base of the toes.

The connecting tissue between the epidermal and dermal layers is then carefully cut with scissors pointed away from the skin. The epidermal layer of the skin is then lifted away from the dermal layer. The separated friction ridge skin is then immersed in warm water for a few seconds and is laid flat to enable further gentle cleansing. A small amount of dishwashing liquid is applied to a very soft-bristled toothbrush, which is then very carefully used to clean out any remaining debris by brushing in the direction of the ridge flow to prevent damage to the ridges. During this process, the skin should be rinsed frequently in clean, warm water. After the skin is sufficiently cleaned and rinsed, it should be carefully blotted dry with paper towels.

To record the friction ridge detail from this skin, an ink roller is lightly coated with ink using an inking plate in the same manner as when recording inked standards from a live person. The friction ridge skin to be recorded is then placed on a hard flat surface, ridge-side up. With gentle pressure, and while the skin is held in place, the ink is rolled onto the skin. The skin is then flipped over, ridge side down, onto a standard 8" x 8" recording card, and while the skin is held in place, the roller is then gently rolled across the skin, pressing the ink onto the card. This method should be repeated until a satisfactory recording is produced.

Fingers and toes can also be recorded in this manner, taking care to remove, label, and examine them separately to prevent confusion. To remove the friction ridge skin from toes and fingers, incisions at the base of the digits, along the extreme sides, and around the insides of the nail are recommended, being careful not to damage any of the pattern areas. The friction ridge skin is then removed by cutting the connecting tissue starting from the base, as with removal of the palm areas. Cleaning, drying, inking, and recording are performed in the same manner as previously described (Rice, 1992, pp 18–25).

4.5 Summary

The methods and techniques described in this chapter for recording living and postmortem friction ridge detail are appropriate for the vast majority of conditions and circumstances. However, it is possible that an unusual circumstance will arise that may require extra patience and skill to achieve the most desirable results. Quality recordings from live subjects are usually not too difficult to obtain, as long as the subject is cooperative. Recording postmortem friction ridge detail, however, may become more of a challenge because of the varying conditions of the friction ridge skin. There are also many levels of difficulty associated with this endeavor, which is why proper training, experience, and determination are essential.

4.6 Reviewers

The reviewers critiquing this chapter were Herman Bergman, Patti Blume, Mike Campbell, Sue Manci Coppejans, Robert J. Garrett, Laura A. Hutchins, Bridget Lewis, Michelle L. Snyder, Lyla A. Thompson, Juliet H. Wood, and Rodolfo R. Zamora.

4.7 References

Cowger, J. F. *Friction Ridge Skin, Comparison and Identification of Fingerprints;* Elsevier Science Publishing Company: New York, 1983.

Federal Bureau of Investigation, U.S. Department of Justice. *The Science of Fingerprints;* U.S. Government Printing Office: Washington, DC, 1979.

Leas, R. L. Program Manager, FBI Disaster Squad—Victim Identification Unit, Quantico, VA. Personal communication, 2006.

Miller, R. D. Recovery of Usable Fingerprint Patterns from Damaged Postmortem Friction Ridge Skin. *J. Forensic Ident.* 1995, *45* (6), 602–605.

Olsen, Sr., R. D., *Scott's Fingerprint Mechanics;* Charles C Thomas: Springfield, 1978.

Rice, K. A. Printing of the Underside of the Epidermal Surface of Decomposed Fingers. *J. Forensic Ident.* 1988a, *38* (3), 98–100.

Rice, K. A. The Re-Hydration and Printing of Mummified Fingers. *J. Forensic Ident.* 1988b, *38* (4), 152–156.

Rice, K. A. Printing the Deceased Who Have Been Subjected to Fire. *J. Forensic Ident.* 1992, *42* (1), 18–25.

Scientific Working Group on Friction Ridge Analysis, Study and Technology. Special Notice—Name Change for Major Case Prints to Complete Friction Ridge Exemplars. *J. Forensic Ident.* 2006, *56* (4), 619–627.

Tomboc, R.; Schrader, M. Obtaining Fingerprint and Palmprint Impressions from Decomposed Bodies or Burn Victims Using the Mikrosil Casting Method. *J. Forensic Ident.* 2005, *55* (4), 471–479.

CHAPTER 5

SYSTEMS OF FRICTION RIDGE CLASSIFICATION

Laura A. Hutchins

CONTENTS

- 3 — 5.1 Introduction to Classification Systems
- 3 — 5.2 Criminal Identification of the Past
- 4 — 5.3 Beginnings of Classification
- 7 — 5.4 Birth of Modern Classification Systems
- 10 — 5.5 Single-Fingerprint Systems
- 12 — 5.6 Footprint and Palmprint Classification Systems
- 18 — 5.7 Computer Automation and Print Classification
- 24 — 5.8 Conclusion
- 24 — 5.9 Reviewers
- 24 — 5.10 References
- 25 — 5.11 Additional Information

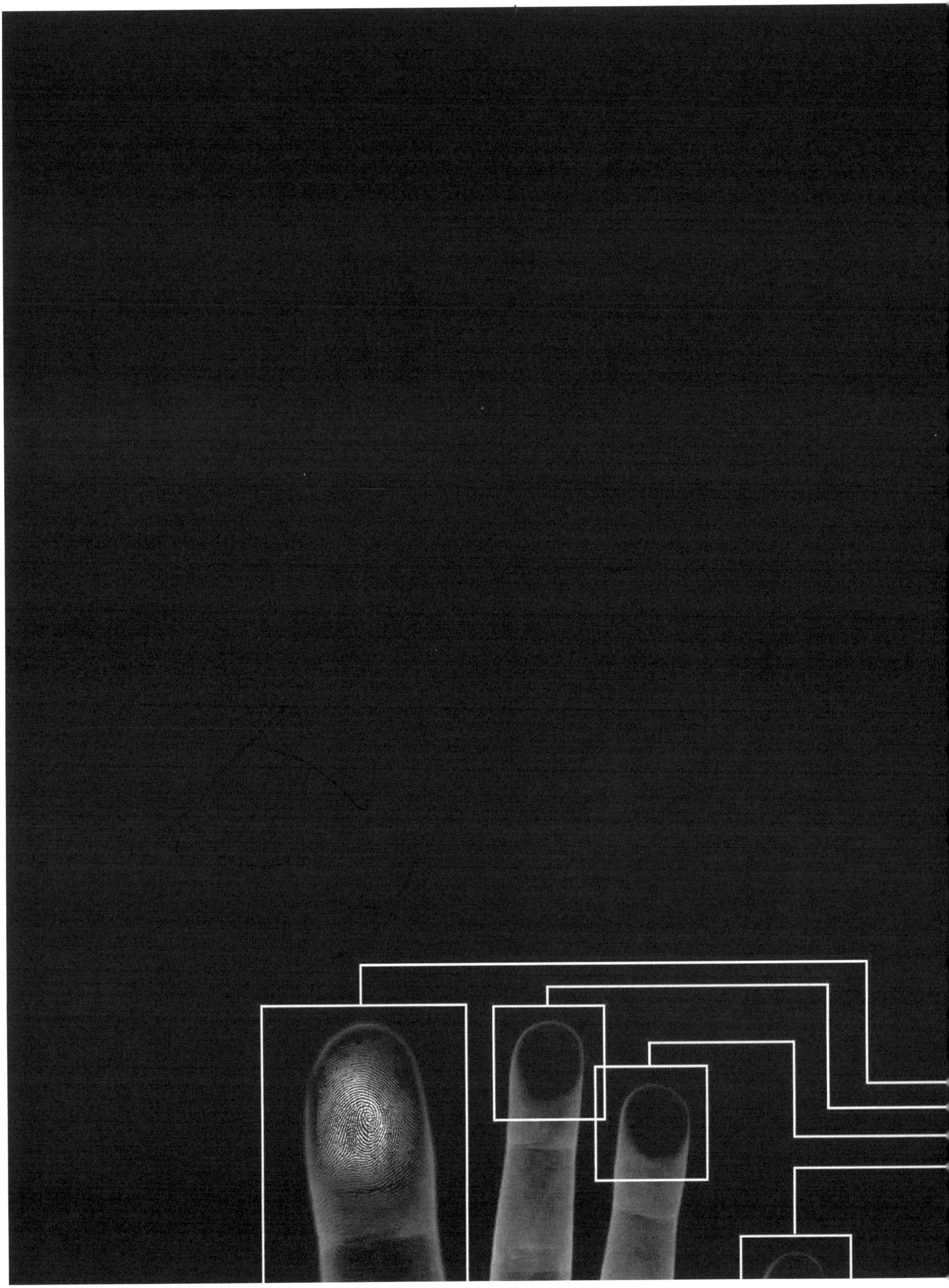

SYSTEMS OF FRICTION RIDGE CLASSIFICATION

Laura A. Hutchins

5.1 Introduction to Classification Systems

The concept of friction ridge individualization as an infallible means of individualization is rooted in the history of man and our inherent need to individualize ourselves, and be individualized, in an ever-expanding world. As populations grew and cities filled with differing classes of people, the populations of jails and prisons grew also. The ability to accurately identify repeat offenders was critical to the effectiveness of criminal justice institutions. It became paramount that an accurate method of individualization be developed.

5.2 Criminal Identification of the Past

Prior to any type of scientific criminal identification, the criminal justice community used purely visible methods to determine identity. These methods involved tattoos or scarification to denote criminals. However, this type of identification was seen as barbaric and inefficient. It was not until the advent of photography that a more humane method of criminal identification was devised.

This method involved taking photographs of all those who were arrested and incorporating the photographs into a compendium of identification, known as a rogues' gallery. (For more on rogues' galleries, see Chapter 8.) The use of the rogues' gallery as means of criminal identification soon proved nonscientific and ineffective because, when offenders were released, they could change their appearance. A simple haircut and change of clothes could render the offender unrecognizable. Additionally, many police departments lacked the insight to standardize the photographs that were taken of those who were arrested (Dilworth, 1977, p 1).

For example, women kept their hats on and veils down, with their heads tilted, when being photographed for the gallery. Yet, for the criminal justice community, photography was the only means of documenting the identity of criminals.

5.2.1 Alphonse Bertillon and Anthropometry*

Alphonse Bertillon began his public service career in 1879 when, having fulfilled his military service in the French army, he joined the Paris Prefecture of Police as a clerk in the Identification Division. He was tasked with the monotonous job of recording on index cards the physical descriptions of individuals who had been arrested. At the time, this was the only method that was available to identify recidivists.

Bertillon's first contribution to the reorganization of the department's criminal files was to incorporate the use of standard photography. Previous photography had been haphazard and inconsistent. Within a month of his appointment as a records clerk, he started an organized and standard system of photography. This system entailed the taking of full-face and profile portraits of the criminals entering the criminal justice system.

In 1882, having contributed greatly to the existing substandard method of criminal identification, Bertillon took on the task of establishing the identity of recidivists through a more scientific means (Rhodes, 1956, pp 71–101). Reflecting upon his family's professions as statisticians, demographers, and physicians, he embarked on the creation of a standard method of identification that was based on the measurement of specific body parts: anthropometry. He believed that by recording the body measurements of a criminal, he was establishing that criminal's body formula which would apply to that one person and would not change.

By 1883, Bertillon believed that he had devised a complete system of criminal identification. The information that was recorded was divided into three sections: (1) descriptive data such as height, weight, and eye color; (2) body marks such as scars, tattoos, and deformities; and (3) body measurements. He chose 11 specific body measurements that he thought could be easily and accurately measured. To create a system of classification that would be manageable and productive, each of the 11 measurements was further subdivided into three variation range groups.

This classification system became the first scientific system that was used to identify criminals. In fact, in 1884, *Bertillonage,* as his system came to be known, identified 241 repeat offenders (Beavan, 2001, p 91). Because of this impressive track record, other European and American criminal justice institutions quickly adopted Bertillonage.

As more police institutions began to maintain Bertillon records, it became apparent that the system was flawed and was merely a band-aid on the still-evident problem of reliable criminal identification. The foremost problem was that measurements taken by different officers were either different enough to preclude future identifications or similar enough to identify two individuals as the same person.

Another problem was that the 243 basic categories in the system were sufficient for an agency handling 5,000 to 10,000 records, but collections that exceeded 10,000 records presented problems; officers found themselves searching through categories that contained an unwieldy amount of cards. The time that was required to check for duplicate records increased from a few minutes to several hours. Additionally, the aging process could affect the accuracy of the measurements, especially if the measurements on record had been taken when the individual was not fully grown.

The realization of these challenges, along with the introduction of fingerprints as a method of identification, would eventually bring an end to use of the Bertillon system. Yet it was not until the early 20th century that anthropometry was completely dismissed as a method of criminal identification in Europe and in the United States.

5.3 Beginnings of Classification

5.3.1 Johannes Evangelist Purkinje

Johannes Evangelist Purkinje was a Czech professor of pathology and physiology at the University of Breslau in Prussia. He was a prolific scientist who made numerous contributions to the field of medicine. He researched sweat pores and skin, introduced the word *plasma*, devised new methods of preparing microscope samples, and researched visual phenomena (Jay, 2000, p 663).

---

* For more information on Bertillon and the other scientists discussed in this chapter, see chapter 1.

In 1823, Purkinje published his most famous medical thesis, *Commentatio de Examine Physiologico Organi Visus et Systematis Cutanei (A Commentary on the Physiological Examination of the Organs of Vision and the Cutaneous System)*. In this thesis, he described nine classifiable fingerprint patterns (Ashbaugh, 1999, p 40): (1) transverse curve, (2) central longitudinal stria, (3) oblique stripe, (4) oblique loop, (5) almond whorl, (6) spiral whorl, (7) ellipse, (8) circle, and (9) double whorl. At this time, this was the only detailed description of fingerprint patterns to appear in the scientific record. Although it is obvious that he recognized the classification element of friction ridge formations, he did not associate them with any type of classification system for use in personal identification (Faulds, 1905, p 33).

5.3.2 Dr. Henry Faulds' Syllabic System of Classification

Dr. Henry Faulds was a Scottish physician and superintendent of Tsukji Hospital in Tokyo, Japan. In the late 1870s, Faulds developed a friendship with the American archaeologist Edward S. Morse. While assisting Morse during an excavation, Faulds noticed the patent impression of a fingerprint in a piece of broken clay. It was at this moment that the connection between fingerprints and individualization was formulated in his mind (Beavan, 2001, p 69).

Faulds devised a method of using ink to record the fingerprint impressions of all 10 fingers on cards and soon had collected thousands of fingerprint cards. His collection became invaluable when the police accused a member of his medical staff of attempted burglary, committed by scaling the hospital wall and entering through a window. He compared a latent print that had been found on the wall with the accused staff member's fingerprints in his collection and determined that the latent print had not been left by his staff member.

Realizing that fingerprints could be the solution to the burgeoning problem of criminal identification, Faulds was determined to prove that fingerprints were the key to accurate and reliable personal individualization. To prove his theory, Faulds researched the permanence and individuality of fingerprints. To prove individuality, he compared the thousands of fingerprint cards he had collected and determined that the fingerprints on each card were unique. To prove permanence, Faulds and his medical students used various means—razors, pumice stones, sandpaper, acids, and caustics—to remove their friction ridges. As he had hoped, the friction ridges grew back exactly as they had been before.

Faulds also needed to prove that fingerprints did not change during the growth process. To this end, he observed the fingerprints of growing children over a period of two years and determined that friction ridges changed only in size and not in uniqueness.

Having determined the individuality and permanence of fingerprints, Faulds published his findings in the journal *Nature* (Faulds, 1880, p 605). In the article, he suggested the use of fingerprints in criminal investigations and the use of printer's ink in obtaining fingerprints. In addition, he mentioned two categories of fingerprint patterns: loops and whorls.

During the next few years, Faulds developed a syllabic system for classifying fingerprints (Faulds, 1912, pp 83–100). He felt that learning this type of classification system would be natural and quite easy for an identification official. His idea was based on his perception that the human brain can quickly associate an object with a sound.

In his system, each hand was represented by five syllables, one syllable for each finger, with each syllable separated by a hyphen. Syllables were constructed from an established list of 21 consonants and 6 vowels representing set fingerprint pattern characteristics (Table 5–1). For example, one hand may be represented and spoken as "RA-RA-RA-RA-RA". (In more complex examples, fingers may be represented by two or more syllables).

Based solely on the primary breakdown of the consonants alone, Faulds produced a classification system that had the potential to create nearly 17 trillion classifications (Beaven, 2001, p 131).

In addition to creating a strand of syllables to represent each hand, Faulds believed that there should be a single-finger index. This index would prove useful in comparing latent prints from a crime scene, provided that the syllable of the latent print could be derived from the known single prints on file.

In 1886, Faulds offered to establish a fingerprinting bureau in Scotland Yard, at his expense, and to institute his fingerprint classification system (Russell, 2004). However, Scotland Yard declined the offer and maintained Bertillonage as the agency's method of criminal identification.

Table 5–1

Faulds' description of syllables.

Consonant	Pattern Description
CH	Hook with short leg facing right
J	Hook with short leg facing left
B	Convex bow with left lineation
P	Convex bow with right lineation
T	Pear-shaped, free-floating
D	Pear-shaped, fixed by stem
K	Spindle with one stem
G	Spindled with stems on both ends
W	Clockwise whorl
V	Counter-clockwise whorl
Q	Large circle/oval w/elements
M	Volcanic mountain peak
N	Flag-staff on mountain top
L	Loop with straight axis
R	Loop with curved axis
S	Sinuous with no angles
Z	Zigzag with angularity
X	Nondescript
F	Aspirate used strictly for pronunciation
H	Aspirate used strictly for pronunciation
Vowel	**Pattern Description**
A	Interior empty, simple
E	Three short ridges/dots
I	Simple detached line/no more than two lines in heart of encircling pattern
O	Small circle/oval/dot in core
U	Fork with 2+ prongs in core
Y	Fork with prongs turning away from concavity

5.3.3 Sir Francis Galton and the Tripartite Classification

Sir Francis Galton, cousin of Charles Darwin, was a noted English scientist. Galton developed an interest in fingerprints in 1888 when he was asked to present a lecture on personal identification. To prepare for the lecture, he researched Bertillonage, the then-current method of personal identification. After investigating the use of anthropometry for criminal identification, he became a critic of the technique. His criticism stemmed from the observation that Bertillon measurements did not take into account the correlation between stature and limb length (Galton, 1889, pp 403–405). He believed that the continued use of Bertillonage as a method of criminal identification would lead to an unacceptably high rate of false identifications. He noted also that the taking of Bertillon measurements was time-consuming and the measurements could vary, depending on who was taking them.

As a result of his distaste for anthropometry, Galton researched the use of fingerprints for personal individualization. His research led him to Faulds' article in *Nature* and a rebuttal letter that same year by Sir William Herschel that stated that he had discovered fingerprint individualization first and had been using it in India since 1860 (Herschel, 1880, p 76). Soon after, Galton began corresponding with Herschel and obtained his collection of fingerprint data.

After four years of intensive study and research, Galton published his famous book *Finger Prints* (1892) in which he established that fingerprints are both permanent and unique. He also realized that for fingerprints to become a viable method of personal individualization, a systematic, understandable, and applicable system of fingerprint classification had to be developed.

In his book, Galton formulated a classification system that was based on the alphabetical enumerations of the three fingerprint patterns: L represented a loop, W represented a whorl, and A represented an arch. To classify a set of fingerprints, the pattern for each finger was labeled with one of these three letters. The letters for the right hand's index, middle, and ring fingers were grouped together, followed by the letters for the left hand's index, middle, and ring fingers. After this string of letters, the letters for the right thumb and right little finger were recorded, followed by the letters for the left thumb and left little finger. For example, a person with the right hand possessing all whorls except for the little finger having a loop, and the left hand having all loops except for the little finger having a whorl, would have the following classification: WWWLLLWLLW. This classification code would then be recorded on a card and the card filed alphabetically by this classification.

Two years after the publication of his book, Galton's elementary fingerprint classification system was incorporated into the Bertillonage files at Scotland Yard. Although this was a success for him, his classification system proved too rudimentary for a large number of files and would not stand on its own as a method of cataloging and classifying criminals.

5.4 Birth of Modern Classification Systems

5.4.1 Juan Vucetich and the Argentine System

Juan Vucetich was born in Croatia and immigrated to Argentina in 1882. Within four years, he was working at the Buenos Aires Police Department, collecting arrest and crime statistics. Within a few more years, Vucetich became head of the Office of Identification.

During his tenure, Vucetich came to the realization that Bertillonage was an ineffective method of criminal identification. Concern regarding the mobility of criminals in and out of Argentina prompted him to search for a more effective method of identification. His search ended when he read the French journal *Revue Scientifique* (1891) detailing Galton's research into the scientific use of fingerprints as a means of individualization. After reading this article, he began his campaign to incorporate the use of fingerprinting into the criminal justice system of Argentina. His campaign paid off, and that same year (1891), fingerprints replaced Bertillonage at the Office of Identification. This was the first occurrence of fingerprint individualization officially usurping anthropometry.

Having achieved a major milestone, Vucetich realized that for the science of fingerprints to be accepted worldwide, a useful and manageable classification system had to be created. Working from Galton's overly general three-pattern classification system, he quickly created a classification system that used subcategories to classify, file, and locate fingerprint cards. He initially called his system *icnofalangométrica*, meaning "finger track measurement". In 1896, he renamed the system *dactiloscopía*, meaning "finger description" (Rodriguez, 2004).

Vucetich's system was an expansion of the three patterns established by Galton: the arch, the loop, and the whorl. However, Vucetich further divided the loop into internal loop (left slope) and external loop (right slope) categories, creating four types of patterns: arch, internal loop, external loop, and whorl.

The classification consisted of four single letters, representing the pattern on the thumb, and four single numbers, representing the patterns on the remaining fingers (Table 5–2). Like Galton's classification system, Vucetich's system started with the right-hand thumb and ended with the left little finger.

Table 5–2

Vucetich's pattern-type symbols.

Pattern	Thumbs	Other Fingers
Arch	A	1
Internal loop	I	2
External loop	E	3
Whorl	V	4

The Vucetich classification system consisted of a basic classification (called the *primary*) and a more descriptive secondary classification using extensions. The primary classification was divided into two groups: the numerator and the denominator. The numerator was termed the *series* and represented the right hand. The denominator was termed the *section* and represented the left hand. The right thumb (called the *fundamental*) and the remaining right-hand fingers (called the *division*) represented the *series*. The left thumb (called the *subclassification*) and the remaining left-hand fingers (called the *subdivision*) represented the *section*. For example, if both the numerator and denominator were A1141, then both the right hand and the left hand had arches in all the fingers except for the ring fingers, which had whorls.

The secondary classification further subdivided the fingerprints into five subtypes: 5, 6, 7, 8, and 9. Each number represented a further description of the pattern, applied to either hand, and was placed as a superscript in parentheses (Table 5–3). When the pattern type was a normal loop variety, the superscript defaulted to ridge count values (Table 5–4).

Table 5–3

Vucetich's secondary classification.

Pattern	Superscript	Description
Arch	5	Vaulted/Normal
	6	Left-inclined
	7	Right-inclined
	8	Tent-shaped
	9	All others
Internal loop	5	Normal flow
	6	Invaded
	7	Interrogatory
	8	Hooked
	9	All others
External loop	Designation same as Internal loop	
Whorl	5	Normal
	6	Sinuous
	7	Ovoid
	8	Hooked
	9	All others

Table 5–4

Vucetich's ridge count values.

Ridge Count Spread	Superscript Value
1–5	5
6–10	10
11–15	15
16–20	20
Over 20	25

For example, a person whose right-hand fingers all have external (right slope) loops and whose left-hand fingers all have internal (left slope) loops would have a Vucetich classification of:

$$\frac{E^{(20)} \; 3^{(10)} \; 3^{(5)} \; 3^{(15)} \; 3^{(10)}}{I^{(10)} \; 2^{(5)} \; 2^{(10)} \; 2^{(10)} \; 2^{(5)}}$$

In 1896, Vucetich published his new classification system in a pamphlet entitled *General Instructions for the Province of Buenos Aires System of Identification.* In 1904, he published the book that would take his classification system across the world: *Dactiloscopía Comparada (Comparative Fingerprinting): The New Argentine System.*

5.4.2 Sir Edward Henry and the Henry Classification System

In the early 1890s, Sir Edward Henry was the new Inspector General of the Bengal District Police in India and was experiencing a common problem of the day: the inability to accurately identify the native people. After reading Galton's *Finger Prints,* he was convinced that he could create a logical and applicable system of fingerprint classification that would enable fingerprints to become the sole system of personal and criminal identification.

Henry returned to England in 1894 and developed a personal and professional relationship with Galton. Galton provided him with his personal research material, along with that of Herschel and Faulds. With this information in hand, Henry returned to India to solve the fingerprint classification problem. Even without a classification system, in 1896 he ordered his police officers to begin taking fingerprints along with anthropometric measurements of Bengali prisoners.

Meanwhile, Henry assigned two of his police officers from the Calcutta Anthropometric Bureau to work on the fingerprint classification project. By 1897, the two officers, Azizul Haque and Hem Chandra Bose, formulated a mathematical method of dividing fingerprint records into a large number of primary groupings that were based on Galton's fingerprint pattern types.

The Henry system began with the formulation of the primary. The primary was determined by assigning a value to each of the 10 fingers, starting with the right thumb and ending with the left little finger. This value was based on the presence of a whorl on a particular finger (Table 5–5). If the finger did not contain a whorl, it was assigned a value of zero.

Table 5–5

Henry's primary values (Henry, 1900, pp 72–73).

Finger	Number	Value if Whorl
Right thumb	1	16
Right index	2	16
Right middle	3	8
Right ring	4	8
Right little	5	4
Left thumb	6	4
Left index	7	2
Left middle	8	2
Left ring	9	1
Left little	10	1

The primary was expressed in ratio form, with the numerator representing the whorl values of the even fingers plus 1 and the denominator representing the whorl values of the odd fingers plus 1. For example, if an individual had a fingerprint record with a pattern series of all whorls, the corresponding primary classification would be 32 over 32. If a person had loops in the right and left index fingers, the primary classification chart would be as follows:

Right thumb	Right index	Right middle	Right ring	Right little
16	0	8	8	4

Left thumb	Left index	Left middle	Left ring	Left little
4	0	2	1	1

The chart is then calculated as follows:

$$\frac{1 + (\text{Sum of Even Finger Values})}{1 + (\text{Sum of Odd Finger Values})} = \frac{1 + (15)}{1 + (29)} = \frac{16}{30}$$

This classification system allowed for 1,024 primary groupings.

To the right of the primary was the secondary. The secondary was determined by the pattern types in the #2 and #7 fingers and was shown in the formula by capital letters representing the pattern (A for arch, T for tented arch, R for radial loop, U for ulnar loop, and W for whorl). To account for the rarity of arches, tented arches, and radial loops in nonindex fingers, these patterns were indicated by lower case letters (a, t, r) and placed after the secondary. If one of these patterns was present in the thumb(s), the small letter was placed to the left of the primary. The subsecondary was to the right of the secondary and represented the ridge counts for loops or ridge tracing for whorls in the remaining fingers.

This new classification system was so successful that in March of 1897, the British Indian government instituted the Henry classification system as the official method of criminal identification. By 1900, the success of the Henry system in India made Scotland Yard review its own identification system. This review resulted in the abandonment of Bertillonage and the adoption of the Henry system. In 1901, Henry was transferred to Scotland Yard, where he set up its first central fingerprint bureau and began training officers in fingerprint classification.

5.4.3 Offshoots of the Henry and Vucetich Classification Systems

Both Vucetich and Henry gained international recognition in the arena of scientific criminal identification. Vucetich traveled the world promoting his book, and Henry gained the backing of the modern European world. Both systems were considered superior to Bertillonage, and both systems had equal recognition in international police and scientific circles.

Table 5–6

Classifications based on Henry and Vucetich systems.

Henry	Australian (Australia)
	Budapest (Budapest)
	Valladares (Portugal)
	Pateer (Amsterdam)
	Windt Kodicek (Germany)
	Spirlet (The Hague)
	Steegers (Cuba)
	Conlay (Federated Malay States Police)
	American (New York City)
	Flak Conley (Newark, NJ)
	RCMP (Canada)
	FBI Extensions (Washington, DC)
Henry-Vucetich	Daae (Norway)
	Protivenski (Prague)
	Olóriz (Madrid)
	Martinez (Mexico)
	Borgerhoff (Belgium)
	Harvey Pacha (Egypt)
	Cabezas (Valparaiso)
	Klatt (Berlin)
	Brussels (Belgium)
	Roscher (Hamburg)
	Japanese National
	Lebedoff (Russia)
	When (Berlin)
	Smallegange (Holland)
	Gasti (Italy)
	Portillo (Barcelona)
	Lyonnese (Lyon)
	Jouenne (Colonial Service in French West Africa)

Table 5–7

Single-fingerprint systems.

Based on Existing Classification Systems	Original Single-Fingerprint Systems
Collins	Born
Larson	Moran
Oloritz	Code
Borgerhoff	Sagredo
Stockis	Dresden
Gasti Register	Barlow
Lyonnese	Jaycox
Neben Register of Roscher	Crosskey
	Battley
	Giraud and Henquel
	Jorgensen
	Monodacylus

As other agencies began to adopt these classification systems, the systems were often modified (Table 5–6). Modifications involved the creation of extensions to produce classification systems that could handle larger populations (McGinnis, 1963, p 115). For example, the United States Federal Bureau of Investigation (FBI) incorporated extensions relating to the ridge counts and whorl tracings of specific fingers to split up the rapidly populating primary and secondary groupings.

5.5 Single-Fingerprint Systems

Although the known-print classification systems were useful for the identification of repeat offenders, they did not aid in the apprehension of criminals by identifying latent prints left at crime scenes. To address this limitation, numerous single-fingerprint classification systems were developed. Some of these systems were based on existing known-print classification systems and some were fully original (Table 5–7). Of all these single-fingerprint classification systems, Chief Inspector Henry Battley and Detective Superintendent Fredrick Cherrill of New Scotland Yard developed the most popular system.

Table 5–8

Battley's subgroup designations (Cherrill, 1954, pp 82–90).

Pattern	Subdivisions	Designation
Arches	Plain arch	1
	Left-sloping	2
	Right-sloping	3
Tented arches	Circle reading (summit of first platform ridge)	A–H
Radial loops	Ridge count between delta and core	#
	Predetermined core definition	A–L
	Circle reading of delta	A–H
Ulnar loops	Ridge count between delta and core	#
	Predetermined core definitions	A–L
	Circle reading of delta	A–H
Whorls / Central pocket loops	Circle reading of first recurving ridge	A–H
	Predetermined core definitions limited to small spirals in "A" circle reading	A.1
		A.2
		A.3
		A.4
	Circle reading of left delta	A–H
	Ridge tracing	I, M, O
	Circle reading of right delta	A–H
	Ridge count between left delta and core	#
	Ridge count between right delta and core	#
Twinned loops	Radial or ulnar slope of descending loop	R, U
	Circle reading of core of descending loop	A–H
	Ridge count between loops	#
	Ridge count between core and delta of descending loop	#
	Circle reading of left delta	A–H
	Ridge tracing	I, M, O
	Circle reading of right delta	A–H
Lateral pocket loop	Radial or ulnar slope of majority of ridges	R, U
	Ridge count between delta and core of innermost loop	#
Composite	No subdivision	
Accidental	No subdivision	
Severely scarred	Cannot classify	

5.5.1 Battley Single-Fingerprint System

In 1929, Battley and Cherrill developed the idea of a single-fingerprint system that did not require all 10 known fingerprints of an individual. They postulated that latent fingerprints found at a crime scene could be individualized using a known print of the same finger of the offender.

The Battley system used 10 main patterns followed by additional subdivisions, depending on the pattern designation (Table 5–8). These additional subdivisions included radial or ulnar inclination, ridge counts, ridge tracings, formation of the core(s), position of the delta(s), and circle readings. A specific subdivision, known as a circle reading, was derived using a special magnifying glass with a plain glass window at the base. This base window consisted of a center circle with a dot in the middle, designated as area A, and seven concentric circles, each 2 mm in width, designated B through H. The center dot was placed over a designated point of the impression, and circle readings were taken that were based on the position of specific formations.

In the system, the known fingerprints from an arrest card would be individually classified according to pattern and established in 10 collections, one for each finger, from the right thumb to the left little finger (i.e., No. 1 collection through No. 10 collection).

Single-fingerprint cards were constructed by mounting the specific fingerprint on a card and filling in particular information in designated areas. This information included the number and name of the digit, the criminal's reference number, the Henry classification, and the Battley classification (Table 5–9).

Table 5–9

Battley index card.

TYPE	CORE	Subgroup Designation
Criminal ID No. Finger No. & Description Henry Classification Adhered Fingerprint From Known Exemplar		Subgroup Designation
		Subgroup Designation
		Subgroup Designation
		Subgroup Designation
		Subgroup Designation
		Subgroup Designation
		Subgroup Designation
		Subgroup Designation
		Subgroup Designation

The Battley system required a great deal of labor to classify and maintain the collections. Eventually, the collections became too large, and it became impossible to accurately and quickly individualize a latent print from a crime scene with a known single print on file.

5.5.2 Additional Single-Print Systems

As previously mentioned, there were single-print systems other than the Battley system. Like Battley, these other systems were based on the classification of individual fingerprints, independent of the other fingers. These systems were frequently based on existing systems or a combination of existing systems and definitions used by those systems.

Similar to Battley, most of the other systems were based on predetermined pattern types (i.e., whorl, arch, and loops) with further subclassifications, such as core formations, delta position, ridge counts, and ridge tracings. Although some systems were similar to the Battley system, they differed in some respects because of added subdivisions (Table 5–10). Some systems went into great detail describing the patterns, some divided each print into sections or zones and recorded the location of ridge characteristics within that area, and some further defined the shapes of deltas (Bridges, 1963, pp 181–213).

5.6 Footprint and Palmprint Classification Systems

The next logical step in the evolution of friction ridge classification systems was the establishment of palmprint and footprint classification systems. Footprints and palmprints were being detected on evidence with enough frequency to warrant the development of classification systems.

5.6.1 Classification of Footprints

Along with the need for a footprint classification system based on latent impression evidence, there was also a need for such a classification system for filing the footprints of newborn babies, military airmen, and people lacking arms. Two main footprint classification systems were developed and used over the years: the Federal Bureau of Investigation system and the Chatterjee system.

5.6.1.1 The FBI's Footprint Classification System. The FBI's classification system was a highly modified version of the system developed by Wentworth and Wilder in their landmark book *Personal Identification* (1918). The basis of the FBI's classification system was the observance of the ball area of the foot, directly below the large toe. This area typically exhibits one of three types of pattern groups: arch, loop, or whorl. Each group was designated by a letter and was further divided by type and ridge count (for loop and whorl patterns only) (FBI, 1985, p 24).

Arch patterns were designated by the letter "O". The O group was further subdivided according to the flow of the ridges. Type 1 subdivision (O1) indicated a vertical ridge flow (i.e., ridges flowing from the big toe to the heel). Type 2 subdivision (O2) indicated a horizontal ridge flow (i.e., ridges flowing from the big toe to the little toe). Looping

Table 5–10

Single-print systems other than Battley (Bridges, 1963, pp 181–213).

Name of Single-Print System	Subdivisions
Collins	Pattern types
	Ridge counts
	Ridge tracing
	Ridge characteristics
Larson	Pattern types
	Inclination of pattern
	Core type
	Ridge characteristics
	Delta type
	Ridge tracing
	Combinations
Oloriz	Primary from Oloriz tenprint system
	Core type
	Limiting lines (type lines)
	Delta type
	Apex angle
Borgerhoff	Pattern types
	Ridge counts
	Ridge tracing
Stockis	Pattern types
	Ridge counts
	Apex angle
	Core type
	Delta type
	Ridge tracing
Gasti	Taken from Gasti (tenprint) classification for each finger
Born	Pattern type
	Zone scheme with marked minutiae
Sagredo	Primary from Oloritz tenprint system
	No delta pattern type
	One delta pattern type
	Two delta pattern type
	Pattern inclination
	Ridge counts
	Ridge tracing
	Delta type
Dresden	Pattern type
	Ridge counts
	Pattern inclination
Neben Register of Roscher	Taken from Roscher tenprint classification for each finger
Lyonnese	Pattern type
	Centro-basal angle from Oloritz
	Ridge tracing
Barlow	Pattern type
	Core type
	Pattern inclination
	Ridge counts
Jaycox	Pattern type
	Pattern inclination
	Core type
	Ridge characteristics of core
Jorgenson	Pattern type
	Pattern inclination
	Ridge counts
	Core type
	Delta position
	Core to delta angle
	Core diameter (whorl)
Crosskey	Pattern type
	Core type
	Ridge counts
	Presence of scar

patterns were designated by the letter "L" and were further subdivided into four types. Type a subdivision (La) indicated a ridge flow entering and exiting toward the toes. Type b and c subdivisions (Lb and Lc) indicated a ridge flow entering and exiting the big toe-side of the foot. (Type b indicated the right foot and Type c indicated the left foot.) Type d subdivision (Ld) indicated a ridge flow entering and exiting toward the heel of the foot.

Whorl patterns were designated by the letter "W" and were further subdivided into three types. Type w subdivision (Ww) indicated a whorl pattern that was either a plain whorl or a central pocket loop whorl. Type d subdivision (Wd) indicated a double loop whorl. Type x subdivision (Wx) indicated an accidental whorl.

Like the Henry classification, the footprint classification was expressed as a fraction, with the right foot as the numerator and the left foot as the denominator. The fraction was made up of the primary, secondary, final, and key. The primary was the pattern group (O, L, or W) and was always expressed as a capital letter. The secondary was the type of subdivision and was placed to the right of the primary (e.g., Ww). The final was the ridge count of the loop or whorl pattern on the right foot and was placed to the right of the secondary (e.g., Ww 25). The key was the ridge count of the loop or whorl pattern on the left foot and was placed to the left of the secondary (e.g., 25 Ww).

A complete footprint classification looked like:

La 32

25 Wd

5.6.1.2 Chatterjee Footprint Classification System. A system developed by Sri Salil Kumar Chatterjee divided the footprint into the following six areas:

Area 1: Ball of the foot, below the big toe.

Areas 2–4: Interspaces below the toes.

Area 5: Center of the foot.

Area 6: Heel.

Chatterjee used an alpha representation for the pattern in Area 1 and a numeric representation for the pattern in the remaining areas (Table 5–11) (Chatterjee, 1953, pp 179–183).

Table 5–11

Alpha and numeric pattern representations (Moenssens, 1971, p 212).

None	O	0
Tented arch	T	2
Upward-slope loop	U	4
Loop with downward slope	D	6
Central pocket loop	C	7
Twin loop	S	8

The Chatterjee footprint classification was also expressed as a fraction, with the right foot as the numerator and the left foot as the denominator. The primary was the Area 1 pattern designation and the secondary was a five-digit number, representing Areas 2 through 6, and was to the right of the primary.

5.6.2 Classification of Palmprints

The classification of palmprints was a worthwhile endeavor because of the frequency of latent palmprints at crime scenes. Three classification systems were established for palmprints: one in Western Australia, one in Liverpool, England, and another in Denmark.

5.6.2.1 Western Australian Palmprint Classification. This classification consisted of a numeric primary and an alpha and numeric secondary in the form of a fraction (Baird, 1959). The classification was based on the tripartite division of the palm into the interdigital, thenar, and hypothenar areas (Figure 5–1).

Table 5–12

Primary value determination (Baird, 1959, pp 21–24).

Area of Consideration	Value
Interdigital #5 finger delta to ulnar edge	1
Interdigital #4 finger delta to #3 finger delta	2
Interdigital #3 finger delta to radial edge	4
Thenar	8
Hypothenar	16
No pattern in area	0

To obtain the primary classification, the three areas were allotted a value based on the ridge flow in that area (Table 5–12). If there was no discernible pattern in the specified area, a value of 0 was given. Notably, the values were the same as those for the primary in the Henry classification; however, this classification was not dependent on the presence of whorls but on the presence of any type of pattern. Because an arch pattern was typically considered to lack a true pattern area because there was no core and delta, this pattern was only given a value when it was present in the interdigital area. As with the Henry classification, a value of 1 was added to the total.

The secondary classification was divided into two parts. The first division was the type of pattern present in the thenar and hypothenar areas. This subdivision was expressed in the form of a fraction, with the thenar as the numerator and the hypothenar as the denominator. The second division, known as the secondary subclassification, concerned the area between the thumb and the index finger and the interdigital area. The thumb to index area was considered as a part of the thenar and was placed in the numerator; the interdigital area was considered as part of the hypothenar and was placed in the denominator.

The classification formula was written as follows:

$$(primary) \frac{(thenar) \ (thumb \ to \ index \ area)}{(hypothenar) \ (interdigital)}$$

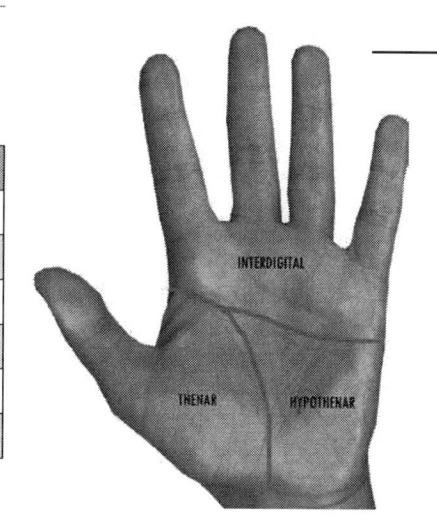

FIGURE 5–1

Tripartite division of the palm.

The Western Australian system used pattern definitions derived from the agencies' known-print classification system, which was a modification of the Henry classification system. The patterns were given specific alpha symbols according to their locations in the palm (Table 5–13). A further subdivision of the secondary classification involved ridge counts and ridge tracings and was expressed as a fraction to the right of the secondary classification.

5.6.2.2 Liverpool Palmprint Classification System. The palmprint classification system that was established in Liverpool, England, was considered a more user-friendly classification system than that used in Western Australia. The Liverpool system also concentrated on the three divisions of the palm.

This system was divided into four parts and consisted of alpha and numeric symbols. The primary division pertained to the cumulative patterns in all three sections: interdigital, thenar, and hypothenar. The secondary division involved patterns in the hypothenar and included a subsecondary classification. The tertiary division involved patterns in the thenar. The quaternary division included patterns in the interdigital section of the palm and had three additional sections: part 1, part 2, and part 3.

This classification used a coding box, where each square contained the alpha or numeric symbol for each part of the classification (Figure 5–2, p 5-17).

Table 5–13

Symbols for secondary classification.

Pattern	Location	Symbol
Arch	Thenar	A
	Thumb-index	None
	Hypothenar	A
	Interdigital	a
Exceptional arch	Thenar	E
	Thumb-index	e
	Hypothenar	E
	Interdigital	e
Joined arch	Thenar	J
	Thumb-index	J
	Hypothenar	J
	Interdigital	J
Joined arch #1	Hypothenar only	J1
Joined arch #2	Hypothenar only	J2
Vertical arch #1	Hypothenar only	V1
Tented arch	Thenar	T
	Thumb-index	t
	Hypothenar	T
	Interdigital	t
Tented arch #1	Hypothenar	T1
Tented arch #2	Hypothenar	T2
Radial loop	Thenar	R
	Thumb-index	r
	Hypothenar	R
	Interdigital	r
Radial loop #1	Hypothenar	R1
Radial loop #2	Hypothenar	R2
Radial loop #3	Hypothenar	R3
Radial loop #4	Hypothenar	R4
Ulnar loop	Thenar	U
	Thumb-index	U
	Hypothenar	U
	Interdigital	U
Ulnar loop #1	Hypothenar	U1
Ulnar loop #2	Hypothenar	U2
Ulnar loop #3	Hypothenar	U3
Ulnar loop #4	Hypothenar	U4
Distal loop*	Interdigital	L
Whorl	Thenar	W
	Thumb-index	w
	Hypothenar	W
	Interdigital	w
Central pocket loop	Thenar	C
	Thumb-index	c
	Hypothenar	C
	Interdigital	c
Double loop	Thenar	D
	Thumb-index	d
	Hypothenar	D
	Interdigital	d
Accidental	Thenar	X
	Thumb-index	x
	Hypothenar	X
	Interdigital	x

* Distal loop only noted when there was another pattern present in the interdigital area.

The primary division was formulated by the sum of set values, as determined by the presence of a pattern in the three palmar sections. The numeral 2 was given for the presence of a pattern in the thenar. The numeral 3 was given for the presence of a pattern in the interdigital area. The numeral 4 was given for the presence of a pattern in the hypothenar. The value of 1 was recorded if the palm was devoid of patterns in all three areas. When a palmar area contained more than one pattern, it was given a single value, as if there was only one pattern in the area. When patterns were present in more than one palmar area, the values were added together. The specific summed values also indicated which palmar area contained a pattern (Table 5–14).

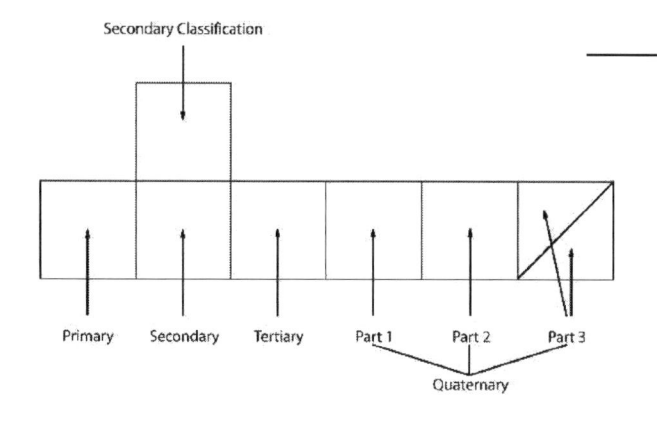

FIGURE 5–2

Coding box for the Liverpool palmprint classification.

Table 5–14

Pattern indication from primary value.

Primary Value	Pattern Indication
1	None
2	Thenar only
3	Interdigital only
4	Hypothenar only
5	Thenar and interdigital only
6	Thenar and hypothenar only
7	Interdigital and hypothenar only
9	Patterns in all three areas

The secondary and subsecondary classification pertained only to the patterns in the hypothenar. Table 5–15 details the patterns and representative symbols that were used in this classification system. If the hypothenar area contained more than one pattern, the coding box was separated by a diagonal line from the lower left corner to the upper right corner, with the left upper half of the box designated for the pattern symbol of the pattern closest to the interdigital area and the lower right half designated for the pattern symbol of the pattern closest to the wrist.

The secondary subclassification involved two distinct subclassifications. For a single loop in the hypothenar, the number of ridge characteristics in the core area was recorded. For a hypothenar devoid of a pattern, the type of delta was recorded (Alexander, 1973, pp 86–90).

Table 5–15

Symbols used in the Liverpool Palmprint Classification System.

Pattern	Symbol
Whorl A (circular)	A
Whorl B (elliptical)	B
Twinned loop	TL
Lateral pocket loop	LP
Central pocket loop	CP
Accidental/composite	ACC
Tented arch	T
Loop core inward	I
Loop core outward	O
Loop core downward	D
Loop core upward	U
Loop core nutant	K
Nondescript	N
Plain arch	N
No pattern	
High carpal delta	H
Low carpal delta	L

The tertiary division pertained to the thenar area of the palm. If there were two patterns in this area, the coding box was again separated by a diagonal line from the lower left corner to the upper right corner, with the left upper half designated for the pattern symbol of the pattern closest to the interdigital area and the lower right half designated for the pattern symbol closest to the wrist.

Part 1 of the quaternary division pertained to the type(s) of pattern in the interdigital area of the palm. If more than one pattern appeared in the interdigital area, the box was separated by three diagonal lines, with the upper left third dedicated for the pattern closest to the index finger and the bottom right third dedicated for the pattern closest to the little finger.

Part 2 of the quaternary division involved a predetermined numerical value indicating the position of the pattern in relation to the fingers (Table 5–16). If more than one pattern was present, the numerals were combined for a single value. If a pattern was between the base of two fingers, the higher value was recorded.

Part 3 of the quaternary division involved the recording of ridge counts for tented arches or loops (inward core, outward core, downward core loops) when only one of these patterns was present in the interdigital area.

5.6.2.3 The Brogger Moller Palmprint Classification System. The Brogger Moller palmprint classification system was formulated by Kaj Brogger Moller of the National Identification Bureau in Copenhagen, Denmark (Moenssens, 1971, p 199). As with the previous two systems, this classification was based on the three defined areas of the palm (i.e., hypothenar, thenar, and base areas). However, this system employed the use of a special measuring glass. This glass contained four separate measuring areas. The areas were defined by three concentric circles measuring 2, 4, and 6 cm from a center dot. Each area was numbered 1 through 4, with 4 marking the area outside the last concentric ring. A second measuring area, known as the 1–6 scale, contained five lines, each 6 cm in length and 3 mm apart. The area between each line was numbered 1 through 6, with 1 representing the top of the scale. A third measuring area, known as the 0–9 scale, looked like a ladder with the right leg missing. This scale contained 10 lines, each 1 cm in length and placed 4 mm apart. Each area between the lines was numbered 0 to 9, with 0 representing the bottom of the scale.

The classification of palm prints under this system was based on the ridge pattern(s) in the three areas of the palm and on the primary, secondary, and tertiary values. The measuring glass was used to determine some of the values (Tables 5–17 to 5–19). The classification was recorded in a table, with the hypothenar on the left, the interdigital in the middle, and the thenar on the right side of the table. For each area, the primary was recorded on the bottom, with the secondary above the primary, followed by the tertiary on the top (Figure 5–3).

5.7 Computer Automation and Print Classification

As federal, state, and local agencies received and retained more and more known exemplars, the need for a more efficient means of known-print individualization became paramount. The identification service divisions of these agencies were tasked with the manual searching of suspect prints with known prints, often taking months to reach a decision of individualization or nonindividualization. This lengthy turnaround time posed an obvious problem if a suspect could not legally be detained pending an answer from the identification division. The solution to this problem came with the invention of the computer.

5.7.1 Birth of Computerized Classification

The first experiment with computer automation of known-print cards took place at the Federal Bureau of Investigation. In 1934, the FBI's Identification Division was starting to feel the effects of a large known-print database that was becoming increasingly difficult to search manually. The FBI's attempt at automation of known prints involved the

Table 5–16

Pattern value for part 2 of the quaternary division.

Under index finger	8
Under ring finger	2

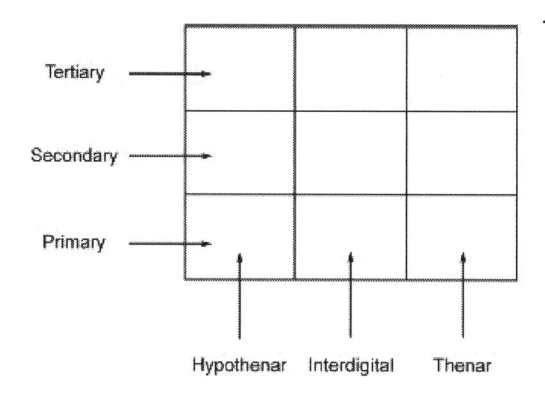

FIGURE 5–3

Brogger Moller palmprint classification box.

Table 5–17

Classification for the hypothenar (Moenssens, 1971, pp 200–205).

Ridge Pattern	Primary	Secondary	Tertiary
No design (carpal delta only)	1	Using circle measurement, dot at carpal delta and read circle where lowest ridge of carpal area falls	None
Distal loop opening toward interdigital, with core pointing to ulnar side	2	Using 0–9 scale, measure distance between carpal delta and core of loop	8 = only when core has distinct inclination toward carpal/radial area
Outward loop opening toward ulnar side, with core pointing toward thenar	3	Using 0–9 scale, measure distance between carpal delta and core of loop	None
Whorls	4	Using 0–9 scale, measure distance between carpal delta and core (for double whorls, using core closest to carpal delta)	None
Double loops	5	Using 0–9 scale, measure distance between two cores	None
Arches	6	1 = arches 2 = tented arches	None
Loops opening toward wrist, with core pointing toward ulnar side of palm	7	Using 0–9 scale, measure distance between core and delta above it	None
Composite patterns (any pattern not conforming to above patterns)	8	None	None

Table 5–18

Classification for the interdigital (Moenssens, pp 206–207).

Ridge Pattern	Primary	Secondary	Tertiary
One loop in base area	1	2 = if loop is between index and middle fingers 3 = if loop is between middle and ring fingers 4 = if loop is between ring and little fingers	Using 1–6 scale, measure height of loop (from deltas to core)
Tented arch	2	1 = arch below index finger 2 = arch below middle finger 3 = arch below ring finger 4 = arch below little finger	Using 1–6 scale, measure height of arch (from base of arch to summit)
Double loops	3	2 = if loop is between index and middle fingers 3 = if loop is between middle and ring fingers 4 = if loop is between ring and little fingers	Using 1–6 scale, measure height of ulnar loop (from deltas to core)
Two loops in same interdigital area and tented arches and loops in other areas	4	2 = if two-loop combination is between index and middle fingers 3 = if two-loop combination is between middle and ring fingers 4 = if two-loop combination is between ring and little fingers	None
Plain arches	5	None	None
One loop and one tented arch	6	2 = if loop is between index and middle fingers 3 = if loop is between middle and ring fingers 4 = if loop is between ring and little fingers	Using 1–6 scale, measure height of loop (from deltas to core)
Three loops or combinations of three loops and tented arches	7	Three loops = height of loop between ring and middle fingers Combination of three loops and tented arches = height of pattern located next to ulnar side of palm	None 2
Long transversal loop below one or several digital deltas	8	None	None
One or several whorls appear alone or in combinations with loops and tented arches	9	2 = if whorl is between index and middle fingers 3 = if whorl is between middle and ring fingers 4 = if whorl is between ring and little fingers	None

Table 5–19

Classification for the thenar (Moenssens, pp 207-209).

Ridge Pattern	Primary	Secondary	Tertiary
No pattern (or plain arch)	1	None	None
Various patterns	2	1 = one proximal loop opens toward radial side with core pointing to web of thumb or center of palm 2 = one proximal loop and one distal loop 3 = one proximal loop and one whorl 4 = one proximal loop and one double loop	Using 0–9 scale, measure distance between core and nearest delta Using 0–9 scale, measure distance between core of proximal loop and nearest delta None None
Patterns with peculiar ridge formations	3	None	None
One distal loop opening toward web of thumb with core pointing downward	4	Using 0–9 scale, measure distance between core and delta (not carpal delta)	None
Three different patterns	5	1 = one single whorl 2 = one whorl and one distal loop 3 = two whorls	None None None
Four different patterns	6	1 = one double loop 2 = one double loop and one distal loop 3 = one double loop and one whorl 4 = two double loops	None None None None
Two collateral distal loops both opening toward web of thumb	7	None	None
Two proximal loops, either both opening toward carpal area or one toward radial area and one toward carpal area	8	None	None
Any pattern not discussed	9	None	None

use of punch cards and sorting machines. Classifications of known-print cards were keyed into the punch cards and sorted according to the information contained on the card. Card-sorting machines could then extract cards containing a specific punched classification, and, from this extraction, examiners could pull the corresponding known-print cards for examination. Although this method was novel at the time, the FBI determined the experiment to be unsuccessful, and it was abandoned (Stock, 1987, p 51).

5.7.2 National Crime Information Center Fingerprint Classification

In 1965, the Federal Bureau of Investigation recognized the country's need for a centralized electronic criminal database. Within two years, the National Crime Information Center (NCIC) was born, connecting 15 metropolitan and state computers with the FBI's NCIC central computer. By 1971, all states and the District of Columbia were connected to NCIC.

The NCIC is made up of millions of records that have been sorted into separate databases. Criminal justice agencies can search these databases for information. One part of the NCIC database is the NCIC fingerprint classification. This alphanumeric classification system is pattern-specific to each individual finger and, unlike the Henry classification system, does not involve the combination of fingers. Like the Henry system, however, NCIC classification can assist only in eliminating or narrowing the search of records for the potential suspect.

The NCIC system consists of a 20-character code, in which each finger—beginning with the right thumb and ending with the left little finger—is represented by two characters (Table 5–20). For example, a person with all plain arches, except tented arches in the index fingers, would have an NCIC classification code of AATTAAAAAAAATTAAAAAA.

5.7.3 First Attempt by FBI To Create an Automated System

In the 1950s, the first commercially available computer came on the market and, by the 1960s, computers had reached the law enforcement community (Ruggles et al., 1994, p 214). Because of previous experience in the use of computer-aided known-print individualization and the continued growth of the fingerprint card databases, an earnest

Table 5–20

NCIC classification codes.

Ulnar loop ridge count (actual ridge count)	01–49
Plain arch	AA
Plain whorl, inner tracing	PI
Plain whorl, meet tracing	PM
Central pocket whorl, outer tracing	CO
Double loop whorl, inner tracing	dI
Double loop whorl, meet tracing	dM
Accidental whorl, outer tracing	XO
Missing or amputated finger	XX

effort was put forth by both local agencies and the Federal Bureau of Investigation to establish a computer program to permanently assist with fingerprint automation.

5.7.4 Automation Research in New York

In 1965, the New York State Information and Identification System began research into the use of minutiae to classify fingerprints (Stock, 1987, p 54). The endeavor began with the manual recording of enlarged fingerprint minutiae on clear overlays and progressed to the use of a magnified rear projection system. The extracted minutiae data was then used for the programming of minutiae extraction software. Shortly after the state contracted with a firm for the development of a minutiae encoding system, budgetary restraints caused the program to be eliminated.

5.7.5 The Royal Canadian Mounted Police Automated System

In 1970, the Royal Canadian Mounted Police (RCMP) initiated an automated classification system that used video images of known-print cards. These video images were filed according to the RCMP Henry classification. When a card was submitted for a known-print search, it was classified and that classification was then searched in the video file. The computer would generate a video file containing all the possible matching known-print cards. This file was then compared on screen with the known print in question.

5.7.6 Automation Research at the FBI

In 1963, the FBI reinitiated its research into the complete automation of its criminal known-print repository. At this time, all attention was directed toward known-print automation and solving the Identification Division's backlog pertaining to its known-print individualization service.

In the mid-1960s, initial research confirmed the feasibility of the project and, by the late 1960s, Cornell Laboratories was chosen to build a prototype automatic fingerprint reader (Stock, 1987, p 55). In 1972, this prototype, known as AIDS (Automated Identification System), was installed in the Identification Division in Washington, DC.

The actual classification of fingerprints went through three different phases during program development. The first phase attempted to emulate the Henry classification system's pattern definitions. It was assumed that if a trained fingerprint technician could easily determine a pattern type by looking at computer-generated ridge flow, so could the computer. However, this proved to be time-consuming, even for the computer, and, in the second phase, the Henry system was replaced with the classification code from NCIC.

In the early 1980s, the third and final phase of automatic fingerprint classification was instituted. The system, called AFIS (Automated Fingerprint Identification System), was based solely on the computerized extraction of minutiae. This extraction, in effect, creates mathematical maps of each impression in a finger block and of the card as a whole. Each map contains the computer-determined pattern type (Table 5–21) and minutiae location and direction.

Table 5–21

AFIS pattern classifications (CJIS, p 2).

Description	AFIS Code
Arch	AU
Left-slant loop	LS
Right-slant loop	RS
Whorl	WU
Amputation	XX
Complete scar	SR
Unable to classify	UC
Unable to print	UP

Thus, the computer scientists created a system whereby numbers could be compared. Today, when a suspect's known-print card is submitted to an automated fingerprint identification system, an algorithm compares one mathematical map to another. The conclusion of the comparison is a list of candidates with the highest matching algorithmic number.

5.7.7 Current Developments in Friction Ridge Automation

The computer software technology that resulted from the research at the Federal Bureau of Investigation has led to numerous companies' creation of software packages for the automation of friction ridge impressions. These software packages are independent of the Federal Bureau of Investigation and are available for purchase by any institution. However, with the inception of the FBI's national Integrated Automated Fingerprint Identification System (IAFIS) in 1999 came mandated standards regarding the transmission of digital information incorporated into IAFIS (Criminal Justice Information Services, 1999; Jain and Pankanti, 2001).

5.7.8 Automated Palmprint Classification Systems

Once again, history is repeating itself. This time it is the need for an automated palmprint identification system (APIS). In response, the biometric software community is aggressively pursuing solutions. Numerous companies are providing software packages containing palmprint individualization systems. Integral to the use of a palmprint system is the digital storage of known palmprint cards.

The FBI is currently converting all of its inked palmprint cards to a digital format in anticipation of integrating an APIS function into IAFIS.

5.8 Conclusion

In any scientific field, the combination of mental acuity and technological innovation always creates the desire for bigger and better things. This is certainly true of friction ridge classification systems. As populations grew, the need for a system that was not dependent upon the limited workforce of the law enforcement community became increasingly important. Rudimentary systems grew into advanced systems that now provide the criminal justice community with a workable solution to the problem of identifying recidivists. Advancements in computer microprocessors and programming, and the marriage of friction ridge impressions and computers, have led the fingerprint community to the current day, where a known-print card can be searched in minutes.

5.9 Reviewers

The reviewers critiquing this chapter were Mike Campbell, Michael Perkins, Charles Richardson, and Lyla A. Thompson.

5.10 References

Alexander, H. *Classifying Palmprints: A Complete System of Coding, Filing, and Searching Palmprints;* Charles C Thomas: Springfield, IL, 1973.

Ashbaugh, D. R. *Quantitative-Qualitative Friction Ridge Analysis: An Introduction to Basic and Advanced Ridgeology;* CRC Press: Boca Raton, FL, 1999.

Baird, A. J. *System Used by the Western Australian Police Force for the Classification and Filing of Palmprints;* 1959 (unpublished).

Beavan, C. *Fingerprints: The Origins of Crime Detection and the Murder Case that Launched Forensic Science;* Hyperion: New York, 2001.

Bridges, B. C. *Practical Fingerprinting;* Funk and Wagnalls: New York, 1963.

Chatterjee, S. K. *Finger, Palm and Sole Prints;* Artine Press: Calcutta, India, 1953.

Criminal Justice Information Services, Federal Bureau of Investigation. *CJIS Informational Letter;* U.S. Department of Justice, U.S. Government Printing Office: Washington, DC, August 20, 1999.

Dilworth, D., Ed. *Identification Wanted: Development of the American Criminal Identification System 1893-1943;* International Association of Chiefs of Police: Gaithersburg, MD, 1977.

Faulds, H. On the Skin—Furrows of the Hand. *Nature* 1880, *22* (October 28), 605.

Faulds, H. *Guide to Finger-Print Identification;* Wood, Mitchell & Co. Ltd.: Hanley, Stoke-On-Trent, U.K., 1905.

Faulds, H. *Dactylography or the Study of Finger-Prints;* Milner and Company: Halifax, London, 1912.

Federal Bureau of Investigation, *Classification of Footprints;* U.S. Department of Justice, U.S. Government Printing Office: Washington DC, 1985. (Revised and reprinted from *Law Enforcement Bulletin,* September 1971.)

Galton, F. *Finger Prints;* MacMillan: New York, 1892.

Galton, F. Human Variety. *Journal of the Anthropological Institute of Great Britain and Ireland* 1889, *18,* 401–419.

Herschel, W. J. Skin Furrows of the Hand. *Nature* 1880, *23* (578), 76.

Jain, A.; Pankanti, S. *Automated Fingerprint Identification and Imaging Systems,* 2nd ed.; CRC Press: New York, 2001.

Jay, V. The Extraordinary Career of Dr. Purkinje. *Archives of Pathology and Laboratory Medicine* 2000, *124* (5), 662–663.

McGinnis, P. D. *American System of Fingerprint Classification;* New York State Department of Correction Division of Identification: New York, 1963.

Moenssens, A. A. *Fingerprint Techniques;* Chilton Book Company: Philadelphia, 1971.

Rhodes, H. *Alphonse Bertillon: Father of Scientific Detection;* Abelard-Schuman: London, 1956.

Rodriguez, J. South Atlantic Crossing: Fingerprints, Science, and the State in Turn-of-the-Century Argentina. *The American Historical Review,* April 2004 [Online], *109.2,* http://www.historycooperative.org/journals/ahr/109.2/rodriguez.html (accessed June 23, 2006).

Ruggles, T.; Thieme, S.; Elman, D. Automated Fingerprint Identification Systems: North American Morpho System. In *Advances in Fingerprint Technology;* Gaensslen, R. E., Lee, H., Eds.; CRC Press: New York, 1994; pp 212–226.

Russell, M. Print Pioneer Identified at Last. *The Herald,* 2004.

Stock, R. M. *An Historical Overview of Automated Fingerprint Identification Systems.* Federal Bureau of Investigation, U.S. Department of Justice, U.S. Government Printing Office: Quantico, VA, 1987; pp 51–60.

5.11 Additional Information

Cherrill, F. R. *The Finger Print System at Scotland Yard: A Practical Treatise on Finger Print Identification for the Use of Students and Experts and a Guide for Investigators when Dealing with Imprints Left at the Scenes of Crime;* Her Majesty's Stationery Office: London, 1954.

Faulds, H. *A Manual of Practical Dactylography: A Work for the Use of Students of the Finger-Print Method of Identification;* The Police Review: London, 1923.

Federal Bureau of Investigation. *The Science of Fingerprints;* U.S. Department of Justice, U.S. Government Printing Office: Washington, DC, 1979.

Herschel, W. J. *The Origin of Finger-Printing;* Oxford University Press: London, 1916.

Henry, E. R. *Classification and Uses of Fingerprints,* 1st ed.; Routledge & Sons: London, 1900.

Purkinje, J. E. *Commentatio de Examine Physiologico Organi Visus et Systematis Cutanei (A Commentary on the Physiological Examination of the Organs of Vision and the Cutaneous System);* Vratisaviae Typis Universitatis: Breslau, Prussia, 1823.

Vucetich, J. *Dactiloscopía Comparada (Comparative Fingerprinting): The New Argentine System;* 1904. (Translation for FBI Laboratories by Patrick J. Phelan, August 27, 1954.)

Wentworth, B.; Wilder, H. H. *Personal Identification;* Gorham Press: Boston, 1918.

CHAPTER 6

AUTOMATED FINGERPRINT IDENTIFICATION SYSTEM (AFIS)

Kenneth R. Moses

CONTRIBUTING AUTHORS
PETER HIGGINS, MICHAEL MCCABE,
SALIL PRABHAKAR, SCOTT SWANN

CONTENTS

- 3 — 6.1 Introduction
- 9 — 6.2 AFIS Operations
- 15 — 6.3 Standards
- 20 — 6.4 Digitization and Processing of Fingerprints
- 31 — 6.5 Summary
- 32 — 6.6 Reviewers
- 32 — 6.7 References
- 33 — 6.8 Additional Information

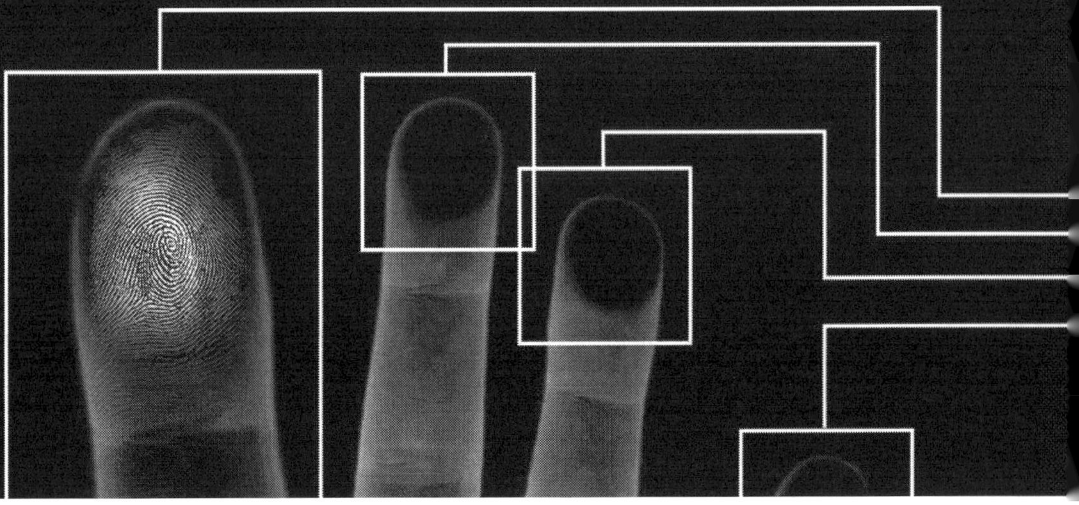

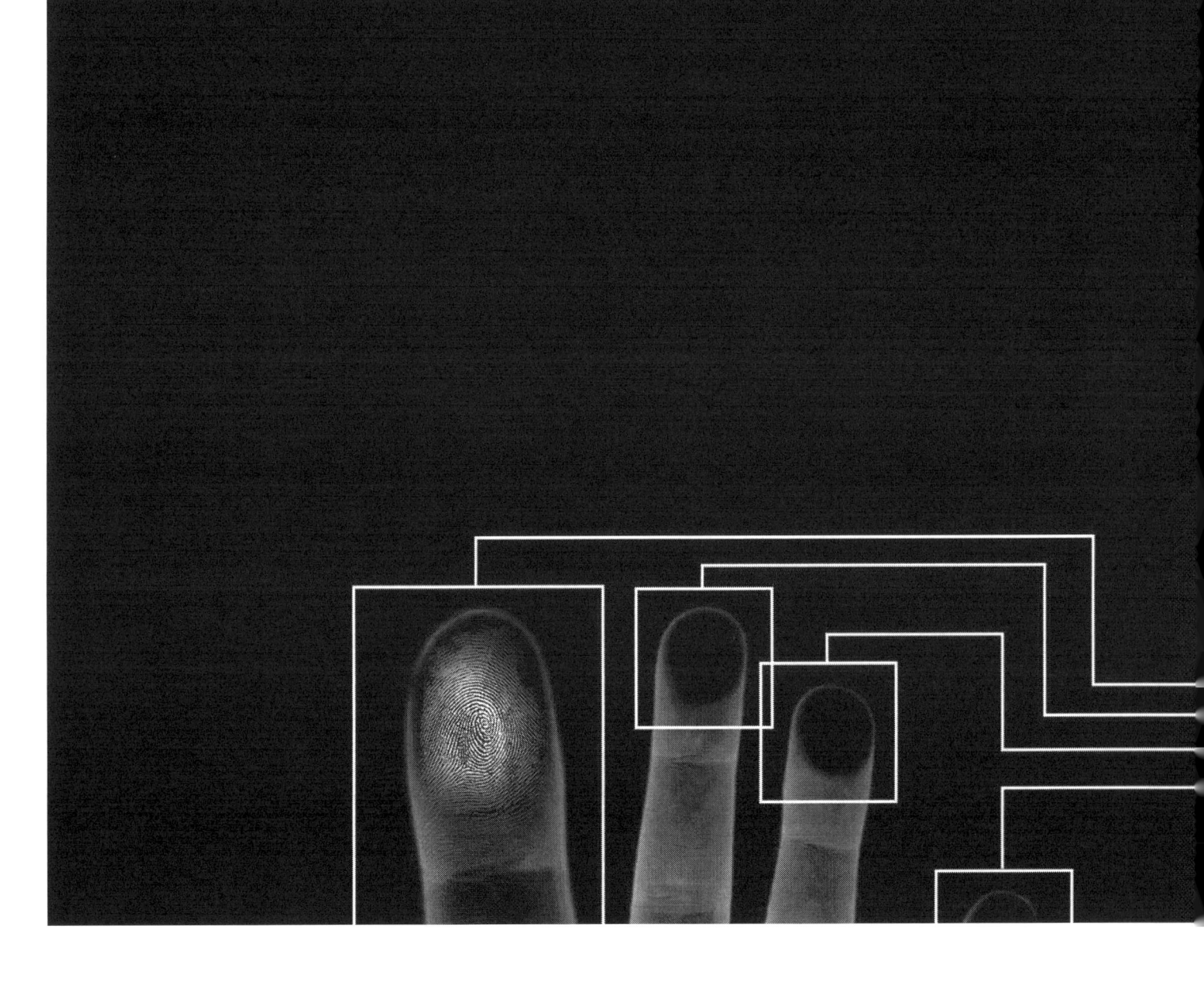

CHAPTER 6

AUTOMATED FINGERPRINT IDENTIFICATION SYSTEM (AFIS)

Kenneth R. Moses

Contributing authors
Peter Higgins, Michael McCabe, Salil Prabhakar, Scott Swann

6.1 Introduction

Prior to the industrial revolution and the mass migrations to the cities, populations lived mostly in rural communities where everyone knew everyone else and there was little need for identification. Indeed, there were no police forces, no penitentiaries, and very few courts. As cities became crowded, crime rates soared and criminals flourished within a sea of anonymity. Newspapers feasted on stories of lawlessness, legislatures quickly responded with more laws and harsher penalties (especially for repeat offenders), and police departments were charged with identifying and arresting the miscreants. Identification systems—rogues' galleries, anthropometry, Bertillon's "portrait parlé", and the Henry system—emerged and quickly spread worldwide at the end of the 19th and beginning of the 20th century.

The late 1960s and early 1970s witnessed another era of civil turmoil and an unprecedented rise in crime rates, but this era happened to coincide with the development of the silicon chip. The challenges inherent in identification systems seemed ready-made for the solutions of automatic data processing, and AFIS—Automated Fingerprint Identification System—was born.

During this same period, The RAND Corporation, working under a national grant, published *The Criminal Investigative Process* (Greenwood et al., 1975), a comprehensive study and critique of the process by which crimes get solved—or do not. Generally critical of traditional methods used by detectives, the study placed any hopes for improvement on physical evidence in general and latent prints in particular. In a companion study, Joan Petersilia concluded that:

> No matter how competent the evidence technician is at performing his job, the gathering of physical evidence at a crime scene will be futile unless such evidence can be properly processed and analyzed. Since fingerprints are by far the most frequently retrieved physical evidence, making the system of analyzing such prints effective will contribute the most toward greater success in identifying criminal offenders through the use of physical evidence. (Petersilia, 1975, p 12)

Though new technology was already in development at the Federal Bureau of Investigation (FBI), it would be a popular movement at the local and state levels that would truly test Petersilia's theory.

6.1.1 Need For Automation

In 1924, the FBI's Identification Division was established by authority of the United States congressional budget appropriation bill for the Department of Justice. The identification division was created to provide a central repository of criminal identification data for law enforcement agencies throughout the United States. The original collection of fingerprint records contained 810,188 records. After its creation, hundreds of thousands of new records were added to this collection yearly, and by the early 1960s the FBI's criminal file had grown to about 15 million individuals. This was in addition to the 63 million records in the civilian file, much of which was the result of military additions from World War II and the Korean conflict.

Almost all of the criminal file's 15 million individuals contained 10 rolled fingerprints per card for a total of 150 million single fingerprints. Incoming records were manually classified and searched against this file using the FBI's modified Henry system of classification. Approximately 30,000 cards were searched daily. The time and human resources to accomplish this daily workload continued to grow. As a card entered the system, a preliminary gross pattern classification was assigned to each fingerprint by technicians. The technicians could complete approximately 100 fingerprint cards per hour. Complete classification and searching against the massive files could only be accomplished at an average rate of 3.3 cards per employee per hour. Obviously, as the size of the criminal file and the daily workload increased, the amount of resources required continued to grow. Eventually, classification extensions were added to reduce the portion of the criminal file that needed to be searched against each card. Nonetheless, the manual system used for searching and matching fingerprints was approaching the point of being unable to handle the daily workload.

Although punch card sorters could reduce the number of fingerprint cards required to be examined based on pattern classification and other parameters, it was still necessary for human examiners to scrutinize each fingerprint card on the candidate list. A new paradigm was necessary to stop the increasing amount of human resources required to process search requests. A new automated approach was needed to (1) extract each fingerprint image from a tenprint card, (2) process each of these images to produce a reduced-size template of characteristic information, and (3) search a database to automatically produce a highly reduced list of probable candidate matches (Cole, 2001, pp 251–252).

6.1.2 Early AFIS Development

In the early 1960s, the FBI in the United States, the Home Office in the United Kingdom, Paris Police in France, and the Japanese National Police initiated projects to develop automated fingerprint identification systems. The thrust of this research was to use emerging electronic digital computers to assist or replace the labor-intensive processes of classifying, searching, and matching tenprint cards used for personal identification.

6.1.3 FBI AFIS Initiative

By 1963, Special Agent Carl Voelker of the FBI's Identification Division realized that the manual searching of the criminal file would not remain feasible for much longer. In an attempt to resolve this problem, he sought the help of engineers Raymond Moore and Joe Wegstein of the National Institute of Standards and Technology (NIST).[1] After describing his problem, he asked for assistance in automating the FBI's fingerprint identification process.

The NIST engineers first studied the manual methods used by human fingerprint technicians to make identifications. These methods were based on comparing the minutiae (i.e., ridge endings and ridge bifurcations) on fingerprint ridges. If the minutiae from two fingerprints were determined to be topologically equivalent, the two fingerprints were declared to be identical—that is, having been recorded from the same finger of the same person. After this review, and after studying additional problems inherent with the inking process, they believed that a computerized solution to automatically match and pair minutiae could be developed that would operate in a manner similar to the techniques used by human examiners to make fingerprint identifications. But to achieve this goal, three major tasks would have to be accomplished. First, a scanner had to be developed that could automatically read and electronically capture the inked fingerprint image. Second, it was necessary to accurately

---

[1] NIST was known as the National Bureau of Standards when the FBI visited Moore and Wegstein.

and consistently detect and identify minutiae existing in the captured image. Finally, a method had to be developed to compare two lists of minutiae descriptors to determine whether they both most likely came from the same finger of the same individual.

The Identification Division of the FBI decided that the approach suggested by Moore and Wegstein should be followed. To address the first two of the three tasks, on December 16, 1966, the FBI issued a Request for Quotation (RFQ) "for developing, demonstrating, and testing a device for reading certain fingerprint minutiae" (FBI, 1966). This contract was for a device to automatically locate and determine the relative position and orientation of the specified minutiae in individual fingerprints on standard fingerprint cards to be used for testing by the FBI. The requirements stated that the reader must be able to measure and locate minutiae in units of not more than 0.1 mm and that the direction of each minutiae must be measured and presented as output in units of not more than 11.25 degrees (1/32 of a full circle). The initial requirements called for a prototype model to process 10,000 single fingerprints (1,000 cards). Contractors were also instructed to develop a proposal for a subsequent contract to process 10 times that number of fingerprints.

The 14 proposals received in response to this RFQ were divided into 5 broad technical approaches. At the conclusion of the proposal evaluation, two separate proposals were funded to provide a basic model for reading fingerprint images and extracting minutiae. Both proposed to use a "flying spot scanner" for capturing the image. But each offered a different approach for processing the captured image data, and both seemed promising. One contract was awarded to Cornell Aeronautical Labs, Inc., which proposed using a general-purpose digital computer to process binary pixels and develop programs for detecting and providing measurement parameters for each identified minutiae. The second contract was awarded to North American Aviation, Inc., Autonetics Division, which proposed using a special-purpose digital process to compare fixed logical marks to the image for identifying, detecting, and encoding each minutia.

While the devices for fingerprint scanning and minutiae detection were being developed, the third task of comparing two minutiae lists to determine a candidate match was addressed by Joe Wegstein (Wegstein, 1969a, 1970, 1972a/b, 1982; Wegstein and Rafferty, 1978, 1979; Wegstein et al., 1968). He developed the initial algorithms for determining fingerprint matches based on the processing and comparison of two lists describing minutiae location and orientation. For the next 15 years, he continued to develop more reliable fingerprint matching software that became increasingly more complex in order to account for such things as plastic distortion and skin elasticity. Algorithms he developed were embedded in AFISs that were eventually placed in operation at the FBI and other law enforcement agencies.

By 1969, both Autonetics and Cornell had made significant progress on their feasibility demonstration models. In 1970, a Request for Proposal (RFP) was issued for the construction of a prototype fingerprint reader to reflect the experience gained from the original demonstration models with an additional requirement for speed and accuracy. Cornell was awarded the contract to deliver the prototype reader to the FBI in 1972. After a year's experience with the prototype system, the FBI issued a new RFP containing additional requirements such as a high-speed card-handling subsystem. In 1974, Rockwell International, Inc., was awarded a contract to build five production model automatic fingerprint reader systems. This revolutionary system was called Finder. These readers were delivered to the FBI in 1975 and 1976. The next 3 years were devoted to using these readers in the conversion of 15 million criminal fingerprint cards (Moore, 1991, pp 164–175).

As it became apparent that the FBI's efforts to automate the fingerprint matching process would be successful, state and local law enforcement agencies began to evaluate this new technology for their own applications. The Minneapolis–St. Paul system in Minnesota was one of the first automated fingerprint matching systems (after the FBI's) to be installed in the United States. Further, while the United States was developing its AFIS technology in the 1960s, France, the United Kingdom, and Japan were also doing research into automatic fingerprint image processing and matching.

6.1.4 French AFIS Initiative

In 1969, M. R. Thiebault, Prefecture of Police in Paris, reported on the French efforts. (Descriptions of work done by Thiebault can be found in the entries listed in the Additional Information section of this chapter.) France's focus was on the solution to the latent fingerprint problem rather than the general identification problem that was the concern in the United States. The French approach incorporated a *vidicon* (a video camera tube) to scan photographic film transparencies of fingerprints. Scanning was done at 400 pixels per inch (ppi), which was less than an optimal scan rate for latent work. This minutiae matching approach was based on special-purpose, high-speed hardware that used an array of logical circuits. The French also were interested in resolving the problem of poor fingerprint image quality. In order to acquire a high-contrast image that would be easy to photograph and process, a technique was developed to record live fingerprint images photographically using a principle of "frustrated total internal reflection" (FTIR). Although not put into large-scale production at that time, 20 years later FTIR became the cornerstone for the development of the modern-day livescan fingerprint scanners. These are making the use of ink and cards obsolete for nonforensic identification purposes today.

By the early 1970s, the personnel responsible for development of France's fingerprint automation technology had changed. As a result, there was little interest in pursuing automated fingerprint identification research for the next several years. In the late 1970s, a computer engineering subsidiary of France's largest financial institution responded to a request by the French Ministry of Interior to work on automated fingerprint processing for the French National Police. Later, this company joined with the Morphologic Mathematics Laboratory at the Paris School of Mines to form a subsidiary called Morpho Systems that went on to develop a functioning. Currently, Morpho Systems is part of Sagem (also known as Group SAFRAN).

6.1.5 United Kingdom AFIS Initiative

During the same period of time, the United Kingdom's Home Office was doing research into automatic fingerprint identification. Two of the main individuals responsible for the United Kingdom's AFIS were Dr. Barry Blain and Ken Millard. (Papers produced by Millard are listed in the Additional Information section of this chapter). Like the French, their main focus was latent print work. By 1974, research was being done in-house with contractor assistance from Ferranti, Ltd. The Home Office developed a reader to detect minutiae, record position and orientation, and determine ridge counts to the five nearest neighbors to the right of each minutia. This was the first use of ridge count information by an AFIS vendor (Moore, 1991).

6.1.6 Japanese AFIS Initiative

Like France and the United Kingdom, Japan's motivation for a fingerprint identification system was directed toward the matching of latent images against a master file of rolled fingerprints. Japan's researchers believed that an accurate latent system would naturally lead to the development of an accurate tenprint system.

By 1966, the Osaka Prefecture Police department housed almost 4 million single fingerprints. An early automation effort by this agency was the development of a pattern classification matching system based on a 17- to 20-digit number encoded manually (Kiji, 2002, p 9). Although this approach improved the efficiency of the totally manual method enormously, it had inherent problems. It required a great deal of human precision and time to classify the latents and single fingerprints; was not fully suitable for latent matching; and produced a long list of candidates, resulting in expensive verifications.

Within a few years, the fingerprint automation focus of Japanese researchers had changed. By 1969, the Identification Section of the Criminal Investigation Bureau, National Police Agency of Japan (NPA), approached NEC to develop a system for the computerization of fingerprint identification. NEC determined that it could build an automated fingerprint identification system employing a similar minutiae-based approach to that being used in the FBI system under development. At that time, it was thought that a fully automated system for searching fingerprints would not be realized for 5 to 10 years. In 1969, NEC and NPA representatives visited the FBI and began to learn about the current state of the art for the FBI's AFIS plans. During the same period, NPA representatives also collaborated with Moore and Wegstein from NIST. Additional AFIS sites were visited where information was acquired regarding useful and worthless approaches that had been attempted. All of this information was evaluated and used in the development of the NEC system.

For the next 10 years, NEC worked to develop its AFIS. In addition to minutiae location and orientation, this system also incorporated ridge-count information present in the local four surrounding quadrants of each minutiae under consideration for pairing. By 1982, NEC had successfully installed its system in the NPA and started the card conversion process. Within a year, latent inquiry searches began.

In 1980, NEC received a U.S. patent for automatic minutiae detection. It began marketing its automated fingerprint identification systems to the United States a few years later.

6.1.7 The Politicization of Fingerprints and the San Francisco Experiment

Early development and implementation of automated fingerprint systems was limited to national police agencies in Europe, North America, and Japan. But the problems associated with huge national databases and the newborn status of computer technology in the 1970s limited the utility of these systems. Government investment in AFIS was justified largely on the promise of efficiency in the processing of incoming tenprint records. But funding these expensive systems on the local level would demand some creativity (Wayman, 2004, pp 50–52).

Following the success of the FBI's Finder, Rockwell took its system to market in the mid-1970s. Rockwell organized a users group for its Printrak system and sponsored an annual conference for customers and would-be customers. Starting with a beta-site in San Jose, California, more than a dozen installations were completed in quick succession. Peggy James of the Houston Police Department, Joe Corcoran from Saint Paul, Donna Jewett from San Jose, and others devoted their energies toward educating the international fingerprint community on the miracle of the minutiae-based Printrak system. Each system that came online trumpeted the solution of otherwise unsolvable crimes and the identity of arrested criminals. A users group newsletter was published and distributed that highlighted some of the best cases and listed the search statistics of member agencies.

Ken Moses of the San Francisco Police Department had attended several of those Printrak conferences and became a staunch crusader for fingerprint automation. In three successive years, he persuaded the Chief of Police to include a Printrak system in the city budget, but each time it was vetoed by the mayor. After the third mayoral veto, a ballot proposition was organized by other politicians. The proposition asked citizens to vote on whether they wanted an automated fingerprint system. In 1982, Proposition E passed with an 80% plurality.

The mayor refused to approve a sole-source purchase from Rockwell, even though it was the only system in the world being marketed. She insisted on a competitive bid with strict evaluation criteria and testing. While on a trade mission to Japan, the mayor learned that the Japanese National Police were working with NEC to install a fingerprint system, but NEC stated that the system was being developed as a public service and the company had no plans to market it. After meeting with key Japanese officials, NEC changed its mind and agreed to bid on the San Francisco AFIS.

When the bids were opened, not only had Printrak and NEC submitted proposals, but a dark horse named Logica had also entered the fray. Logica had been working with the British Home Office to develop a system for New Scotland Yard.

San Francisco retained systems consultant Tim Ruggles to assist in constructing the first head-to-head benchmark tests of competing in-use fingerprint systems. The test was most heavily weighted toward latent print accuracy, and a set of 50 latent prints graded from poor to good from actual past cases was searched against a prescribed tenprint database. All tests were conducted at the respective vendor's home site.[2] NEC was awarded the contract and installation was completed in December 1983.

Besides being the first competitive bid on 1980s technology, what differentiated the San Francisco system from those that had gone before was organizational design. AFIS was viewed as a true system encompassing all aspects of friction ridge identification—from the crime scene to the courtroom. The AFIS budget included laboratory and crime scene equipment, training in all phases of forensic evidence, and even the purchase of vehicles. In 1983, a new crime scene unit was organized specifically with the new system as its centerpiece. Significant organizational changes were put into effect:

1. All latents that met minimum criteria would be searched in AFIS.

2. A new unit called Crime Scene Investigations was created and staffed on a 24/7 schedule.

3. Department policies were changed to mandate that patrol officers notify crime scene investigators of all felonies with a potential for latent prints.

---

[2] The results of the earliest competitive benchmark tests were published by the International Association for Identification in 1986 (Moses, 1986). Thereafter, some vendors often demanded that the results of benchmark tests be kept secret, and law enforcement agencies generally acquiesced to those demands. This has made it extremely difficult for researchers and prospective purchasers to evaluate competing systems. The veil of secrecy has generally carried over to the sharing of AFIS operational performance data by agency personnel who often develop a strong sense of loyalty to their AFIS vendor.

CHAPTER 6 | AFIS

4. All crime scene investigators who processed the crime scenes were trained in the use of the system and encouraged to search their own cases.

5. Performance statistics were kept from the beginning, and AFIS cases were tracked through the criminal justice system to the courts.

The result of the San Francisco experiment was a dramatic 10-fold increase in latent print identifications in 1984. The district attorney demanded and got five new positions to prosecute the AFIS cases. The conviction rate in AFIS-generated burglary cases was three times higher than in burglary cases without this type of evidence (Figure 6–1; Bruton, 1989).

At a time when burglary rates were steeply rising in cities across the nation, the burglary rate plummeted in San Francisco (Figure 6–2; Bruton, 1989). Reporters, academics, and police administrators from around the world inundated the San Francisco Police Department for demonstrations and information.

The importance of politics and publicity was not lost on other agencies. Los Angeles even enlisted the backing of film stars to stir up public support. The identification of serial killer Richard Ramirez, the infamous Night Stalker, through a search of the brand-new California State AFIS made worldwide headlines and guaranteed the future funding of systems in California.

6.1.8 AFIS Proliferation

The widely publicized success in San Francisco provided the spark for the rapid proliferation of new AFIS installations along with a methodology of benchmark testing to evaluate the claims of the growing number of competing vendors. Governments quickly provided funding so that, by 1999, the International Association for Identification's (IAI's) *AFIS Directory of Users* identified 500 AFIS sites worldwide (IAI, 1999).

The burgeoning market in these multimillion-dollar systems put forensic identification on the economic map. Commercial exhibits at IAI's conferences that had formerly featured companies hawking tape and powder now expanded to digital image enhancement, lasers and forensic light sources, and the latest in new developments from Silicon Valley. The San Francisco Crime Lab received its first digital imaging system in 1986. This 3M/Comtal system was dedicated to friction ridge enhancement. Fingermatrix installed the first livescan device in the San Francisco Police Identification Bureau in 1988. AFIS brought crime scene and forensic identification out of the basement; no local or state law enforcement administrator wanted to be accused of being left behind.

However, the frenzied expansion of AFIS was not always logical and rational. By the early 1990s, the four biggest vendors—Printrak, NEC, Morpho, and Cogent—were in

FIGURE 6–1

Tracking latent hits through the courts. (Bruton, 1989.)

DISPOSITIONS OF ADULT FELONY ARRESTS

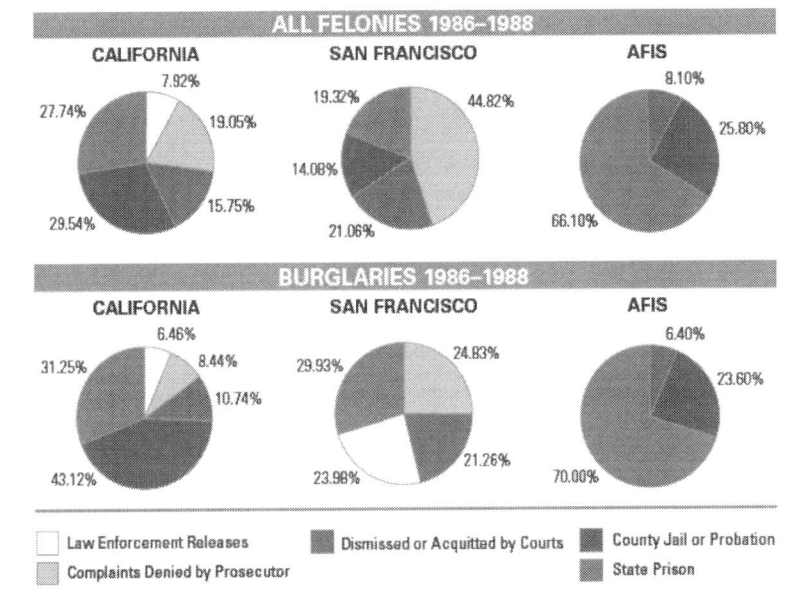

ALL FELONIES 1986–1988

CALIFORNIA: 7.92%, 19.05%, 15.75%, 29.54%, 27.74%
SAN FRANCISCO: 19.32%, 44.82%, 14.08%, 21.06%
AFIS: 8.10%, 25.80%, 66.10%

BURGLARIES 1986–1988

CALIFORNIA: 6.46%, 8.44%, 10.74%, 43.12%, 31.25%
SAN FRANCISCO: 24.83%, 21.26%, 23.98%, 29.93%
AFIS: 6.40%, 23.60%, 70.00%

- Law Enforcement Releases
- Complaints Denied by Prosecutor
- Dismissed or Acquitted by Courts
- County Jail or Probation
- State Prison

FIGURE 6–2

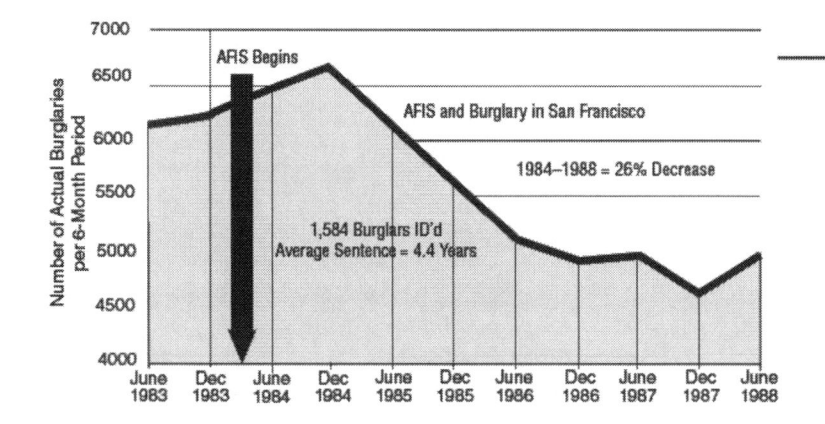

Statistical study of AFIS hits vs. burglaries in San Francisco, 1984–1988. (Bruton, 1989.)

competition, each offering proprietary software that was incompatible with the others, especially in latent print searching.

Expansion was often based on political considerations and competing mission priorities. Local and state agencies expressed differences in priorities in terms of system design, with states generally emphasizing criminal identification or tenprint functions, while cities and counties focused on crime solving or latent print functions. Generally, the demands of latent print processing on computer resources far exceeded the requirements of tenprint processing, and states balked at the additional expense and technical complexity. As a result, cities, counties, and states often went their separate ways, installing dissimilar systems that could not communicate with neighboring jurisdictions or with the central state repository. Vendors eagerly encouraged this fragmentation in an attempt to gain market share and displace competitors whenever possible. The evolution of electronic transmission standards (see section 6.3) ameliorated this problem for tenprint search but not for latent search.

6.2 AFIS Operations

6.2.1 AFIS Functions and Capabilities

Identification bureaus are legislatively mandated to maintain criminal history records. Historically, this meant huge file storage requirements and cadres of clerks to maintain and search them. Demographic-based criminal history computers were established well ahead of AFIS, first as IBM card sort systems and then as all-digital information systems with terminals throughout the state and, via the National Crime Information Center (NCIC) network and the National Law Enforcement Teletype System (Nlets), throughout the nation. These automated criminal history systems became even more labor-intensive than the paper record systems they supposedly replaced. In many systems, more paper was generated and placed into the history jackets along with the fingerprint cards, mug shots, warrants, and other required documents.

AFIS revolutionized state identification bureaus because it removed from the paper files the last document type that could not previously be digitized—the fingerprint card. State identification bureaus could now bring to their legislatures cost–benefit analyses that easily justified the purchase of an automated fingerprint system through the reduction of clerical personnel.

Local and county jurisdictions did not usually enjoy the economic benefits of state systems. Pre-AFIS personnel levels were often lower and controlled more by the demands of the booking process than by file maintenance. AFIS generally increased staffing demands on the latent and crime-scene-processing side because it made crime scene processing dramatically more productive. Local and county AFIS purchases were usually justified on the basis of their crime-solving potential.

6.2.1.1 Technical Functions. Law enforcement AFISs are composed of two interdependent subsystems: the tenprint (i.e., criminal identification) subsystem and the latent (i.e., criminal investigation) subsystem. Each subsystem operates with a considerable amount of autonomy, and both are vital to public safety.

The tenprint subsystem is tasked with identifying sets of inked or livescan fingerprints incident to an arrest or citation or as part of an application process to determine whether a person has an existing record.

In many systems, identification personnel are also charged with maintaining the integrity of the fingerprint and criminal history databases. Identification bureau staffs are generally composed of fingerprint technicians and supporting clerical personnel.

An automated tenprint inquiry normally requires a minutiae search of only the thumbs or index fingers. Submitted fingerprints commonly have sufficient clarity and detail to make searching of more than two fingers unnecessary. Today's AFIS can often return a search of a million records in under a minute. As databases have expanded across the world, some AFIS engineers have expanded to searching four fingers or more in an effort to increase accuracy.

The latent print or criminal identification subsystem is tasked with solving crimes though the identification of latent prints developed from crime scenes and physical evidence. Terminals used within the latent subsystem are often specialized to accommodate the capture and digital enhancement of individual latent prints. The latent subsystem may be staffed by latent print examiners, crime scene investigators, or laboratory or clerical personnel. The staff of the latent subsystem is frequently under a different command structure than the tenprint subsystem and is often associated with the crime laboratory.

The search of a latent print is more tedious and time-consuming than a tenprint search. Latent prints are often fragmentary and of poor image quality. Minutiae features are normally reviewed one-by-one before the search begins. Depending on the portion of the database selected to be searched and the system's search load, the response may take from a few minutes to several hours to return.

Most law enforcement AFIS installations have the ability to perform the following functions:

- Search a set of known fingerprints (tenprints) against an existing tenprint database (TP–TP) and return with results that are better than 99% accurate.[3]

- Search a latent print from a crime scene or evidence against a tenprint database (LP–TP).

- Search a latent from a crime scene against latents on file from other crime scenes (LP–LP).

- Search a new tenprint addition to the database against all unsolved latent prints in file (TP–LP).

Enhancements have been developed to allow other functions that expand AFIS capabilities, including:

- Addition of palmprint records to the database to allow the search of latent palmprints from crime scenes.

- Interfacing of AFIS with other criminal justice information systems for added efficiency and "lights out"[4] operation.

- Interfacing of AFIS with digital mug shot systems and livescan fingerprint capture devices.

- Addition of hand-held portable devices for use in identity queries from the field. The query is initiated by scanning one or more of the subject's fingers, extracting the minutiae within the device, and transmitting to AFIS, which then returns a hit or no-hit (red light, green light) result. Hit notification may be accompanied by the thumbnail image of the subject's mug shot.

- Multimodal identification systems, including fingerprint, palmprint, iris, and facial recognition, are now available.

6.2.2 System Accuracy

Most dedicated government computer systems are based on demographic data such as name, address, date of birth, and other information derived from letters and numbers. For example, to search for a record within the motor vehicle database, one would enter a license number or operator data. The success of the search will be dependent on the accuracy with which the letters and numbers were originally perceived and entered. The inquiry is straightforward and highly accurate at finding the desired record.

Automated fingerprint systems are based on data extracted from images. Although there is only one correct spelling for a name in a motor vehicle database, a fingerprint image can be scanned in an almost infinite number of ways. Success in searching fingerprints depends on the clarity of the images and the degree of correspondence between

---

[3] This figure is based on requirements found in award documents and benchmark testing rather than operational observation.

[4] "Lights out" generally refers to the ability of the system to operate without human intervention.

the search print and the database print (compression and algorithms are two other factors that can affect accuracy). In the case of searching a new tenprint card against the tenprint database, there is usually more than enough image information present to find its mate 99.9% of the time in systems with operators on hand to check respondent lists (rather than true "lights out" operations).

A latent print usually consists of a fragmentary portion of a single finger or piece of palm, though the quality of some latent impressions can exceed their corresponding images of record. The amount of information present in the image is usually of lesser quality and often is contaminated with background interference. Entering latents into the computer has a subjective element that is based on the experience of the operator. Based on latent print acceptance test requirements commonly found in AFIS proposals and contracts, the chances of a latent print finding its mate in the database is about 70 to 80%. Naturally, the better the latent image, the higher the chances of success. Inversely, the chance of missing an identification, even when the mate is in the database, is 25%. Especially in latent print searches, failure to produce an identification or a hit does not mean the subject is not in the database. Other factors beyond the knowledge and control of the operator, such as poor-quality database prints, will adversely affect the chances of a match.

Because of the variability of the images and the subjectivity of the terminal's operator, success is often improved by conducting multiple searches while varying the image, changing operators, or searching other systems that may contain different copies of the subject's prints. It is common that success comes only on multiple attempts.

6.2.3 Peripheral Benefits

6.2.3.1 Community Safety. There is no national reporting mechanism for the gathering of AFIS (or latent print) statistics, so the measurable benefits are illusive. However, to provide some recognition of those benefits, the author of this chapter conducted a survey of latent hits in the 10 largest states by population for the year 2005 (Table 6–1). Prior attempts to provide this type of information have revealed inconsistencies in how identifications are counted and how the hit rate is determined (Komarinski, 2005, pp 184–189).

Based on the author's survey, an estimated 50,000 suspects a year in the United States are identified through AFIS latent searches. In conducting the survey, if the contacted state bureaus did not have statewide figures, attempts were made to also contact the five largest cities in that state. (In no instance was it possible to contact every AFIS-equipped jurisdiction in a state, so the total hits are the minimum number of hits.) Also, only case hits or suspect hits were counted, depending on what data each agency kept. (When agencies reported multiple hits to a single person, this was not included in data presented.)

Extrapolating from the table, if the remaining 40 states and all agencies of the federal government each had just one latent hit per day, the total estimate of latent hits for the entire United States would surpass 50,000.

Table 6–1

Minimum hits (cases or persons identified) from 10 largest states by population for 2005.

1	California	8,814
3	New York	2,592
5	Illinois	1,224
7	Ohio*	1,495
9	Georgia	980
	Total	29,178

* Cleveland not available.
** Detroit not available.

Few studies have been done to measure what effect, if any, a dramatic increase in the rate of suspect latent print identifications from AFIS has had on public safety overall. The burglary data from San Francisco in the late 1980s (Figure 6–2) is probative but must be narrowly construed. FBI Uniform Crime Reports show a steady decline in most serious offenses that coincide with the proliferation of AFIS, but no cause-and-effect relationship has been explored by academia or government. During the 1990s, many states passed "three strikes" laws increasing the punishment for felony offenses that some theorists have held are responsible for the decline in crime. But before harsher penalties can be applied, perpetrators must be identified and apprehended.

Burglary is the offense most impacted by AFIS. Assume that an active burglar is committing two offenses per week when he is apprehended on the basis of an AFIS hit. He is convicted and, based on harsh sentencing laws, sent to prison for 5 years. In this case, that one AFIS hit will have prevented 100 crimes per year over the course of the 5 year sentence. If this one arrest is then multiplied by some fraction of the totals from the table above, a truer appreciation of the impact that AFIS is having on society can be gained.

6.2.3.2 Validation of Friction Ridge Science. There are many ways to test the efficacy of a theoretical proposition. Corporate and academic laboratories pour tremendous resources into building models that they hope will closely duplicate performance in the real world. Even after successfully passing such testing, theories fail and products get recalled after weathering the rigors of the real world. In-use models invariably trump laboratory models.

During the past 100 years, many models have been constructed to test the theory that no two friction ridge images from different areas of palmar surfaces are alike and to determine what minimum number of minutiae is sufficient to support an individualization decision.

Automated fingerprint systems have been effectively testing identification theory millions of times a day every day for more than 20 years. These systems tend to validate what friction ridge examiners have propounded since Galton first set forth his standards. AFIS has also served as a catalyst to help examiners expand their image-processing knowledge and skills.

Some errors occur every year in both manual and automated systems, and it is through the study of errors that both systems can be improved in the future. According to Dr. James Wayman, Director of the National Biometrics Test Center, "Error rates (in friction ridge identification) are difficult to measure, precisely because they are so low" (Wayman, 2000)

6.2.4 IAFIS

The Integrated Automated Fingerprint Identification System, more commonly known as IAFIS, is the world's largest collection of criminal history information. Fully operational since July 28, 1999, IAFIS is maintained by the FBI's Criminal Justice Information Services (CJIS) Division in Clarksburg, WV, and contains fingerprint images for more than 64 million individuals. The FBI's CJIS Division system's architecture and the identification and investigative services provided by the division form an integrated system-of-services (SoS) concept. These identification and information services enable local, state, federal, tribal, and international law enforcement communities, as well as civil organizations, to efficiently access or exchange critical information 24 hours a day, 365 days per year. The SoS provides advanced identification and ancillary criminal justice technologies used in the identification of subjects.

The systems within the CJIS SoS, including IAFIS, have evolved over time, both individually and collectively, to add new technological capabilities, embrace legislative directives, and improve the performance and accuracy of their information services. During its first year of inception, IAFIS processed nearly 14.5 million fingerprint submissions. Today, IAFIS processes similar tenprint volumes in as little as 3 to 4 months. Although designed to respond to electronic criminal transactions within 2 hours and civil transactions within 24 hours, IAFIS has exceeded these demands, often providing criminal search requests in less than 20 minutes and civil background checks in less than 3 hours. Likewise, IAFIS provides the latent print examiners with a superlative investigative tool, allowing fingerprint evidence from crime scenes to be searched in approximately 2 hours rather than the 24-hour targeted response time. Although declared a successful system early within its deployment, IAFIS continues to improve as a vital asset to law enforcement agencies more than 10 years later. Today's transient society magnifies the need for an economic, rapid, positive identification process for both criminal and noncriminal justice background checks. IAFIS processes are regularly improved to allow for a quick and accurate fingerprint-based records check, whether related to terrorists trying to enter the United States or applicants seeking positions of trust. Figure 6–3 illustrates the states that currently interface with IAFIS electronically.

The increasingly complex requirements of the SoS architecture demand a well-structured process for its operations and maintenance. Each of these systems has multiple segments consisting of computer hardware and software that provide the operating systems and utilities, database management, workflow management, transaction or

FIGURE 6–3

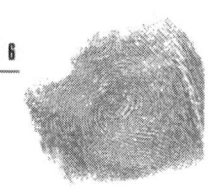

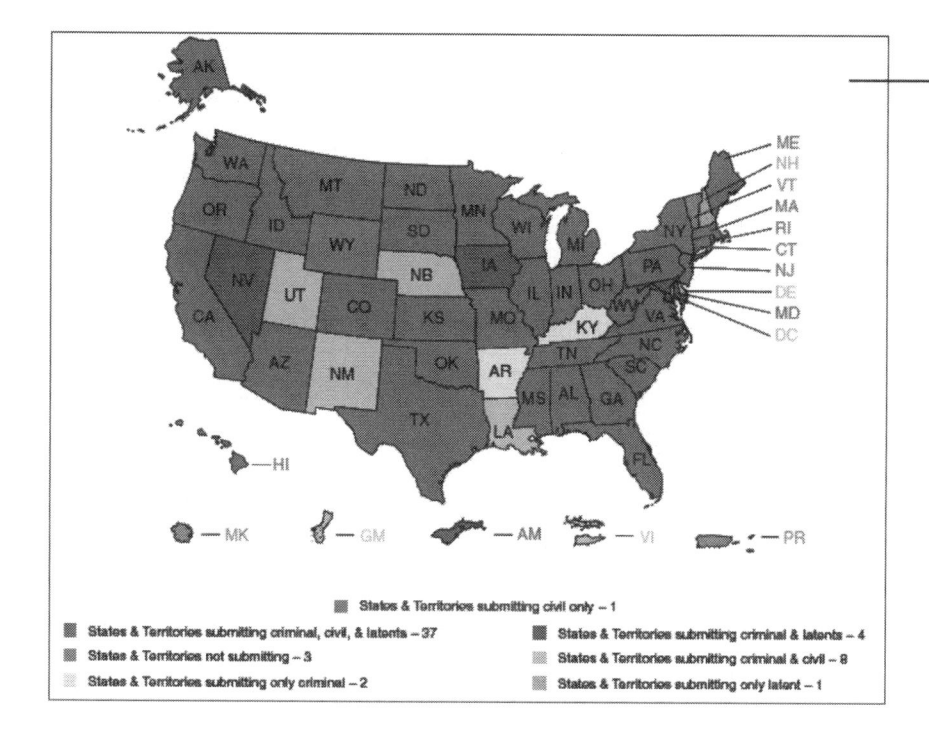

Electronic submissions to IAFIS. (Illustration from the Federal Bureau of Investigation.)

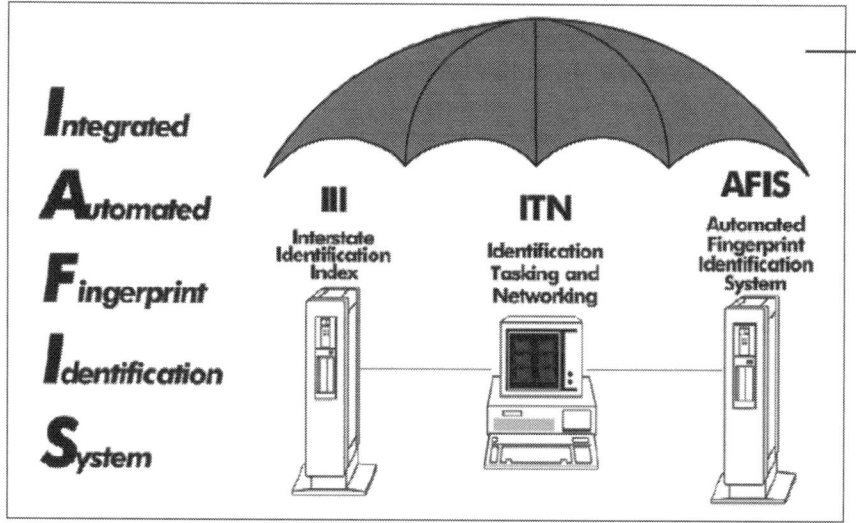

- States & Territories submitting civil only – 1
- States & Territories submitting criminal, civil, & latents – 37
- States & Territories submitting criminal & latents – 4
- States & Territories not submitting – 3
- States & Territories submitting criminal & civil – 8
- States & Territories submitting only criminal – 2
- States & Territories submitting only latent – 1

FIGURE 6–4

IAFIS segments. (Illustration from the Federal Bureau of Investigation.)

Integrated **A**utomated **F**ingerprint **I**dentification **S**ystem

- III — Interstate Identification Index
- ITN — Identification Tasking and Networking
- AFIS — Automated Fingerprint Identification System

messaging management, internal and external networking, communications load balancing, and system security. IAFIS consists of three integrated segments: the Identification Tasking and Networking (ITN) segment, the Interstate Identification Index (III), and AFIS (Figure 6–4).

Within IAFIS, the ITN segment acts as a "traffic cop" for the fingerprint system, providing workflow/workload management for tenprint, latent print, and document processing. The ITN provides the human–machine interfaces, the internal interfaces for communications within the IAFIS backbone communications element, the storage and retrieval of fingerprint images, the external communications interfaces, the IAFIS back-end communications element, and user fee billing. The III provides subject search, computerized criminal history, and criminal photo storage and retrieval. The AFIS searches the FBI fingerprint repository for matches to tenprint and latent fingerprints. Supporting IAFIS is the CJIS-wide area network (WAN), providing the communications infrastructure for the secure exchange of fingerprint information to and from external systems. The external systems are the state control

FIGURE 6–5

IAFIS networked architecture. (Illustration from the Federal Bureau of Investigation.)

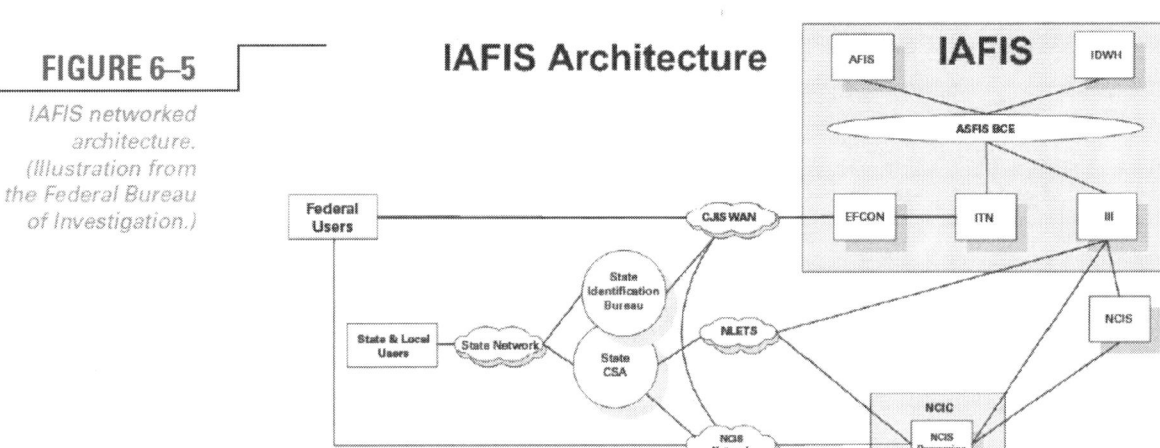

terminal agencies, state identification bureaus, and federal service coordinators.

Also submitting fingerprint information to IAFIS is the Card Scanning Service (CSS). The CSS acts as a conduit for agencies that are not yet submitting fingerprints electronically. The CSS makes the conversion of fingerprint information from paper format to electronic format and submits that information to IAFIS. Another system providing external communications for IAFIS is Nlets. The purpose of Nlets is to provide interstate communications to law enforcement, criminal justice, and other agencies involved in the enforcement of laws. Figure 6–5 depicts the high-level IAFIS architecture. Users wishing to interface with IAFIS electronically must comply with the FBI's Electronic Fingerprint Transmission Specification (EFTS).

Electronic access to and exchange of fingerprint information with the world's largest national repository of automated criminal and civil records is fulfilling the CJIS mission:

> The CJIS Division mission is to reduce terrorist activities by maximizing the ability to provide timely and relevant criminal justice information to the FBI and to qualified law enforcement, criminal justice, civilian, academic, employment, and licensing agencies concerning individuals, stolen property, criminal organizations and activities, and other law enforcement-related data.

6.2.4.1 IAFIS Status as of Early 2006. Because of the evolutionary changes to the American National Standards Institute (ANSI)/NIST standard in 1997, 2000, and 2006, the FBI has not always had the financial resources or corporate commitment to update IAFIS and keep it current. One area where it has moved forward is the acceptance and processing of "segmented slaps" for civil transactions. These transactions use a modified livescan platen that is 3 inches high so the four fingers of each hand can be placed as a "slap" in a straight up-and-down position. Similarly, both thumbs can be captured simultaneously for a total of three images (type 4 or type 14 as defined in sections 6.3.2.1 and 6.3.3). The resultant transaction's three-image files are easy to segment with the capture device software. The three images and relative location of the segmented fingers within the images are all transmitted. This dramatically reduces collection time and improves the captured-image quality from a content perspective due to the flat, straight, 3-inch placement.

One drawback to IAFIS is that it cannot store and search palmprints, though several production AFISs can do so. Also, at least one foreign production and several domestic AFIS sites accept and store 1,000-pixels-per-inch tenprint images—IAFIS cannot yet do this.

The FBI recognizes its need to expand its services and has (1) tested small palm systems and (2) started a project known as the Next Generation Identification Program (NGI). Driven by advances in technology, customer requirements, and growing demand for IAFIS services, this program will further advance the FBI's biometric identification services, providing an incremental replacement of current IAFIS technical capabilities while introducing new functionality. NGI improvements and new capabilities will be introduced across a multiyear time frame within a phased approach. The NGI system will offer state-of-the-art biometric identification services and provide a flexible framework of core capabilities that will serve as a platform for multimodal functionality.

6.2.4.2 Universal Latent Work Station. AFISs that are fully ANSI/NIST compliant can send image-based transactions from site to site. But in the latent community, most practitioners want to edit the images and extract the minutiae themselves, that is, perform remote searches rather than submittals. This model also plays well with the ability of most agencies to provide the skilled labor required for imaged-based submittals from other agencies.

The FBI CJIS Division addressed this issue by working closely with Mitretek and the four major AFIS vendors to develop a set of tools that would permit the creation of remote searches for any of their automated fingerprint identification systems and for IAFIS. The result is a free software product called the Universal Latent Workstation (ULW). This software can run on a stand-alone PC with either a flatbed scanner or a digital camera interface. It can also run on vendor-provided latent workstations. At a minimum, when specifying an AFIS in a procurement, one should mandate that the AFIS be able to generate remote searches to IAFIS. It is further recommended that the procurer ask for the ability to perform the ULW function so the vendors can integrate ULW into their systems.

The ULW also provides the ability to launch latent print image searches into IAFIS without the need to manually encode minutiae when working with high-quality latent prints.

6.3 Standards

6.3.1 Background

Standards are mutually agreed upon attributes of products, systems, communication protocols, and so forth. Standards are what permit people to purchase light bulbs made in Hungary, the United States, or Japan and know they will fit in a standard lamp socket. Industries and governments establish standards not just for the convenience of the consumer but to permit competition for the same product.

Each nation has its own standards bureau or management body. In the United States, it is ANSI. At the international level, there are several such bodies. They include the United Nation's International Labor Organization (ILO) and International Civil Aviation Organization (ICAO), the International Criminal Police Organization (Interpol), the International Standards Organization (ISO), and the International Electrotechnical Commission (IEC).

Other than the United Nations and Interpol, these standards bodies do not "invent" or "create" standards but rather provide processes that authorized bodies can use to propose standards for approval at the national level and then at the international level. The United Nations and Interpol tend to build on these national and international standards bodies' standards rather than starting from scratch.

ANSI has offices in both New York and Washington, DC. ANSI has authorized more than 200 bodies to propose standards. If all the procedures are followed correctly and there are no unaddressed objections, then the results of the efforts of these bodies become ANSI standards. The 200 organizations include the following:

- The Department of Commerce's NIST

- IAI

- The American Association of Motor Vehicle Administrators

- The International Committee for Information Technology Standards (INCITS)

6.3.2 Fingerprint Standards

Law enforcement agencies around the world have had standards for the local exchange of inked fingerprints for decades. In 1995, Interpol held a meeting to address the transfer of ink-and-paper fingerprint cards (also known as forms) between countries. The local standards naturally had different text fields, had different layouts of text fields, were in different languages, and were on many different sizes of paper. Before that effort could lead to an internationally accepted fingerprint form, Interpol moved to the electronic exchange of fingerprints.

In the ink-and-paper era, the standards included fiber content and thickness of the paper, durability of the ink, size of the "finger boxes", and so forth. With the move in the early 1990s toward near real-time responses to criminal fingerprint submittals, there came a new set of standards.

The only way to submit, search, and determine the status of fingerprints in a few hours from a remote site is through electronic submittal and electronic responses. The source can still be ink-and-paper, but the images need to be digitized and submitted electronically to address the growing demand for rapid turnaround of fingerprint transactions.

The FBI was the first agency to move to large-scale electronic submission of fingerprints from remote sites. As part of the development of IAFIS, the FBI worked very closely with NIST to develop appropriate standards for the electronic transmission of fingerprint images.

Starting in 1991, NIST held a series of workshops with forensic experts, fingerprint repository managers, industry representatives, and consultants to develop a standard, under the ANSI guidelines, for the exchange of fingerprint images. It was approved in November 1993, and the formal title was "Data Format for the Interchange of Fingerprint Information (ANSI NIST-CSL 1-1993)". This standard was based on the 1986 ANSI/National Bureau of Standards minutiae-based standard and ANSI/NBS-ICST 1-1986, a standard that did not address image files.

This 1993 NIST standard (and the later revisions) became known in the fingerprint technology world simply as the "ANSI/NIST standard". If implemented correctly (i.e., in full compliance with the standard and the FBI's implementation), it would permit fingerprints collected on a compliant livescan from any vendor to be read by any other compliant AFIS and the FBI's yet-to-be-built (at that time) IAFIS.

The standard was deliberately open to permit communities of users (also known as domains of interest) to customize it to meet their needs. Some of the customizable areas were image density (8-bit gray scale or binary) and text fields associated with a transaction (e.g., name, crime). The idea was that different communities of users would write their own implementation plans. The mandatory parts of the ANSI/NIST standard were the definitions of the record types, the binary formats for fingerprint and signature images and, within certain record types, the definition of "header" fields such as image compression type.

6.3.2.1 Record Types. For a transaction to be considered ANSI/NIST compliant, the data must be sent in a structured fashion with a series of records that align with ANSI/NIST record types as implemented in a specific user domain (e.g., Interpol).

- All transmissions (also known as transactions) have to start with a type 1 record that is basically a table of contents for the transmission, the transaction type field (e.g., CAR for "criminal tenprint submission—answer required"), and the identity of both the sending and receiving agencies.

- Type 2 records can contain user-defined information associated with the subject of the fingerprint transmission (such as name, date of birth, etc.) and the purpose of the transaction (arrest cycle, applicant background check, etc.). These fields are defined in the domain-of-interest implementation standard (e.g., the FBI's EFTS). Note that type 2 records are also used for responses from AFISs. They fall into two sets: error messages and search results. The actual use is defined in the domain specification.

- Types 3 (low-resolution gray scale), 4 (high-resolution gray scale), 5 (low-resolution binary), and 6 (high-resolution binary) were set up for the transmission of fingerprint images at different standards (500 ppi for high resolution and 256 ppi for low resolution) and image density (8 bits per pixel for grayscale) or binary (1 bit per pixel for black and white). Note that all images for records type 3 through 6 are to be acquired at a minimum of 500 ppi; however, low-resolution images are down-sampled to 256 ppi for transmission. There are few, if any, ANSI/NIST implementations that support type 3, 5, or 6 images (see explanation below). None of these three record types are recommended for use by latent examiners and fingerprint technicians.

- Type 7 was established for user-defined images (e.g., latent images, faces) and, until the update of the ANSI/NIST standard in 2000, it was the record type for exchanging latent images. This record type can be used to send scanned copies of identity documents, and so forth. Again, the domain specification determines the legitimate uses of the type 7 record.

- Type 8 was defined for signatures (of the subject or person taking the fingerprints), and it is not used in many domains.

- Type 9 was defined for a minimal set of minutiae that could be sent to any AFIS that was ANSI/NIST-compliant.

The first such implementation plan was the FBI's EFTS issued in 1994. The EFTS limited what record types, of the nine defined in the ANSI/NIST standard, the FBI would use, and defined the type 2 data fields. The key decision the FBI made was that it would only accept 500-ppi gray-scale images or, in ANSI/NIST parlance, type 4 images. As a result of that decision, all law enforcement systems since then have specified type 4 images and do not accept types 3, 5, or 6, which as a result have fallen into disuse for these applications in the United States.

The type 4 records start out with header information in front of the image. The headers tell the computer which finger the image is from, whether it is from a livescan or an inked card, the image size in the number of pixels of width and height, and whether the image is from a rolled impression or a flat or plain impression.

6.3.2.2 Image Quality. Both the ANSI/NIST standard and the EFTS lacked any metrics or standards for image quality. The FBI then appended the EFTS with an image quality standard (IQS) known as Appendix F. (Later, a reduced set of image quality specifications were added as Appendix G because the industry was not uniformly ready to meet Appendix F standards.) The IQS defines minimal acceptable standards for the equipment used to capture the fingerprints. There are six engineering terms specified in the IQS. They are:

1. Geometric image accuracy—the ability of the scanner to keep relative distances between points on an object (e.g., two minutiae) the same relative distances apart in the output image.

2. Modulation transfer function (MTF)—the ability of the scanning device to capture both low-frequency (ridges themselves) and high-frequency (ridge edge details) information in a fingerprint at minimum standards.

3. Signal-to-noise ratio—the ability of the scanning device to digitize the information without introducing too much electronic noise (that is, with the pure white image parts appearing pure white and the totally black image parts appearing totally black).

4. Gray-scale range of image data—avoiding excessively low-contrast images by ensuring that the image data are spread across a minimal number of shades of gray.

5. Gray-scale linearity—as the level of gray changes in a fingerprint capture, the digital image reflects a corresponding ratio of gray level across all shades of gray.

6. Output gray-level uniformity—the ability of the scanning device to create an image with a continuous gray scale across an area on the input image (tested using a special test image) that has a single gray level.

Interestingly, only two of these six image quality standards apply to latent scanning devices: geometric image accuracy and MTF. In fact, the FBI does not certify (see below for a discussion of certified products) scanners for latent use but recommends that latent examiners purchase equipment they are comfortable with using from an image-quality perspective. But EFTS Appendix F does mandate that latent images be captured at 1,000 ppi.

There are no standards for the quality of the actual fingerprint, but livescan and AFIS vendors have rated fingerprint quality for years. They know that fingerprint quality is possibly the strongest factor in the reliability of an AFIS's successfully matching a fingerprint to one in the repository. These ratings are often factored into the AFIS algorithms.

In a paper titled "The Role of Data Quality in Biometric Systems" (Hicklin and Khanna, 2006), the authors wrote the following:

> Note that this definition of data quality goes beyond most discussions of biometric quality, which focus on the concept of sample quality. Sample quality deals with the capture fidelity of the subject's physical characteristics and the intrinsic data content of those characteristics. However, an equally important issue for any operational system is metadata quality: databases need to be concerned with erroneous relationships between data elements, which generally come from administrative rather than biometric-specific causes.

Although no standard exists for fingerprint image quality, NIST has researched the relationship between calculated image quality (using algorithms similar to those employed by AFIS vendors) and successful match rates in automated fingerprint identification systems. This led NIST to develop and publish a software utility to measure fingerprint image quality.

The software is entitled NIST Fingerprint Image Software 2. It was developed by NIST's image group for the FBI and the U.S. Department of Homeland Security and is available free to U.S. law enforcement agencies as well as to biometrics manufacturers and researchers. The CD contains source code for 56 utilities and a user's guide.

The following summary is from the NIST Web site in 2007:

> New to this release is a tool that evaluates the quality of a fingerprint scan at the time it is made. Problems such as dry skin, the size of the fingers and the quality and condition of the equipment used can affect the quality of a print and its ability to be matched with other prints. The tool rates each scan on a scale from 1 for a high-quality print to 5 for an unusable one. "Although most commercial fingerprint systems already include proprietary image quality software, the NIST software will for the first time allow users to directly compare fingerprint image quality from scanners made by different manufacturers," the agency said.

6.3.2.3 Certified Products List. To assist the forensic community to purchase IQS-compliant equipment, the FBI established a certification program. The vendors can self-test their equipment and submit the results to the FBI where, with the technical assistance of Mitretek, the results are evaluated. If the results are acceptable, a letter of certification is sent to the vendor. It is important to know that, for capture devices, it is a combination of the optics (scanner), image processing software, and the operating system that is tested. Therefore, letters of certification are not issued for a scanner but for a scanner and PC configuration that includes a specific scanner model, connected to a PC running a specific operating system, and any image-enhancement scanner drivers used.

At the rate at which manufacturers upgrade scanners, it can be hard to purchase previously certified pieces of equipment. A complete list of all certified equipment is maintained on the FBI's Web site under the CJIS section.

6.3.2.4 Compression. About the same time as the writing of the EFTS, the FBI decided on the compression standard for ANSI/NIST transmissions. Given that the data rate (bandwidth) of telecommunications systems was very low in 1993 compared to today's rates and that the cost of disk storage was quite high, the FBI elected to compress fingerprint images using a technique called wavelet scalar quantization (WSQ).

The initial plan was for tenprint transmissions to be compressed with WSQ at 20:1 and for latent images to remain uncompressed. An FBI fingerprint card in the early 1990s had a surface area for fingerprints that was 8 inches wide and 5 inches high for a total of 40 square inches. Scanning at 500 ppi in both the 8-inch direction (X) and the 5-inch direction (Y) yielded a total of 10 million bytes of information (10 MB). Compression at 20:1 would produce a half (0.5) MB file that was much easier to transmit and store.

At the 1993 IAI Annual Training Conference in Orlando, Fl, the IAI Board of Directors expressed its concerns to the IAFIS program director about the proposed compression rate of 20:1. The FBI agreed to support an independent assessment of the impact of compression on the science of fingerprint identification by the IAI AFIS committee, under the Chairmanship of Mike Fitzpatrick of Illinois (IAI AFIS Committee, 1994). As a result of the study, the FBI agreed to reduce the average compression to 15:1 (Higgins, 1995, pp 409–418).[5]

As other domains of interest adopted the ANSI/NIST standard around the world (early adopters included the Royal Canadian Mounted Police and the United Kingdom Home Office), they all used the EFTS as a model and all incorporated the IQS standard by reference. With one or two exceptions, they also adopted WSQ compression at 15:1.

With the move to higher scan rates for tenprint transactions, the compression technology of choice is JPEG 2000, which is a wavelet-based compression technique. Currently (as of 2007), there are at least five 1000-ppi tenprint, image-based automated fingerprint identification systems using JPEG 2000. Both Cogent and Motorola have delivered 1000-ppi systems. It is anticipated that the other vendors will deliver such systems as the demand increases. Given that older livescan systems operating at 500 ppi can submit transactions to these new automated fingerprint identification systems, it is important that they be capable of working in a mixed-density (500-ppi and 1000-ppi) environment.

All four major AFIS vendors demonstrated the capability to acquire, store, and process 1000-ppi tenprints and palmprints during the 2005 Royal Canadian Mounted Police AFIS Benchmark. It is important to note that these systems acquire the known tenprint and palm images at 1000 ppi for archiving but down-sample them to 500 ppi

---

[5] The study showed that expert latent print examiners were unable to differentiate original images from those compressed at either 5:1 or 10:1 when presented with enlargements on high-quality film printers. One possible implication of that study was that latent images might safely be compressed at 2:1 (or possibly even more) for transmission, with no loss of information content. Currently, there are no agencies reporting the use of compression with latent images.

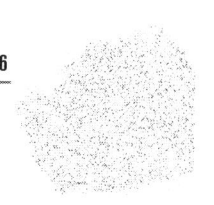

for searching and creating an image to be used in AFIS. Currently, 1000-ppi images are used primarily for display at latent examiner workstations. As automated fingerprint identification systems move to using third-level features, it is assumed that the higher resolution images will play a role in the algorithms.

6.3.3 Updates to the ANSI/NIST Standard

Since 1993, the ANSI/NIST standard has been updated three times, most recently in 2007 and 2008. The key changes are as follows:

- In 1997, type 10 transactions were added to permit facial, scar marks, and tattoo images to be transmitted with fingerprint transactions. The title of the document was changed to reflect that: "Data Format for the Interchange of Fingerprint, Facial & SMT (Scar, Mark, and Tattoo) Information (ANSI/NIST-ITL 1a-1997)".

- In 2000, types 13 through 16[6] were added to support higher density images, latent images in a new format, palm images, and test images, respectively (ANSI/NIST-ITL 1-2000).

- NIST held two workshops in 2005 to determine whether there were any new areas that should be added. The major changes desired were the addition of standard record types for biometric data types beyond fingers and faces (e.g., iris images) and the introduction of XML data in the type 2 records. Several other changes and additions were also proposed. (See the 2007 and 2008 revisions, ANSI/NIST–ITL 1–2007 and 2–2008.)

6.3.4 Early Demonstrations of Interoperability

By 1996, the IAI AFIS Committee was organizing and managing (under the chairmanships of Mike Fitzpatrick, Peter Higgins, and Ken Moses) a series of demonstrations of interoperability of tenprint-image transactions originating from Aware software, Comnetix Live Scan, and Identix Live Scan and going to Cogent Systems, Printrak (now Motorola), and Sagem Morpho automated fingerprint identification systems. The second year of these demonstrations (1998) saw the same input being submitted between operational AFIS sites from the same three AFIS vendors all over the Nlets network (AFIS Committee Report, 1998, p 490).

6.3.5 Latent Interoperability

When IAFIS was being developed, the FBI established (in the EFTS) two ways for latent impressions to be run through IAFIS from outside agencies.

6.3.5.1 Remote Submittals. The agency with the latent impression can send (electronically or via the mail) the impression (as an image in the case of electronic submittal) to the FBI, and FBI staff will perform the editing, encoding, searching, and candidate evaluation. The FBI will make any identification decision and return the results to the submitting agency. This process mimics the pre-IAFIS workflow but adds the option of electronic submittal.

6.3.5.2 Remote Searches. The agency with the latent impression performs the editing and encoding and then sends (electronically) a latent fingerprint features search (LFFS) to IAFIS for lights-out searching. IAFIS then returns a candidate list, including finger images, to the originating agency to perform candidate evaluation. The submitting agency makes any identification decision. To support LFFS remote search capability, the FBI published the "native" IAFIS feature set definition.

Many civil agencies and departments have wanted to be able to offer remote tenprint searches, but the feature sets for the major AFIS vendors are proprietary. In 2006, NIST performed a study on interoperability of the native feature set level of many AFIS and livescan companies and compared those with the performance of INCITS 378 fingerprint template standard minutiae (the basic set A and the richer set B).

The MINEX report (Grother et al., 2006) shows that minutiae-based interoperability is possible (with some loss of reliability and accuracy) for single-finger verification systems. The report is careful to point out that the use of INCITS 378 templates for remote criminal tenprint and latent searches is unknown and cannot safely be extrapolated from the report.

Because most AFISs (other than IAFIS) do not have remote LFFS functionality (as of 2007), latent interoperability at the image level usually requires labor on the part of the searching agency. The desire to move that labor burden to the submitting agency is natural because many have some level of excess capacity that could possibly support remote latent searches during off-hours.

---

[6] Types 11 and 12 were set aside for a project that never came to fruition and are not used in the standard AFIS Committee Report, 1998.

6.4 Digitization and Processing of Fingerprints

6.4.1 Algorithms

Demands imposed by the painstaking attention needed to visually match the fingerprints of varied qualities, the tedium of the monotonous nature of the manual work, and increasing workloads due to a higher demand on fingerprint recognition services prompted law enforcement agencies to initiate research into acquiring fingerprints through electronic media and to automate fingerprint individualization based on digital representation of fingerprints. As a result of this research, a large number of computer algorithms have been developed during the past three decades to automatically process digital fingerprint images. An algorithm is a finite set of well-defined instructions for accomplishing some task which, given an initial state and input, will terminate in a corresponding recognizable end-state and output. A computer algorithm is an algorithm coded in a programming language to run on a computer. Depending upon the application, these computer algorithms could either assist human experts or perform in lights-out mode. These algorithms have greatly improved the operational productivity of law enforcement agencies and reduced the number of fingerprint technicians needed. Still, algorithm designers identified and investigated the following five major problems in designing automated fingerprint processing systems: digital fingerprint acquisition, image enhancement, feature (e.g., minutiae) extraction, matching, and indexing/retrieval.

6.4.2 Image Acquisition

Known fingerprint data can be collected by applying a thin coating of ink over a finger and rolling the finger from one end of the nail to the other end of the nail while pressing the finger against a paper card. This would result in an inked "rolled" fingerprint impression on the fingerprint card. If the finger was simply pressed straight down against the paper card instead of rolling, the resulting fingerprint impression would only contain a smaller central area of the finger rather than the full fingerprint, resulting in an inked "flat" or "plain" fingerprint impression.

The perspiration and contaminants on the skin result in the impression of a finger being deposited on a surface that is touched by that finger. These "latent" prints can be chemically or physically developed and electronically captured or manually "lifted" from the surface by employing certain chemical, physical, and lighting techniques. The developed fingerprint may be lifted with tape or photographed. Often these latent fingerprints contain only a portion of the friction ridge detail that is present on the finger, that is, a "partial" fingerprint.

Fingerprint impressions developed and preserved using any of the above methods can be digitized by scanning the inked card, lift, item, or photograph. Digital images acquired by this method are known as "off-line" images. (Typically, the scanners are not designed specifically for fingerprint applications.)

Since the early 1970s, fingerprint sensors have been built that can acquire a "livescan" digital fingerprint image directly from a finger without the intermediate use of ink and a paper card. Although off-line images are still in use in certain forensic and government applications, on-line fingerprint images are increasingly being used. The main parameters characterizing a digital fingerprint image are resolution area, number of pixels, geometric accuracy, contrast, and geometric distortion. CJIS released specifications, known as Appendix F and Appendix G, that regulate the quality and the format of fingerprint images and FBI-compliant scanners. All livescan devices manufactured for use in forensic and government law enforcement applications are FBI compliant. Most of the livescan devices manufactured to be used in commercial applications, such as computer log-on, do not meet FBI specifications but, on the other hand, are usually more user-friendly, compact, and significantly less expensive. There are a number of livescan sensing mechanisms (e.g., optical, capacitive, thermal, pressure-based, ultrasound, and so forth) that can be used to detect the ridges and valleys present in the fingertip. However, many of these methods do not provide images that contain the same representation of detail necessary for some latent fingerprint comparisons. For example, a capacitive or thermal image may represent the edges and pores in a much different way than a rolled ink impression. Figure 6–6 shows an off-line fingerprint image acquired with the ink technique, a latent fingerprint image, and some livescan images acquired with different types of commercial livescan devices.

The livescan devices often capture a stream of fingerprint images from a single scan instead of just one image. Depending on the application for which the livescan device was designed, it may run one or more algorithms using

AFIS | CHAPTER 6

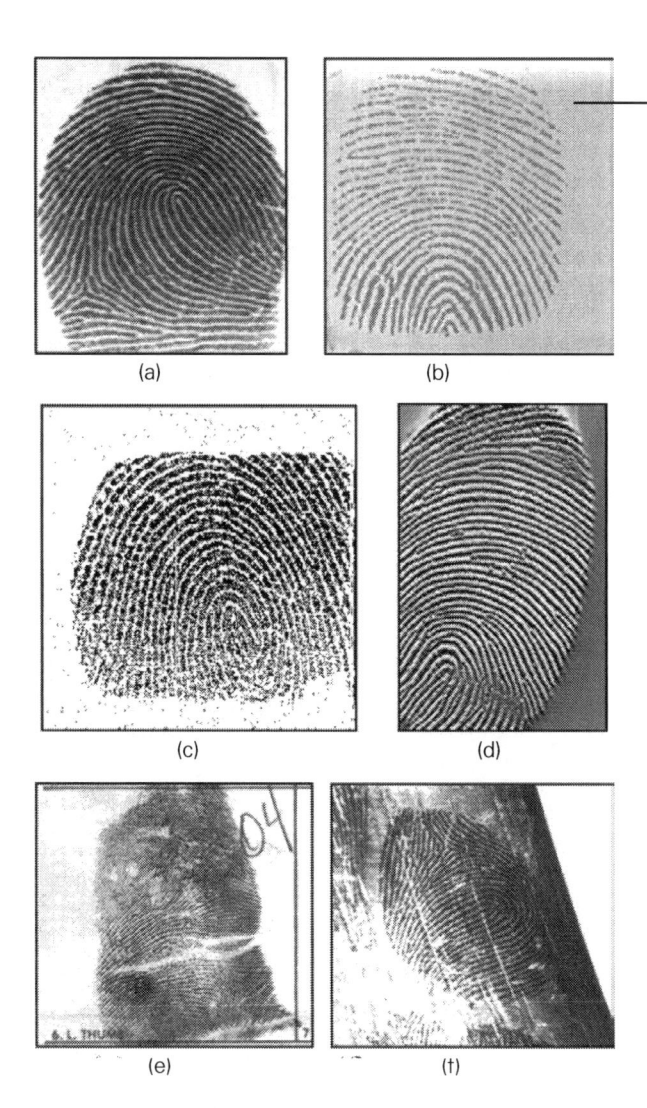

FIGURE 6–6

*Fingerprint images from
(a) a livescan FTIR-based optical scanner;
(b) a livescan capacitive scanner;
(c) a livescan piezoelectric scanner;
(d) a livescan thermal scanner;
(e) an off-line inked impression;
(f) a latent fingerprint.*

either a resource-limited (memory and processing power) microprocessor on-board or by using an attached computer. For example, the livescan booking stations usually run an algorithm that can mosaic (stitch) multiple images acquired as a video during a single rolling of a finger on the scanner into a large rolled image. Algorithms also typically run on an integrated booking management system to provide real-time previews (graphical user interface and zoom) to assist the operator in placing or aligning fingers or palms correctly. Typically, a fingerprint image quality-checking algorithm is also run to alert the operator about the acquisition of a poor-quality fingerprint image so that a better quality image can be reacquired from the finger or palm. Typical output from such an automatic quality-checker algorithm is depicted in Figure 6–7.

Although optical scanners have the longest history and highest quality, the new solid-state sensors are gaining great popularity because of their compact size and the ease with which they can be embedded into laptop computers, cellular phones, smart pens, personal digital assistants (PDAs), and the like. Swipe sensors, where a user is required to swipe his or her finger across a livescan sensor that is wide but very short, can offer the lowest cost and size. Such sensors image a single line or just a few lines (slice) of a fingerprint, and an image-stitching algorithm is used to stitch the lines or slices to form a two-dimensional fingerprint image (Figure 6–8).

Depending on the application, it may be desirable to implement one or more of the following algorithms in the livescan device:

CHAPTER 6 | AFIS

FIGURE 6–7

(a) A good-quality fingerprint;
(b) A medium-quality fingerprint with creases;
(c) A poor-quality fingerprint;
(d) A very poor-quality fingerprint containing a lot of noise.

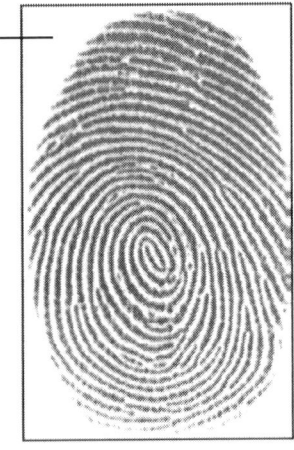

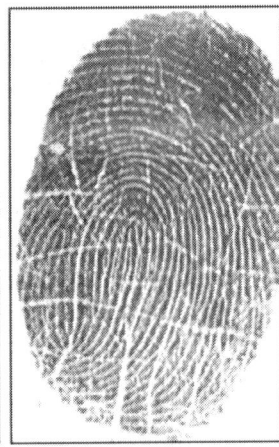

(a) Quality index = 0.9   (b) Quality index = 0.7

(c) Quality index = 0.4   (d) Quality index = 0.2

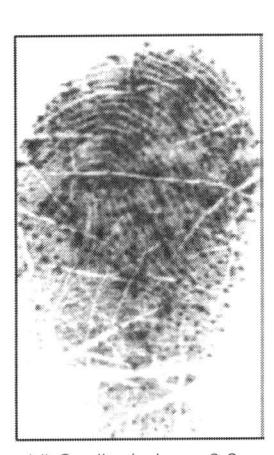

- Automatic finger-detection algorithm—The scanner automatically keeps looking for the presence of a finger on its surface and, as soon as it determines that there is a finger present on its surface, it alerts the system.

- Automatic fingerprint-capture algorithm—Immediately after the system has been alerted that a finger is present on the surface of the scanner, it starts receiving a series of images, and the fingerprint-capture algorithm automatically determines which frame in the image sequence has the best image quality and grabs that frame from the video for further image processing and matching.

- Vitality detection algorithm—The scanner can determine whether the finger is consistent with deposition by a living human being.

- Image data-compression algorithm—Compressed image will require less storage and bandwidth when transferred to the system.

- Image-processing algorithms—Certain applications will benefit from feature extraction carried out on the sensor itself; the transfer of the fingerprint features will also require less bandwidth than the image.

- Fingerprint-matching algorithm—Certain applications would like the fingerprint matching to be performed on the sensor for security reasons, especially for on-board sequence checking.

- Cryptographic algorithms and protocol(s)—Implemented in the scanner to carry out secure communication.

FIGURE 6-8

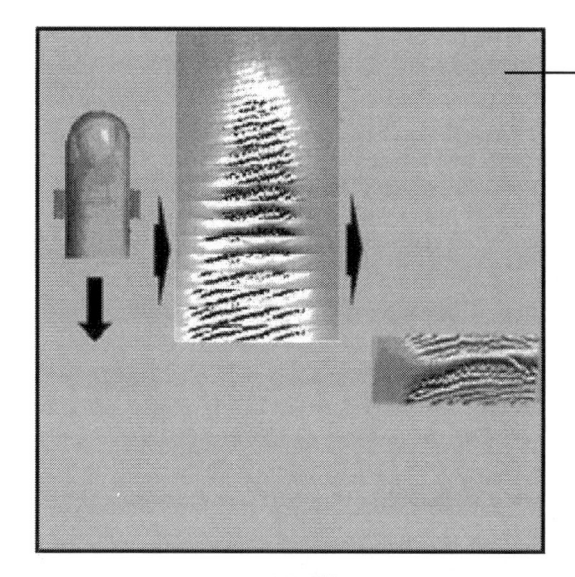

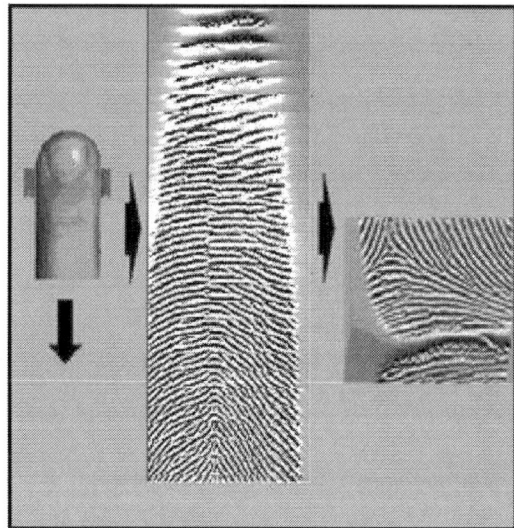

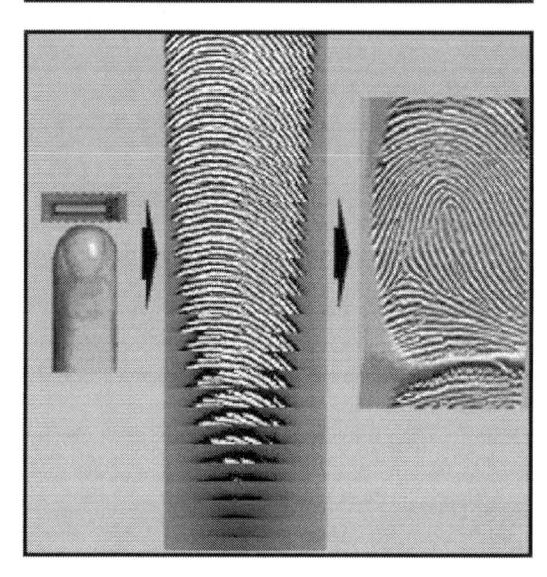

As the user sweeps his or her finger on the sensor, the sensor delivers new image slices, which are combined into a two-dimensional image.

6.4.3 Image Enhancement

Fingerprint images originating from different sources may have different noise characteristics and thus may require some enhancement algorithms based on the type of noise. For example, latent fingerprint images can contain a variety of artifacts and noise. Inked fingerprints can contain blobs or broken ridges that are due to an excessive or inadequate amount of ink. Filed paper cards may contain inscriptions overlapping the fingerprints and so forth. The goal of fingerprint enhancement algorithms is to produce an image that does not contain artificially generated ridge structure that might later result in the detection of false minutiae features while capturing the maximum available ridge structure to allow detection of true minutiae. Adapting the enhancement process to the fingerprint capture method can yield the optimal matching performance over a large collection of fingerprints.

A fingerprint may contain such poor-quality areas that the local ridge orientation and frequency estimation algorithms are completely wrong. An enhancement algorithm that can reliably locate (and mask) these extremely poor-quality areas is very useful for the later feature detection and individualization stages by preventing false or unreliable features from being created.

Fingerprint images can sometimes be of poor quality because of noise introduced during the acquisition process. For example: a finger may be dirty, a latent print may be lifted from a difficult surface, the acquisition medium (paper card or livescan) may be dirty, or noise may be introduced during the interaction of the finger with the sensing surface (such as slippage or other inconsistent contact). When presented with a poor-quality image, a forensic expert would use a magnifying glass and try to decipher the fingerprint features in the presence of the noise. Automatic fingerprint image-enhancement algorithms can significantly improve the quality of fingerprint ridges in the fingerprint image and make the image more suitable for further manual or automatic processing. The image enhancement

FIGURE 6–9

An example of local area contrast enhancement. The algorithm enhances the entire image by enhancing a large number of small square local areas.

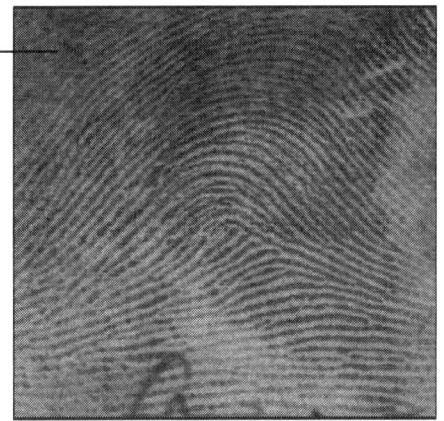

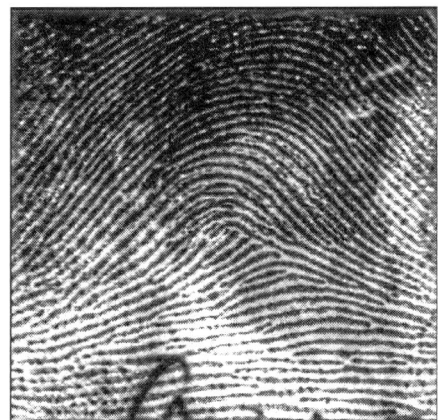

algorithms do not add any external information to the fingerprint image. The enhancement algorithms use only the information that is already present in the fingerprint image. The enhancement algorithms can suppress various types of noise (e.g., another latent print, background color) in the fingerprint image and highlight the existing useful features. These image enhancement algorithms can be of two types.

6.4.3.1 Enhancement of Latent Prints for AFIS Searching. In the case of latent searches into the forensic AFISs, the enhancement algorithm is interactive, that is, live feedback about the enhancement is provided to the forensic expert through a graphical user interface. Through this interface, the forensic expert is able to use various algorithms to choose the region of interest in the fingerprint image, crop the image, invert color, adjust intensity, flip the image, magnify the image, resize the image window, and apply compression and decompression algorithms. The forensic expert can selectively apply many of the available enhancement algorithms (or select the parameters of the algorithm) based on the visual feedback. Such algorithms may include histogram equalization, image intensity rescaling, image intensity adjustments with high and low thresholds, local or global contrast enhancement, local or global background subtraction, sharpness adjustments (applying high-pass filter), background suppression (low-pass filter), gamma adjustments, brightness and contrast adjustments, and so forth. An example of local area contrast enhancement is shown in Figure 6–9. In this example, the fingerprint image enhancement algorithm enhances only a small, square, local area of the image at a time but traverses over the entire image in a raster scan fashion such that the entire image is enhanced. Subsequent fingerprint feature extraction can then be either performed manually or through automatic fingerprint feature extraction algorithms.

6.4.3.2 Automated Enhancement of Fingerprint Images. In the case of lights-out applications (frequently used in automated background checks and commercial applications for control of physical access), human assistance does not occur in the fingerprint individualization process. Enhancement algorithms are used in the fully automated mode to improve the fingerprint ridge structures in poor-quality fingerprint images.

An example of a fully automated fingerprint image-enhancement algorithm is shown in Figure 6–10. In this example, contextual filtering is used that has a low-pass (smoothing) effect along the fingerprint ridges and a band-pass (differentiating) effect in the direction orthogonal to the ridges to increase the contrast between ridges and valleys. Often, oriented band-pass filters are used for such filtering. One such type of commonly used filters is known as Gabor filters. The local context is provided to such contextual filters in terms of local orientation and local ridge frequency.

6.4.4 Feature Extraction

Local fingerprint ridge singularities, commonly known as *minutiae points,* have been traditionally used by forensic experts as discriminating features in fingerprint images. The most common local singularities are ridge endings and ridge bifurcations. Other types of minutiae mentioned in the literature, such as the lake, island, spur, crossover, and so forth (with the exception of dots), are simply composites of ridge endings and bifurcations. Composite minutiae, made up of two to four minutiae occurring very close to each other, have also been used. In manual latent print processing, a forensic expert would visually locate the minutiae in a fingerprint image and note its location, the orientation of the ridge on which it resides, and the minutiae

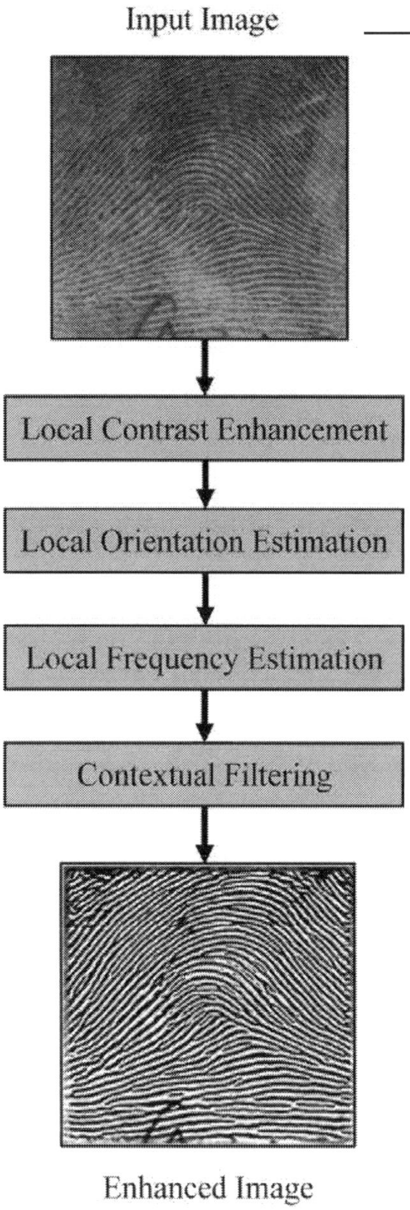

FIGURE 6–10

Stages in a typical contextual filtering-based fingerprint image enhancement algorithm.

One common approach followed by the fingerprint feature extraction algorithms is to first use a binarization algorithm to convert the gray-scale-enhanced fingerprint image into binary (black and white) form, where all black pixels correspond to ridges and all white pixels correspond to valleys. The binarization algorithm ranges from simple thresholding of the enhanced image to very sophisticated ridge location algorithms. Thereafter, a thinning algorithm is used to convert the binary fingerprint image into a single pixel width about the ridge centerline. The central idea of the thinning process is to perform successive (iterative) erosions of the outermost layers of a shape until a connected unit-width set of lines (or skeletons) is obtained. Several algorithms exist for thinning. Additional steps in the thinning algorithm are used to fill pores and eliminate noise that may result in the detection of false minutiae points.

The resulting image from the thinning algorithm is called a *thinned image* or *skeletal image.* A minutiae detection algorithm is applied to this skeletal image to locate the x and y coordinates as well as the orientation (theta) of the minutiae points. In the skeletal image, by definition, all pixels on a ridge have two neighboring pixels in the immediate neighborhood. If a pixel has only one neighboring pixel, it is determined to be a ridge ending and if a pixel has three neighboring pixels, it is determined to be a ridge bifurcation.

Each of the algorithms used in fingerprint image enhancement and minutiae extraction has its own limitation and results in imperfect processing, especially when the input fingerprint image includes non-friction-ridge noise. As a result, many false minutiae may be detected by the minutiae detection algorithm. To alleviate this problem, often a minutiae postprocessing algorithm is used to confirm or validate the detected minutiae. Only those minutiae that pass this postprocessing algorithm are kept and the rest are removed. For example, if a ridge length running away from the minutia point is sufficient or if the ridge direction at the point is within acceptable limits, the minutia is kept.

type. Automatic fingerprint feature-extraction algorithms were developed to imitate minutiae location performed by forensic experts. However, most automatic fingerprint minutiae-extraction algorithms only consider ridge endings and bifurcations because other types of ridge detail are very difficult to automatically extract. Further, most algorithms do not differentiate between ridge endings and bifurcations because they can be indistinguishable as a result of finger pressure differences during acquisition or artifacts introduced during the application of the enhancement algorithm.

FIGURE 6–11

Stages in a typical fingerprint minutiae extraction algorithm.

Enhanced Image → Ridge Location → Ridge Thinning → Minutiae Detection → Postprocessing → Minutiae points

The postprocessing might also include an examination of the local image quality, neighboring detections, or other indicators of nonfingerprint structure in the area. Further, the image can be inverted in gray scale, converting white to black and black to white. Reprocessing of this inverted image should yield minutiae endings in place of bifurcations, and vice versa, allowing a validity check on the previously detected minutiae. The final detected minutiae are those that meet all of the validity checks. Figure 6–11 shows the steps in a typical fingerprint feature-extraction algorithm; the extracted minutiae are displayed overlapping on the input image for visualization.

Note that the stages and algorithms described in this section represent only a typical fingerprint minutiae-extraction algorithm. A wide variety of fingerprint minutiae-extraction algorithms exist and they all differ from one another, sometimes in how they implement a certain stage and sometimes in the stages they use and the order in which they use them. For example, some minutiae extraction algorithms do not use a postprocessing stage. Some others do not use a ridge-thinning stage, and the minutiae detection algorithm works directly on the result of the ridge location algorithm. Some work directly on the enhanced image, and some even work directly on the raw input image. Additional stages and algorithms may also be used.

Many other features are often also extracted in addition to minutiae. These additional features often provide useful information that can be used in the later matching stages to improve the fingerprint-matching accuracy. For example, minutiae confidence, ridge counts between minutiae, ridge count confidence, core and delta locations, local quality measures, and so forth, can be extracted. These additional features may be useful to achieve added selectivity from a minutiae-matching process. Their usefulness for this purpose may be mediated by the confidence associated with each such feature. Therefore, it is important to collect confidence data as a part of the image-enhancement and feature-extraction process to be able to properly qualify detected minutiae and associated features.

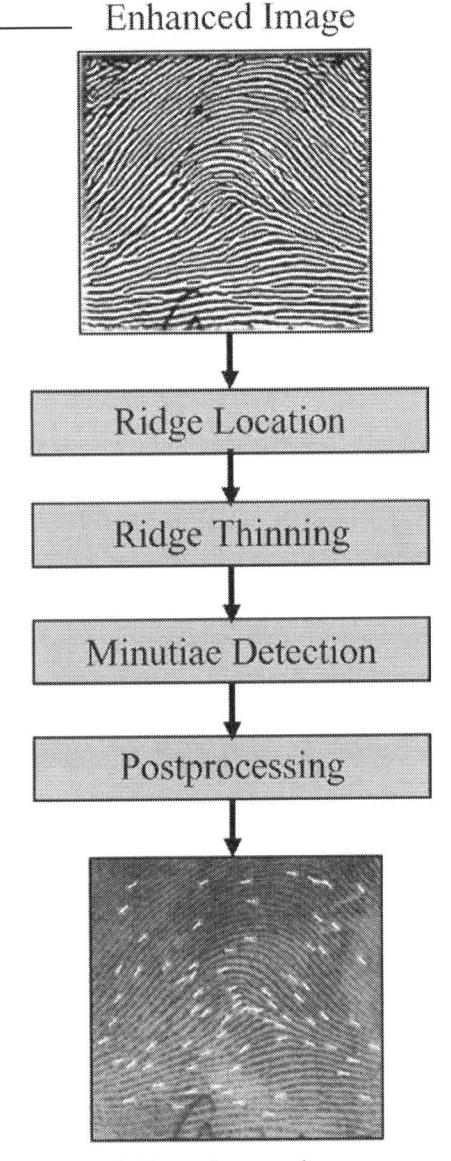

The early fingerprint feature-extraction algorithms were developed to imitate feature extraction by forensic experts. Recently, a number of automatic fingerprint feature-extraction (and matching) algorithms have emerged that use non-minutiae-based information in the fingerprint images. For example, sweat pores, which are very minute details in fingerprints, smaller than minutiae points, have been successfully extracted by algorithms from high-resolution fingerprint images. Other non-minutiae-based features are often low-level features (for example, texture features) that do not have a high-level meaning, such as a ridge ending or bifurcation. These features are well suited for machine representation and matching and can be used in place of minutiae features. Often, a combination of minutiae and non-minutiae-based features can provide the best accuracy in an automatic fingerprint individualization system. Forensic experts use such fine features implicitly, along with normal ridge endings and bifurcations features, during examination.

6.4.5 Matching

Fingerprint matching can be defined as the exercise of finding the similarity or dissimilarity in any two given fingerprint images. Fingerprint matching can be best visualized by taking a paper copy of a file fingerprint image with its minutiae marked or overlaid and a transparency of a search fingerprint with its minutiae marked or overlaid. By placing the transparency of the search print over the paper copy of the file fingerprint and translating and rotating the transparency, one can locate the minutiae points that are common in both prints. From the number of common minutiae found, their closeness of fit, the quality of the fingerprint images, and any contradictory minutiae matching information, it is possible to assess the similarity of the two prints. Manual fingerprint matching is a very tedious task. Automatic fingerprint-matching algorithms work on the result of fingerprint feature-extraction algorithms and find the similarity or dissimilarity in any two given sets of minutiae. Automatic fingerprint matching can perform fingerprint comparisons at the rate of tens of thousands of times each second, and the results can be sorted according to the degree of similarity and combined with any other criteria that may be available to further filter the candidates, all without human intervention.

It is important to note, however, that automatic fingerprint-matching algorithms are significantly less accurate than a well-trained forensic expert. Even so, depending on the application and the fingerprint image quality, the automatic-fingerprint-matching algorithms can significantly reduce the work for forensic experts. For example, in the case of latent print matching where only a single, very poor quality partial fingerprint image is available for matching, the matching algorithm may not be very accurate. Still, the matching algorithm can return a list of candidate matches that is much smaller than the size of the database; the forensic expert then needs only to manually match a much smaller number of fingerprints. In the case of latent print matching when the latent print is of good quality, or in the case of tenprint-to-tenprint matching in a background check application, the matching is highly accurate and requires minimal human expert involvement.

Automatic fingerprint-matching algorithms yield imperfect results because of the difficult problem posed by large intraclass variations (variability in different impressions of the same finger) present in the fingerprints. These intraclass variations arise from the following factors that vary during different acquisition of the same finger: (1) displacement, (2) rotation, (3) partial overlap, (4) nonlinear distortion because of pressing of the elastic three-dimensional finger onto a rigid two-dimensional imaging surface, (5) pressure, (6) skin conditions, (7) noise introduced by the imaging environment, and (8) errors introduced by the automatic feature-extraction algorithms.

A robust fingerprint-matching algorithm must be able to deal with all these intraclass variations in the various impressions of the same finger. The variations in displacement, rotation, and partial overlap are typically dealt with by using an alignment algorithm. The alignment algorithm should be able to correctly align the two fingerprint minutiae sets such that the corresponding or matching minutiae correspond well with each other after the alignment. Certain alignment algorithms also take into account the variability caused by nonlinear distortion. The alignment algorithm must also be able to take into consideration the fact that the feature extraction algorithm is imperfect and may have introduced false minutiae points and, at the same time, may have missed detecting some of the genuine minutiae points. Many fingerprint alignment algorithms exist. Some may use the core and delta points, if extracted, to align the fingerprints. Others use point pattern-matching algorithms such as Hough transform (a standard tool in pattern recognition that allows recognition of global patterns in the feature space by recognition of local patterns in a transformed parameter space), relaxation, algebraic and operational research solutions, "tree pruning," energy minimization, and so forth, to align minutiae points directly. Others use thinned ridge matching or orientation field matching to arrive at an alignment.

Once an alignment has been established, the minutiae from the two fingerprints often do not exactly overlay each other because of the small residual errors in the alignment algorithm and the nonlinear distortions. The next stage in a fingerprint minutiae-matching algorithm, which establishes the minutiae in the two sets that are corresponding

CHAPTER 6 | AFIS

FIGURE 6–12

Stages in a typical fingerprint minutiae matching algorithm.

and those that are noncorresponding, is based on using some tolerances in the minutiae locations and orientation to declare a correspondence. Because of noise that is introduced by skin condition, recording environment, imaging environment, and the imperfection of automatic fingerprint feature-extraction algorithms, the number of corresponding minutiae is usually found to be less than the total number of minutiae in either of the minutiae sets in the overlapping area. So, finally, a score computation algorithm is used to compute a matching score. The matching score essentially conveys the confidence of the fingerprint matching algorithm and can be viewed as an indication of the probability that the two fingerprints come from the same finger. The higher the matching score, the more likely it is that the fingerprints are mated (and, conversely, the lower the score, the less likely there is a match). There are many score computation algorithms that are used. They range from simple ones that count the number of matching minutiae normalized by the total number of minutiae in the two fingerprints in the overlapping area to very complex probability-theory-based, or statistical-pattern-recognition-classifier-based algorithms that take into account a number of features such as the area of overlap, the quality of the fingerprints, residual distances between the matching minutiae, the quality of individual minutiae, and so forth. Figure 6–12 depicts the steps in a typical fingerprint matching algorithm.

Note that the stages and algorithms described in this section represent only a typical fingerprint minutiae-matching algorithm. Many fingerprint minutiae-matching algorithms exist and they all differ from one another. As with the various extraction algorithms, matching algorithms use different implementations, different stages, and different orders of stages. For example, some minutiae-matching algorithms do not use an alignment stage. These algorithms instead attempt to prealign the fingerprint minutiae so that alignment is not required during the matching stage. Other algorithms attempt to avoid both the prealignment and alignment during matching by defining an intrinsic coordinate system for fingerprint minutiae. Some minutiae-matching algorithms use local alignment, some use global alignment, and some use both local and global alignment. Finally, many new matching algorithms are totally different and are based on the non-minutiae-based features automatically extracted by the fingerprint feature-extraction algorithm, such as pores and texture features.

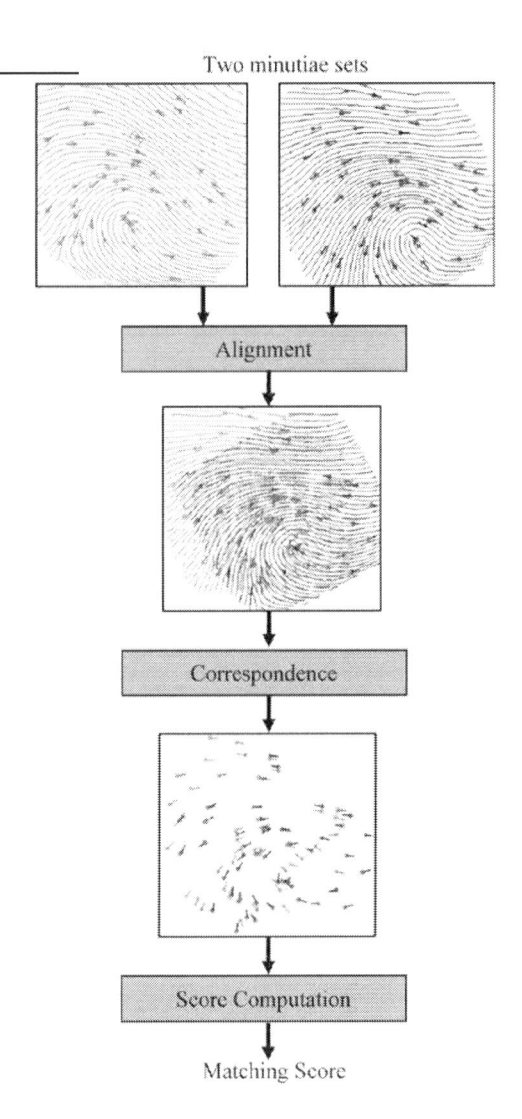

6.4.6 Indexing and Retrieval

In the previous section, the fingerprint matching problem was defined as finding the similarity in any two given fingerprints. There are many situations, such as controlling physical access within a location or affirming ownership of a legal document (such as a driver's license), where a single match between two fingerprints may suffice. However, in a large majority of forensic and government applications, such as latent fingerprint individualization and background checks, it is required that multiple fingerprints (in fact, up to 10 fingerprints from the 10 fingers of the same person) be matched against a large number of fingerprints present in a database. In these applications, a very large amount of fingerprint searching and matching is needed to be performed for a single individualization. This is very time-consuming, even for automatic fingerprint-matching algorithms. So it becomes desirable (although not necessary) to use automatic fingerprint indexing and retrieval algorithms to make the search faster.

Traditionally, such indexing and retrieval has been performed manually by forensic experts through indexing of fingerprint paper cards into file cabinets based on fingerprint pattern classification information as defined by a particular fingerprint classification system.

Similar to the development of the first automatic fingerprint feature extraction and matching algorithms, the initial automatic fingerprint indexing algorithms were developed to imitate forensic experts. These algorithms were built to classify fingerprint images into typically five classes (e.g., left loop, right loop, whorl, arch, and tented arch) based on the many fingerprint features automatically extracted from fingerprint images. (Many algorithms used only four classes because arch and tented arch types are often difficult to distinguish.)

Fingerprint pattern classification can be determined by explicitly characterizing regions of a fingerprint as belonging to a particular shape or through implementation of one of many possible generalized classifiers (e.g., neural networks) trained to recognize the specified patterns. The singular shapes (e.g., cores and deltas) in a fingerprint image are typically detected using algorithms based on the fingerprint orientation image. The explicit (rule-based) fingerprint classification systems first detect the fingerprint singularities (cores and deltas) and then apply a set of rules (e.g., arches and tented arches often have no cores; loops have one core and one delta; whorls have two cores and two deltas) to determine the pattern type of the fingerprint image (Figure 6–13). The most successful generalized (e.g., neural network-based) fingerprint classification systems use a combination of several different classifiers.

Such automatic fingerprint classification algorithms may be used to index all the fingerprints in the database into distinct bins (most implementations include overlapping or pattern referencing), and the submitted samples are then compared to only the database records with the same classification (i.e., in the same bin). The use of fingerprint pattern information can be an effective means to limit the volume of data sent to the matching engine, resulting in benefits in the system response time. However, the automatic fingerprint classification algorithms are not perfect and result in errors in classification. These classification errors increase the errors in fingerprint individualization because the matching effort will be conducted only in a wrong bin. Depending on the application, it may be feasible to manually confirm the automatically determined fingerprint class for some of the fingerprints where the automatic algorithm has low confidence. Even so, the explicit classification of fingerprints into just a few classes has its limitations because only a few classes are used (e.g., five), and the fingerprints occurring in nature are not equally distributed in these classes (e.g., arches and tented arches are much more rare than loops and whorls).

Many of the newer automatic fingerprint classification algorithms do not use explicit classes of fingerprints in distinct classifications but rather use a continuous classification of fingerprints that is not intuitive for manual processing but is amenable to automatic search algorithms. In continuous classification, fingerprints are associated with numerical vectors summarizing their main features. These feature vectors are created through a similarity-preserving transformation, so that similar fingerprints are mapped into close points (vectors) in the multidimensional space. The retrieval is performed by matching the input fingerprint with those in the database whose corresponding vectors are close to the searched one. Spatial data structures can be used for indexing very large databases. A continuous classification approach allows the problem of exclusive membership of ambiguous fingerprints to be avoided and the system's efficiency and accuracy to be balanced by adjusting the size of the neighborhood considered. Most of the continuous classification techniques proposed in the literature use the orientation image as an initial feature but differ in the transformation adopted to create the final vectors, and in the distance measure.

Some other continuous indexing methods are based on fingerprint minutiae features using techniques such as geometric hashing. Continuous indexing algorithms can also be built using other non-minutiae-based fingerprint features such as texture features.

FIGURE 6–13

The six commonly used fingerprint classes: (a) whorl, (b) right loop, (c) arch, (d) tented arch, (e) left loop, and (f) double loop whorl.

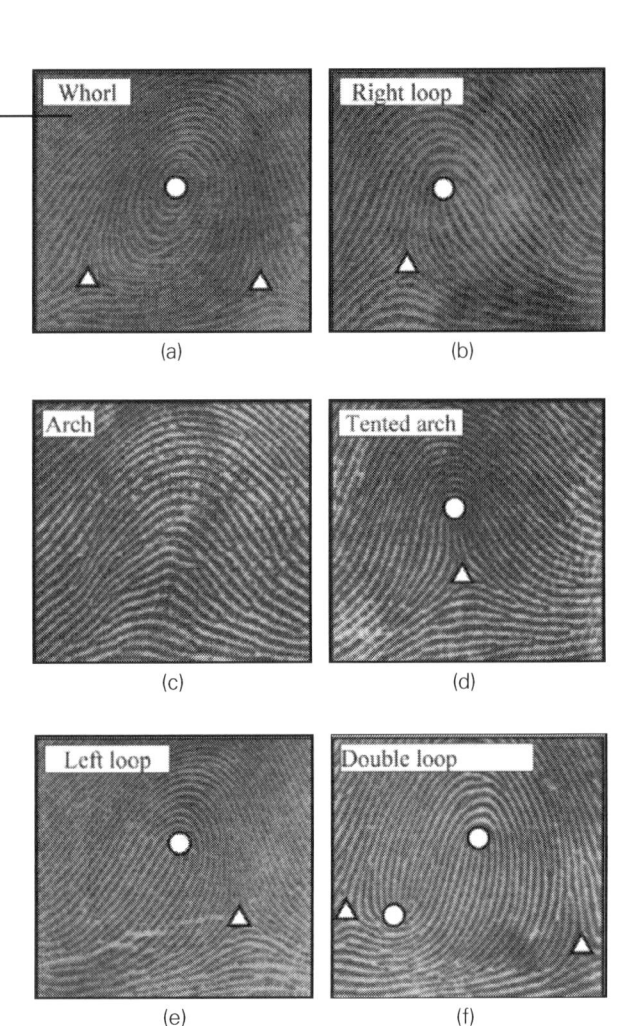

Choosing an indexing technique alone is usually not sufficient; a retrieval strategy is also usually defined according to the application requirements, such as the desired accuracy and efficiency, the matching algorithm used to compare fingerprints, the involvement of a human reviewer, and so on. In general, different strategies may be defined for the same indexing mechanism. For instance, the search may be stopped when a fixed portion of the database has been explored or as soon as a matching fingerprint is found. (In latent fingerprint individualization, a forensic expert visually examines the fingerprints that are considered sufficiently similar by the minutiae matcher and terminates the search when a true correspondence is found.) If an exclusive classification technique is used for indexing, the following retrieval strategies can be used:

- Hypothesized class only—Only fingerprints belonging to the class to which the input fingerprint has been assigned are retrieved.

- Fixed search order—The search continues until a match is found or the whole database has been explored. If a correspondence is not found within the hypothesized class, the search continues in another class, and so on.

- Variable search order—The different classes are visited according to the class likelihoods produced by the classifier for the input fingerprint. The search may be stopped as soon as a match is found or when the likelihood ratio between the current class and the next to be visited is less than a fixed threshold.

Finally, many system-level design choices may also be used to make the retrieval fast. For example, the search can be spread across many computers, and special-purpose hardware accelerators may be used to conduct fast fingerprint matching against a large database.

6.4.7 Accuracy Characterization

Although manual fingerprint matching is a very tedious task, a well-trained forensic expert is not likely to make individualization mistakes, especially when the fingerprint image quality is reasonable. Automatic fingerprint algorithms, on the other hand, are not nearly as accurate as forensic experts and have difficulty in dealing with the many noise sources in fingerprint images. Accuracy of fingerprint algorithms is crucial in designing fingerprint systems for real-world usage. The matching result must be reliable because many real-world decisions will be based on it. Algorithm designers usually acquire or collect their own fingerprint database and test the accuracy of their fingerprint algorithms on this database. By testing new algorithms, or changes in the old algorithm, or changes in algorithm parameters on the same database, they can know whether the new algorithm or changes improve the accuracy of the algorithm. Further, the algorithms' developers look closely at the false-positive and false-nonmatch errors made by their algorithms and get a better understanding of the strengths and limitations of their algorithms. By comparing the errors made by different algorithms or changes, the algorithm designers try to understand whether a change improves false positives, false nonmatches, both, or neither, and why. The algorithms' designers can then come up with algorithmic techniques to address the remaining errors and improve their algorithms' accuracy. It is desirable to have as large a database of fingerprints as possible from as large a demography as possible so that the algorithms are not overly adjusted to any certain variety of fingerprints and the accuracy obtained in the laboratory generalizes well in the field. Public organizations (e.g., NIST) perform periodic testing of fingerprint algorithms from different vendors on a common database to judge their relative accuracy.

There is a trade-off between the false positives and false-nonmatch error rates in fingerprint matching. Either of these two errors can be lowered at the expense of increasing the other error. Different applications have different requirements for these two types of errors. Interestingly, different fingerprint algorithms may perform differently, depending on the error rates. For example, algorithm A may be better than algorithm B at a low false-positive rate, but algorithm B may be better than algorithm A at a low false-nonmatch rate. In such cases, the algorithm designers may choose a certain algorithm or specific parameters to be used, depending on the application.

6.5 Summary

Fingerprint technology has come a long way since its inception more than 100 years ago. The first primitive live-scan fingerprint readers introduced in 1988 were unwieldy beasts with many problems as compared to the sleek, inexpensive, and relatively miniscule sensors available today. During the past few decades, research and active use of fingerprint matching and indexing have also advanced our understanding of individuality, information in fingerprints, and efficient ways of processing this information. Increasingly inexpensive computing power, less expensive fingerprint sensors, and the demand for security, efficiency, and convenience have led to the viability of automatic fingerprint algorithms for everyday use in a large number of applications.

There are a number of challenges that remain to be overcome in designing a completely automatic and reliable fingerprint individualization system, especially when fingerprint images are of poor quality. Although automatic systems have improved significantly, the design of automated systems do not yet match the complex decision-making of a well-trained fingerprint expert as decisions are made to match individual fingerprints (especially latent prints). Still, automatic fingerprint matching systems hold real promise for the development of reliable, rapid, consistent, and cost-effective solutions in a number of traditional and newly emerging applications.

Research in automatic fingerprint recognition has been mostly an exercise in imitating the performance of a human fingerprint expert without access to the many underlying information-rich features an expert is able to glean by visual examination. The lack of such a rich set of informative features in automatic systems is mostly because of the unavailability of complex modeling and image-processing techniques that can reliably and consistently extract detailed features in the presence of noise. Perhaps using the human, intuition-based manual fingerprint recognition approach may not be the most appropriate basis for the design of automatic fingerprint recognition systems. There may be a need for exploring radically different features rich in discriminatory information, robust methods of fingerprint matching, and more ingenious methods for combining fingerprint matching and classification that are amenable to automation.

6.6 Reviewers

The reviewers critiquing this chapter were Patti Blume, Christophe Champod, Wayne Eaton, Robert J. Garrett, Laura A. Hutchins, Peter D. Komarinski, and Kasey Wertheim.

6.7 References

AFIS Committee Report. International Association for Identification: Mendota Heights, MN, 1994.

AFIS Committee Report. *J. Forensic Ident.* 1998, *48* (4), 489–500.

American National Standards for Information Systems—Data Format for the Interchange of Fingerprint Information; ANSI/NIST-CSL 1-1993; National Institute of Standards and Technology, U.S. Government Printing Office: Washington, DC, 1993.

American National Standard for Information Systems—Data Format for the Interchange of Fingerprint, Facial & SMT (Scar, Mark, and Tattoo) Information; ANSI/NIST-ITL 1a-1997; National Institute of Standards and Technology, U.S. Government Printing Office: Washington, DC, 1997.

American National Standard for Information Systems—Data Format for the Interchange of Fingerprint, Facial, & & Scar Mark & Tattoo (SMT); ANSI/NIST-ITL 1-2000, NIST Special Publication #500-245; National Institute of Standards and Technology, U.S. Government Printing Office: Washington, DC, 2000.

American National Standards for Information Systems—Data Format for the Interchange of Fingerprint, Facial, & Other Biometric Information—Part 1 (Traditional Format); ANSI/NIST-ITL 1-2007, NIST Special Publication #500-271; National Institute of Standards and Technology, U.S. Government Printing Office: Washington, DC, 2007. Available online at http://www.nist.gov/customcf/get_pdf.cfm?pub_id=51174.

American National Standards for Information Systems—Data Format for the Interchange of Fingerprint, Facial, & Other Biometric Information—Part 2 (XML Version); ANSI/NIST-ITL 2-2008, NIST Special Publication #500-275; National Institute of Standards and Technology, U.S. Government Printing Office: Washington, DC, 2008. Available online at http://www.nist.gov/customcf/get_pdf.cfm?pub_id=890062.

Bruton, T. *Annual Report of the Crime Scene Investigations Unit;* San Francisco Police Department: San Francisco, CA, 1989.

Cole, S. *Suspect Identities;* Harvard University Press: Cambridge, MA, 2001.

FBI Request for Quotation No. 66-1, December 16, 1966.

Greenwood, P. W.; Chaiken, J. M.; Petersilia, J. *The Criminal Investigative Process* (Vols. 1–3); Technical Report R-1777-DOJ; RAND Corporation: Santa Monica, CA, 1975.

Grother, P.; McCabe, M.; et al. *MINEX: Performance and Interoperability of INCITS 378 Fingerprint Template;* NISTIR 7296; National Institute of Standards and Technology, March 21, 2006.

Hicklin, A.; Khanna, R. *The Role of Data Quality in Biometric Systems;* Mitretek Systems: Falls Church, VA, 2006.

Higgins, P. Standards for the Electronic Submission of Fingerprint Cards to the FBI. *J. Forensic Ident.* 1995, *45* (4), 409–418.

International Association for Identification. *AFIS Directory of Users;* IAI: Mendota Heights, MN, 1999.

Kiji, K. *AFIS 30-Year History;* NEC Internal Corporate Report; NEC Solutions: Tokyo, Japan, 2002.

Komarinski, P. *Automated Fingerprint Identification Systems;* Elsevier: New York, 2005.

Moore, R. T. Automatic Fingerprint Identification Systems. In *Advances in Fingerprint Technology*, 1st ed.; Lee, H. C.; Gaensslen, R. E., Eds.; Elsevier, NY, 1991; pp 163–191.

Moses, K. R. Consumer's Guide to Fingerprint Systems. *Ident. News* 1986, *36* (6), 5–7, 10.

National Institute for Standards and Technology. *MINEX: Performance and Interoperability of INCITS 378 Fingerprint Template (NISTIR 7296);* March 6, 2005.

Petersilia, J. *The Collection and Processing of Physical Evidence;* WN-9062-DOJ; RAND Corporation: Santa Monica, CA, 1975.

Wayman, J. *Biometric Systems.* Springer: New York, 2004.

Wegstein, J. H. *A Computer Oriented Single-Fingerprint Identification System;* Technical Note 443; National Bureau of Standards, U.S. Department of Commerce: Washington, DC, 1969a.

Wegstein, J. H. *A Semi-Automated Single Fingerprint Identification System;* Technical Note 481; National Bureau of Standards, U.S. Department of Commerce: Washington, DC, 1969b.

Wegstein, J. H. *Automated Fingerprint Identification;* Technical Note 538; National Bureau of Standards, U.S. Department of Commerce: Washington, DC, 1970.

Wegstein, J. H. *The M40 Fingerprint Matcher;* Technical Note 878; National Bureau of Standards, U.S. Department of Commerce: Washington, DC, 1972a.

Wegstein, J. H. *Manual and Automated Fingerprint Registration;* NBS Technical Note 730; National Bureau of Standards, U.S. Department of Commerce: Washington, DC, 1972b.

Wegstein, J. H. *An Automated Fingerprint Identification System;* NBS Special Publication 500-89; National Bureau of Standards, U.S. Department of Commerce: Washington, DC, 1982.

Wegstein, J. H.; Rafferty, J. F. *The LX39 Latent Fingerprint Matcher;* Special Publication 500-36; National Bureau of Standards, U.S. Department of Commerce: Washington, DC, 1978.

Wegstein, J. H.; Rafferty, J. F. The Automated Identification of Fingerprints. In *Dermatoglyphics—Fifty Years Later;* March of Dimes: Washington, DC, 1979.

Wegstein, J. H.; Rafferty, J. F.; Pencak, W. J. *Matching Fingerprints by Computer;* Technical Note 466; National Bureau of Standards, U.S. Department of Commerce: Washington, DC, 1968.

6.8 Additional Information

Asai, K.; Kato, Y.; Hoshino, Y.; Kiji, K. Automatic Fingerprint Identification; In *Proceedings of the SPIE, vol. 182—Imaging Applications for Automated Industrial Inspection and Assembly,* 1979; pp 49–56.

Lee, H. C.; Gaensslen, R.E., Eds. *Advances in Fingerprint Technology;* 2nd ed.; CRC Press: Washington, D.C., 2001.

Millard, K. An Approach to the Automatic Retrieval of Latent Fingerprints; In *Proceedings of Carnahan Conference on Electronic Crime Countermeasures,* Lexington, KY, 1975; pp 45–51.

Millard, K. Development on Automatic Fingerprint Recognition; In *Proceedings of the Carnahan Conference on Security Technology,* Zurich, Switzerland, 1983; pp 173–178.

Prabhakar, S.; Jain, A.; Maltoni, D.; Maio, D. *Handbook of Fingerprint Recognition;* Springer-Verlag: New York, 2003.

Ratha, N.; Bolle, R., Eds. *Automated Fingerprint Recognition Systems;* Springer-Verlag: New York, 2004.

Roberts, D. F. Dermatoglyphics and Human Genetics. In *Dermatoglyphics—Fifty Years Later;* Birth Defects Original Article Series; Wertelecki, W., Plato, C., Paul, N. W., Eds.; Alan R. Liss Inc.: New York, 1979; pp 475–494.

Thiebault, R. Automatic Process for Automated Fingerprint Identification; In *Proceedings of the International Symposium on Automation of Population Register Systems,* 1967; pp 207–226.

Thiebault, R. An Automatic Procedure for Identifying Fingerprints. *International Criminal Police Rev.* 1970, *25,* 2–10.

Uchida, K. Fingerprint Identification. *NEC J. Advanced Technology* 2005, *2* (1), 19–27.

Wayman, J.; Jain, A.; Maltoni, D.; Maio, D., Eds. *Biometric Systems,* Springer-Verlag: New York, 2005.

CHAPTER 7

LATENT PRINT DEVELOPMENT

BRIAN YAMASHITA AND
MIKE FRENCH

CONTRIBUTING AUTHORS
STEPHEN BLEAY, ANTONIO CANTU,
VICI INLOW, ROBERT RAMOTOWSKI,
VAUGHN SEARS, AND MELISSA WAKEFIELD

CONTENTS

3	7.1 Introduction		28	7.10 Fluorescence Examination
6	7.2 The Composition of Latent Print Residue		34	7.11 Vacuum Metal Deposition
11	7.3 Latent Print Powders		37	7.12 Blood Enhancement Techniques
14	7.4 Ninhydrin and Analogues		42	7.13 Aqueous Techniques
18	7.5 1,8-Diazafluoren-9-one (DFO)		53	7.14 Formulations for Chemical Solutions
20	7.6 1,2-Indanedione		55	7.15 Reviewers
22	7.7 5-Methylthioninhydrin (5-MTN)		55	7.16 References
22	7.8 Modifications for Use on Chemically Treated Papers		66	7.17 Additional Information
23	7.9 Cyanoacrylate Fuming			

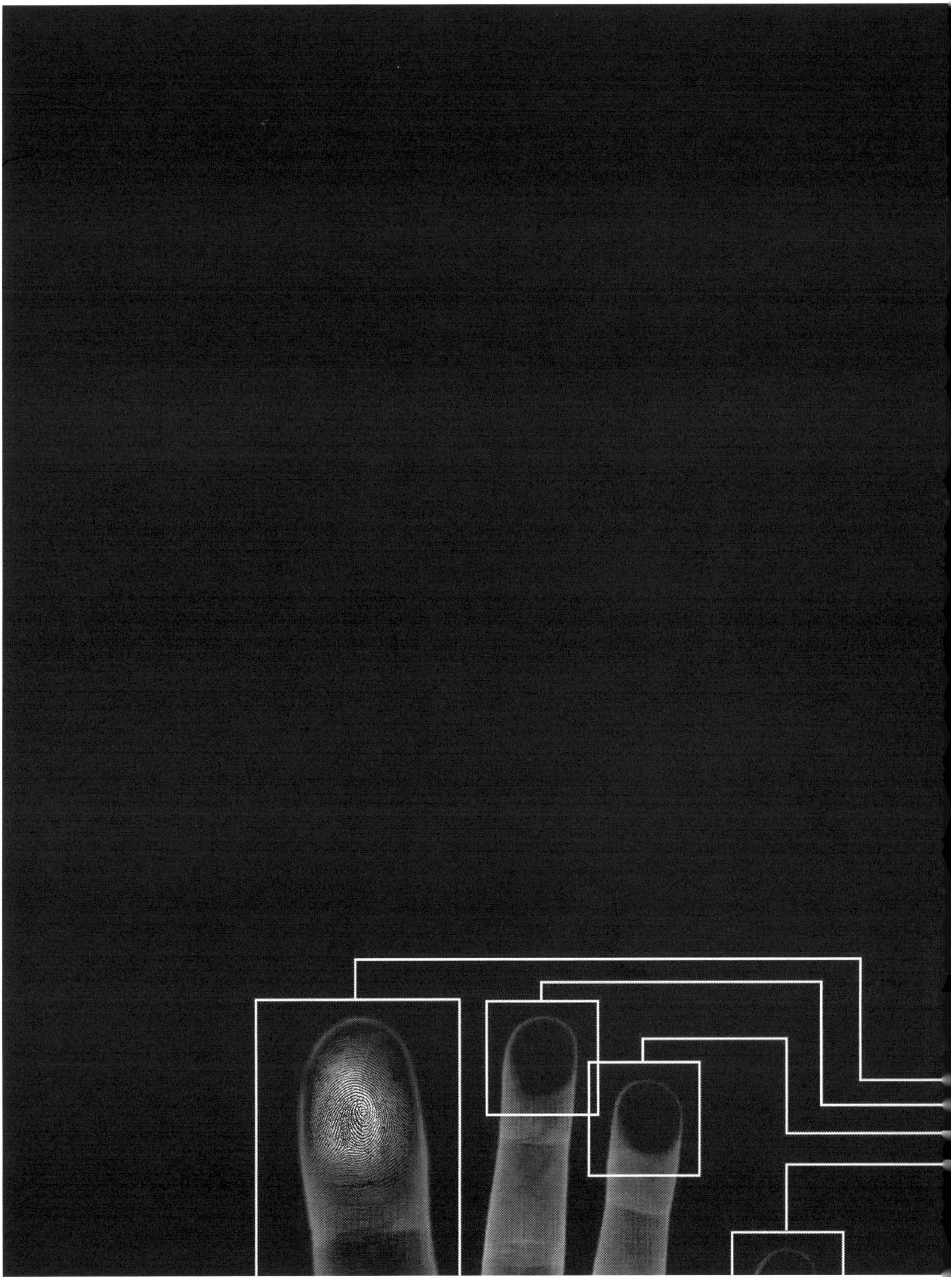

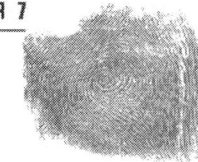

LATENT PRINT DEVELOPMENT

BRIAN YAMASHITA AND MIKE FRENCH

CONTRIBUTING AUTHORS
STEPHEN BLEAY,
ANTONIO CANTU, VICI INLOW,
ROBERT RAMOTOWSKI,
VAUGHN SEARS, AND
MELISSA WAKEFIELD

7.1 Introduction

Latent fingerprint development may be achieved with a wide array of optical, physical, and chemical processes, most having evolved during the past century. Because some techniques are often intricately related and continuously changing, it is imperative that those involved in laboratory and crime scene processing are well trained and well practiced (Trozzi et al., 2000, pp 4–9; Kent, 1998).

For those involved in crime scene and laboratory work, safety is paramount. It is important to follow safe work practices when using the processes described in this chapter. This can be accomplished by observing manufacturer warnings, reading material safety data sheets, and observing one's own institutional policies regarding evidence handling and fingerprint development. It is also important for those working with potentially hazardous materials or equipment to wear the appropriate personal protective equipment, such as gloves, lab coats, eye protection, and respirators; to use engineering controls such as fume hoods; and to practice proper laboratory procedures to reduce exposure to pathogens or harmful chemicals. (Masters, 2002).

7.1.1 Types of Prints

Fingerprints found at crime scenes or developed in the laboratory are categorized by some examiners as patent, latent, or plastic impressions (Lee and Gaennslen, 2001, p 106), although all three types are routinely associated with the term *latent print*.

A patent print is simply a visible print. Many of these types of prints are wholly visible to the unaided eye, and only some form of imaging is needed for preservation. A good example of a patent print would be a greasy impression left on a windowpane. Patent prints can also be left in blood, paint, ink, mud, or dust. Lighting is a very important consideration in the search for this type of fingerprint; a good flashlight or forensic light source is especially useful in the hunt for patent impressions.

The word *latent* means hidden or unseen. Latent prints are undetectable until brought out with a physical or chemical process designed to enhance latent print residue. Many of these processes and techniques are discussed in the remainder of this chapter.

A plastic print is created when the substrate is pliable enough at the time of contact to record the three-dimensional aspects of the friction skin. These impressions are formed when the raised friction ridges are physically pushed into the substrate, creating a mold of the friction skin ridge structure. Clay, putty, soft wax, melted plastic, heavy grease, and tacky paint are all substrates conducive to forming and retaining plastic impressions. Plastic impressions are usually photographed under oblique lighting that enhances the contrast of the ridges and furrows. These prints may also be preserved with silicone-type casting materials.

7.1.2 Deposition Factors

Deposition factors that influence the quality, or even the presence, of latent prints include the conditions surrounding the contact between friction skin and those objects that are touched. These conditions are described as follows:

Pre-transfer conditions include the condition or health of the donor's friction skin and the amount and type of residue on the skin (Olsen, 1978, pp 118–120). These conditions are affected by age, gender, stimuli, occupation, disease, and any substances the subject may have touched prior to deposition.

Transfer conditions also dictate whether a suitable impression will be left (Olsen, 1978, pp 117–122). These are the conditions of the surface (substrate) being touched, including texture, surface area, surface curvature or shape, surface temperature, condensation, contaminants, and surface residues. The pressure applied during contact (deposition pressure), including lateral force, also contributes to transfer conditions.

Post-transfer conditions, also called environmental factors, are forces that affect the quality of latent prints after deposition (Olsen, 1978, pp 121–122). Examples of these factors are physical contact from another surface, water, humidity, and temperature.

7.1.3 Surface Types

Correctly identifying the type of surface expected to bear a fingerprint is an important step toward successful development. Surfaces are generally separated into two classes: porous and nonporous. This separation is required to select the proper technique or reagent and the appropriate sequential order for processing.

Porous substrates are generally absorbent and include materials like paper, cardboard, wood, and other forms of cellulose. Fingerprints deposited onto these media absorb into the substrate and are somewhat durable. Amino acid techniques are particularly useful here because the amino acids tend to remain stationary when absorbed and do not migrate (Almog, 2001, p 178).

Nonporous surfaces do not absorb. These surfaces repel moisture and often appear polished. They include glass, metal, plastics, lacquered or painted wood, and rubber. Latent prints on these substrates are more susceptible to damage because the fingerprint residue resides on the outermost surface. Cyanoacrylate (CA), dye stains, powders, and vacuum metal deposition are usually the best choices to use on these surfaces.

A type of substrate that does not easily fit into the first two categories but should be mentioned is considered semiporous. Semiporous surfaces are characterized by their nature to both resist and absorb fingerprint residue. Fingerprint residue on these surfaces may or may not soak in because of the absorbent properties of the substrate and the variable viscous properties of the fingerprint residue. These surfaces include glossy cardboard, glossy magazine covers, some finished wood, and some cellophane. Semiporous surfaces should be treated with processes intended for both nonporous and porous surfaces.

Textured substrates can be porous or nonporous and present the problem of incomplete contact between the friction ridge skin and the surface being touched. (An example might be the pebbled plastic of some computer monitors.) This often results in fingerprints being discontinuous and lacking fine detail when developed. Additionally, these surfaces often do not respond well to a conventional brush and powder. The brushing action and tape lift typically develop the texture of the substrate, leaving fingerprints difficult or impossible to visualize.

Various techniques, such as the use of very fine powder or flexible lifting media, may be used to reduce the problems caused by textured surfaces (Guerrero, 1992; Kelly et al., 2001, pp 7–12; Knaap and Adach, 2002, pp 561–571).

7.1.4 Process Selection

Fingerprint reagents and development techniques are generally intended to be used in combination and sequential order. These methods are often specific to either porous or nonporous substrates; however, some techniques have universal applications. Deviation from the recommended order could render subsequent processes ineffective. Refer to Trozzi et al. (2000), Kent (1998), and Champod et al. (2004, pp 217–225) for examples of guidelines for sequential ordering, and to Champod et al. (2004, pp 105–179) for a recent review that includes many fingerprint development techniques. The following general procedures are appropriate during a systematic search for latent fingerprint evidence:

- Visual inspection with a bright light, forensic light source, or laser
- Sequential latent print processing
- Documentation of developed prints at each step

It is important to note that not all processes are used invariably. Some discretion will remain with individual agencies and practitioners both at the crime scene and in the laboratory. The following factors may influence the choice of development techniques as well as the level of resources used in any situation:

- Type of latent print residue suspected
- Type of substrate
- Texture of substrate
- Condition of substrate (clean, dirty, tacky, sticky, greasy, etc.)
- Environmental conditions during and following latent print deposition
- Length of time since evidence was touched
- Consequences of destructive processing methods
- Subsequent forensic examinations
- Sequential ordering of reagents
- Seriousness of the crime

7.1.5 Evidence Handling

Proper evidence handling begins with the use of latex, nitrile, PVC, or other suitable gloves. Some glove manufacturers or safety supply distributors will list gloves recommended for use with various chemicals. The use of gloves protects the evidence from contamination and the user from exposure to pathogens or hazardous chemicals. It does not, however, guarantee that latent prints will be preserved because even a gloved hand may destroy fragile latent prints on contact. This is especially true on nonporous surfaces where the latent print resides on the extreme surface of the evidence. To prevent damage to fingerprints on these surfaces, evidence should be handled in areas not normally touched or on surfaces incapable of yielding viable fingerprints. It should also be noted that the use of gloves does not preclude the transfer of friction ridge detail from the examiner to the exhibit (Willinski, 1980, pp 682–685; St-Amand, 1994, pp 11–13; Hall, 1991, pp 415–416).

7.1.6 Packaging

Packaging helps ensure the integrity of the evidence by keeping contaminants away, keeping trace evidence intact, and helping to guarantee chain of custody. Cardboard boxes, paper bags, and plastic bags are the most common forms of evidence packaging. Most experts recommend paper packaging because it is breathable and cost effective, although plastic bags are also widely used. Any items that have been wet should be allowed to air-dry prior to packaging because excess moisture trapped in any package will increase the probability of destructive fungal growth. Moisture can also be trapped in plastic bags when evidence is gathered in high-humidity environments.

Items of nonporous evidence should not be allowed to rub together. Nonporous evidence should be stored singly, secured inside an appropriately sized package in a manner that prevents shifting and rubbing. Under no circumstances should fillers such as shredded paper, wood shavings, or packing peanuts be used inside the package with the evidence because they may easily wipe off fragile fingerprints. (However, they can be used outside the evidence container, inside the mailing container.) Porous evidence can be secured in boxes, bags, and envelopes and can be stored together because latent prints are not likely to rub off on contact. Once evidence is secured, the package should be sealed with evidence tape so that there are no entry points. The tape should be signed by the person securing the evidence, and the appropriate identifying information should be placed on the package as specified by the agency responsible for collection.

The remainder of this chapter is intended to describe, in some detail, the nature of latent print residue and the most commonly used fingerprint development techniques. Experimental and novel techniques have not been included, nor have processes considered by the authors to be redundant, impractical, or overly hazardous. However, the omission of reference to a particular technique does not indicate its unsuitability as a fingerprint development technique. Several formulations for various chemical solutions have been collected in Section 7.14.

7.2 The Composition of Latent Print Residue

7.2.1 Introduction

The composition of sweat that is deposited when friction ridge skin makes contact with a surface is a complex mixture (Ramotowski, 2001, pp 63–104; Bramble and Brennan, 2000, pp 862–869). Recent studies have identified hundreds of compounds present in human sweat (Bernier et al., 1999, pp 1–7; Bernier et al., 2000, pp 746–756). A considerable number of studies into the nature of sweat have been performed by both the dermatology and forensic science communities. In particular, a number of studies have investigated how the chemical composition of these residues changes with time, which is a critical problem for the fingerprint examiner. Although knowledge of the composition of sweat produced in the various glands throughout the body is of interest and provides a baseline for comparison purposes, this information does not accurately represent what is actually going on in the deposited print at a crime scene. Studies have shown that significant changes begin to occur in the latent print almost immediately after deposition. If the latent print is to be successfully visualized, a thorough understanding of these changes is needed.

This section will begin with a very brief overview of skin anatomy, which will be necessary to gain a better understanding of how the chemical compounds in a latent print are secreted onto the surface of friction ridge skin. Next, there will be a detailed look at the chemical composition of the secretions from each of the glands responsible for contributing to latent print residue. Another section will cover how the composition of some of these secretions changes as the donor ages. Finally, recent studies that have investigated how latent print residue changes with time will be summarized.

7.2.2 Anatomy of Skin

This topic is covered in more detail elsewhere in this sourcebook, so the treatment here will be very brief. Readers are directed to Ramotowski (2001, pp 63–104) for more detail.

Skin is the largest organ in the human body (Odland, 1991). The total area of skin on the body exceeds 2 m^2; yet, on most parts of the body, the thickness is no more than 2 mm. Skin serves several functions, including regulation of body temperature, moisture retention, protection from invasive organisms (e.g., viruses, bacteria), and sensation. It is composed of two primary and distinct layers, the epidermis and dermis.

The epidermis is composed of several distinct layers (Ramotowski, 2001, pp 63–104; Odland, 1991). The layer situated just above the dermis is the stratum germinativum (basal cell layer), and the top layer is the stratum corneum (cornified layer). In this stratum, eleiden is converted to keratin, which is continually sloughed off the surface of the epidermis, resulting in a constant need to replenish the keratin that is lost. A cell beginning in the stratum germinativum typically travels through to the stratum corneum in about 28 days.

The dermis is composed of a variety of different connective tissues, including collagen, elastin fibers, and an interfibrillar gel composed of glycosamin–proteoglycans, salts, and water (Odland, 1991). This layer also contains the two major sudoriferous and sebaceous glands.

7.2.3 The Production of Sweat

Three primary glands contribute to the production of sweat. These are the sudoriferous glands (eccrine and apocrine) and the sebaceous glands. Each gland contributes a unique mixture of chemical compounds. These compounds either exude from pores onto the friction ridges or are transferred to the friction ridges through touching an area (e.g., the forehead, underarm, etc.).

The eccrine gland is one of two types of sudoriferous (or "sweat") glands present in the body. Several million of these glands are distributed throughout the body, most commonly on the palms of the hands and soles of the feet and least numerous on the neck and back (Anderson et al., 1998, p 1561). These glands produce a secretion that is mostly water but contains many compounds in trace quantities (Brusilow and Gordes, 1968, pp 513–517; Mitchell and Hamilton, 1949, p 360; Sato, 1979, pp 52–131; Bayford, 1976, pp 42–43; Olsen, 1972, p 4). The average quantity of secretions produced during a typical 24-hour period varies between 700 and 900 grams. The pH of sweat has been reported to vary from 7.2 (extracted directly from the gland), to 5.0 (recovered from the skin surface at a low sweat rate), to between 6.5 and 7.0 (recovered from the skin surface at a high sweat rate) (Kaiser and Drack, 1974, pp 261–265).

The eccrine gland also secretes organic compounds. Of primary importance to the development of latent print ridge detail are the amino acids. Table 7–1 summarizes the average values of abundance for the amino acids listed (Hadorn et al., 1967, pp 416–417; Hamilton, 1965, pp 284–285; Oro and Skewes, 1965, pp 1042–1045). Serine is the most abundant amino acid, and thus all other values are normalized to a value of 100 for that compound. Proteins are also found in eccrine sweat (Nakayashiki, 1990, pp 25–31; Uyttendaele et al., 1977, pp 261–266). One study found more than 400 different polypeptide components present (Marshall, 1984, pp 506–509).

Lipids have also been detected in eccrine sweat. There is some difficulty in accurately determining the amounts of these compounds present in eccrine secretions because sweat often mixes with sebaceous compounds on the skin surface. However, one study reported detectable amounts of both fatty acids and sterol compounds (Boysen et al., 1984, pp 1302–1307).

Other miscellaneous compounds, including drugs, have been found in eccrine secretions (Sato, 1979, pp 52–131; Lobitz and Mason, 1948, p 908; Förström et al., 1975, pp 156–157). One study reported the presence of sulfonamides, antipyrine, and aminopyrine (Johnson and Maibach, 1971, pp 182–188). Another reported that L-dimethylamphetamine and its metabolite L-methamphetamine had been detected (Vree et al., 1972, pp 311–317). Ethanol has also been detected in eccrine sweat (Naitoh et al., 2000, pp 2797–2801), which has led to the suggestion of using

Table 7–1

Relative abundance of amino acids in sweat.

Serine	100
Ornithine–Lysine	45
Alanine	30
Threonine	15
Valine	10
Glutamic acid	8
Phenylalanine	6
Tyrosine	5

sweat as a means of noninvasively determining a person's serum ethanol concentration (Hawthorne and Wojcik, 2006, pp 65–71). Acetaminophen has also been reported in a person's sweat a day after taking the medication (Mong et al., 1999).

The other sudoriferous gland present in skin is the apocrine gland. These sweat glands are associated with the coarse hair of the armpits and pubic area. They are larger than eccrine glands and secrete a thicker fluid (Anderson et al., 1998, p 1561). The gland's duct typically empties into a hair follicle (above where a sebaceous gland duct would be) before the secretions reach the skin's surface (Robertshaw, 1991). Because the contents of the apocrine gland often mix with sebaceous secretions prior to reaching the skin's surface, it is difficult to obtain uncontaminated "pure" apocrine secretions for analysis. One of the few published studies of apocrine secretions described them as milky in appearance and stated that they dried to a plasticlike solid, which fluoresced and had an odor (Shelley, 1951, p 255). Compounds reported to have been isolated from apocrine secretions include proteins, carbohydrates, cholesterol, iron (Knowles, 1978, pp 713–721), C_{19}-steroid sulfates, and Δ16-steroids (Toth and Faredin, 1985, pp 21–28; Labows et al., 1979, pp 249–258).

Sebaceous glands are relatively small saclike organs and can be found in the dermis layer of skin. They are found throughout the body and are associated with body hair. They are particularly abundant on the scalp, face, anus, nose, mouth, and external portions of the ear (Anderson et al., 1998, p 1464). They are not found on the palms of the hands or soles of the feet. The secretions from the sebaceous gland typically empty into a hair follicle before reaching the skin's surface, although in some regions they do reach the skin's surface directly (e.g., lips). The purpose of sebaceous secretions appears to be to help prevent sweat evaporation (and thus retain body heat) and to lubricate hair and surrounding skin.

The primary compounds present in sebaceous secretions are lipids. Table 7–2 lists the approximate percentage values for the various lipid classes present in sebaceous secretions, as reported by Goode and Morris (1983). Knowles (1978, pp 713–721) reported similar concentration ranges.

Table 7–2

The approximate percentage of lipids in sebaceous secretions.

Lipid	Percentage
Glycerides	33
Fatty acids	30
Wax esters	22
Cholesterol esters	2
Cholesterol	2
Squalene	10

Free fatty acids in sebum are derived primarily from the hydrolysis of triglycerides and wax esters. About half of the fatty acids are saturated, with straight chain C16 and C14 being the most common (Green, 1984, pp 114–117). Monounsaturated fatty acids comprise about 48% of sebum, and polyunsaturated acids comprise the remaining 2–3% (Nicolaides and Ansari, 1968, pp 79–81). Branched chain fatty acids have also been reported (Green, 1984, pp 114–117).

Wax esters comprise about 20–25% of sebum. These compounds contain a fatty acid that has been esterified with a fatty alcohol. A significant percentage of these compounds (≈27%) have been reported to contain branched chain fatty acids (Nicolaides et al., 1972, pp 506–517). Sterol esters are thought to be produced secondarily by certain strains of bacteria (Puhvel, 1975, pp 397–400). Squalene, which comprises about 10% of sebum, is a major precursor for steroid production in the body (including the steroid alcohols, lanosterol and cholesterol).

7.2.4 Variation in Sebum Composition with the Age of the Donor

The free fatty acid composition in sebum changes dramatically with age of the donor (Ramasastry et al., 1970, pp 139–144). The approximate percentage of fatty acids in newborns (approximately 5 days old) has been reported to be only about 1.5% of the overall sebum composition. This value rises dramatically to about 20–23% in young children (age 1 month to 4 years). The value then stabilizes to 16–19% for adolescent and postadolescent subjects (up to approximately 45 years of age).

Triglycerides also vary significantly. Newborns were found to have triglycerides making up approximately 52% of their sebum. This value decreased to 38% in infants (1 month to 2 years of age). Subsequently, the value peaked at 50% in young children (ages 2–4 years) and then slowly decreased to 41% in postadolescent subjects.

In newborns, 26.7% of sebum was composed of wax esters. This value began to decrease in infants (17.6%) and continued until reaching a low of 6.9% in subjects between the ages of 4 and 8 years. The values then began to increase in preadolescents (17.8%) and continued to rise until reaching a maximum of 25% in postadolescents (up to 45 years of age).

The value of cholesterol in sebum tended to peak in preadolescents (7.2%). Newborns were reported to have 2.5% cholesterol in their sebum, whereas postadolescents had the lowest values, 1.4%. Cholesterol ester composition tended to vary in an unpredictable way. A value of 6.1% was reported for newborns, which increased to 10.3% for infants (1 month to 2 years of age). This value then decreased to 8.9% for young children (ages 2–4 years) and then increased to 14.6% in subjects of ages 4–8 years. This value then decreased dramatically to 5.7% in preadolescent children and continued to decline to 2.1% in postadolescent subjects (up to 45 years of age).

Although squalene composition changes with donor age, the range is not very significant. The concentration of squalene begins at 9.9% for newborns and reaches a low of 6.2% in children of ages 2–4 years. The concentration then slowly begins to rise in children 4–8 years in age (7.7%) and peaks at a value of 12% in postadolescents.

7.2.5 Latent Print Residue

A latent print is a mixture of some or all of the secretions from the three types of glands. The amount of material contained in a latent print deposit is rather small, typically less than 10 µg, and has an average thickness of about 0.1 µm (Scruton et al., 1975, pp 714–723). The latent print secretion is a complex emulsification of these numerous and varying compounds. When deposited on a surface, nearly 99% of the print is composed of water. As this water begins to evaporate rapidly from the deposit, the print begins to dry out. This process begins to alter certain reagents' ability to visualize the print. Fingerprint powder, for example, will not work as well on a dried-out latent print, but other processes, like ninhydrin and physical developer, have developed prints several years old (McDiarmid, 1992, pp 21–24).

Latent print residue is generally divided into two basic categories, water-soluble and water-insoluble. The water-soluble portion of the print deposit is typically composed of eccrine secretions like salts (e.g., NaCl) and amino acids (e.g., serine, glycine). Chemicals like ninhydrin (which reacts with amino acids) and silver nitrate (which reacts with sodium chloride) are effective reagents for visualizing this water-soluble portion of the residue. However, an eccrine-rich latent print that is exposed to water most likely will not be recovered with these methods. This is why, before the introduction of physical developer in the 1970s, there was no reliable method for recovering prints from water-soaked documents.

The water-insoluble portion can really be divided into two subcategories. One fraction of this residue is composed of large, water-insoluble molecules (e.g., proteins) and the other fraction is composed mainly of nonpolar lipids (e.g., fatty acids). Reagents like physical developer are thought to react with compounds similar to the first fraction, and reagents like Oil Red O or Nile Red react with lipids from the second fraction.

7.2.6 Aging of Latent Print Residue

A number of laboratories have looked into studying the changes in the composition of latent print residue and have determined that the composition of latent print residue can change dramatically over time. The foundation work in this area was conducted during the 1960s and 1970s by the U.K. Home Office Scientific Research and Development Branch and Central Research Establishment (Bowman et al., 2003, pp 2–3). Additional studies have been conducted by some of the Home Office Forensic Science Service laboratories and several Department of Energy National Laboratories.

7.2.7 Home Office Scientific Development Branch (U.K.)

The U.K. Home Office sponsored a number of research efforts, which were carried out by two groups: the Scientific Research and Development Branch (also known as the Police Scientific Development Branch [PSDB] and currently known as the Scientific Development Branch) and the Central Research Establishment. A number of studies conducted in the mid- to late 1960s looked at determining the amount of certain inorganic compounds (chlorides) (Cuthbertson, 1969) as well as lipids (Wilson and Darke, 1978) in latent print residue. These studies did not address the changes in composition with time. However, one study monitored the change in chlorides, amino acids (as leucine), and urea concentration in a deposit over the course of 236 days (Knowles, 1978, pp 713–721). After 236 days, the chloride concentration had changed from 0.223 µg/cm^2 to 0.217 µg/cm^2. The amino acid content had changed from 0.083 µg/cm^2 to 0.046 µg/cm^2, and the urea content from 0.083 µg/cm^2 to 0.028 µg/cm^2.

The PSDB recently sponsored some work in this area (Fitzgerald, 2003). A project was started in February 2002 between the University of Lincoln and PSDB to look into the gas chromatography–mass spectroscopy (GC–MS) analysis of the composition of latent print residue and how it changes over time.

7.2.8 Home Office Forensic Science Service (U.K.)

The U.K. Home Office Forensic Science Service (FSS) has also been active in the area of latent print chemistry. The FSS conducted an early preliminary study in conjunction with the University of Lausanne in 1999 (Jacquat, 1999). This study compared the aging of prints exposed to light and darkness over the period of 1 month. The six most abundant peaks found in the residue were oleic acid, palmitic acid, cholesterol, squalene, and two wax esters. Data were collected from four donors at the time of deposition (t = 0), after 2 weeks, and finally after 4 weeks. Palmitic acid in a print kept in the dark and squalene in a print kept in the light showed a significant decrease over the first 2 weeks and then stabilized. Cholesterol and oleic acid showed a regular decrease in prints stored in the dark. No other observable trends were detected for the other compounds.

A recent study funded by the Technical Support Working Group (TSWG), an interagency working group that funds projects related to counter-terrorism, looked at the changes in lipid content of a print over time and under different environmental conditions (Jones et al., 2001a). The FSS study used methyl-N-trimethylsilyltrifluoroacetamide as a derivitizing agent. Samples were analyzed at selected intervals and stored in either light or dark conditions at 25 °C and 20% relative humidity. Several general trends were observed. Squalene was found to degrade rather quickly and was rarely detected in older prints. In some cases, certain fatty acid concentrations initially increased before tending to decrease over time. This may have been due to the breakdown of wax esters, which may have contributed fatty acids to the residue before the compounds began to break down. Similar trends were observed for samples stored in the dark; however, the decreases were less rapid than for samples stored in the light. The FSS is currently continuing to investigate this topic with a research grant issued by the U.K. Engineering and Physical Sciences Research Council.

Another effort conducted by the FSS involved the use of microfluidic systems for the chemical analysis of latent print residues (Valussi, 2003). The objective of this work was to develop a microfluidic device, based on capillary electrophoresis (CE), that would enable sampling, preconcentration, and analysis of latent print residues. The proposed micro-TAS (total analytical system) used microchip technology to allow for ultrafast and highly efficient separations. The analysis involved placing a print directly onto a gel-coated CE chip. An applied voltage caused polar components of the residue to migrate into the chip. After preconcentration, the residue was separated and then analyzed. The project demonstrated that the CE chip method is capable of separating certain components of latent print residue; however, additional refinements will be necessary to separate specific compounds (or groups of compounds) of interest.

7.2.9 Pacific Northwest National Laboratory

The Pacific Northwest National Laboratory (PNNL) performed a series of aging experiments for latent prints deposited on glass fiber filter paper (Mong et al., 1999). This TSWG-funded R&D effort was done during the late 1990s. The results obtained from the aging experiments were generally as expected. Most of the unsaturated lipids (e.g., squalene and fatty acids such as oleic and palmitoleic acids) diminished significantly during the 30-day study period. The saturated compounds (e.g., palmitic and stearic acids) remained essentially stable during the same 30-day period. Overall, as the sample print aged, there was a tendency to form more lower molecular weight breakdown products (e.g., octanoic and nonanoic acids) over time. It was hypothesized that these low molecular weight compounds would either break down further or evaporate.

7.2.10 Savannah River Technical Center

The Savannah River Technical Center (SRTC), in a project jointly funded by the Department of Energy and TSWG, also studied how latent print residue changes with time (Walter, 1999). This study focused on what changes occur as lipids in the print begin to age. The ultimate goal was to determine whether any of the breakdown products would be suitable for visualization by chemical reagents. A limited number of conditions (e.g., UV exposure, indoor and outdoor conditions, addition of a catalyst) were also evaluated as part of this study.

The primary breakdown products for the lipids studied by SRTC were found to be a class of compounds known as hydroperoxides. The standard mixture used in this experiment involved a combination of cholesterol, triglycerides, fatty acids, wax esters, cholesterol esters, and a catalyst, protoporphyrin IX dimethyl ester (approximately 0.01% of the overall mixture). This mixture was then exposed to the various environmental conditions. As with the PNNL study, the SRTC found that unsaturated compounds were rapidly depleted from the samples, even ones stored in relatively cool, dark conditions. One experiment that looked at the aging of squalene on a glass slide found that after 1 month of exposure to ambient laboratory conditions, 10% of the sample had been converted to hydroperoxides. The SRTC was going to pursue chemiluminescent methods for visualizing these hydroperoxides. However, because hydroperoxides themselves are somewhat unstable, it is not known how long these compounds remain in aged print residues and whether additional compounds found in actual prints would speed up their breakdown.

7.2.11 Conclusion

The chemistry of latent print residue is very complex, yet its physical characteristics and properties are due to more than just the hundreds (or potentially thousands) of chemical compounds that comprise the residue. These compounds form a complex three-dimensional matrix, an emulsion of water and organic and inorganic compounds. The interaction of all of these different compounds as they are exposed to a variety of environmental conditions over a period of time can produce dramatic changes in the physical properties of the latent print. These changes can explain why some reagents, like powders, and iodine fuming, tend to work on relatively fresh prints, whereas a reagent like physical developer has been known to develop decades-old prints.

It is only by obtaining a better understanding of the chemical composition of latent print residue and how it changes with time that we can make improvements to existing reagents and design novel compounds for specialized conditions or surfaces. Such data will also assist in better understanding how latent print development reagents actually work (as well as what they actually react with in the residue). Only then can we develop a methodical approach for reagent design that will yield useful new techniques in the future for visualizing latent print residues.

7.3 Latent Print Powders

7.3.1 Background

Latent print visualization with powder, or "dusting", involves the application of finely divided particles that physically adhere to the aqueous and oily components in latent print residue on nonporous surfaces (Sodhi and Kaur, 2001, pp 172–176). This technique is one of the oldest and most common methods of latent print detection, with one of the earliest references dating back to 1891 (Forgeot, 1891, pp 387–404). Early practitioners used a variety of locally available ingredients to make their own dusting powders, including charcoal, lead powder, cigar ashes (Moenssens, 1971, pp 106–107), powdered "washing blue", powdered iron, soot (Lightning Powder Inc., 2002, pp 2–3), and talc (Olsen, 1978, pp 212–214).

7.3.2 Theory

Fingerprint dusting is relatively simple and relies on the adherence of powder to the latent print residue to provide good visibility and definition of fingerprint detail. Latent print powder has an affinity for moisture and preferentially clings to the residue deposited by friction ridge skin. It is well accepted that the mechanical attraction between these particles and the moisture and oily components in a print causes adhesion, with absorption being a factor (Olsen, 1978, pp 212–214; Lee and Gaensslen, 2001, pp 108–109). Particle size, shape, relative surface area (Olsen, 1978, pp 212–214), and charge (Menzel, 1999, p 143) appear to play roles as well.

Most commercial powders rely on at least two essential elements to provide adhesion to latent print residue without "painting" the substrate. These elements are referred to as pigment and binder. The pigment in fingerprint powder provides for effective visualization, offering contrast and definition against the background surface. The binder (also referred to as the carrier in some applications) provides for maximum and preferential adhesion to latent print residue (Menzel, 1999, p 143). Some pigment powders offer enough adhesion to be used individually. Background painting occurs when an undesirable amount of powder adheres to the substrate as well as the latent print, hindering detection.

Visualization will occur via reflected light (light powders), absorbed light (dark powders), and luminescence (fluorescent powders). Sometimes powders are combined for effectiveness on both light and dark substrates. This is the case with bichromatic powder, which uses highly reflective aluminum powder mixed with black powder to achieve visualization on both light and dark surfaces. A disadvantage of mixing different types of pigment particles is that extremely faint impressions, with few particles adhering to the print, may suffer from having only a fraction of the necessary pigment needed for visualization. This problem can be overcome by tagging a single type of pigment particle with a fluorescent dye stain, thus creating a particle with dual uses rather than combining different types of particles.

Commercial powder manufacturers tend to label powders by color, such as black, white, silver, gray, and so forth, rather than labeling the ingredients. Particles that serve as good fingerprint powders include carbon black (colloidal carbon), lamp black, talc, kaolin, aluminum, metal flake, and dolomite (Lee and Gaensslen, 2001, pp 108–109), among others. Good binders include iron powder (Lee and Gaennslen, 2001, pp 108–109), lycopodium, corn starch, rosin, and gum arabic (Menzel, 1999, p 143).

One of the most common latent print powders, known for its versatility and effectiveness, is carbon black. When mixed with a carrier, this powder works on a wide range of surfaces and causes little substrate painting (Cowger, 1983, pp 79–80). Carbon black mixtures produce a dark gray-black image that can be visualized on varying colored surfaces. This type of powder will also show up on glossy black surfaces, conversely appearing light in color (Cowger, 1983, pp 79–80). Interestingly, black fingerprint powder can also be prepared or "tagged" with a fluorescent dye stain (Thornton, 1978, pp 536–538), giving it the dual purpose as a photoluminescent technique as well.

Other effective and widely used latent print powders are flake metal powders made from aluminum, zinc, copper, brass, stainless steel, iron, cobalt, and nickel. Some data indicate that flake powders are more sensitive than nonflake powders (Kent, 1998). However, flake powders also sometimes tend to "paint" the substrate more than nonflake particles do.

Flake powders are manufactured by ball-milling spherical metallic particles into flakes ranging from 1 to 50 µm in diameter (James et al., 1991, pp 1368–1375). The increased surface area of the flake relative to the weight of the particle contributes to this powder's adhesion. It appears that commercially available flake powder with a mean diameter of 10 µm and an average thickness of 0.5 µm is optimum for latent print development. It is also important to note that the addition of stearic acid, intended to influence flake morphology during milling, increases the adhesion value of the flakes as well (James et al., 1990, pp 247–252). Aluminum flake powder that was washed of its stearic acid content resulted in poor fingerprint development, whereas aluminum flakes produced with approximately 10 weight-percent of stearic acid produced good results (James et al., 1991, pp 1368–1375). Another study indicated that a range of flake metals produced optimum results with 3–5 weight-percent of stearic acid levels (James et al., 1993, pp 391–401).

7.3.3 Application

All manufacturer warnings, including those in material safety data sheets, should be heeded when using fingerprint powder. Although commercial suppliers of latent print powder have discontinued using known hazardous ingredients such as lead, mercury, and cadmium, it is strongly recommended that the practitioner wear a dust mask or work on a downdraft table as minimum precautions while using any powder.

Powders are typically applied to nonporous surfaces with a soft brush. Powdering is not recommended for porous or highly absorbent surfaces such as uncoated paper or raw wood because other chemical treatments outperform powder on these surfaces. The softness of the bristles is particularly important to prevent damage to fragile latent print residue. Latent prints with a high moisture or oil content are easily damaged by a brush that is too stiff or is used with excessive force. Conventional brushes are typically made with animal hair, fiberglass filaments, or sometimes feathers. Although fingerprint brushes are largely taken for granted these days, a study of brushes has been carried out (Bandey, 2004).

Powders applied with a traditional filament brush consist of very fine particles and are usually low density or "fluffy" in nature. This enables particles to be easily picked up or "loaded" onto the brush filaments. The low density of this powder also allows it to easily become airborne during the dusting process, making a dust mask or respirator necessary at the crime scene.

It is important to keep brushes clean, dry, and relatively free of tangles. To apply fingerprint powder with a conventional brush, the filament tips are lightly dipped into a sterile, wide-mouth container holding a small amount of powder. This is called "loading" the brush. Excess powder is then shaken, spun, or tapped from the brush. The powder is then applied evenly to all areas of the substrate.

An area of the surface (or a substrate similar in nature) should be tested before fully processing the item. This is done to establish the optimum amount of powder to be used on that substrate and to avoid background painting. Brushing is accomplished with light and even strokes that resemble painting. It is important always to begin by lightly powdering and slowly building to heavier applications to minimize fingerprint damage.

When latent prints appear, they can be lightly brushed by adding powder and subsequently brushing excess powder away. This is done in the direction of the ridge flow to prevent damage to the impression.

Another type of powder, called magnetic or magna powder, allows for application with a magnetized rod that has no bristles. This type of powder can be light, dark, or fluorescent and utilizes the ferromagnetic properties of iron powder mixed with pigment powders. The magnetized applicator (magna brush) is dipped into the powder, picking up a ball of the iron and particle mixture, essentially forming its own brush (Figure 7–1). This ball serves as an effective carrier for pigment particles and is passed back and forth over the substrate to develop latent impressions.

It is important to note that the magnetic powder ball formed with a magna brush is much softer than conventional filament brushes and typically causes less damage to fragile latent prints (MacDonell, 1961, pp 7–15). Magnetic powders are usually less effective on ferromagnetic substrates such as steel or nickel and are therefore not recommended on those substrates. The magnetic attraction may cause contact between the applicator and substrate, damaging latent prints in the process. In addition, magnetized particles from the powder will cling to the substrate and resist removal.

There are two ways to record or preserve a powdered impression. The most common and simplest method is lifting. To lift a print, good-quality transparent tape is placed onto the surface bearing a powdered impression. Common tape size for fingerprint lifting is 1.5–2 in. wide. While it is being applied, the tape is rubbed to remove air bubbles and to ensure good adhesion to the latent prints. It is then removed and placed on a backing card that contrasts with the color of the powder. Probably the most common lift is of black fingerprint powder placed on a white backing card. Other adhesive lifting media are hinge lifters, where the adhesive square is attached to the backing card by a hinge; opaque adhesive gel lifters, typically black or white; and silicon-type materials that are spread onto the surface and allowed to harden to a flexible rubbery medium before lifting. Care must be taken during the comparison process to note which lifting techniques cause the print to appear reversed.

If the impression will be photographed in situ, the importance of powder color increases. Documenting powdered impressions this way requires combining proper selection of powder and photographic lighting that will produce ample contrast against the substrate.

Another type of powder that produces excellent results on a wide variety of surfaces is fluorescent powder. Fluorescent powder relies on the principle of luminescence to provide contrast between fingerprint and background. Fluorescent powders are typically created by adding a laser dye in solution to a binder and allowing the mixture to evaporate (Menzel, 1999, pp 62–65). The resulting dried mass is then ground into latent print powder.

Fluorescent powdering is highly sensitive when used with a good forensic light source and the appropriate barrier filters. In theory, luminescent fingerprint powder should be more sensitive than conventional methods (Menzel, 1999,

FIGURE 7–1

Magnetic applicator.

pp 4–7). It is important to test tape and lift cards used with fluorescent powders for any inherent fluorescence because fluorescence caused by lifting media will interfere with the quality of the impression.

Another use of fingerprint powder, or the components of fingerprint powder, is in a suspension, for use on wet surfaces or on adhesive tapes. Conventional small-particle reagent, for developing fingerprints on wet, nonporous surfaces, uses molybdenum disulphide in suspension, but other reagents have been developed (Frank and Almog, 1993, pp 240–244). A similar suspension, Sticky-side powder (Burns, 1994, pp 133–138), used to develop prints on the adhesive side of tape, has also been reformulated using fingerprint powder (Bratton et al., 1996, p 28; Wade, 2002, pp 551–559).

Finally, a word of caution may be in order. Although using fingerprint powder is quick and inexpensive, concerns have been raised recently concerning the possibility of contamination due to the transfer of DNA through the use of fingerprint brushes (van Oorschot et al., 2005, pp 1417–1422). Crime scene examiners are being warned to be aware of this possibility.

7.4 Ninhydrin and Analogues

7.4.1 Ninhydrin History

Ninhydrin was first described in 1910 when Siegfried Ruhemann mistakenly prepared the compound (Ruhemann, 1910a, pp 1438–1449). Ruhemann observed that the new compound reacted with skin and amino acids to produce a purple product (Ruhemann, 1910b, pp 2025–2031), and he published a series of papers detailing this and other reactions (Ruhemann, 1911a, pp 792–800; 1911b, pp 1306–1310; 1911c, pp 1486–1492). He proposed a structure for the deeply colored product (Ruhemann, 1911c, pp 1486–1492), today known as Ruhemann's purple, and commented on the possible application of the reaction to the detection of trace amounts of amino acids and protein products in biological samples (Ruhemann, 1911a, pp 792–800).

Following Ruhemann's discovery, ninhydrin found widespread use in analytical chemistry and biochemistry applications. As early as 1913, the reaction with amino acids was an important diagnostic test for the presence of protein and amine compounds in biological samples (Crown, 1969, pp 258–264; Friedman and Williams, 1974, pp 267–280). With the advent of chromatography, the reaction became even more useful for the location of amino acids on paper chromatograms or in fractions produced by liquid chromatography (Crown, 1969, pp 258–264; Smith and Agiza, 1951, pp 623–627).

Ruhemann's purple and other by-products of the ninhydrin and amino-acid reaction were also used to quantitatively measure amino acid content of samples (Yemm et al., 1955, 209–214; Smith and Agiza, 1951, pp 623–627). The reagent was so powerful and versatile that some authors suggested it was the most widely used reaction in analytical laboratories (Friedman and Williams, 1974, pp 267–280).

This use of ninhydrin was frequently accompanied by warnings to avoid contact between bare skin and any surfaces to come into contact with the reagent (Crown, 1969, pp 258–264). This was due to the strong reaction between ninhydrin and sweat, which would cause the appearance of fingerprints on chromatograms (Crown, 1969, pp 258–264; Odén and von Hofsten, 1954, pp 449–450). Despite these warnings, which clearly indicated the ability of ninhydrin to develop fingerprints, the reagent was not applied in a forensic context until 1954 (Odén and von Hofsten, 1954, pp 449–450).

Following this initial report, ninhydrin rapidly became indispensable tool in the detection of latent fingerprints, with widespread use among jurisdictions being documented as early as 1959 (Speaks, 1964, pp 11–13, 23). The technique is now amongst the most popular methods for fingerprint detection on paper and other porous substrates (Champod et al., 2004, pp 114–136). This method has limitations, however, and chemists have addressed these limitations by the synthesis of analogues—compounds structurally related to ninhydrin that exhibit similar reactions with amino acids—to improve the clarity of the developed fingerprint (Almog, 2001, pp 177–209). Several of these analogues were highly successful (e.g., 1,8-diazafluoren-9-one [DFO], 1,2-indanedione, and 5-methylthioninhydrin), although none have been able to completely replace ninhydrin as the most frequently used technique (Almog, 2001, pp 177–209).

7.4.2 Theory

7.4.2.1 Fingerprint Detection by Amino Acid Reagents. Some fingerprints are created by the deposition of sweat from the fingers when they come into contact with a surface. This sweat consists mainly of aqueous components,

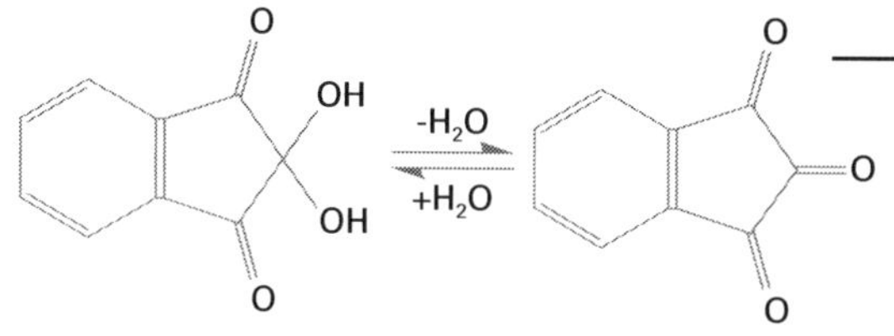

FIGURE 7–2

Equilibrium between hydrated and anhydrous ninhydrin structures.

which comprise 98% of the volume of a fingerprint (Pounds and Jones, 1983, pp 180–183). These aqueous deposits contain a small, but detectable, amount of amino acids, averaging about 250 ng per fingerprint (Hansen and Joullié, 2005, pp 408–417). After the water evaporates from the surface, the amino acids remain as solid material (Knowles, 1978, pp 713–720).

For porous surfaces such as paper, amino acids are desirable targets for fingerprint development reagents (Almog, 2001, pp 177–209). Although uncontrollable variables (such as the total amount of sweat deposited by the finger, the amino acid concentration of the individual's excretions, and the age of the fingerprint) influence the amount of amino acids transferred to the paper (Everse and Menzel, 1986, pp 446–454), amino acids are always present in perspiration in some amount (Speaks, 1970, pp 14–17). On contact with paper, these amino acids impregnate the surface of the paper, where they are retained by their high affinity for cellulose (Champod et al., 2004, p 114; Almog, 2001, pp 177–209; Hansen and Joullié, 2005, pp 408–417).

Because of this affinity, amino acids do not migrate significantly from their initial deposition sites; however, the amount of amino acids retained in the fingerprint decreases gradually over time (Knowles, 1978, pp 713–720). Furthermore, amino acids react with a wide variety of chemicals to produce colored compounds (Hansen and Joullié, 2005, pp 408–417). These qualities have been exploited to produce clear, sharp images of fingerprints that were up to 40 years old (Champod et al., 2004, p 114).

At least 14 amino acids may be present in fingerprint residues (Knowles, 1978, pp 713–720; Hier et al., 1946, pp 327–333). To produce the best-developed fingerprint, the ideal reagent must be nonspecific to a particular amino acid (i.e., reacts well with all).

Ninhydrin is one of many chemicals that acts as a nonspecific amino acid reagent and is, therefore, highly suitable for fingerprint development (Champod et al., 2004, p 114; Almog, 2001, pp 177–209).

7.4.2.2 Properties of Ninhydrin. Ninhydrin is a crystalline solid that is colorless to pale yellow in color and is highly soluble in polar solvents such as water and methanol (McCaldin, 1960, pp 39–51). When heated, the solid becomes pink to red in color at approximately 125 °C (Almog, 2001, pp 177–209), melts at 130–140 °C, and decomposes at 241 °C. The compound is found as the stable hydrate in the presence of any water but will assume a triketone structure in anhydrous conditions (Hansen and Joullié, 2005, pp 408–417). This equilibrium is illustrated in Figure 7–2.

7.4.2.3 Reaction of Ninhydrin with Amino Acids. The first observation of ninhydrin's reaction with skin to form a deep purple compound was reported in 1910 (Ruhemann, 1910a, pp 1438–1449). Subsequent studies indicated that the purple color resulted from the reaction between ninhydrin and amino acids and described the product of this reaction as diketohydrindylidene–diketohydrindamine (Ruhemann, 1910b, pp 2025–2031; 1911a, pp 792–800; 1911c, pp 1486–1492), which is now known as Ruhemann's purple. By-products of this reaction include an aldehyde derivative of the amino acid and carbon dioxide (Friedman and Williams, 1974, pp 267–280; Yemm et al., 1955, pp 209–214).

Multiple attempts have been made to determine the mechanism of this reaction (Friedman and Williams, 1974, pp 267–280; Hansen and Joullié, 2005, pp 408–417; McCaldin, 1960, pp 39–51; Retinger, 1917, pp 1059–1066; Bottom et al., 1978, pp 4–5; Grigg et al., 1986, pp 421–422; Grigg et al., 1989, pp 3849–3862; Joullié et al., 1991, pp 8791–8830; Schertz et al., 2001, pp 7596–7603). The mechanism that is most accepted today is the one proposed by Grigg et al. (1989, pp 3849–3862) and illustrated briefly in Figure 7–3. Acid and water are other reagents required for this reaction to occur.

Structural studies of the reaction product have confirmed that Ruhemann's original product structure was correct and that the reaction with amino acids produces the ammonium salt of Ruhemann's purple (Ruhemann, 1911c, pp 1486–1492; Grigg et al., 1986, pp 421–422; 1989, pp 3849–3862).

This reaction is complex and requires a finely tuned set of conditions in order to progress at a reasonable rate. The pH of the reaction must be above 4 (Friedman and Williams, 1974, pp 267–280; Bottom et al., 1978, pp 4–5) and ideally should be between 4.5 and 5.2 (Grigg et al., 1989, pp 3849–3862). Development in a high-humidity environment is of utmost importance (Champod et al., 2004, pp 116–117; Almog, 2001, pp 177–209) because water is a necessary reactant. Finally, because Ruhemann's purple is known to degrade in the presence of light and oxygen, the treated fingerprint should be stored in a dark, cool place (Friedman and Williams, 1974, pp 267–280; Joullié et al., 1991, pp 8791–8830). Ninhydrin-treated fingerprints are colored purple and exhibit excellent contrast and clarity of detail (Champod et al., 2004, p 117; Almog, 2001, pp 177–209).

7.4.2.4 Optical Enhancement of Ninhydrin-Developed Fingerprints. Ninhydrin treatment provides excellent contrast under ideal conditions (e.g., fresh fingerprints on white paper). On colored paper or with aged fingerprints, however, the results can often be less than optimal (Crown, 1969, pp 258–264; Everse and Menzel, 1986, pp 446–454; Speaks, 1970, pp 14–17; Grigg et al., 1989, pp 3849–3862; German, 1981, pp 3–4; Herod and Menzel, 1982a, pp 200–204; Lennard et al., 1986, pp 323–328).

Several methods have been developed to increase the contrast between ninhydrin-developed fingerprints and a colored substrate or to enhance weakly developed fingerprints. The UV-to-visible light spectrum of Ruhemann's purple shows two *absorption maxima*—wavelengths of light that are strongly absorbed by the compound. These maxima, at $\lambda = 407$ nm and $\lambda = 582$ nm (Lennard et al., 1986, pp 323–328), can be used to increase the contrast between the developed fingerprint and a nonabsorbing background. When lasers became available to the forensic community in the late 1970s to early 1980s, a treatment with zinc chloride was described for enhancing weak ninhydrin prints by using the light of an argon ion laser (German, 1981, pp 3–4; Herod and Menzel, 1982a, pp 200–204). This method was capable

FIGURE 7–3

Accepted reaction mechanism of ninhydrin with amino acids.

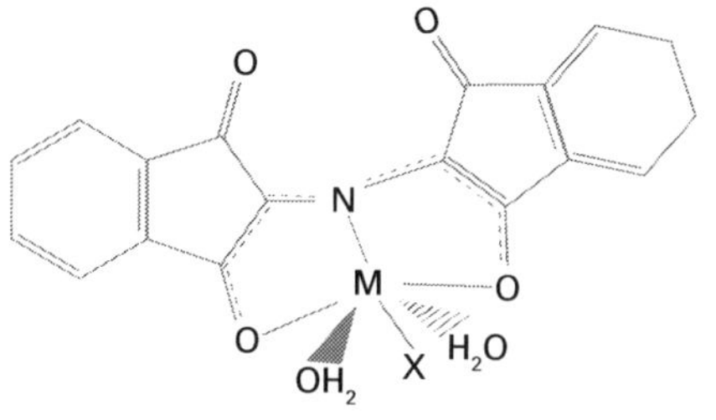

FIGURE 7–4

Structure of Ruhemann's purple–metal salt complex.

M: Cadmium or zinc
X: Anion from the metal salt

of drastically increasing the number of identifiable latent fingerprints developed by the ninhydrin process. With the current ubiquity of forensic light sources, both absorption bands of Ruhemann's purple can be exploited to produce high-contrast fingerprints (Champod et al., 2004, p 117).

7.4.2.5 Post-Treatment with Metal Salts. The reaction between Ruhemann's purple and metal salts such as zinc, cadmium, cobalt, and copper was used in a biochemical context to preserve ninhydrin spots on chromatograms (Kawerau and Wieland, 1951, pp 77–78). Formation of a metal-salt complex alters the color of Ruhemann's purple from deep violet to red or orange, depending upon the salt used (Stoilovic et al., 1986, pp 432–445). The lighter hue may provide a greater contrast against a dark-colored background, especially when observed at 490–510 nm, where the metal–Ruhemann's purple complex has an absorption maximum (Stoilovic et al., 1986, pp 432–445).

It has been reported that viewing zinc-complexed ninhydrin-treated fingerprints under an argon ion laser could induce fluorescence of even weakly developed prints (Herod and Menzel, 1982b, pp 513–518). This discovery had a profound impact on fingerprint development because fluorescent reagents are more sensitive than chromogenic ones and can be viewed more clearly against colored backgrounds (Champod et al., 2004, p 120). Subsequent studies revealed that intense laser light was not necessary if the zinc-treated samples were cooled to the temperature of liquid nitrogen (-196 °C or 77 K); the fluorescence could be observed under a xenon arc lamp. This technique required submersion of the document in liquid nitrogen, a glass plate being placed between the sample and the light source and camera, and a heat source to prevent condensation on the glass (Kobus et al., 1983, pp 161–170). Later research showed that cadmium complexes provided an improved luminescence under these conditions (Stoilovic et al., 1986, pp 432–445).

Structural studies of the Ruhemann's purple–metal salt complexes have identified the structure in Figure 7–4 (Lennard et al., 1987, pp 597–605; Davies et al., 1995a, pp 565–569; 1995b, pp 1802–1805).

7.4.3 Application

7.4.3.1 Ninhydrin Formulations. Several ninhydrin formulations have been reported in the literature (Crown, 1969, pp 258–264; Odén and van Hofsten, 1954, pp 449–450; Speaks, 1964, pp 11–13, 23; Champod et al., 2004, pp 117–120; Almog, 2001, pp 177–209; Everse and Menzel, 1986, pp 446–454; Clay, 1981, pp 12–13). Ninhydrin solutions are typically prepared in two steps: first, a stock solution is prepared that has a high proportion of polar solvent to facilitate the stability of the mixture; second, a portion of the stock solution is diluted with a nonpolar carrier solvent to produce a reagent suitable for application to evidential items.

Application of ninhydrin working solutions can be performed by dipping, spraying, or brushing (Odén and van Hofsten, 1954, pp 449–450; Speaks, 1964, pp 11–13, 23), with the dipping method preferred in most instances. The item to be examined is briefly submerged in the working solution and allowed to air-dry to evaporate the solvent (Champod et al., 2004, pp 116–117).

Following treatment with ninhydrin solution, development should ideally proceed at room temperature, in a dark and humid environment (50–80% humidity), for a period of 1–2 days (Champod et al., 2004, pp 116–117). If ambient humidity is low, development in a specialized, humidity-controlled fingerprint development chamber may be necessary (Almog, 2001, pp 177–209). The development may be accelerated by the application of steam or heat, but this may result in a greater degree of background development, reducing the clarity and contrast of the resulting fingerprints (Almog, 2001, pp 177–209). Steaming can be achieved by holding a steam iron above the exhibit; heat can be delivered in a press, oven, fingerprint development cabinet, or by a microwave oven and should not exceed 80 °C (Almog, 2001, pp 177–209).

Ninhydrin crystals may be ground in a mortar and pestle to form a fine powder and applied directly to the fingerprints with a fingerprint brush (Almog, 2001, pp 177–209). This method is slow and produces only faint prints but may be suitable for some types of heat- or solvent-sensitive paper (Wakefield and Armitage, 2005). Ninhydrin may also be applied by a fuming method; a forensic fuming cabinet is used to heat the ninhydrin until it sublimes, allowing gaseous ninhydrin to deposit on the fingerprint residues (Schwarz and Frerichs, 2002, pp 1274–1277). The reagent is most suited to paper, although any porous substrate may give visible results, and some nonporous substrates have been reported to produce visible fingerprints (Herod and Menzel, 1982a, pp 200–204; Speaks, 1966, pp 3–5).

7.4.3.2 Metal Salt Post-Treatment. The application of zinc or cadmium salts to ninhydrin-developed fingerprints will result in an immediate color change from purple to orange or red, respectively (Lennard et al., 1987, pp 597–605). Note that the use of zinc is preferred to cadmium because of cadmium's toxicity. Dipping the exhibit into the solution is preferred over spraying because of the toxicity of some of the reagents. If humidity is low, a short blast of steam may be required to produce development. However, the humidity must be carefully controlled if zinc salts are used because high moisture levels cause the formation of an unstable, nonfluorescent, red complex that will reduce the contrast of the resulting fingerprint (Stoilovic et al., 1986, pp 432–445; Davies et al., 1995a, pp 565–569).

Post-treated fingerprints may be further enhanced by viewing under 490 nm light (for zinc-treated residues) or 510 nm light (for cadmium-treated residues) (Champod et al., 2004, p 120; Stoilovic et al., 1986, pp 432–445). Fluorescence may be induced by submerging the article in liquid nitrogen and exciting the treated fingerprint with the above-mentioned wavelengths of light. The fluorescent emissions should be viewed using a 550–570 nm band-pass filter or a 550 nm long-pass filter (Champod et al., 2004, pp 121–124).

7.5 1,8-Diazafluoren-9-one (DFO)

7.5.1 History

1,8-Diazafluoren-9-one (DFO) was first prepared in 1950 (Druey and Schmidt, 1950, pp 1080–1087), but its reaction with amino acids was not explored until 1990, when it was first applied as a fingerprint development reagent. The preliminary results of this study were promising; DFO treatment resulted in faint red or pink fingerprints that were intensely fluorescent at room temperature (Pounds et al., 1990, pp 169–175; Grigg et al., 1990, pp 7215–7218). This presented clear advantages over the metal complexation-induced fluorescence of ninhydrin-developed fingerprints, and DFO was rapidly identified as the best fluorescent reagent for fingerprint development (Almog, 2001, pp 177–209). The reagent is now widely used in sequence with ninhydrin to develop fingerprints on porous surfaces (Wilkinson et al., 2005).

7.5.2 Theory

Although DFO is not a direct analogue of ninhydrin (Hansen and Joullié, 2005, pp 408–417), the structures of the two compounds, and the outcome of their reactions with amino acids, are similar (Grigg et al., 1990, pp 7215–7218; Wilkinson, 2000a, pp 87–103). Like ninhydrin, DFO contains a central ketone center activated by the nearby presence of electron-withdrawing groups. The structure of DFO is illustrated in Figure 7–5; the nitrogenous rings act similarly to the flanking ketone groups in ninhydrin (Hansen and Joullié, 2005, pp 408–417).

Mechanistic studies of DFO's reaction with amino acids have shown that the presence of methanol is essential. This allows the DFO to form a hemiketal (Figure 7–6), which is less stable than the parent structure and therefore more reactive, producing a more sensitive response to amino acid residues in fingerprints (Wilkinson, 2000a, pp 87–103). The red reaction product has been fully characterized and resembles Ruhemann's purple (Grigg et al., 1990, pp 7215–7218; Wilkinson, 2000a, pp 87–103).

The product of this reaction is pink to red in color with λ_{max} of approximately 560 nm and a weaker absorption at 520 nm (Pounds et al., 1990, pp 169–175; Wilkinson, 2000a, pp 87–103). Under excitation by either of these wavelengths, the product is strongly fluorescent at room temperature, emitting intense light of 576 nm (Stoilovic, 1993, pp 141–153). An illustration of a DFO-developed fingerprint in

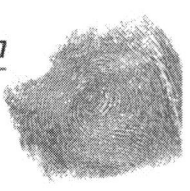

FIGURE 7–5

Structure of 1,8-diazafluoren-9-one (DFO).

FIGURE 7–6

Hemiketal formation and reaction with amino acids.

both white light and under fluorescent conditions appears in Figure 7–7.

Unlike the ninhydrin reaction, the DFO reaction requires a high-temperature, low-humidity environment (Pounds et al., 1990, pp 169–175). Post-treatment with metal salts and subsequent cooling to liquid nitrogen temperatures does not significantly affect the intensity of the DFO product's fluorescence (Conn et al., 2001, pp 117–123).

DFO is reported to be a more sensitive fingerprint development reagent than ninhydrin, producing a greater number of identifiable latent fingerprints (Wilkinson et al., 2005; Stoilovic, 1993, pp 141–153; Cantu et al., 1993, pp 44–66). This sensitivity is due to the fact that a weakly fluorescing fingerprint is easier to see than a weakly colored fingerprint (Almog, 2001, pp 177–209). Despite this observation, if ninhydrin is applied after DFO treatment, additional development occurs, producing Ruhemann's purple. The conventional explanation for this phenomenon is that, although DFO-developed fingerprints are more visible when fluorescing, DFO does not react to completion with every amino acid in the fingerprint residue, thus leaving some amino acids available to react with ninhydrin (Wilkinson, 2000a, pp 87–103). The combination of DFO followed by ninhydrin develops more latent fingerprints than DFO or ninhydrin alone (Wilkinson et al., 2005), and this is the recommended sequence of examinations for porous surfaces such as paper (Champod et al., 2004, pp 128–131; Almog, 2001, 177–209).

7.5.3 Application

Several DFO formulations have been reported in the literature (Champod et al., 2004, pp 230–231; Almog, 2001, pp 177–209; Pounds et al., 1990, pp 169–175; Grigg et al., 1990, pp 7215–7218; Wilkinson et al., 2005; Wilkinson, 2000a, pp 87–103; Stoilovic, 1993, pp 141–153; Didierjean et al., 1998, pp 163–167). DFO solution can be applied to specimens by dipping, spraying, or brushing, although dipping is the preferred method (Champod et al., 2004, pp 128–131). The exhibit is allowed to dry and then heated to promote development. Several heating methods are suitable: heating in a 100 °C oven for 10–20 minutes (Champod et al., 2004, p 128; Almog, 2001, pp 177–209; Pounds et al., 1990, pp 169–175; Didierjean et al., 1998, pp 163–167), applying a 160 °C iron for 20–30 seconds (Stoilovic, 1993, pp 141–153), or applying a 180 °C ironing press for 10 seconds (Almog, 2001, pp 177–209; Stoilovic, 1993, pp 141–153). The reaction must be carried out in a dry environment with low humidity because moisture interferes with the development reaction (Champod et al., 2004, p 129; Almog, 2001, pp 177–209; Wilkinson, 2000a, pp 87–103).

After DFO application and heating, developed fingerprints can be observed using 530 nm excitation light and a 590 nm barrier filter, or 555 nm excitation light and a 610 nm barrier filter (Almog, 2001, pp 177–209). The exhibit may then be treated with ninhydrin as previously described.

7.6 1,2-Indanedione

7.6.1 History

The fingerprint-developing capabilities of 1,2-indanedione were first considered after a related compound, 6-methyl-thio-1,2-indanedione, was found to produce fluorescent fingerprints (Hauze et al., 1998, pp 744–747). This prompted researchers to synthesize the parent compound and several other analogues and to evaluate their utility as fingerprint reagents (Ramotowski et al., 1997, pp 131–139). The results were similar to DFO in that a faint, pink-colored product was produced that fluoresced brightly at room temperature (Ramotowski et al., 1997, pp 131–139). Further research indicated that these reagents are more sensitive than other current methods and, because of the ease of synthesis, can be a cheaper alternative (Cava et al., 1958, pp 2257–2263; Dayan et al., 1998, pp 2752–2754; Joullié and Petrovskaia, 1998, pp 41–44). In the eight years following these discoveries, 1,2-indanedione has become a standard reagent in Israeli laboratories and has been investigated for use in many other countries (Almog, 2001, pp 177–209).

7.6.2 Theory

1,2-Indanedione is a close analogue of ninhydrin and is theorized to react with amino acids in a very similar fashion (Petrovskaia et al., 2001, pp 7666–7675). The structure of 1,2-indanedione has been characterized (Wilkinson, 2000b, pp 123–132) and is illustrated in Figure 7–8(A).

Mechanistic studies of 1,2-indanedione's reaction with amino acids have indicated that the presence of methanol desensitizes the reagent (Wilkinson, 2000b, pp 123–132). Like DFO, indanedione forms a hemiketal with methanol; however, unlike DFO, this hemiketal is more stable than the parent compound and thus its formation prevents the reaction with amino acids. Because 1,2-indanedione is completely converted to the less sensitive hemiketal (Wilkinson, 2000b, pp 123–132), some suggest that alcohols should be avoided in any indanedione formulations (Wilkinson et al., 2005; Wiesner et al., 2001, pp 1082–1084). Other studies have not corroborated this lack of sensitivity in methanolic solution (Roux et al., 2000, pp 761–769). Similar ambiguity exists on the addition of acetic acid (Lennard et al., 2005, p 43); some authors have found that a small amount of acetic acid improves the results (Hauze et al., 1998, pp 744–747; Joullié and Petrovskaia, 1998, pp 41–44), whereas others have experienced blurry, unclear fingerprints when using acidified solutions (Almog, 2001, pp 177–209; Wiesner et al., 2001, pp 1082–1084; Kasper et al., 2002). These discrepancies have been linked to the acid content of the paper produced in the authors' various countries (Wilkinson et al., 2005).

FIGURE 7–7

DFO-developed fingerprint. Left, under ambient light. Right, excited by a forensic light source and viewed through the proper viewing filter.

Production of the compound shown in Figure 7–8(B) during the reaction between amino acids and 1,2-indanedione has been confirmed. However, this compound does not fully explain the coloration of the developed print or its fluorescence. The possibility of a Ruhemann's purple analogue has not been ruled out (Petrovskaia et al., 2001, pp 7666–7675); such a compound is illustrated in Figure 7–8(C). Further studies are currently under way to elucidate the structure of the fluorescent species, which is expected to be polymeric (Wallace-Kunkel et al., 2005).

Whether or not metal salt post-treatment enhances the fluorescence of the developed fingerprint is another point of contention amongst authors. The varied results with each step of the indanedione development process indicate the influence that environmental conditions have upon the technique, and each research group should establish an optimal formula for use in its laboratory (Wilkinson et al., 2005; Lennard et al., 2005, p 43).

7.6.3 Application

Because of regional variations in humidity, acid content of paper, and other environmental factors, a single 1,2-indanedione formulation cannot be recommended. Application of the 1,2-indanedione reagent can be carried out by immersion of the exhibit or by spraying of the reagent. Development can occur at room temperature but may require 4–5 days (Roux et al., 2000, pp 761–769). In light of the established fact that heat treatment does not cause excessive background development, it is recommended that steam heat be applied to the treated fingerprints to expedite development (Almog, 2001, pp 177–209; Ramotowski et al., 1997, pp 131–139; Joullié and Petrovskaia, 1998, pp 41–44; Roux et al., 2000, pp 761–769). This heat can be applied in a humidity oven (100 °C at 60% relative humidity) (Wiesner et al., 2001, pp 1082–1084; Roux et al., 2000, pp 761–769; Almog et al., 1999, pp 114–118), by steam iron (Ramotowski et al., 1997, pp 131–139; Joullié and Petrovskaia, 1998, pp 41–44), or by a heat press (100 °C for 2–5 minutes [Kasper et al., 2002] or 165 °C for 10 seconds [Lennard et al., 2005, p 43]).

Fluorescence can be observed under 520 nm illumination and viewed through a 590 nm filter (Joullié and Petrovskaia, 1998, pp 41–44). Zinc salt post-treatment can be applied to enhance the color of the developed fingerprint (Roux et al., 2000, pp 761–769) and may increase the fluorescent intensity (Almog, 2001, pp 177–209; Hauze et al., 1998, pp 744–747; Ramotowski et al., 1997, pp 131–139; Lennard et al., 2005, p 43; Almog et al., 1999, pp 114–118).

1,2-Indanedione develops more fingerprints than DFO, ninhydrin, or the DFO–ninhydrin sequence combined (Wiesner et al., 2001, pp 1082–1084; Lennard et al., 2005, p 43). The indanedione-DFO sequence is capable of visualizing even more latent fingerprints than 1,2-indanedione alone (Roux et al., 2000, pp 761–769), and indanedione can also enhance ninhydrin-developed fingerprints (Kasper et al., 2002). However, ninhydrin treatment of indanedione-developed prints does not afford further enhancement (Wiesner et al., 2001, pp 1082–1084).

Finally, on a somewhat negative note, Wilkinson et al. had very poor results with indanedione for a study carried out across Canada (Wilkinson et al., 2003, pp 8–18).

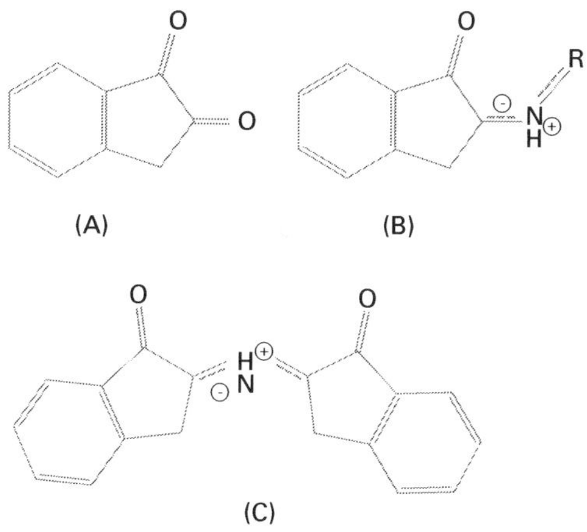

FIGURE 7–8

Structure of (A) 1,2-indanedione; (B) a known product of the reaction between 1,2-indanedione and amino acids; (C) a possible Ruhemann's purple analogue produced by the reaction.

7.7 5-Methylthioninhydrin (5-MTN)

5-Methylthioninhydrin (5-MTN) was first prepared and applied as a fingerprint reagent in 1990 as part of a U.S. Secret Service project (Cantu et al., 1993, pp 44–46). This analogue reacts with amino acids in a manner identical to ninhydrin because the reactive, chromogenic core of the molecule is not changed by the addition of the sulfur group (Figure 7–9) (Elber et al., 2000, pp 757–760). As a result, 5-MTN-developed fingerprints are a shade of purple similar to ninhydrin-developed fingerprints.

Development of 5-MTN-treated fingerprints requires heat and humidity, much the same as ninhydrin development. This can be delivered in the same manner described previously for ninhydrin or by microwaving the treated exhibit for 2–3 minutes alongside a container of water (Almog et al., 1992, pp 688–694). Care must be taken to avoid overheating the sample because significant background development may occur. The resulting fingerprint should appear deep purple in color, similar to a ninhydrin-developed fingerprint.

On treatment with a zinc salt, the 5-MTN-developed fingerprint changes color from purple to pink (Almog et al., 1992, pp 688–694). Accompanying this change is a strong fluorescence at room temperature when excited by light at 520 nm and viewed through a 590 nm filter (Cantu et al., 1993, pp 44–66; Almog et al., 1992, pp 688–694), with an intensity that is comparable to that of DFO. This is an obvious advantage over the continued use of ninhydrin (Cantu et al., 1993, pp 44–66). A recent study confirmed that 5-MTN could outperform ninhydrin but produced poorer fluorescent results than DFO or 1,2-indanedione (Wallace-Kunkel et al., 2006, pp 4–13). The fluorescence becomes even more intense if the exhibit is cooled to liquid nitrogen temperatures, but this step is not necessary (Almog et al., 1992, pp 688–694).

5-MTN can be synthesized in small-scale operations in the forensic laboratory following methods reported in the literature (Heffner and Joullié, 1991, pp 2231–2256; Della et al., 1999, pp 2119–2123). Alternatively, it can be sourced from commercial forensic suppliers. However, some suppliers provide the ethanolic hemiketal of 5-MTN, which dissolves more readily but may require some alteration of the given formulation (Section 7.14) to ensure the appropriate concentration of 5-MTN in the solution (BVDA, 2010).

7.8 Modifications for Use on Chemically Treated Papers

7.8.1 Chemically Treated Papers

Chemically treated paper is a class that encompasses thermal paper and carbonless specialty papers (Stimac, 2003a, pp 185–197). These papers cannot be treated with the conventional amino acid reagent formulations described previously because the polar solvents react unfavorably with the chemical treatments applied to the paper during manufacture. This undesired interaction frequently causes the surface of the paper to blacken, obliterating the documentary evidence the paper contained (Stimac,

FIGURE 7–9

Structure of 5-methylthioninhydrin and its reaction product with amino acids.

2003a, pp 185–197). To address this limitation, several solvent-free or low-polarity formulations have been devised for the treatment of these difficult substrates.

7.8.2 Application of DFO to Chemically Treated Paper

DFO may be applied to chemically treated paper by a process known as "DFO-Dry" (Bratton and Juhala, 1995, pp 169–172). This technique does not require the application of a solvent to the exhibit under examination. Instead, filter paper is impregnated with a solution of 1 g DFO in 200 mL methanol, 200 mL ethyl acetate, and 40 mL acetic acid. The dried filter paper is applied to the exhibit, a towel is placed on top, and a steam iron filled with 5% acetic acid solution is applied for one minute. This transfers DFO onto the exhibit and provides the heat for development. This technique results in a less prominent color change but equal fluorescence to solvent-based methods (Bratton and Juhala, 1995, pp 169–172).

7.8.3 Ninhydrin Techniques

7.8.3.1 "Nin-Dry". This method was described in 1996 (McMahon, 1996, pp 4–5) and is similar to the previously described "DFO-Dry" process. Blotter or filter paper is soaked in a solution of 30–50 g ninhydrin dissolved in 1.5 L acetone and allowed to dry. An exhibit is placed between two sheets of the impregnated paper and then sealed into a plastic bag for 3 days to 1 week. This technique develops high-contrast fingerprints while preserving the integrity and appearance of the document and is applicable to any fragile paper types, including chemically treated papers.

7.8.3.2 Ninhydrin Fuming. The method proposed by Schwarz and Frerichs (2002, pp 1274–1277), and described above, can be applied to chemically treated papers with no loss of document detail.

7.8.3.3 Nonpolar Solution. A ninhydrin solution can be prepared in a mixture of the nonpolar solvents HFE 71IPA and HFE 7100. The exhibit is immersed in the working solution and allowed to develop in dark, humid conditions for 2–3 days, avoiding high temperatures (Stimac, 2003a, pp 185–197).

7.8.4 Indanedione Formulation

Indanedione is sufficiently soluble in nonpolar solvents that it can be effectively applied to thermal paper without causing any blackening (Stimac, 2003b, pp 265–271). The exhibit is immersed in the prepared solution and allowed to develop for at least 1 day in dark, cool conditions. Fluorescence is induced as described previously.

7.8.5 2-Isononylninhydrin (INON)

2-Isononylninhydrin, also known as INON, or commercially as ThermaNin, is a derivative of ninhydrin with greatly increased solubility in nonpolar solvents (Takatsu et al., 1991; Joullié, 2000). This compound, which is a product of the reaction between 3,5,5-trimethyl-1-hexanol and ninhydrin (Almog, 2001, pp 177–209; Hansen and Joullié, 2005, pp 408–417; Takatsu et al., 1992), has the chemical structure shown in Figure 7–10.

Solutions of this reagent do not have a long shelf life, so working solutions should be prepared as needed (BVDA, 2010).

The 2-isononylninhydrin solution is applied to the chemically treated paper by immersing the exhibit in the solution in an aluminum or plastic tray. The exhibit is allowed to dry and develop in dark, humid conditions for 24–48 hours. Under these conditions, the ninhydrin hemiketal reacts with water absorbed by the paper to form ninhydrin and 3,5,5-trimethyl-1-hexanol. The freed ninhydrin reacts slowly with the residues in the fingerprint to develop a fingerprint that is somewhat less intensely colored than a traditionally ninhydrin-developed print. This may be due to the relatively lower concentration of ninhydrin present after the hydrolysis reaction occurs (Al Mandhri and Khanmy-Vital, 2005).

7.9 Cyanoacrylate Fuming

7.9.1 Background

The liquid commercial adhesive, super glue, was inadvertently developed in the 1950s by researchers who were trying to develop an acrylic polymer for the aircraft industry. Besides its use as a glue, CA adhesive also found use as a field dressing in Vietnam in the 1960s, although it never received FDA approval for this use. In the late 1970s, researchers in Japan and the United Kingdom almost simultaneously discovered the latent fingerprint development capabilities of the fumes of the liquid adhesive. Shortly thereafter, latent print examiners from the U.S. Army Criminal Investigation Laboratory in Japan and the Bureau of Alcohol, Tobacco, and Firearms introduced this technique to North America. Once CA fuming proved practical, with the introduction of methods to make the technique faster

FIGURE 7–10

Structure of 2-isononylninhydrin (INON).

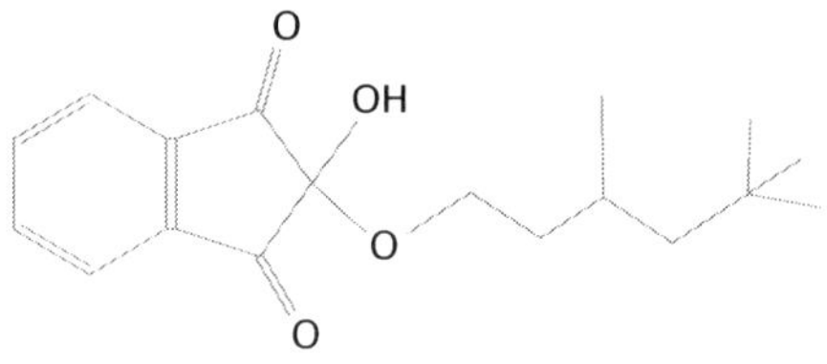

FIGURE 7–11

Ethyl cyanoacrylate monomer.

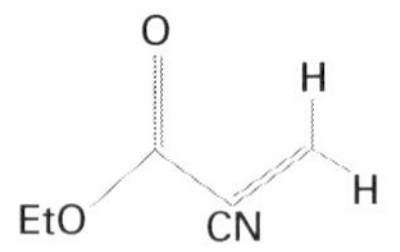

and more effective, it quickly gained acceptance worldwide (German, 2005; Jueneman, 1982, p 15).

Since those early discoveries, innumerable crimes have been solved through the routine use of CA ester (usually methyl or ethyl) fuming of evidence, and a substantial amount of research has been aimed at identifying the ideal environment for the technique.

Today, CA fuming continues to be a versatile and effective development technique on virtually all nonporous surfaces, including glass, metal, coated papers, and all forms of plastics. The method is particularly effective on rough surfaces where physical contact with a fingerprint brush tends to develop the texture of the material along with the latent fingerprints. CA vapors are extremely sensitive to fingerprint residue, adaptable to many different crime scene and laboratory situations, and are relatively inexpensive to employ.

Studies into the explicit polymerization initiators and the role of water in the development of latent prints are ongoing. These studies should eventually lead to a better understanding of latent print polymerization as it relates to latent print composition, pH, aging, and humidity.

7.9.2 Theory

Super glue or CA development of latent prints is best explained as a three-stage process to produce polymer growth, thus enabling latent print visualization.

The first stage occurs when fumes of CA ester monomers (see diagram of ethyl CA monomer in Figure 7–11) are introduced to latent fingerprints and quickly bond with initiators in the residue. In the second stage, the monomer on the fingerprint residue reacts with another CA monomer in the vapor phase to form a dimer on the print. This reacts with yet another monomer, and another, eventually forming a polymer, a long chain of CA molecules. The final phase is when the polymer chain reaction is terminated. The overall development time is fast, especially when volatilization of the liquid glue is accelerated (Lewis et al., 2001, pp 241–246). The polymerization process may, however, be restarted later if fingerprints prove to be underdeveloped with the first exposure to fumes.

Fully developed CA prints are a white three-dimensional matrix, often visible to the unaided eye, and can be further enhanced with a variety of techniques. CA-developed impressions are generally more durable than untreated fingerprints because of the plasticization of the print. Because of this, some authorities recommend CA treatment in the field before evidence packaging to protect otherwise fragile fingerprints during transportation and storage (Perkins and Thomas, 1991, pp 157–162).

For normal eccrine sweat fingerprints, CA polymerized under ambient laboratory environmental conditions appears as noodlelike, fibrous structures when viewed with a scanning electron microscope (SEM) (Figure 7–12). These polymer morphologies change, however, when variables such as the age of the latent print, the residue composition, and environmental conditions are altered.

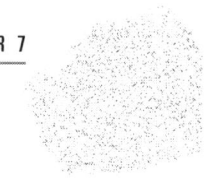

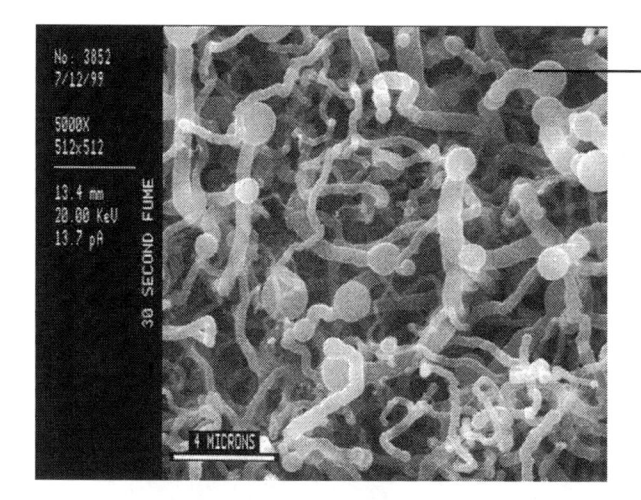

FIGURE 7–12

Scanning electron microscopy of cyanoacrylate polymerized eccrine residue. (Reprinted, with permission from the Journal of Forensic Sciences, 46 (2), copyright ASTM International, 100 Barr Harbor Drive, West Conshohocken, PA 19428.)

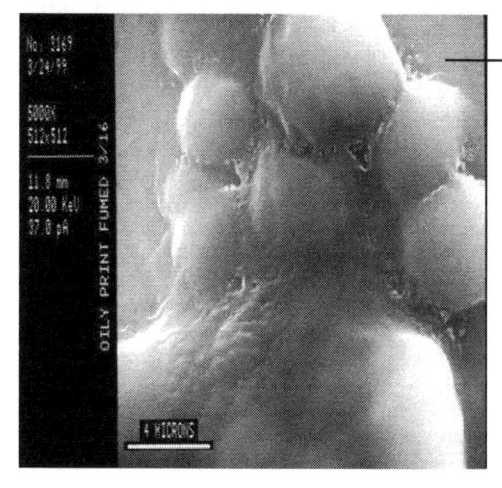

FIGURE 7–13

Scanning electron microscopy of cyanoacrylate polymerized oily residue. (Reprinted with permission from the Journal of Forensic Sciences, 46 (2), copyright ASTM International, 100 Barr Harbor Drive, West Conshohocken, PA 19428.)

Lewis et al. (2001, pp 241–246) observed differences between clean and oily latent print residues and the effects of aging on each. Latent prints lacking sebum (clean prints) tended to suffer from the effects of aging to a far greater extent than prints containing sebum (oily prints, Figure 7–13). After 1 day of aging, clean prints showed a trend away from the previously mentioned fibrous morphology toward polymer structures that appeared rounded under SEM. Clean prints also became difficult, if not impossible, to develop after a period of only 2 weeks, whereas prints contaminated with sebum produced distinguishable polymer growth for periods of up to 6 months. Lewis et al. (2001, pp 241–246) also observed that a low-humidity environment during latent print aging had a noticeable and adverse impact on development with CA, whereas prints aged under high humidity lasted longer and produced higher quality polymerization.

Interestingly, latent prints developed in a vacuum chamber also produce smooth spherical or capsule-type formations observed with SEM and tend to be more translucent to the unaided eye (Watkin et al., 1994, pp 545–554). This may be due in part to exposing the print to the near zero-humidity environment of the vacuum, presumably removing moisture from the fingerprints. The role of humidity in CA development of latent prints is not understood at this time. During the mid-1990s, Kent empirically observed that humid environments outperformed vacuum environments in the CA development of latent prints (Kent and Winfield, 1995; Kent, 2005, pp 681–683), whereas Lewis et al. (2001, pp 241–246) observed that humidity during the latent print aging process had a greater effect than during polymerization. Clearly, the role of humidity during aging and polymerization must be examined further.

The actual initiators that cause latent print polymerization are just recently being understood. Originally, it was believed that CA primarily reacted with the water in fingerprint residue (Jueneman, 1982, p 15). However, current research indicates that water-soluble amines and carboxylic groups in latent print residue are the primary initiators of CA polymerization. These two groups each produce significantly higher molecular weights of polymer growth than water alone. Furthermore, amines and carboxylic acid will polymerize in the absence of any water, leaving the role of water during the aging and development process unclear (Wargacki et al., 2005).

The pH of the humidity to which the latent prints are exposed prior to CA treatment may also play an important role by rejuvenating latent prints prior to the polymerization process. Latent prints that are exposed to acetic acid vapors and then CA fumed have shown higher molecular weights than those not exposed. Conversely, basic humidity produced with ammonia vapors also appears to enhance CA development. Present research makes it clear that acidic and basic humidity environments will both individually enhance latent print polymer growth, with acidic enhancement proving more effective. Although the actual mechanism is not fully understood, it is currently thought that exposure to ammonia vapors primarily enhances the functionality of the amine groups, whereas acetic acid vapors favorably influence the more robust carboxylic initiators (Wargacki et al., 2005).

7.9.3 Application

It is important to mention that liquid CA and its fumes can cause acute damage to skin, eyes, and mucous membranes, and the long-term effects of exposure are not fully known. The user must take care to use appropriate ventilation and personal protective equipment and to always practice safe handling. All manufacturer's warnings, including those given in material safety data sheets, must be heeded during use.

The ideal result of CA development is polymerization on the latent print that sufficiently scatters light and does not coat the background, making the white impression slightly visible against the substrate. This type of "minimal" development produces the greatest amount of detail, especially when used in conjunction with fluorescent dye stains (Figure 7–14). Overfuming will leave prints appearing "frosty" with a lack of edge detail, making them difficult to differentiate from a background also coated with CA polymer.

Sometimes, depending on latent composition and environmental conditions, developed impressions will appear translucent or glassy in nature and will be very difficult to detect without specific lighting or fluorescent dye staining.

In fact, most impressions will be aided by some form of enhancement before recording.

Fuming with CA can be as simple and inexpensive as vaporizing the glue in a fish tank with a tight-fitting lid or as elaborate as using a commercially designed chamber with dynamic temperature and humidity controls. Both systems are intended to achieve the same result: vaporizing liquid glue in an environment suitable for polymerization of CA on latent prints.

A common and effective approach to the volatilization of CA is to warm a small amount of liquid glue (approximately 0.5 g or less) in an aluminum evaporation dish on a heating block or coffee cup warmer. An aluminum dish is preferred because it inhibits polymerization (Olenik, 1983, pp 9–10). The warm fumes rise but soon fall to the bottom of the chamber as cooling sets in. Therefore, a circulation fan is often used during fuming to keep the vapors evenly dispersed around the evidence at all levels of the tank. Prints that are later determined to be underfumed can be fumed again, in effect restarting the polymerization process.

A second approach to vaporizing CA utilizes a commercially available fuming wand. These wands typically use butane fuel to heat a small brass cartridge containing ethyl CA (Weaver and Clary, 1993, pp 481–492). Fumes from the heated cartridge on the end of the wand can be directed toward the evidence or used to fill a chamber. The disadvantage of using a fuming wand in an open environment is that air currents easily sweep the CA vapors away from the evidence, making development difficult to control. The use of a fuming wand outside a fume hood also presents some health and safety challenges that must be considered (Froude, 1996, pp 19–31).

Vaporization can also be achieved without an external heat source. Instead, chemical acceleration is produced by the exothermic reaction that can be achieved by pouring liquid glue on a pad of high cellulose content pretreated with sodium hydroxide. Pretreatment simply involves a cotton ball prepared with a few drops of NaOH solution.

CA fuming without acceleration can be achieved by increasing the total surface area of the liquid glue, thereby increasing the rate of evaporation. One way to achieve this is to sandwich a bead of liquid glue between two sheets of aluminum foil (Olenik, 1989, pp 302–304). The sheets are then pressed together and an ink roller is used to evenly disperse the glue into a thin layer across the entire inside

FIGURE 7–14

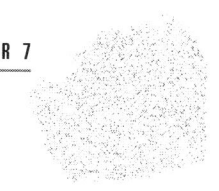

(A) Cyanoacrylate (CA) polymerized print on a plastic wrapper. (B) CA print stained with RAM* and viewed at 475 nm with an orange barrier filter.

*RAM is a fluorescent stain mixture of rhodamine 6G, Ardrox, and 7-(p-methoxybenzylamino)-4-nitrobenz-2-oxa-1,3-diazole (MBD).

of the foil surfaces. These sheets are then opened and placed inside a chamber, exposing the relatively volatile layers of glue to the air. CA development time using this method will vary significantly with the size of the chamber.

Fuming in a vacuum chamber has also been suggested as a method of increasing the volatility of CA (Campbell, 1991, pp 12–16; Yamashita, 1994, pp 149–158; Harvey et al., 2000, pp 29–31; Bessman et al., 2005, pp 10–27). The reduced atmospheric pressure lowers the boiling point of the liquid glue and may vaporize it more rapidly at room temperature. The negative pressure also eliminates humidity in the tank, affecting the overall appearance of the developed impressions. Prints developed in a vacuum environment often appear translucent, making them hard to detect without liquid dye stains (Watkin et al., 1994, pp 545–554). Some researchers have found, however, that this practice is less effective overall than the use of controlled humidity environments (Kent and Winfield, 1995; Kent, 2005, pp 681–683).

Although CA development in a laboratory chamber is preferred, makeshift chambers in the field can also be easily created. Chambers include cardboard boxes, small frames with clear plastic sheeting, large tents, vehicle interiors, and even entire rooms (Weaver, 1993, pp 135–137; Bandey and Kent, 2003). The most common of these field chambers is probably the automobile interior. One method of fuming involves placing a hot plate (reaching approximately 60 °C) in the center of the vehicle, with approximately 1 gram of glue in an evaporation dish. The interior is then sealed off by closing all the doors and windows. The fumes from the heated glue rapidly fill the vehicle interior, developing impressions throughout. This process takes approximately 10–30 minutes, although the length of time is variable. In some cases, so as not to destroy the entire vehicle, parts of the vehicle may be removed and fumed separately (e.g., steering wheel, mirror).

In some instances, CA fuming of a firearm may interfere with subsequent firearms examinations. The firearms examiners may have to be consulted before any CA processing (Rosati, 2005, pp 3–6).

Fuming times depend on the size of the chamber, the quantity of glue, the temperature of the heat source, and the nature of the substrate and latent print residue. Under all conditions, fuming should be terminated shortly after the first signs of the appearance of fingerprints. Some examiners will place a test strip with fingerprints in the chamber to watch for the development of prints. This not only helps to determine when processing should cease but also acts to ensure that the equipment is functioning properly. Fuming can be restarted later if impressions appear underdeveloped.

7.9.4 Enhancement

Once prints have been developed, they can be enhanced optically with oblique, axial, reflected, and transmitted lighting techniques; chemically enhanced with fluorescent dye stains; and physically enhanced with the application of fingerprint powder, in that order. Fluorescent dye staining and examination with a laser or forensic light source usually produces the most dramatic results; however, not all CA-polymerized prints will accept dye stains.

Dye staining simply requires preparing a commercially available fluorescent stain in solution and applying it to the polymerized fingerprints. For a comprehensive reference of fluorescent dye stain recipes, see the FBI *Processing Guide for Developing Latent Prints* (Trozzi et al., 2000) or the Home Office manual (Kent, 1998, 2004). Once a dye solution is chosen, it is applied to the nonporous surfaces treated with CA fumes by dipping or using a wash bottle to spray it. It is thought that dye-staining polymerized prints works like a molecular sieve, where the dye molecules get stuck in the polymer by filling voids in the compound (Menzel, 1999, p 162). For this reason, it is important to adequately rinse the surface bearing the fingerprints with the dye stain. The result is a print that produces intense fluorescence when viewed with a forensic light source or laser (Figure 7–14). At this stage, proper photography can go beyond simply documenting the image to enhance the visibility of the fluorescing print by recording detail imperceptible to the unaided eye.

Powdering is also a good way to visualize and document polymerized impressions. Oftentimes, impressions are durable enough that they may be repeatedly brushed with fingerprint powder and lifted with tape until the right contrast is achieved in the lift (Illsley, 1984, p 15).

7.9.5 Conclusion

CA fuming is a proven and effective method of developing latent print impressions containing eccrine and sebaceous residues that has been in use since the late 1970s. The CA molecules bond to residue via polymerization to form a visible and durable compound that can be enhanced and recorded by fluorescence, photography, and lifting. Research is ongoing into the actual chemistry and mechanics of the CA reaction. Currently, the heat-accelerated technique in controlled high humidity (60–80% relative humidity) is most often the suggested method of application. It is also recommended that CA development be done shortly after fingerprint deposition for maximum results. Although CA fuming has proven effective for considerable durations of time after deposition, CA fuming prior to evidence packaging can also be an effective means of stabilizing fragile latent impressions during storage and transportation.

7.10 Fluorescence Examination

7.10.1 Background

As early as 1933, fluorescence examination with UV light was suggested as a method of visualizing latent prints dusted with anthracene powder on multicolored surfaces (Inbau, 1934, p 4). Before the late 1970s, UV fluorescent powder was used occasionally and appears to have been the only credible fluorescent method of latent print detection. In 1976, researchers at the Xerox Research Centre of Canada discovered inherent latent print fluorescence via continuous wave argon ion laser illumination. Shortly thereafter, the first latent print in a criminal case was identified, using inherent luminescence via laser excitation (fingerprint on black electrical tape) (Menzel and Duff, 1979, p 96).

Since the late 1970s, advancements in the technology of fluorescence detection have greatly aided the hunt for many types of forensic evidence. Today, evidence that would be barely perceptible or even invisible under normal lighting is routinely intensified by fluorescence. Bloodstains, semen, bruises, bone fragments, questioned documents, flammable residues, fibers, and fingerprints all merit examination with a forensic light source or laser.

7.10.2 Theory

Visible light consists of electromagnetic radiation of different colors and wavelengths. When light passes through a prism, it is separated spatially according to wavelengths, resulting in the classic colors of the rainbow. Violet light has the highest energy and the shortest wavelength (approximately 400 nm, where a nanometer is one-billionth of a meter), whereas red light has the lowest energy and the longest wavelength (approximately 700 nm), with green, yellow, and orange being intermediate in energy and wavelength (Champod et al., 2004, pp 41–76).

Atoms and molecules have different unique arrangements of electrons around their nuclei, corresponding to different discrete "energy levels". When light falls on a surface, a photon of light is absorbed if the energy of the photon exactly matches the difference in energy between two of the energy levels of the molecules of the surface substance. If light of a particular color or energy does not match the difference in energy, it is reflected. The color of the surface is made up of the colors of light that are reflected and is not the color corresponding to the wavelengths of light that are absorbed. Objects that are different colors are absorbing and reflecting different wavelengths of light. For example, chlorophyll, which gives leaves their green color, absorbs strongly at the red and blue ends of the visible spectrum, but reflects green light. We see the world by observing the wavelengths of light reflecting off objects all around us.

After a molecule absorbs light and is raised to a higher energy level, it tends to relax back to the lowest level or "ground state" by giving off energy as heat, usually through collisions with other molecules. In some molecules, however, the excess absorbed energy is given off in the form of light. This is photoluminescence. If the emission is immediate, it is termed fluorescence. If it is long-lived, it is phosphorescence. Fluorescence stops within nanoseconds when the forensic light source is turned off, whereas phosphorescence will continue. The glowing numbers of a darkroom timer are an example of phosphorescence.

The excited molecule will lose some of its energy before it emits light as photoluminescence. As a result, the emitted light is of a different color or wavelength than the excitation light (Figure 7–15). The fluorescence is said to be "red-shifted", meaning that it is to the red side of the electromagnetic spectrum in relation to the incident light from the forensic light source. The difference in the wavelengths of the exciting and emitted light is called the Stokes shift. When using fluorescence to view a fingerprint, the viewing or barrier filter blocks the reflected wavelengths of light from the light source while allowing the fluorescent wavelengths to pass through.

Fluorescence examination of latent prints is extremely sensitive (Menzel, 1999, p 5). By using the correct barrier filters that will block out the light from the forensic light source being used, but not the fluorescence, a very high signal-to-noise ratio may be observed. If there is fluorescent chemical only on the fingerprint, the background will give off no signal, and the print will be easily seen glowing against a black background.

Fingerprint examinations may produce fluorescence from four sources:

- Native constituents in latent print residue

- Foreign substances picked up by the hand and transferred through deposition

- Intentional chemical enhancement

- Substrate (background) fluorescence

Some research has been aimed at identifying "native" or inherent luminescence within fingerprint residue. This fluorescence is typically weak and is thought to come from compounds such as riboflavin and pyridoxin (Dalrymple et al., 1977, p 106). Foreign contaminants in fingerprint residue, such as food or drug residue, also may appear luminescent. Treatment by chemical and physical means designed to produce fluorescence, however, is generally considered to be the most productive. Dramatic results are routinely achieved through the use of fluorescent powders, dye stains, and chemical reagents.

7.10.3 Application

The use of lasers and forensic light sources pose real and sometimes irreversible health hazards. Lasers can generate enough intensity that even incidental or reflected light may damage the unprotected eye. Filtered lamps also produce intense light and, in addition, some will generate hazardous UV radiation. The appropriate eye protection must be used in coordination with the excitation wavelengths being employed. Please read all manufacturer warnings before using any forensic light source.

CHAPTER 7 | Latent Print Development

FIGURE 7–15

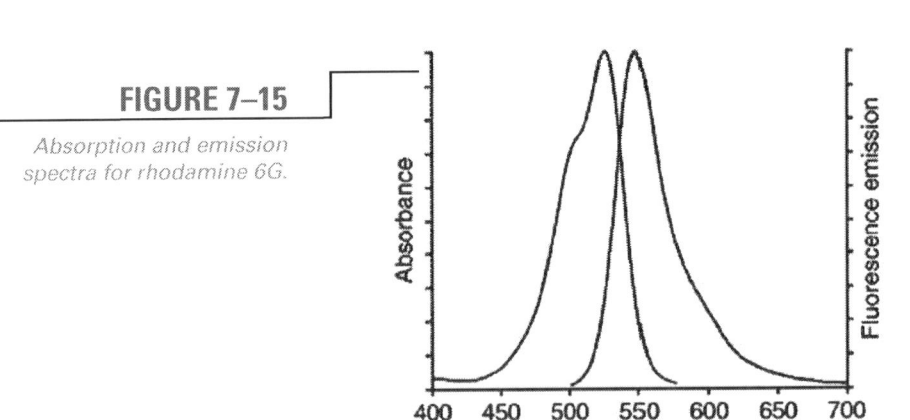

Absorption and emission spectra for rhodamine 6G.

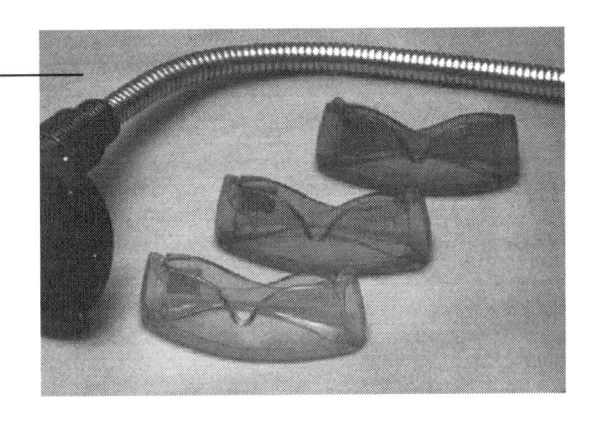

FIGURE 7–16

Goggles.

To visualize latent prints via fluorescence, a specific bandwidth of radiation must be shone on either an untreated latent print or one treated with a fluorescent chemical. The wavelengths chosen will be determined by the chemical involved and the luminescent nature of the substrate. The evidence is then examined through viewing goggles (Figure 7–16) or filter plates that block the incident light from the forensic light source. These goggles act as a barrier filter and are fundamental in separating the incident light generated by the light source and the weak fluorescing signal emitted by the latent print. This separation of incident and emitted light signals gives fluorescence examination its sensitivity. It is important to use the correct goggles to get the optimum results as well as for health and safety considerations.

UV-only excitation does not necessarily require viewing goggles because of the invisibility to the human eye of the incident lighting; however, protective goggles, which can include clear polycarbonate lenses, should be worn during evidence examination to protect the eyes from reflected UV radiation. Not all UV light sources produce pure UV, and a yellow viewing filter will be required if visible light is present. Photography of UV-only excited fluorescence may also require the correct UV barrier filter on the camera because some films and digital media may be sensitive to the incident lighting even when the human eye is not. Protective clothing should be worn to minimize skin exposure to UV radiation.

In general, yellow filters are used for incident light wavelengths from UV to 445 nm, orange filters for light sources of 445–515 nm, and red filters for 515–550 nm. Specific goggles and filters will vary in transmission values and should be matched to the light source being used. Viewing goggles are available through laser and forensic light source companies and most forensic supply houses.

Once a fluorescing image is observed, it can sometimes be "tuned" by adjusting the excitation wavelengths emitted by the light source, and the barrier filter used for viewing, to minimize background fluorescence and maximize contrast. The resulting image must be photographed using a photographic filter that transmits the same wavelengths as the filter used for viewing.

7.10.4 Light Sources

The light sources used to generate these narrow bandwidths come in several different varieties, including UV lamps, filtered lamps, and lasers. Each of these light sources has advantages and disadvantages, depending on the intended purpose and one's budget.

Recently, "alternate" or "forensic" light sources (filtered lamps) have become heavily relied on in laboratories and at crime scenes because of improvements in power output, versatility, portability, and affordability when compared to lasers. These high-intensity lamps use long-pass, short-pass, and band-pass filters in front of a metal halide or xenon bulb to produce the desired wavelength ranges for examining evidence (Wilkinson and Watkin, 1994, pp 632–651; Wilkinson et al., 2002, pp 5–15). Recently, hand-held forensic "flashlights" have been introduced, many based on light-emitting diode (LED) technology (Wilansky et al., 2006).

Lasers, on the other hand, have in the past been less portable and affordable but generated considerably more power than filtered lamps. Lasers are desirable when only very weak fluorescence is observed. Some examples of weak fluorescence include the inherent fluorescence of latent fingerprint residue or fingerprints developed with reagents such as crystal violet that emit a very weak fluorescent signal. New lasers (532 nm), which are air-cooled and portable, have recently come on the market. For a more comprehensive discussion of laser types, functionality, uses, and theory, see Menzel's *Fingerprint Detection with Lasers* (Menzel, 1999, pp 3–21) or the Home Office publication, *Fingerprint Detection by Fluorescence Examination* (Hardwick et al., 1990).

Besides simply detecting evidence, a forensic light source or laser is often an effective means of image enhancement as well. This enhancement may come from intentionally causing a background to fluoresce to increase the contrast between a fingerprint and its substrate, or from muting a background pattern by selecting a wavelength range that reduces the background color.

Bloody impressions are a good example of enhancement through absorption at a discrete wavelength. The maximum absorption wavelength for dried blood is approximately 420 nm. Illumination at this wavelength makes the blood-stained ridges appear darker. If the background fluoresces in this wavelength range, the bloody impression will be significantly enhanced (Figure 7–17) (Stoilovic, 1991, pp 289–296; Vandenberg and van Oorschot, 2006, pp 361–370).

7.10.5 Fluorescent Powders, Dye Stains, and Reagents

Many fluorescent processes have been developed to aid the forensic examiner with tools that go far beyond using a light source alone. Fluorescent powders are abundant and widely available at forensic supply companies, with most companies marketing their own particular brand name.

Dye stains such as MBD [7-(*p*-methoxybenzylamino)-4-nitrobenz-2-oxa-1,3-diazole], rhodamine 6G (R6G), Ardrox, basic yellow, and basic red can be prepared in the lab and are extremely effective for enhancing fingerprints developed with cyanoacrylate. Some of these dye stains can be combined to produce a stain that will fluoresce across a broad spectrum. One such stain is RAM, a combination of R6G, Ardrox, and MBD. Because RAM can be used at various wavelengths, the practitioner can often "tune out" problematic backgrounds by selecting a wavelength that maximizes fingerprint fluorescence and suppresses background fluorescence.

Treatments for paper are equally effective as those used on nonporous surfaces and include ninhydrin toned with zinc chloride and the ninhydrin analogues: DFO, 1,2-indanedione, and 5-MTN (5-methylthioninhydrin).

Four excellent references containing recipes and instructions for fluorescent reagents are the FBI *Processing Guide for Developing Latent Prints* (Trozzi et al., 2000), the Home Office *Manual of Fingerprint Development Techniques* (Kent, 1998, 2004), *Fingerprints and Other Ridge Skin Impressions* (Champod et al., 2004, pp 142–145, 228–229), and *Advances in Fingerprint Technology* (Lee and Gaensslen, 2001, pp 105–175).

Table 7–3 is a list of common reagents and their corresponding wavelengths of peak absorption and emission. Precise adherence to a peak excitation and absorption wavelength is not always possible (depending on the available light source) and not always advisable because many substrates may interfere with visibility at these wavelengths. Because the absorption bands are generally quite wide, the excitation wavelength can differ from the absorption maximum and still induce significant fluorescence.

FIGURE 7–17

Composite image of a bloody fingerprint on copy paper. The left side was photographed at 415 nm. The right side was photographed under daylight-balanced photographic lighting.

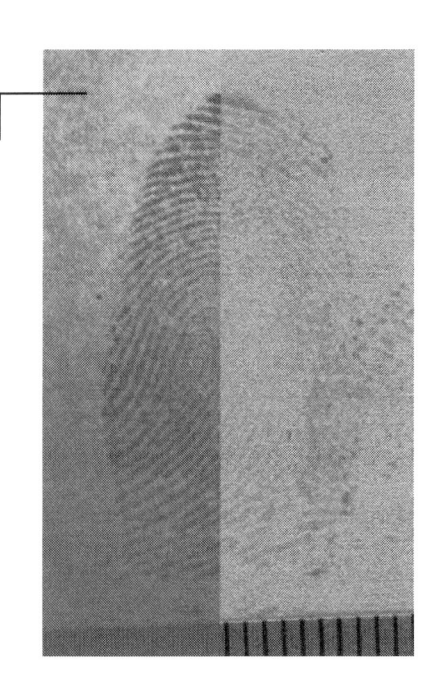

7.10.6 Time- and Phase-Resolved Imaging

As mentioned earlier, background fluorescence may be generated intentionally to better visualize a fingerprint that is faintly absorbing light but not fluorescing. This condition will increase contrast by brightening the background, making the darker fingerprint stand out. However, background fluorescence is more often a hindrance, competing with a fluorescing fingerprint for visualization.

Time-resolved imaging has been advocated as one possible means to solve this problem. This technique takes advantage of the difference between the time of emission of the substrate and the fluorescing fingerprint (Menzel, 1999, p 126). Early devices utilized a light source with a gated, rotating wheel that "chops" the light to exploit these differences in emissions. The light shines on the fingerprint and substrate when an opening in the wheel is in front of the light. The light source is then effectively turned off when a blade in the wheel passes in front of the light source. Shortly thereafter, an opening in the wheel passes in front of a detector. The size of the openings in the wheel, and the speed with which it turns, will determine the length of time that the print is exposed and the delay between excitation and detection. If the background fluorescence decays faster than the fluorescence of the chemical on the latent fingerprint, the background can be eliminated by adjusting the delay time (Menzel, 2001, p 216; Campbell, 1993, pp 368–377).

Later designs proved more practical by using an electronic light chopper in conjunction with a gateable charge-coupled device (CCD) camera, each component controlled by a computer with the image displayed on a monitor (Menzel, 1999, p 126). Time-resolved imaging is still considered impractical for widespread application. Phase-resolved imaging stands to be the next technological advance and is currently used in other fields of spectroscopy (Menzel, 2001, p 216).

7.10.7 Conclusion

Fluorescence examination is firmly grounded in everyday latent print detection and imaging techniques. The sensitivity of this technique warrants application on all forms of forensic evidence. Specific bandwidths of radiation are shone on untreated prints as well as prints treated with powders and chemical reagents. When viewed with the appropriate barrier filters, sensitivity via photoluminescence detection may be achieved down to nearly the single photon. Absorption at discrete wavelengths, absent fluorescence, is also a beneficial enhancement technique on substances such as the purple impressions from ninhydrin or dried blood, rendering them darker and easier to view and photograph. Because background fluorescence is the biggest hindrance to fluorescence examination, experimental concepts such as time- and phase-resolved imaging have been proposed to address this problem.

Table 7-3

Common reagents and their wavelengths of peak absorption and emission.

Reagent/Substance	Absorption Maximum (nm)	Emission Maximum (nm)
DFO	560 (Champod et al., 2004, pp 129–130)	580 (Champod et al., 2004, pp 129–130)
1,2-Indanedione	515	
5-MTN	550 (Wallace-Kunkel et al., 2006, pp 4–13)	
Ninhydrin	415–560* (Champod et al., 2004, pp 117–118)	
Ninhydrin/ZnCl	490	540 (Champod et al., 2004, pp 120–124)
Ardrox	380	500 (Lee and Gaennslen, 2001, p 124)
Basic Yellow 40	445 (Champod et al., 2004, pp 142–145, 228–229) 440 (Lee and Gaennslen, 2001, p 124)	495 (Champod et al., 2004, pp 142–145, 228–229) 490 (Lee and Gaennslen, 2001, p 124)
MBD	465	515 (Lee and Gaennslen, 2001, p 124)
Basic Red 28	495	585 (Champod et al., 2004, pp 142–145, 228–229; Lee and Gaennslen, 2001, p 124)
Rhodamine 6G	490–530 (Champod et al., 2004, pp 142–145, 228–229) 525 (Lee and Gaennslen, 2001, p 124)	565 (Champod et al., 2004, pp 142–145, 228–229) 555 (Lee and Gaensslen, 2001, p 124)
Crystal Violet	532**	
Acid Yellow 7	527	550 (Sears et al., 2005, pp 741–763)
Acid Yellow 7 + Blood	445–480	485–500 (Sears et al., 2005, pp 741–763)
Untreated Dried Blood	415* (Champod et al., 2004, p 168)	

* Does not fluoresce but appears dark.

** Weak fluorescence requiring laser illumination.

CHAPTER 7 | Latent Print Development

7.11 Vacuum Metal Deposition

7.11.1 History

Vacuum metal deposition (VMD) is a long-established industrial technique for the application of metal coatings to components such as glass to form a mirror. In 1964, physics professor Samuel Tolansky (Royal Holloway College, University of London) noted that the deposition of silver in a vacuum system developed latent fingerprints accidentally deposited on a glass component. An investigation into the process as a fingerprint development technique was proposed. However, this was not pursued at the time by the U.K. Home Office because other techniques for fingerprint detection on glass were considered cheaper, easier to use, and sufficiently effective.

In 1968, French workers reported (Theys et al., 1968, p 106) that VMD of a mixture of zinc, antimony, and copper powder was capable of developing latent prints on paper. As a consequence of this article, interest in the technique was revived in the United Kingdom, and Tolansky initiated a research program to investigate the optimum conditions and the potential applications for VMD. One of the early objectives of the research was to establish why the French composition was effective. Closer examination of deposited metal coatings produced by the French laboratory indicated that the coating was almost entirely zinc, the presence of antimony and copper not being necessary to develop prints (Hambley, 1972).

The research program initiated by Tolansky (Hambley, 1972) investigated the deposition characteristics of a range of metals on paper substrates, identifying single metals and metal combinations giving the optimum print development. Research was also conducted into the ability of the technique to detect latent prints on fabrics. These experiments showed that although some print development was obtained by the use of single metals (e.g., gold, silver, copper, zinc, and cadmium), in general, the best results were obtained by the use of a combination of metals, typically gold or silver followed by cadmium or zinc. Initially, the gold and cadmium combination was selected as the optimum, although subsequent health and safety issues have resulted in the gold and zinc combination being recommended instead. Gold was preferred over silver as the initial deposition metal because silver can be degraded by fingerprint secretions and atmospheric pollutants.

The early experimental work was carried out on small-scale equipment with a bell jar, but research continued to develop larger equipment suitable for use in a fingerprint laboratory. By the mid-1970s, systems modified from standard industrial equipment had been developed (Kent, 1982) and were in use in several police forces and forensic providers within the United Kingdom. Later, manufacturers made refinements, increasing the size of the vacuum chamber and adding controls specific to the fingerprint development process. In the 1990s, the technique made its way from Europe to North America (Murphy, 1991, pp 318–320; Misner, 1992, pp 26–33; Masters and DeHaan, 1996, pp 32–45). Specially constructed VMD equipment is now supplied by several manufacturers worldwide.

Although VMD was originally investigated as a fingerprint development technique for use on paper and fabrics, it was established that other processes are capable of giving better results on paper. However, VMD was found to give excellent results on nonporous substrates and in comparative studies was found to outperform all other techniques in developing marks on plastic bags (Misner, 1992, pp 26–33; Kent et al., 1975, 1978; Reynoldson and Reed, 1979). The process was also found to develop marks on substrates exposed to water and conditions of high humidity, giving substantial advantages over techniques such as CA fuming for articles that have been exposed to these conditions.

Few modifications have been made to the process itself since the change in the second deposition metal from cadmium to zinc in the late 1970s. Recently, there has been further research on VMD in Australia, looking in detail at the various print development regimes that can be followed on different grades of polyethylene (Jones et al., 2001c, pp 73–88) and how the surfaces could be "reactivated" to develop prints if excess metal deposition had occurred initially (Jones et al., 2001d, pp 5–12). The work was extended to investigate other polymer substrates, including polypropylene, polyvinylchloride, and polyethylene terephthalate (Jones et al., 2001b, pp 167–177), and different deposition conditions were recommended for each class of polymer, in particular the amount of gold deposited prior to zinc deposition (polyethylene terephthalate and polyvinylchloride require significantly more gold to develop prints than polymer or polypropylene).

However, there are situations where the performance of VMD leaves much to be desired. It is believed that the effectiveness of VMD can be detrimentally affected by the

FIGURE 7–18

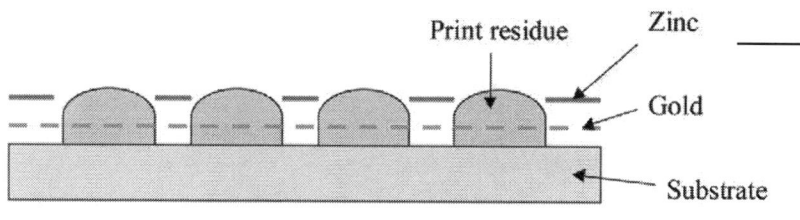

Schematic diagram of normal development, showing zinc depositing where gold nuclei are available on the surface.

presence of body fluids (Batey et al., 1998, pp 165–175) and drug residues (Magora et al., 2002, pp 159–165). It has also been difficult to develop prints on heavily plasticized polymers (such as clingfilm and plasticized vinyl) using the VMD process. Recent work has indicated that deposition of silver as a single metal may give improved detection rates over the gold and zinc combination for these types of substrates, and the silver deposition process has now been published for operational use (Home Office Scientific Development Branch, 2005, pp 8–9).

7.11.2 Theory

There is general agreement on the theory associated with normal development of prints by the VMD method. The reason that the metal combinations are postulated to work well is due to the condensation characteristics of zinc (and cadmium). These metals will not condense on grease, such as that found in fingerprint residues, even when the oily residues are present only as a monolayer. However, zinc will deposit on small nuclei of metal, and this is the reason that gold or silver deposition is carried out first. Gold and silver can be deposited over the entire surface and begin to form nuclei, the morphology of which depends on the nature of the surface (surface energy, chemical species present) upon which they are being deposited. The resultant gold coating is very thin (several nanometers only) and discontinuous. However, in the regions coated with the fatty residues of the latent fingerprint, the gold diffuses into the fat and hence there are no gold nuclei close to the surface. As a consequence, when zinc is subsequently deposited, it will condense on the regions of gold nuclei (i.e., the background substrate) but not on the regions of the fatty deposit (i.e., the fingerprint ridges). This theory of nucleation was discussed in more detail by Stroud (1971, 1972). The normal development process is depicted schematically in Figure 7–18, and a photograph of a mark produced by normal development is shown in Figure 7–19.

Tests carried out to determine which components of the latent print were most likely to be responsible for inhibiting metal deposition identified several substances, including stearic acid, palmitic acid, cholesterol oleate, glycerol trioleate, and amino acids L-arginine monohydrochloride, L-leucine, and DL-threonine. Most of these substances are non-water-soluble or long-chain fats or acids with low vapor pressure, which determines their stability and non-migration over the surface during the VMD process. These findings were in accord with the observation that VMD was capable of developing prints on substrates exposed to water. Experiments to study the diffusion of gold into thin films of stearic acid (Thomas, 1978, pp 722–730) demonstrated that 60% of the gold penetrated the stearic acid to a depth greater than the detection depth of the electron spectroscopy for the chemical analysis (ESCA) surface analysis technique and hence would probably not be sufficiently close to the surface for zinc to nucleate on it.

Electron microscopy has also been used to confirm that the size and distribution of gold nuclei formed during the deposition process varied greatly according to the substrate and the chemical species present (Kent, 1981, p 15). It was this difference in nuclei size and distribution, coupled with diffusion of gold into the fatty deposits, that subsequently delineated the print during VMD.

In practice, many prints developed using VMD may be "reverse developed" (i.e., zinc preferentially deposits on the fingerprint ridges rather than the background). There are differences in opinion as to why this arises (Jones et al., 2001b, pp 167–177; 2001c, 73–78; Kent et al., 1976, p 93), but none of the theories have been categorically proven, and in some cases reverse and normal development may be observed on the same substrate (although it is stated that this is most common for [if not exclusive to] low-density polyethylene substrates). Figure 7–20 shows a reverse-developed mark on a polyethylene bag.

CHAPTER 7 | Latent Print Development

FIGURE 7–19

Photograph of a normally developed mark on a polyethylene bag.

FIGURE 7–20

Photograph of a reverse-developed mark on a polyethylene bag.

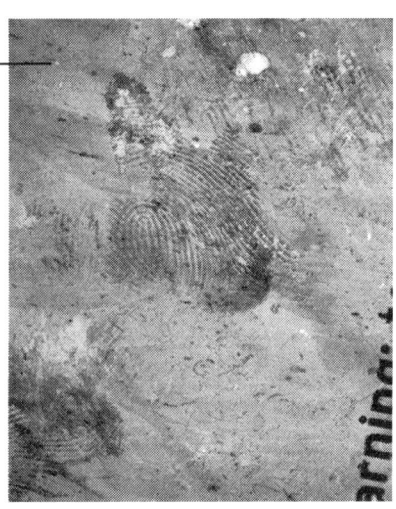

7.11.3 Application

The equipment used for VMD may vary according to manufacturer, but the essential elements of the system are the same. The equipment consists of a vacuum chamber capable of being pumped down to very low pressure ($< 3 \times 10^{-4}$ mbar), filaments for evaporation of gold and zinc, and a viewing window so that the deposition of zinc can be monitored. The chamber may also contain a "cold finger", chilled to low temperature to help reduce pump downtimes by condensing some of the vapor in the chamber. Articles to be coated are attached to the inside circumference of the vacuum chamber, above the coating filaments. A typical system is illustrated in Figure 7–21.

The filaments ("boats") used for deposition of gold and zinc are typically formed from thin sheets of molybdenum. The gold filament usually consists of a shallow dimple in a thin strip of molybdenum. Gold deposition takes place when the chamber has reached a pressure of 3×10^{-4} mbar or lower, and the current to the filament is increased until the filament reaches a yellow-to-white heat. Deposition of gold should be complete within 10 seconds, but if any residue is observed on the filament as the current is reduced, the temperature should be increased again until all gold has been evaporated.

Once gold deposition is completed, the pressure in the chamber is increased to ~5×10^{-4} mbar and the current to the zinc deposition filament(s) is turned on. The reason for increasing the pressure in the chamber is to reduce the speed of zinc deposition by introducing more air molecules with which the zinc may collide. Some substrates can coat very quickly, so the slower deposition process gives the operator more control. The zinc deposition filaments are larger and significantly deeper than the gold filament, and the quantity of zinc added is greater, typically 1 g per run. For zinc deposition, the current is increased until the

FIGURE 7–21

Typical vacuum metal deposition equipment.

filament glows a cherry-red to dull orange color. Once this occurs, the operator should observe the deposition process through the viewing window, ceasing deposition as soon as marks become visible on the substrate. After zinc deposition, the gold filament should be briefly heated to yellow-to-white heat to burn off any zinc contamination. The process is described in more detail elsewhere (Kent, 2004).

There is great variability in the speed at which different substrates coat, and it may take more than 10 minutes to obtain a suitable coating on some types of material. In some cases, it may be necessary to carry out multiple deposition runs in order to obtain satisfactory results or to develop all the marks present. The presence of surface contamination, release agents, or plasticizers may mean that it is not possible to obtain a zinc coating at all; in these circumstances, the deposition of 60 mg of silver, using the same deposition conditions for gold, may yield additional marks.

The VMD technique was initially adopted as an operational technique for the detection of latent prints on thin polyethylene sheets, and it was shown to be superior to other processes developed subsequent to the initial comparison trials. VMD has now been used operationally for many years and has been shown to be an effective technique for a wider range of materials than polyethylene. Recent results have shown VMD to produce results on a range of substrates (e.g., a ticket coated with ferromagnetic ink, and on expanded polystyrene) (Suzuki et al., 2002, pp 573–578). The use of the technique has also begun to increase in North America, and successful results have been obtained from plastic bags, in some cases several years old and exposed to moisture (Batey et al., 1998, pp 165–175).

The range of specimens that have been successfully treated using VMD is extensive and includes:

- Plastic bags and packaging.
- Glass and plastic bottles.
- Firearms.
- Glossy card, photographic paper, and magazine covers.
- Clean leather items (including handbags and shoes).
- Adhesive tapes (nonsticky side).

It is evident that there is much overlap between the types of articles that can be treated with VMD and those that are treated using CA fuming. In many cases, the deciding factor as to which technique is to be used is whether the article has been wetted because VMD remains effective on wetted items, whereas CA fuming does not. In practice, it is possible to use the two processes in sequence, and more marks may be detected in this way because the two processes work on different fingerprint constituents. However, at present, there still seems to be some debate as to which of the two techniques should be done first.

7.12 Blood Enhancement Techniques

7.12.1 History

Blood is one of the most common known contaminants of fingerprints found at scenes of crime. The use of blood evidence in the history of forensic investigation dates back over 150 years. The earliest tests were of two types, both relying on the presence of the heme group: those that produced crystals and those that relied on its catalytic nature.

The crystal or confirmatory tests were formulated by Teichmann in 1850 (Thorwald, 1966, p 23) and Takayama in 1912 (Gerber and Saferstein, 1997, pp 18–19). However, these tests require the blood to be scraped from the surface and, therefore, give no regard to the forms of physical evidence such as fingerprints, footwear impressions, or spatter patterns.

Catalytic or presumptive tests that attempted to keep much of the physical evidence intact were produced by Van Deen and Day in 1862 and were based on guaiacol (Gerber and Saferstein, 1997, pp 18–19); by Schönbein in 1863, using hydrogen peroxide; and by Adler and Adler around 1900, using benzidine (Thorwald, 1966, p 23). Adler and Adler pioneered the use of leucomalachite green in 1904 (Eckert and James, 1989, p 2); Medinger modified their method in 1931 to make it more sensitive (Söderman and O'Connell, 1935, p 226).

Other presumptive tests for blood were developed by Kastle and Sheed in 1901 and Kastle and Meyer in 1903, using phenolphthalein; by Ruttan and Hardisty in 1912, using o-tolidine; by Specht in 1937, using luminol (3-aminophthalhydrazide); and by Gershenfeld in 1939, using o-toluidine (Eckert and James, 1989, p 2).

In 1911, Abderhalden and Schmidt (1911, p 37) reported the development of fingerprints on the bottle label of triketohydrindene hydrate (ninhydrin). This discovery was not exploited for the detection of fingerprints or blood until 1954, when Odén (Odén and von Hofsten, 1954, p 449) produced his ninhydrin formulation based on acetone. The use of this method for the enhancement of fingerprints in blood revolutionized thinking in this area of forensic investigation. The emphasis was shifted away from presumptive tests for heme, which generally require expert opinion to interpret the test results correctly, and onto easier-to-use reagents that produce intensely colored products with other components of blood, usually protein or its breakdown products.

Use of the protein dye, amido black (acid black 1), quickly became popular with forensic investigators. Its use by the Metropolitan Police Laboratory, in a solvent base of methanol and acetic acid, was discussed at a forensic science symposium in 1961 by Godsell (1963, p 79). This formulation, with a change in the method for fixing blood— from the use of heat to immersion in methanol (Faragher and Summerscales, 1981), along with a water-based formulation of the same dye (Hussain and Pounds, 1989a)— continued to be recommended for the enhancement of fingerprints in blood by the U.K. Home Office until 2004 (Kent, 2004), when a new formulation by Sears and Prizeman (2000, p 470) was adopted.

Many other protein stains for the enhancement of both fingerprints and footwear impressions in blood have also been proposed: coomassie blue (acid blue 83) and Crowle's double stain (acid blue 83 and acid red 71) by Norkus and Noppinger in 1986 (Norkus and Noppinger, 1986, p 5); fuchsin acid (acid violet 19, Hungarian Red), patent blue V (acid blue 1), and tartrazine (acid yellow 23) by Barnett and colleagues in 1988 (Barnett et al., 1988); benzoxanthene yellow and acid violet 17 by Sears and colleagues in 2001 (Sears et al., 2001, p 28); and acid yellow 7 by Sears and colleagues in 2005 (Sears et al., 2005, p 741).

Although the use of protein dyes became most popular for enhancing fingerprints in blood, research on presumptive enhancement methods continued and, in 1976, Garner et al. (1976, p 816) proposed the use of tetramethylbenzidene (TMB) as safer and just as reliable as benzidine. Suggestions for other presumptive tests continue: tetraamino-biphenyl (TAB) and diaminobenzidine (DAB) in 1989 by Hussain and Pounds (1989b); fluorescein in 1995 by Cheeseman and DiMeo (1995, p 631); and leucocrystal violet (LCV) in 1996 by Bodziak (1996, p 45).

In addition, many modifications have been made to ninhydrin formulations to increase its effectiveness and safety: by Crown in 1969 (Crown, 1969, p 258) and Morris and Goode in 1974 (Morris and Goode, 1974, p 45). Further changes were forced on the fingerprint community because of "The Montreal Protocol on Substances That Deplete the Ozone Layer" (United Nations Environ Programme, 1999), and new formulations were proposed by Watling and Smith in 1993 (Watling and Smith, 1993, p 131) and Hewlett and colleagues in 1997 (Hewlett et al., 1997, p 300). The use of transition metal toners to change the color or make the reaction product between amines and ninhydrin fluoresce has also been proposed by Morris in 1978 (Morris, 1978), Everse and Menzel in 1986 (Everse and Menzel, 1986, p 446), and Stoilovic and colleagues in 1986 (Stoilovic et al., 1986, p 432).

It was also suggested that the use of one of several ninhydrin analogues would improve sensitivity, and many have been proposed: benzo(f)ninhydrin in 1982 by Almog et al. (1982, p 912), 5-methoxyninhydrin in 1988 by Almog and Hirshfeld (1988, p 1027), DFO in 1990 by Grigg et al. (1990, p 7215), and indanedione in 1997 by Ramotowski et al. (1997, p 131).

In the late 1970s and early 1980s, those developing high-intensity light sources observed that shorter wavelengths of light in the UV and violet regions of the spectrum make surfaces fluoresce strongly. This can give extra detail if a fingerprint is in a strongly light-absorbing material such as blood (Hardwick et al., 1990). This is an especially valuable method for the enhancement of fingerprints in blood, as the heme group absorbs light throughout much of the visible part of the spectrum (Kotowski and Grieve, 1986, p 1079).

All these developments meant that by the late 1990s, there were so many reagents and formulations for the enhancement of blood-contaminated fingerprints and footwear impressions, with little or no comparative data, that it was causing immense confusion amongst practitioners. Also, the emergence of DNA analysis heaped even more uncertainty onto which techniques could or should be used for the enhancement of blood, such that vital evidence was likely to be lost by the wrong choices. Therefore, the U.K. Home Office set out to clarify the situation and began a program of work to review and compare the most commonly used of these techniques (Sears and Prizeman, 2000, p 470; Sears et al., 2001, p 28; 2005, p 741). Resulting from this colossal task were a number of key findings that were incorporated in a comprehensive update to *The Manual of Fingerprint Development Techniques* in 2004 (Kent, 2004).

7.12.2 Theory

Blood consists of red cells (erythrocytes), white cells (leukocytes), and platelets (thrombocytes) in a proteinaceous fluid called plasma, which makes up roughly 55% of whole blood volume. The red cells principally contain the hemoglobin protein but also have specific surface proteins (agglutinogens) that determine blood group. The white cells, which form part of the immune system, have a nucleus that contains DNA.

Hemoglobin makes up roughly 95% of red cells' protein content and is made of four protein subunits, each containing a heme group. The heme group is made of a flat porphyrin ring and a conjugated ferrous ion.

Chemical blood enhancement methods fall broadly into two types—those that use the heme grouping to prove or infer the presence of blood and those that react with proteins or their breakdown products. The latter are not at all specific for blood; however, because of the high content in blood of protein and protein breakdown products, these techniques are the most sensitive available to the forensic investigator (Sears et al., 2005, p 741).

7.12.3 Tests for Heme

Two kinds of tests use the heme group in hemoglobin: crystal tests and catalytic tests.

Crystal tests are specific or confirmatory for the presence of heme, but not whether the blood is human or not. The two best-known crystal tests are those formulated by Teichmann and Takayama. The Teichmann test results in the formation of brown rhombohedral crystals of hematin, and the Takayama test results in red-pink crystals of pyridine hemochromogen (Palenik, 2000, p 1115; Ballantyne, 2000, p 1324). Both these tests have to be carried out ex situ so are of no use for fingerprint enhancement.

The catalytic tests are only presumptive or infer the presence of heme because they are subject to false-positive and false-negative reactions caused by a variety of nonblood substances. Consequently, individual results require careful interpretation by experts. These tests all rely on the peroxidase activity of the heme group (i.e., the ability to reduce hydrogen peroxide to water and oxygen). This reaction may then be coupled to the oxidation of colorless reduced dyes (e.g., phenolphthalein, leucocrystal violet, tetramethylbenzidine, and fluorescein) that, when oxidized, form their colored counterparts (Ballantyne, 2000, p 1324).

$$H_2O_2 + \text{colorless reduced dye} \rightarrow H_2O + \text{colored oxidized dye}$$

(Lee and Pagliaro, 2000, p 1333).

The luminol test also relies on the peroxidase activity of the heme group but uses sodium perborate instead of hydrogen peroxide. This then produces a product that luminesces in the presence of blood. The bluish-white chemiluminescence is faint and must be viewed in the dark by an operator who is fully dark-adapted to gain the best from this test. Even with careful application of luminol, it is all too easy to damage the fine detail of blood-contaminated fingerprints. This technique should be used only when fine detail is not required and when other techniques might be compromised by surface type or impracticality, such as dark or patterned carpets (Sears et al., 2005, p 741).

The major concern with the catalytic tests for blood is that they can produce false-positive results in the presence of chemical oxidants and catalysts; salts of heavy metals such as copper, nickel, and iron; and plant peroxidases such as those found in horseradish, citrus fruits, and numerous root vegetables (Lee and Pagliaro, 2000, p 1334). A two-stage test can obviate this. The reduced colorless dye is applied initially and if no color change is observed, then the hydrogen peroxide is added. A color change at this point is more likely to indicate the presence of blood.

It is generally accepted that a negative result with a catalytic test proves the absence of blood; however, strong reducing agents, such as ascorbic acid, may inhibit such tests (Eckert and James, 1989, p 121).

7.12.4 Tests for Protein and Its Breakdown Products

There are two types of techniques for proteins—those that stain proteinaceous material and those that react with amines. Blood contains more protein than any other material, so these techniques are inherently more sensitive than those for heme, although they are not at all specific for blood.

The most effective protein dyes for the enhancement of fingerprints in blood are a group known as acid dyes. They are often characterized by the presence of one or more sulphonate ($-SO_3$) groups, usually the sodium (Na^+) salt. These groups function in two ways: first, they provide for solubility in water or alcohol, the favored major solvents from which to apply these dyes; and, second, they assist the reaction by virtue of their negative charge (anionic). If acidic conditions are used (acetic acid being the favored option), the blood protein molecules acquire a positive charge (cationic) and this attracts the acid dye anions. Also, hydrogen bonding and other physical forces, such as van der Waals, may play a part in the affinity of acid dyes to protein molecules (Christie et al., 2000, pp 19–20). The presence of a short-chain alcohol in the dyeing solution helps to prevent the blood from diffusing during the dyeing stage (Sears and Prizeman, 2000, p 470). Ethanol is preferred because this offers lower toxicity and flammability than methanol. The use of water as the major solvent gives the solution a flash point of around 30 °C, enabling this formulation (containing water, ethanol, and acetic acid) to be used at crime scenes with a few simple precautions (Kent, 2004).

If acid dye formulations are applied directly to fingerprints in blood without a fixing stage, the blood will solubilize and ridges will diffuse or be completely washed away. A number of different fixing agents have been used, but the most effective are 5-sulphosalicylic acid and methanol. Which one is used depends on the major solvent used in the dyeing process: if water is the main solvent, then a solution of 5-sulphosalicylic acid is most effective, whereas if the main dyeing solvent is methanol, then methanol is the best fixing agent (Sears and Prizeman, 2000, p 470). These fixing agents act in different ways; the 5-sulphosalicylic acid precipitates basic proteins, and methanol dehydrates the blood.

The use of solutions based on methanol has waned for a number of reasons, including its toxicity, flammability, and tendency to cause damage to surfaces (e.g., paints, varnishes, and some plastics), which has a negative effect on fingerprint development. This fixing stage gives the protein dyes another advantage over the presumptive tests for blood: as well as being a more sensitive test, it often produces more sharply defined fingerprint ridges and the detail is clearer.

A washing stage is required post-dyeing. On nonporous surfaces, this just removes excess dye; however, on porous surfaces, this also acts as a destainer, removing dye that has been absorbed by the background surface. The wash solution has to be carefully constructed so that it solubilizes the dye, does not diffuse or wash away the dyed fingerprint, and retains the intensity of color of the dye in the fingerprint. For this reason, the same solvent mix as that used for the dyeing process, or some small variation of it, is generally most effective (Sears and Prizeman, 2000, p 470).

Ninhydrin and DFO react with amines and are the two most widely used techniques to develop latent fingerprints on porous surfaces (Figure 7–22). They are also very effective for the enhancement of blood (Sears et al., 2005, p 741). They both react with amino acids similarly to form products that contain two deoxygenated molecules of the starting product, bridged by a nitrogen atom that is donated from the amine (McCaldin, 1960, p 39; Wilkinson, 2000a, p 87).

Although the reaction mechanisms and products have similarities, the method of their visualization is entirely different. Ninhydrin, under the right conditions, produces an intensely colored product (Ruhemann's purple), and DFO

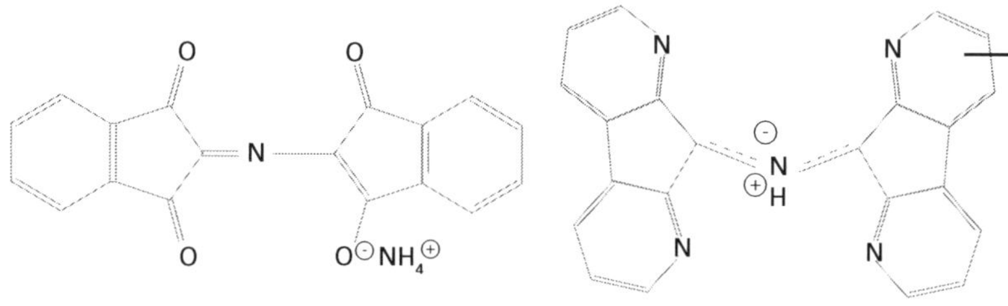

FIGURE 7–22

The reaction products for the reaction of ninhydrin (left) and DFO (right) with amines.

produces a pale pink, extremely fluorescent product. Ruhemann's purple can be made to fluoresce by complexing it with metal salts, but this additional process is still not as sensitive as DFO (Stoilovic, 1993, p 141). DFO requires heat for the reaction to proceed (Hardwick et al., 1993, p 65), whereas ninhydrin will react at room temperature, provided moisture is available, although the process proceeds much faster at elevated temperatures and humidities.

7.12.5 Fluorescence

The use of fluorescence to enhance fingerprints in blood can be extremely effective. There are two ways this may be achieved: (1) by exciting fluorescence in the background surface on which the blood is deposited or (2) by treatment with a chemical that either breaks the heme group or turns the blood into a fluorescent species, or does both of these.

Many materials fluoresce when excited by high-intensity light in the UV and violet regions of the spectrum. This is coincidentally where the heme group is most absorbent, with a peak around 421 nm (known as the Soret Band) (Kotowski and Grieve, 1986, p 1079). This absorbency is why blood-contaminated fingerprints will appear dark against a light background. Fluorescence examination may be used before any other fingerprint enhancement techniques because it is nondestructive, and if long-wave UV or violet light (350–450 nm) (Hardwick et al., 1990) is used, then DNA typing is also unaffected (Kent, 2004). The use of ninhydrin, acid black 1, or acid violet 17 can further intensify the contrast between fingerprint and background by increasing the light absorption properties of the blood.

The use of a strong organic acid in conjunction with hydrogen peroxide breaks up the heme group so that it is no longer as effective at absorbing light. Then, when excited by green (500–550 nm) light, it will fluoresce orange. This effect has also been noted as blood ages.

DFO and acid yellow 7 both produce fluorescent species with blood that can be excited by green (510–570 nm) and blue (420–485 nm) light, respectively. Both can be less effective on heavy deposits of blood because the heme group retains its ability to absorb both the excitation light and that emitted as fluorescence.

7.12.5.1 Application. Currently it is considered that fluorescence examination, two amino acid reagents, and three acid dyes are the most effective means of enhancing fingerprints in blood (Sears et al., 2005, p 741). The most appropriate techniques to use for maximum effectiveness, either individually or in sequential order, depend on the porosity of the surface to be treated. This applies to both latent fingerprint development and enhancement of blood-contaminated fingerprints.

Testing of the surface for fluorescence should always be carried out before any other technique. High-intensity light sources with outputs between 350 and 450 nm are most effective. When the blood-contaminated or latent fingerprints are on porous surfaces, the most effective sequence of techniques is DFO, ninhydrin, either acid black 1 or acid violet 17 (after carrying out a spot test to see which is most suitable), and then finally physical developer (Sears et al., 2005, p 741).

When the blood-contaminated or latent fingerprints are on nonporous surfaces, the most effective sequence of techniques is VMD, powders, acid yellow 7, acid violet 17, then finally either physical developer or solvent black 3 (sudan black). Superglue may be used instead of VMD or powders, but this will inhibit the dyeing process for blood by preventing the dye from reaching the blood (Sears et al., 2005, p 741).

DFO and ninhydrin working solution should be applied by dipping or by brushing with a soft brush on larger articles or surfaces. It is recommended that DFO be heated to 100 °C for 20 minutes; however, when this is not possible, temperatures as low as 50 °C may be used, but the rate of reaction is much slower (Hardwick et al., 1993, p 65). It is recommended that ninhydrin-treated articles or surfaces be heated to 80 °C and humidified to 65% RH. However, the reaction will proceed at room temperature and humidity, but more slowly.

High-intensity light sources capable of emitting wavelengths between 510 and 570 nm must be used to excite fluorescence from blood reacted with DFO. The fluorescence emitted is between 550 and 650 nm. Benefit may also be gained by using shorter wavelengths, between 350 and 450 nm, to excite background fluorescence after ninhydrin treatment.

The three recommended acid dyes, acid black 1 (CI 20470), acid violet 17 (CI 42650), and acid yellow 7 (CI 56205), should all be applied to blood fixed for at least 5 minutes with a solution of 5-sulphosalicylic acid. Dyeing of fixed blood is most effective if the area of interest is immersed in the dyeing solution for at least 3 minutes for acid black 1 and acid violet 17 and for at least 5 minutes in the case of acid yellow 7. Areas heavily contaminated with blood require longer dyeing times. If it is not possible to immerse the bloodied fingerprints, then the dyeing solution should be applied above the area of interest and allowed to flow down over it, keeping the area damp for the specified time. A well may be constructed around the area of interest on horizontal surfaces, which may be flooded and drained as appropriate.

Areas of interest will then need to be washed or destained to remove excess dye. The most effective solution for doing this is the same solvent composition as the dye solution, washing as required to remove excess dye or de-stain the background.

High-intensity light sources capable of emitting wavelengths between 420 and 485 nm must be used to excite fluorescence from blood dyed with acid yellow 7. The fluorescence emitted is between 480 and 550 nm. The use of shorter wavelengths between 350 and 450 nm, to excite background fluorescence after acid black 1 or acid violet 17 treatment, may be beneficial.

Work carried out by the U.K. Home Office has demonstrated that positive DNA identification may be made after fluorescence examination and any single chemical treatment, provided that simple guidelines are followed. If more than one fingerprint development technique is used in sequence, then the chances of successfully carrying out DNA identification are much reduced (Kent, 2004).

The U.K. work has shown that the most effective formulation for the acid dyes is as follows (Sears et al., 2005, p 741):

Fixing Solution—46 g 5-sulphosalicylic acid dehydrate dissolved in 1 L water.

Staining Solution—1 g acid dye dissolved in 700 mL distilled water, 250 mL ethanol, and 50 mL acetic acid.

Washing Solution—700 mL water, 250 mL ethanol, and 50 mL acetic acid.

The staining and washing solutions are flammable. Safety precautions must be taken if these solutions are used outside a fume cupboard with ambient temperatures above 28 °C (Kent, 2004).

7.13 Aqueous Techniques

This section covers four commonly used aqueous metal deposition methods: those involving silver nitrate reagents, silver physical developers, multimetal deposition processes, and gun blueing reagents. Each of these methods involves reagents with metal salts dissolved in an aqueous carrier (or an alcohol, as in the case of some silver nitrate reagents). These reagents reveal water-resistant latent prints such as sebaceous prints (except for the silver nitrate reagents used on porous surfaces that target salt). Here, the metal ions are reduced to metal particles on the latent print residue (except for the case of latent prints on metal, where the print residue resists the deposition).

7.13.1 Silver Nitrate Reagents

7.13.1.1 History and Background. One of the first reagents used for developing latent prints on porous surfaces was a 1–3% aqueous solution of silver nitrate, $AgNO_3$. It was used as early as 1891 for this purpose (Forgeot, 1891; Rhodes, 1940, p 10). Most formulations now include an alcohol to hasten drying and to increase the wetness (reduce the surface tension) (Lee and Gaensslen, 2001, pp 105–175). The silver ions in silver nitrate react with the chloride ions in salt (sodium chloride, NaCl) contained in the latent print residue to form silver chloride (AgCl), a highly insoluble salt ($K_{sp} = 1.8 \times 10^{-10}$) (Dean, 1985).

$$Ag^+ + Cl^- \rightleftharpoons AgCl \rightarrow K_{formation} = 1/K_{dissociation} = 1/K_{sp} = 5.6 \times 10^7$$

There are at least two reasons the silver nitrate treatment works well on porous surfaces. One is that the precipitation process is much faster than the dissolution process; that is, the reaction to form the insoluble AgCl is quicker than the ability of the aqueous carrier to dissolve away the soluble NaCl salt. The second reason is that the insoluble AgCl gets trapped within the structure or "micro-roughness" (Kerr et al., 1981, pp 209–214) of the porous surface; that is, the fresh latent print residue is in an aqueous or semiaqueous form that soaks into the porous surface, carrying its constituents with it.

An ethanol-based 3% (w/v) silver nitrate reagent (90% ethanol and 10% water) develops prints on water-repelling surfaces such as waxed paper, cardboard with a wax finish, and Styrofoam (Trozzi et al., 2000). Here, the ethanol is used to reduce the dissolution of the NaCl in the fingerprint residue, to better wet the surface (because these surfaces are usually water-repellent), and to give faster evaporation. As expected, because of the low porosity of such surfaces, developed prints on these surfaces are more fragile than those on porous surfaces like paper and wood.

Under ordinary room light, the silver chloride gradually converts by photo-reduction to elemental silver; however, this is hastened with UV radiation. The most efficient development occurs with short-wavelength UV radiation (254 nm); however, the safer, long-wavelength UV radiation (366 nm) also develops prints, but less efficiently (Goode and Morris, 1983).

$$AgCl + h\nu \rightleftharpoons Ag + \tfrac{1}{2}Cl_2$$

The elemental silver formed is colored dark brown to black (not a silver color). The reason for this is that the silver deposits as an aggregate of tiny (colloidal-size) silver particles, which makes for a highly porous surface that traps much of the light that strikes it. The formation of dark, light-trapping silver happens because the silver ions are reduced very quickly.

7.13.1.2 Application (Porous and Water-Repelling Surfaces). The silver nitrate reagent is usually applied to specimens by dipping them in the solution or by spraying the solution on the specimens. The FBI (Trozzi et al., 2000, pp 38–39) recommends the 3% $AgNO_3$ water-based formulation for porous surfaces and the 3% $AgNO_3$ ethanol-based formulation for water-repellent surfaces.

Champod et al. (2004, pp 153–154) recommend the 2% $AgNO_3$ methanol-based reagent for porous surfaces. After drying, the specimens are exposed to a high-intensity light source, UV light, or sunlight to develop the prints. As soon as the prints develop, they are photographed and the specimens are stored in the dark. Over time, the background darkens because of the gradual reduction of any residual silver nitrate in the specimens (this reduction is accelerated if exposed to light). Rinsing the specimens after development and then drying them in the dark does little to slow down the background development.

Goode and Morris (1983) reported in 1983 that immersing specimens in disodium ethylenediaminetetracetic acid (Na_2EDTA) complexes excess silver ions, which are then easily rinsed away with water. Their modified silver nitrate (MSN) procedure uses a 1% aqueous silver nitrate solution that also contains 5% Na_2EDTA and 3% K_2CO_3. The MSN procedure involves (1) treating the specimens with this modified reagent for just enough time to wet the surface, (2) transferring them to a 1% (w/v) Na_2EDTA solution and leaving them in for 1 minute, (3) removing and washing thoroughly with distilled water, and finally (4) placing this in a 5% thiourea solution containing 1% KOH for about 30 seconds to 2 minutes. The first step creates the silver chloride from the chloride ions in the latent print, and the last step converts this to black silver sulfide. Later in 1998, Price and Stow (1998, pp 107–110) recommended dipping the specimens in a "stopping solution" consisting of an aqueous solution of 40% methanol, 20% acetic acid, and 2% glycerol to suppress the further development of the background.

7.13.1.3 Enhancement. According to Lennard and Margot (1988, pp 197–210), weakly developed prints could be enhanced by treating the specimens with a diluted silver physical developer solution. The dilution factor is 1:10. Goode and Morris (1983) discuss a radioactive enhancing method that converts a silver print to a radioactive, β-emitting silver sulfide print, which is then imaged using radiographic film (this image-recording process is sometimes called autoradiography or β-radiography). If the original silver nitrate treatment did not significantly stain the background with silver, then this method will bring out only the developed prints with little or no interfering background. The process, described by Goode and Morris (1983) and reviewed by Cantu (2001, pp 29–64), involves converting the silver in the silver image to silver bromide (AgBr), using brominating (bleaching) methods, and then treating this with either sodium sulfide or thiourea (where the sulfur is radioactive ^{35}S) to convert AgBr to $Ag_2{}^{35}S$. The process is called radioactive toning. If the MSN procedure is used, which yields a silver sulfide print, then radioactive thiourea is used to form $Ag_2{}^{35}S$.

Cons

7.13.1.4 Limitation. The major drawback of the silver nitrate method is that the chloride ions in the latent print residue diffuse over time, and humidity accelerates this diffusion. This will affect the resolution (ridge detail) of the developed print. Normally, prints no older than 1 week will develop well; however, one should attempt to examine the evidence as soon as possible to avoid this diffusion. According to Goode and Morris (1983), in an indoor environment in the United Kingdom, prints on porous surfaces last longer (months) in the winter than in the summer (days to weeks). However, they state that these effects depend on factors such as the type of surface (prints last longer on paper than on raw wood) and, of course, the relative humidity. For this reason, the silver nitrate reagent is used now in special cases. The silver physical developer and multimetal deposition methods are more commonly used for water-insoluble components but do not target chlorine ions.

7.13.1.5 Use of Silver Nitrate on Metals. The discussion so far has been on the use of silver nitrate on porous and certain glossy (water-repellent) surfaces to develop chloride-bearing prints. Silver nitrate has also been used on certain metal surfaces, such as cartridge cases, to develop prints by depositing silver everywhere (giving a gray-to-black metallic appearance) except where the latent print sits (Olsen, 1978; Cantu et al., 1998, pp 294–298). That is, the silver nitrate brings out "lipid-bearing prints" because such prints protect the metal surface on which they lie from reacting with the silver nitrate. (If chloride ions are present in the latent print residue, silver chloride is formed; however, the contrast of the print against the background remains and may even be enhanced upon the reduction of silver chloride to dark silver.) The usual reaction of the silver ions (Ag^+) with the metal surface is

$$nAg^+ + M \rightleftharpoons nAg + M^{n+}$$

Here, M represents the metal and M^{n+} is a corresponding ion. Silver is said to displace the metal M. By observing the placement of the silver in the electromotive series (see Table 7–4), we see that silver can displace copper, iron, nickel, zinc, lead, and aluminum.

$$2Ag^+ + Cu \rightleftharpoons 2Ag + Cu^{2+} \quad E^°_{redox} = 458 \text{ mV}$$

$$3Ag^+ + Al \rightleftharpoons 3Ag + Al^{3+} \quad E^°_{redox} = 2461.6 \text{ mV}$$

Here, for example, $E^°_{redox}$ (Ag^+/Ag; Cu/Cu^{2+}) = $E^°_{red}$ ($Ag^+ + e^- \rightleftharpoons Ag$) + $E^°_{ox}$ ($Cu \rightleftharpoons Cu^{2+} + 2e^-$) is computed from the standard reduction potentials (Table 7–4) (Dean, 1985; Weast, 1986). A positive value of $E^°_{redox}$ indicates that the redox reaction is thermodynamically favorable but does not say anything about the rate or speed of the reaction. Another consideration is that these metals oxidize, some more readily than others, and this creates an oxide film on the metal surface. If a print was placed before the metal oxidized, the print may naturally show up, given enough time (some refer to this as the "print getting etched" on the metal). However, if it was placed after the oxide film formed, it is often difficult for the silver nitrate reagent to further oxidize the metal in this oxide film; thus, the deposition of silver and subsequent development of the print may occur but not as readily. The formation of a protective, impermeable oxide layer is called passivation (Atkins, 1990, p 927).

Table 7–4

Standard reduction potentials of several ionic and molecular species.

($E^°$) in mV	Half Reaction Standard Potential
$H_2O_2 + 2H^+ + 2e^- \rightleftharpoons 2H_2O$	+ 1776
$Au^{3+} + 3e^- \rightleftharpoons Au$	+ 1498
$2Cl_2 + 2e^- \rightleftharpoons 2Cl^-$	+ 1358
$OCl^- + H_2O + 2e^- \rightleftharpoons Cl^- + 2OH^-$	+ 810
$Ag^+ + e^- \rightleftharpoons Ag$	+ 799.6
$Fe^{3+} + e^- \rightleftharpoons Fe^{2+}$	+ 771
$H_2SeO_3 + 4H^+ + 4e^- \rightleftharpoons Se + 3H_2O$	+ 740
$Ag(NH_3)_2^+ + e^- \rightleftharpoons Ag + 2NH_3$	+ 373
$Cu^{2+} + 2e^- \rightleftharpoons Cu$	+ 341.9
$Ag_2O + H_2O + 2e^- \rightleftharpoons 2Ag + 2OH^-$	+ 342
$2H^+ + 2e^- \rightleftharpoons H_2$	0.0
$Fe^{3+} + 3e^- \rightleftharpoons Fe$	– 37
$Pb^{2+} + 2e^- \rightleftharpoons Pb$	– 126.2
$Ni^{2+} + 2e^- \rightleftharpoons Ni$	– 257
$Fe^{2+} + 2e^- \rightleftharpoons Fe$	– 447
$Zn^{2+} + 2e^- \rightleftharpoons Zn$	– 761.8
$Al^{3+} + 3e^- \rightleftharpoons Al$	– 1662

7.13.2 Silver Physical Developers

7.13.2.1 History and Background. The silver physical developer originated in photographic chemistry as an alternate method to the chemical developer for developing film (Cantu, 2001, pp 29–64; Bunting, 1987, p 85; Cantu and Johnson, 2001, pp 242–247). Exposing silver bromide or silver iodide crystals to light causes specks of silver to form on the crystal surface (Walls and Attridge, 1977, pp 104–108). These become "developing centers" (or "triggering sites") for either chemical or physical development. A silver physical developer deposits silver on exposed silver bromide crystals, whereas a chemical developer reduces the exposed silver bromide to silver. The fixing bath, in the former case, removes the unexposed silver bromide crystals and also the exposed silver bromide crystals (leaving behind the silver deposited on them) whereas, in the latter case, it only removes the unexposed silver bromide because the exposed silver bromide has been converted to silver.

Because of this process, the silver physical developer soon became known as one of the most sensitive reagents for detecting trace amounts of silver (Feigl and Anger, 1972, pp 423–424). Latent print examiners (Collins and Thomas) in the United Kingdom recognized this during the early 1970s (Goode and Morris, 1983) and applied it first to prints submitted to vacuum metal deposition. Then they expanded its use to other substances like fabrics and paper. It was found early on that the silver physical developer works better on porous than nonporous surfaces. Also, no one really knew which substances in latent print residue were responsible for causing the silver physical developer to work. That is, no one knew what was in fingerprint residue that acted as a developing center or triggering site (like the silver specks). It was not until recently that some plausible or reasonable explanations emerged.

A silver physical developer is an aqueous solution containing silver ions and a reducing agent that reduces the silver ions to silver, but it also contains two other sets of chemicals: one set keeps the reducing agent from reducing the silver ions to elemental silver unless a "triggering substance" is present (e.g., exposed silver bromide crystals in photographic film), and the other set keeps the solution stable. The first set suppresses the reducing ability of the reducing agent to the point that reduction occurs only when triggering sites are present. It, therefore, *suppresses the formation* of elemental silver in solution. However, due to this delicate balance, some spontaneous reduction occurs whereby colloidal-sized silver particles (nanoparticles) are formed in solution and, because these are triggering sites (i.e., they are silver specks), they grow. They grow in an autocatalytic way; that is, the silver that is formed triggers the reduction of more silver. Thus, the second set of chemicals suppresses this growth.

The silver physical developer currently used for latent print development on porous surfaces contains silver ions (silver nitrate) and ferrous ions (ferrous ammonium sulfate) as the principal components; citric acid and ferric ions (ferric nitrate) as the set of chemicals that *suppress the formation* of spontaneously formed colloidal silver particles; and a cationic and non-ionic surfactant as the set of chemicals that suppress the growth of such particles.

The net equation for the silver-deposition reaction is

$$Ag^+ + Fe^{2+} \rightleftharpoons Ag + Fe^{3+} \rightarrow \rightarrow \quad E^\circ_{redox} = 28.6 \text{ mV}$$

E°_{redox} is computed from Table 7–4.

Adding citric acid reduces the concentration of ferric ions through the formation of ferric citrate and shifts the equilibrium of $Ag^+ + Fe^{2+} \rightleftharpoons Ag + Fe^{3+}$ to the right (forming elemental silver),

$$Fe^{3+} + H_3Cit \rightleftharpoons FeCit + 3H^+ \rightarrow \rightarrow \quad K_{formation} = 0.398 \text{ at } 25\ °C$$

However, for every ferric citrate molecule formed, three protons are released and these drive the equilibrium to the left (suppression of the formation of elemental silver). The overall reaction is

$$Ag^+ + Fe^{2+} + H_3Cit \rightleftharpoons Ag + FeCit + 3H^+ \quad E^\circ_{redox} = 5.0 \text{ mV}$$

Thus, adding citric acid reduces the E°_{redox} from 28.6 mV to 5 mV. This reduction facilitates adjusting the concentrations of the components (citric acid and the ferric, ferrous, and silver salts) so that the reduction of silver ions to elemental silver nanoparticles occurs only on the triggering sites and not in solution. However, even with this suppression of their formation rate, those that do form become nucleating (triggering) sites for further deposition of silver (the process is autocatalytic) and consequently grow until they precipitate. This will eventually deplete most of the silver ion solution (depending on the concentration of ferrous ions initially present).

To bring stability to the solution, the silver particles formed must somehow have their triggering ability blocked. This is where surfactants become important.

When silver nanoparticles are spontaneously formed, they get surrounded by citrate ions (each of which carries three negative charges) in solution and thus acquire a negative charge. The main surfactant used to suppress the growth of any spontaneously formed silver nanoparticles is a positively charged cationic surfactant, n-dodecylamine acetate. The reason for choosing a cationic surfactant is that it helps suppress the negative charge of the silver nanoparticles formed. This will then reduce the attraction of positive silver ions toward the particles and thus reduce the possibility of their growth (by the reduction of silver on their surface). The cationic surfactant surrounds the negatively charged silver particle in a staggered way, with as many positive ends pointing toward the particle as pointing away from the particle (Cantu, 2001, pp 29–64; Cantu and Johnson, 2001, pp 242–247; Jonker et al., 1969, pp 38–44). This surfactant-encapsulated particle is said to be encased in a *micelle*. A non-ionic surfactant, Synperonic-N, is used in conjunction with n-dodecylamine acetate to aid the dissolution of the latter.

On exposed photographic film or paper, the silver physical developer works by reducing its silver ions on the silver specks (nucleating sites) found on the surface of exposed silver bromide crystals and nowhere else. Being an autocatalytic process, the deposition of silver on the nucleating sites continues until it is stopped, for example, by removing the sample from the solution and rinsing it with water. The surfactant-stabilized silver physical developer remains stable and active for several weeks. If silver ions come in contact with hydroxyl ions, insoluble silver hydroxide (AgOH) is formed, which converts to brownish-black silver oxide (Ag_2O). Today, most paper is alkaline (basic) because it contains calcium carbonate ($CaCO_3$) as filler. When wet, it is basic and will turn black when dipped in a silver nitrate solution and will dry to a brownish-black color. Consequently, alkaline paper must be neutralized before submitting it to silver physical development. Any acid that does not furnish chlorides (which react with silver to form insoluble AgCl) will neutralize the $CaCO_3$. The neutralization reaction involves the release of carbon dioxide bubbles:

$$CaCO_3 + 2H^+ \rightarrow Ca^{2+} + H_2O + CO_2 \text{ (gas)}$$

The following are the rudiments of some concepts that help explain how the silver physical developer visualizes latent prints on porous surfaces.

The Charge of Latent Print Residue (at low pH). It is fortuitous that the silver physical developer is acidic, with a pH of about 1.38 because this helps explain why it works in developing latent prints on porous surfaces. It is known (Saunders, 1989) that when latent print residue (on a porous or nonporous substrate) is immersed in a colloidal gold solution of pH < 3, colloidal gold nanoparticles selectively deposit on the residue. This suggests that at pH < 3, the latent print residue acquires a positive charge. It is also known that colloidal gold at low pH is used to "stain" proteins and this happens because, at low pH, the amine groups (e.g., $R-NH_2$) in proteins acquire a positive charge upon protonation ($R-NH_3^+$). Therefore, one possibility is that latent print residue contains proteins that initially were dispersed in latent print residue but, after drying, became nondispersible. It is also known that alkenes (olefins) can acquire a positive charge in an acidic environment (either a carbonium ion or a protonated alcohol is formed). Therefore, another possibility is that latent print residue contains olefins.

The Surface Area of Proteins in Porous Surfaces and Their Binding to Cellulose. It was recognized early on that the silver physical developer works best on porous surfaces, particularly cellulose-based surfaces such as paper and cardboard. When latent print residue is placed on such surfaces, the surfaces' porosity causes the residue to penetrate and thus cover a large surface area; this then exposes more nucleating (triggering) sites for silver physical development than if it did not spread out (as in a nonporous surface). Furthermore, if amines are present (as in proteins), they can form hydrogen bonds with the hydroxyl groups in the cellulose.

The Deposition of Silver Particles on Latent Print Residue. In the silver physical developer, a newly formed silver nanoparticle is negatively charged (due to adhered citric acid ions) and attracts the positive amine "head" ($R-NH_3^+$) of several surfactant molecules, which eventually envelop the entire particle (in the staggered configuration mentioned above). However, the nanoparticle also gets attracted to the positively charged latent print residue. Once one of these nanoparticles reaches the residue, it gets neutralized. The avalanche of silver particle deposition occurs on this initial particle (because each silver particle is now a nucleating site—the autocatalytic effect) and it grows. The final result is an agglomeration of numerous "grown" particles (about 10–40 μm in diameter) along the latent print residue.

Formulation. The formulation of the silver physical developer reagent provided in Section 7.14 is the original British formulation (Kent, 1998), which is very close to the Dutch formulation (Jonker et al., 1969, pp 38–44) used in the photofabrication of circuit boards. The procedure for visualizing prints on porous surfaces, however, involves three steps: a pretreatment step, the silver physical development step, and a post-treatment step.

Other formulations for the silver physical developers exist (Cantu, 2001, pp 29–64), but one that is currently used by many is based on using high-purity water, such as that produced by water purification units that use reverse osmosis and deionizing technologies (the water is referred to as RO/DI water). By using such water, less detergent is needed (2.8 g of each, instead of 4.0 g) (Kent, 1998), although the performance is adversely affected. However, Burow et al. (2003, pp 1094–1100) showed that one can also reduce the amount of several other components and end up with a reagent that performs as well or better than the traditional reagent (it does, however, involve adding malic acid to the reagent); the cost reduction is about 16%. Seifert, Burow, and Ramotowski (from the U.S. Secret Service forensic laboratory) showed (unpublished results) that Tween 20 can be used instead of Synperonic-N.

The hypochlorite step is an enhancing step. It does two things: it lightens (bleaches) the paper and darkens the silver print. The print becomes darker through the formation of silver oxide (OCl$^-$ + 2Ag $\rightleftharpoons$ Ag$_2$O + Cl$^-$ E$^o_{redox}$ = 550 mV; see Table 7–4). Other enhancement methods are treated by Cantu (2001, pp 29–64) as well as bleaching methods. One bleaching method, used successfully in bringing out a developed print found on highly patterned printing, converts the silver print to a whitish silver iodide print and darkens the background through the starch–iodine reaction (Cantu et al., 2003, pp 164–168).

7.13.2.2 Application. The procedure for using the silver physical developer involves three treatments in sequence and *in the same glass tray*. The latter point is important in that it simplifies the process and saves time. It is based on the fact that residual reagent from one treatment does not affect the performance of the next treatment. The three treatments are the acid pretreatment, the silver physical developer treatment, and the hypochlorite post-treatment. Occasionally, a distilled water pretreatment precedes these to remove any dirt or soil from the specimens. This, as well as the other treatments, removes any prints developed with ninhydrin, and writing or printing made with water-soluble inks (e.g., some roller ball pen inks and inkjet printing inks). Also, a tap water post-treatment is done between the silver physical development and the hypochlorite post-treatment. Again, all this is done in one glass tray.

Water Pretreatment—This is designed to remove dirt and soil, if present.

Acid Pretreatment—This reacts with calcium carbonate in alkaline paper, causing release of carbon dioxide as bubbles, and neutralizes the paper.

Silver Physical Developer Treatment—This is done in subdued light to avoid the photo-reduction of silver ions to elemental silver (which results in background development and weakens the reagent). The tray is rocked back and forth; within 10 minutes, prints begin to develop and continue with increasing contrast. Good development occurs within 10–30 minutes.

Water Post-Treatment—This is done with running tap water for about 5 minutes to remove excess silver physical developer (and any silver chloride that may form).

Hypochlorite Post-Treatment—The treatment time is about 2–3 minutes. This lightens the background and darkens the silver print.

Washing and Drying—The specimens are washed in tap water and dried (e.g., by using a photodryer or by air-drying on blotter paper).

7.13.3 Multimetal Deposition Methods

7.13.3.1 History and Background. In the late 1980s, Dr. George Saunders, then with the Los Alamos National Laboratory in Los Alamos, NM, visited the U.S. Secret Service forensic laboratory to share ideas about techniques for latent fingerprint development. He presented a novel idea that he initially called a Universal Process for Fingerprint Detection and later, because it involved the deposition of two metals, the multimetal deposition (MMD) method. He based his idea on an existing method used for staining proteins, antibodies, and other macromolecules (e.g., proteins separated on membranes or gels). This method involved staining with colloidal gold (whereby colloidal gold binds to the macromolecule) and enhancing (or amplifying) this gold "signal" or stain with a silver physical developer.

The binding of colloidal gold to proteins was first observed in 1939 by Kausche and Ruska (1939, pp 21–24). In 1971, Faulk and Taylor (1971, pp 1081–1083) used this property to bind rabbit anti-Salmonella antiserum, and the resulting coated colloid was then used to label the surface of Salmonella bacteria. The labeling mechanism was detectable through the electron microscopic image of the gold. In 1983, DeMey (1983, pp 82–112) used uncoated gold to directly stain proteins on membrane surfaces. Also in 1983, Holgate et al. (1983, pp 938–944) showed that a gold stain can be intensified with silver staining. They basically recognized that gold colloids are (1) highly negatively charged particles that bind to many macromolecules and (2) activation (triggering) sites for silver physical development. The colloidal gold particles acquire their negative charge through the adsorption of citrate ions (each carries three negative charges) on their surface (the citrate ions come from the sodium citrate used in the formulation).

Saunders knew that fingerprint residue contains macromolecules like proteins and lipoproteins and, therefore, should be able to be visualized through the staining and enhancing ability of the colloidal gold and physical developer technique. He formulated his own colloidal gold solution using the Frens method (Frens, 1973, pp 20–22) and silver physical developer. He called the latter the *modified* physical developer to distinguish it from the traditional silver physical developer used to visualize latent prints on porous surfaces. By formulating his own reagents, he was able to optimize them. The process was soon found to visualize latent prints on porous and nonporous surfaces; the latter includes surfaces like glass, metal, ceramic, and plastic, whether they are dark or light.

Thus, the MMD process is basically a silver physical development process that is preceded by a colloidal gold treatment; the gold treatment provides the latent print residue with the nucleating sites (gold colloids) for silver physical development. Like the silver physical developer, the MMD process develops the water-insoluble components of latent print residue (e.g., the sebaceous portion of the residue).

For visualizing latent prints on porous surfaces with the MMD process, Saunders provided two important comments for the users. One is that, on porous surfaces, extensive rinsing must be done after the colloidal gold treatment to reduce possible background development. This is because colloidal gold particles get trapped in the pores and become triggering sites for silver physical development. The other is that the zinc salt treatment, sometimes done after the ninhydrin process, should be avoided. Divalent ions such as Zn^{2+} have a tendency to bind to colloidal gold and, therefore, trapped divalent ions in the surface's pores attract the colloidal gold particles and the entire surface is subject to silver physical development.

7.13.3.2 Formulation (MMD). The MMD process involves two reagents used in sequence: the colloidal gold solution and the modified silver physical developer.

There are two points of note regarding the modified silver physical developer: One is that Tween 20, a non-ionic surfactant, is used instead of a more stabilizing cationic surfactant. Cantu and Johnson (2001, pp 242–247) speculate that this may be because a cationic surfactant would surround bound gold particles (that still carry some negative charge) and therefore hinder the physical development process on them. The second point is that the silver ion concentration of the working solution is only 0.2%, and this is apparently low enough that no "blackening" (formation of silver oxide) occurs on the surface of alkaline (basic) paper. Thus, no acid pretreatment is needed to neutralize such paper (which normally contains calcium carbonate). The colloidal gold solution has a pH of about 2.8 and, therefore, causes some neutralization of such paper, but the divalent calcium ions that are generated apparently do not significantly destabilize the gold solution (they may on the surface where they are formed). Examples of latent prints developed (on a variety of surfaces) using the MMD process are found in Figure 7–23.

7.13.3.3 Formulation (MMD II). In 1993, Dr. Bernard Schnetz presented his work, carried out at the Institut de Police Scientifique et de Criminologie of the University of Lausanne, on biochemical techniques for amplifying colloidal gold-treated latent prints. He treated latent prints with colloidal gold, attached a protein to the colloidal gold particles (already bound to latent print residue), and amplified these with enzymes or stains that form colored or fluorescent products (Schnetz, 1993). In 1997, he reported on an update to this work and also on his variation of the multimetal deposition (MMD II) process (Schnetz, 1997), and in 2001, he and Margot published their work on its optimization (Schnetz and Margot, 2001, pp 21–28). Like the MMD process, this is a two-step process, but it uses siliconized glassware, colloidal gold with a particle size of 14 nm diameter (compared to 30 nm for the Saunders colloidal gold), and a silver physical developer quite different from the Saunders modified silver physical developer.

Dr. John Brennan, recently retired from the Forensic Science Service (London, U.K.), has successfully used the

FIGURE 7–23

Latent prints visualized by the MMD process on a variety of surfaces. Top left: revolver cartridge case. Top middle: adhesive side of black Mylar tape. Top right: adhesive side of heavy-duty strapping tape. Middle: plastic and metal surfaces of a computer disk. Bottom left: paper label of computer disk. Bottom right: plastic credit card. Notice that the developed prints appear dark on light-colored surfaces and light on dark-colored surfaces.

MMD and MMD II processes on several evidence types and tends to favor the MMD II (J. Brennan, private communication). Dr. Naomi Jones presented her doctoral thesis several metal deposition methods; she also found that the MMD II process surpassed the MMD process in performance (Jones, 2002).

7.13.4 Gun Blueing Reagents

7.13.4.1 History and Background. Gun blueing is used to refinish gun barrels with a bluish sheen. One is warned not to leave fingerprints on the barrel because the gun blueing solution will not work there (Angier, 1936, p 6). The Bundeskriminalamt (BKA) in Germany discovered that this was also true on bullet cartridges (Cantu et al., 1998, pp 294–298). Thus was the birth of gun blueing solutions for visualizing latent prints on metal surfaces, particularly those of bullet cartridges.

7.13.4.2 Metal Deposition and Etching. Gun blueing of metals involves the simultaneous deposition of two metals, selenium and copper, on a metal surface. The bimetal deposited is blue-black in color.

As discussed previously for silver nitrate, the sebaceous print resists the deposition, and silver deposits (as a gray-to-black metal) everywhere, except where the fingerprint exists. To be more precise about what is occurring, we should note that the deposition process is always accompanied by an etching process. For silver on copper, silver ions deposit (the deposition or reduction process) as cupric ions are removed (the etching or oxidation process). There are, however, etching processes that do not involve metal deposition (e.g., etching with acidified hydrogen peroxide) (Cantu et al., 1998, pp 294–298), and these processes are also hindered by sebaceous material.

Other one-metal deposition methods for revealing latent prints on cartridge cases include the use of palladium (Migron and Mandler, 1997, pp 986–992) and selenium (Bentsen et al., 1996, pp 3–8). Besides showing that palladium can reveal sebaceous prints on metal, Migron and Mandler did an extensive analytical study of how the deposition process works on brass surfaces containing sebaceous prints. The work by Bentsen and colleagues on the deposition of selenium is similar to what gun blueing does and is, therefore, discussed below, along with gun blueing.

7.13.4.3 General Composition. There are several manufacturers of gun blueing solutions, and no two solutions have exactly the same formulation, but all contain the three necessary active ingredients: selenious acid, a cupric salt, and an acid. An acidified solution of selenious acid is a relatively strong etching (oxidizing) reagent, as noted by the oxidation potential (Table 7–4):

$$H_2SeO_3 + 4H^+ + 4e^- \rightleftharpoons Se + 3H_2O \quad E° = +740 \text{ mV}$$

Note that acid (H⁺) is needed, and this is why the blueing solution also contains an acid. Table 7–4 shows that an acidic solution of selenious acid can oxidize and etch copper, lead, nickel, zinc, and aluminum. A solution of cupric ions is also a strong etching (oxidizing) reagent capable of oxidizing lead, nickel, zinc, and aluminum.

As *each* of these reagents etches, the metal ions get deposited on what is etched. For example, on aluminum, the oxidation and reduction (etching and deposition) reaction is

$$3H_2SeO_3 + 12H^+ + 4Al \rightleftharpoons 3Se + 9H_2O + 4Al^{3+}$$

$$E°_{redox} = 2402 \text{ mV}$$

$$3Cu^{2+} + 2Al \rightleftharpoons 3Cu + 2Al^{3+} \quad E°_{redox} = 2003.9 \text{ mV}$$

If *both* reagents are present together, as in the gun blueing solution, then the ratio of Cu to Se that deposits depends on the speed (kinetics) of each of the two competing reactions; it is possible that a 1:1 Cu–Se alloy is formed, but it is not certain. The final result is a blue-black metallic coating (everywhere except where a sebaceous latent print exists).

The composition of some gun blueing solutions is given in Table 7–5. Note that all involve selenious acid (one involves selenium dioxide, which is the anhydrous form of selenious acid), a cupric salt, and an acid. Interestingly, Bentsen et al. (1996, pp 3–8) used a 0.4% selenious acid solution (without cupric ions or acid) to develop prints on metal surfaces such as spent cartridge cases. This deposits selenium metal on the metal being treated and this solution, along with the vacuum cyanoacrylate ester treatment, was rated highly among other methods tested.

7.13.4.4 Formulations. Cantu et al. (1998, pp 294–298) recommend a 1:80 dilution of a commercial gun blueing solution. Leben and Ramotowski (1996, pp 8, 10) recommend a stronger solution (a 1:40 dilution) and indicate that an improvement over just using the diluted gun blueing reagent is to treat the metallic specimens first (e.g., cartridge cases) with CA fumes. Table 7–6 is a summary of their recommendations.

7.13.4.5 Application. Since its introduction by the BKA, gun blueing is now used in several laboratories because of its ease. As mentioned above, a CA ester treatment prior to gun blueing improves the detection of latent prints on metal. After treatment, there is a tendency for the gun blueing solution to continue its deposition, and several arresting methods have been proposed (Cantu et al., 1998, pp 294–298). These include dipping in a sodium bicarbonate solution, dipping in clear varnish (Bentsen et al., 1996, pp 3–8), applying a lacquer spray (private communication from Anton Theeuwen and Josita Limborgh, Netherlands Ministry of Justice, Forensic Science Laboratory), and using fingernail polish (private communication from Vici Inlow, U.S. Secret Service forensic laboratory).

If overdevelopment occurs, then acidified hydrogen peroxide is recommended for removing excess gun blue deposit (Cantu et al., 1998, pp 294–298). If we assume the copper–selenium alloy is a 1:1 adduct, then the net reaction for its removal is

$$3H_2O_2 + 2H^+ + Cu–Se \rightleftharpoons H_2SeO_3 + Cu^{2+} + 3H_2O$$

A suggested composition for the acidified hydrogen peroxide solution is 5 volumes of household vinegar (5% acetic acid) and 7 volumes of household hydrogen peroxide (3% hydrogen peroxide). This is based on stoichiometry of the above equation. However, a 1:1 mixture also works well.

7.13.4.6 Comments on Etching. Etching without metal deposition can also reveal prints on metal surfaces by the contrast formed between the etched background and the unetched latent print. From Table 7–4 it can be seen that acid can displace iron, lead, nickel, zinc, and aluminum. Acidified hydrogen peroxide, however, will also displace copper. Cantu et al. (1998, pp 294–298) noted that acidified hydrogen peroxide visualizes prints rather well on many metal surfaces. They provide a lengthy discussion and explanation of why the etching process should be carefully watched: the metals that are etched out as ions can redeposit as the process continues.

Schütz et al. (2000, pp 65–68) compared etching and gun blueing methods with the multimetal deposition method on their ability to develop latent prints on cartridge cases. They found that (1) gun blueing excelled in visualizing sebaceous prints on brass cartridge cases, (2) for aluminum cartridge cases, MMD worked best (the modified physical developer step, performed after the colloidal gold step, brought out the print contrast), and (3) nothing worked well for lacquered steel cartridge cases. For the latter, they recommend CA fuming.

7.13.5 Sudan Black B

7.13.5.1 History and Background. Sudan black B (herein referred to as Sudan black) was initially used in laboratories for biological testing or chemical screening for fatty components (Figure 7–24). The reaction produces a blue-black product or image. Sudan black was initially reported for use as a friction ridge development technique in 1980 by Mitsui, Katho, Shimada, and Wakasugi of the Criminal Science Laboratory in Nagoya-shi, Japan (Mitsui et al., 1980, pp 9–10; 1981, pp 84–85).

Table 7–5

Composition of some gun blueing solutions*

	Manufacturer	Birchwood-Casey						Brownells	Outers	E. Kettner
	Trade name	Perma Blue Liquid Gun Blue PB22	Perma Blue Immersion Blue PBIM	Perma Blue Paste Gun Blue SBP 2	Super Blue Extra Strength	Brass Black Metal Touch Up BB2	Aluminum Black PAB 17	Formula 44/40 Instant Gun Blue	Gunslick Gun Blue	Waffen-Brünierung
	Used for	Steel	Steel	Steel	Steel	Brass, Bronze, Copper	Aluminum	Steel	Steel	Steel
Selenium Compounds	Selenious Acid	3	4	2	5	3	4	6		
	Selenium Dioxide								3	
Cupric Salt	Cupric Chloride			3						
	Cupric Nitrate				4					
	Cupric Sulfate	3	4			4	8	8	2	
Zinc Salt	Zinc Sulfate					5				
Nickel Salt	Nickel Sulfate						1		2	
Acid	Hydrochloric									
	Nitric	3	2		4					
	Phosphoric		4	4	4	8	3			
	Fluoboric						2			
	Amido sulfonic							12		
Solution pH (dilution factor)		2.3 (1/40)	N/A (1/40)	1.5	2.3 (1/80)	2.3 (1/40)	2.3 (1/80)	1.8 (1/80)	3.3 (1/40)	2.3 (1/80)
Other	Polyethylene Stearyl Ether			15						
	Octylphenoxy Polyethoxyethanol				1					
	Ammonium Molybdate					4				
	Ammonium Bifluoride			1						

*All concentrations are as maximum percent. Except for pH, all information is obtained from Material Safety Data Sheets.

CHAPTER 7 | Latent Print Development

Table 7–6

Summary of recommended protocols for treating cartridge cases.

Nickel Plated Brass	Brass Black	1 mL GB in 40 mL distilled water	Other solutions also worked well on these casings.
Lacquered Steel	Super Glue Only		None of the gun blue solutions produced identifiable detail.

Sudan black is a dye stain used for the detection of sebaceous components of friction ridge skin residue on nonporous and some semiporous substrates (e.g., latex gloves and some ceramics) (Figure 7–25). This dye stain also detects friction ridge skin detail where the friction ridge skin or the substrate has been contaminated with grease, food residue, or dried deposits of soda or sweetened (e.g., by fructose or sucrose) drinks. It has also been used to enhance friction ridge detail previously treated by the CA fuming technique.

The color and porosity of the substrate will need to be considered. Porous substrates tend to absorb the dye, resulting in a lack of contrast between the friction ridge detail and the item background. Because of the blue-black color of the dye stain, there will be a lack of contrast between the friction ridge detail and dark-color items. It is recommended that other processing techniques be used on these items (Stone and Metzger, 1981, pp 13–14).

Dried Sudan black-processed prints have been lifted using conventional lifting tape (as used with the powder processing technique). It has been successful on waxy coated, glossy, and smooth substrates. However, it has been less successful on heavily contaminated, uneven, and semiporous substrates.

7.13.5.2 Validation of Reagent and Application Technique. As in the application of all reagents and processes, it is suggested that the Sudan black solution be validated before use. To validate the solution, contaminate a nonporous substrate with the targeted matrix (e.g., sebaceous-, grease-, fructose-, sucrose-, or food-contaminated friction ridge detail or material), then apply the Sudan black solution to the substrate in the manner noted below. If no reaction is observed, the solution or the validation matrix will require further evaluation. It is sound practice to be familiar with the application technique and the reaction(s) with the substrate and matrix before applying them to evidence.

Review the material safety data sheets for safety, handling, and storage information.

7.13.5.3 Reagent Solution. The reagent solution consists of 15 g of Sudan black dissolved in 1 L of ethanol or methanol, creating a blue-black color solution, which is

FIGURE 7–24

The chemical structure of sudan black.

FIGURE 7–25

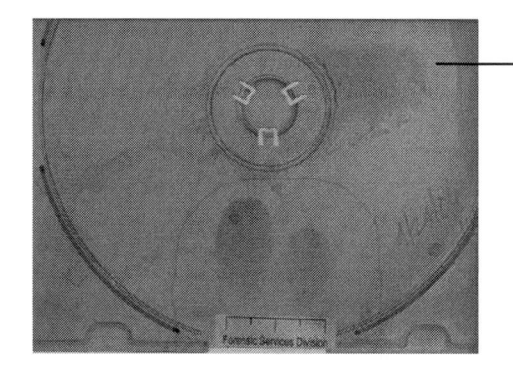

Sebaceous friction ridge detail on a plastic substrate processed with sudan black.

then added to 500 mL of distilled water and stirred until completely mixed. The shelf life of the solution is indefinite.

7.13.5.4 Sequential Methodology and Processing Technique. Before processing with sudan black, view the item with a forensic light source to detect any inherent fluorescence of the friction ridge residue or the substrate. Photograph any visible detail.

- Place the Sudan black solution in a clean glass or metal dish, pouring in a sufficient amount to submerge the item being processed. The solution can also be applied by spraying. It is recommended that the immersion technique be used to prevent inhalation of airborne particulate spray.

- Allow item to be immersed in the solution for approximately 2 minutes. If the item has been previously processed using the CA fuming technique, the item may require longer immersion time in the solution.

- Rinse item under cool or cold, slow-running tap water, or place item in a clean dish containing cool or cold water until excess dye is removed from the background.

- Allow item to dry at room temperature.

- View the developed blue-black image; faint images have been improved by a second treatment with the Sudan black solution (follow the previous application steps). It is suggested that the item be viewed with a forensic light source after Sudan black processing because the background may fluoresce, creating enhanced contrast.

- Any developed images will need to be photographed for comparison, documentation, and archival purposes.

7.14 Formulations for Chemical Solutions

7.14.1 Ninhydrin (Kent, 1998; Champod et al., 2004, p 239)

Stock Solution: 25 g ninhydrin dissolved in 225 mL absolute ethanol, 10 mL ethyl acetate, 25 mL glacial acetic acid.

Working Solution: 52 mL of stock solution diluted to 1000 mL with HFE 7100.

7.14.2 Zinc Chloride Solution (Champod et al., 2004, p 240)

Stock Solution: 8 g zinc chloride dissolved in 180 mL ethanol, 20 mL glacial acetic acid.

Working Solution: 6 mL of stock solution diluted to 100 mL with carrier solvent (e.g., HFE 7100).

7.14.3 1,8-Diazafluoren-9-one (DFO) (Kent, 1998; Champod et al., 2004, p 230)

0.25 g of DFO dissolved in 30 mL methanol and 20 mL glacial acetic acid. Add this to 725 mL HFE 7100 and 275 mL HFE 71DE.

7.14.4 Nonpolar Ninhydrin (Stimac, 2003a, pp 185–197)

Stock Solution: 1.5 g ninhydrin dissolved in 100 mL HFE 71IPA (may require refluxing at low temperature).

Working Solution: 15 mL of stock solution diluted with 100 mL HFE 7100.

CHAPTER 7 | Latent Print Development

7.14.5 1,2-Indanedione

0.25 g 1,2-indanedione dissolved in 90 mL ethyl acetate and 10 mL glacial acetic acid. Add this to 1 L of HFE 7100 (Merrick et al., 2002, pp 595–605).

or

2 g 1,2-indanedione dissolved in 70 mL ethyl acetate. Add this to 1 L HFE 7100 (Almog et al., 1999, pp 114–118).

7.14.6 5-Methylthioninhydrin (5-MTN) (Wallace-Kunkel et al., 2006, pp 4–13)

1.7 g 5-MTN dissolved in 52.5 mL ethyl acetate, 50 mL methyl tert-butyl ether, 12.5 mL absolute ethanol, and 5 mL glacial acetic acid. Add this to 360 mL HFE 7100.

7.14.7 2-Isononylninhydrin (INON, Thermanin) (Al Mandhri and Khanmy-Vital, 2005)

4–5 g INON dissolved in 15 mL ethyl acetate, 5 mL isopropanol, and 980 mL HFE 7100.

7.14.8 Silver Nitrate (Trozzi et al., 2000, pp 38–39)

Dissolve 30 g silver nitrate in 1 L distilled water.

or

Dissolve 30 g silver nitrate in 100 mL distilled water and add to 1 L ethanol.

7.14.9 Physical Developer (Kent, 1998)

Acid Pretreatment: 30 g of maleic acid is dissolved in 1 L distilled water. Indefinite shelf life.

Stock Solution #1: 30 g ferric nitrate nonahydrate dissolved in 900 mL distilled water. 80 g ferrous ammonium sulfate hexahydrate dissolved in this solution. 20 g anhydrous citric acid dissolved in this solution. Shelf life may be several months.

Stock Solution #2: 4 g n-Dodecylamine acetate dissolved in 1 L distilled water. 4 g (4 mL) Synperonic N added to this solution. Indefinite shelf life.

Stock Solution #3: 20 g silver nitrate dissolved in 100 mL distilled water. Indefinite shelf life.

Working Solution: 900 mL stock solution #1. Add 40 mL of stock solution #2 and stir for 5 minutes. Add 50 mL of stock solution #3 and stir for 5 minutes. Shelf life is 1–2 weeks.

Hypochlorite Post-Treatment Solution: 100 mL of household chlorine bleach (~6% NaOCl) is mixed with 100 mL water.

7.14.10 Multimetal Deposition (Saunders, 1989, 1996, 1997)

Colloidal Gold Solution

Stock Solution #1: 10% (w/v) tetrachlorauric acid (HAuCl$_4$.3H$_2$O) in high-purity (RO/DI) water.

Stock Solution #2: 1% (w/v) trisodium citrate (Na$_3$Cit.2H$_2$O) in high-purity water.

Stock Solution #3: 0.5 M (10.5% w/v) citric acid (H$_3$Cit.H$_2$O) in high-purity water.

Stock Solution #4: 1% Polyethylene glycol.

Working Solution: Add 1 mL of stock solution #1 to 1 L of high-purity water and bring to a boil. Rapidly add 10 mL of stock solution #2 and boil gently for 10 minutes. Add 5 mL of Tween 20 (or Tween 80) and mix well. Add 10 mL of stock solution #4 to the cooled solution and adjust the pH to 2.7 using stock solution #3. Restore total volume to 1 L with high-purity water. Shelf life is 3 months.

Modified Silver Physical Developer Solution

Stock Solution #1: Dissolve 33 g ferric nitrate nonahydrate in 1 L of high-purity water. Add 89 g of ferrous ammonium sulfate hexahydrate to the solution. Add 22 g of citric acid to the solution. Add 1 mL of Tween 20 to the solution.

Stock Solution #2: 20% (w/v) silver nitrate in high-purity water.

Working Solution: Add 1 part of stock solution #2 to 99 parts of stock solution #1. Only stable for 15 minutes.

Application

Prewashing: Porous items should be washed several times in high-purity water.

Colloidal Gold: Soak items in colloidal gold solution for 30–120 minutes, but avoid overdevelopment.

In-Between Rinsing: Rinse items in high-purity water. For porous items, use several water changes for 15 minutes or more.

Silver Physical Developer: Place items into freshly made solution. Silver amplification occurs within 10–15 minutes.

Postwashing: Rinse with tap water. Air dry.

7.14.11 MMD II (Schnetz and Margot, 2001, pp 21–28)

Silanization of Glassware

Soak glassware for 8 hours in 10% Extran MA 01 alkaline liquid (Merck). Rinse with high-purity hot water, then high-purity cold water. Dry in an oven at 100 °C. Soak for 5 seconds in 2% (v/v) 3-aminopropyltriethoxysilane in acetone. Rinse twice with acetone, then water. Dry in an oven at 42 °C for 8 hours.

Colloidal Gold Solution

Stock Solution #1: 10% (w/v) tetrachlorauric acid in high-purity water.

Stock Solution #2: 1% (w/v) sodium citrate in high-purity water.

Stock Solution #3: 0.5 M citric acid in high-purity water.

Stock Solution #4: 1% (w/v) tannic acid in high-purity water.

Working Solution #1: Add 0.5 mL of stock solution #1 to 400 mL of high-purity water. Heat to 60 °C.

Working Solution #2: Add 20 mL of stock solution #2 and 0.1 mL of stock solution #4 to 75 mL of high-purity water. Heat to 60 °C.

Once both solutions reach 60 °C, rapidly add working solution #2 to working solution #1 and mix vigorously. Heat the mixture to boiling, cool, and adjust to 500 mL with high-purity water. Solution can be stored in a plastic bottle at 4 °C. Before use, bring to room temperature, add 0.5 mL Tween 20 (or Tween 80), and adjust pH to 2.7 with stock solution #3.

Silver Physical Developer Solution

Stock Solution #1: 24 parts 25.5% (w/v) citric acid solution, 22 parts 23.5% sodium citrate solution, and 50 parts high-purity water. Adjust to pH 3.8 with additional citric acid or sodium citrate solution.

Stock Solution #2: 0.2% (w/v) silver acetate solution.

Stock Solution #3: 0.5% (w/v) hydroquinone in stock solution #1.

Rinsing Solution: 0.25% (w/v) hydroquinone (1 part stock solution #3 and 1 part high-purity water).

Working Solution: One part stock solution #2 and one part stock solution #3. Unstable, so prepare just before use.

Application

Prewashing: Porous items should be washed with high-purity water for 2 minutes. Nonporous items need only brief washing in high-purity water.

Colloidal Gold: Soak items in colloidal gold solution for 5–15 minutes with mild agitation.

In-Between Rinsing: Rinse briefly in high-purity water.

In-Between Hydroquinone Rinsing: Rinse for 2–5 minutes in hydroquinone rinsing solution.

Silver Physical Development: Place items in silver physical developer for about 18 minutes.

Postwashing: Rinse with high-purity water.

Fixing: Fix with 1:9 dilution of photographic fixer for 2–5 minutes, rinse with tap water, air dry.

7.15 Reviewers

The reviewers critiquing this chapter were Christophe Champod, Sue Manci Coppejans, Christine L. Craig, Robert J. Garrett, Deborah Leben, Bridget Lewis, Jon T. Stimac, Juliet H. Wood, and Rodolfo R. Zamora.

7.16 References

Abderhalden, E.; Schmidt, H. Utilization of Triketohydrindene Hydrate for the Detection of Proteins and Their Cleavage Products. *Z. Physiologische Chem.* 1911, *72*, 37.

Al Mandhri, A.; Khanmy-Vital, A. Detection of Fingerprints on Paper with 2-Isononyl-Ninhydrin. Presented at the 17th Meeting of the International Association of the Forensic Sciences. Hong Kong, 2005.

Almog, J. Fingerprint Development by Ninhydrin and Its Analogues. In *Advances in Fingerprint Technology;* Lee, H. C., Gaensslen, R. E., Eds.; CRC Press: Boca Raton, FL, 2001.

Almog, J.; Hirshfeld, A. 5-Methoxyninhydrin: A Reagent for the Chemical Development of Latent Fingerprints That Is Compatible with the Copper Vapour Laser. *J. Forensic Sci.* 1988, *33* (4), 1027–1030.

Almog, J.; Hirshfeld, A.; Klug, J. T. Reagents for the Chemical Development of Latent Fingerprints: Synthesis and Properties of Some Ninhydrin Analogues. *J. Forensic Sci.* 1982, *27* (4), 912–917.

Almog, J.; Hirshfeld, A.; Frank, A.; Grant, H.; Harel, Z.; Ittah, Y. 5-Methylthio Ninhydrin and Related Compounds: A Novel Class of Fluorogenic Fingerprint Reagents. *J. Forensic Sci.* 1992, *37* (3), 688–694.

Almog, J.; Springer, E.; Wiesner, S.; Frank, A.; Khodzhaev, O.; Lidor, R.; Bahar, E.; Varkony, H.; Dayan, S.; Razen, S. Latent Fingerprint Visualization by 1,2-Indanedione and Related Compounds: Preliminary Results. *J. Forensic Sci.* 1999, *44* (1), 114–118.

Anderson, K. N.; Anderson, L. E.; Glanze, W. D., Eds. *Mosby's Medical, Nursing, and Allied Health Dictionary,* 5th ed.; Mosby, Inc.: St. Louis, MO, 1998.

Angier, R. H. *Firearm Blueing and Browning;* Arms and Armour: London, 1936.

Atkins, P. W. *Physical Chemistry,* 4th ed.; W. H. Freeman and Co.: New York, 1990.

Ballantyne, J. Serology: Overview. In *Encyclopedia of Forensic Science;* Siegel, J., Saukko, P., Knupfer, G., Eds.; Academic Press: London, 2000; pp 1322–1331.

Bandey, H. L. *The Powder Process, Study 1: Evaluation of Fingerprint Brushes for Use with Aluminum Powder;* HOPSDB Report 54/2004; Home Office Police Scientific Development Branch: Sandridge, U.K., 2004.

Bandey, H. L.; Kent, T. *Superglue Treatment of Crime Scenes—A Trial of the Effectiveness of the Mason Vactron SUPERfume Process;* HOPSDB Report 30/2003; Home Office Police Scientific Development Branch: Sandridge, U.K., 2003.

Barnett, K. G.; Bone, R. G.; Hall, P. W.; Ide, R. H. *The Use of Water Soluble Protein Dye for the Enhancement of Footwear Impressions in Blood on Non-Porous Surfaces—Part I;* Technical Note 629; Forensic Science Service: Birmingham, U.K., 1988.

Batey, G.; Copeland, J.; Donnelly, D.; Hill, C.; Laturnus, P.; McDiarmid, C.; Miller, K.; Misner, A. H.; Tario, A.; Yamashita, A. B. Metal Deposition for Latent Print Development. *J. Forensic Ident.* 1998, *48* (2), 165–176.

Bayford, F. Sweat. *Fingerprint Whorld* 1976, *1,* 42–43.

Bentsen, R. K.; Brown, J. K.; Dinsmore, A.; Harvey, K. K.; Kee, T. G. Post Firing Visualization of Fingerprints on Spent Cartridge Cases. *Sci. Justice* 1996, *36* (1), 3–8.

Bernier, U. R.; Booth, M. M.; Yost, R. A. Analysis of Human Skin Emanations by Gas Chromatography/Mass Spectrometry: 1. Thermal Desorption of Attractants for the Yellow Fever Mosquito (Aedes Aegypti) from Handled Glass Beads. *Anal. Chem.* 1999, *71* (1), 1–7.

Bernier, U. R.; Kline, D. L.; Barnard, D. R.; Schreck, C. E.; Yost, R. A. Analysis of Human Skin Emanations by Gas Chromatography/Mass Spectrometry: 2. Identification of Volatile Compounds That Are Candidate Attractants for the Yellow Fever Mosquito (Aedes Aegypti). *Anal. Chem.* 2000, *72* (4), 747–756.

Bessman, C. W.; Nelson, E.; Lipert, R. J.; Coldiron, S.; Herrman, T. R. A Comparison of Cyanoacrylate Fuming in a Vacuum Cabinet to a Humidity Fuming Chamber. *J. Forensic Ident.* 2005, *55* (1), 10–27.

Bodziak, W. J. Use of Leuco-Crystal Violet to Enhance Shoeprints in Blood. *Forensic Sci. Int.* 1996, *82* (1), 45–52.

Bottom, C. B.; Hanna, S. S.; Siehr, D. J. Mechanism of the Ninhydrin Reaction. *Biochem. Educ.* 1978, *6* (1), 4–5.

Bowman, V., Sears, V., Bandey, H., Hart, A., Bleay, S., Gibson, A., Fitzgerald, L., Eds. What Is the Oldest Fingerprint You Have Developed? In *Fingerprint Development and Imaging Update.* Home Office Scientific Development Branch: Sandridge, U.K., 2003; pp 2–3.

Boysen, T. C.; Yanagawa, S.; Sato, F.; Sato, K. A Modified Anaerobic Method of Sweat Collection. *J. Applied Physiol.* 1984, *56* (5), 1302–1307.

Bramble, S. K.; Brennan, J. S. Fingerprints (Dactyloscopy): Chemistry of Print Residue. In *Encyclopedia of Forensic Science;* Siegel, J., Saukko, P., Knupfer, G., Eds.; Academic Press: London, 2000; pp 862–869.

Bratton, R. M.; Juhala, J. A. DFO-Dry. *J. Forensic Ident.* 1995, *45* (2), 169–172.

Bratton, R. M.; Gregus, J.; Juhala, J. A. A Black Powder Method to Process Adhesive Tapes. *Fingerprint Whorld* 1996, *22* (83), 28.

Brusilow, S. W.; Gordes, E. H. Ammonia Secretion in Sweat. *American J. Physiol.* 1968, *214* (3), 513–517.

Bunting, R. K. *The Chemistry of Photography;* Photoglass Press: Normal, IL, 1987.

Bureau voor Dactyloscopische Artikelen (BVDA). Product Information for 5-Methylthioninhydrin and Thermanin. http://www.bvda.com (accessed Jan 5, 2010).

Burns, D. S. Sticky-Side Powder: The Japanese Solution. *J. Forensic Ident.* 1994, *44* (2), 133–138.

Burow, D.; Seifert, D.; Cantu, A. A. Modifications to the Silver Physical Developer. *J. Forensic Sci.* 2003, *48* (5), 1094–1100.

Campbell, B. M. Vacuum Chamber Cyanoacrylate Technique Evolution. *RCMP Gazette* 1991, *53* (12), 12–16.

Campbell, B. M. Time-Resolved Photography of Latent Prints on Fluorescent Backgrounds. *J. Forensic Ident.* 1993, *43* (4), 368–377.

Cantu, A. A. Silver Physical Developers for the Visualization of Latent Prints on Paper. *Forensic Sci. Rev.* 2001, *13* (1), 29–64.

Cantu, A. A.; Johnson, J. L. Silver Physical Development of Latent Prints. In *Advances in Fingerprint Technology;* Lee, H. C., Gaensslen, R. E., Eds.; CRC Press: Boca Raton, FL, 2001; pp 242–247.

Cantu, A. A.; Leben, D. A.; Joullié, M. M.; Heffner, R. J.; Hark, R. R. A Comparative Examination of Several Amino Acid Reagents for Visualizing Amino Acid (Glycine) on Paper. *J. Forensic Ident.* 1993, *43* (1), 44–66.

Cantu, A. A.; Leben, D. A.; Ramotowski, R.; Kopera, J.; Simms, J. R. Use of Acidified Hydrogen Peroxide to Remove Excess Gun Blue from Gun Blue-Treated Cartridge Cases and to Develop Latent Prints on Untreated Cartridge Cases. *J. Forensic Sci.* 1998, *43* (2), 294–298.

Cantu, A. A.; Leben, D. A.; Kelley, W. Some Advances in the Silver Physical Development of Latent Prints on Paper. *Int. Soc. Opt. Eng. (SPIE)* 2003, *5071,* 164–168.

Cava, M. P.; Little, R. L.; Napier, D. R. Condensed Cyclobutane Aromatic Systems: V. The Synthesis of Some a-Diazo-Indanones: Ring Contraction in the Indane Series. *J. Am. Chem. Soc.* 1958, *80* (9), 2257–2263.

Champod, C.; Lennard, C.; Margot, P.; Stoilovic, M. *Fingerprints and Other Ridge Skin Impressions;* CRC Press: Boca Raton, FL, 2004.

Cheeseman, R.; DiMeo, L. A. Fluorescein as a Field-Worthy Latent Bloodstain Detection System. *J. Forensic Ident.* 1995, *45* (6), 631–646.

Christie, R. M.; Mather, R. R.; Wardman, R. H. *The Chemistry of Colour Application;* Blackwell Science, Ltd.: Oxford, 2000.

Clay, W. E. Fluorisol: The Solvent of Choice for Ninhydrin Detection of Latent Fingerprints. *Ident. News* 1981, *31* (4), 12–13.

Conn, C.; Ramsay, G.; Roux, C.; Lennard, C. The Effect of Metal Salt Treatment on the Photoluminescence of DFO-Treated Fingerprints. *Forensic Sci. Int.* 2001, *116* (2), 117–123.

Cowger, J. F. *Friction Ridge Skin, Comparison and Identification of Fingerprints;* Elsevier Science: New York, 1983.

Crown, D. A. The Development of Latent Fingerprints with Ninhydrin. *J. Crim. Law Criminol. Police Sci.* 1969, *60* (2), 258–264.

Cuthbertson, F. *The Chemistry of Fingerprints;* AWRE Report No. 013/69; United Kingdom Atomic Weapons Establishment: Aldermaston, U.K., 1969.

Dalrymple, B.; Duff, J. M.; Menzel, E. R. Inherent Fingerprint Fluorescence-Detection by Laser. *J. Forensic Sci.* 1977, *22* (1), 106–115.

Davies, P. J.; Kobus, H. J.; Taylor, M. R.; Wainwright, K. P. Synthesis and Structure of the Zinc(II) and Cadmium(II)

Complexes Produced in the Photoluminescent Enhancement of Ninhydrin Developed Fingerprints Using Group 12 Metal Salts. *J. Forensic Sci.* 1995a, *40* (4), 565–569.

Davies, P. J.; Taylor, M. R.; Wainwright, K. P.; Kobus, H. J. Zinc(II) Chloride-Methanol Complex of 2-[(1,3-Dihydro-1,3-dioxo-2H-inden-2-ylidene)amino]-1H-indene-1,3(2H)- dionate(1-) Sodium Salt: A Complex of Ruhemann's Purple. *Acta Crystallogr., Sect. C: Cryst. Struct. Commun.* 1995b, *51* (9), 1802–1805.

Dayan, S.; Almog, J.; Khodzhaev, O.; Rozen, S. A Novel Synthesis of Indanediones Using the HOF.CH3CN Complex. *J. Org. Chem.* 1998, *63* (8), 2752–2754.

Dean, J. A. *Lange's Handbook of Chemistry,* 13th ed.; McGraw-Hill: New York, 1985.

Della, E. W.; Janowski, W. K.; Pigou, P. E.; Taylor, B. Synthesis of Fingerprint Reagents: Aromatic Nucleophilic Substitution as a Route to 5-Substituted Ninhydrins. *Synthesis* 1999, *12,* 2119–2123.

DeMey, J. Colloidal Gold Probes in Immunocytochemistry. In *Immunohistochemistry: Practical Applications in Pathology and Biology;* Polak, J. M., Van Noorden, S., Eds.; John Wright and Sons Ltd.: London, 1983; pp 82–112.

Didierjean, C.; Debart, M.; Crispino, F. New Formulations of DFO in HFE7100. *Fingerprint Whorld* 1998, *24* (94), 163–167.

Druey, J.; Schmidt, P. Phenanthrolinchinone und Diazafluorene. *Helv. Chim. Acta* 1950, *33* (4), 1080–1087.

Eckert, W. G.; James, S. H. *Interpretation of Bloodstain Evidence at Crime Scenes;* Elsevier Science: New York, 1989.

Elber, R.; Frank, A.; Almog, J. Chemical Development of Latent Fingerprints: Computational Design of Ninhydrin Analogues. *J. Forensic Sci.* 2000, *45* (4), 757–760.

Everse, K. E.; Menzel, E. R. Sensitivity Enhancement of Ninhydrin-Treated Latent Fingerprints by Enzymes and Metal Salts. *J. Forensic Sci.* 1986, *31* (2), 446–454.

Faragher, A.; Summerscales, L. *Fingerprint Enhancement Using the Amido Black Technique after Chemical Fixation;* Technical Note 240; Forensic Science Service: Birmingham, U.K., 1981.

Faulk, W. P.; Taylor, G. M. An Immunocolloid Method for the Electron Microscope. *Immunochemistry* 1971, *8* (11), 1081–1083.

Feigl, F.; Anger, V. *Spot Tests in Inorganic Analysis;* Elsevier: Amsterdam, 1972.

Fitzgerald, L. Development of a GC-MS Method for the Analysis of Latent Fingerprint Components. Presented at the International Fingerprint Research Group Meeting, St. Albans, U.K., 2003.

Forgeot, R. Etude medico-legale des empreintes peu visibles ou invisibles et revelees par des procedes speciaux. *Archives d'anthropologie criminelle et des sciences penales* 1891, *6,* 387–404.

Förström, L.; Goldyne, M. E.; Winkelmann, R. K. IgE in Human Eccrine Sweat. *J. Investigative Derm.* 1975, *64* (3), 156–157.

Frank, A.; Almog, J. Modified SPR for Latent Fingerprint Development on Wet, Dark Objects. *J. Forensic Ident.* 1993, *43* (3), 240–244.

Frens, G. Controlled Nucleation for the Regulation of the Particle Size in Monodisperse Gold Suspensions. *Nature* 1973, *241* (105), 20–22.

Friedman, M.; Williams, L. D. Stoichiometry of Formation of Ruhemann's Purple in the Ninhydrin Reaction. *Bioorg. Chem.* 1974, *3,* 267–280.

Froude, Jr. J. H. The Super Glue Fuming Wand: A Preliminary Evaluation. *J. Forensic Ident.* 1996, *46* (1), 19–31.

Garner, D. D.; Cano, K. M.; Peimer, R. S.; Yeshion, T. E. An Evaluation of Tetramethylbenzidine as a Presumptive Test for Blood. *J. Forensic Sci.* 1976, *21* (4), 816–821.

Gerber, S. M.; Saferstein, R. Eds. *More Chemistry and Crime: From Marsh Arsenic Test to DNA Profile;* American Chemical Society: Washington, DC, 1997.

German, E. R. You Are Missing Ninhydrin Developed Prints. *Ident. News* 1981, *31* (9), 3–4.

German, E. R. Cyanoacrylate (Superglue) Fuming Tips. *2005.* http://www.onin.com/fp (accessed Jan 5, 2010).

Godsell, J. Fingerprint Techniques. *J. Forensic Sci.* Soc. 1963, *3* (2), 79.

Goode, G. C.; Morris, J. R. *Latent Fingerprints: A Review of Their Origin, Composition, and Methods for Detection;* AWRE Report No. 022/83; United Kingdom Atomic Weapons Research Establishment: Aldermaston, U.K., 1983.

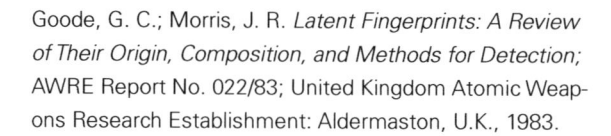

Green, S. C.; Stewart, M. E.; Downing, D. Variation in Sebum Fatty Acid Composition Among Adult Humans. *J. Investigative Dermatol.* 1984, *83* (2), 114–117.

Grigg, R.; Malone, J. F.; Mongkolaussavaratana, T.; Thianpatanagul, S. Cycloaddition Reactions Relevant to the Mechanism of the Ninhydrin Reaction. X-Ray Crystal Structure of Protonated Ruhemann's Purple, a Stable 1,3-Dipole. *J. Chem. Soc., Chem. Commun.* 1986, 421–422.

Grigg, R.; Malone, J. F.; Mongkolaussavaratana, T.; Thianpatanagul, S. X=Y-ZH Compounds as Potential 1,3 Dipoles. Part 23 Mechanisms of the Reactions of Ninhydrin and Phenalene Trione with a-Amino Acids. X-Ray Crystal Structure of Protonated Ruhemann's Purple, a Stable Azomethine Ylide. *Tetrahedron* 1989, *45* (12), 3849–3862.

Grigg, R.; Mongkolaussavaratana, T.; Pounds, C. A.; Sivagnanam, S. 1,8-Diazafluorenone and Related Compounds. A New Reagent for the Detection of a-Amino Acids and Latent Fingerprints. *Tetrahedron Lett.* 1990, *31* (49), 7215–7218.

Guerrero, M. B. L. The Transparent, Liquid Adhesive, Latent Print Lifter. *J. Forensic Ident.* 1992, *42* (2), 101–105.

Hadorn, B.; Hanimann, F.; Anders, P.; Curtius, H.; Halverson, R. Free Amino Acids in Human Sweat from Different Parts of the Body. *Nature* 1967, *215* (99), 416–417.

Hall, M. M. Ridge Detail Through Latex Gloves. *J. Forensic Ident.* 1991, *41* (6), 415–416.

Hambley, D. S. The Physics of Vacuum Evaporation Development of Latent Fingerprints. Ph.D. Thesis, The Royal Holloway College, University of London, 1972.

Hamilton, P. B. Amino-Acids on Hands. *Nature* 1965, *205*, 284–285.

Hansen, D. B.; Joullié, M. M. The Development of Novel Ninhydrin Analogues. *Chem. Soc. Rev.* 2005, *34*, 408–417.

Hardwick, S. A.; Kent, T.; Sears, V. *Fingerprint Detection by Fluorescence Examination: A Guide to Operational Implementation;* White Crescent Press, Ltd.: Luton, U.K., 1990.

Hardwick, S. A.; Kent, T.; Sears, V.; Winfield, P. Improvements to the Formulation of DFO and the Effects of Heat on the Reaction with Latent Fingerprints. *Fingerprint Whorld* 1993, *19* (73), 65–69.

Harvey, K. K.; Dinsmore, A.; Brown, J. K.; Burns, D. S. Detection of Latent Fingerprints by Vacuum Cyanoacrylate Fuming—An Improved System. *Fingerprint Whorld* 2000, *26*, 29–31.

Hauze, D. B.; Petrovskaia, O.; Taylor, B.; Joullie, M. M.; Ramotowski, R.; Cantu, A. A. 1,2-Indanediones: New Reagents for Visualizing the Amino Acid Components of Latent Prints. *J. Forensic Sci.* 1998, *43* (4), 744–747.

Hawthorne, J. S.; Wojcik, M. H. Alcohol Measurement: A Review of the Literature. *Can. Soc. Forensic Sci. J.* 2006, *39* (2), 65–71.

Heffner, R. J.; Joullié, M. M. Synthetic Routes to Ninhydrins. Preparation of Ninhydrin, 5-Methoxyninhydrin, and 5-(Methylthio)ninhydrin. *Synth. Commun.* 1991, *21* (21), 2231–2256.

Herod, D. W.; Menzel, E. R. Laser Detection of Latent Fingerprints: Ninhydrin. *J. Forensic Sci.* 1982a, *27* (1), 200–204.

Herod, D. W.; Menzel, E. R. Laser Detection of Latent Fingerprints: Ninhydrin Followed by Zinc Chloride. *J. Forensic Sci.* 1982b, *27* (3), 513–518.

Hewlett, D. F.; Sears, V.; Suzuki, S. Replacements for CFC113 in the Ninhydrin Process: Part 2. *J. Forensic Ident.* 1997, *47* (3), 300–305.

Hier, S. W.; Cornbleet, T.; Bergeim, O. The Amino Acids of Human Sweat. *J. Biol. Chem.* 1946, *166* (1), 327–333.

Holgate, C. S.; Jackson, P.; Cowen, P. N.; Bird, C. C. Immunogold–Silver Staining: New Method of Immunostaining with Enhanced Sensitivity. *J. Histochem. and Cytochem.* 1983, *31* (7), 938–944.

Home Office Scientific Development Branch. Silver VMD. *HOSDB Fingerprint Development and Imaging Newsletter,* Oct 2005, *47/05,* 8–9.

Hussain, J. I.; Pounds, C. A. T*he Enhancement of Fingerprints in Blood, Part II: A Modified Amido Black Staining Technique;* HOCRE Report 649; Forensic Science Service: Birmingham, U.K., 1989a.

Hussain, J. I.; Pounds, C. A. *The Enhancement of Marks Made in Blood with 3,3',4,4'-Tetraaminobiphenyl;* CRSE Report 653; Forensic Science Service: Birmingham, U.K., 1989b.

Illsley, C. P. Superglue Fuming and Multiple Lifts. *Ident. News* 1984, *34* (1), 6, 15.

Inbau, F. E. Scientific Evidence in Criminal Cases, Part III: Finger-Prints and Palm-Prints. *Sparks From the Anvil* 1934, *2* (12), 4.

Jacquat, A. *Evolution des substances grasses des empreintes digitales au cours du temps. Analyse par TLC et GC-MS.;* University of Lausanne: Lausanne, Switzerland, 1999.

James, J. D.; Wilshire, B.; Cleaver, D. Laboratory Simulation of Commercial Brass Flake Manufacture. *Powder Metal.* 1990, *33* (3), 247–252.

James, J. D.; Pounds, C. A.; Wilshire, B. Flake Metal Powders for Revealing Latent Fingerprints. *J. Forensic Sci.* 1991, *36* (5), 1368–1375.

James, J. D.; Pounds, C. A.; Phil, M.; Wilshire, B. Magnetic Flake Powders for Fingerprint Development. *J. Forensic Sci.* 1993, *38* (2), 391–401.

Johnson, H. L.; Maibach, H. I. Drug Excretion in Human Eccrine Sweat. *J. Investigative Dermatol.* 1971, *56* (3), 182–188.

Jones, N. Metal Deposition Techniques for the Detection and Enhancement of Latent Fingerprints on Semi-Porous Surfaces. Ph.D. Thesis, University of Technology, Sydney, NSW, Australia, 2002.

Jones, N. E.; Jickells, S.; Charles, Y.; Elliott, J. *Chemical Analysis of Latent Print Residue;* Forensic Science Service: London, 2001a.

Jones, N.; Mansour, D.; Stoilovic, M.; Lennard, C.; Roux, C. The Influence of Polymer Type, Print Donor and Age on the Quality of Fingerprints Developed on Plastic Substrates Using Vacuum Metal Deposition. *Forensic Sci. Int.* 2001b, *124* (2–3), 167–177.

Jones, N.; Stoilovic, M.; Lennard, C.; Roux, C. Vacuum Metal Deposition: Factors Affecting Normal and Reverse Development of Latent Fingerprints on Polyethylene Substrates. *Forensic Sci. Int.* 2001c, *115* (1–2), 73–88.

Jones, N.; Stoilovic, M.; Lennard, C.; Roux, C. Vacuum Metal Deposition: Developing Latent Fingerprints on Polyethylene Substrates After the Deposition of Excess Gold. *Forensic Sci. Int.* 2001d, *123* (1), 5–12.

Jonker, H.; Molenaar, A.; Dippel, C. J. Physical Development Recording System: III. Physical Development. *Photographic Sci. and Eng.* 1969, *13* (2), 38–44.

Joullié, M. M. New Reagents for the Development of Latent Fingerprints. U.S. Department of Justice Grant Report 92-IJ-CX-K0154, Jan 17, 2000. http://www.ncjrs.gov/pdffiles1/nij/grants/179287.pdf.

Joullié, M. M.; Petrovskaia, O. A Better Way to Develop Fingerprints. *CHEMTECH* 1998, *28* (8), 41–44.

Joullié, M. M.; Thompson, T. R.; Nemeroff, N. H. Ninhydrin and Ninhydrin Analogs: Syntheses and Applications. *Tetrahedron* 1991, *47* (42), 8791–8830.

Jueneman, F. B. Stick It to 'Em. *Ident. News* 1982, *32* (6), 5, 15.

Kaiser, D.; Drack, E. Diminished Excretion of Bicarbonate from the Single Sweat Gland of Patients with Cystic Fibrosis of the Pancreas. *Eur. J. Clin. Investigation* 1974, *4* (4), 261–265.

Kasper, S. P.; Minnillo, D. J.; Rockhold, A. M. Validating IND (1,2-Indanedione). *Forensic Sci. Commun.* 2002, *4* (4).

Kausche, G. A.; Ruska, H. Die Sichtbarmachung der Adsorption von Metallkolloiden an Eiweißkörper: I. Die Reaktion kolloides Gold—Tabakmosaikvirus. *Kolloid-Z.* 1939, *89* (1), 21–26.

Kawerau, E.; Wieland, T. Conservation of Amino-Acid Chromatograms. *Nature* 1951, *168* (4263), 77–78.

Kelly, G.; Bird, D.; Burt, D.; Massey, S.; Morhart, B.; Swiderski, D. Use of Children's Glue as an Aid in Fingerprint Lifting. *Ident. Canada* 2001, *24* (4), 7–12.

Kent, T. Latent Fingerprints and Their Detection. *J. Forensic Sci. Soc.* 1981, *21* (1), 15–22.

Kent, T. *User Guide to the Metal Deposition Process for the Development of Latent Fingerprints;* HOPSDB Publication No. 24; Home Office Police Scientific Development Branch: Sandridge, U.K., 1982.

Kent, T., Ed. *Manual of Fingerprint Development Techniques,* 2nd ed.; Home Office Police Scientific Development Branch: Sandridge, U.K., 1998.

Kent, T., Ed. *Manual of Fingerprint Development Techniques,* 2004 update; Home Office Police Scientific Development Branch: Sandridge, U.K., 2004.

Kent, T. [Letter to the Editor]. A Comparison of Cyanoacrylate Fuming in a Vacuum Cabinet to a Humidity Fuming Chamber. *J. Forensic Ident.* 2005, *55* (6), 681–683.

Kent, T.; Winfield, P. Superglue Fingerprint Development— Atmospheric Pressure and High Humidity, or Vacuum Evaporation? In *Proceedings of the International Symposium on Fingerprint Detection and Identification;* Ne'urim, Israel, 1995.

Kent, T.; Thomas, G. L.; East, H. W. *Application of the Metal Deposition Technique to the Development of Fingerprints on Polythene;* HOPSDB Technical Note; Home Office Scientific Development Branch: Sandridge, U.K., 1975.

Kent, T.; Thomas, G. L.; Reynoldson, T. E.; East, H. W. A Vacuum Coating Technique for the Development of Latent Fingerprints on Polythene. *J. Forensic Sci. Soc.* 1976, *16* (2), 93–101.

Kent, T.; Gillett, P. C.; Lee, D. *A Comparative Study of Three Techniques: Aluminium Powdering, Lead Powdering and Metal Deposition for the Development of Latent Fingerprints on Polythene;* HOPSDB Technical Memo; Home Office Police Scientific Development Branch: Sandridge, U.K., 1978.

Kerr, F. M.; Westland, A. D.; Haque, F. Observations on the Use of Silver Compounds for Fingerprint Visualization. *Forensic Sci. Int.* 1981, *18,* 209–214.

Knaap, W.; Adach, E. The Knaap Process: Lifting Two-Dimensional Footwear and Fingerprint Impressions Using Dental Stone. *J. Forensic Ident.* 2002, *52* (5), 561–571.

Knowles, A. M. Aspects of Physicochemical Methods for the Detection of Latent Fingerprints. *J. Phys. E: Sci. Instrum.* 1978, *11* (8), 713–721.

Kobus, H. J.; Stoilovic, M.; Warrener, R. N. A Simple Luminescent Post-Ninhydrin Treatment for the Improved Visualisation of Fingerprints on Documents in Cases Where Ninhydrin Alone Gives Poor Results. *Forensic Sci. Int.* 1983, *22* (2–3), 161–170.

Kotowski, T. M.; Grieve, M. C. The Use of Microspectrophotometry to Characterize Microscopic Amounts of Blood. *J. Forensic Sci.* 1986, *31* (3), 1079–1085.

Labows, J. N.; Preti, G.; Hoelzle, E.; Leyden, J.; Kligman, A. Steroid Analysis of Human Apocrine Secretion. *Steroids* 1979, *34* (3), 249–258.

Leben, D. A.; Ramotowski, R. Evaluation of Gun Blueing Solutions and Their Ability to Develop Latent Fingerprints on Cartridge Casings. *Chesapeake Examiner* 1996, *34* (2), 8–10.

Lee, H. C.; Gaensslen, R. E. Methods of Latent Fingerprint Development. In *Advances in Fingerprint Technology,* 2nd ed.; Lee, H. C., Gaensslen, R. E., Eds.; CRC Press: Boca Raton, FL, 2001; pp 105–175.

Lee, H.C.; Pagliaro, E.M. Serology: Blood Identification. In *Encyclopedia of Forensic Science;* Siegel, J., Saukko, P., Knupfer, G., Eds.; Academic Press: London, 2000; pp 1331–1338.

Lennard, C. J.; Margot, P. A. Sequencing of Reagents for the Improved Visualization of Latent Fingerprints. *J. Forensic Ident.* 1988, *38* (5), 197–210.

Lennard, C. J.; Margot, P.; Stoilovic, M.; Warrener, R. N. Synthesis of Ninhydrin Analogues and Their Application to Fingerprint Development: Preliminary Results. *J. Forensic Sci. Soc.* 1986, *26* (5), 323–328.

Lennard, C. J.; Margot, P.; Sterns, M.; Warrener, R. N. Photoluminescent Enhancement of Ninhydrin Developed Fingerprints by Metal Complexation: Structural Studies of Complexes Formed Between Ruhemann's Purple and Group IIB Metal Salts. *J. Forensic Sci.* 1987, *32* (3), 597–605.

Lennard, C. J.; Wallace-Kunkel, C.; Roux, C.; Stoilovic, M. B25: 1,2-Indanedione: Is it a Useful Fingerprint Reagent? In *Proceedings of the 2005 American Academy of Forensic Science Meeting;* New Orleans, LA, 2005; p 43.

Lewis, L. A.; Smithwick, R.; Devault, G.; Bolinger, B.; Lewis, S. A. Processes Involved in the Development of Latent Fingerprints Using the Cyanoacrylate Fuming Method. *J. Forensic Sci.* 2001, *46* (2), 241–246.

Lightning Powder Inc. Dusting for Latents. *Minutiae,* Jan–Feb 2002, *70,* 2–3.

Lobitz, W. C.; Mason, H. L. Chemistry of Palmar Sweat: VII. Discussion of Studies on Chloride, Urea, Glucose, Uric Acid, Ammonia–Nitrogen, and Creatinine. *Arch. Dermatol. Syphilol.* 1948, *57,* 907–915.

MacDonell, H. L. Bristleless Brush Development of Latent Fingerprints. *Ident. News* 1961, *11* (3), 7–15.

Magora, A.; Azoury, M.; Geller, B. Treatment of Cocaine Contaminated Polythene Bags Prior to Fingerprint Development by Cyanoacrylate Fuming. *J. Forensic Ident.* 2002, *52* (2), 159–165.

Marshall, T. Analysis of Human Sweat Proteins by Two-Dimensional Electrophoresis and Ultrasensitive Silver Staining. *Anal. Biochem.* 1984, *139* (2), 506–509.

Masters, N. *Safety for the Forensic Identification Specialist*, 2nd ed.; Lightning Powder Inc.: Salem, OR, 2002.

Masters, N.; DeHaan, J. D. Vacuum Metal Deposition and Cyanoacrylate Detection of Older Latent Prints. *J. Forensic Ident.* 1996, *46* (1), 32–45.

McCaldin, D. J. The Chemistry of Ninhydrin. *Chem. Rev.* 1960, *60* (1), 39–51.

McDiarmid, C. Does Haste Make Waste? *RCMP Gazette* 1992, *54* (6), 21–24.

McMahon, P. Procedure to Develop Latent Prints on Thermal Paper. *Ident. Canada* 1996, *19* (3), 4–5.

Menzel, E. R. *Fingerprint Detection with Lasers*, 2nd ed.; Marcel Dekker, Inc.: New York, 1999.

Menzel, E. R. *Fingerprint Detection with Photoluminescent Nanoparticles*, 2nd ed.; Lee, H. C., Gaensslen, R. E., Eds.; CRC Press: Boca Raton, FL, 2001.

Menzel, E. R.; Duff, J. M. Laser Detection of Latent Fingerprints—Treatment with Fluorescers. *J. Forensic Sci.* 1979, *24* (1), 96–100.

Merrick, S.; Gardner, S. J.; Sears, V.; Hewlett, D. F. An Operational Trial of Ozone-Friendly DFO and 1,2-Indanedione Formulations for Latent Fingerprint Detection. *J. Forensic Ident.* 2002, *52* (5), 595–605.

Migron, Y.; Mandler, D. Development of Latent Fingerprints on Unfired Cartridges by Palladium Deposition: A Surface Study. *J. Forensic Sci.* 1997, *42* (6), 986–992.

Misner, A. Latent Fingerprint Detection on Low Density Polyethylene Comparing Vacuum Metal Deposition to Cyanoacrylate Fuming and Fluorescence. *J. Forensic Ident.* 1992, *42* (1), 26–33.

Mitchell, H. H.; Hamilton, T. S. The Dermal Excretion under Controlled Environmental Conditions of Nitrogen and Minerals in Human Subjects, with Particular Reference to Calcium and Iron. *J. Biol. Chem.* 1949, *178* (1), 345–361.

Mitsui, T.; Katho, H.; Shimada, K.; Wakasugi, Y. Development of Latent Prints Using a Sudan Black B Solution. *Ident. News* 1980, *30* (8), 9–10.

Mitsui, T.; Katho, H.; Shimada, K.; Wakasugi, Y. Development of Latent Prints Using a Sudan Black B Solution. *Fingerprint Whorld* 1981, *6* (24), 84–85.

Moenssens, A. A. *Fingerprint Techniques;* Chilton Book Company: Philadelphia, 1971.

Mong, G. M.; Petersen, C. E.; Clauss, T. R. W. *Advanced Fingerprint Analysis Project. Fingerprint Constituents;* PNNL Report No. 3019; Pacific Northwest National Laboratory: Richland, WA, 1999.

Morris, J. R. *Extensions to the NFN Reagent for the Development of Latent Fingerprints;* AWRE Report; Atomic Weapons Research Establishment: Aldermaston, U.K., February 1978.

Morris, J. R.; Goode, G. C. NFN an Improved Ninhydrin Reagent for the Detection of Latent Fingerprints. *Police Research Bull.* 1974, *24,* 45–53.

Murphy, M. A Vacuum Metal Identification. *J. Forensic Ident.* 1991, *41* (5), 318–320.

Naitoh, K.; Inai, Y.; Hirabayashi, T. Direct Temperature-Controlled Trapping System and Its Use for the Gas Chromatographic Determination of Organic Vapor Released from Human Skin. *Anal. Chem.* 2000, *72* (13), 2797–2801.

Nakayashiki, N. Sweat Protein Components Tested by SDS-Polyacrylamide Gel Electrophoresis Followed by Immunoblotting. *The Tohoku J. Exp. Med.* 1990, *161* (1), 25–31.

Nicolaides, N.; Ansari, M. N. A. The Dienoic Fatty Acids of Human Skin Surface Lipid. *Lipids* 1968, *4* (1), 79–81.

Nicolaides, N.; Fu, H. C.; Ansari, M. N. A.; Rice, G. R. The Fatty Acids of Wax Esters and Sterol Esters from Vernix

Caseosa and from Human Skin Surface Lipid. *Lipids* 1972, *7* (8), 506–517.

Norkus, P.; Noppinger, K. New Reagents for the Enhancement of Fingerprints in Blood. *Ident. News* 1986, *36* (4), 5,15.

Odén, S.; von Hofsten, B. Detection of Fingerprints by the Ninhydrin Reaction. *Nature* 1954, *173* (4401), 449–450.

Odland, G. F. Structure of the Skin. In *Physiology, Biochemistry, and Molecular Biology of the Skin,* 2nd ed.; Goldsmith, L., Ed.; Oxford University Press: New York, 1991.

Olenik, J. Super Glue, A Modified Method. *Ident. News* 1983, *33* (1), 9–10.

Olenik, J. H. Cyanoacrylate Fuming: An Alternative Non-Heat Method. *J. Forensic Ident.* 1989, *39* (5), 302–304.

Olsen, Sr., R. D. The Chemical Composition of Palmar Sweat. *Fingerprint and Ident. Magazine* 1972, 3–23.

Olsen, Sr., R. D. *Scott's Fingerprint Mechanics;* Charles C Thomas: Springfield, IL, 1978.

Oro, J.; Skewes, H. B. Free Amino-Acids on Human Fingers: The Question of Contamination in Microanalysis. *Nature* 1965, *207* (1), 1042–1045.

Palenik, S. Microchemistry. In *Encyclopedia of Forensic Science;* Siegel, J., Saukko, P., Knupfer, G., Eds.; Academic Press: London, 2000; pp 1111–1116.

Perkins, D. G.; Thomas, W. M. Cyanoacrylate Fuming Prior to Submission of Evidence to the Laboratory. *J. Forensic Ident.* 1991, *41* (3), 157–162.

Petrovskaia, O.; Taylor, B.; Hauze, D. B.; Carroll, P.; Joullié, M. M. Investigations of the Reaction Mechanisms of 1,2-Indanediones with Amino Acids. *J. Org. Chem.* 2001, *66* (23), 7666–7675.

Pounds, C. A.; Jones, R. J. Physicochemical Techniques in the Development of Latent Fingerprints. *Trends in Anal. Chem.* 1983, *2* (8), 180–183.

Pounds, C. A.; Grigg, R.; Mongkolaussavaratana, T. The Use of 1,8-Diazafluoren-9-one (DFO) for the Fluorescent Detection of Latent Fingerprints on Paper. A Preliminary Evaluation. *J. Forensic Sci.* 1990, *35* (1), 169–175.

Price, D.; Stow, K. A Method for Stopping Overdevelopment of Silver Nitrate Treated Finger and Footwear Marks. *Fingerprint Whorld* 1998, *24,* 107–110.

Puhvel, S. M. Esterification of (4-14C) Cholesterol by Cutaneous Bacteria (Staphylococcus Epidermis, Propionibacterium Acnes, and Propionibacterium Granulosum). *J. Investigative Dermatol.* 1975, *64* (6), 397–400.

Ramasastry, P.; Downing, D.; Pochi, P. E.; Strauss, J. S. Chemical Composition of Human Surface Lipids from Birth to Puberty. *J. Investigative Dermatol.* 1970, *54* (2), 139–144.

Ramotowski, R. Composition of Latent Print Residue. In *Advances in Fingerprint Technology,* Lee, H. C., Gaensslen, R. E., Eds.; CRC Press: Boca Raton, FL, 2001; pp 63–104.

Ramotowski, R.; Cantu, A. A.; Joullié, M. M.; Petrovskaia, O. 1,2-Indanediones: A Preliminary Evaluation of a New Class of Amino Acid Visualizing Compounds. *Fingerprint Whorld* 1997, *23* (90), 131–139.

Retinger, J. M. The Mechanism of the Ninhydrin Reaction. A Contribution to the Theory of Color of Salts of Alloxantine-Like Compounds. *J. Am. Chem. Soc.* 1917, *39* (5), 1059–1066.

Reynoldson, T. E.; Reed, F. A. *Operational Trial Comparing Metal Deposition with Small Particle Reagent for the Development of Latent Prints on Polyethylene;* SRDB Report; Home Office Scientific Development Branch: Sandridge, U.K., 1979.

Rhodes, H. *Forensic Chemistry;* Chapman & Hall, Ltd.: London, 1940.

Robertshaw, D. Apocrine Sweat Glands. In *Physiology, Biochemistry, and Molecular Biology of the Skin,* 2nd ed.; Goldsmith, L., Ed.; Oxford University Press: New York, 1991.

Rosati, B. B. Does Superglue Hinder Traditional Firearms Identification? *AFTE J.* 2005, *37,* 3–6.

Roux, C.; Jones, N.; Lennard, C.; Stoilovic, M. Evaluation of 1,2-Indanedione and 5,6-Dimethoxy-1,2-Indanedione for the Detection of Latent Fingerprints on Porous Surfaces. *J. Forensic Sci.* 2000, *45* (4), 761–769.

Ruhemann, S. Cyclic Di- and Tri-Ketones. *J. Chem. Soc. Trans.* 1910a, *97,* 1438–1449.

Ruhemann, S. Triketohydrindene Hydrate. *J. Chem. Soc. Trans.* 1910b, *97*, 2025–2031.

Ruhemann, S. Triketohydrindene Hydrate, Part III: Its Relation to Alloxan. *J. Chem. Soc. Trans.* 1911a, *99*, 792–800.

Ruhemann, S. Triketohydrindene Hydrate, Part IV: Hydrindantin and Its Analogues. *J. Chem. Soc. Trans.* 1911b, *99*, 1306–1310.

Ruhemann, S. Triketohydrindene Hydrate, Part V: The Analogues of Uramil and Purpuric Acid. *J. Chem. Soc. Trans.* 1911c, *99*, 1486–1492.

Sato, K. The Physiology, Pharmacology, and Biochemistry of the Eccrine Sweat Gland. *Rev. Physiol., Biochem. Pharmacol.* 1979, *79*, 51–131.

Saunders, G. Multimetal Deposition Method for Latent Fingerprint Development. Presented at the 74th Conference of the International Association for Identification, Pensacola, FL, 1989.

Saunders, G. *Fingerprint Chemistry I, Final Report to U.S. Secret Service;* U.S. Secret Service: Washington, DC, 1996.

Saunders, G. *Fingerprint Chemistry II, Final Report to the U.S. Secret Service;* U.S. Secret Service: Washington, DC, 1997.

Schertz, T. D.; Reiter, R. C.; Stevenson, C. D. Zwitterion Radicals and Anion Radicals from Electron Transfer and Solvent Condensation with the Fingerprint Developing Agent Ninhydrin. *J. Org. Chem.* 2001, *66* (23), 7596–7603.

Schnetz, B. Latent Fingerprint and Colloidal Gold: New Reinforcement Procedures. Abstract for the International Association of Forensic Science Conference, Dusseldorf, Germany, 1993.

Schnetz, B. Latent Fingerprint, Colloidal Gold, and Biochemical Techniques. Abstract for the European Network of Forensic Science Institutes (ENFSI) Meeting, Lausanne, Switzerland, 1997.

Schnetz, B.; Margot, P. Latent Fingerprints, Colloidal Gold and Multimetal Deposition (MMD). Optimisation of the Method. *Forensic Sci. Int.* 2001, *118*, 21–28.

Schütz, F.; Bonfanti, M.; Champod, C. La révélation des traces papillaires sur les douilles par les techniques de etching et de blueing et comparaison avec la déposition multimétallique. *Can. Soc. Forensic Sci. J.* 2000, *33* (2), 65–81.

Schwarz, L.; Frerichs, I. Advanced Solvent-Free Application of Ninhydrin for Detection of Latent Fingerprints on Thermal Paper and Other Surfaces. *J. Forensic Sci.* 2002, *47* (6), 1274–1277.

Scruton, B.; Robins, B. W.; Blott, B. H. The Deposition of Fingerprint Films. *J. Phys. D: Appl. Phys.* 1975, *8* (6), 714–723.

Sears, V.; Prizeman, T. M. The Enhancement of Fingerprints in Blood, Part I: The Optimization of Amido Black. *J. Forensic Ident.* 2000, *50* (5), 470–480.

Sears, V.; Butcher, C.; Prizeman, T. M. The Enhancement of Fingerprints in Blood, Part II: Protein Dyes. *J. Forensic Ident.* 2001, *51* (1), 28–38.

Sears, V.; Butcher, C.; Fitzgerald, L. A. Enhancement of Fingerprints in Blood, Part III: Reactive Techniques, Acid Yellow 7, and Process Sequences. *J. Forensic Ident.* 2005, *55* (6), 741–763.

Shelley, W. B. Apocrine Sweat. *J. Investigative Dermatol.* 1951, *17*, 255.

Smith, A. M.; Agiza, A. H. The Determination of Amino-Acids Colorimetrically by the Ninhydrin Reaction. *Analyst* 1951, *76*, 623–627.

Söderman, H.; O'Connell, J. J. *Modern Criminal Investigation;* Funk & Wagnalls Co.: New York, 1935.

Sodhi, G. S.; Kaur, J. Powder Method for Detecting Latent Fingerprints: A Review. *Forensic Sci. Int.* 2001, *120* (3), 172–176.

Speaks, H. A. The Use of Ninhydrin in the Development of Latent Fingerprints. *Finger Print and Ident. Magazine* 1964, *45* (3), 11–13, 23.

Speaks, H. A. Ninhydrin Prints from Rubber Gloves. *Finger Print and Ident. Magazine* 1966, *48* (3), 3–5.

Speaks, H. A. Ninhydrin Development of Latent Prints. *Finger Print and Ident. Magazine* 1970, *52* (2), 14–17.

St-Amand, F. Fingerprints from Latex Gloves. *Ident. Canada* 1994, *17* (4), 11–13.

Stimac, J. Thermal and Carbonless Papers—A Fundamental Understanding for Latent Friction Ridge Development. *J. Forensic Ident.* 2003a, *53* (2), 185–197.

Stimac, J. Thermal Paper: Latent Friction Ridge Development via 1,2-Indanedione. *J. Forensic Ident.* 2003b, *53* (3), 265–271.

Stoilovic, M. Detection of Semen and Blood Stains Using Polilight as a Light Source. *Forensic Sci. Int.* 1991, *51*, 289–296.

Stoilovic, M. Improved Method for DFO Development of Latent Fingerprints. *Forensic Sci. Int.* 1993, *60* (3), 141–153.

Stoilovic, M.; Kobus, H. J.; Margot, P.; Warrener, R. N. Improved Enhancement of Ninhydrin Developed Fingerprints by Cadmium Complexation Using Low Temperature Photoluminescence Techniques. *J. Forensic Sci.* 1986, *31* (2), 432–445.

Stone, R. S.; Metzger, R. A. Comparison of Development Techniques Sudan Black B Solution/Black Magna Powder for Water-Soaked Porous Items. *Ident. News* 1981, *31* (1), 13–14.

Stroud, P. T. *Some Comments on Finger Print Development by Vacuum Deposition;* AWRE Nuclear Research Note 5/71; Atomic Weapons Establishment (AWRE): Aldermaston, U.K., 1971.

Stroud, P. T. *Further Comments on Finger Print Development by Vacuum Deposition;* AWRE Nuclear 10/72; Atomic Weapons Establishment (AWRE): Aldermaston, U.K., 1972.

Suzuki, S.; Suzuki, Y.; Ohta, H. Detection of Latent Fingerprints on Newly Developed Substances Using the Vacuum Metal Deposition Method. *J. Forensic Ident.* 2002, *52* (5), 573–578.

Takatsu, M.; Kageyama, H.; Hirata, K.; Akashi, S.; Yoko Ta, T.; Shiitani, M.; Kobayashi, A. Development of a New Method to Detect Latent Fingerprints on Thermal Paper with o-Alkyl Derivative of Ninhydrin. *Rep. Natl. Res. Inst. Police Sci.* 1991, *44* (1), 1–6.

Theys, P.; Lepareux, A.; Chevet, G.; Ceccaldi, P. F. New Technique for Bringing Out Latent Fingerprints on Paper: Vacuum Metallisation. *Int. Criminal Police Rev.* 1968, *217*, 106–109.

Thomas, G. L. The Physics of Fingerprints and Their Detection. *J. Phys. E: Sci. Instrum.* 1978, *11* (8), 722–730.

Thornton, J. I. Modification of Fingerprint Powder with Coumarin 6 Laser Dye. *J. Forensic Sci.* 1978, *23* (3), 536–538.

Thorwald, J. *Crime and Science: The New Frontier in Criminology;* Brace and World, Inc: New York, 1966.

Toth, I.; Faredin, I. Steroid Excreted by Human Skin: II. C 19-Steroid Sulphates in Human Axillary Sweat. *Acta Medica Hungarica* 1985, *42* (1–2), 21–28.

Trozzi, T.; Schwartz, R.; Hollars, M. *Processing Guide for Developing Latent Prints;* Federal Bureau of Investigation, Laboratory Division, U.S. Department of Justice, U.S. Government Printing Office: Washington, DC, 2000.

United Nations Environ Programme. *The Montreal Protocol on Substances That Deplete the Ozone Layer;* United Nations Environ Programme: Nairobi, Kenya, 1999. http://www.un-documents.net/mpsdol.htm (accessed Jan 5, 2010).

Uyttendaele, K.; De Groote, M.; Blaton, V.; Peeters, H. Analysis of the Proteins in Sweat and Urine by Agarose-Gel Isotachophoresis. *J. Chromatogr.* 1977, *132* (2), 261–266.

Valussi, S. Microfluidics Systems for the Chemical Analysis of Fingerprint Residues. Presented at the International Fingerprint Research Group Meeting, St. Albans, U.K., 2003.

van Oorschot, R. A. H.; Treadwell, S.; Beaurepaire, J.; Holding, N. L.; Mitchell, R. J. Beware of the Possibility of Fingerprinting Techniques Transferring DNA. *J. Forensic Sci.* 2005, *50* (6), 1417–1422.

Vandenberg, N.; van Oorschot, R. A. H. The Use of Polilight in the Detection of Seminal Fluid, Saliva, and Bloodstains and Comparison with Conventional Chemical-Based Screening Tests. *J. Forensic Sci.* 2006, *51* (2), 361–370.

Vree, T. B.; Muskens, A.; Van Rossum, J. M. Excretion of Amphetamines in Human Sweat. *Archives Internationales de Pharmacodynamie et de Therapie* 1972, *199* (2), 311–317.

Wade, D. C. Development of Latent Prints with Titanium Dioxide (TiO_2). *J. Forensic Ident.* 2002, *52* (5), 551–559.

Wakefield, M. A.; Armitage, S. Canberra Institute of Technology, Canberra, Australia. Unpublished Results, 2005.

Wallace-Kunkel, C.; Stoilovic, M.; Lennard, C.; Roux, C. A0571: 1,2-Indanedione as a Finger Mark Reagent Optimisation and Characterisation. Presented at the 17th Meeting of the International Association of the Forensic Sciences, Hong Kong, 2005.

Wallace-Kunkel, C.; Lennard, C. J.; Stoilovic, M.; Roux, C. Evaluation of 5-Methylthioninhydrin for the Detection of Fingermarks on Porous Surfaces and Comparison. *Ident. Canada* 2006, *29* (1), 4–13.

Walls, H. J.; Attridge, G. G. *Basic Photo Science: How Photography Works;* Focal Press: London, 1977.

Walter, S. *Latent Print Visualization of Aged Lipid Residues;* Status Report, April 1999; Savannah River Technical Center: Aiken, SC, 1999.

Wargacki, S.; Dadmun, M. D.; Lewis, L. Identifying the True Initiator in the Cyanoacrylate Fuming Method. Presented at the 2005 International Association for Identification Conference, Dallas, TX, 2005.

Watkin, J. E.; Wilkinson, D.; Misner, A. H.; Yamashita, A. B. Cyanoacrylate Fuming of Latent Prints: Vacuum Versus Heat/Humidity. *J. Forensic Ident.* 1994, *4* (5), 545–554.

Watling, W. J.; Smith, K. O. Heptane: An Alternative to the Freon Ninhydrin Mixture. *J. Forensic Ident.* 1993, *43* (2), 131–134.

Weaver, D. E. Large Scale Cyanoacrylate Fuming. *J. Forensic Ident.* 1993, *43* (2), 135–137.

Weaver, D. E.; Clary, E. J. A One-Step Fluorescent Cyanoacrylate Fingerprint Development Technology. *J. Forensic Ident.* 1993, *43* (5), 481–492.

Weast, R. C., Ed. *CRC Handbook of Chemistry and Physics,* 67th ed.; CRC Press: Boca Raton, FL, 1986.

Wiesner, S.; Springer, E.; Sasson, Y.; Almog, J. Chemical Development of Latent Fingerprints: 1,2-Indanedione Has Come of Age. *J. Forensic Sci.* 2001, *46* (5), 1082–1084.

Wilansky, M.; Jomphe, A.; Kovacs, G.; Lawrence, J.; LeBlanc, D.; St-Pierre, M.; Wilkinson, D.; Yamashita, A. B. *A Comparison of Hand-Held Forensic Light Sources;* FIRS Technical Report #16; Royal Canadian Mounted Police: Ottawa, 2006.

Wilkinson, D. Study of the Reaction Mechanism of 1,8-Diazafluoren-9-one with the Amino Acid, L-Alanine. *Forensic Sci. Int.* 2000a, *109* (2), 87–103.

Wilkinson, D. Spectroscopic Study of 1,2-Indanedione. *Forensic Sci. Int.* 2000b, *114*, 123–132.

Wilkinson, D.; Watkin, J. E. A Comparison of the Forensic Light Sources: Polilight, Luma-Lite, and Spectrum 9000. *J. Forensic Ident.* 1994, *44* (6), 632–651.

Wilkinson, D.; Yamashita, A. B.; Annis, K. A Comparison of Forensic Light Sources: Luma-Lite, Mini-Crimescope 400, Omniprint 1000A, Polilight PL500, and Quaser 2000/30. *Ident. Canada* 2002, *25* (1), 5–15.

Wilkinson, D.; Mackenzie, E.; Leech, C.; Mayowski, D.; Bertrand, S.; Walker, T. The Results from a Canadian National Field Trial Comparing Two Formulations of 1,8-Diazafluoren-9-one (DFO) with 1,2-Indanedione. *Ident. Canada* 2003, *26* (2), 8–18.

Wilkinson, D.; Rumsby, D.; Babin, B.; Merrit, M.; Marsh, J. *The Results from a Canadian National Field Trial Comparing 1,8-Diazafluoren-9-one (DFO) with Ninhydrin and the Sequence DFO Followed by Ninhydrin;* Technical Report TR-03-2005; Canadian Police Research Centre: Ontario, 2005.

Willinski, G. Permeation of Fingerprints Through Laboratory Gloves. *J. Forensic Sci.* 1980, *25* (3), 682–685.

Wilson, J. D.; Darke, D. J. *The Results of Analyses of the Mixtures of Fatty Acids on the Skin: Part I. Commentary;* AERE Report No. G-1154; Atomic Energy Research Establishment: ca 1978.

Yamashita, A. B. Use of a Benchtop Desiccator for Vacuum Cyanoacrylate Treatment of Latent Prints. *J. Forensic Ident.* 1994, *44* (2), 149–158.

Yemm, E. W.; Cocking, E. C; Ricketts, R. E. The Determination of Amino-Acids with Ninhydrin. *Analyst* 1955, *80*, 209–214.

7.17 Additional Information

Almog, J.; Gabay, A. A Modified Super Glue Technique—The Use of Polycyanoacrylate for Fingerprint Development. *J. Forensic Sci.* 1986, *31* (1), 250–253.

Beecroft, W. Enhancement of PD Prints. *RCMP Gazette*, 1989, *21*, 17.

Boniforti, L.; Passi, S.; Caprilli, F.; Nazzaro-Porro, M. Skin Surface Lipids. Identification and Determination by Thin-Layer Chromatography and Gas-Liquid Chromatography. *Clin. Chim. Acta* 1973, *47* (2), 223–231.

Burns, T. D.; Brown, J. K.; Dinsmore, A.; Harvey, K. K. Base-Activated Latent Fingerprints Fumed with a Cyanoacrylate Monomer: A Quantitative Study Using Fourier-Transform Infra-Red Spectroscopy. *Anal. Chim. Acta* 1998, *362* (2), 171–176.

Champod, C.; Egli, N.; Margot, P. A. Fingermarks, Shoesole and Footprint Impressions, Tire Impressions, Ear Impressions, Toolmarks, Lipmarks, Bitemarks—A Review: 2001 to 2004. In *Proceedings of the 14th Interpol Forensic Science Symposium;* Lyon, France, 2004; pp 227–244.

Forgeot, R. *Des empreintes digitales étudiées au point de vue médico-judiciaire;* A. Storck: Lyon, France, 1891.

Hamm, E. D. Chemical Developers in Footwear Prints. *Fingerprint Whorld* 1984, *9*, 117–118.

Loveridge, F. H. Shoe Print Development by Silver Nitrate. *Fingerprint Whorld* 1984, *10* (38), 58.

Morton, S. Shoe Print Development by PD Treatment. *Fingerprint Whorld* 1983, *9* (34), 60–61.

Siegel, J., Saukko, P., Knupfer, G., Eds.; *Encyclopedia of Forensic Sciences;* Academic Press: London, 2000.

Yong, A. S. J. *Detection of Latent Fingerprints with Cyanoacrylates: New Techniques Involving Coloured and Photoluminescent Compounds;* Australian National University: Canberra, ACT, Australia, 1986.

CHAPTER 8

THE PRESERVATION OF FRICTION RIDGES

Laura A. Hutchins

Contributing author
Robert E. May

CONTENTS

- 3   8.1 Introduction
- 3   8.2 History of Photography
- 5   8.3 Photography in the Criminal Justice Community
- 6   8.4 The Fingerprint Camera
- 7   8.5 Modern Photography
- 16   8.6 Other Methods of Friction Ridge Preservation
- 19   8.7 Conclusion
- 20   8.8 Reviewers
- 20   8.9 References

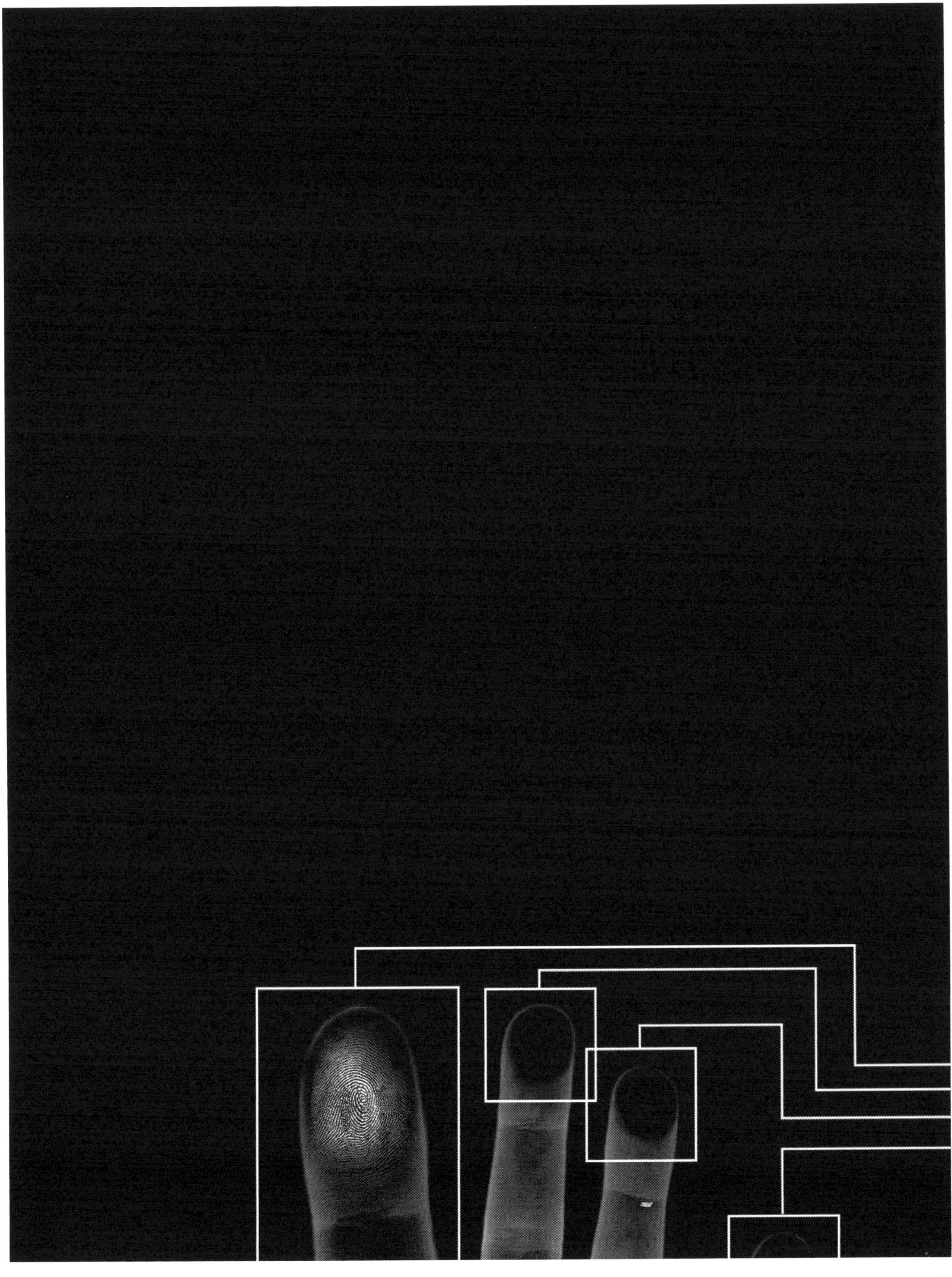

CHAPTER 8

THE PRESERVATION OF FRICTION RIDGES

Laura A. Hutchins

Contributing author
Robert E. May

8.1 Introduction

Inherent in the criminal justice community, and specifically the crime laboratory, is the policy that the information derived from evidence must be preserved to the extent possible. With regard to friction ridge detail, methods of preservation include film and digital photography, latent print lifts, and the use of casting material. Although the two latter methods do create secondary evidence in the form of a lift or cast, the photographing of the friction ridge detail on the lift or the cast is still important to generate additional secondary evidence. Certainly with respect to state and national labs, evidence submitted with a case must be returned to the contributor. With this in mind, the preservation of all relevant friction ridge information derived from evidence is mandatory, and the production of an archival image enables most of that information to be retained within the case file.

8.2 History of Photography

Photography dates back to the time of Aristotle and his study of light, specifically his reference to the passing of light through a pinhole and the creation of a reverse image on the ground (London, 2005, p 368). In the 10th century, the Arabian scholar Alhazen described in detail the discovery of the camera obscura, meaning "dark chamber" (London, 2005, p 368). He explained how light could pass through a single hole in a wall of a dark room and project inverted images from the outside onto the opposite wall of the darkened room. Alhazen made specific references to the ability to view a solar eclipse by this method. Eventually, the camera obscura became the size of a box, and a lens for focusing and a mirror for adjusting the light were incorporated. The original use of the camera obscura was for artists as an aid for drawing in perspective (Davenport, 1999, p 4).

The word photography (derived from two ancient Greek words, *phos*, meaning light, and *graphos*, meaning to write) was coined by Sir John Herschel in 1839 (Redsicker, 1994, p 1). The first application of recording images by the action of light on a sensitive material was 12 years prior to Herschel's use of the word. It was in 1827 when the French inventor Joseph Nicéphore Niépce took the first successful sun-exposure picture. Pewter coated with a mixture of bitumen of Judea (an asphaltlike substance) and lavender oil was placed inside a camera obscura that was aimed at the courtyard outside his window. After 8 hours, the pewter plate was removed from the camera obscura and was rinsed in lavender oil. The bitumen mixture had hardened on areas of the plate that had been exposed to light, whereas the bitumen mixture on the areas not exposed remained soluble and was washed away in the rinse (London, 2005, p 368). The result was a permanent scene of the view outside Niépce's window on the pewter plate.

In 1829, Niépce formed a partnership with a chemist, Louis Jacques Mandé Daguerre. The partnership was formed in order to improve the process discovered by Niépce. Unfortunately, after four years of unfruitful experimentation, Niépce died of a stroke. Daguerre continued experimenting in order to find a way to reduce the necessary exposure time and permanently fix the photographic image. By 1837, Daguerre had discovered that by coating a copper plate with silver and exposing it to iodine crystals, a chemical reaction took place, producing a light-sensitive silver iodide compound. The plate was put inside a camera obscura and was exposed, and a latent image was recorded on the plate. The plate was then removed and exposed to mercury vapors that caused an alloy to form where the silver iodide had been exposed to light. The unexposed silver iodide was washed away in a salt fixer solution, leaving the bare metal. The resulting plate contained an image; the silver alloy formed the light areas of the picture and the bare metal formed the dark areas (London, 2005, p 369). He named the end result a *daguerreotype* (Figure 8–1). Obviously, the use of a single plate for photography posed another problem: how did one make copies?

This question was answered by Englishman William Henry Fox Talbot. Talbot was experimenting with photography at the same time as Daguerre; however, Talbot was using paper instead of copper plates. Talbot used paper sensitized with silver chloride, a compound formed by combining table salt with silver nitrate and gallic acid. The sensitized paper was exposed for a couple of minutes, producing a latent image. This image was visualized by treating the paper with silver nitrate and gallic acid and was fixed in a solution of potassium iodide of hypo (Davenport, 1999, p 9). This *negative* was then was placed over another light-sensitive piece of paper and exposed, creating a *positive* image. This technique, known as a calotype, was the first negative-positive process (London, 2005, p 370). Unfortunately, the sharpness of the final image paled in comparison with that of the daguerreotype, and the daguerreotype continued to thrive.

In 1851 another Englishman, F. Scott Archer, discovered the use of wet *collodion* in photography. This process was a blend of the *calotype* (a negative and positive image print on paper) and the daguerreotype (with its sharpness). This technique used glass plates coated in collodion, which is *guncotton* (nitrocellulose, a flammable compound) dissolved in ether or alcohol. The glass plates were sensitized, exposed, and developed, all while the collodion was still

FIGURE 8–1

Early daguerreotype of the United States Capitol, ca 1846.

(Reprinted from Library of Congress collection, available online at www.memory.loc.gov.)

wet (Davenport, 1999, pp 18–19). Although the technique was complicated by the fact that the glass plates had to remain wet, it was much cheaper than the Daguerre method, produced negatives that were much sharper than calotypes, and reduced exposure time to a few seconds. Because Archer never patented his discovery, the use of this type of photography was adopted worldwide and supplanted the previous two methods. For the next 20 years, the wet method of photography continued to thrive.

In 1871, Richard Leach Maddox produced the first viable dry plate that retained light sensitivity (Davenport, 1999, pp 22–23). Maddox's discovery was prompted by health problems caused by overexposure to the ether vapor used in the wet collodion process. Being an enthusiast of photography, he searched for an alternate method of adhering the silver salts to the glass plate. He discovered that instead of using wet collodion, he could coat the glass with an emulsion of gelatin that the sensitizing material adhered to and the glass would still retain its light-sensitive properties (Harrison, 1888, p 61).

As more and more photographers began using this method, the desire for the process to be more available to amateur photographers and the general public became the focal point of one man, George Eastman. By 1888, Eastman had initiated a method of mass producing dry paper film rolls contained within a simple box camera, called the Kodak.

8.3 Photography in the Criminal Justice Community

8.3.1 Identifying the Criminal: Rogues' Galleries of the Past

With the coming of the second Industrial Revolution (1871–1914), city populations became flooded with people coming and going on steam-powered ships and railways. As cities grew, so did the criminal element. It was an easy time to be a criminal. The criminal justice community had no established method of recognizing repeat offenders. It was very easy for recidivists to deny their true identity by merely giving the authorities another name. In fact, at the time, the only method of criminal recognition was the memory of police officers. When the daguerreotype was discovered, the criminal justice community quickly implemented the photograph as a way of documenting criminals.

Collections of photographs of criminals for identification purposes became known as *rogues' galleries*. Rogues' galleries were displayed in police departments for reference while checking in suspects and, after the invention of photographic negatives, served as the template for "wanted" posters. By the late 1800s, extensive rogues' galleries could be found in many police departments. Eventually, Alphonse Bertillon (see Chapter 1, p 8) incorporated *portraits parlé*, now known as mug-shots (Figure 8–2), into his system of identification (Phillips, 1997, p 20). From this standard front and side mug-shot technique, books were produced. In essence, the rogues' gallery from the wall became a pocket book.

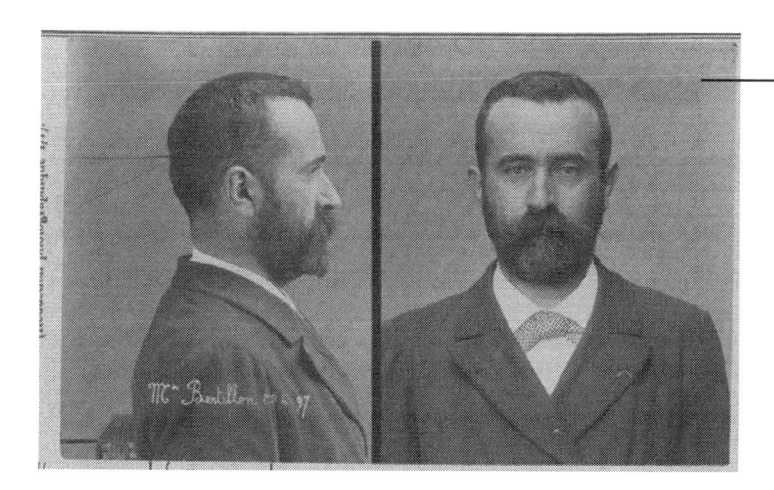

FIGURE 8–2

Portraits parlé of Alphonse Bertillon taken in 1897.

(Reprinted with permission from the R.A. Reiss photographic collection at the Institut de Police Scientifique, Université de Lausanne.)

8.3.2 Documenting the Crime

The advantages of the camera went beyond the mere accumulation of rogues' galleries. It was a natural progression from documenting the criminal to documenting the crime itself (Figure 8–3). The value of permanently recording a true and accurate depiction of a crime came to be an invaluable investigative tool. Not only could the photographs say what a witness could not, but they were seen as objective recordings (Buckland, 2001, p 27). As early as 1859, photographs began to appear in the courtroom, ranging from photographs comparing forged and nonforged signatures to photographs establishing the true identity of a corpse (Moenssens).

With the advent of the crime laboratory, evidence that was photographed at the crime scene could be analyzed and photographed in a controlled environment. By the 1930s, full-service crime laboratories were springing up across the world (e.g., FBI Laboratory in 1932, London's Metropolitan Police Forensic Laboratory in 1935). The advent of the crime laboratory occurred in conjunction with several forensic science milestones. The 1930s witnessed the ushering in of typewriter standard files, fraudulent check files, automotive paint files, firearms reference collections, use of the polygraph, the first use of the ABO blood testing on forensic evidence, metallurgical services, gunshot residue analysis, DNA secretor analysis, luminol as a presumptive test for blood, and the establishment of the Single Fingerprint Section at the FBI. As methods of forensic detection were established in crime laboratories, the recording of results through photography became standard procedure.

8.4 The Fingerprint Camera

The first camera designed specifically for fingerprint work was made by Folmer & Schwing Manufacturing Company of New York in the early 20th century. The camera was self-sufficient, providing a fixed focus lens and lighting contained within an oblong box (Figure 8–4). The lens was positioned at a fixed point that produced a focused life-size

FIGURE 8–3

Daguerreotype taken after President Lincoln's assassination.

(Reprinted from www.civilwarphotos.net.)

FIGURE 8–4

Self-contained fingerprint camera.

(Courtesy of the South Wales Police Museum.)

image on the negative (1:1) and the lamps were activated by the movement of the shutter, thus exposing the 2" x 3" glass plate (Lightning Powder Co., Inc., 2003, p 5). A photograph was taken by positioning the open end of the oblong camera over the print and pressing the exposure button. The creation of this type of camera enabled a person who was not trained in the art of photography to take photographs of latent prints.

This type of fingerprint camera remained in existence until the 1970s. Technological advances were incorporated into the design over the years, but the basic concept and ease of use continued. Advances involved additional lens types, variable shutter speeds, adjustable apertures, electronic flash bulbs, and the use of roll film or Polaroid-type films of sizes varying from 2 1/4" x 3 1/4" to 4" x 5" (Olsen, 1978, p 178).

8.5 Modern Photography

As with any type of specific-use technology, the cost of specialized equipment leads to the need for more affordable equipment that can also be used for other purposes. Smaller police departments could not afford to purchase a fingerprint camera, so they began to outfit the cameras they owned with attachments for fingerprint photography (Olsen, 1978, p 147). A general-purpose camera could be adapted for fingerprint work with the use of a camera stand, proper lighting, and an appropriate lens. Another factor that allowed for the easy transition to traditional camera usage was the ease with which irregularly shaped objects could be photographed. The fingerprint camera was perfectly suited to flat evidence, but evidence that was irregular in shape posed depth of field problems. Additionally, although the fingerprint camera was appropriate to basic fingerprint processing techniques such as powdering, the advent of forensic light sources demanded the use of nonspecific camera equipment.

8.5.1 Film Photography

Modern film is composed of plastic sheets that are coated with an emulsion containing silver halide salts bonded by gelatin. The grain size of the silver halide salt determines the sensitivity of the film and the resulting resolution. Film with a smaller grain size, known as *slow film,* requires a longer exposure but produces a photograph of finer detail. When the silver halide salts are exposed to a form of light, an invisible image is recorded on the film. Film-developing chemicals are then applied to the exposed film in order to visualize the latent images. This process causes the conversion of the silver halide salts to metallic silver. The metallic silver blocks the transmission of light and forms the black portion of a negative.

There are generally three camera formats available: small, medium, and large. In photography, the term "format" refers to the size of the film that is used in the camera. Small format cameras use film that is 35 mm and smaller. The main disadvantage of using a small format camera is that the small negative must be enlarged in the printing process. A medium format camera uses film that is fixed at 6 cm in width but varies in length, ranging from 4.5 cm to 7 cm. Large format cameras use film that is 4" x 5" or larger. The advantage of having a larger format camera is the higher resolution that is achieved.

8.5.2 Digital Photography

The history of the digital camera is rooted in the technology that gave rise to the television and the first videotape recorder. This technology allowed for the conversion of information into electrical impulses that could be recorded onto magnetic tape. In 1970, Willard Boyle and George Smith of AT&T Bell Labs invented the *charge coupled device* (CCD) (Boyle, 1970). Essentially, a CCD is an image recording sensor containing picture elements, commonly referred to as *pixels,* on a grid (Bidner, 2000, p 25). The pixels on the sensor record light electronically (i.e., light is converted into electrons). Generally, the greater the number of pixels on the CCD, the sharper the image. This electronically recorded light is then converted into digital data.

With regard to photography, a digital camera records the image with a CCD instead of recording the image on film (Ippolito, 2003, p 36). Specifically, an image is focused on the sensor through the lens. The sensor for the digital camera contains millions of CCD cells (pixels) on a grid. Each CCD records a color and a brightness (tonal) value that is stored as a series of numbers in the camera's memory. These stored numbers are then reassembled and sent as an image to a printer or a computer screen. Because of the volume of pixels on the grid, the human eye views the recorded image as continuous tones, just as one would view a photograph (London, 2005, p 200).

Key to the understanding of digital camera technology is pixel resolution. Pixel resolution refers to the number of pixels in an image. For example, a 1000 x 1000 pixel image printed in a one-inch square would have 1000 pixels per inch (PPI).

Traditional film photography cameras are based upon film format; digital camera file format is based upon the storage of data. Most digital cameras offer a choice of file formats for saving images. There are two main types of formats: compressed and uncompressed. Compressed file formats produce smaller image files that allow for more storage space. Images are reduced in size by the discarding, or loss, of pixel information. Every time an image is saved in a compressed format, information is lost. Because of this loss, compression file formats are referred to as *lossy*. The most common type of lossy compression format is JPEG (Joint Photographic Experts Group).

Uncompressed file formats are those in which no pixel values are lost and the image can be retrieved in its original form (Federal Bureau of Investigation, 2004, p 14). Uncompressed file formats include TIFF (tagged information file format) and RAW formats (i.e., the camera's native or unprocessed file format). Both formats store an image in its original form, thus requiring more storage space. For the purpose of recording friction ridge impressions, the use of TIFF or RAW images in digital photography is valuable to ensure that the integrity of the evidence is preserved.

A vital aspect of maintaining the integrity of the evidence is the acquisition of a digital camera that meets or exceeds the guidelines set forth by the Scientific Working Group on Friction Ridge Analysis, Study and Technology (SWGFAST) (SWGFAST, 2009) and the National Institute of Standards and Technology (NIST). NIST has established that the minimal resolution of an image taken by a digital camera that is used for latent impression evidence be 1000 PPI at 1:1 (SWGIT, 2002; SWGFAST, 2009, p 2).

Another key aspect to digital photography in relation to the criminal justice community is the maintenance of the original digital image. The original image must be stored in an unaltered state. The original images can be stored on the following media: silver-based film negative, write-once compact disk-recordable (CD-R), and digital versatile disk-recordable (DVD-R) (SWGIT, 2006, pp 3-4). If digital processing is needed, it must be performed on a duplicate image.

In addition to the acquisition of fingerprint impressions with a digital camera, impressions on relatively flat surfaces may be digitized through the use of a flatbed scanner and the image(s) can be imported into a computer. A flatbed scanner consists of a flat piece of glass, known as a *platen*, a light source under the platen and in the lid, and a CCD image recording sensor on a track underneath the platen. Items to be scanned are placed face down on the platen, and the CCD sensor track moves beneath the item, recording the image(s). The type of item to be scanned dictates the location of the light source for the scan (opaque versus transparent lifts). For opaque items, the light on the tract below the platen is used. As the tract moves below the item, the CCD sensor records the light that is reflected off the item. This is known as *reflective scanning*. *Transmissive scanning* is used to record image(s) on a transparent item. With transmissive scanning, the light from the lid is transmitted through the item and onto the CCD. Like the digital camera, the flatbed scanner must be able to produce the PPI requirement for latent impressions set forth by NIST, and the original images should be recorded on the appropriate medium.

8.5.3 Properties of Light

Photography is the recording of images on sensitive material by the reaction of light, and the photographer will benefit by knowing something about its properties and how to control it.

Light travels as waves. Light waves ordinarily travel in straight lines, passing through some substances, and being absorbed or reflected by others. Forms of energy transmitted by waves of any nature are classified according to their wavelength into a system called the *electromagnetic spectrum*. This classification is important because it allows the assignment of a given wavelength to each form of energy with which photography is concerned. For fingerprint photography, the wavelengths that are most important are those in the invisible short- and long-wave ultraviolet light and the visible light *spectrum*.

The term spectrum refers to the entire range of electromagnetic radiation. In their basic nature, there are no differences between light waves and other kinds of electromagnetic waves. The various types of electromagnetic waves that make up the electromagnetic spectrum are gamma rays, x-rays, ultraviolet radiation, visible light, infrared radiation, radar, and radio waves (Figure 8–5) (Langford, 1973, p 23).

8.5.3.1 Luminescence. When certain materials, such as some solids, liquids, or gases, are subjected to electromagnetic radiation, such as ultraviolet radiation or monochromatic light, they will emit light of a longer wavelength (Miller, 1998, p 205). This occurrence is called *luminescence*. The two particular types of luminescence are known as *fluorescence* and *phosphorescence*. If the luminescence ceases within a fraction of a second (i.e., less than 10^{-6} second) (Menzel, 1980, p 68) after removing the exciting radiation, the phenomenon is called fluorescence. Although fluorescence ceases almost immediately after removing the exciting radiation, some substances continue to emit luminescence for some time. This phenomenon is called phosphorescence (Miller, 1998, p 205). For most fingerprint imaging purposes, the differences between fluorescence and phosphorescence are inconsequential.

Invisible ultraviolet radiation (UV) is that portion of the electromagnetic spectrum that can induce visible luminescence in certain materials. *Invisible long-wave ultraviolet radiation* in the electromagnetic spectrum ranges from 320 nm to 390 nm. *Visible light* is that portion of the electromagnetic spectrum that normally stimulates sight. Visible light in the electromagnetic spectrum ranges from 390 nm to 700 nm. When materials absorb light and re-emit this light at longer wavelengths, the difference between absorption and emission is known as *Stokes shift* (Figure 8–6) (Menzel, 1980, p 9).

8.5.3.2 Filters Used in Luminescent Photography. A *barrier filter* of optical photographic quality and particular absorption and transmission properties is needed to visualize and photograph luminescing latent prints. The barrier filter will absorb or reflect most of the excitation and will transmit the sufficiently longer wavelength to enable photographic imaging (Figure 8–7). Without the barrier filter, the excitation light tends to compete with and wash out luminescing friction ridge detail. In some instances, a barrier filter may help block interfering fluorescence. Modern forensic light sources come with an array of nanometer choices and barrier filters that allow for the visualization and resulting photography of luminescing latent prints (Table 8–1). For most forensic light sources (e.g., laser, alternate lightsource, LEDs), the customary barrier filters are orange (amber), yellow, and red.

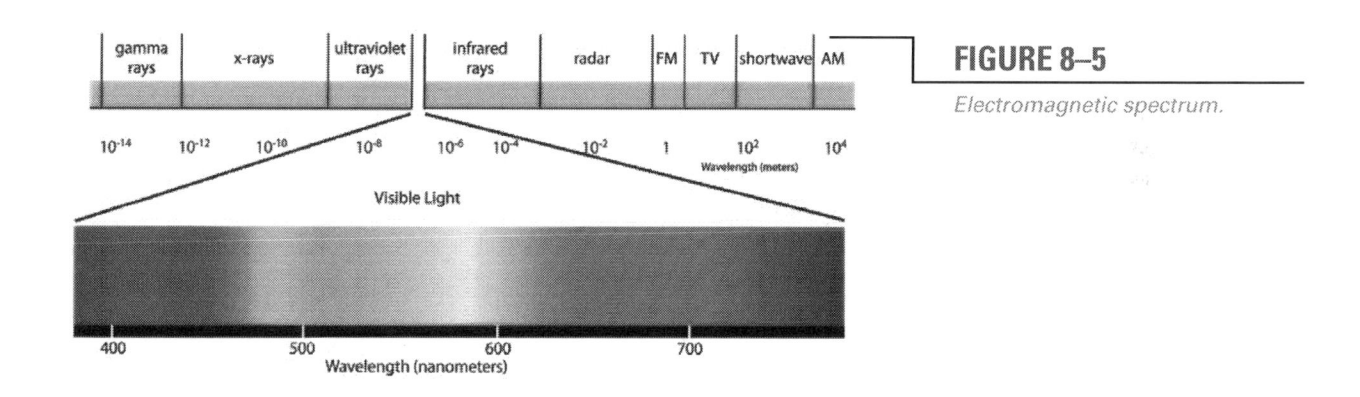

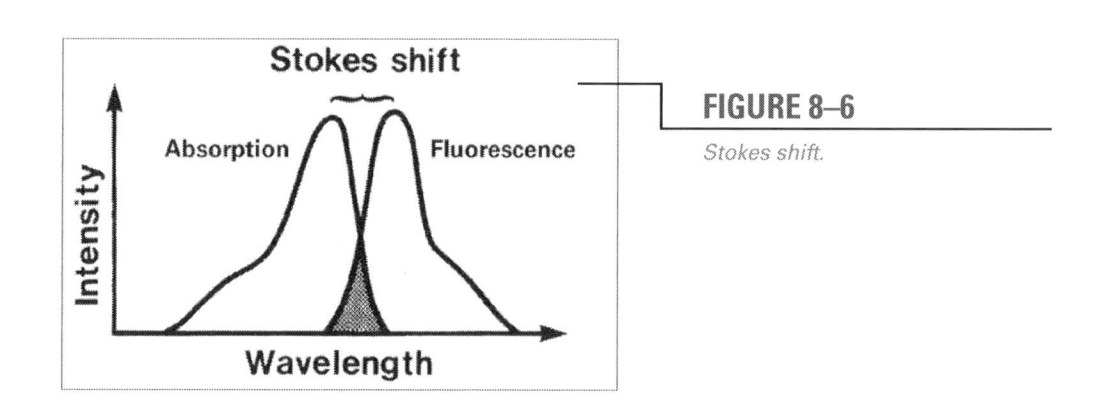

FIGURE 8–5
Electromagnetic spectrum.

FIGURE 8–6
Stokes shift.

CHAPTER 8 | The Preservation of Friction Ridges

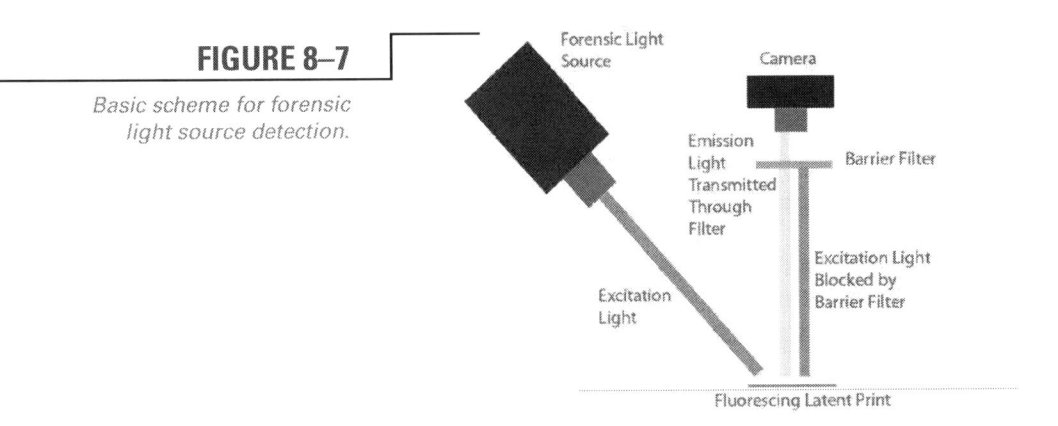

FIGURE 8–7

Basic scheme for forensic light source detection.

Table 8–1

Emitted light and corresponding filter selections (Hardwick, 1990, p 21; Eastman Kodak Company, 1990, p 4).

Emitted Light (Color)	Corresponding Nanometers	Barrier Filter (Color)	Common Barrier Filter
Invisible Ultraviolet	320–400	Pale Yellow	390, 405, 415
Violet/Blue	350–469	Yellow	476
		Yellow/Orange	510, 515
		Orange	529, 550
		Red	593
Blue	352–519	Yellow/Orange	510, 515
		Orange	529, 550
		Red	593
Blue/Green	468–526	Orange	529, 550
		Red	593
Green	473–546	Orange	549
		Red	593
Green/Yellow	503–591	Red	593

Using long-wave ultraviolet radiation, latent impressions developed with chemical treatments, dye stains, and fluorescent powders are often visible without the use of a filter. However, when photographing latent impressions that luminesce, with black and white film or a digital format, using a UV barrier filter will block the invisible light that the film or the digital sensor is sensitive to, thus eliminating the chance of distortion or overexposure of an image.

8.5.4 Close-Up Photography Equipment

Medium and small format cameras need a *macro lens* in order to take close-up photographs. A macro lens is classified as a *flat field lens*, meaning that the images are produced on an even plane, thereby maintaining the sharpness on the edges (Eastman Kodak Company, 1988, p 41). Conversely, a standard lens is classified as a *curved field lens,* meaning the images are produced on a bowed plane. This makes a standard lens less desirable for close-up photography because the edges will lose their sharpness.

Additional methods for achieving close-up photography are *close-up lenses, reversing ring adaptors,* and *bellows units*. Close-up lenses are clear glass lenses that are used to increase the magnification of the standard lens. Close-up lenses screw into the filter mounting threads on the front of the lens. The lenses are numbered from 1 to 10, with the higher number representing the increased strength of the lens. A reversing ring adaptor allows the lens to be turned so that the rear element of the lens faces toward the subject. This increases the distance between the film plane and the lens, thereby increasing the image size. A flexible bellows unit extends the lens forward, allowing closer focusing.

8.5.5 The Use of Filters

The use of black and white film in latent print photography allows for the use of color filters for heightened contrast. These filters will lighten or darken the images and are dependent upon the background color; a colored filter will lighten the tone of the same color and darken the tone of a complementary color (Table 8–2).

8.5.6 Lighting

8.5.6.1 Equipment. The source of the illumination may be a photographic laboratory lamp, photographic slide viewer, electronic flash, forensic light source, or photographic negative viewing light. A *diffuser* is used in order to provide an even illumination of the entire object being photographed. Any type of translucent covering (e.g., plexiglass or thin white paper) can be used as a diffuser. The diffuser is placed between the object being photographed and the light source, about 6 to 12 inches away from the light source. (When the diffuser and the light are too close, the light will be brighter in the center of the area.)

8.5.6.2 Lighting Techniques. The type of evidence that is to be photographed determines the type of lighting technique employed. For example, evidence that is reflective will require a lighting technique far different from evidence that is transparent. In order to take accurate and clear photographs, the photographer must have an understanding of the varied lighting techniques that are available.

Table 8–2

Contrast adjusting filters.

Blue	Blue	Red
Green	Green	Red or Blue
Yellow	Yellow	Blue

CHAPTER 8   The Preservation of Friction Ridges

FIGURE 8–8

Direct lighting.

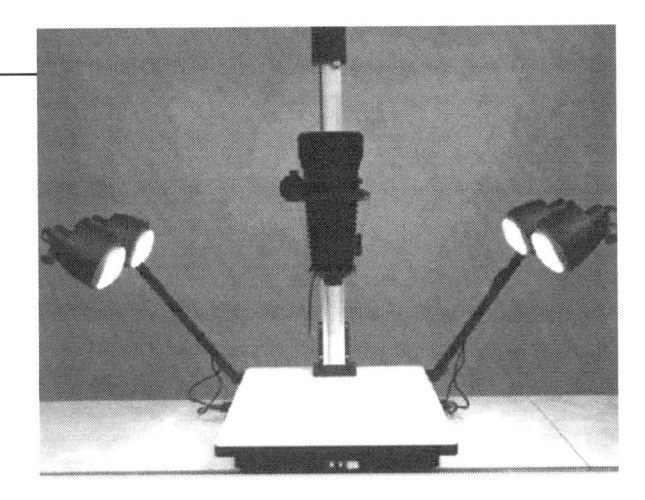

FIGURE 8–9

Front directional lighting.

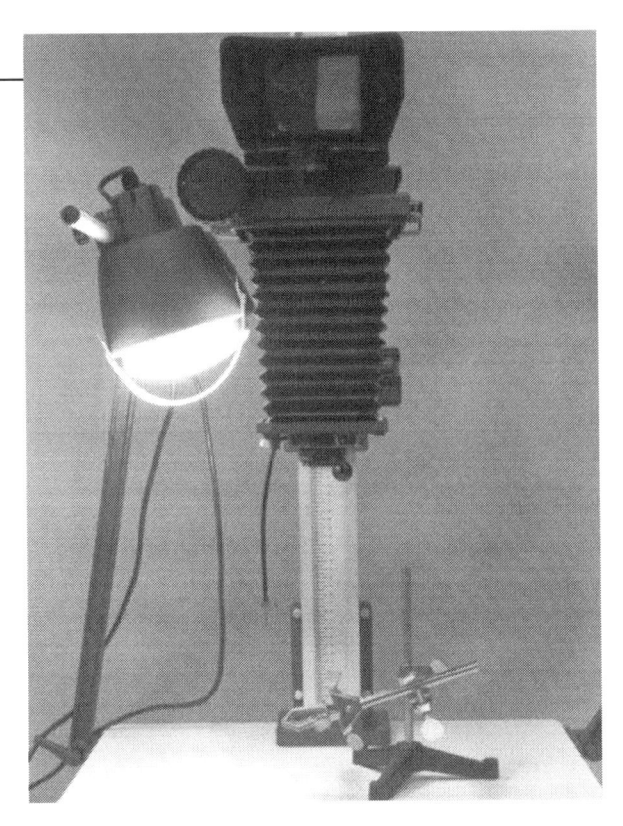

Direct Lighting. Direct lighting provides strong lighting from a source without the light first having been reflected off another surface. This type of lighting produces substantial contrast between the light and dark areas of the object being photographed. Direct lighting is set up with two or four lights equally balanced and set 45 degrees above the object, with the light shining directly onto the object (Figure 8–8).

Direct Reflection Lighting. Direct reflection lighting uses one light source set approximately 10 degrees from the object, with the object set at approximately 10 degrees from the camera lens. This technique can only be used on flat surfaces and creates very high contrast. Latent prints developed with black, gray, or silver powder will always photograph dark (black) on a light gray (white) background (Figure 8–9).

8–12

FIGURE 8–10
Direct reflection lighting.

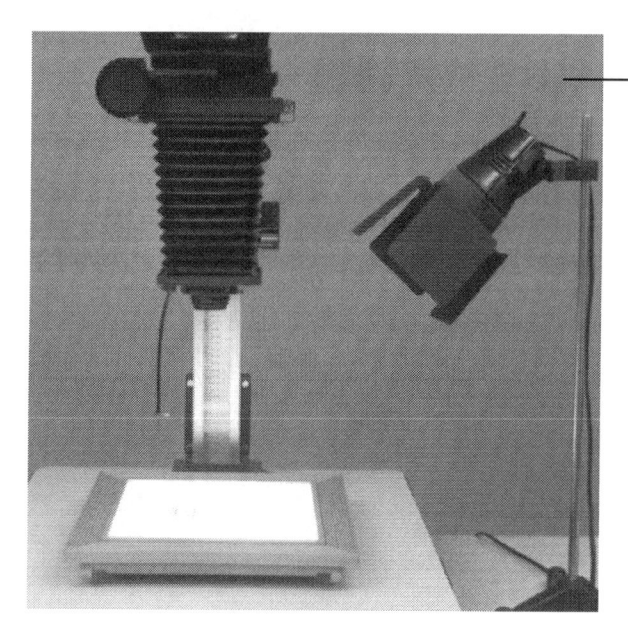

FIGURE 8–11
Transmitted lighting.

Front Directional Lighting. Front directional lighting (axial or axis lighting) uses one light source set at 90 degrees from the axis of the camera lens. The object to be photographed is mounted directly under the camera lens. A piece of glass is placed in the axis of the camera lens at a 45-degree angle to reflect the light down onto the object. Front directional lighting is used when photographing latent prints on mirrors or prints inside curved items (e.g., glasses or cups) (Figure 8–10).

Transmitted Lighting. Transmitted lighting is also referred to as *back lighting*. When employing this technique, the illuminator is placed behind the object being photographed, with the light from the illuminator directed through the evidence toward the camera (Figure 8–11). Transmitted lighting is used when photographing an object that is transparent or translucent. Another distinct advantage for transmitted lighting is the recording of watermarks in paper.

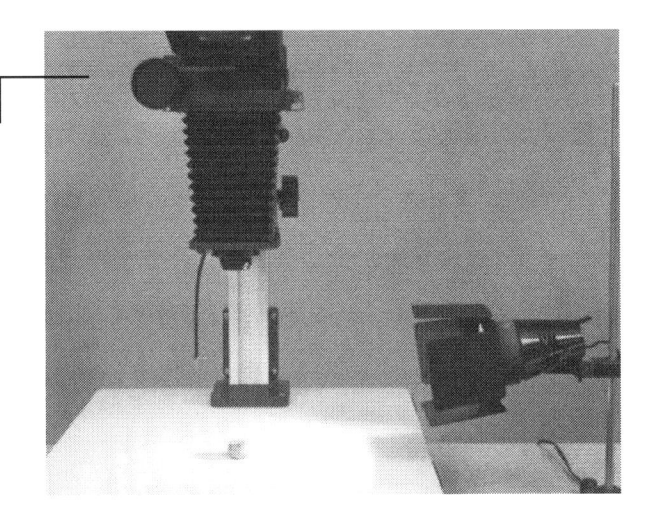

CHAPTER 8 | The Preservation of Friction Ridges

FIGURE 8–12
Oblique lighting.

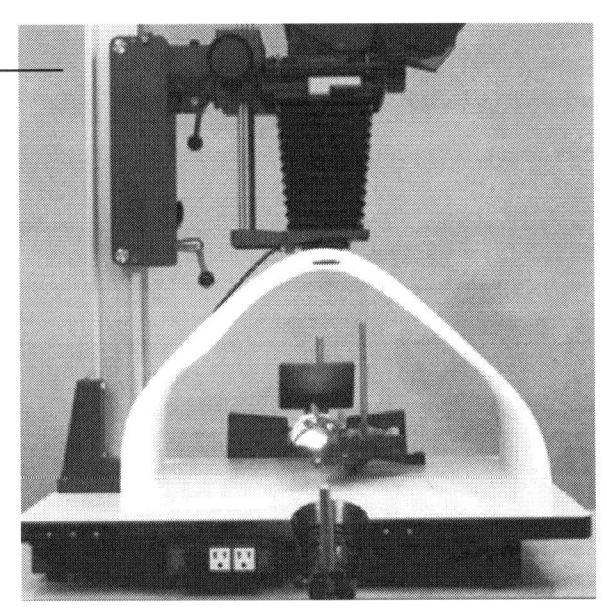

FIGURE 8–13
Bounced lighting.

Oblique Lighting. Oblique lighting is also called *side lighting* or *cross lighting*. Oblique lighting uses low-angle illumination to show detail by creating shadows. For this type of lighting, a single light source should be positioned at a low angle to skim across the surface, highlighting the raised portions (Figure 8–12). If shadows become a problem, a second light is required. When two lights are used, they are placed opposite each other to light up both sides of the impressed area. The proper angle for the light source can be found by viewing the item through the view finder and adjusting the height of the light source.

Bounced Lighting. Bounced light is light that does not travel directly from the illumination source to the object being photographed but is reflected off another surface (Figure 8–13). Bounced lighting illuminates the object with a shadow-reducing softer light. Bounced lighting is ideal for photographing objects that are concave or convex.

8.5.7 Processing and Evidence-Dependent Photography

The key to latent print photography is the proper usage of the equipment in relation to the type of evidence being photographed and the processing that was performed. For example, knowing the best lighting technique for a certain type of evidence can mean the difference between excellent photographic evidence and evidence that needs to be re-photographed.

8.5.7.1 Ninhydrin Impressions. The ability to adjust color is based upon the components of color and how a change in one color component affects other colors. A color wheel aids in the determination of color change (Figure 8–14). Looking at the color wheel, if a color is to be darkened (more contrast), an increase in the opposite color achieves this effect. If a color is to be lightened, or decreased, colors adjacent to that color are added.

Latent impressions processed with ninhydrin (a chemical reagent) develop in the visible red range. Looking at the color wheel, the color opposite red is green. Green (#58) and yellow-green (#11) filters have been found to enhance latent impressions developed with ninhydrin. Additionally, ninhydrin impressions should be photographed using balanced direct lighting.

8.5.7.2 Superglued Impressions on Multicolored Objects. Multicolored smooth objects (e.g., magazines, photographs, and product packaging) often pose a problem when it comes to photographing latent impressions that cross over background color variations. A solution to this is a reflected ultraviolet imaging system (RUVIS), which eliminates the multicolored background by absorbing UV light. Using the RUVIS, fingerprint residue treated with superglue may appear light or dark, untreated sebaceous prints may appear as black, and untreated sweat prints reflect white (Lin, 2006, pp 2137–2153).

8.5.7.3 Luminescent Photography. When exposing an item with luminescent latent impression(s) to a forensic light source, the luminescence of the latent impressions may diminish or completely disappear. This phenomenon is called *photodecomposition* or *photodegradation* and can occur within seconds. Because of this, objects with luminescent latent impression(s) should not be exposed to a forensic light source for longer than necessary (Hardwick, 1990, p 38). Sometimes the latent impression(s) can be redeveloped to make them luminesce again. This is normally not the case if the latent impression(s) are inherently luminescing.

8.5.7.4 Impressions on Reflective Surfaces. Latent impressions on reflective surfaces (e.g., chrome, silver, or nickel) are usually processed with gray or light-colored powder because the reflective surface photographs black or dark gray when employing direct lighting. Direct lighting photography used with reflective surfaces produces light ridges on a dark background and therefore the negative may be color reversed.

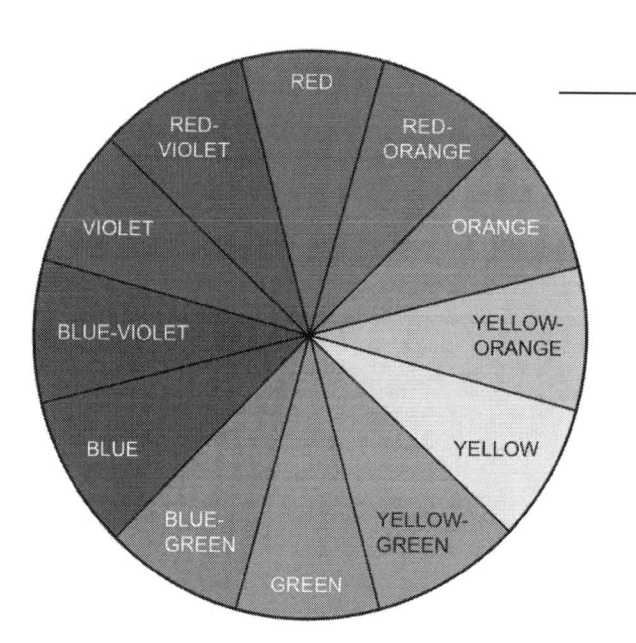

FIGURE 8–14

The color wheel.

Bounced lighting may also be used when photographing flat reflective surfaces. A distinct advantage of using bounced lighting over direct lighting for photographing reflective surfaces is that bounced lighting normally produces dark ridges on a light background. This is because bounced lighting highlights the object and not the ridges.

8.5.7.5 Indented Impressions. Oblique lighting is primarily used for photographing "plastic" impressions (e.g., those in putty, casting material, wax, grease, butter, dust, blood, or any pliable surface). The use of this technique allows shadows to be cast into the areas impressed by the ridges. Care should be exercised when photographing this type of evidence to prevent heat generated by the lights from degrading the impressions.

8.5.7.6 Impressions on Irregular Surfaces. Latent prints on concave or convex surfaces often pose a problem for the photographer. Because of the curvature of the surface, total illumination of the latent prints and adequate depth of field is difficult to achieve. Even illumination of the latent print with bounced lighting can overcome this problem. A distinct advantage to this is that friction ridges will be depicted black or dark gray and the furrows and background will be white or light gray.

When using bounced lighting to illuminate latent prints for photographic purposes, the lens of the camera should be extended through the center of a pliable white matte surface material. A filter adaptor ring may be used to hold the matte in place. Once the matte material surrounds the camera lens, the material is positioned as a concave reflector partially surrounding the object being photographed. With the camera and reflective matte material in place, the photographic light is then positioned to illuminate the concave matte material. The light will reflect off the matte material and back onto the surface of the object being photographed.

8.5.7.7 Transparent Latent Print Lifts. Transparent tape can be used to lift latent impressions developed with any color of fingerprint powder. Transparent tape that is mounted on either a white or black backing card is photographed using direct lighting or may be digitally recorded using a scanner. Transparent tape that is mounted onto clear plastic may be photographed using direct lighting if the lift is placed on contrasting material before being photographed.

Another option for photographing transparent lifts is using transmitted lighting. Using transmitted lighting has two benefits: improved contrast is achieved and the spoiling effects of excessive powder on the lifts are decreased. When items are processed with powder, there is a possibility that excess powder will adhere to the background and will be lifted along with the latent impressions. By using transmitted lighting, the light transmits through the thinner background powder but is not transmitted through the thicker powder adhering to the latent impression(s). Transparent lifts may also be used as a photographic negative for recording through direct contact with unexposed film or photographic paper on a darkroom enlarger or similar setup.

8.6 Other Methods of Friction Ridge Preservation

As mentioned previously, latent print preservation is also achieved through the use of latent print lifts and casting material. Typically, these types of preservation methods are used at the crime scene. Often the evidence that needs to be processed for latent prints is too large to be removed or is immovable and must be processed in the field. Another factor dictating the use of latent print lifts and casting material is when photography cannot adequately record the latent impression(s). When this occurs, the impression should be imaged insofar as possible before lifting or casting procedures are used, to retrieve the latent print detail. At this point, the lift or cast can be imaged again for additional preservation.

8.6.1 Fingerprint Lifters

Fingerprint lifters are used after the application of fingerprint powders. The powder clings to latent print deposits or contaminants already on a substance. A lift is usually made with tape or a similar lifting material having the correct amount of adhesive to remove enough of the fingerprint powder without destroying the original item. Fingerprint lifters come in a variety of types that vary in color, size, flexibility, and tackiness (stickiness).

In general, there are four types of commercially produced fingerprint lifts: (1) transparent tape lifters (Figures 8–15 and 8–16), (2) hinge lifters, (3) rubber-gelatin lifters, and (4) lifting sheets.

The tape may be clear or frosted and is dispensed from a roll. The tape should be unrolled in one continuous motion to the desired length. If the tape is pulled in stages, the

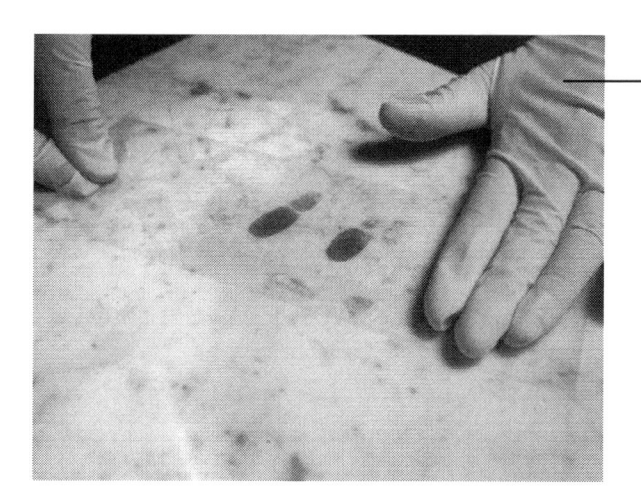

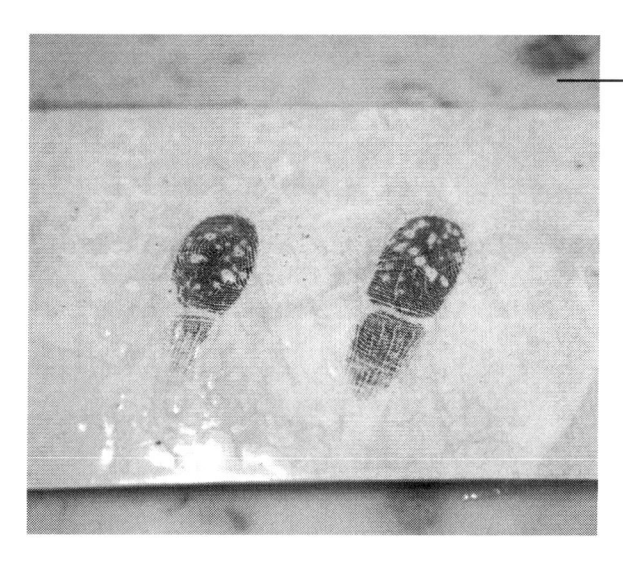

FIGURE 8–15
Transparent tape.

FIGURE 8–16
Tape attached to backing card.

tape will contain hesitation marks where each pull was stopped. Such marks may obscure lifted impressions.

The color of the powder that is used determines the color of the backing to which the tape is adhered. The chosen backing should contrast adequately with the color of the powder that was used. When a transparent backing is used, it is up to the photographer to use an appropriately contrasting background. An advantage of using transparent tape lifters is the fact that the latent impressions on the lift will be in the proper viewing position.

Some stretchable polyethylene tapes are formulated to lift latent prints off textured surfaces. These tapes are thicker and more pliable and are able to lift powder from the contours of the textured surface, whereas traditional lifting tape only lifts powder from the top of the textured surface.

8.6.1.2 Hinge Lifters. As the name implies, the hinge lifter is composed of lifting tape and a backing card hinged together on one side. The adhesive side of the hinge lifter is protected by a plastic cover. When preparing to lift a latent impression, the divider is removed and discarded. The exposed adhesive is then placed on the latent impression, lifted off the surface, and then folded back onto the hinged backer (Figures 8–17 and 8–18). Hinge lifters are manufactured in various sizes and contain markings that indicate the correct side for viewing when used as designed. Hinge lifters are available with white, black, or transparent backings.

CHAPTER 8 The Preservation of Friction Ridges

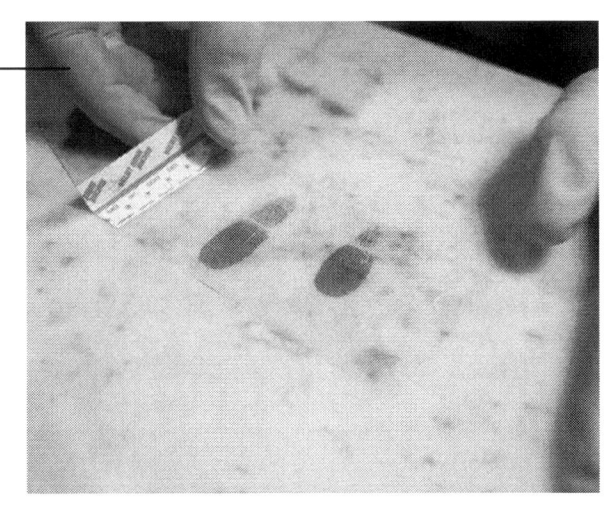

FIGURE 8–17
Hinge lifter.

FIGURE 8–18
Hinge lifter.

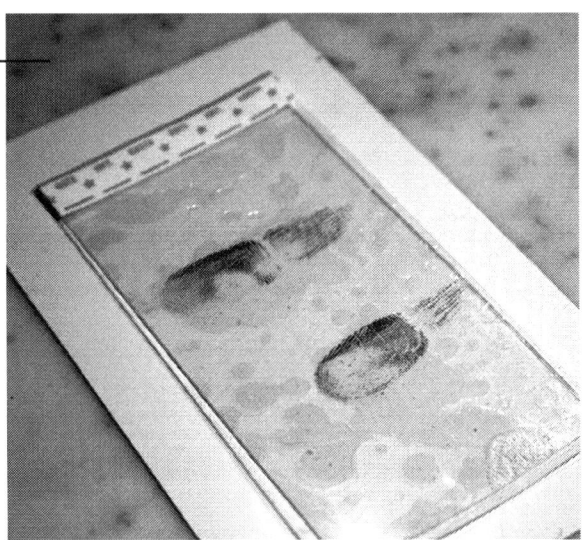

8.6.1.3 Rubber-gelatin Lifters. Of the different types of lifters, rubber-gelatin lifters tend to be the least tacky and most pliable. This type of lifter is commonly chosen when a latent impression is on a surface that is considered either fragile (peeling paint from a wall) or irregularly shaped (e.g., doorknob). Rubber-gelatin lifters include a cover sheet, a low-adhesion gelatin layer, and a high-quality elastic sheet of rubber (Lightning Powder Co., Inc., 2000). These types of lifters are available in various sizes in black, white, or transparent sheets.

The rubber sheet contains adhesive material and is applied to the powdered latent impression. Once it is removed from the surface, the clear and clean plastic covering is reapplied (Figures 8–19 and 8–20). Because the latent impression adheres to the rubber and is viewed through the covering, the print will be in reverse position.

8.6.1.4 Lifting Sheets. Lifting sheets are made specifically for the recording of forensic impressions and are commonly used in the processing of human remains. The sheets are flexible and have a smooth adhesive coating. The sheets come in various sizes and can be cut according to need.

For processing human remains, sheets are cut slightly larger than the size of the finger-block on a standard fingerprint card. Because of the slight elasticity of the material,

8–18

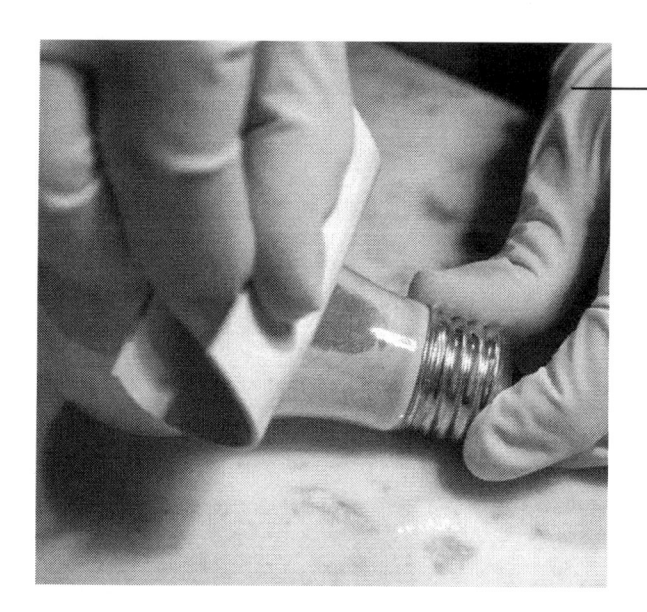

FIGURE 8–19
Rubber-gelatin lifter.

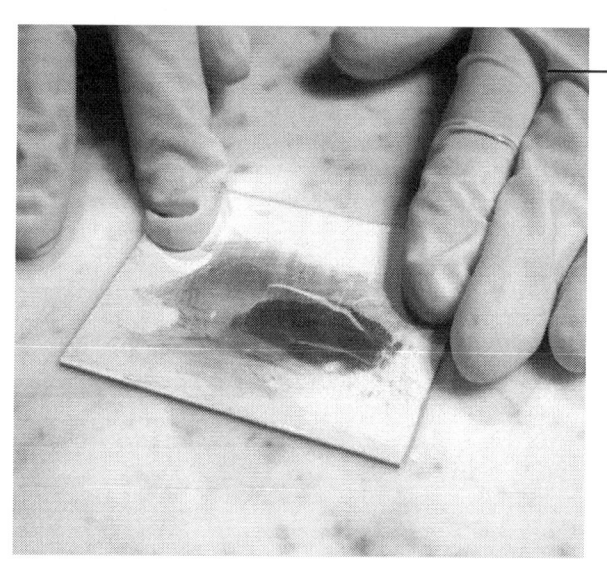

FIGURE 8–20
Rubber-gelatin lifter.

it is easy to wrap the material around a finger that has been lightly coated with fingerprint powder. Once a print is obtained, the lifter is cut down to finger block size and is placed in the correct location on the back of a transparency that has had a standard fingerprint card printed on it. When the transparency is viewed from the front, the printed friction ridges are in the correct position, with the correct color, in the appropriate finger-block.

8.6.2 Casting Material

Casting material is advantageous when dealing with patent impressions, powdered latent impressions on textured surfaces, or when processing the friction ridges of deceased individuals. Casting materials are available in several colors and have been manufactured to dry quickly and release easily.

In addition to use in photographic recording, casting material can be powdered or inked and then lifted or impressed on lifting sheets. The resulting image will be a reverse position image of the friction ridges.

8.7 Conclusion

The recording of friction ridge detail dates back to the early 1900s. From the very beginning, the value of accurate preservation was realized, and preservation methods improved as new technologies and techniques were introduced to the forensic community. The forensic science community has witnessed the discovery of groundbreaking fingerprint detection and preservation techniques, ranging from the simple to the complex. Throughout, innovation has been the norm in crime laboratories.

8.8 Reviewers

The reviewers critiquing this chapter were Herman Bergman, Jeri Eaton, Robert J. Garrett, Alice Maceo, Kenneth O. Smith, Jr., Kasey Wertheim, and Juliet H. Wood.

8.9 References

Bellis, M. George Eastman—History of Kodak and Rolled Photographic Film. http://www.inventors.about.com/od/estartinventors/ss/George_Eastman.htm, accessed July 17, 2006.

Bidner, J. *Digital Photography: A Basic Guide to New Technology. The Kodak Workshop Series;* Silver Pixel Press: New York, 2000.

Boyle, W. S.; Smith, G. E. Charge-Coupled Semiconductor Devices. *Bell Systems Technical Journal* 1970, *49*, 587.

Buckland, G.; Evans, H. *Shots in the Dark: True Crime Pictures;* Bulfinch Press: New York, 2001.

Davenport, A. *The History of Photography;* University of New Mexico Press: Alubquqerque, NM, 1999, p 4.

Eastman Kodak Company. *Handbook of Kodak Photographic Filters (Publication B-3);* Eastman Kodak Company: Rochester, NY, 1990.

Eastman Kodak Company. *Photography with Large Format Cameras;* Eastman Kodak Company: Rochester, NY, 1988.

Federal Bureau of Investigation. *Latent Print Operations Manual, Standard Operation Procedures for Digital Images;* Federal Bureau of Investigation, U.S. Department of Justice: Washington, DC, 2004.

Hardwick, S. A.; Kent, T.; Sears, V. *Fingerprint Detection by Fluorescence Examination: A Guide to Operational Implementation;* White Crescent Press, Ltd.: Luton, 1990.

Harrison, W. J. A *History of Photography Written as a Practical Guide and an Introduction to its Lastest Developments.* The County Press: London, 1888.

Ippolito, J. A. *Understanding Digital Photography;* Thomson/Delmar Learning: New York, 2003, p 36.

Langford, M. J. *Basic Photography,* 3rd ed.; The Focal Press: Woburn, 1973.

Leggat, R. *A History of Photography from Its Beginnings Till the 1920's.* http://www.rleggat.com/photohistory (accessed July 2, 2006).

Lightning Powder Co., Inc. Fingerprint Camera. *Minutiae,* 2003, *74*, 5.

Lightning Powder Company, Inc. Rubber-Gelatin Lifters: Technical Note 1-2072; Lightning Powder Company, Inc.: Jacksonville, FL, 2000.

Lin, S. S.; Yemelyanov, K. M.; Pugh, Jr. E. N.; Engheta, N. Polarization-Based and Specular-Reflection-Based Noncontact Latent Fingerprint Imaging and Lifting. *J. Opt. Soc. Am.* 2006, *23* (9), 2137-2153.

London, B.; Upton, J.; Stone, J.; Kobre, K.; Brill, B. *Photography;* Prentice Hall: Upper Saddle River, 2005.

Menzel, E. R. *Fingerprint Detection with Lasers,* 1st ed.; Marcel Dekker, Inc: New York, 1980.

Miller, L. S. *Police Photography,* 4th ed.; Anderson Publishing Company: Cincinnati, 1998.

Moenssens, A. A. The Origin of Legal Photography. http://www.forensic-evidence.com/site/EVID/LegalPhotog.html (accessed September 10, 2010).

Olsen Sr., R. D. *Scott's Fingerprint Mechanics;* Charles C. Thomas: Springfield, 1978.

Phillips, S. S.; Haworth-Booth, M.; Squires, C. *Police Pictures: The Photograph as Evidence;* San Francisco Museum of Modern Art and Chronicle Books: San Francisco, 1997.

Redsicker, D. R. Principles in Photography. In *The Practical Methodology of Forensic Photography*; Redsicker, D. R., Ed.; CRC Press: Boca Raton, Fla., 1994.

Scientific Working Group on Friction Ridge Analysis, Study and Technology (SWGFAST). Standard for Friction Ridge Digital Imaging (Latent/Tenprint). 2009. Available online at http://www.swgfast.org/documents/imaging/090914_Standard_Imaging_1.1.pdf

Scientific Working Group on Imaging Technology (SWGIT). General Guidelines for Capturing Latent Impressions Using a Digital Camera, Version 1.2, December 6, 2001. *Forensic Sci. Communications* 2002, *4* (2) (online journal).

SWGIT. Overview of SWGIT and the Use of Imaging Technology in the Criminal Justice System, Version 3., 2006, pp 1-8. Available online at http://www.theiai.org.

CHAPTER 9

EXAMINATION PROCESS

John R. Vanderkolk

CONTENTS

- 3 9.1 Introduction
- 7 9.2 Fundamentals of Comparison
- 12 9.3 ACE-V Examination Method
- 17 9.4 Decision Thresholds
- 19 9.5 The Examination
- 20 9.6 Simultaneous, Adjacent, or Aggregate Fingerprints
- 20 9.7 Summary
- 21 9.8 Reviewers
- 21 9.9 References
- 22 9.10 Additional Information

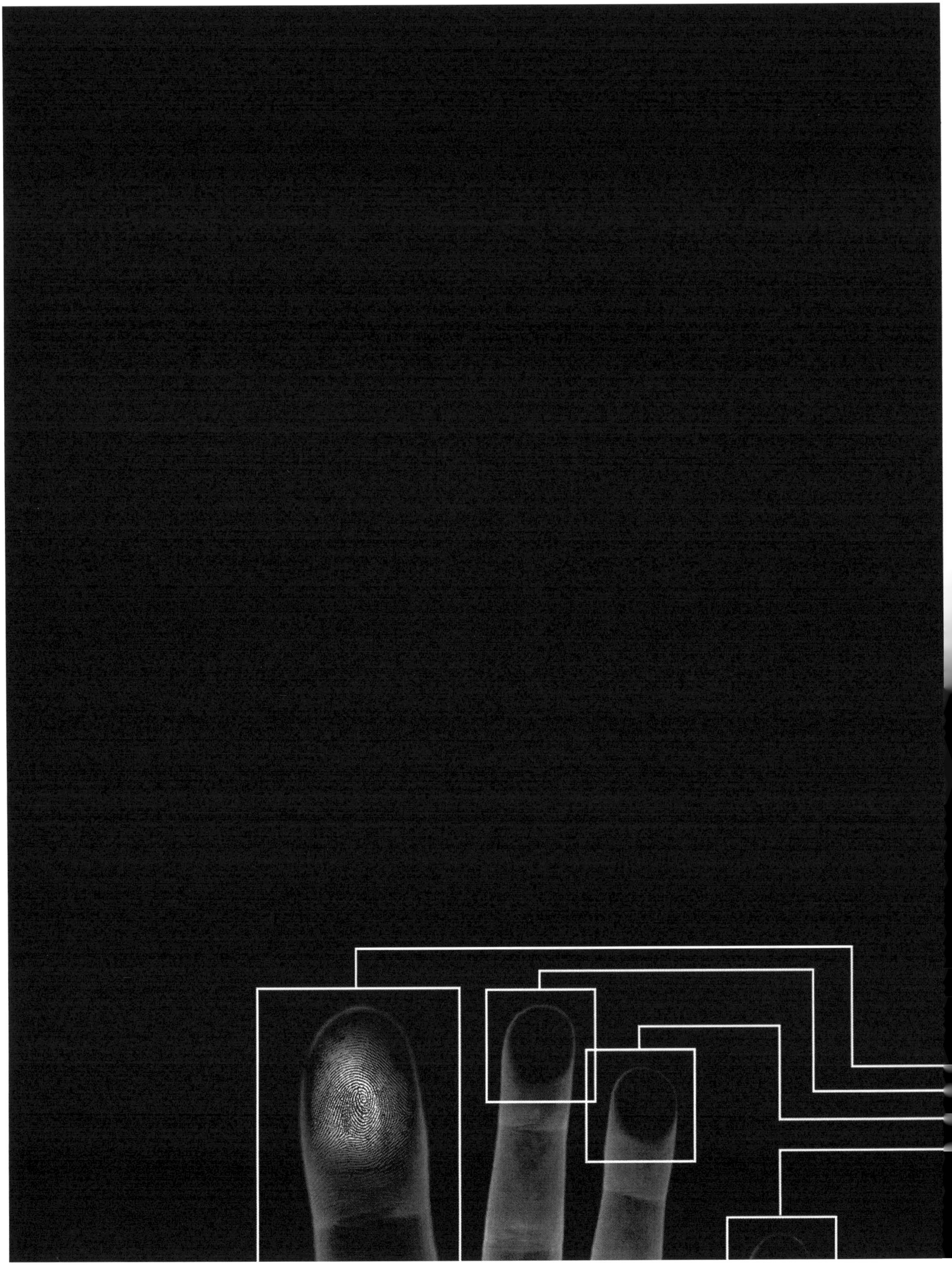

CHAPTER 9

EXAMINATION PROCESS

John R. Vanderkolk

9.1 Introduction

The purpose of an examination is to determine or exclude the *source* of a *print*.* This chapter will discuss a method used by examiners to determine a print's source by looking at and comparing the general ridge flow in two fingerprints, the sequences and configurations of ridge paths, and if needed, the sequences and configurations of morphological details of a particular ridge and nearby ridges. This chapter also addresses the philosophies of perception and decision-making that all fingerprint examiners need to understand before turning to the mechanics of a comparison.

Many authors (Seymour, 1913; Bridges, 1942; Osterburg; 1977; Stoney, 1985; Stoney and Thornton, 1986; and Hare, 2003) have sought to describe an examination method or thresholds of sufficiency for source determination [Olsen, 1983, pp 4–15; Stoney, 1985; 1986, pp 1187–1216; Hare, 2003, 700–706]. These explanations usually involve visual aids or physical tools that demonstrate a sequence or configuration of a number of points (e.g., details of ridge endings, bifurcations, and dots). Some of these involve the use of transparent grids, tracings, overlaid prints, pinholes through photographic enlargements of the specific points in the prints, or an enlarged chart documenting corresponding points. These efforts attempt to (and in some instances do) help to illustrate portions of the examination process.

The examination method of analysis, comparison, evaluation, followed by verification (ACE-V) is the established method for perceiving detail in two prints and making decisions. A thorough understanding of the sufficiency threshold within the method is essential. Merely arriving at a predetermined, fixed mathematical quantity of some details of a friction ridge impression (i.e., point counting) is a simplistic and limited explanation for why two prints originated from the same unique and persistent source or originated from different unique and persistent sources.

---

* For the purposes of this chapter, the term *print* refers to any recording of the features of friction ridge skin (i.e., unintentional recordings such as evidence prints and intentionally recorded impressions from any palmar and plantar surface). Unless indicated otherwise, *source* in this chapter will refer to a specific area of friction ridge skin. The source can be the palms or soles, the fingers or toes, specific areas of ridges, or a specific area of one ridge.

There is much more to prints than the arrangement of Galton points. The examiner must use knowledge and understanding gained from training and experience to make judgments about the features of the sources and details in prints to reach a conclusion about the origin of the print in question.

Cognitive science explains the processes of perception, decision-making, and development of expertise. Research in cognitive science is helping to explain how experienced examiners differ from novices [Palmer, 1999; Busey and Vanderkolk, 2005]. A philosophy of how examiners can determine or exclude a source of a print must be established for an examination method to be effective. Examiners draw from many philosophies to develop a particular examination method.

9.1.1 Philosophy of Uniqueness

Pattern formations in nature are never repeated in their morphological structures (or, as the saying goes, "nature never repeats itself") [Kirk, 1963; McRoberts, 1996]. This statement is supported and explained in part by biology, chemistry, and physics, and through practice and experience of observing natural patterns [Ball, 1999]. The morphogenesis of friction skin and the many developmental factors that influence the unique arrangement of friction ridges prior to birth provide the fundamental explanation of why volar skin is unique.

Basic print minutiae are defined and used in mathematical formulas for traditional classification, statistical modeling, and automated fingerprint identification systems (AFIS). These formulas consider some of the variations in friction ridge skin arrangements, but not all of the detail that is present. In spite of these limitations, no model and application has provided evidence that prints are *not* unique. Instead, the study of pattern formations in nature, and pattern formations in friction ridge skin in particular, have determined the formations in friction ridge skin to be unique. The friction ridge skin features of creases, furrows, scars, cuts, and natural imperfections are also unique.

9.1.2 Philosophy of Persistency

The morphological surface structure of friction ridge skin is persistent. Often, the friction ridge arrangement (ridge flow and minutiae) has been described as permanent. However, the cellular surface of the friction ridge skin is not permanent. Surface cells are replaced on a regular basis. The competing forces of regenerating skin cells and the effort of maintaining the form and function of the organ of skin produces a persistent, *not* permanent, naturally patterned surface with all of its minute and microscopic features. In other words, the process strives to reproduce, but cannot perfectly reproduce, the patterns of the preceding cells so that the arrangements of replacement cells can follow the form and function of the replaced cells. Microscopic variations do occur. Aging of skin is an example of persistency; although patterns in friction ridge skin are not perfectly permanent, they are remarkably persistent over time.

For friction ridge skin to be valuable for the examination of two prints, the unique features of ridges, creases, scars, and imperfections in the skin that had been recorded as details in two prints must be persistent between the two occurrences when each print was made. Persistency is all that is needed, not permanency.

9.1.3 Philosophy of Examination Logic

Deduction, induction, and abduction are three types of logic [Burch, 2001; McKasson and Richards, 1998, pp 73-110] an examiner can use to determine answers to questions in friction ridge examinations. A simple explanation of logic and inference could be found in the statements:

if A and B, therefore C

if B and C, therefore A

or

if A and C, therefore B

Replacing "A" with "Case", "B" with "Rule" and "C" with "Result", the examiner can explain which logic is used.

9.1.3.1 Deductive Logic. "Case and Rule, therefore Result" becomes "The two prints came from the same source and individualization is possible because the features of friction ridge skin are unique and persistent, therefore, the details in the two sufficient prints agree." Deductive logic starts with and infers the general and ends with the particular. Deductive logics infers that the particular of the details between two prints agree if the examiner knows the two sufficient prints did come from the same source, or a specific area of skin, and that friction ridge skin is unique and persistent. Deductive logic is used in training examiners. The trainer and trainees know the two prints came from the same source, the trainer and trainees know the rule of uniqueness and persistency of friction ridge skin, and so the trainer and trainees know the details in these two prints agree. Deductive logic helps the examiner understand tolerance for variations in appearance or distortion of two prints from the same source. With variations in appearances or distortions of the two prints, deductive logic is used during training exercises to learn agreement of details in sequences and configurations from the same source and to learn disagreement of details from different sources.

9.1.3.2 Inductive Logic. "Case and Result, therefore Rule" becomes "The two prints came from the same source and the details in the two sufficient prints agree, therefore, individualization is possible because the features of friction ridge skin are unique and persistent." Going from the particular to the general, or from results and case determination toward the rule, is an example of inductive logic. Determining that the details in two sufficient prints agree and making a conclusion that they originated from the same source supports the rule of friction ridge skin being unique and persistent. The determination that the details in two sufficient prints disagree and that they originated from different sources also supports the rule of friction ridge skin being unique and persistent. Studying all known sources is impossible. Examiners can thus never prove uniqueness of the source through inductive logic; it can only be inferred.

9.1.3.3 Abductive Logic. "Rule and Result, therefore Case" becomes "Individualization is possible because the features of friction ridge skin are unique and persistent and the details in the two sufficient prints agree, therefore, the two prints came from the same source." In actual case work, examiners start with the fundamental principles of friction ridge skin being unique and persistent, conduct an examination to determine agreement or disagreement of details in two sufficient prints, and make the determination whether the prints came from the same source. Starting with a rule, determining a result of comparison, and reaching a conclusion in a particular case is abductive logic. As one author explains:

> Notice how both deduction and induction are involved in abduction: induction helps to generate the formulation of the given and deduction helps to show a logical relation of the premises of the given. Further, when abductive logic generates a Case, deductive logic explains the logical relation of Rule and Result, and inductive logic provides a relation of the Case to the Rule. If, by the performance of this logic, the scientist can show a universal truth, the scientist claims an adductive logic. Abductive reasoning treats the particular; adductive treats the *universal*.

> Recall that "universal" does not mean "absolute." Universal refers to the breadth of the truth of the rule, its result and its case, as determined by the scientific community reviewing it: all who should know, agree. ("Absolute", on the other hand, refers to the quality of the truth of the rule and demands that the rule be unconditional, or "perfectly true".) Universal is a term that implies "everyone" when what we mean is "everyone who takes the same given," or for "the world" when what we mean is "the real world in which I and my colleagues operate." Universality involves subjective consensus: it is what "everyone knows" and accepts and is the basis for such hypotheses as "identity exists." It is our "given" by which we proceed to investigate the observations we are making. [McKasson and Richards, 1998, p 80]

If the rule of all pattern formations in nature being unique could definitely be demonstrated as false, or falsified, the rule would have to be altered. This falsification has never occurred. Based on observation, experimentation, and knowledge of pattern formations in nature (volar skin, other natural pattern formations, and their prints), the rule of law in forensic comparative sciences is: pattern formations in friction ridge skin cannot be replicated, and their prints can be individualized.

9.1.4 Philosophy of Belief

> The general context of belief is the collaboration of mankind in the advancement and the dissemination of knowledge. For if there is such a collaboration, then men not only contribute to a common fund of knowledge but also receive from it. But while they contribute in virtue of their own experience, understanding, and judgment, they receive not an immanently generated but a reliably communicated knowledge. That reception is belief, and our immediate concern is its general context. [Lonergan, 1992, p 725]

Because collaboration is a fact, because it is inevitable, because it spreads into a highly differentiated network of interdependent specialties, the mentality of any individual becomes a composite product in which it is impossible to separate immanently generated knowledge and belief. [Lonergan, 1992, p 727]

One expert cannot generate all knowledge about everything that is used in examinations of prints. The expert must rely on valid collaboration and beliefs.

In order to know and have confidence in a conclusion, the examiner must be tolerant for variations in appearances of the two prints, because each independent deposition of a print does not produce a perfect replication of a previously deposited print. With each independent touching of a substrate (the surface being touched), there are always variations in appearances or distortions of the source friction ridge skin. The less clear a print, the more tolerant for variations the examiner must be. The clearer the print, the less tolerant for variations the examiner should be. The examiner must not stretch tolerance too far. Tolerance for variations in appearances, or distortions, must be within the limits of the substrate, the pliability of the skin, the effects of friction, and the motion of touching of friction ridge skin to the substrate. The examiner must study distorted friction ridge skin and its prints to understand tolerances for variations in appearances of prints.

Doubt must be overcome when determining actual agreement or disagreement between the details of the two prints. The examiner starts with no knowledge whether agreement or disagreement exists, begins doubting whether sufficient agreement or disagreement actually exists, continues the examination and works through doubt, and then makes a determination whether the details in the two prints actually agree or disagree. As the examiner works through doubt by asking and answering all relevant and appropriate questions [Lonergan, 1992, pp 296–300], predictions start to take place. The examiner predicts to find agreement or disagreement of details. Once reliable prediction [Wertheim, 2000, p 7] takes place by correctly predicting then validly determining the details, and all relevant questions have been asked and answered correctly based on ability, training, experience, understanding, and judgments, the examiner removes the irritation of doubt about actual agreement or disagreement of details and can make a determination whether the prints originated from the same source. The examiner must prevent prediction from becoming a bias that improperly influences the determination of agreement or disagreement. All relevant questions must have been asked and answered correctly for the

prediction to be reliable. The examiner transitions through the examination by analyzing, comparing, and evaluating the details of the prints through critical and objective comparative measurements of the details of general ridge flow, specific ridge paths and ridge path lengths, the sequences and configurations of ridge paths and their terminations, and the sequences and configurations of edges or textures and pore positions along ridge paths.

The examiner makes a transition from insufficient knowledge, through doubt, to knowing and belief. The examiner bases this knowing on the previous training, experience, understanding, and judgments of self and a belief in the legitimacy of the training, experience, understanding, and judgments of the collaborated community of scientists. The examiner critically asks all relevant and appropriate questions about the subject (prints), correctly answers all the relevant questions about the subject, knows the determination, removes the irritation of doubt, and becomes fixated on belief [Peirce, 1877, 1–15]. Some of the relevant and appropriate questions involve the uniqueness and persistency of the friction ridge skin, the substrate, the matrix, distortion of the friction ridge skin, deposition pressure, deposition direction, development technique, clarity of details, quantity of details, sufficiency of sequence of details, threshold to determine sufficiency, and examination method. The scientific or examination method asks questions throughout the process to remove doubt from the examiner's conclusion. The examiner is seeking the truth or reality of the relationship between the two prints. By asking all relevant and appropriate questions; correctly answering all relevant questions based upon previous training, experience, understanding, and judgments of self and others within the collaboration of forensic scientists; and removing the irritation of doubt, the examiner knows what is believed as truth.

The collaboration of scientists and dissemination of knowledge is what science is about. The collaboration of scientists and dissemination of knowledge generate the relevant questions that need to be asked and determine the correctness of the answers. This process parallels the description of scientific method by making observations, forming hypotheses, asking questions, collecting data, testing data, reaching a conclusion, sharing the conclusion, and being able to replicate the conclusion.

If two examiners reach opposing conclusions of individualization and exclusion about the source of the same unknown print, one of the examiners has failed to ask and correctly answer relevant and appropriate questions about the prints. One of the examiners is wrong. As these rare dilemmas occur, part of the conflict resolution needs to determine whether all relevant and appropriate questions about the prints had been asked and correctly answered by the examiners. Humans can and do make mistakes. The resolution needs to confront the training, experience, understanding, judgments, and knowledge and beliefs of the examiners and their collaborators. Science must learn from mistaken beliefs through inquiry and collaboration of the scientists. Something has led the erroneous examiner to his or her mistaken belief. If the inquiry and collaboration fail to determine the cause for the mistaken belief, that belief will continue, for there is no reason to change. [Lonergan, 1992, pp 735–736]

9.2 Fundamentals of Comparison

Examiner understanding of friction ridge skin and the associated features of ridges, furrows, creases, scars, cuts, warts, wrinkles, blisters, and imperfections is needed before examination of prints takes place. In order to reach conclusions from the examination process, fundamental principles of the source, or skin, must be established. Uniqueness and persistency of skin are the fundamental principles [SWGFAST, 2002a, p 1; SWGFAST, 2004, p 1].

Every science has nomenclature that is needed for communication purposes. Adequately describing something that is unique is a difficult challenge. After all, unique implies nothing else is just like it. Labels are attached to the features of friction ridges and details of their prints for communication and classification purposes. Whorls, loops and arches, ending ridges, bifurcations, and dots are some of the generic labels used to generally describe the morphological structures of friction ridges and the details in prints. Examiners need to be attentive to the actual uniqueness of the features of the ridge and not allow the use of generalized descriptive labels to diminish the examiner's understanding of the actual value of the feature. If an examiner is looking for just ridge endings or bifurcations, the examiner might only see a ridge that ends or bifurcates. Conversely, if an examiner looks for the overall inherent morphology of the ridge, the shapes and dimensions of the ridge, where it starts, the path it takes, where it ends, the widths, the edges, the pore positions, and the morphology of the neighboring ridges, the examiner will become more perceptive of the details within the prints. Pattern formations in nature can never be completely described through the use of commonly labeled unique features [Grieve, 1990, p 110; Grieve, 1999; Vanderkolk, 1993].

Often, prints of the same source are recorded at two significantly different times, before and after trauma to the skin. As an example, scars might be present in a more recent print and not in a previous recording of the same source. By having a basic understanding of the biology, healing, and regeneration of skin, the examiner will understand the persistency issues related to the source that made the two prints. As long as there is sufficient persistency of any natural, traumatic, or random unique feature of the skin between the times of deposition of the two prints, the details of any unique and persistent features of the skin can be used in conjunction with the details of other unique and persistent features. There is no reason to ignore any of the details of any of the unique and persistent features in the source.

9.2.1 Variations in Appearances

Examiner understanding of variations in appearances among prints is needed before examination of a print takes place. Each independent print from the source will vary in appearance from every other independent print from the same source. Many factors influence the variations in appearances of prints.

The surface areas of the friction ridge skin that touch substrates influence the variations in appearances. The exact surface area of skin touching the first substrate will not be the exact surface area of skin that touches the second substrate. Each time the skin touches a substrate, the surface area will vary.

The manner in which friction ridge skin touches a substrate influences the variations in appearance. Each independent touching has different influences that cause variations in the appearances of the prints. Flat touching, rolling, sliding, or twisting will influence the skin's pliability, causing distortions. Studying the manners of touching and distortion will aid the examiner in examination of prints.

The substrates or surfaces being touched influence the variations in appearance. Each independent touching of differing substrates has different influences that cause variations. The cleanliness, texture, contour, or porous nature of the substrate will influence the prints.

The matrices, or residues, on the friction ridge skin when the skin touches a substrate influence the variations in appearance. Sweat, oil, and blood are common matrices that cause variations. The matrices on the substrate that is touched by friction ridge skin also influence the variations. Oils, dust, blood, or other residues are common matrices on substrates. The types and amounts of matrices and their interactions will influence variations with each touching of the substrate. The actual transfers of matrices between skin and substrate will vary because each independent touching has different influences that cause variations.

Variations in temperature, humidity, or weather before, during, and after independent touching of substrates influence the matrices upon a given substrate. These variations also influence the transfers of matrices between skin and substrate.

As skin is traumatized with imperfections and regenerates, variations in the morphology of the skin can occur. The healing process occurs over time. Realizing the persistency issues of healing and aging of various features is thus needed to understand variations.

Variations in different latent print processing or development techniques, and variations in the application of these techniques, will influence variations in appearances of an unknown or latent print. Heavy or light powdering, cyanoacrylate fuming, chemical processing, or fluorescent processing will cause variations in appearance.

The same is true for variations in different standard print capturing techniques, and variations in the application of these techniques. The components and amounts of inks, chemicals, powders, substrates, or electronics used to capture, record, or print known or standard prints influence variations in appearance.

The handling, packaging, or storing of an undeveloped or nonfixed print can further influence its appearance. The matrix might evaporate, rub off, get scratched, transfer to the package, or blend into the substrate. Surface contact, environment, temperature, humidity, and light all can influence the appearance of a captured print, just as they can with a latent print.

Additionally, the techniques used to view or enlarge prints will influence variations in appearance. Magnification, photographic equipment, computers, facsimile or copy machines, and other media used for printing, viewing, copying, and enlarging prints can cause variations.

The plethora of influences that occur during independent touching, processing, capturing, recording, storing, and viewing of unknown and known prints will cause each independent print to vary in appearance from every other recording. The examiner needs to realize this when examining prints. Each print will have various quality and quantity of details of recorded features. These variations do not necessarily preclude determination or exclusion of the source of the print. Rather, they are expected. Just as pattern formations in nature are unique, the prints made by each independent touching will produce a pattern that is just not like any other, as depicted in Figure 9–1. There is no such thing as a perfect or exact match between two independent prints or recordings from the same source. Each print is unique; yet, an examiner can often determine whether unique prints originated from the same unique source.

9.2.2 Levels of Detail in Prints

A way to describe features by using three levels of detail in prints was introduced by David Ashbaugh [Ashbaugh, 1999, pp 95–97, 136–144]. McKasson and Richards talk of levels as sets, subsets, and sub-subsets [McKasson and Richards, 1998, pp 94–100]. Levels of detail in prints are simple descriptions of the different types of information throughout the print. Depending on the clarity of the print, various levels may be detectable.

9.2.2.1 First Level Detail. First level detail of friction ridge features is the general overall direction of ridge flow in the print. First level detail is not limited to a defined classification pattern. Every impression that is determined to be a friction ridge print has a general direction of ridge flow, or first level detail. Impressions of fingers, phalanges, tips, sides, palms, or soles have first level detail. The perceived general direction of ridge flow is not considered to be unique. General direction is shared by many other sources. Figure 9–2 depicts three prints showing general direction of ridge flow.

9.2.2.2 Second Level Detail. Second level detail is the path of a specific ridge. The actual ridge path includes the starting position of the ridge, the path the ridge takes, the length of the ridge path, and where the ridge path stops. Second level detail is much more than the specific location of where a ridge terminates at a ridge ending or bifurcation, or its Galton points. Sequences and configurations with other ridge paths are part of second level detail.

FIGURE 9–1

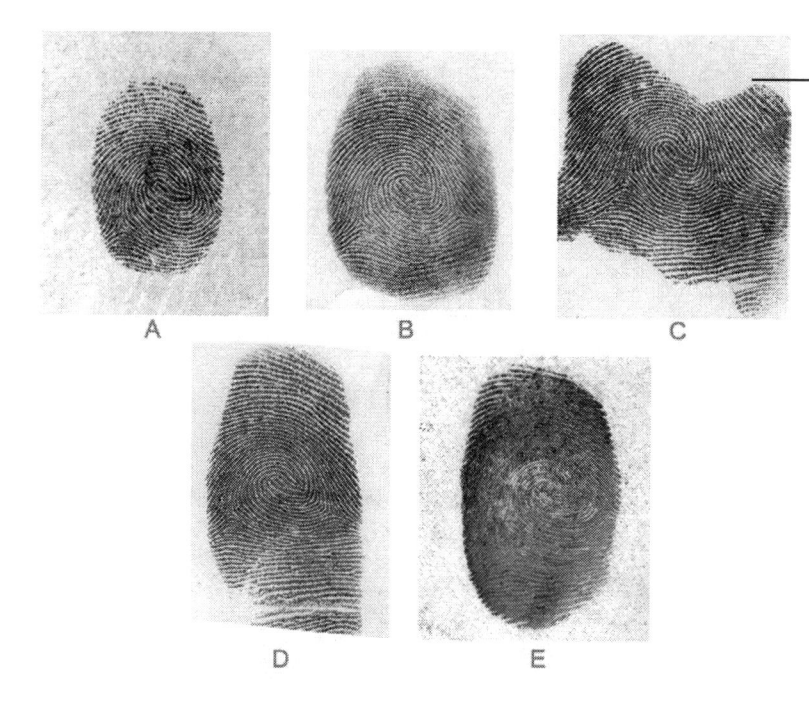

Right thumbprint with differing factors demonstrated in inked impressions: (a) a typical impression, (b) more pressure exerted, causing a color reversal and recording a larger area; (c) an impression rolled from one side to the other; (d) an impression with some pressure toward the top of the finger and rolled forward to record more of the tip; (e) an impression with excessive pressure, resulting in a poorly recorded print.

The ridge path and its length with terminations are unique. The sequences and configurations of a series of ridge paths are also unique. Second level details in a print cannot exist without first level details. The general direction of ridge flow must exist for a specific ridge path to exist. Figure 9–3 depicts three prints with first and second levels of details.

9.2.2.3 Third Level Detail. Third level details are the shapes of the ridge structures. This level of detail encompasses the morphology (edges, textures, and pore positions) of the ridge. Fingerprint scientists Edmund Locard and Salil Chatterjee contributed to the field's awareness of the edges and pores of the ridge [Chatterjee, 1953, pp 166–169]. The features of third level details are unique in their shapes, sequences, and configurations. Clarity of the print might limit an examiner's ability to perceive the morphology, sequences, and configurations of third level details. Third level details cannot exist without first and second levels of detail. The general direction of ridge flow and a specific ridge path must exist for morphology or pore positions of a ridge to be visibly present as third level detail in a print. Figure 9–4 depicts three prints with first, second, and third levels of detail.

9.2.2.4 Levels of Detail of Other Features. First, second, and third levels of detail can also describe other features (e.g., creases, scars, incipient ridges, and other imperfections) from volar skin represented in a print. First level details describe the general directions and positions of the features. Figure 9–5 depicts the general direction of creases, scars, and imperfections.

Second level details of creases, scars, or imperfections are the actual paths of the specific features. The actual path includes the starting position of the detail, the path it takes, the length of the path, and where the path stops. A second level detail is much more than the location where a feature stops or bifurcates. Second level details of these features do not require the path termination to occur. A continuous path from one end of the print to the other end of the print is included within the definition of second level details. Second level details of other features cannot exist without first level details of the same features. Figure 9–6 depicts general direction and specific paths of creases, scars, and imperfections.

Third level details of creases, scars, or imperfections are the morphologies or shapes within their structures. This level of detail encompasses the morphological edges and textures along or upon the feature. Third level details of a crease, scar, or imperfection cannot exist without first and second levels of these details. Specific shapes and edges of creases, scars, and imperfections are depicted in Figure 9–7.

FIGURE 9–2
General ridge flow is visible.

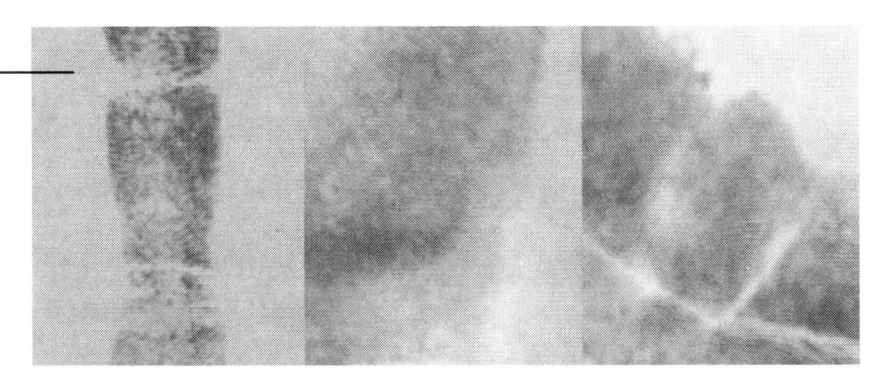

FIGURE 9–3
First and second levels of detail.

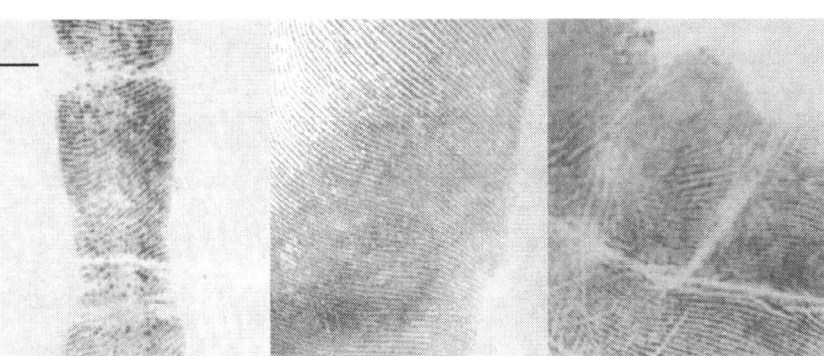

FIGURE 9–4
Prints with first, second, and third levels of detail.

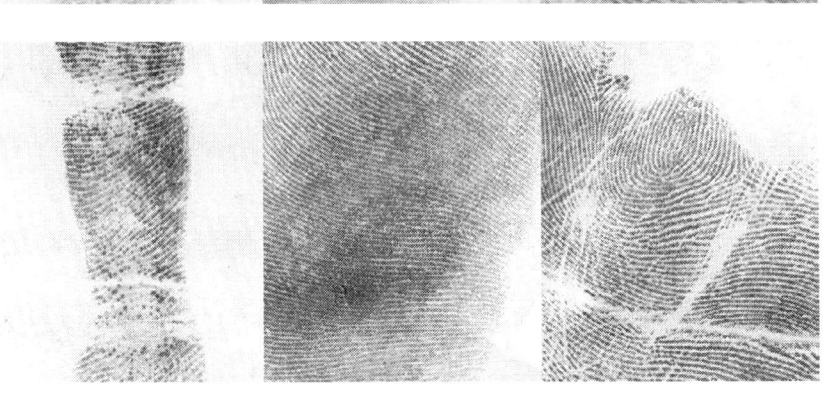

An emphasis needs to be placed on persistency. No matter which unique feature is considered, persistency of the feature on the source must be sufficient between the two events of touching for details of the feature to be significant in an examination.

9.2.3 Ranges of Clarity

The ability to completely describe the clarity of a print is difficult, if not impossible, because there are ranges of clarity within each level of detail, and levels of detail are not equally clear throughout each level within a print. The ranges of clarity within each level of detail exist because the clarity within each level varies within each print [Vanderkolk, 2001]. Clear first level details have more significance than less clear first level details. Likewise, clear second level details have more significance than less clear second level details and clear third level details have more significance than less clear third level details. As clarity improves, the power or significance of the details within each level improves.

Ranges of clarity and their significance within each of the three levels of detail are depicted in Figure 9–8 [Vanderkolk, 2001]. The quality axis represents the clarity of details of the friction ridge features. Quality can approach perfectly clear recordings of the friction ridge features, but will never reach perfect clarity. The axis approaches, but does not reach, 100% recorded quality of the features of the source.

FIGURE 9–5

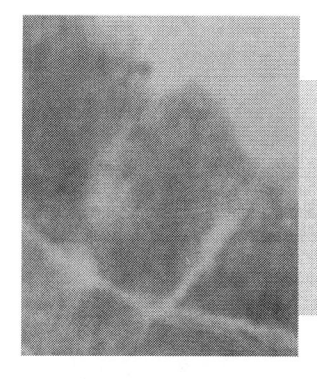

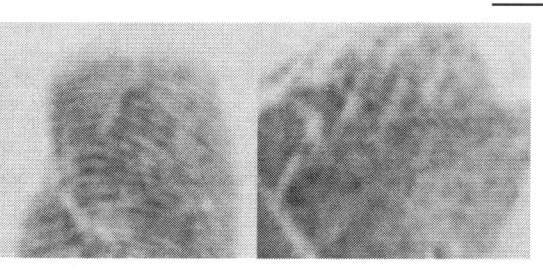

General direction of creases, scars, and imperfections.

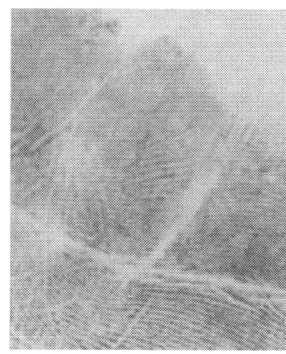

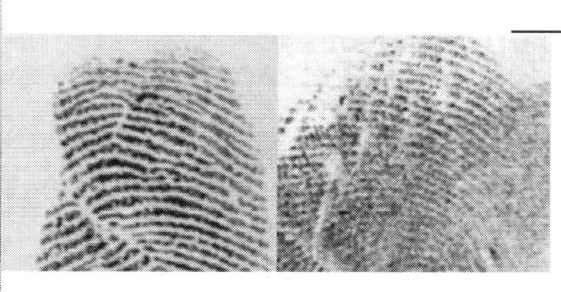

FIGURE 9–6

General direction and specific paths of creases, scars, and imperfections.

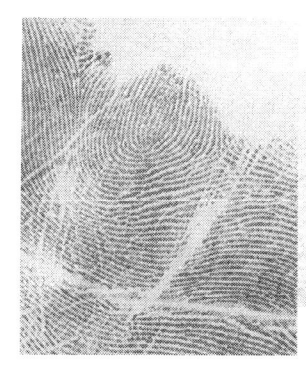

FIGURE 9–7

General direction, specific paths, and specific shapes and edges of creases, scars, and imperfections imperfections.

Quality is difficult to accurately quantify. That is why no numerical scale is placed on the quality axis. This scale simply depicts the relationship between quality and significance. As the quality of the print increases, the significance of the detail observed increases.

Quality also cannot exist without a quantity of details. Any figure depicting the quality aspect should also include a quantity of those details. As those details are observed and comparatively measured, the quantity of details increases across the horizontal axis and the quality of those same details are represented with the vertical axis. (For more on the relationship between quality and quantity, see section 9.4.)

The bottom of Figure 9–8 starts at 0. There is no image, no details, no significance. The diagram is separated into first, second, and third levels. An undefined width of quantity of details exists across the horizontal axis. Heights occur within each level, depicting the undefined increments that detail will have as the quality of the image increases. All first level details are not equally clear. All second level details are not equally clear. All third level details are not equally clear. The details within each level and among the levels have different significance or power, depending upon their clarities. As clarity increases, the significance of the details increases. As clarity decreases, the significance of the details decreases. Notice that there is no top to third

FIGURE 9–8

Ranges of clarity and their significance in the three levels of detail. *(Adapted from Vanderkolk, 2001, p 462.)*

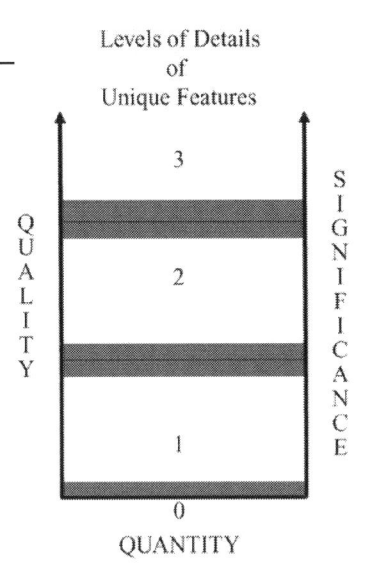

level details. Again, the clarity of the image and third level details can approach, but never reach, perfect recording of the features of the skin.

An undefined breadth of gray area in Figure 9–8 separates each level. These gray areas represent expertise and doubt by the examiner. The black lines within the gray areas represent reality. The examiner cannot perfectly determine when the clarity of details transitions from one level to the next; doubt exists. The examiner must default to lower significance when in doubt. Just as importantly, the examiner must not give too much significance to details within a white level area. Too much significance must not be given to any particular detail [Grieve, 1988; Ashbaugh, 1999, pp 95–97, 143, 217–226; Vanderkolk, 1999; Vanderkolk, 2001].

As in ranges of clarity within levels of details of friction ridge features, there are ranges of clarity within first, second, and third levels of details of crease, scar, and imperfection features.

9.3 ACE-V Examination Method

The examination method of analysis, comparison, evaluation (ACE) and verification (V) has a history of progression [Huber, 1959 60; Huber, 1972; Cassidy, 1980; Tuthill, 1994; Ashbaugh, 1999; Vanderkolk, 2004]. ACE V is the examination method described in the Scientific Working Group for Friction Ridge Analysis, Study, and Technology (SWGFAST) documents [SWGFAST, 2002a, p 2]. Variations of the descriptions used elsewhere parallel the phases of ACE

in other scientific applications [Palmer, 1999, pp 413–416] and ACE-V in other forensic disciplines [McKasson and Richards, 1998, pp 131–138]. ACE is a simple explanation of the phases involved in perception and decision-making. ACE gives the expert specific phases of examination that can be used to document the perception, information-gathering, comparison, and decision-making that takes place during an examination of prints. Scientific method is often described as observation, hypothesis formulation, experimentation, data analysis, and conclusion. ACE is one description of a method of comparing print details, forming a hypothesis about the source, experimenting to determine whether there is agreement or disagreement, analyzing the sufficiency of agreement or disagreement, rendering an evaluation, and retesting to determine whether the conclusion can be repeated.

Describing information-gathering and decision-making is difficult. ACE is a structured approach to gathering information about the details in prints. ACE is not a linear method in which analysis is conducted once, comparison is conducted once, and then a decision is made once in the evaluation. ACE can and does recur during information-gathering and decision-making. However, the three phases of ACE need to be discussed independently. The analysis and comparison must be conducted so that the comparative measurements and sequences can be accurately determined to reach a valid evaluation. The examiner must avoid allowing biases to influence each phase of the examination. Improper adjustments of determinations in the analysis and comparison phases because of biases do not validate a conclusion made in the evaluation. Thus, improper determinations can result from biases [Dror, 2005, pp 799–809; Dror, 2006, pp 74–78; Dror, 2006, pp 600–610; Byrd, 2005].

9.3.1 Analysis

Analysis is the assessment of a print as it appears on the substrate. The analysis of the print proceeds by systematically separating the impression into its various components. The substrate, matrix, development medium, deposition pressure, pressure and motion distortion, and development medium are analyzed to ascertain the variations in appearances and distortions. An analysis of clarity establishes the levels of detail that are available to compare and the examiner's tolerance for variations [Ashbaugh, 1999, pp 94]. The examiner makes a determination, based upon previous training, experience, understanding, and judgments, whether the print is sufficient for comparison with another print. If one of the prints is determined to be insufficient, the examination is concluded with a determination that the print is insufficient for comparison purposes. If the known print is insufficient, better known standards are needed for further comparison.

9.3.2 Comparison

The direct or side-by-side comparison of friction ridge details to determine whether the details in two prints are in agreement based upon similarity, sequence, and spatial relationship occurs in the comparison phase [Ashbaugh, 1999, pp 109–136, SWGFAST, 2002a, p 3]. The examiner makes comparative measurements of all types of details and their sequences and configurations. This comparative measurement is a mental assessment of details, not just a series of physical measurements using a fixed scale. The comparative assessments consider tolerance for variations in appearances caused by distortions. Because no print is ever perfectly replicated, mental comparative measurements must be within acceptable tolerance for variations. Comparative measurements of first, second, and third level details are made along with comparisons of the sequences and configurations of ridge paths. To repeat, comparative measurement involves mentally measuring the sequences and configurations of the elements of all levels and types of details of the first print with the same elements of the second print.

As stated earlier, because each independent touching of a substrate produces a unique print with a variation in appearance, comparative measurement tolerance must be considered during the comparison phase. The less clear or more distorted either print is, the more tolerant for variations the examiner must be. The clearer and less distorted either print is, the less tolerant for variations the examiner must be. Because the examiner is more tolerant for variations in poor-quality prints, the examiner will require more details when making an agreement or disagreement determination. Because the examiner is less tolerant for variations in good-quality prints, the examiner can make a determination using fewer details. And, also as previously stated, understanding the causes for distortion will support the explanations for variations in appearances. The examiner needs to study a variety of known distorted prints to understand acceptable tolerance for variations in appearances in prints.

Actual agreement or disagreement of similar details in sequences and configurations between two prints is the determination sought by the examiner during the comparison. Because the prints will vary in appearance, judgments must be made throughout the process. After determinations of actual agreement or disagreement of first, second, or third levels of details in the comparison phase, evaluation is the next step.

9.3.3 Evaluation

"Evaluation is the formulation of a conclusion based upon analysis and comparison of friction ridge skin" (prints) [SWGFAST, 2002a, p 3]. Whereas in the comparison phase, the examiner makes determinations of agreement or disagreement of individual details of the prints in question, in the evaluation phase the examiner makes the final determination as to whether a finding of individualization, or same source of origin, can be made.

During the evaluation, the examiner cannot determine two prints originated from the same source with agreement of only first level details. If the examiner determines sufficient agreement of first and second level details, or of first, second, and third levels of detail, after analysis and comparison, an evaluation of individualization is made. Figure 9–9 represents two prints with first, second, and third levels of agreement. (Not all details are marked in Figure 9–9.)

FIGURE 9–9

Two prints with first, second, and third levels of agreement.

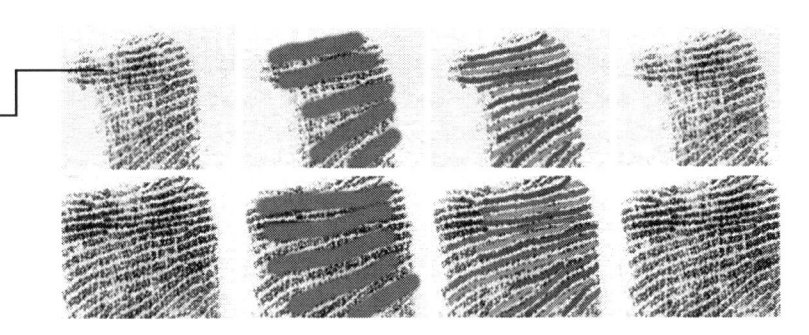

If a determination is made that first, second, or third level details actually disagree, evaluation of the analysis and comparison results in an exclusion determination as depicted in Figures 9–10 to 9–12. It is important to note that excluding a finger as having made the unknown print is not the same as excluding a person as having made the unknown print. The examiner needs to indicate whether the source being excluded is a person, a hand or foot, a finger or toe, or ridges. Sufficiently complete and clear recordings of detail from the volar surfaces is needed to make any exclusion.

The inability to determine actual disagreement does not result in a determination of individualization. Instead, if after analysis and comparison no determination of sufficient agreement or disagreement of details can be made, an inconclusive determination is warranted [SWGFAST, 2002a, p 4]. The details might seem like they could agree or like they could disagree, but there is doubt. The examiner cannot determine whether the details agree or disagree, or perhaps cannot even determine whether the sequences and configurations of details are sufficient to decide. This could be due to insufficiency of the unknown print, insufficiency of the known print, or a combination of both. The examiner cannot determine which factor is insufficient, and must default to an inconclusive determination.

9.3.4 Recurring, Reversing, and Blending Application of ACE

The human mind is much too complex to only conduct one linear and single application of analysis, comparison, and evaluation during an examination. Figure 9–13 represents a model to help explain and illustrate the complexity of the variety of perceptual phases that occur and recur during an examination. The critical application of ACE is represented in the model by red area A, green area C, and blue area E.

There are no arrows in the model. The examination starts with analysis, then comparison, then evaluation. However, the examiner can change the phases with little effort. The phases of the examination often recur. The examiner often re-analyzes, re-compares, and re-evaluates during the examination. The recurring application of each phase is a natural occurrence.

The examiner can easily change directions in the examination. If unable to determine the significance of the examination with the details and information gathered in the current phase, the examiner can reverse the direction of application and return to a previous phase.

The actual phases of the examination cannot be completely isolated from the other phases. After analysis of the first print, the analysis of the second print starts. During this second analysis, the examiner begins to mentally compare the details in the first print to the details being determined in the second print. As this second analysis takes place, a mental comparison begins; the analysis and comparison phases seem to blend together. Even while analyzing and comparing the second print, an evaluation of the analysis and comparison phases starts to take place. The evaluation is blended into the analysis, which is blended with the comparison. This happens within all phases of the examination. The blending of phases is most apparent when quickly excluding a source as having made both prints when the first level details are extremely different. During the comparison, re-analyzing takes place. As critical comparative measurements are made, the detail is re-analyzed to verify the previous analysis. During the comparison, evaluations start to take place. During the evaluation, re-analyzing and re-comparing takes place. All these processes seem to occur at the same time in the mind of the examiner.

The examiner needs to critically examine the prints while in each phase and understand the recurring, reversing, and blending potential of each phase. Biases can potentially influence the perceptions taking place in each phase. The examiner must resist using what is determined to be present in one print as justification for finding that detail in

FIGURE 9–10

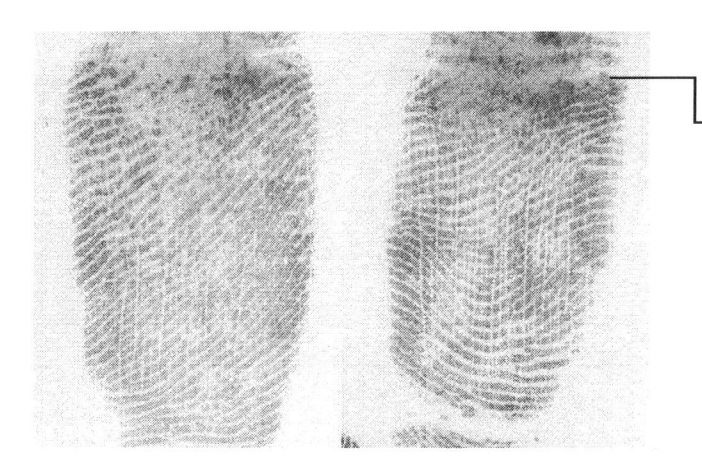

First level details not in agreement.

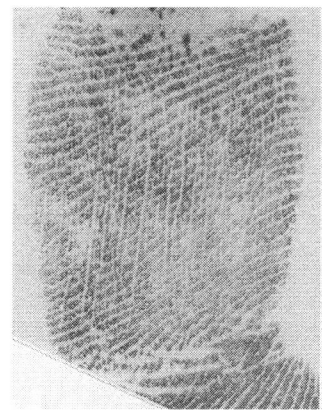

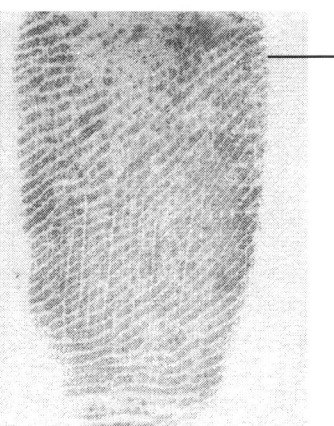

FIGURE 9–11

Second level detail not in agreement.

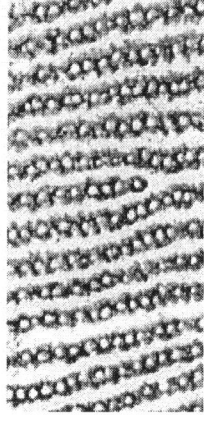

FIGURE 9–12

Third level detail not in agreement.

the other print. The analyses, comparisons, and evaluations must not be contaminated by the examiner's justification of details that do not exist. The details must be determined from proper analyses of the first print followed by proper analyses of the second print. As comparisons are taking place, the analyses will be reconsidered. As evaluations are taking place, the analyses and comparisons will be reconsidered. The examiner must consciously apply each independent phase of ACE. Critical perception needs to take place in the separate phases of ACE, and critical decisions must be made within each phase as well.

The examiner needs to critically attend to the prints during the examination. The actual examination is represented in the model by the three smaller circles with capital A, C, and E in the red, green, and blue parts of the circles. The colors of the circles represent the attention dedicated to

CHAPTER 9 | Examination Process

FIGURE 9–13

The recurring, reversible, and blending primary phases of ACE are represented by the small interlocking circles with the following colors: A = red; C = green; E = blue. The blending phases of A/C = yellow; C/E = blue/green; A/E = magenta; A/C/E = white.

The recurring, reversible, and blending complementary phases of ACE expertise are represented by the larger interlocking circles with the following colors: a = red; c = green; e = blue. The blending phases of a/c = yellow; c/e = blue/green; a/e = magenta; a/c/e = white.

The black dot in the center represents the subconscious processing of detail in which perception can occur. The gray (that encircles the ACE/ace circles) represents other expert knowledge, beliefs, biases, influences, and abilities. The white that encircles the gray represents the decision has been made.

(Reprinted from the *Journal of Forensic Identification*, 2004, *54* (1), p 49.)

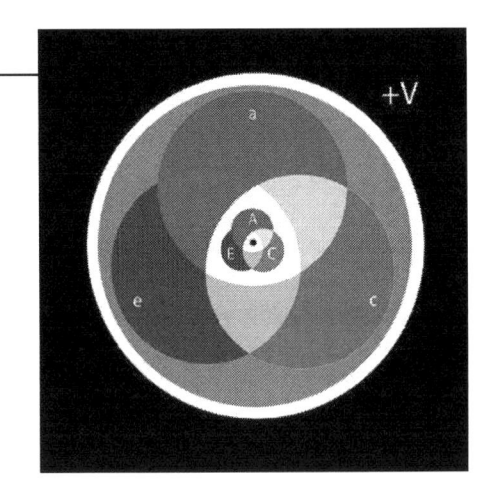

the examination. The black dot in the middle of the model represents subconscious perception. The white center area represents a blended ACE that occurs very quickly. Yellow, cyan, and magenta also represent blended phases. Conscious, critical perception and decisions need to be made during the examination, represented by the red, green, and blue parts of the phases.

The examiner bases decisions made during the examination upon expertise or the knowledge and beliefs from previous training, experience, understanding, and judgments of his or her own and in collaboration with other scientists. This expertise is represented by the larger colored and overlapping circles labeled with lower case letters of a, c, and e that encircle the smaller current examination of colored circles. The current examination takes place within the larger expertise circles.

Each ACE examination is based on knowledge gained in previous ones. In the diagram, the current examination happens within the blended phases of previous analyses, comparisons, and evaluations. Also, each of the three phases of the current ACE examination is analyzed (a), compared (c), and evaluated (e) in consideration of previous examinations and training, experience, understanding, and judgments to determine the print's significance or sufficiency. That is why the model represents the current examination taking place within the white overlapping area of the larger expert phases of the model.

Numerous analyses, comparisons, and evaluations take place within the ACE phases. The first print (the unknown or latent print) is analyzed numerous times as needed. Then the second print (usually the known or standard print) is analyzed numerous times, as needed. Then, the first print is compared with the second print numerous times, as needed. Many comparative measurements take place to determine the agreement or disagreement of various levels of details. Many evaluations take place. Eventually, the final analysis and comparison lead to the final evaluation.

Many influences can affect the current ACE examination. Knowledge and beliefs of uniqueness, persistency, and impression evidence in other types of forensic comparative sciences can influence the examination. Biases, pressures, or expectations can influence the examination. The examiner needs to be aware of other influences and conduct the examination so that these influences do not negatively affect the examination. These other influences are represented by the gray that encircles the colored circles.

The white around the circles represents the decision made after critical analysis, comparison, and evaluation examination of the prints. After sufficient ACE examination within expertise and influences, the examiner makes a determination.

9.3.5 Verification

"Verification is the independent examination by another qualified examiner resulting in the same conclusion" [SWGFAST, 2002a, p 4]. In Figure 9–13, verification is represented by +V. Having a second examiner apply the ACE methodology between the unknown and known prints without indications of a previous conclusion by the original examiner is one method of applying verification. Reworking the case with indications of decisions made by the original examiner is another method of applying verification. Conducting an examination between two enlarged and charted prints provided by the original examiner is another method of applying verification. There are many methods of applying the verification phase of an examination beyond these examples. The method of verification must be selected so that the verifier is not improperly influenced by the original examiner's decisions or work products. The verifier must be able to reach an unbiased conclusion.

SWGFAST states verification is required for all individualizations. Verification is optional for exclusion or inconclusive determinations [SWGFAST, 2002a, p 4].

9.4 Decision Thresholds

Each print examined must have sufficient details or recording of the features of the skin to determine or exclude the source. Lack of clarity in the prints diminishes the examiner's ability to determine or exclude a source of the print. Because the prints have reduced quality of details, the prints must have sufficient quantity of details of these features to determine or exclude a source.

Decisions must be made within each phase of ACE. Whether to go forward, backward, or to stop in the examination must be decided. Selecting a threshold of sufficiency is the challenge. During the last 100 years, various models of sufficiency have been presented. Locard presented his tripartite rule in 1914; he indicated that more than 12 clear minutiae establishes certainty [Champod, 1995, p 136]. In 1924, the New Scotland Yard adopted a policy (with some exceptions) of requiring 16 points [Evett, 1996, pp 51–54]. At some time prior to 1958, the Federal Bureau of Investigation abandoned the practice of requiring a set number of points [Hoover, 1958]. During the 1970 conference of the International Association for Identification (IAI), a resolution was passed to form a committee for the purpose of determining "the minimum number of friction ridge characteristics which must be present in two impressions in order to establish positive identification" [McCann, 1971, p 10]. Three years later, that committee reported that "no valid basis exists at this time for requiring that a predetermined minimum number of friction ridge characteristics must be present in two impressions in order to establish positive identification" [McCann, 1973, p 14]. The standardization committee report has been reaffirmed and continues to date as the IAI position, and has been reaffirmed in various other forums [Grieve, 1995, pp 580–581; SWGFAST, 2004, p 1]. In North America, the prevailing threshold of sufficiency is the examiner's determination that sufficient quantity and quality of detail exists in the prints being compared.

This is the quantitative–qualitative threshold (QQ), and can be explained simply as: For impressions from volar skin, as the quality of details in the prints increases, the requirement for quantity of details in the prints decreases. As the quantity of details in the prints increases, the requirement for quality of details decreases. So, for clearer prints, fewer details are needed and for less clear prints, more details are needed. This follows the law of uniqueness in pattern formations in nature. When challenged to predetermine how much is needed to individualize, it depends on how clear the prints are and how many details are present.

QQ represents the most natural threshold for recognition of details of unique features. Natural recognition relies upon how clear a print is and how many details are in the print. The QQ threshold can be used in all forensic comparative sciences that rely upon uniqueness and persistency in the source to make determinations. Artificial, predetermined quantities of limited and generically labeled details of unique features of the source are not adequate for

FIGURE 9–14

Quality-quantity curves.

(Adapted from the *Journal of Forensic Identification*, 2001, 51 (5), p 464.)

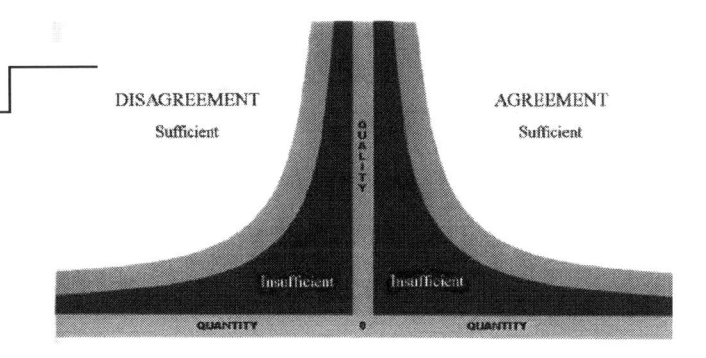

explaining agreement. Sufficiency for same source determinations depends on a quality/quantity relationship.

Figure 9–14 depicts the QQ threshold curves [Vanderkolk 1999, Vanderkolk 2001]. For any impression from volar skin, quality relies upon quantity just as quantity relies upon quality. Under the curve is insufficiency. Insufficiency is represented by black. Upon leaving the black and interfacing with the gray curve, sufficiency is reached. This sufficiency threshold is based on the value of 1. (X times Y = 1, or Q times Q = 1, is the curve.) One unit of uniqueness in agreement is the theoretical minimum needed to determine the prints had been made by the same unique and persistent source. One unit of uniqueness in disagreement is the minimum needed to determine the two prints had been made by different unique and persistent sources. This is why the threshold model is based on the value of quality times quantity equaling one. However, the examiner cannot determine the actual threshold of absolute minimum sufficiency of one unit of uniqueness. Therefore, the examiner must go beyond the theoretical minimum threshold of one, through the gray doubt area to the curves, and transition to knowing and believing the determination. An understanding of sufficiency becomes fixated beyond the gray doubt, in the white area.

Defining the physical attributes of one unit of uniqueness using common terms is difficult, if not impossible, because each unit of uniqueness is itself unique. Less clarity of many details increases the need to have more quantity of details to equal one unit. Sequences and alignments of details and features must be studied to develop expertise and understand uniqueness. The understanding of the physical attributes of uniqueness is based on previous training, experience, understanding, and judgments of the expert and the beliefs of the collaborating scientific community.

The gray quality and quantity axes intersect at zero. If the QQ curves were to intersect with either axis, there would be no print: A print with no quality of details could not exist. Neither could a print with no quantity of details. The QQ curves continue along both axes. The prints can approach perfect and complete recording of all the details of all the features of the skin, but will never reach perfection. Since nature is unique, there can never be a perfect and complete print, or replication of uniqueness. If complete replication of uniqueness would occur, uniqueness would cease.

The curves stop in the model because the examiner can only perceive details to a practical level. The curves actually continue. The quality axis approaches, but cannot reach, 100% clarity of the original source. The quantity axis approaches, but cannot reach, complete recording of all features within the recorded area of the skin. The model depicts reality and practicality at the same time.

The curve on the right side represents sufficiency of agreement of details for the evaluation phase. This curve also represents sufficiency of details in the analysis and comparison phases. The curve on the left side represents sufficiency of disagreement of details for the comparison and evaluation phases. These are two separate and distinct positive curves, mirror images of each other. The curves must be separate and distinct. Actual agreement and disagreement of unique details in two prints from unique and persistent source(s) cannot exist at the same time. Two prints from different unique and persistent sources cannot have two, four, six, or any number of details that actually match. (If an examiner states this is possible, the examiner is confused about uniqueness, confused about persistency, confused about actual agreement, confused about actual disagreement, or a combination of all of these.)

The ability to perceive agreement or disagreement is limited by a combination of the imperfectly recorded prints and human beings' perceptual abilities. If sufficiency does not exist for source determination or exclusion, the examiner cannot determine whether the details of unique features of the source(s) agree or disagree. Therefore, gray doubt exists between, or connects, the two insufficient areas under the QQ curves of agreement and disagreement. The examiner cannot determine whether the details of unique and persistent features of the skin actually agree or disagree. The examiner cannot determine the sufficiency of sequences and configurations of the details that are perceived.

The model also depicts the three decisions that can be reached after conducting analyses, comparisons, and evaluations:

- Agreement (white area): Sufficient details agree and support a determination that the prints came from the same source.

- Disagreement (white area): Sufficient details disagree and warrant a determination that the prints came from different sources.

- Inconclusive (gray and black areas): The examiner cannot determine whether the details actually agree or disagree, or cannot determine sufficiency of sequences and configurations.

The interface position between black and gray is fixed. The black area under each curve is also fixed. The black is insufficiency, less than the value of 1. The width of the gray varies. The upper limit of the gray can expand away from the black to represent less expertise or more doubt, or contract toward the black to represent more expertise or less doubt. Each examiner varies in their width of the gray. The width varies with expertise, training, experience, understanding, and judgments of their own and of others. The width of the gray also represents individual daily variations within the examiner.

The examiner must avoid examinations when unable to properly attend to the examination. The human factor must be considered when making determinations. The examiner must remember, "when in doubt, don't" and "do not be wrong". The gray also represents the interaction of the examiner with the method and threshold. The examiner is part of the method and makes the determinations using the QQ threshold as a model.

9.5 The Examination

An ACE examination starts with the analysis of the first print. The examiner then selects and stores some of the details of the first print as a target group in memory. The size or area of the print that contains the target group should not be too large because the examiner cannot perfectly store all the details of a large group in memory. These details are most likely some of the first level of general direction with, possibly, limited sequences and configurations of some second- and third-level details. Details of ridges, creases, scars, and imperfections can also be included within the first selected target group. Persistency of the features of the skin must be considered when selecting and then searching for a target. The examiner normally selects targets that are distinct and occur near the delta, core, or interfaces of details of ridges, creases, scars, and imperfections, because it should be easy to determine whether these exist in the second print.

Next, the analysis of the second set of prints starts. An example would be a tenprint card. Definitely different prints are quickly excluded based on very different first level direction of general ridge flow. This is an example of analysis, comparison, and evaluation blending. During the analysis of the second print, the target group of the first print's details is recalled as comparisons and evaluations start to take place. The first level ridge flow and sequences and configurations of the target group of details of the first print are searched in the second print. If a potential target group is not located in the second print, a second target group in the first print is then selected. This second target group is then searched in the second print. As always, the selection of a number of target groups of first, second, and, if needed, third levels of details of ridges, creases, scars, or imperfections is based on expertise of training, experience, understanding, and judgments of previous searching.

Once a similar target group is located in the second image, critical and recurring comparative measurements of sequences and configurations of first and second or third levels of details take place. If sufficiency is determined for actual agreement in the target and neighboring details, the examiner determines the two prints were produced by the same source.

If the target groups from the first image cannot be found in the second print, and the examiner determines the details of the persistent features actually cannot exist in

FIGURE 9–15

Each latent impression is marked with uppercase letters and its corresponding known print is marked with a corresponding lowercase letter. The first and third columns show the unannotated individual impressions. The second and fourth columns have colored markings to show the corresponding ridge flow and details.

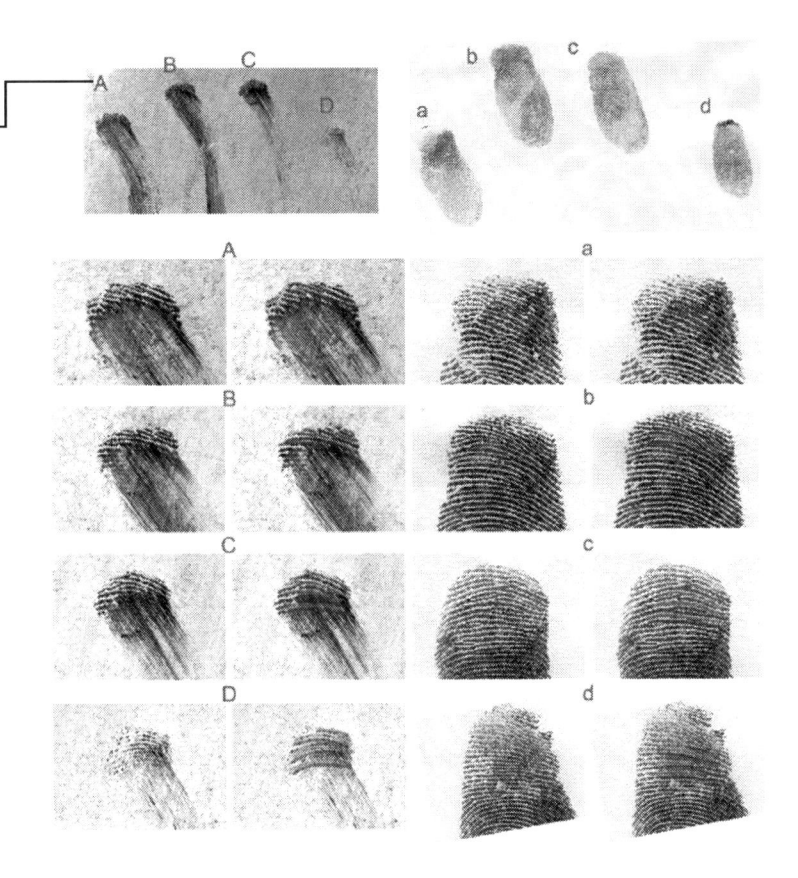

the source of the second print, after recurring analyses and comparisons of various sufficient target groups, exclusion of the particular source is warranted.

If the target groups from the first print seem to be found in the second print, but the determination of agreement or disagreement of comparative measurements of all levels of available details throughout the prints cannot be determined between the two prints, or the target groups of the first print cannot be actually excluded from occurring in the features of the source of the second print, an inconclusive evaluation is warranted. If the examiner is unable to explain the variations of appearances, distortions, discrepancies, differences, agreement, or disagreement between the two prints, the inconclusive determination is similarly warranted.

9.6 Simultaneous, Adjacent, or Aggregate Prints

If a group of unknown prints are analyzed and determined to have been deposited within tolerance for simultaneity from one person—based on substrate, matrix, pressure, motion, and quality and quantity of levels of details in the prints—the prints can be analyzed, compared, and evaluated as an aggregate unit from one person. The individual prints within the aggregate are from individual areas or ridge sources, all from the one aggregate source of one person.

As in many aspects of forensic comparative science, challenges are made about aggregate prints. Just as with individual prints, the examiner needs to be able to defend the aggregate based on research, training, experience, understanding, and judgments. Whether the source can be determined depends on the quality and quantity of details and the examiner's expertise with aggregate prints [Ashbaugh, 1999, pp 134–135; FBI, pp 3–4; Cowger, pp 154–158; SWGFAST, 2002b; Black, 2006]. Figure 9–15 depicts the examination of details in an aggregate to reach a decision.

9.7 Summary

An expert conducts an examination based upon knowledge and beliefs from training, experience, understanding, and judgments. An acceptable explanation of a method to document expert perception is analysis, comparison, and evaluation, and the demonstration of repeatable determinations with verification.

Levels of clarity exist within all prints made by a unique and persistent source. A description of first, second, and third levels of detail of the features of the source is used to describe the clarity. Ranges of clarity exist within each of the three levels of details. Details in prints have various significances based on clarity.

Decisions are made throughout the perceptual process. A threshold, based on unique detail and expertise, is used to make decisions throughout the process. Quality of details of unique features of the source need a corresponding quantity of details to go beyond doubt to sufficiency in the QQ threshold. Likewise, quantity of details of unique features of the source need a corresponding quality of details to go beyond doubt in the QQ threshold.

The examination method needs the examiner to make decisions throughout the process. The examiner needs to ask and correctly answer all relevant questions to reach the proper conclusion in the examination. The examiner transitions from not knowing, through the irritation of doubt, to knowing and believing. The examiner does not simply make a leap of faith. What is needed is for scientists to collaborate more to better explain the foundations and processes examiners experience when making judgments throughout this process. There is more to print comparisons than counting to a predetermined threshold of a limited number of generically labeled parts within the wonderfully unique tapestries of skin and prints.

9.8 Reviewers

The reviewers critiquing this chapter were Debbie Benningfield, Herman Bergman, Patti Blume, Leonard G. Butt, Mike Campbell, Brent T. Cutro, Sr., Robert J. Garrett, Laura A. Hutchins, Alice Maceo, Charles Richardson, Jon T. Stimac, Kasey Wertheim, and Rodolfo R. Zamora.

9.9 References

Ashbaugh, D. R. *Quantitative-Qualitative Friction Ridge Analysis: An Introduction to Basic and Advanced Ridgeology;* CRC Press: Boca Raton, 1999.

Ball, P. The *Self-Made Tapestry: Pattern Formation in Nature;* Oxford University Press: New York, 1999.

Black, J. Pilot Study: The Application of ACE-V to Simultaneous (Cluster) Impressions. *J. Forensic Ident.* 2006, *54* (6), 933–971.

Byrd, J. S. Confirmation Bias, Ethics, and Mistakes in Forensics. *J. Forensic Ident.* 2006, *56* (4), 511–523.

Burch, R. Charles Sanders Peirce. In *The Stanford Encyclopedia of Philosophy,* Fall 2001 ed.; Zalta, E., Ed.; 2001.

Busey, T.; Vanderkolk, J. Behavioral and Electrophysiological Evidence for Configural Processing in Fingerprint Experts. *Vision Res.* 2005, *45* (4), 431–448.

Cassidy, M. J. *Footwear Identification;* Public Relations Branch of the Royal Canadian Mounted Police: Ottawa, 1980.

Champod, C. Edmond Locard–Numerical Standards and "Probable" Identifications. *J. Forensic Ident.* 1995, *45* (2), 136–163.

Chatterjee, S. K. *Finger, Palm and Sole Prints;* Artine Press: Calcutta, 1953, pp 166–169.

Cowger, J. F. *Friction Ridge Skin, Comparison and Identification of Fingerprints;* Elsevier Science: New York, 1983.

Dror, I. E.; Péron, A. E.; Hind, S.; Charlton, D. When Emotions Get the Better of Us: The Effect of Contextual Top-Down Processing on Matching Fingerprints. *Applied Cognitive Psychol.* 2005, *19* (6), 799–809.

Dror, I. E.; Charlton, D.; Peron, A. E. Contextual Information Renders Experts Vulnerable to Making Erroneous Identifications. *Forensic Sci. Int.* 2006, *156* (1), 74–78.

Dror, I. E.; Charlton, D. Why Experts Make Errors. *J. Forensic Ident.* 2006, *56* (4), 600–616.

Evett, I.; Williams, R. L. A Review of the Sixteen Points Fingerprint Standard in England and Wales. *J. Forensic Ident.* 1996, *46* (1), 49–73.

Federal Bureau of Investigation. An Analysis of Standards in Fingerprint Identification. *FBI Law Enforcement Bull.* 1972, *46* (6), 1–6.

Grieve, D. L. The Identification Process: Attitude and Approach. *J. Forensic Ident.* 1988, *38* (5), 211–224.

Grieve, D. L. Reflections on Quality Standards—An American Viewpoint. *Fingerprint Whorld* 1990, 110.

Grieve, D. Symposium Report. *J. Forensic Ident.* 1995, *45* (5), 578–584.

Grieve, D. L. The Identification Process: TWGFAST and the Search for Science. *Fingerprint Whorld* 1999, *25* (98), 315–325.

Hare, K. Proportional Analysis: The Science of Comparison. *J. Forensic Ident.* 2003, *53* (6), 700–706.

Hoover, J. E. Re: Points of Identity in Latent Prints. (Letter to Lt. James Blake, Dated March 12, 1958.) *The Print* 1994, *10* (7), 7.

Huber, R. A. Expert Witness. *Criminal Law Quarterly* 1959, *2*, 276-295.

Huber, R. A. The Philosophy of Identification. RCMP *Gazette*, 1972, pp 9–14.

Kirk, P. L. The Ontogeny of Criminalistics. *J. Criminal Law, Crimin. and Police Science* 1963, *54*, 235–238.

Lonergan, B. *Insight: A Study of Human Understanding*, 5th ed.; University of Toronto Press: Toronto, 1992.

McCann, P. Interim Report of the Standardization Committee of the International Association for Identification. *Ident. News* 1971, *21* (10), 10–13.

McCann, P. Report of the Standardization Committee of the International Association for Identification. *Ident. News* 1973, *23* (8), 13–14.

McKasson, S.; Richards, C. *Speaking as an Expert—A Guide for the Identification Sciences From the Laboratory to the Courtroom*; Charles C Thomas: Springfield, 1998.

McRoberts, A. Nature Never Repeats Itself. *The Print* 1996, *12* (5), 1–3.

Olsen Sr., R. D. *Problem Solving Techniques in Latent Print Identification*; Federal Bureau of Investigation, U.S. Department of Justice, U.S. Government Printing Office: Washington, D.C., 1983.

Palmer, S. E. *Vision Science–Photons to Phenomenology*; The MIT Press: Cambridge, 1999.

Peirce, C. S. The Fixation of Belief. *Popular Sci. Monthly* 1877, *12* (November), 1–15.

Stoney, D. A. A Quantitative Assessment of Fingerprint Individuality; Ph.D. Thesis, University of California, 1985.

Stoney, D. A.; Thornton, J. I. A Critical Analysis of Quantitative Fingerprint Individuality Models. *J. Forensic Sci.* 1986, *31* (4), 1187–1216.

SWGFAST. *Friction Ridge Examination Methodology for Latent Print Examiners*, 2002a.

SWGFAST. *Training to Competency for Latent Print Examiner*. 2002b.

SWGFAST. Standards for Conclusions. *J. Forensic Ident.* 2004, *54* (3), 358–359.

Thornton, J. I. The Snowflake Paradigm. *J. Forensic Sci.* 1986, *31* (2), 399-401.

Tuthill, H. *Individualization: Principles and Procedures in Criminalistics*; Lightning Powder Co.: Salem, MA, 1994.

Vanderkolk, J. R. Class Characteristics and "Could Be" Results. *J. Forensic Ident.* 1993, *43* (2), 119–125.

Vanderkolk, J. R. Forensic Individualization of Images Using Quality and Quantity of Information. *J. Forensic Ident.* 1999, *49* (3), 246–256.

Vanderkolk, J. R. Levels of Quality and Quantity of Detail. *J. Forensic Ident.* 2001, *51* (5), 461–468.

Vanderkolk, J. R. ACE+V : A Model. *J. Forensic Ident.* 2004, *54* (1), 45–51.

Wertheim, P. Scientific Comparison and Identification of Fingerprint Evidence. *The Print* 2000, *16* (5), 1–8.

9.10 Additional Information

IAI-Resolution VII. *Ident. News* 1979, *29* (8), 1.

IAI-Resolution VII Amended. *Ident. News* 1980, *30* (8), 3.

A False Impression. *Fingerprint Whorld* 1983, *8* (32), 107.

The Science of Fingerprints: Classification and Uses; Federal Bureau of Investigation, U.S. Department of Justice; U.S. Government Printing Office: Washington, D.C., 1984.

Ashbaugh, D. R. Edgeology. *RCMP Gazette,* 1982.

Ashbaugh, D. R. Identification Specialist and Trainer. *RCMP Gazette,* 1982.

Ashbaugh, D. R. Ridgeoscopy—The Time is Now. *Fingerprint Whorld,* 1982, *8* (30), 36–38.

Ashbaugh, D. R. Ridgeology: Our Next Evaluative Step. *RCMP Gazette,* 1983.

Ashbaugh, D. R. Fingerprint Identification Today. *Ident. News* 1983, *33* (8-9, 14–15).

Ashbaugh, D. R. The Key to Fingerprint Identification. *Ident. News* 1985, *35* (7), 13–15.

Ashbaugh, D. R. Poroscopy. *Ident. Canada* 1986, *9* (1), 3.

Ashbaugh, D. R. Palmar Flexion Creases Identification. *J. Forensic Ident.* 1991, *41* (4), 255–273.

Ashbaugh, D. R. Ridgeology. *J. Forensic Ident.* 1991, *41* (1), 16–64.

Ashbaugh, D. R. Incipient Ridges and the Clarity Spectrum. *J. Forensic Ident.* 1992, *42* (2), 106–114.

Ashbaugh, D. R. Defined Pattern, Overall Pattern and Unique Pattern. *J. Forensic Ident.* 1992, *42* (6), 503–512.

Ashbaugh, D. R. The Premise of Friction Ridge Identification, Clarity, and the Identification Process. *J. Forensic Ident.* 1994, *44* (5), 499–516.

Balshy, J. C. The Fingerprint Did Not Lie. *Ident. News* 1976, *26* (3), 3–4.

Berry, J. Editor's Observations. *Fingerprint Whorld* 1980, *5,* 103–104.

Berry, J. The Map Reference. *Ident. News* 1985, *35* (9), 12–13.

Blake, J. W. Identification of the Newborn by Flexure Creases. *Ident. News* 1959, *9* (9), 3–5.

Blank, J. P. The Fingerprint that Lied. *Reader's Digest* 1975, pp 81–85.

Bridges, B. C. *Practical Fingerprinting;* Funk & Wagnalls Company: New York, 1942.

Brown, W. Here We Go Again. *Finger Print Mag.* 1947, pp 5–8.

Butler, M. Criminals Use Their Loaf. *Fingerprint Whorld* 1979, 89.

Champod, C.; Lennard, C.; Margot, P. Alphonse Bertillon and Dactyloscopy. *J. Forensic Ident.* 1993, *43* (6), 604–625.

Chapel, C. E. *Fingerprinting: A Manual of Identification;* Coward McCann: New York, 1941.

Chatterjee, S. K. *Speculation in Fingerprint Identification;* Srijib Chatterjee: Calcutta, India, 1983.

Chatterjee, S. K.; Hague, R. V. *Fingerprints or Dactyloscopy and Ridgeoscopy;* Srijib Chatterjee: Calcutta, India, 1988.

Clark, J. D. ACE-V: Is it Scientifically Reliable and Accurate? *J. Forensic Ident.* 2002, *52* (4), 401–408.

Clements, W. W. *The Study of Latent Fingerprints;* Charles C Thomas: Springfield, IL, 1987.

Cook, T. A Wise Decision. *Finger Print and Ident. Mag.* 1974, 2.

Cowger, J. F. Moving Towards Professionalization of Latent Print Examiners. *J. Forensic Sci.* 1979, *24* (3), 591–595.

Cummins, H.; Midlo, C. *Finger Prints, Palms and Soles: An Introduction to Dermatoglyphics,* 3rd ed.; Research: South Berlin, MA, 1976.

Davis, J. E. Pressure Distortion in Latent Prints. *Finger Print and Ident. Mag.* 1946, 3–5.

Davis, J. E. Further Thoughts on Fingerprint Comparisons. *Finger Print and Ident. Mag.* 1955.

Deutscher, D.; Leonoff, H. *Identification Evidence;* Carswell: Toronto, 1991.

Dillon, D. J. The Identification of Impressions of Nonfriction-Ridge-Bearing Skin. *J. Forensic Sci.* 1963, *8* (4), 576–582.

Dondero, J. *Comparing Finger Prints for Positive Identification;* Faurot, Inc: New York, 1944.

Enklaar, F. Principles and Problems in the Process of Identification. *Ident. News* 1964, *14* (8), 4–10.

Galton, F. *Finger Prints;* MacMillan: New York, 1892.

Galton, F. *Decipherment of Blurred Finger Prints;* Mac-Millan: London, 1893.

Gregory, R. L. *Eye and Brain, The Psychology of Seeing;* McGraw-Hill: New York, 1981.

Gribben, A. A. Fingerprint Testimony in Court. *The Literary Dig.* 1919.

Grieve, D. L. The Identification Process: Traditions in Training. *J. Forensic Ident.* 1990, *40* (4), 195–213.

Grieve, D. L. The Identification Process: The Quest for Quality. *J. Forensic Ident.* 1990, *40* (3), 109–113.

Grieve, D. L. Decision: Responsibility or License. *J. Forensic Ident.* 1993, *43* (6), 559–562.

Grieve, D. L. Faulds, Faults, and Forensic Fundamentals. *J. Forensic Ident.* 1994, *44* (4), 353–356.

Grieve, D. L. Eliminate the Impossible. *J. Forensic Ident.* 1994, *44* (3), 245–250.

Grieve, D. L. Long Road to Deadwood. *J. Forensic Ident.* 1995, *45* (4), 347–372.

Grieve, D. L. Rarely Pure, and Never Simple. *J. Forensic Ident.* 1995, *45* (3), 245–249.

Gupta, S. R. Statistical Survey of Ridge Characteristics. *Int. Criminal Police Rev.* 1968, *218* (130).

Halle, L. *Out of Chaos;* Houghton Mifflin Co.: Boston, 1977.

Hazen, R. J.; Phillips, C. E. *The Expert Fingerprint Witness;* Federal Bureau of Investigation, U.S. Department of Justice, U.S. Government Printing Office: Washington, DC, 1981.

Henry, E. R. *Classification and Uses of Fingerprints,* 1st ed.; Routledge & Sons: London, 1900.

Hepburn, D. The Papillary Ridges on the Hands and Feet of Monkeys and Men. *The Scientific Transactions of the Royal Dublin Society* 1895, *5* (2), 525–537.

Hough, W. Thumb Marks. *Sci. Mag.* 1886, p 166.

Huberman, M. J. Anatomy of a Problem: Proving the Identity of Fingerprints in Limiting Situations. *The Advocate* 1983, *41* (2).

Jevons, W. S.; Nagel, E. *The Principles of Science–A Treatise on Logic and Scientific Method;* Dover: New York, 1958.

Johnson, R. W. Manufactured Fingerprints. *Fingerprint Whorld* 1978, 61.

Johnson, R. W. Fraudulent Fingerprints. *Police Product News,* 1984, p 58.

Jolly, J. S. Is This Enough. *Ident. News* 1986, 36 (11), 11–12.

Kilkuchi, S. Concerning the Appearance of Linear Dots in Fingerprints. *Finger Print and Ident. Mag.*, 1977.

Kingston, C. R. Probabilistic Analysis of Partial Fingerprint Patterns. University of California, 1964.

Kingston, C. R.; Kirk, P. L. The Use of Statistics in Criminalistics. *J. Criminal Law and Crimin.* 1964, *55,* 514–516.

Kingston, C. R. Applications of Probability Theory in Criminalistics-II. *J. Am. Statistical Assoc.* 1965, *60* (312), 1028–1034.

Kingston, C. R.; Kirk, P. L. Historical Development and Evaluation of the "12 Point Rule" in Fingerprint Identification. *Int. Criminal Police Rev.* 1965, 20 (186), 62–69.

Krupowicz, T. E. Frictional Ridges, Characteristics, the Identity Factor. *Ident. News* 1986, 36 (3), 3, 6–9.

Lanigan, R. *The Human Science of Communicology: A Phenomenology of Discourse in Foucault and Merleau-Ponty;* DuQuesne University Press: Pittsburgh, 1992.

Larkin, J.; McDermott, J.; Simon, D.; Simon, H. Expert and Novice Performance in Solving Physics Problems. *Science* 1980, *208* (4450), 1335–1342.

Lee, H. C.; Gaensslen, R. E. *Advances in Fingerprint Technology,* 2nd ed.; CRC Press: Washington, DC, 2001.

Lohnes, R. C. Infant Footprint Identification By Flexure Creases. Quantico, VA, 1987.

Mairs, G. T. Identification of Individuals by Means of Fingerprints, Palmprints, and Soleprints. *Scientific Monthly* 1918, *7* (4), 299–319.

Mairs, G. T. Novel Method of Print Comparison. *Finger Print Magazine,* 1948, 20–23.

Massey, S. L. Persistence of Creases of the Foot and Their Value for Forensic Identification Purposes. *J. Forensic Ident.* 2004, *54* (3), 296–315.

Moenssens, A. A. *Fingerprints and the Law;* Chilton Book Company: Philadelphia, PA, 1969.

Moenssens, A. A. Poroscopy–Identification by Pore Structure. *Finger Print and Ident. Mag.* 1970.

Moenssens, A. A. *Fingerprint Techniques;* Chilton Book Company: Philadelphia, 1971.

Moenssens, A. A. Testifying as a Fingerprint Witness. *Ident. News* 1972, 22 (8, 9), 5.

Moenssens, A. A.; Starrs, J. E.; Henderson, C. E.; Inbau, F. E. *Scientific Evidence in Civil and Criminal Cases,* 4th ed.; The Foundation Press, Inc.: Westbury, CT, 1995.

Montgomery, G. Seeing with the Brain. *Discover Mag.,* 1988.

Montgomery, R. B. Sole Prints of Newborn Babies. *Am. J. Med. Sci.* 1925, *169* (6), 830.

Montgomery, R. B. Sole Patterns–A Study of the Footprints of Two Thousand Individuals. *The Anatomical Record* 1926, 33 (2).

Morfopoulos, V. Anatomy of Evidence. *Ident. News* 1970, *20* (12), 10–11.

Myers, H. J. I. The First Complete and Authentic History of Identification in the United States. *Finger Print and Ident. Mag.* 1938, 3–31.

Myers, H. J. I. Supplemental History of Identification in the United States. *Finger Print and Ident. Mag.* 1942, 3–28.

Myers, H. J. I. A Third History of Identification in the United States. *Finger Print and Ident. Mag.* 1948.

Newell, A.; Simon, H. *Human Problem Solving;* Prentice-Hall, Inc.: Englewood, NJ, 1972.

Nielson, J. P. The Identification Process. *Ident. News* 1986, *36* (9), 5–9.

Oatess, R. Elbow Print Identification. *J. Forensic Ident.* 2000, *50* (2), 132–137.

O'Hara, C. E.; Osterburg, J. W. *An Introduction to Criminalistics;* MacMillan: New York, 1949.

Olsen Sr., R. D. *Scott's Fingerprint Mechanics;* Charles C Thomas: Springfield, IL, 1978.

Olsen Sr., R. D. Friction Ridge Characteristics and Points of Identity: An Unresolved Dichotomy of Terms. *Ident. News* 1981, *31* (11), 12–13.

Olsen Sr., R. D. Cult of the Mediocre. *Ident. News* 1982, *32* (9), 3–6.

Osterburg, J. W. An Inquiry into the Nature of Proof: The Identity of Fingerprints. *J. Forensic Sci.* 1964, *9* (4), 413–427.

Osterburg, J. W. *The Crime Laboratory;* Indiana University Press: Bloomington, 1968.

Osterburg, J. W. Fingerprint Probability Calculations Based on the Number of Individual Characteristics Present. *Ident. News* 1974, 24 (10), 3–9.

Osterburg, J. W.; Parthasarathy, T.; Raghaven, T. E. S.; Sclove, S. L. Development of a Mathematical Formula for the Calculation of Fingerprint Probabilities Based on Individual Characteristics. *J. Am. Statistical Assoc.* 1977, *72* (360), 772–778.

Padney, S. N. Muzzle Printometry in Bovines. Indian *J. Animal Sci.* 1979, *49* (12), 1038–1042.

Padney, S. N. Note on Muzzle Printometry for Determining Age of Cattle. Indian *J. Animal Sci.* 1982, *52* (11), 1102–1104.

Padney, S. N. Note on the Ridges of Cattle Muzzle Prints. Indian *J. Animal Sci.* 1982, *52* (11), 1104–1107.

Peirce, C. S. How to Make Our Ideas Clear. *Popular Sci. Monthly* 1878, *12* (January), 286–302.

Peirce, C. S. Deduction, Induction, and Hypothesis. *Popular Sci. Monthly* 1878, *13* (June), 470–482.

Peirce, C. S. *Selected Writings (Values in a Universe of Chance);* Dover: New York, 1958.

Plater, D. Suspicion of Foolproof Fingerprints. *The Fire and Arson Investigator* 1985, *36* (1), 29–30.

Putter, P. J. Nose Prints on Cattle. *Fingerprint Whorld* 1981, *6* (24), 90–91.

Putter, P. J. An Investigation to Ascertain Whether Muzzle-prints of Cattle Can Be Individualized by Applying the Same

Techniques as Those Used in Dactyloscopy. *Fingerprint Whorld* 1982, *6* (27), 55–59.

Santamaria, F. A New Method for Evaluating Ridge Characteristics. *Finger Print and Ident. Mag.* 1955, *36* (11), 3–6.

Schmidt, S. Non-Logical Processes in Science and Elsewhere. *Analog* 1981, *51* (February), 5–11.

Seymour, L. *Fingerprint Classification;* Private: Los Angeles, 1912.

Solis, J. A.; Maala, C. P. Muzzle Printing as a Method for Identification of Cattle and Carabaos. *Philippine J. Veterinary Med.* 1975, *14* (1), 7.

Sorrentino, U. Identity of Digital Prints. *Finger Print and Ident. Mag.* 1960, 3–5.

Steinwender, E. Dactyloscopic Identification. *Finger Print and Ident. Mag.*, 1960.

Taylor, R. A. Flexure Creases–Alternative Method for Infant Footprint Identification. *Ident. News* 1979, *29* (9), 12–14.

Thompson, D. W. *On Growth and Form;* Dover: New York, 1992.

Thornton, J. I. The One-Dissimilarity Doctrine in Fingerprint Identification. *Int. Criminal Police Rev.* 1977, *306* (March), 89.

Tiller, C. D. Identification of Fingerprints–How Many Points Are Required? *RCMP Gazette.*

Tiller, C. D. That's Him But. *Ident. Newsletter* 1979, *2* (4).

Tiller, C. D. Are You a Professional? *Ident. Newsletter* 1980, *3* (4).

Tiller, C. D. Identification by Fingerprints–The Real Anatomy. *Advocate* 1983, *41* (4).

Triplett, M.; Cooney, L. The Etiology of ACE-V and its Proper Use: An Exploration of the Relationship Between ACE-V and the Scientific Method of Hypothesis Testing. *J. Forensic Ident.* 2006, *56* (3), 345–355.

Tsuchihashi, Y. Studies on Personal Identification by Means of Lip Prints. *Forensic Sci.* 1974, *3* (3), 233–248.

Tuthill, H. Analysis, Comparison, Evaluation: The Philosophy and Principles of Identification. *Ontario Police College* 1987, (July), 2.

Vanderkolk, J. R. Ridgeology—Animal Muzzle Prints and Human Fingerprints. *J. Forensic Ident.* 1991, *41* (4), 274–284.

Vanderkolk, J. R. Correction: Ridgeology—Animal Muzzle Prints and Human Fingerprints. *J. Forensic Ident.* 1991, *41* (5), 317.

Vanderkolk, J. R. Forensic Science, Psychology and Philosophy. *J. Forensic Ident.* 2002, *52* (3), 252–253.

Wertheim, P. A. Explaining Fingerprints to the Layman. *Bulletin of the Oklahoma Division IAI* 1987 (April).

Wertheim, P. A. The Ability Equation. *J. Forensic Ident.* 1996, *46* (2), 149–159.

Wilder, H. H.; Wentworth, B. *Personal Identification;* The Gorham Press: Boston, 1918.

Wilton, G. *Fingerprints;* Wm Hodge: London, 1938.

Ziman, J. *The Force of Knowledge; The Scientific Dimension of Society;* Cambridge University Press: New York, 1976.

CHAPTER 10

DOCUMENTATION OF FRICTION RIDGE IMPRESSIONS: FROM THE SCENE TO THE CONCLUSION

Alice V. Maceo

CONTENTS

- 3   10.1 Introduction
- 5   10.2 Primary Custody Documentation
- 17   10.3 Secondary Custody Documentation
- 18   10.4 Tertiary Custody Documentation
- 19   10.5 Conclusion
- 20   10.6 Reviewers
- 20   10.7 References

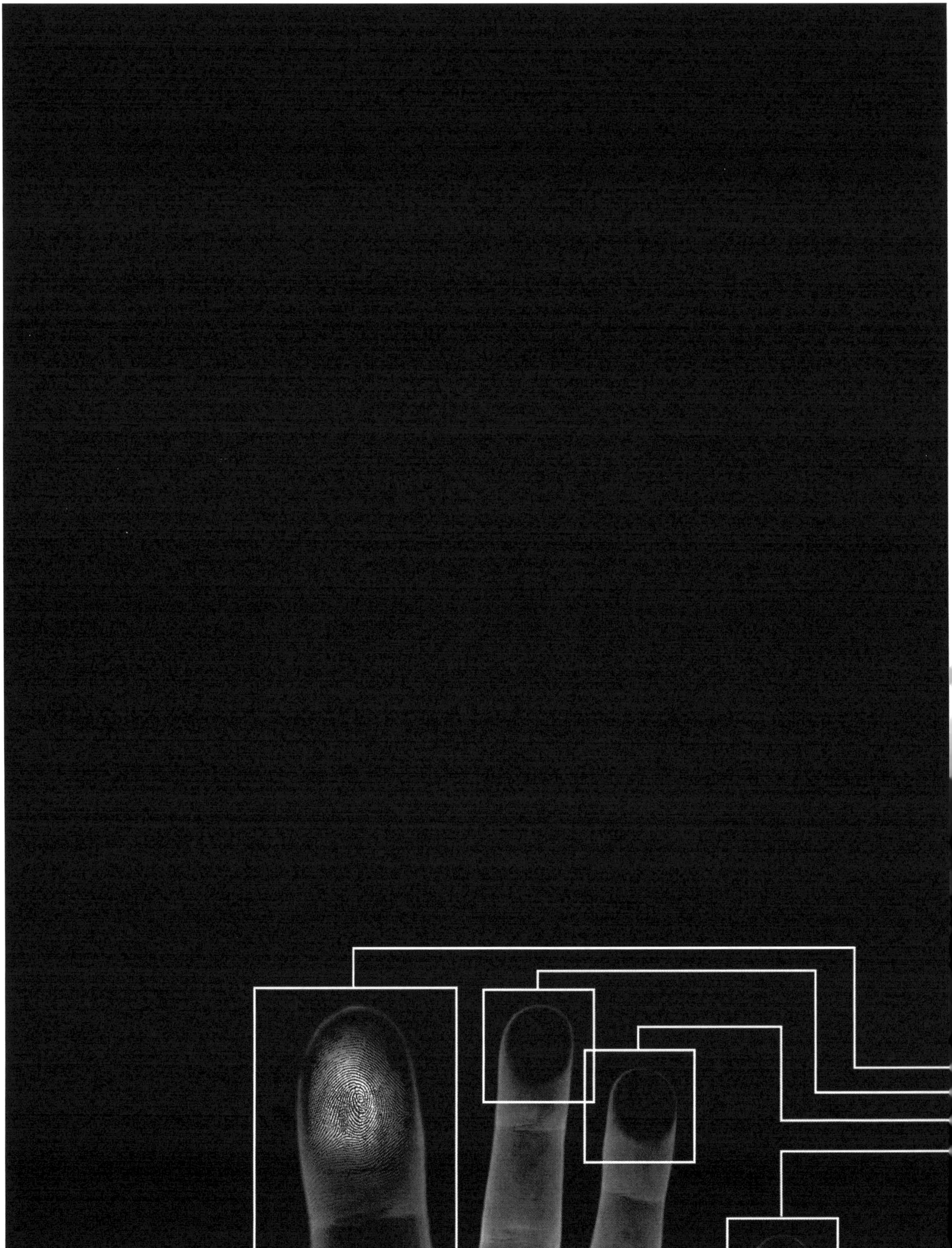

DOCUMENTATION OF FRICTION RIDGE IMPRESSIONS: FROM THE SCENE TO THE CONCLUSION

ALICE V. MACEO

10.1 Introduction

The goal of documentation, regardless of the jurisdiction or even the subject matter, is to provide transparency of information. Activities, data, methods, standards, and results are documented to provide the collector of the information with a detailed history that does not rely on memory and allows another person to review the information.

10.1.1 Analytical and Experimental Laboratories

In science, documentation is crucial to evaluate results and to test the validity of experimental research. Laboratories operate in two realms: (1) using established methods under standard operating procedures to answer routine questions or (2) using experimentation to develop new methods to answer novel questions. An example of the former laboratory would be an analytical laboratory that routinely tests water samples for the concentration of dissolved oxygen. This laboratory uses established methods and procedures for each sample and reports the results. An example of the latter type of laboratory would be a research laboratory that develops a new, more efficient method for testing the concentration of dissolved oxygen. This new method, once validated, may be implemented by the analytical laboratory.

Depending on the type of laboratory, analytical or research, the level of documentation will vary. Analytical laboratories typically have a reference collection of methods and procedures. Documentation of analysis centers around the activities and data associated with each sample: origin of the sample, preservation of the sample, chain of custody of the sample, controls, and results of analysis.

Research laboratories, however, must document the basis and the development of the method. This level of documentation will include how the method was derived, the theoretical hypothesis predicting the feasibility of the method, the data used to test the method, the results of testing, and the evaluation of the theoretical hypothesis with the results of testing. If the results of rigorous testing support the theoretical hypothesis, a new method has emerged. The method must be published and validated before an analytical laboratory will adopt it.

10.1.2 Forensic Laboratories

Most of forensic science operates in the analytical realm. Established methods and procedures are detailed in technical or operational manuals. Analysts are responsible for documenting the activities, methods, and results of their examinations in the case record. Because anything can potentially become evidence, forensic science must occasionally enter the realm of research to test novel procedures. Experimentation must follow accepted scientific research practices and demonstrate reliability prior to implementation.

The examination of friction ridge impressions follows the ACE-V model—analysis, comparison, evaluation, and verification—and falls into the analytical category. Latent prints are examined following an established method outlined in the technical or operational manuals for the laboratory. The activities and data are documented in the case record. Unlike other analytical processes, the examination of friction ridge impressions is nondestructive and the samples (latent prints and exemplars) are not consumed. The original samples can be maintained in the case record, permitting re-examination. If the original samples cannot be retained, examination-quality reproductions or legible copies of the samples can be maintained.

Development, recovery, and examination of friction ridge impressions must follow the accepted methods in the technical and operational manuals of the laboratory. Documentation must permit transparency of all activities and data generated, must support the reported conclusions, and must contain sufficient detail, "such that, in the absence of the examiner(s), another competent examiner or supervisor could evaluate what was done and interpret the data" (ASCLD/LAB, 2005, p 32).

10.1.3 Tiers of Documentation

Law enforcement agencies have adopted many administrative protocols for the recovery and examination of friction ridge impressions. In some agencies, one person responds to the crime scene, processes all the evidence for patent and latent impressions, and examines the prints. In other agencies, one person responds to the scene and collects items of evidence, another person processes the evidence for latent prints, a third person photographs the latent prints, and a final person examines the latent prints.

For ease of explanation, documentation will be approached from three different starting points. These starting points will be referred to in a manner that generally reflects when the latent print examiner (LPE) enters the chain of custody: *primary custody, secondary custody,* and *tertiary custody.*

Primary Custody. Primary custody refers to the situation in which an LPE maintains custody of the latent print evidence from its discovery through its examination. In this situation, the LPE responds to a crime scene, recovers latent prints from the scene, and transports items of evidence back to the laboratory for latent print development and recovery. The LPE is the first link in the chain of custody for all latent prints generated in the case.

Secondary Custody. Secondary custody refers to the situation in which an LPE receives items of evidence secured by other personnel, such as a crime scene analyst (CSA), who responded to the crime scene. The LPE develops and recovers latent prints from evidence collected and secured by someone else. The LPE starts the chain of custody for the recovered latent prints but does not start the chain of custody for the item of evidence.

Tertiary Custody. Tertiary custody refers to the situation in which an LPE receives latent prints recovered by other personnel. For instance, a CSA develops and recovers all of the latent prints associated with a case and submits the photographs and lifts to an LPE for examination. The LPE does not start the chain of custody for the latent prints and typically does not see the original surfaces from which the latent prints were recovered.

10.1.4 Case-Wide Documentation

Case-wide documentation of friction ridge impressions, regardless of when the LPE enters the chain of custody, must include the significant information and activities related to the impressions. Case-wide documentation should include:

- Information linking the latent prints to the appropriate surface or item of evidence related to the crime scene.

- Condition of the item or surface processed for latent prints (e.g., the ledge was dusty, the tire iron was rusty).

- Development and recovery techniques used to visualize the latent prints.

- Quality controls used during development of the latent prints.

- Chain of custody for the items of evidence.

- Chain of custody for the latent prints.

- Information referencing the exemplars used for comparison.

- Automated Fingerprint Identification System (AFIS) database searches.

- Conclusions of the examination of each latent print.

- Verified conclusions.

- Disposition of evidence (items of evidence and latent prints).

If more than one person is involved in the recovery and examination of the latent prints (e.g., a CSA and an LPE), their combined documentation should detail the history of the latent print from its discovery to the conclusions rendered from the examination.

Different agencies have different criteria for documentation. For instance, some agencies require that examination-quality photographs be taken of all latent prints developed with powders prior to lifting, whereas others do not. Even within an agency, the standard may vary with the circumstances, for instance, with the type of crime. Additionally, the manner in which the documentation resides in the case record varies among agencies. Some agencies use the original lift cards or photographs as part of the case record and place all of the documentation related to the latent prints on the lift cards or photographs. Some agencies use worksheets or forms and may only retain legible copies of the latent prints and known prints in the case record because the original lift cards and photographs must be returned to a submitting agency.

The purpose of this chapter is not to address every possible agency-based documentation criterion and case record requirement. Appropriate documentation for the primary, secondary, and tertiary custody scenarios will be addressed from the perspective of the LPE. The goal is to give generalized information with examples.

The documentation for the three custody scenarios will overlap in some areas. Special considerations and generalities will be noted, and sometimes the reader will be directed to a previous section containing the information.

10.2 Primary Custody Documentation

10.2.1 General Crime Scene Documentation

Documentation of friction ridge impressions begins at the crime scene. General crime scene documentation is accomplished through a combination of photographs, sketches, and notes. The case notes typically begin with:

- The case number.

- The crime scene address.

- The name of the victim.

- The dates and times the LPE arrived at and departed from the scene.

- The name of the LPE.

The LPE should document pertinent information regarding the crime from the first responder. This initial information will guide the LPE to areas or items at the scene that may have latent print evidence. Each page of the crime scene notes should contain the case number, page number, total number of pages (e.g., 2/3 or 2 of 3), and the initials of the LPE.

10.2.2 Collecting Items of Evidence

Documentation should indicate where items of evidence were located in the scene and the condition of the evidence prior to collection. For example, if the victim was assaulted with a knife and a bloody knife (potentially holding latent prints) was found in a hallway, the knife should be documented in its original location, orientation, and condition. Documentation may include sketches, measurements, and photographs of the knife, showing the general location (Figure 10–1), orientation (Figure 10–2), and condition (Figure 10–3). It is recommended that an

FIGURE 10–1

Photograph documenting the general location of evidence.

FIGURE 10–2

Photograph documenting the orientation of evidence.

evidence marker be included with the case number and item number in the orientation and condition photographs. After documentation, the item can be recovered and preserved for additional analysis in the laboratory.

Items recovered from the scene can be placed in a temporary storage container for transport. The temporary storage container should have a label, either on the container or inside the container, that contains the case number, item number, and date and time of recovery. The LPE should have some method for ensuring that all evidence taken from the scene is protected from loss or deterioration. Packaging, sealing, and labeling typically occur after the evidence has been examined by the LPE at the laboratory or before it is submitted to other personnel (e.g., an evidence control section for entry into an electronic evidence tracking system).

10.2.3 Latent Print Development and Recovery on Scene

Latent prints that are of sufficient value for recovery must be documented. When processing a crime scene or an item of evidence, it may be difficult to determine whether the latent print contains sufficient quality and quantity of detail (i.e., of value) for comparison. The LPE generally cannot perform a critical analysis until the photographs and lifts are examined in the proper setting at the laboratory. Latent prints that are of sufficient value may later be deemed insufficient for comparison. This is to be expected in a conservative approach that ensures all possible evidence is preserved.

10.2.3.1 Documenting the Surface Prior to Processing. If not already annotated in the general crime scene documentation (photos, sketches, or notes), the LPE should document the areas of the scene to be processed for latent

FIGURE 10-3

Photograph documenting the condition of evidence.

FIGURE 10-4

Photograph documenting the exterior of a patio door.

prints prior to applying latent print development techniques. For example, if a patio door was the point of entry, its original orientation and condition (e.g., opened, closed, damaged, dusty) should be documented. Figure 10–4 demonstrates photo documentation of the exterior of a patio door.

10.2.3.2 Designating and Labeling Latent Prints on the Surface. There are many administrative ways to designate latent prints on a surface or item. The key is to make sure that the LPE can reconstruct the location and orientation of the latent prints recovered. In addition to referencing the surface or item from which the latent print was recovered, the location and orientation of a latent print may provide the following valuable information:

(1) The manner in which a surface or item was touched.

(2) An explanation for any distortion in the latent print.

(3) The anatomical source of the latent print (e.g., which area of the hand touched the surface).

One method of designation is to choose a sequential numbering or lettering system (e.g., L1, L2, L3, etc.). The notes, sketches, photographs, and lifts reference each latent print by its designator. Often, there are multiple latent prints in a small area that are photographed or lifted together. In these instances, the designator may actually refer to two or more latent prints.

Depending on agency policy, if there is more than one suitable latent print on a lift or photograph, each suitable latent print may be attributed a subdesignator. For example, if L2 has three impressions, they may be designated A, B, and C. L2A would reference print A on photograph (or lift) L2.

The LPE may choose to label the latent prints on the surface as part of the photographic documentation. Labeling latent prints can be accomplished two ways: marking directly on the surface or using a label. The nature of the surface or agency policy may dictate how latent prints are labeled.

FIGURE 10–5

Location of patent print L1.

10.2.3.3 Patent Prints. The LPE should first examine surfaces at the scene for visible impressions (patent prints). The surfaces that were examined and the results of the examination should be documented. Returning to the patio door in Figure 10–4, if there were no impressions of sufficient value for recovery, it should be noted (e.g., *"Visual inspection: No patent prints of value were noted on the interior or exterior of the patio door"*). If there were no impressions, it should be noted (e.g., *"Visual inspection: No patent prints were visible on the interior or exterior of the patio door"*).

10.2.3.4 Location and Orientation of Patent Prints. If there are patent prints of sufficient value for recovery, they should be assigned designators and their location and orientation documented through photography, sketches, or notes. A sample note may say, *"Visual inspection: L1 on exterior glass of patio door."* A location photograph containing a label (Figure 10–5) is an effective method to document the location of the patent print.

10.2.3.5 Examination-Quality Photographs. Because patent prints must be recovered through photography, it is imperative to be able to establish the dimensions or scale for the photographs. This is normally accomplished by including a scale in the photograph. Notes should reflect that examination-quality photographs were taken and include the designator for each print photographed.

10.2.3.6 Development Techniques. The LPE should document which surfaces were processed, which technique(s) were applied, and the results. For example, the notes may reflect, *"Kitchen counter top was processed with black powder; no latent prints of value developed."*

Returning to the patio door in Figure 10–4, if the LPE decides to use powder to process the door, his or her notes should reflect the results of the processing and display the designator of any latent prints photographed or lifted. The LPE may use a combination of notes, sketches, and photography to document the location and orientation of the designated latent prints. The LPE may note, *"Patio door processed with black powder: L1 developed further; L2 developed on exterior of glass; L3 developed on exterior door knob."* The LPE should note whether any examination-quality images were taken and whether lifts were made; for example, *"L1, L2, and L3 photographed and lifted after development with black powder."* Figures 10–6 and 10–7 demonstrate the photographic documentation of the location of developed latent prints.

For each processing technique applied at the scene, the documentation should include:

- The development technique applied.

- The surfaces or items to which the technique was applied.

- An indication of whether no latent prints, no latent prints of value, or latent prints of value were developed.

- The location and orientation of the developed latent prints.

- The method of recovery.

10.2.4 Marking Photographs and Lifts

The photographs and lifts recovered from the scene must be marked in a manner that reflects the origin of the

Documentation of Friction Ridge Impressions: From the Scene to the Conclusion **CHAPTER 10**

FIGURE 10–6

Location of developed latent prints L1, L2, and L3.

FIGURE 10–7

Location of developed latent print L3.

latent print lift or photograph. The lift or photograph should include:

- The case number.
- The date recovered.
- The address of the investigation.
- The surface or item from which the latent print was obtained.
- The name or a unique marking of the LPE (e.g., initials).
- The development technique (if a photograph).
- The latent designator.

Figure 10–8 is an example of a latent lift card containing the recommended information. The "up" designation indicates the orientation of the latent prints to the surface.

10.2.5 Exemplars Prepared by the Latent Print Examiner

It is sometimes necessary for the LPE to prepare known prints of certain individuals connected to the scene, typically victims or witnesses. Regardless of how the exemplars are recorded, they should bear:

- The name of the donor.
- An identifier for the donor (e.g., date of birth).
- The donor's signature.
- The area of friction ridge skin recorded (e.g., left hand, right hand, or finger name or number).
- The case number, the date, and the name (and signature or initials) of the LPE.

FIGURE 10–8

Annotated lift card.

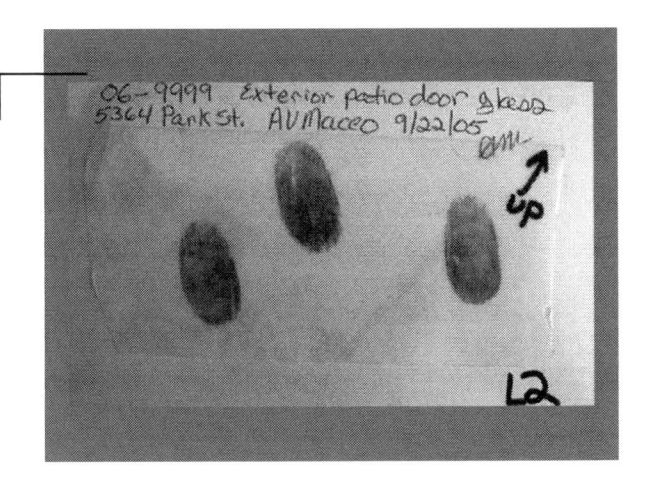

FIGURE 10–9

Documentation of known prints taken at the scene.

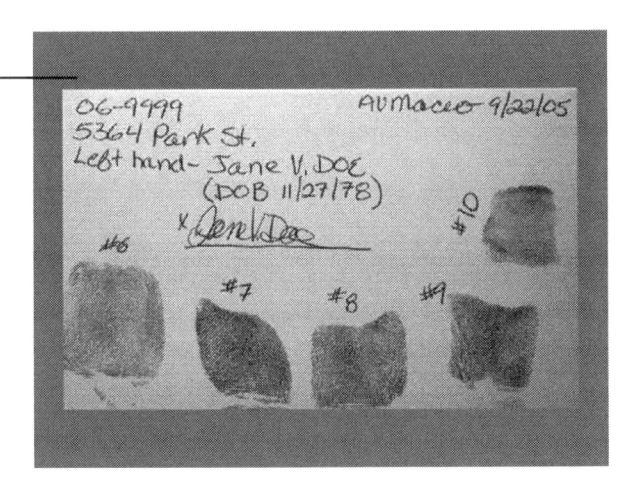

At the completion of the case, the LPE may retain the exemplars in the case record. Figure 10–9 is an example of known prints taken from the left hand of the victim at the scene.

10.2.6 Latent Print Development on Items of Evidence

Completion of the crime scene response often segues into latent print processing of critical items of evidence at the laboratory. The LPE must be cognizant of the presence of additional types of evidence, such as DNA, trace evidence, or indented writing on an item. In some laboratories, the LPE is responsible for the documentation and collection of the additional evidence prior to latent print processing. In other laboratories, the LPE may need to coordinate with analysts from other sections to document and collect the additional evidence. In either case, the LPE should note who evaluated the item, whether any samples were collected, and the disposition of the collected samples.

10.2.6.1 General Notes. Many agencies use worksheets or free-form notes to document the latent print development activities and observations by the LPE. The date(s) of the activities should be recorded, and each page of the notes should contain the case number, page number, total number of pages, and the initials of the LPE. The latent print processing notes generated at the lab may be a continuation of the notes started at the crime scene or may be a separate set of notes. Separation of the notes depends on whether the agency reports the crime scene response in a separate report from that for the latent print development and examination at the laboratory.

10.2.6.2 Description and Condition of the Evidence. The notes typically begin with the item number and description of the evidence (e.g., *"Item 1: J. P. Schmenckels International kitchen knife"*). Items that have serial numbers, such as firearms, should contain the serial number in the description.

FIGURE 10–10
Location and orientation of L4.

FIGURE 10–11
Examination-quality photograph of L4 after CA processing.

The LPE should indicate the condition of the item. The condition may include whether a surface is smooth or textured and whether the item is dusty, rusty, or contains any residue.

10.2.6.3 Initial Observations. Prior to using any development techniques, the item should be carefully examined for the presence of any patent impressions. If there are no impressions of value noted during the initial observations, the notes should reflect that no patent prints or no patent prints of value were observed.

If patent impressions of value are present, their location and orientation on the item should be documented (through notes, sketches, or photographs) and an examination-quality photograph should be taken. Once again, the LPE must establish the scale for the examination-quality photographs.

10.2.6.4 Latent Print Development and Recovery. Once the initial observations are complete, the LPE must select and determine the sequence of development techniques appropriate for the item. The notes should reflect the techniques used and the observations of the LPE after each technique. In some laboratories, the LPE may also need to document the lot numbers of the chemicals used and the results of any controls processed concurrently with the evidence.

Item 1, the knife mentioned above that was recovered from the crime scene, was processed with cyanoacrylate (CA) and a fluorescent dye stain (RAM). Figure 10–10 is photographic documentation of the location and orientation of latent print L4 developed on the knife after CA processing. Figure 10–11 is an examination-quality photograph of L4 after CA processing. Figure 10–12 is an examination-quality photograph of L4 after RAM processing. The notes for Item 1 may include the following:

Item 1: J. P. Schmenckels International kitchen knife

Visual: Possible blood on blade of knife; sample of blood from right side of blade obtained and retained by DNA Analyst Watson. Handle has slightly rough surface.

CHAPTER 10 Documentation of Friction Ridge Impressions: From the Scene to the Conclusion

FIGURE 10–12

Examination-quality photograph of L4 after RAM processing.

No patent prints of value visible on the blade; no patent prints visible on handle.

CA: Photo L4 on left side of blade near handle; no latent prints of value developed on handle.

RAM: Re-photo L4; no additional latent prints of value developed on blade; no latent prints of value developed on handle.

10.2.6.5 Marking Items of Evidence. Once processing of the items collected from the crime scene is complete, each item of evidence should be marked for identification prior to final packaging and sealing (ASCLD/LAB, 2005, p 20). The LPE may write the case number and item number directly on the item to serve as a unique identifier. The knife in Figure 10–10 could be marked "06-9999/1" indicating case number 06-9999 and item number 1. The manner in which evidence is marked should be detailed in the technical or procedural manual of the LPE's agency.

If the item is too small or writing directly on the item will alter or destroy any evidentiary value, the item may be placed inside a container. The container should then be marked with the unique identifier (ASCLD/LAB, 2005, p 21). For example, if a bullet casing was taken from the scene, the casing could be placed in an envelope that is marked with a unique identifier (e.g., case number and item number). The casing, inside the marked envelope, can then undergo final packaging and sealing.

10.2.6.6 Disposition of the Evidence. Once the evidence has been properly packaged and sealed, the LPE should document its final disposition. The LPE should document the date the evidence was released and to whom or where the evidence was released. For some agencies, the evidence is placed in long-term storage by the LPE. For other agencies, the LPE releases the evidence to other personnel responsible for storing the evidence.

10.2.6.7 Marking Photographs and Lifts. If latent prints were recovered from evidence processed at the laboratory by the LPE, the photographs and lifts should contain the same information as those recovered from the crime scene:

- The case number.
- The date recovered.
- The address of the scene (may be omitted because the address is the laboratory).
- The surface or item from which the latent print was obtained.
- The name and a unique marking of the LPE.
- The development technique (if a photograph).
- The latent designator.

Figure 10–13 is an example of a labeled photograph.

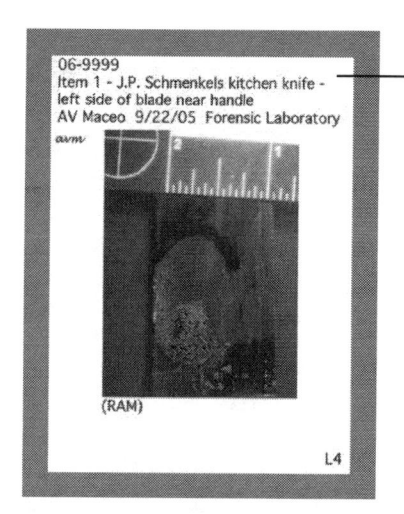

FIGURE 10–13

Labeled photograph of L4.

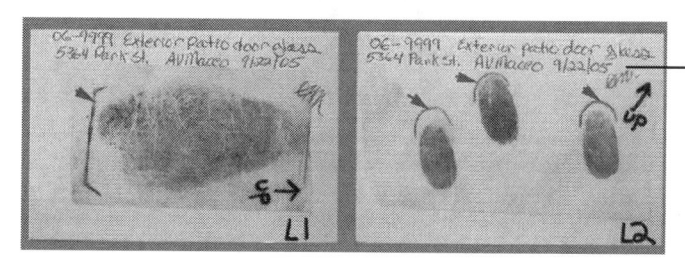

FIGURE 10–14

Analysis notes documented on lift cards L1 and L2. Blue arrows point to analysis symbols.

10.2.7 Examination of Friction Ridge Impressions

10.2.7.1 General Notes. After all of the latent prints associated with a case have been properly labeled, the LPE enters the examination phase: analysis, comparison, evaluation, and verification (ACE-V) of the latent prints. The level of documentation can vary among agencies; however, the key is to make sure the LPE indicates:

- Which latent prints are suitable for comparison.
- The source of known prints to be compared.
- The results of the comparisons.
- Who verified any conclusions.

10.2.7.2 Elements of Analysis. The elements to be considered in the analysis of friction ridge impressions should be detailed in the technical or operational manual for the laboratory. Elements of the analysis should include (SWGFAST, 2002, pp 2–3):

- The existence and clarity of level-one, level-two, and level-three detail.

- The possible anatomical source.
- The factors influencing the clarity of the impressions.

The quality of level-one, level-two, and level-three detail is influenced by the following factors: pressure distortion, deposition pressure, development medium, matrix, and substrate (Ashbaugh, 1999, p 109).

Minimal Documentation of Analysis. Documentation of analysis may be minimal, using symbols to mark directly on the lift cards and photographs. This is particularly effective when the original lifts or photographs are part of the case record. If symbols are used to document the analysis, the proper use and meaning of the symbols should be detailed in the technical or operational manual. Figure 10–14 is an example of analysis notes documented directly onto lift cards L1 and L2; the blue arrows point to the analysis symbols used by the LPE.

If L1 and L2 are part of the case record, they should contain all of the basic elements of the analysis. L1 and L2 are black powder lifts (that is, black powder is the developmental medium) and indicate the location from which the latent prints were recovered (substrate). The latent prints deemed suitable for comparison are marked with symbols. The

CHAPTER 10 Documentation of Friction Ridge Impressions: From the Scene to the Conclusion

FIGURE 10–15

Latent print L2A containing analysis annotations.

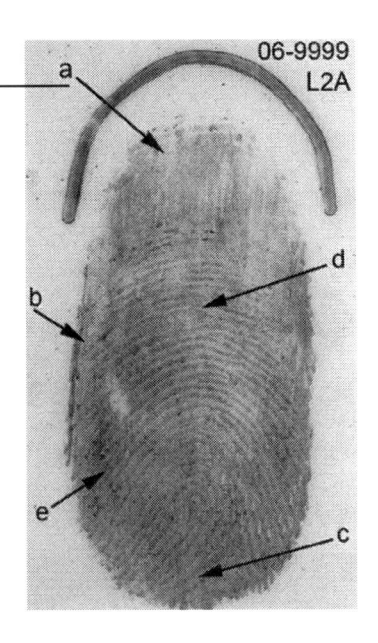

symbols also indicate the anatomical source and orientation of each impression. L1 has a bracket delineating the base of a palm impression. L2 has an arch over the top of each finger impression. It is understood that the LPE considered all of the elements of analysis and factors of quality detailed in the technical or operational manual in order to make the determination of suitability for comparison.

Expanded Documentation of Analysis. Worksheets or free-form notes may be used to document the analysis. The notes must contain enough detail to discern which photograph or lift was examined and the results of the analysis of the latent prints. The amount of information to be included on the worksheets or notes should be outlined in an agency's technical or procedural manual.

If the original lifts or photographs are not retained as part of the case record, the LPE needs to be able to connect which latent prints were suitable for comparison on each latent lift and photograph. Without the original or legible reproductions of the original latent lifts and photographs in the case record, this connection would not be possible. The notes for L1 and L2 in Figure 10–14 may be as follows:

L1–Exterior patio door glass

Analysis:

Black powder lift: One palm impression suitable for comparison, appears to be a left hypothenar, normal matrix, average deposition pressure, no discernible pressure distortion.

L2–Exterior patio door glass

Analysis:

Black powder lift: Three finger impressions suitable for comparison (A, B, & C) are consistent with simultaneous #7, #8, & #9* fingers, normal matrix, average deposition pressure, pressure distortion caused by apparent downward movement of fingers on surface.

Expanded documentation of the analysis of a complex impression may include photographic enlargements of the impression and detailed notes regarding all of the elements of analysis and factors of quality. Figure 10–15 is an image of a latent print from lift L2 in Figure 10–14. The latent print in Figure 10–15 is referred to as L2A (latent print A from lift L2).

Expanded documentation of the analysis of latent print L2A in Figure 10-15 may include the marked photographic enlargement and the following notes:

L2–Exterior patio door glass

Analysis:

Black powder lift: Three finger impressions suitable for comparison (A, B, & C) are consistent with simultaneous #7, #8, & #9 fingers.

---

* #1 is right thumb, and #10 is left little finger.

10–14

L2A analysis:

Substrate: The appearance of the latent lift is consistent with the indicated substrate glass from a patio door.

Anatomical aspect: Based on adjacent impressions, L2A is consistent with an impression of a left index finger.

Matrix: Consistent with normal residue.

Deposition pressure: Average deposition pressure across the entire impression, possibly a bit lighter toward the tip of the finger.

Pressure distortion: Caused by apparent downward movement of fingers on surface. Indicators of pressure distortion are marked in the photographic enlargement as a, b, c, d, and e. The original touch of the finger is indicated as "a". As the finger slid across the surface, the detail in this area was obliterated. The direction of travel is noted in the striations present in the impression; one such striation is marked "b". Another indication of pressure distortion is the change in furrow width across the impression. The furrows are widest at the base of impression "c" (also an indication of downward movement). The furrows are slightly narrowed toward the top of impression "d" and are barely discernible on the left side of impression "e".

Level One: Good clarity; small count, left-slant loop; approximately 4 ridges from delta to core.

Level Two: Good clarity overall—ridge paths discernible through most of the impression; some become unclear along the edges of the impression. Ridge paths are difficult to follow just above the core of the impression.

Level Three: Areas of good, fair, and poor quality throughout the impression.

Whether minimal or expanded, the case record should reflect which latent lifts and photographs were analyzed, who analyzed the latent prints and photographs, and the results of the analysis. The amount of detail in the documentation of the analysis will be dependent on the requirements outlined in the applicable technical or operational manual.

10.2.7.3 Comparison. The next phase of the examination involves the comparison of the unknown friction ridge impressions (latent or patent prints) to the exemplars. The LPE must have some means to document the source of the known prints compared and the evaluation of each comparison. The exact method by which the exemplars are documented should be detailed in the technical or operational manual.

At a minimum, the case record should indicate the name and an identifier for each source of exemplars compared. This is sometimes annotated in a list in the case notes or on the envelope or packet containing the latent lifts and photographs. For example, some agencies may place all latent prints developed by the LPE in a preprinted envelope. The envelope and its contents are considered part of the case record. The exterior of the envelope typically contains the basic case information and may include a section that lists the names and identifiers of the exemplars compared. The names and identifiers of the exemplars may also be listed in the case notes.

Original or legible copies of the exemplars to be compared should be maintained with the case record or be readily available. This is particularly critical for exemplars associated with one or more of the latent prints (i.e., used to determine an individualization). The original or legible copies of the exemplars may be included in the case notes or placed in the envelope with the latent lifts and photographs. The LPE should also indicate in the case record if additional or better quality exemplars are needed from any of the individuals compared.

The LPE should document which, if any, latent prints were searched through AFIS. Documentation should be sufficient to indicate:

- Which latent prints were searched.
- Which AFIS databases were searched.
- The date(s) the searches were completed.
- Who launched the search.
- Who evaluated the results.

10.2.7.4 Evaluation. The LPE should document the conclusion of each comparison conducted. This documentation may be minimal or quite detailed, depending on the agency's requirements.

Minimum Documentation of Evaluation. Minimum documentation for individualizations should include annotation on the notes, lifts, or photographs with the following:

- The name and identifier of the source of the impression.
- The anatomical source (e.g., which finger or palm).

FIGURE 10–16

Minimum documentation of individualizations annotated on lift L2.

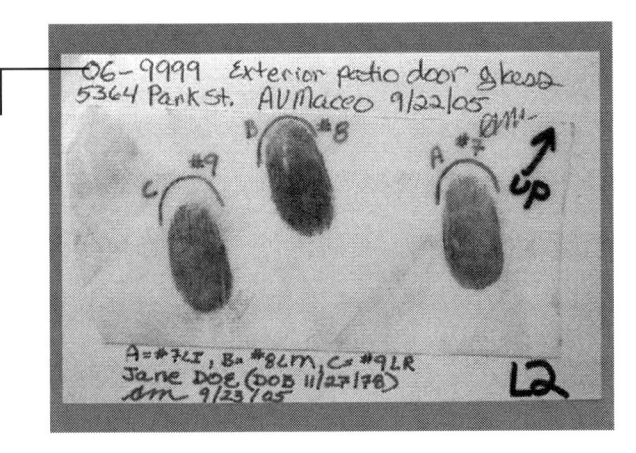

- The identifier (e.g., initials) of the LPE.
- The date the conclusion was rendered.

Figure 10–16 is an example of minimum documentation of individualizations on lift L2.

In lieu of, or in addition to, making the lift or photograph, comparisons may be documented in the notes as follows:

John DOE (ID# 123456): negative 9/22/05.

Susana SMITH (ID# 987654): negative 9/22/05.

Jane DOE (DOB 11/27/78): L2A = #7 LI, L2B = #8 LM, L2C = #9 LR, 9/23/05.

Under minimum documentation, impressions that are compared but not individualized are typically documented in a default manner without markings. In other words, the individualizations are annotated and, by default, all other comparison results (exclusion and inconclusive) in the case are not. Frequently, wherever the LPE lists the names and identifiers of the sources of the exemplars, there is a reference as to whether the person was identified. As in Figure 10–16, the notes, lifts, and photographs containing the annotations are the case documentation by which latent prints were associated with the exemplars. If there are no associations indicated on the lift or photograph, all persons listed were compared with negative results, as recorded in the notes.

Expanded Documentation of Evaluation. The case notes (worksheets or free-form notes) may also contain expanded documentation of the conclusions. The notes must document the conclusion of the comparison of each latent print with each exemplar. The information included on the worksheets or notes should be outlined in the technical or procedural manual. If the original lifts or photographs are not retained as part of the case record, the LPE should retain legible reproductions of the original latent lifts and photographs in the case record.

Case note documentation of the comparison of L2 with the exemplars of three individuals may be as follows:

L2–Exterior patio door glass

Analysis:

Black powder lift: Three finger impressions suitable for comparison (A, B, & C) are consistent with simultaneous #7, #8, & #9 fingers, normal matrix, average deposition pressure, pressure distortion caused by apparent downward movement of fingers on surface.

Expanded documentation of an individualization may include enlargements demonstrating a subset of the data used to support the LPE's conclusions. Figure 10–17 is an example of an enlargement demonstrating a limited portion of the level-one, level-two, and level-three detail of a different comparison to support an individualization.

Exemplars Compared and Conclusions:

John DOE (ID# 123456): negative 9/22/05.

Susana SMITH (ID# 987654): negative 9/22/05.

Jane DOE (DOB 11/27/78): L2A = #7 LI, L2B = #8 LM, L2C = #9 LR, 9/23/05.

FIGURE 10-17

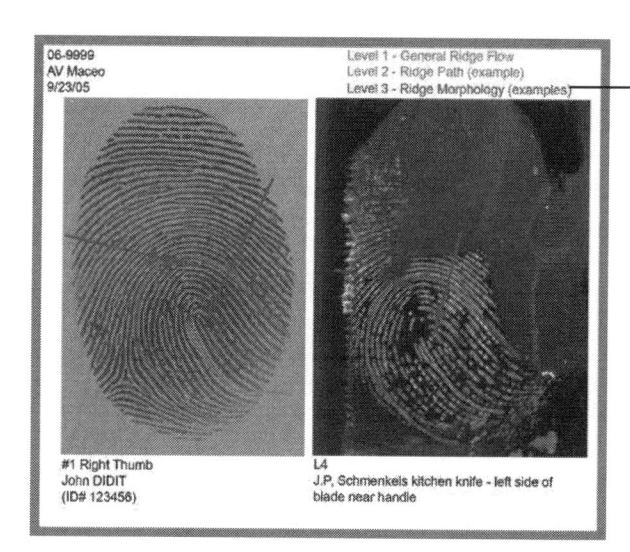

Enlargements of L4 and exemplar, demonstrating subset of detail used to conclude individualization.

Whether minimal or expanded, the goal of documentation is to ensure that the LPE or a person reviewing the case can discern:

- Which latent prints are suitable for comparison.
- The source of the exemplars compared to the suitable latent prints.
- The conclusions reached from each comparison.

The activities and results of the examination by the LPE should be clear and understandable.

10.2.7.5 Verification. Verification of any conclusions should be documented in the case record. The technical or procedural manual should indicate which conclusions must be verified and how the verification is documented. (Instances where blind verification is required may require special documentation procedures to preclude the verifier from knowing the original examiner's results.) For some agencies, only the individualizations are verified; for other agencies, all conclusions are verified. Sometimes, verification of all conclusions is dependent on certain criteria, such as the type of case.

The person verifying the conclusions should place his or her personal marking and date in the case record. The personal marking and date may go on each lift containing verified conclusions, on the envelope containing the latent prints, or in the case notes.

10.2.7.6 Disposition of Lifts and Photographs. The LPE should indicate the disposition of the latent lifts and photographs after the examination is complete. In some agencies, it is only necessary to indicate if the latent lifts and photographs are not secured in the normal manner. For instance, it may be standard procedure that the latent prints are stored in a secured file cabinet and that the LPE must indicate on the envelope the date that the envelope was secured in the file cabinet. It may also be standard procedure that digital images are stored on a CD in the case file or in an image management database. As long as the standard procedures are followed, no notations are required.

If the original latent lifts and photographs are released to a submitting agency, there should be documentation in the case record as to when the latent prints were released and to whom the latent prints were released.

10.3 Secondary Custody Documentation

11.3.1 Latent Print Development on Items of Evidence

When an LPE receives an item of evidence recovered from a crime scene by other personnel (e.g., a crime scene analyst), additional documentation is needed concerning the chain of custody for the evidence and the packaging of the evidence.

General notes and documentation regarding the description and condition of the evidence, initial observations, latent print development and recovery, marking items of evidence, disposition of evidence, and marking photographs and lifts is detailed in section 10.2.6, Latent Print Development on Items of Evidence.

10.3.1.1 Chain of Custody. The LPE should indicate the date the items were received and from whom. The LPE may receive the item directly from responding personnel or from a secured storage facility.

10.3.1.2 Packaging of the Evidence. The LPE should indicate whether the items were packaged and sealed properly.

For example, the notes may reflect that Items 6, 7, and 8 were received in a sealed brown paper bag. The LPE should also note whether there is any internal packaging. The notes may contain the information as follows:

> Sealed brown paper bag received from vault 6/2/06 containing Items 6, 7, and 8. Inside sealed brown paper bag: Item 7 in a manila envelope and Item 8 in a plastic vial; no inner packaging for Item 6.

There are times when an LPE may receive evidence prior to final packaging by the personnel who responded to the scene. This may occur when there is concern that packaging may destroy the latent print evidence. In this circumstance, the LPE should document who delivered the evidence and the date and condition in which the evidence was delivered. After the LPE has completed the latent print development and recovery, the item should undergo final packaging and sealing. The LPE may package and seal the evidence, or the evidence may be returned to the person who initially recovered the item from the scene. Either circumstance must be indicated in the notes.

10.3.2 Examination of Friction Ridge Impressions

The examination of the friction ridge impressions recovered by the LPE from items of evidence submitted by other personnel follows the same documentation discussed in section 10.2.7, Examination of Friction Ridge Impressions.

10.4 Tertiary Custody Documentation

When an LPE receives photographs and lifts of latent prints recovered by other personnel (e.g., a crime scene analyst), additional documentation is necessary to establish the chain of custody for the evidence.

10.4.1 Chain of Custody

Latent lifts and photographs are considered evidence and should be properly packaged and have a chain of custody. The LPE should document all of the pertinent information:

- The case number.
- The address.
- Who recovered the latent prints. The date the latent prints were recovered.
- An inventory of what was received (e.g., the number of lifts, photographs, any sketches or notes, and any elimination prints submitted).

10.4.2 Marking Lifts and Photographs With a Unique Identifier

Each latent lift and photograph should be marked with a unique identifier. The submitted latent lifts and photographs should already bear the case number, which should be annotated on each photograph and lift by the person who recovered the latent prints. The LPE may choose to include a sequential alphabetical or numerical designator to serve as the unique identifier for each lift and photograph. The LPE's initials followed by a sequential number is an effective method for marking the photographs and lifts (e.g., avm 1, avm 2, avm 3, etc.).

It is sometimes helpful to have one system of labeling latent prints developed by the LPE (L1, L2, L3, etc.) and another system of labeling latent prints submitted by other personnel (dbf 1, dbf 2, dbf 3, etc.). Within one case, the LPE may be responsible for examining latent prints he or she recovered, and the LPE may be responsible for examining latent prints recovered by other personnel. A different labeling system readily distinguishes the two in the case record.

10.4.3 Examination of Friction Ridge Impressions

After documenting the chain of custody and placing a unique identifier on the lifts and photographs, the examination of the latent prints proceeds. The documentation of examination (analysis, comparison, evaluation, and verification) of the friction ridge impressions is discussed in section 10.2.7, Examination of Friction Ridge Impressions.

10.5 Conclusion

In order to properly review a case record, the case record should contain sufficient information to illuminate the activities and the results of any conclusions. Documentation of friction ridge impressions begins at the crime scene. A surface or item of evidence should be documented at the scene. The location and orientation of any latent prints developed at the scene should be documented in a manner that connects the latent print to the original surface.

Subsequent development of latent prints on items recovered from the scene should demonstrate the location and orientation of any latent prints developed on the item.

Examination of the recovered latent prints should contain sufficient information that a person reviewing the case record can discern:

- The origin of the latent prints.
- Which latent prints are of sufficient value for comparison.

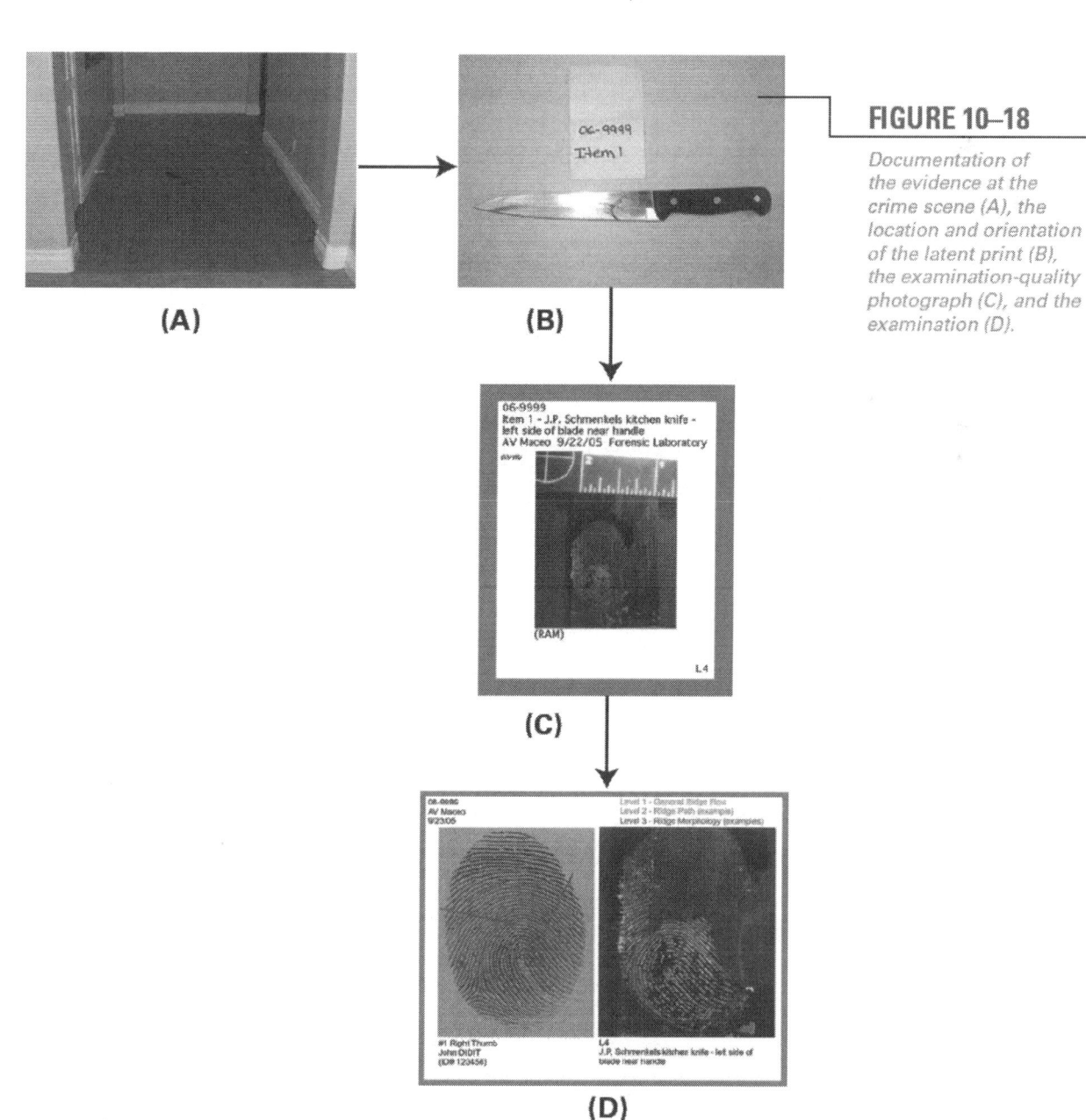

FIGURE 10–18

Documentation of the evidence at the crime scene (A), the location and orientation of the latent print (B), the examination-quality photograph (C), and the examination (D).

- The donor of the exemplars compared to the latent prints.
- The conclusions reached.

Figure 10–18 is an example of how photography may be used to connect all of the elements of documentation for one case.

Latent print examiners should follow the policies and procedures outlined in the technical or operational manual of their agency. It is important that these policies and procedures follow sound scientific practices and are sufficiently detailed to permit an accurate review of the case record. Proper documentation is often the critical component in the admissibility of the evidence.

10.6 Reviewers

The reviewers critiquing this chapter were Leonard G. Butt, Brent T. Cutro, Sr., Robert J. Garrett, and Michael Perkins.

10.7 References

American Society of Crime Laboratory Directors/Laboratory Accreditation Board (ASCLD/LAB). *ASCLD/LAB Manual;* American Society of Crime Laboratory Directors/Laboratory Accreditation Board: Garner, NC, 2005.

Ashbaugh, D. R. *Quantitative-Qualitative Friction Ridge Analysis: An Introduction to Basic and Advanced Ridgeology;* CRC Press: Boca Raton, FL, 1999.

Scientific Working Group on Friction Ridge Analysis, Study and Technology (SWGFAST). *Friction Ridge Examination Methodology for Latent Print Examiners;* Scientific Working Group on Friction Ridge Analysis, Study and Technology, 2002.

CHAPTER 11

EQUIPMENT

Julieanne Perez-Avila

CONTENTS

- 3 11.1 Introduction
- 3 11.2 Crime Scene Equipment
- 7 11.3 Laboratory Equipment
- 12 11.4 Conclusion
- 12 11.5 Credits and Reviewers
- 12 11.6 References
- 13 11.7 Equipment Suppliers

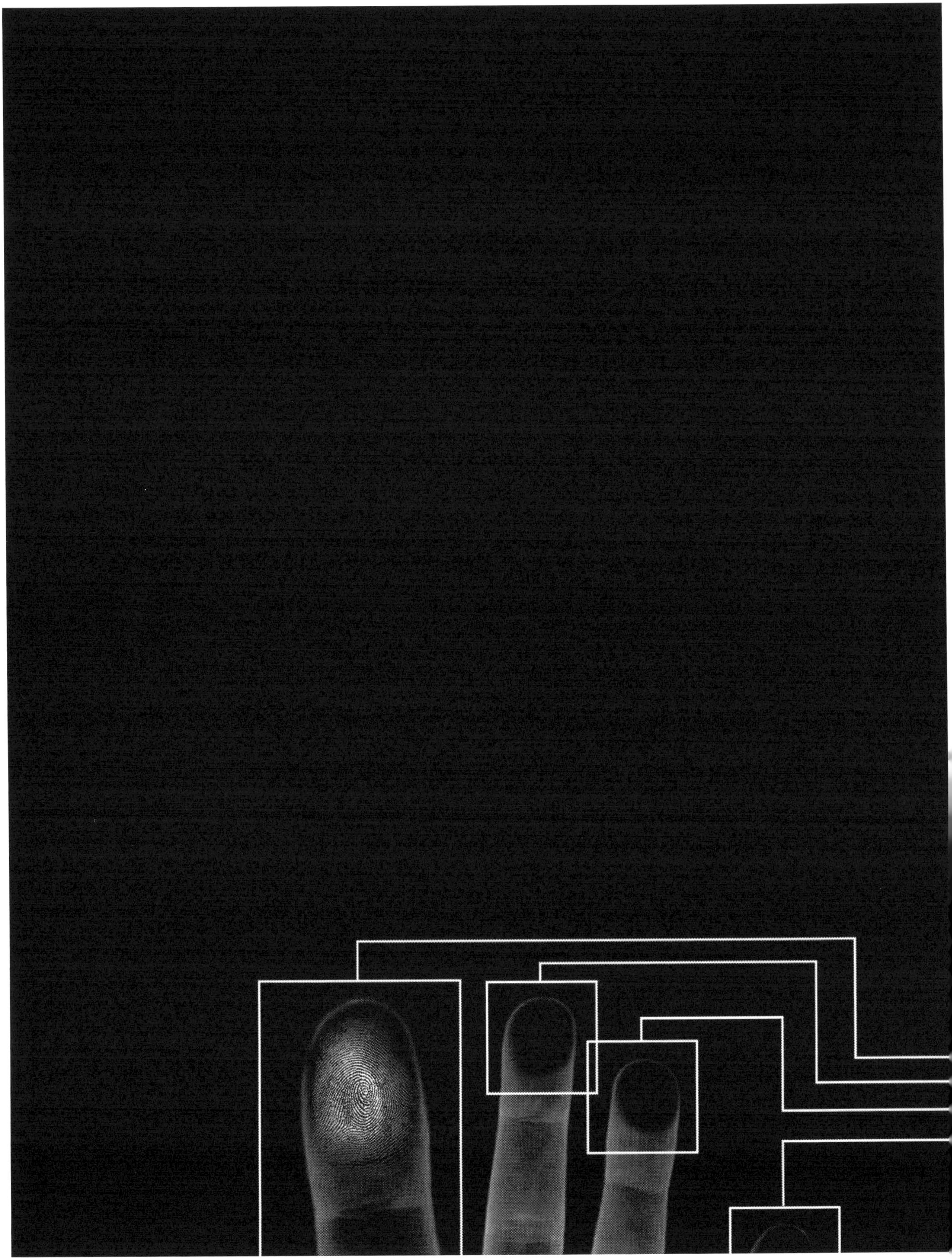

CHAPTER 11

EQUIPMENT

Julieanne Perez-Avila

11.1 Introduction

Fingerprints, although they may be found 50 years after being deposited on a piece of paper, are at the same time very fragile and easily destroyed. The arrival of a fingerprint technician at a crime scene marks a critical point in an investigation. It is what he or she decides to do, even unwittingly, that may affect the success or failure of fingerprint evidence collection. A technician must be knowledgeable about the equipment that is available both in the field and in the laboratory. With this knowledge, the technician will be able to select the best method for developing and preserving a print.

This chapter focuses on equipment that can be used easily in the field and equipment that would be found in the laboratory setting. There will, of course, be some overlap between the crime scene and laboratory equipment.

11.2 Crime Scene Equipment

11.2.1 Light Sources

A light source may include any item that produces electromagnetic radiation of any wavelength (from ultraviolet to infrared). Light sources are indispensable to a crime scene responder and a variety of them are useful.

11.2.1.1 Flashlight. A flashlight is an important item that should be in every fingerprint kit. It should be of good quality and produce a strong, even light. A flashlight is typically handheld, lightweight, and powered with batteries. It can be held at an angle to any surface that is being examined.

11.2.1.2 Forensic Light Sources. In the early 1980s, a modified xenon arc lamp* was developed by the Forensic Science Research Unit of Australia, the "Quasar" light source was developed by the Scientific Research Branch of

---

* The xenon arc lamp was introduced as an alternative to lasers and was commonly referred to as an *alternate light source* or ALS. Later, alternate light sources became known as *forensic light sources*.

the United Kingdom's Home Office, and the "Lumaprint" light was developed by the National Research Council of Canada. Currently, there are many types of forensic light sources (Lee and Gaensslen, 2001, pp 152–153). Many delivery systems using diffraction gratings or filters with various lamps provide a variety of configurations and models. In more recent years, several forensic light sources have been designed to use light-emitting diodes instead of lamps.

The principle for all forensic light sources is basically the same: a high-powered lamp produces a white light consisting of a wide range of wavelengths. An investigator selects certain wavelengths of light through the use of a filter or a diffraction grating. The selected wavelengths pass through an aperture to produce a beam, or the light is directed through the use of an optical device (e.g., fiber optics, liquid light guides). This ability to select various wavelengths can be a benefit not found in most lasers. (For more on lasers, see section 11.3.3.)

The intensity of a forensic light source (FLS) is not as strong as a laser; however, an FLS does have the benefit of being less expensive and more easily transported than a laser (Wilkinson and Watkin, 1994, pp 632–651; Fisher, 1993, p 111).

Forensic light sources are used by shining the light over the evidence or room to help investigators detect latent prints. Contaminants in, and constituents of, a latent print will sometimes cause an inherent luminescence when exposed to certain wavelengths. Certain chemicals and powders can also be used to make latent prints visible. Not all substances become visible at the same wavelength (Fisher, 1993, p 111).

Investigators should wear goggles with filters when using any FLS. The type of goggle needed depends on the type of light used (Masters, 1995, pp 133–142).

11.2.2 Fingerprint Powder Applicators

11.2.2.1 Traditional Fingerprint Powder Applicators. Fingerprint powder applicators come in many shapes, sizes, and fiber components. They may be made from camel hair, squirrel hair, goat hair, horse hair, feathers, synthetic or natural fibers, carbon filaments, or fiberglass. These brushes are used to lightly apply powder to a surface; soft brushes reduce the risk of damaging the fragile print (Fisher, 1993, pp 101–104).

11.2.2.2 Magnetic Fingerprint Powder Applicators. The magnetic brush, or *magna brush,* was developed by Herbert MacDonell in 1961 (MacDonell, 1961, p 7). Since his early design, many variations have been manufactured (Figure 11–1), from large wide-headed applicators to applicators that have a plastic disposable cover for use in situations where potentially hazardous material could contaminate an application (James, Pounds, and Wilshire, 1992, pp 531–542; Lightning Powder Company, 1999, p 3). Most have a similar design: a magnetized steel rod within a nonmagnetic case. The magnetic rod is moveable and can be retracted within the case. When the rod is not retracted, the head of the applicator is magnetized.

To use the magnetic applicator, it is lowered into the magnetic powder. The magnet allows the fingerprint powder to cling to the end of the applicator. The powder that adheres to the applicator will create a bristlelike brush consisting of only powder. This very soft brush is then carefully brushed

FIGURE 11–1

Fingerprint powder applicators.

across the desired surface. The ends of the powder will adhere to the constituents of the latent print and make the print visible. Care should be exercised to touch only the ends of the suspended powder, not the applicator itself, to the surface being processed. This provides a very delicate brush with minimal abrasion to fragile prints.

Excess powder can be removed by first retracting the magnetic rod and releasing the unused powder from the applicator back into the powder jar (or appropriate disposal container, if the powder has become contaminated) and then passing the applicator over the area again to allow any excess powder to re-adhere to the magnet.

11.2.3 Latent Print Backing Cards and Lifting Materials

11.2.3.1 Latent Print Backing Cards. Latent print backing cards are used for recording prints that have been lifted with tape. They typically have a glossy side and a non-glossy side and come in either white or black. The card is usually preprinted with areas for information about the lift (date, case number, location, who made the lift, etc.) and space where a sketch may be recorded.

11.2.3.2 Lifting Tape and Hinge Lifters. Over the years, different types of tapes to lift latent prints have been developed. Aside from the standard clear and frosted tapes, there is a polyethylene tape that has some stretch to it, allowing for lifts to be more easily taken from curved surfaces. Tapes that are thicker than the clear and frosted tapes were developed to conform better to textured surfaces, allowing for more of the print to be lifted. Adhesive tape from a roll may be torn or cut to any length and then affixed to the developed print. Care should be exercised to remove a suitable length of tape in one continuous motion to avoid lines that are created by intermittent stops during the removal of the tape from the roll. (Many examiners prefer not to detach the piece of tape from the roll but instead use the roll as a secure handle for the tape.)

After an item has been processed with powder, the edge of the lifting device (e.g., end of the tape) is pressed onto the surface adjacent to the latent print and the device is carefully smoothed over the print. The tape is then peeled off and placed on a backing card of contrasting color to the powder.

There are also precut hinge lifters of various sizes. These are small pieces of backing material with a same-size piece of adhesive tape attached. They allow an examiner to place the adhesive tape on an impression and then press it directly onto the attached backing to mount it.

11.2.3.3 Rubber/Gel Lifters. Rubber/gel lifters come in precut elastic sheets. They have a low-tack adhesive gelatin layer on the backing material, which is covered with clear acetate. The low-tack adhesive and flexibility of the backing material make these lifters desirable for lifting prints off curved and delicate surfaces such as light bulbs, doorknobs, and paper. The lifters are available in white, black, and with transparent backing material. The transparent lifters can be affixed directly to a lift card, whereas lifters with either a black or white backing material are instead protected with a clear cover sheet and compared as a reversed (mirrored) image.

11.2.4 Casting Materials

When the surface of an item is rough or textured, a casting material can be used to fill the crevices, providing a greater chance of lifting the entire print. Casting material can also be useful to preserve and record fingerprint impressions in semisolid surfaces (e.g., fresh putty used to secure panes of glass in a window) (Bay, 1998, pp 130–132). Casting material is available in a variety of compounds (e.g., silicone, putty, rubber) and colors. A color that will contrast with the print powder should be selected (Morris, 2005).

11.2.5 Cameras

Any type of camera that has accessories for close-up work can be used in fingerprint and palmprint photography (Moenssens, 1971, p 151). However, a camera system with a lens for macrophotography works best. Photographic flood lights or an off-camera flash system for lighting is necessary. These, in combination, form a system that can be used to photograph evidence in the laboratory or in the field. The press or view camera using 4" x 5" sheet film was the most commonly used camera until it was replaced by easy-to-use 35 mm cameras. The newer high-resolution digital single-lens reflex cameras are also suitable for fingerprint photography (Dalrymple, Shaw, and Woods, 2002, pp 750–761; Crispino, Touron, and Elkader, 2001, pp 479–495).

11.2.6 Tenprint Cards

Tenprint cards are included as a part of the standard equipment for on-scene print recording. Often, investigators collect latent prints from a scene without obtaining the victim's elimination prints. In most cases, elimination prints can be easily obtained at the scene, but often they are overlooked. If the time is taken to obtain the elimination prints, comparisons can be made and lab personnel are less likely to need to run victim prints through the FBI's Automated Fingerprint Identification System or the Integrated Automated Fingerprint Identification System.

11.2.7 Miscellaneous Equipment

Additional items that should be included in a crime scene evidence kit (Figure 11–2):

1. Retractable tape measure

2. Rulers (metal machine ruler and small plastic rulers; a laser ruler may be helpful as well)

3. Scales to indicate dimensions in photographs (nonadhesive and adhesive for placing on walls, if necessary)

4. Packaging containers (to preserve the evidence in the condition it is found and to prevent contamination)

    a. Paper bags

    b. Boxes of various sizes

    c. Manila envelopes of various sizes

    d. Plastic evidence bags

    e. Evidence tubes (for holding knives, screwdrivers, etc.)

5. Packaging and tamper-resistant evidence tape (for sealing the packaging containers)

6. Warning labels (for biohazard and chemically processed evidence)

7. Dust masks (for use with powders, especially in an enclosed area) and respirators (for use with chemical reagents that require protection)

8. Clear goggles for use with powder (in addition to goggles with filters for use with FLS)

9. Disposable gloves

10. Handheld magnifier

11. Pens and permanent markers

12. Plastic sleeves for tripod legs (in case of contaminated scenes)

Sometimes evidence needs to be collected for processing at the laboratory. Tools to help the technician collect evidence include:

1. Screwdrivers

2. Socket wrenches

3. Reciprocating saw

4. Pry bar

FIGURE 11–2

Evidence kit (with rulers, manila envelopes, and other items).

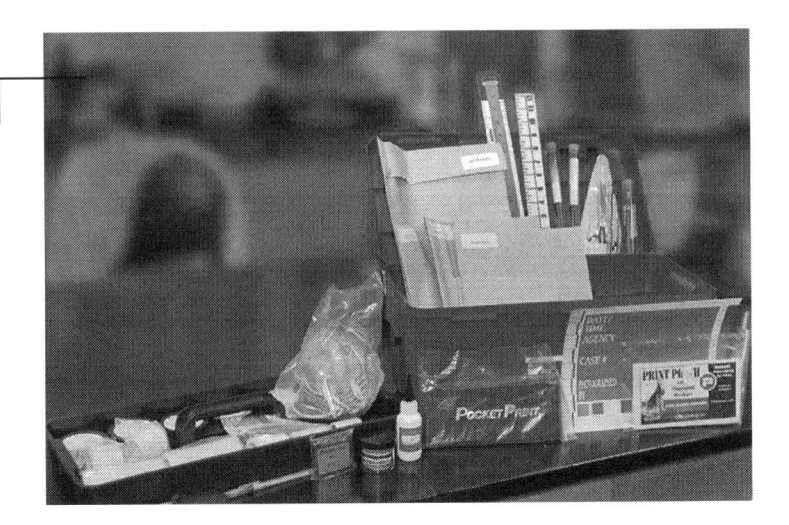

As a technician gains experience and finds what works and what does not, he or she can modify his or her personal kit as needed.

11.3 Laboratory Equipment

11.3.1 Cyanoacrylate Fuming Chambers

Cyanoacrylate ester (CA or CAE) fuming, commonly referred to as *superglue fuming,* was introduced into the United States in the early 1980s as a way to develop latent fingerprints (Norkus, 1982, p 6; Kendall, 1982, pp 3–5). The prints are developed when CA vapor molecules react with components in the latent print residue. As these molecules collect, they begin to form clusters, often becoming visible to the naked eye. These clusters may then be photographed or processed with powder or chemicals.

Cyanoacrylate fuming chambers have two basic equipment requirements in addition to glue. First, the fumes must be contained. Anything from a commercially made chamber (Figure 11–3) to a simple plastic bag, garbage can, or fish tank (Figure 11–4) can be used. The second requirement is proper ventilation. Both of these requirements are used to contain the fumes and limit the operator's exposure to them, since they may be irritating to eyes and mucous membranes.

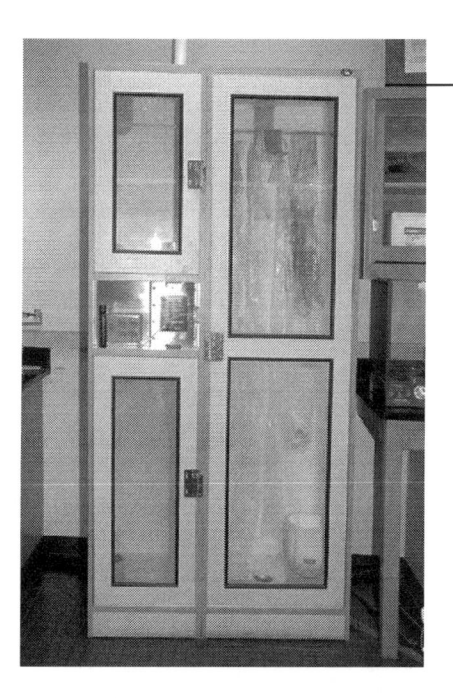

FIGURE 11–3

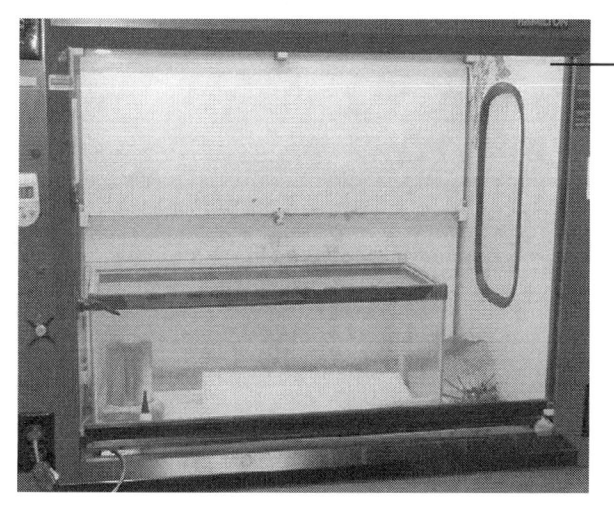

Fuming cabinet.

FIGURE 11–4

Fish tank in fume hood.

The development process may be accelerated by adding a heat source, such as a coffee cup warmer. This heat causes the glue to vaporize, thereby developing the latent print more rapidly (Lee and Gaensslen, 2001, p 119). Small containers, known as *boats*, are used to contain the liquid CA for placement on the heat source. The chamber should also include a system to separate and suspend the specimens that are being processed.

The vacuum fuming chamber (Figure 11–5) was developed by the Identification Division of the Royal Canadian Mounted Police, and a description of its usage and results was published in the early 1990s (Lee and Gaensslen, 2001, pp 119–120). This chamber vaporizes fumes from cyanoacrylate under vacuum conditions without the white buildup of residue that might typically occur when fuming in a conventional chamber. In addition, unlike with ordinary containers, there is no need to spread out items to be processed when they are placed in the chamber; everything will still be fumed evenly (McNutt, 2004, p 6). The use of this chamber also makes overfuming less likely, avoiding the possibility of excessive buildup of the residue.

11.3.2 Vacuum Metal Deposition Chamber

A vacuum metal deposition chamber, used for developing latent prints, is typically a steel cylindrical chamber with a door at one end. The chamber is attached to a system of valves and vacuum pumps that work to reduce the pressure to a level where the evaporation of metals may occur. Theys, Turgis, and Lepareux first reported in 1968 that the "selective condensation of metals under vacuum" settles on the sebum (fat) films, revealing latent prints. This procedure sequentially evaporates small amounts of gold or zinc in a vacuum chamber, and a very thin metal film is deposited onto the latent print, making it visible (Lee and Gaensslen, 2001, p 140). This procedure is effective on smooth, nonporous surfaces (e.g., plastic bags).

11.3.3 Laser

The word *laser* is an acronym for "light amplification by stimulated emission of radiation." According to Fisher (1993, p 111), "Not all lasers are suitable for fingerprint work. The color or wavelength of the output, as well as the light intensity or power output, is important."

The concept for the laser was first noted in 1957 by Gordon Gould, a Columbia University graduate student (Taylor, 2000, pp 10–11). It took him until 1988 to resolve a complex patent dispute and legal battle regarding this remarkable invention (Taylor, 2000, p 284). An article by Dalrymple, Duff, and Menzel (1977, pp 106–115) introduced the use of the laser to fingerprint examiners around the world (Ridgely, 1987, pp 5–12). This article described how natural components in some latent fingerprints luminesce under laser illumination.

There are various types of lasers, but they all basically work the same way. To understand how they work, one must understand the basics of atoms. In simplified terms, atoms

FIGURE 11–5

Vacuum fuming chamber.

Table 11–1

Relative humidity from dry and wet bulb thermometer readings

t – t' / t	2.0	2.5	3.0	3.5	4.0	4.5	5.0	5.5
68	83	78	74	70	66	–	–	–
69	83	78	74	70	66	–	–	–
70	83	79	75	71	67	–	–	–
71	83	80	76	72	68	–	–	–
72	83	80	76	72	68	65	–	–
73	84	80	76	72	69	65	–	–
74	84	80	76	72	69	65	–	–
75	84	80	77	73	69	66	–	–
76	84	81	77	74	70	67	–	–
77	84	81	77	74	70	67	–	–
78	84	81	77	74	70	67	–	–
79	85	81	78	74	71	67	–	–
80	85	82	78	75	71	68	65	–
81	85	82	78	75	71	68	65	–
82	85	82	78	75	72	69	65	–
83	85	82	78	75	72	69	65	–
84	86	82	79	76	72	69	66	–
85	86	82	79	76	72	69	66	–
86	86	83	79	76	73	70	67	–
87	86	83	79	76	73	70	67	–
88	86	83	80	77	73	70	67	65
89	86	83	80	77	73	71	68	65
90	86	83	80	77	74	71	68	65

The left column is the dry bulb reading (t). The top horizontal row is the difference between the dry bulb reading and the wet bulb reading (t – t'). Find the cell at the intersection of the dry bulb reading and the difference of the bulb readings. For example, if the dry reading is 85° and the wet bulb reading is 81°, the difference is 4. Look at the chart and find 85° on the far left and 4 on the top row. Read down and across to meet at 72; that is the relative humidity.

have a nucleus containing protons and neutrons, encircled by an electron cloud. Within the cloud, electrons exist at various energy levels (levels of excitation), depending on the amount of energy to which the atom is exposed by heat, light, or electricity. When the atom gets excited by a specific quantity (*quantum*) of energy, the electrons are excited from their ground state energy level to higher energy states or levels (*orbitals*). When electrons drop back into the ground state energy level, the atom releases energy in the form of a particle of light (*photon*).

A laser contains a mirror at each end that is used to reflect photons. As the photons bounce back and forth between the two mirrors, they stimulate other atoms to release more photons of the same wavelength. This is called *stimulated emission*. One mirror is only partially reflective. This allows a portion of the coherent radiation (a *laser beam*) to be emitted (Menzel, 1980, pp 1–21).

11.3.4 Humidity Chamber

Humidity chambers (also known as *environmental chambers*) (Figure 11–6) regulate the moisture and temperature inside them so optimum conditions for a specific process (e.g., ninhydrin processing) can be achieved. A very basic way to determine humidity is simply to have one wet bulb thermometer and one dry bulb thermometer inside the chamber. The wet bulb thermometer has a piece of muslin tightly wrapped about its bulb. This cloth is dampened with distilled water; as the water evaporates, the thermometer cools. The rate of cooling depends on how much water vapor is in the air. The dry bulb thermometer measures the surrounding air temperature in the chamber. Table 11–1 provides an easy way to determine relative humidity based on the readings of the wet and dry bulb thermometer measurements (Olsen, 1978, pp 197–199). Experience and research have determined that the best prints obtained from treatment with ninhydrin are those that have been exposed to relative humidity of 65–80% (Kent, 1998; Nielson, 1987, p 372). Digital thermo-hygrometers are also available to monitor the processing of humidity and temperature.

In the absence of a humidity chamber, some technicians will use a common household iron to provide a warm and moist environment to accelerate the development of ninhydrin prints. Although this technique is frequently used with success, excessive moisture could damage the prints being developed.

CHAPTER 11 Equipment

11.3.5 Cameras

As in field work (see section 11.2.5), most cameras and accessories that are capable of close-up photography should be suitable for fingerprint photography in the lab. Special-purpose fingerprint cameras were developed that employed a fixed focus and were placed directly over the print to be photographed. These cameras were equipped with batteries and small bulbs for illumination. They primarily used 2.25" x 3.25" or 4" x 5" sheet film. Press and view cameras (e.g., 4" x 5" Crown and Speed Graphics) were also used and had the advantage of being useful for general crime scene photography.

During the 1960s, the Polaroid Corporation introduced the MP-3 copy camera and, later, the MP-4 (Figure 11–7). The MP-4 became a widely used tool for fingerprint photography within the laboratory setting because it allowed for the use of glass plate holders, sheet film holders, roll film adapters, film pack holders, and ground glass focusing. The use of 4" x 5" sheet film to record fingerprints at a life-size scale on the negative is still common in some agencies. However, the trend of using 35mm and digital equipment (cameras and scanners) is becoming more common.

Digital equipment is convenient and produces results that are instantly viewable. Issues of quality are measured in many ways, with resolution and bit depth being two

FIGURE 11–6
Humidity chamber.

FIGURE 11–7
MP-4 camera.

important issues. "Friction ridge impressions should be captured (color or grayscale) at 1000 ppi or higher resolution. Grayscale digital imaging should be at a minimum of 8 bits. Color digital imaging should be at a minimum of 24 bits" (SWGFAST, 2002, p 277).

11.3.6 Comparison Tools

The customary tools used to perform comparisons include a magnifier, ridge counters, and a comfortable working environment with good lighting. Additional tools that are useful are a light box, a comparator, and an image enhancement system.

11.3.6.1 Magnifiers. A magnifier (Figure 11–8) is a basic piece of equipment for comparing latent prints. A good fingerprint magnifier is a solidly built magnifying glass that has an adjustable eyepiece to allow for individual eyesight variations. Magnification is typically 4.5X with the use of good lighting (Olsen, 1978, pp 171–175).

The magnifier's purpose is to allow the examiner to see sufficient ridge characteristics while still keeping a sufficient field of view. This allows the examiner to evaluate the qualities of ridge details while considering the position of these ridge characteristics relative to one another. Some examiners use two magnifiers (one for each of the prints being compared) and switch their attention (view) back and forth between the prints being compared. Other examiners fold the photograph or latent lift card along the edge of the print in question so that it may be placed adjacent to the exemplar print underneath a single magnifier.

Some magnifiers allow for a *reticle* to be inserted in the base. These discs have a line, or lines, going through them that can be placed over the core and delta of the print to help when doing classifications (Olsen, 1978, pp 171–175).

11.3.6.2 Ridge Counters. A ridge counter (or teasing needle) is a pencil-like instrument with a thick needle attached to one end (Figure 11–8). Other similar instruments with retractable pins are also commercially available.

Ridge counters are used to maintain a point of reference during the examination process. They help an examiner keep track of where he or she is when examining or classifying a print. The proper use of ridge counters requires a light touch to avoid pricking the tape on latent lift cards or damaging exemplars.

11.3.6.3 Light Box. A light box contains a light source and has a semitransparent top made of plastic or glass. It is used for evaluating photographic negatives and transparent lifters (Olsen, 1978, pp 184–185).

11.3.6.4 Comparator. A fingerprint comparator is a desktop projection system that has a light source that magnifies and displays images on a screen. Known and unknown prints (which have been placed on platforms) are displayed side-by-side on a split screen. This allows the examiner to study both prints and is especially helpful during training and when multiple examiners are reviewing and discussing prints. Analog and digital imaging systems were introduced to the fingerprint community during the early 1980s (German, 1983, pp 8–11), and by 1985, numerous laboratories had initiated their use (German, 1985, p 11). Side-by-side fingerprint

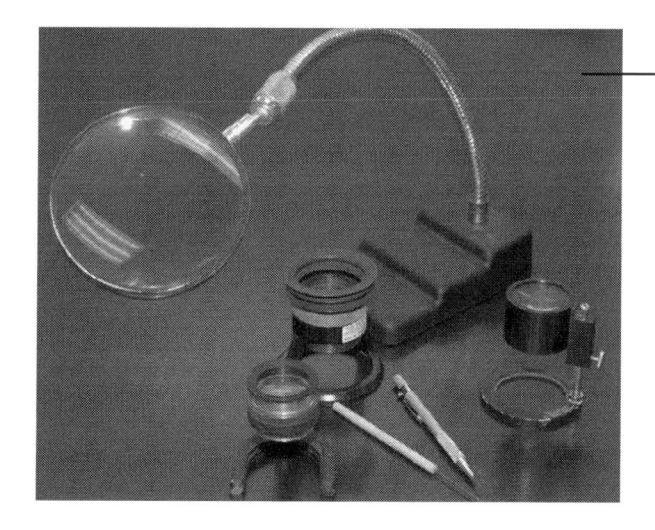

FIGURE 11–8
Magnifiers and ridge counters.

examinations are now also accomplished using a standard computer with readily available image-editing software.

11.4 Conclusion

Whether processing a crime scene or processing evidence in a laboratory, it is important to have a good working knowledge of the equipment and what it can do to obtain the best possible results in each case.

11.5 Credits and Reviewers

All photographs by Aaron Matson, Imaging Specialist, Wisconsin State Crime Laboratory, Milwaukee, WI.

The reviewers critiquing this chapter were Robert J. Garrett, Bridget Lewis, Michael Perkins, and Juliet H. Wood.

11.6 References

Bay, A. L., Jr. Additional Use for Mikrosil Casting Material. *J. Forensic Ident.* 1998, *48* (2), 130–132.

Crispino, F.; Touron, P.; Elkader, A. A. Search for a Digital Enhancement Protocol for Photoshop Software. *J. Forensic Ident.* 2001, *51* (5), 479–495.

Dalrymple, B. E.; Duff, J. M.; Menzel, E. R. Inherent Fingerprint Fluorescence—Detection by Laser. *J. Forensic Sci.* 1977, *22* (1), 106–115.

Dalrymple, B.; Shaw, L.; Woods, K. Optimized Digital Recording of Crime Scene Impressions. *J. Forensic Ident.* 2002, *52* (6), 750–761.

Fisher, B. A. J., Ed. *Techniques of Crime Scene Investigation,* 5th ed.; CRC Press: Washington, DC, 1993.

German, E. R. Analog/Digital Image Processing. *Ident. News* 1983, *33* (11), 8–11.

German, E. R. Electronic Latent Print Detection: A 1985 Update. Presented at 70th Annual Conference of the International Association for Identification, Savannah, GA, July 1985.

James, J. D.; Pounds, C. A.; Wilshire, B. New Magnetic Applicators and Magnetic Flake Powders for Revealing Latent Fingerprints. *J. Forensic Ident.* 1992, *42* (6), 531–542.

Kendall, F. G. Super Glue Fuming for the Development of Latent Fingerprints. *Ident. News* 1982, *32* (5), 3–5.

Kent, T., Ed. *Manual of Fingerprint Development Techniques,* 2nd ed.; Home Office, Police Scientific Development Branch: Sandridge, U.K., 1998.

Lee, H.; Gaensslen, R. E., Ed. *Advances in Fingerprint Technology,* 2nd ed.; CRC Press: Washington, DC, 2001.

Lightning Powder Company. Disposable Magnetic Brush. *Minutiae* 1999, *53* (March-April), 3.

MacDonell, H. L. Bristleless Brush Development of Latent Fingerprints. *Ident. News* 1961, *11* (3), 7–9, 15.

Masters, N. E. *Safety for the Forensic Identification Specialist;* Lightning Powder Company: Salem, OR, 1995.

McNutt, J. Advancement in Latent Print Processing: Vacuum Cyanoacrylate Fuming. *The Print* 2004, *20* (2), 6–7.

Menzel, E. R. *Fingerprint Detection With Lasers;* Marcel Dekker, Inc.: New York, 1980.

Moenssens, A. A. *Fingerprint Techniques;* Chilton Book Company: Philadelphia, 1971.

Morris, M. Casting a Wide Net: Lifting Fingerprints From Difficult Surfaces. *Forensic Magazine* 2005, *4* (2), 8–12.

Nielson, J. P. Quality Control for Amino Acid Visualization Reagents. *J. Forensic Sci.* 1987, *32* (2), 370–376.

Norkus, P. M. Glue It. *Ident. News* 1982, *32* (5), 6.

Olsen R. D., Sr. *Scott's Fingerprint Mechanics;* Charles C Thomas: Springfield, IL, 1978.

Ridgely, J. E., Jr. Latent Print Detection by Laser. *Ident. News* 1987, *37* (4), 5–12.

Scientific Working Group on Friction Ridge Analysis, Study and Technology (SWGFAST). Friction Ridge Digital Imaging Guidelines, version 1.0. *J. Forensic Ident.* 2002, *52* (3), 276–278. [Version 1.1, effective 9/14/09, available online at http://www.swgfast.org/CurrentDocuments.html.]

Taylor, N. *LASER: The Inventor, the Nobel Laureate, and the Thirty-Year Patent War;* Simon & Schuster: New York, 2000.

Wilkinson, D. A.; Watkin, J. E. A Comparison of the Forensic Light Sources: Polilight, Luma-Lite, and Spectrum 9000. *J. Forensic Ident.* 1994, *44* (6), 632–651.

11.7 Equipment Suppliers

Armor Forensics
Lightning Powder Company, Inc.
13386 International Parkway
Jacksonville, FL 32218
(800) 852 0300
(904) 485 1836
http://www.redwop.com

Arrowhead Forensic Products
11030 Strang Line Road
Lenexa, KS 66215
(913) 894 8388
(800) 953 3274
info@arrowheadforensics.com
http://www.crime-scene.com

BVDA International b.v.
Postbus 2323
2002 CH Haarlem
The Netherlands
+31 (0)23 5424708
info@bvda.nl
http://www.bvda.com/EN/index.html

CSI Equipment Ltd.
Locard House
Deethe Farm Estate
Cranfield Road
Woburn Sands
United Kingdom
MK17 8UR
+44 (0)1908 58 50 58
info@csiequipment.com
sales@csiequipment.com

CSI Forensic Supply
P.O. Box 16
Martinez, CA 94553
(925) 686 6667
(800) 227 6020
http://www.csiforensic.com

Evident Crime Scene Products
739 Brooks Mill Road
Union Hall, VA 24176
(800) 576 7606
contact@evident.cc
http://www.evidentcrimescene.com

Faurot Forensic Products
P.O. Box 99146
Raleigh, NC 27624
(919) 556 9670
http://www.faurotforensics.com

Lynn Peavey Company
P.O. Box 14100
Lenexa, KS 66285
(913) 888 0600
(800) 255 6499
lpv@peaveycorp.com
http://www.lynnpeavey.com

Morris Kopec Forensics, Inc.
631 Palm Springs Drive, Suite 107
Altamonte Springs, FL 32701
(407) 831 9921
rjkopec@aol.com or mkforensics@aol.com

QPST
P.O. Box 8408
Warnbro 6169
Western Australia
+61 (0) 8 9524 7144
info@qpst.net
http://www.qpst.net

Sirchie Finger Print Laboratories, Inc.
100 Hunter Place
Youngsville, NC 27596
(919) 554 2244
(800) 356 7311
sirchieinfo@sirchie.com
http://www.sirchie.com

SPEX Forensics
19963 W. 162nd Street
Olathe, KS 66062
(800) 657 7739
(913) 764 0117
questions@mail.spexforensics.com
http://www.spexforensics.com

CHAPTER 12

QUALITY ASSURANCE

M. Leanne Gray

CONTENTS

- 3   12.1 Introduction
- 4   12.2 Quality Assurance Program
- 9   12.3 Additional Quality Assurance Measures That May Be Added to a Quality Assurance Program
- 11 12.4 Conclusion
- 11 12.5 Reviewers
- 11 12.6 References
- 11 12.7 Additional Information

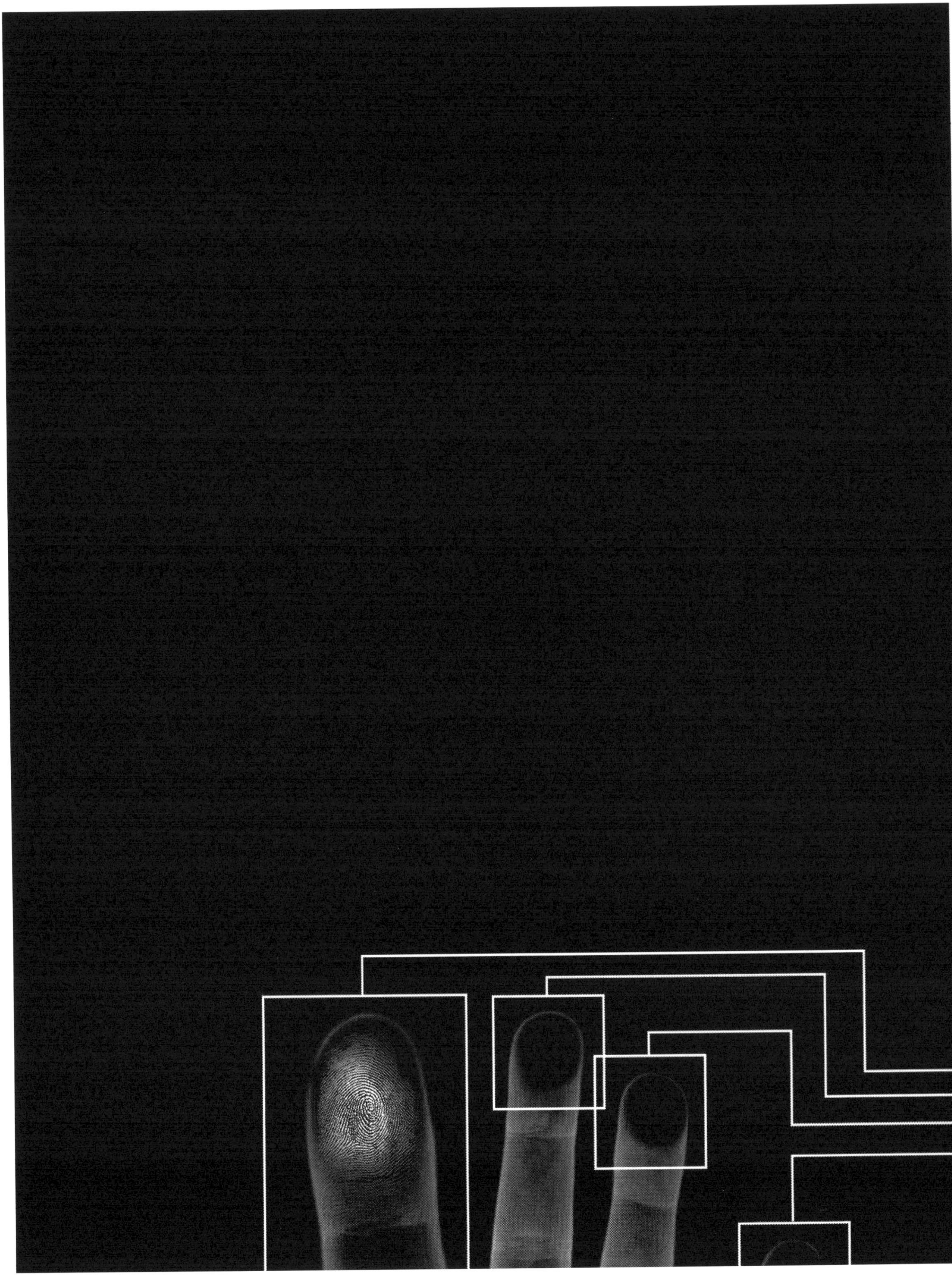

CHAPTER 12

QUALITY ASSURANCE

M. Leanne Gray

12.1 Introduction

The purpose of a quality assurance program is to ensure that all examiners meet the quality standards set by the discipline and by the individual laboratory. A quality assurance program includes "those planned and systematic actions necessary to provide sufficient confidence that a laboratory's product or service will satisfy given requirements for quality" (ASCLD/LAB, 2005, p 66). A quality assurance program sets the guidelines for development and implementation of standards that address examiner qualifications, report writing, document control, quality control measures, procedural validation and documentation, organizational structure, infrastructure requirements, and evidence control.

There are two fundamental principles in friction ridge examination: (1) all latent print examiners must be trained and found to be competent to perform casework prior to beginning independent casework, and (2) all individualizations (i.e., identifications) must be verified by another competent and qualified examiner (SWGFAST, 2006, p 122).

The processing of evidence to develop and preserve latent prints can involve various processing techniques and preservation methods. Although no standard sequence can be applied to all items to be processed, standardized sequences within an agency should be established for particular circumstances (e.g., type of evidence, type of case). Friction ridge examination requires that an examiner analyze and determine the suitability of the ridge detail, compare the ridge detail with known exemplars, and evaluate the sufficiency of visual information to reach a conclusion. Possible conclusions are individualizations (identifications), exclusions, or inconclusives (SWGFAST, 2004, pp 358–359).

Quality issues that arise from inconsistencies, clerical or administrative errors, or erroneous conclusions may occur.

A quality assurance program will allow for the tracking of any of these quality issues. A quality assurance program will ensure that all examiners are following proper protocol in order to minimize the number of issues that are produced.

Because the forensic science community is constantly growing and changing, and, therefore, the rules governing quality assurance continue to change, this chapter will discuss generalities of a quality assurance program. For specific guidelines and the most up-to-date resources, please refer to the appendix of related references on quality assurance programs and accreditation and certification organizations, section 12.6.

12.2 Quality Assurance Program

12.2.1 Quality Assurance Documents

A quality assurance program should be written and contained in a set of documents or in a single document (e.g., quality manual). Included in the quality manual should be documentation for the following areas: processing techniques; preparation, use, and storage of chemicals; laboratory safety procedures; material safety data sheets; evidence handling procedures; proficiency testing; minimum notation requirements on examination worksheets; report wording guidelines; technical and administrative case reviews; training and competency records; equipment calibration and maintenance logs; validation records; policy and procedure manuals for electronic fingerprint systems; and testimony reviews (SWGFAST, 2006, pp 117–118).

A quality manual should also outline the responsibilities of personnel regarding adherence to the quality assurance program and delineate the procedures to follow when dealing with quality issues. In addition, documents may address such areas as minimum standards and controls, qualifications of a verifier, organization and management requirements, personnel requirements, and facility requirements.

12.2.2 Competency Testing

An agency must have a method to initially test for competency when an examiner first joins the agency or an examiner completes an internal training program. This initial competency testing may include oral, written, or practical tests. If an agency is large and has multiple worksites, any required tests should be consistent from one worksite to another. This will ensure that each examiner's overall quality and minimum level of competency are consistent throughout the agency. No examiner should be allowed to begin independent casework until he or she has satisfied all aspects of the initial competency testing phase.

12.2.3 Evidence Handling and Quality Audits

Each agency must establish a policy for the handling of all evidence within its control. A chain of custody shall be maintained from the time that the evidence is collected or received until it is released. Procedures shall establish how evidence is collected, received, and stored. The procedures shall preserve the identity, integrity, condition, and security of the item. The policy should include information about how evidence is to be packaged, seal requirements, and what to do when evidence is lost or if there is a discrepancy. Included in this policy should be periodic audits of all evidence within the agency's control. The time frame for these audits to occur (e.g., monthly, quarterly, semi-annually, or annually), as well as what percentage of evidence will be examined and who will conduct the audit, should be established.

In addition, an agency should establish a policy for auditing all other aspects of the agency's quality system, including a time frame for these audits to occur as well as who will conduct these audits. An agency may choose to bring in auditors from outside agencies or have internal auditors conduct the inspections.

12.2.4 Preparation, Use, and Storage of Chemicals

An agency must have a policy in place describing proper procedures for preparation, use, and storage of all chemicals that are maintained within the agency. This policy may address such issues as markings required on the chemicals when received, length of time a chemical can be kept and used if commercially purchased, shelf life of each reagent solution that is prepared within the agency, and a list of chemicals and reagent solutions that must be tested prior to use with casework. An agency should create and maintain a list of all chemicals and reagent solutions that are used in each section of the agency. In addition, an agency should have a plan for proper disposal of chemicals and reagent solutions, including contact information for any outside vendors that may be needed to implement the disposal of outdated or no longer used chemicals or reagent solutions.

12.2.5 Processing Techniques

An agency must have a policy in place to delineate what validated processing techniques are sanctioned by the agency. Any changes, updates, or deletions to a processing technique must be made available to all agency examiners. An agency may wish to include a guideline for examiners to follow that details what processing techniques are appropriate at each step of an examination. However, any list should be viewed as merely a guide.

12.2.6 Policies and Procedure Manuals for Electronic Fingerprint Systems

An agency must have policies and procedure manuals delineating the requirements for use, maintenance, and updates to any electronic fingerprint systems that are accessible to examiners within the agency. These policies and procedure manuals should be reviewed routinely to ensure that any changes, updates, or deletions are current.

These policies and procedure manuals may include, but are not limited to, such things as training that an examiner must successfully complete prior to having access to the electronic fingerprint system(s); documentation requirements, such as paperwork or images that must be maintained; and report wording requirements when an electronic fingerprint system is used in casework.

12.2.7 Examination Procedures

An agency must establish procedures for the processing and examination of evidence, note taking, and report writing. These procedures should describe established protocols and types of examinations performed. Additionally, they shall require that at the time of collection (whether in the field or in the laboratory), all latent print evidence shall be marked with minimal information (i.e., a unique case identifier, personal markings) and when relevant, information to explain the orientation or position of the latent. The substrate information should also be included. This may include the use of a diagram.

An agency must establish procedures for the comparison of friction ridge detail (SWGFAST, 2002, p 324). These procedures should describe established protocols (e.g., Are all latents to be compared or should the comparisons be concluded after the first latent is individualized?).

12.2.8 Verification

An agency should establish rules governing the qualifications that are needed to be a verifier. These qualifications may include a minimum number of hours of training, a minimum number of continuing education credits, or a minimum number of cases completed without quality issues. It is important to remember that, when setting a standard for the qualifications of a verifier, the number of years of service is not as important as the quality of work that has been produced.

12.2.8.1 Verification. Verification of a latent print comparison is "the confirmation of an examiner's conclusion by another competent examiner" (SWGFAST, 2006, p 122). An agency must establish rules governing the verification process. These rules may be limited to individualizations but may also include exclusions or inconclusives.

12.2.8.2 Blind Verification. "Blind verification is the confirmation of an examiner's conclusion by another competent examiner who has no expectation or knowledge of the prior conclusion" (SWGFAST, 2006, p 122). This process would require that the initial case examiner not place any markings of any kind, including conclusion notations, on any of the evidence needed for the verification examination, thus assuring that another examiner given the same evidence will be unaware of the initial examiner's findings.

The Scientific Working Group on Friction Ridge Analysis, Study and Technology (SWGFAST) recommends blind verification "in cases involving an individualization, exclusion, or inconclusive of a person based on only a single latent print" (SWGFAST, 2006, p 122). An agency should establish policies regarding what cases require using a blind verification process.

12.2.9 Conflict Resolution

Because of the inherent variables (e.g., skill, experience) and the possibility of examiner error, an examiner and a subsequent verifier may provide results that are not consistent. An agency shall define what constitutes an inconsistency and conduct a quality review to resolve all inconsistencies in examination results.

The quality review must ensure that all policies are followed and that personal preferences are not allowed to take precedence over minimum standards and controls or policy interpretation. Some quality reviews may resolve the inconsistencies by having the affected examiners document their analyses, followed by an unmediated discussion of the issue(s). The documented analyses should become a permanent addition to the case file. If the inconsistency is resolved following the examiner discussion, the decision should be documented in the case file and reported to management. If the inconsistency is not resolved at this level, an agency may need to use another examiner or may create a committee with representatives from both management and peer examiners to review the analyses and the case file. The committee would then attempt to resolve the inconsistency. Some agencies may need or elect to have a complete reexamination of the case made by an independent external examiner or agency.

To determine the root cause of the inconsistency, it may be necessary to review training records, the training program, and prior work performance.

All quality reviews should be documented and provide a determination of the correct results, the root cause(s) of the inconsistency, and whether the inconsistency would require any corrective action. Some quality reviews may be minor tasks that require a quick review, determination, and very little documentation. However, other quality reviews may require a great deal of effort to complete and may result in complex decisions.

12.2.10 Training

If an agency decides to establish an internal training program, the depth and scope of the training program must be included. In addition, any training that an agency provides should be in compliance with generally accepted practices and processing techniques within the scientific community. Copious records must be maintained of all training received by each examiner to aid in establishing competency records.

A formal training program should include a detailed description of the training to be provided to each trainee. For a training program to be successful, qualified trainers must be identified and given ample time and resources to create and maintain the training program.

A training program must also exist if an examiner who has already been trained to competency needs remedial training. An agency that has not established an internal training program must have a mechanism in place for examiners already trained to competency to receive required remedial training from a reliable source.

Care should also be taken when interviewing and hiring trainees. Some agencies emphasize that the trainee must have a solid educational background in science and math. However, it is also essential that the trainee be evaluated for aptitude and ability to work in a highly structured environment that requires detailed analysis and where work is often accomplished autonomously. Although the testing to date is limited, it might be helpful to test prospective trainees for pattern recognition ability (Byrd, 2003, pp 329–330). It may also be beneficial to regularly test new trainees and current employees for visual acuity and overall eye health to ensure continued excellence and quality of work.

An agency that wishes to develop an internal training program is encouraged to review the SWGFAST *Training to Competency for Latent Print Examiners* document and contact agencies that have established training programs.

12.2.11 Proficiency Tests

To measure individual performance and provide demonstrative evidence of each examiner's comparison ability, each agency must establish proficiency testing requirements. These requirements shall include that each latent print examiner be tested at least annually (SWGFAST, 2009, p 679). This policy should delineate the type of testing and how often it must be completed. As part of the proficiency testing policy, documentation requirements should be delineated and maintained. The proficiency testing policy should also indicate whether the tests are to be taken independently and whether verifications of individualizations are required.

The test design may include agency procedures such as documentation, evidence handling, and related administrative actions. Test designs can include open testing (examiners are aware they are being tested), blind testing (examiners are unaware they are being tested), or double-blind testing (the agency and examiners are unaware they are being tested).

12.2.11.1 Internal Proficiency Tests. The internal proficiency test, after being created, should be reviewed by either a senior section member of the agency's staff or an outside source prior to distribution of the test. This review will ensure that the quality of the test is commensurate with cases that are routinely analyzed.

A quality assurance program should set parameters for internal proficiency tests, including that they shall contain multiple latent friction ridge impressions and known standards (SWGFAST, 2009, p 678). These parameters may also include the additional requirement of evaluating nonsuitable prints.

12.2.11.2 External Proficiency Tests. The use of a commercially prepared external proficiency test has the advantage of being nonbiased because the agency purchasing the test has no input into the makeup of the test and no advance notice of the test answers prior to submission of the test for grading. External proficiency testing ensures that the examiner is compared against the manufacturer's validated results. The results can also be compared with the results of other test takers.

12.2.11.3 Blind Proficiency Tests. An agency may use blind proficiency tests to verify the quality of an examiner's work without his or her knowledge. The agency may generate mock evidence and then assign it as a regular case. The case examiner may never know that he or she worked a blind proficiency test, unless the quality of work that was produced required a quality review.

12.2.11.4 Double-Blind Proficiency Tests. Having another agency submit mock evidence as a regular case can provide a double-blind test to evaluate the performance of the individual(s) completing the case and the agency's overall performance with respect to that case.

12.2.12 Technical Case Review

A technical case review is a useful tool to regularly determine the quality of casework and ensure reliable results. An agency must establish what constitutes a technical review, who shall conduct technical case reviews, and the frequency of the reviews. The American Society of Crime Laboratory Directors/Laboratory Accreditation Board (ASCLD/LAB) defines a technical review as a "review of notes, data and other documents which form the basis for scientific conclusion" (ASCLD/LAB, 2005, p 68). SWGFAST further explains that "these reviews concentrate on whether the appropriate tests and examinations have been performed to support the results and conclusions reported and on whether sufficient supporting documentation is present. They also focus on whether the conclusions are consistent with the documentation and are within accepted practices" (SWGFAST, 2006, pp 124–125).

A technical review may include a partial or complete reworking of the case, and, therefore, technical case reviews must be conducted by another qualified latent print examiner.

12.2.13 Administrative Review

An agency must establish what constitutes an administrative review and who shall conduct administrative reviews. ASCLD/LAB defines an administrative review as "a procedure used to check for consistency with laboratory policy and for editorial correctness" (ASCLD/LAB, 2005, p 61). SWGFAST indicates that "administrative reviews shall be conducted by a supervisor or designee" (SWGFAST, 2006, p 125). An administrative review may include reviewing all documentation within a case file for technical accuracy or may simply be a review of the documentation verifying that no clerical errors, such as typographical errors, are on the worksheet or written report.

An agency must have a mechanism in place for dealing with cases in which an administrative review identifies a quality issue. If the issue is minor, then communication between the reviewer and the original case examiner may be sufficient to correct the issue. If the issue is major and the individual conducting the administrative review is not management, then management should be notified immediately. Management should then notify the quality manager and the quality reviewer (when applicable) to begin a formal review process to determine whether the error is singular in nature or systemic.

An agency may outline specific provisions in the quality manual regarding confidentiality when dealing with issues. An examiner identified as having an issue has a right for that issue not to become public knowledge among his or her coworkers. If nonmanagement personnel discover a quality issue, the agency may mandate that the original administrative reviewer cease involvement in any additional quality reviews that result from the initial issue being identified. In addition, the administrative review examiner should be required to maintain confidentiality regarding the issue and the original case examiner indefinitely, unless given specific permission by management to discuss these facts.

12.2.14 Testimony Review

Each agency should have a mechanism in place to review the testimony of each examiner within that agency. SWGFAST recommends that testimony reviews be done annually (SWGFAST, 2006, p 126). This review should encompass both the technical accuracy of the testimony and the overall presentation and ability of the examiner to provide an accurate and articulate accounting of all examinations conducted and any conclusions or opinions noted.

An agency may require that the reviewer be a manager (preferably one with a background in the specialty being testified to), an individual from the training department (when applicable), or a peer. An agency may allow for a verbal or written contract with court officials. An agency may also incorporate the use of a preprinted evaluation survey containing specific questions that can be provided to either or both of the attorneys involved, as well as the judge, as another means of determining the quality of the testimony provided by the examiner.

12.2.15 Corrective Action

It may be necessary to take corrective action to remedy an issue related to the quality of the work product and to prevent further related issues. An agency must have a general description of what corrective action is appropriate according to the type of issue identified. This corrective action may include such options as removing an examiner from casework responsibility, a review of prior casework, requiring an examiner to receive and complete additional training in the area the issue was made, or reviewing additional casework completed by the examiner to determine whether the issue was singular in nature or systemic.

Corrective actions should not be construed as disciplinary actions. They are an important part of any quality review to detect and remedy any errors or issues relating to the quality of the work product.

12.2.16 Laboratory Safety Procedures

Each agency must establish safety procedures and policies for its system. The safety procedures and policies should be in compliance with Occupational Safety and Health Administration (OSHA) and state regulations. The safety procedures and policies should include such areas as personal protective equipment use, safe storage and disposal of chemicals, and how access to the facility is controlled. (See also section 12.2.4 on storing chemicals.) An agency may wish to include policies on blood-borne pathogens and chemical hygiene in its safety procedures.

12.2.16.1 Designation of a Safety Manager. An agency should designate a safety manager (irrespective of other responsibilities) who "has the defined authority and obligation to ensure that the requirements of the safety system are implemented and maintained" (ASCLD/LAB, 2005, p 67). Policies should be stated regarding the scope and depth of responsibilities for the safety manager. The requirements for and duties expected of the safety manager should be outlined in the safety documents and may contain such information as the qualifications of the safety manager; time limits, if any, that a person shall be designated as safety manager; reviewing and updating any written safety policies; disseminating all safety policies and updates to all examiners and management; maintaining all safety records; tracking all safety issues; and producing a written report annually detailing the safety record of the agency.

12.2.16.2 Material Safety Data Sheets. Material safety data sheets are provided by or can be acquired from all companies selling chemicals. Each agency must design a program for the collection, storage, and maintenance of the material safety data sheets for all chemicals purchased or used within the agency. Material safety data sheets provide vital safety information about chemicals and are a valuable tool to maintain safety within an agency.

12.2.17 Equipment Calibration and Maintenance

Performance checks are used by agencies to ensure that equipment and instruments are functioning to established criteria. An agency must establish a system to verify that each piece of analytical equipment is examined regularly to ensure proper working order. All equipment that requires calibration should have written documentation, such as a logbook, to verify the date that the equipment was examined, the person or business that examined the equipment, and any adjustments or calibrations that were performed on that instrument. An agency may establish a schedule that requires regular internal inspections, such as quarterly reviews, and an annual external review.

12.2.18 Method Validation Records

Each processing procedure must be validated and documentation must be maintained prior to use in casework. An agency must establish internal minimum standards for the validation process and sequence of processing techniques. An agency may decide to accept an outside agency's published validation study. An agency may adopt another agency's or laboratory's procedure but must still demonstrate the protocol works as intended. This means that the agency must demonstrate that agency examiners using available equipment and instruments can achieve the established requirements.

Processing techniques should be reviewed periodically to ensure that the techniques are current and still effective. This review will allow for updates and revisions to be made to the processing procedure. Each agency must establish an appropriate time frame for these reviews (e.g., one year, five years).

12.2.19 Continuing Education

An agency should create and maintain a policy outlining and encouraging all examiners to pursue additional educational opportunities. These educational opportunities may include such coursework as undergraduate or postgraduate classes or degrees, academic or service-related seminars, and educational conferences provided by professional organizations (e.g., the International Association for Identification (IAI), the Canadian Identification Society, and the Fingerprint Society).

An agency may wish to include in this policy the tracking of individual requests or attendance at any of the above-mentioned continuing education opportunities. By tracking these requests and attendance records, an agency may better identify which individuals strive to further their knowledge about their profession, which may be acknowledged during a performance review.

12.3 Additional Quality Assurance Measures That May Be Added to a Quality Assurance Program

In addition to the basic components, an agency can add other components to its quality assurance program.

12.3.1 Quality Manager

A quality assurance program may have one individual who "has the defined authority and obligation to ensure that the requirements of the quality system are implemented and maintained" (ASCLD/LAB, 2005, p 66). In a large organization, this person may have the job title of quality manager and this may be his or her primary function at that agency. For smaller agencies, the quality manager may be a part-time position. The quality manager may have casework responsibilities along with managing the quality assurance program.

It is important that an agency document the specific requirements and duties expected of this position. These may include, but are not limited to, qualifications of the quality manager; time limits, if any, that a person shall be designated as quality manager; reviewing and updating the quality manual; disseminating quality assurance program policies and updates to all examiners and management; completing all case file reviews or overseeing the work produced by quality reviewers; maintaining all quality records; tracking all quality issues; and producing a written report annually detailing the quality record of the agency.

12.3.2 Minimum Standards and Controls

An agency may establish a set of minimum standards and controls to ensure that all analysts within the agency understand exactly what is expected regarding the quality of casework being produced. These minimums should be clear and precise to allow for easy understanding and should include all requirements for evidence handling, evidence examination, evidence preservation, examination documentation, evidence disposition, and report wording.

If an agency establishes minimum standards and controls, it must establish a policy for reevaluating them. This reevaluation should include a timetable to ensure that all standards and controls are accurate and current with generally accepted scientific practices.

Minimum standards and controls for each aspect of casework should be documented either in the agency's quality manual or in the agency's procedures manual, when applicable.

12.3.3 Organization and Management Requirements

An agency may establish organization and management requirements for all staff members. Organization and management requirements may include the delineation of organizational structure, administrative practices, and delegation of authority. Organization and management requirements should be documented either in the agency's quality manual or in the agency's overall policy manual.

12.3.4 Personnel Requirements

An agency may establish personnel requirements for all staff members. These requirements may include minimum educational requirements, specific undergraduate or post-baccalaureate class-specific requirements, and employee development by attending professional organization meetings and seminars. Personnel requirements should be documented either in the agency's quality manual or in the agency's overall policy manual.

12.3.5 Facility Requirements

An agency should ensure that the working facility is designed for maximum case productivity while maintaining the highest level of safety available. This policy should address safety showers, eye wash stations, fire extinguishers, fume hood air flow requirements, and time frames for verifying the working condition of these safety features.

In addition, a facility requirement policy should contain specific time frames and conditions, such as the minimum number of staff required onsite to ensure the safety of staff when engaging in certain activities, such as chemical processing or laser examination. Specific safety requirements and guidelines can be found by contacting OSHA. State regulations should also be identified and followed. Facility requirements should be documented either in the agency's quality manual, safety manual (if such a manual exists), or overall policy manual.

12.3.6 Use of External Laboratory Services

Agencies may find it necessary, because of large backlogs or the inability to perform a specific service, to pursue the use of external laboratory services. If that is the case, it is the agency's responsibility to ensure that any external laboratory service with which it initiates a contract adheres to all of the agency's quality assurance policies and procedures regarding all aspects of casework, including evidence handling and evidence processing.

12.3.7 Agency Accreditation and Certification

Examiner certification and laboratory accreditation have become demonstrative measures of quality within the forensic disciplines. These programs have been promoted to provide the criminal justice system with generally accepted methods for quality assurance. Examiner certification demonstrates a level of competency and ability for the individual, and accreditation demonstrates agency compliance with accepted policies and procedures for quality assurance.

12.3.7.1 International Association for Identification — Latent Print Certification Program. The IAI established the program in 1977. This certification program requires a minimum of two years' experience and a bachelor's degree. (Years of experience can be substituted for the educational requirement.) Basic testing requirements include a written test, a fingerprint pattern interpretation test, and a comparison test.

12.3.7.2 American Society of Crime Laboratory Directors/Laboratory Accreditation Board (ASCLD/LAB) Legacy Program. The ASCLD/LAB Legacy Program has an extensive process to accredit agencies. This accreditation process involves reviewing an agency's written policies, procedures, and casework and then inspecting that agency to confirm that it is following minimum accreditation standards and the policies it has set forth. ASCLD/LAB evaluates an agency according to three criteria: essential, important, and desirable. The definition of essential is "standards which directly affect and have fundamental impact on the work product of the laboratory or the integrity of the evidence" (ASCLD/LAB, 2005, p 63). The definition of important is "standards which are considered to be key indicators of the overall quality of the laboratory, but may not directly affect the work product nor the integrity of the evidence" (ASCLD/LAB, 2005, p 64). The definition of desirable is "standards which have the least affect on the work product or the integrity of the evidence but which nevertheless enhance the professionalism of the laboratory" (ASCLD/LAB, 2005, p 63).

In addition, ASCLD/LAB has set new standards on many issues that continue to push the forensic community to a higher level of quality. An ASCLD/LAB accreditation must be renewed every five years. This renewal involves the same process as the initial accreditation process and is outlined extensively by ASCLD/LAB in its manual.

12.3.7.3 International Organization for Standardization (ISO). ISO works in conjunction with the International Electrotechnical Commission (IEC) to create a worldwide standardization system. ISO is the world's largest developer of standards. ISO's principal activity is the development of technical standards. ISO has created a technical standard (17025) for any testing and calibration laboratory; this standard is applicable to forensic laboratories. The function of ISO does not include accreditation programs. It sets standards that allow agencies to pursue ISO accreditation through accrediting bodies. Currently, ASCLD/LAB and Forensic Quality Services (FQS) have programs that allow forensic agencies to pursue accreditation that is based on ISO/IEC standard 17025.

The ASCLD/LAB International Accreditation Program is based on the requirements of ISO/IEC 17025, plus supplemental requirements that are based on the International Laboratory Accreditation Cooperation (ILAC) Guide 19 (Guidelines for Forensic Science Laboratories) and the ASCLD/LAB Legacy Program requirements.

Forensic Quality Services-International's (FQS-I) accreditation program is based on the requirements of ISO/IEC 17025, ILAC Guide 19, and FQS-I field-specific criteria. The field-specific criteria include "Forensic Requirements for Agencies that Perform Latent Print Testing", developed by a technical advisory committee of latent print examiners specifically for the FQS-I program (FQS-I, 2006).

12.4 Conclusion

The forensic science community must continue to push for higher standards of forensic excellence. An examiner must always remember that the work produced in a forensic agency has the potential to have a dramatic effect not only on a suspect in a criminal case, but also on the victim and both the suspect's and victim's families. As examiners, we owe it to the community we serve to produce a quality work product each time we work a case, no matter what the offense.

12.5 Reviewers

The reviewers critiquing this chapter were Patti Blume, Deborah Friedman, Alice Maceo, Kenneth O. Smith, Jr., Lyla A. Thompson, and Juliet H. Wood.

12.6 References

American Society of Crime Laboratory Directors/Laboratory Accreditation Board. *ASCLD/LAB Manual*. ASCLD/LAB: Garner, NC, 2005.

Byrd, J.; Bertram, D. Form-blindness. *J. Forensic Ident.* 2003, *53* (3), 315–341.

Forensic Quality Services-International. *Forensic Requirements for Agencies that Perform Latent Print Testing*. FQS-I: Largo, FL 2006.

Scientific Working Group on Friction Ridge Analysis, Study and Technology (SWGFAST). Friction Ridge Examination Methodology for Latent Print Examiners. *J. Forensic Ident.* 2002, *52* (3), 324–328.

SWGFAST. Standards for Conclusions. *J. Forensic Ident.* 2004, *54* (3), 358–359.

SWGFAST. Quality Assurance Guidelines for Latent Print Examiners. *J. Forensic Ident.* 2006, *56* (1), 117–127.

SWGFAST. Guidelines for Latent Print Proficiency Testing Programs. *J. Forensic Ident.* 2009, *59* (6), 677–680.

12.7 Additional Information

Arter, D. R. *Quality Audits for Improved Performance*, 3rd ed.; ASQ Quality Press: Milwaukee, WI, 2003.

Bauer, J. E.; Duffy, G. L.; Westcott, R. T., Eds. *The Quality Improvement Handbook*, 2nd ed.; ASQ Quality Press: Milwaukee, WI, 2006.

Benbow, D. W.; Elshennawy, A. K.; and Walker, F. *The Certified Quality Technician Handbook;* ASQ Quality Press: Milwaukee, WI, 2003.

Clark, T. J. *Success Through Quality: Support Guide for the Journey to Continuous Improvement;* ASQ Quality Press: Milwaukee, WI, 1999.

Crosby, P. B. *Philip Crosby's Reflections on Quality;* McGraw-Hill: New York, 1996.

Crosby, P. B. *Quality Is Free;* McGraw-Hill: New York, 1979.

Crosby, P. B. *Quality Is Still Free;* McGraw-Hill: New York, 1996.

Griffiths, D. N. *Management in a Quality Environment;* ASQ Quality Press: Milwaukee, WI, 1995.

Hartman, M. G., Ed. *Fundamental Concepts of Quality Improvement;* ASQ Quality Press: Milwaukee, WI, 2002.

Okes, D.; Westcott, R. T., Eds. *The Certified Quality Manager Handbook*, 2nd ed; ASQ Quality Press: Milwaukee, WI, 2000.

Russell, J. P. *The Internal Auditing Pocket Guide;* ASQ Quality Press: Milwaukee, WI, 2003.

Russell, J. P., Ed. *The ASQ Auditing Handbook,* 3rd ed.; ASQ Quality Press: Milwaukee, WI, 2006.

Singer, D. C., Ed. *A Laboratory Quality Handbook of Best Practices and Relevant Regulations;* ASQ Quality Press: Milwaukee, WI, 2001.

Singer, D. C.; Upton, R. P. *Guidelines for Laboratory Quality Auditing;* Marcel Dekker: New York, 1993.

St. Clair, J. *Crime Laboratory Management;* Elsevier: New York, 2003.

SWGFAST. *Training to Competency for Latent Print Examiners.* http://www.swgfast.org/documents/qualifications-competency/020822_Competency_Latent_2.1.pdf.

Tague, N. R. *The Quality Toolbox,* 2nd ed.; ASQ Quality Press: Milwaukee, WI, 2004.

CHAPTER 13

FINGERPRINTS AND THE LAW

Andre A. Moenssens and
Stephen B. Meagher

CONTENTS

- 3   **13.1 Introduction**
- 4   **13.2 The Expert and the Rules of Evidence**
- 11   **13.3 Daubert Challenges to "Fingerprinting"**
- 22   **13.4 Historical Account of Fingerprints, Palmprints, and Footprints in U.S. Courts**
- 25   **13.5 Conclusion**
- 26   **13.6 Reviewers**
- 26   **13.7 References**

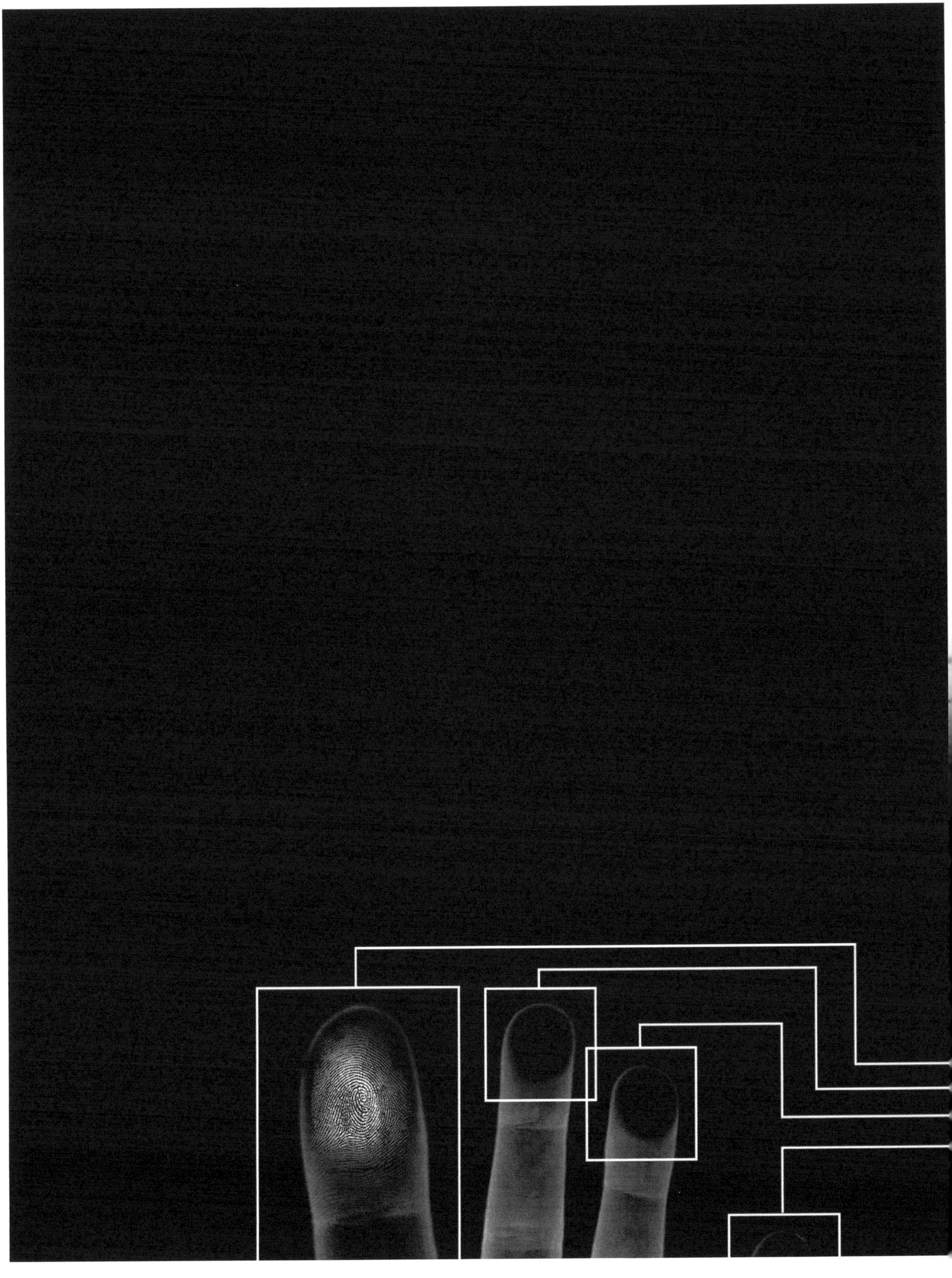

CHAPTER 13

FINGERPRINTS AND THE LAW

ANDRE A. MOENSSENS AND
STEPHEN B. MEAGHER

13.1 Introduction

Fingerprints, palmprints, and impressions of bare soles have been widely recognized and accepted as a reliable means to identify a person. A reproduction of the friction ridge arrangements on a fingerprint, palmprint, or footprint may be left on an object when it is touched. This permits the impression to be used for the personal identification of individuals in criminal investigations. Thus, the forensic science of fingerprints, palmprints, and footprints is utilized by law enforcement agencies in support of their investigations to positively identify the perpetrator of a crime. This forensic science is also used for exculpatory or elimination purposes.

This chapter will address the laws and rules of evidence as they apply to friction ridge impression evidence. Historical court decisions and recent appellate and United States Supreme Court rulings will be addressed. This chapter will primarily address federal court decisions and the Federal Rules of Evidence, which may not be applicable to all states.

The term "friction ridge impression" will be used to refer to any impression made from human friction ridge skin (e.g., the skin on the palm side of fingers and hands and the soles of the feet). There are two different types of friction ridge impressions: those of known individuals intentionally recorded, and impressions from one or more unknown persons on a piece of evidence from a crime scene or related location; the latter are generally referred to as latent prints.

The scope of this chapter will include legal aspects associated with experts and evidence, and legal challenges to the admissibility of friction ridge impression evidence. The basis of the material will be the U.S. legal system at the federal level. The text makes occasional references to laws or court decisions of specific states or foreign countries when notable. The reader is strongly encouraged to consult those legal sources that more particularly govern the jurisdiction in which the expert will be testifying.

13.2 The Expert and the Rules of Evidence

13.2.1 Introduction

The term "forensic science" implies the use of a scientifically based discipline as it intersects with and provides evidence for legal proceedings. The Federal Rules of Evidence (FRE) set out the framework within which evidence is admitted into court. The primary rules that apply to expert witnesses are FRE 702, Testimony by Experts; and FRE 703, Bases of Opinion Testimony by Experts.

FRE 701, Opinion Testimony by Lay Witnesses, permits a better understanding of the distinction between opinion testimony offered by an expert and those instances where even a lay witness may offer opinions in a court of law.

How these rules affect examiners of friction ridge impressions will be discussed later. At this point, the discussion is limited to defining the terms the law of evidence uses in connection with legal proceedings.

13.2.2 Federal Rules of Evidence — Rule 702

The definition and uses of expert testimony, which are also applicable to persons performing forensic friction ridge impression examinations, are expressed in FRE 702. Currently, the rule provides:

> If scientific, technical, or other specialized knowledge will assist the trier of fact to understand the evidence or to determine a fact in issue, a witness qualified as an expert by knowledge, skill, experience, training, or education, may testify thereto in the form of an opinion or otherwise, if (1) the testimony is based upon sufficient facts or data, (2) the testimony is the product of reliable principles and methods, and (3) the witness has applied the principles and methods reliably to the facts of the case. (As amended Apr. 17, 2000, eff. Dec. 1, 2000.) (FRE, 2004, p 13)

The rule encompasses a number of issues. In the order of their mention in the rule, each will be discussed, first in a general sense, and then as they apply to the expert in friction ridge impression examinations. The key purpose of Rule 702 is to determine whether a witness warrants expert status and will be permitted to offer opinion testimony.

13.2.2.1 Qualifications of the Expert Witness. A witness who will be offering opinion testimony must first be shown to be qualified as an expert. That step involves the expert taking the stand, being sworn to tell the truth, and providing answers to questions posed by an attorney relating to the witness's competence. At the conclusion of direct testimony, the counsel proffering the witness will ordinarily move that the witness be recognized by the court as an expert. Opposing counsel is given an opportunity to question the witness to challenge his or her expert qualifications. At the conclusion of this process, the judge decides whether the witness may offer opinion testimony as an expert. In deciding, the judge may limit the extent to which the expert will be permitted to testify. The jury has no role in this preliminary step; the determination whether a proffered witness qualifies as an expert is a legal decision. (The process is sometimes referred to as the voir dire of an expert.)

13.2.2.2 Testimony about the Facts of a Case. It is only after the preliminary stage of qualifying the witness as an expert is completed that the witness can offer opinions about the case in which the witness was called to court. In a jury trial, the jurors act as the arbiters of the facts. When facts are in dispute, the jurors decide what they believe happened. When the experts testify, the jurors ultimately decide also whether they will accept the opinions expressed by the experts as true facts. Before the jury deliberates, the judge will instruct them that they are free to either believe or disbelieve, in whole or in part, the testimony of any witness, including an expert. The credibility instruction on lay and expert witnesses shows how important it is for the expert to offer concise, credible, understandable, and convincing testimony.

13.2.2.3 Is the Examination of Friction Ridge Impressions a Science? The first seven words of FRE 702, "If scientific, technical or other specialized knowledge…", evoke an immediate question for the expert: Is a forensic friction ridge impression examination scientific, technical, specialized knowledge, or a combination of two or three of these choices? The question can be logically followed with several more: Is it important to distinguish between them and choose just one? Does the court require the expert to state under which aspect of the rule the expert purports to testify?

These questions have been answered by the U.S. Supreme Court in its decision in *Kumho Tire Co.* v *Carmichael*, 526 U.S. 137, 119 S. Ct. 1167 (1999). The court clearly stated that the same criteria used in *Daubert* v *Merrell Dow Pharmaceuticals, Inc.*, 509 U.S. 579, 113 S. Ct. 2786 (1993), to determine whether testimony offered as scientific knowledge is reliable should also govern the admissibility of testimony under the "technical" and "other specialized knowledge" prongs of Rule 702 to the extent these criteria may be applicable to them. (*Daubert* and *Kumho Tire* are discussed more in depth in sections 13.3.1.3 and 13.3.1.4.) Therefore, distinguishing between science, applied science, technology, or experience-based expertise is not paramount or even required. (These two important cases will be revisited later in a discussion of challenges to the admissibility of fingerprint evidence.)

Though the "science versus experience" issue may not be important under Rule 702, it is nevertheless an intriguing question that warrants further discussion. If one postulates that the discipline of forensic friction ridge impression examination represents "science", then *Daubert* requires a showing of the scientific underpinnings that make the discipline reliable. Is forensic friction ridge impression examination a scientific endeavor such as, for instance, chemistry or biology? Or is it more of an applied technical field based in several sciences?

The Scientific Working Group on Friction Ridge Analysis, Study, and Technology (SWGFAST), a recognized body charged with formulating guidelines for the friction ridge impression examiners' discipline, posits that forensic friction ridge impression examination "is an applied science based upon the foundation of biological uniqueness, permanence, and empirical validation through observation" (SWGFAST, Press Kit). This is logical when one understands that the fundamental premises on which friction ridge impression "individualizations" (identifications) rest are (1) friction ridge uniqueness and (2) persistence of the friction ridge arrangements. Without an understanding of the biological aspects underlying the formation of friction ridges prenatally, experts would never be justified in reaching a conclusion, reliable or otherwise, that an individualization has been effected (i.e., a positive identification of one individual who was the source of an impression to the exclusion of all other possible persons). The SWGFAST position thus supports the claim that forensic friction ridge impression examination is scientific.

But is it possible that forensic friction ridge impression examination is also technical? Furthermore, does it also require specialized knowledge and training on the part of the expert? Any expert trained to competency in forensic friction ridge impression examinations will certainly admit that, in addition to its scientific underpinnings, the task at hand also requires specialized technical knowledge if one is to achieve a reliable conclusion. Therefore, forensic friction ridge impression examinations can be proffered as any or all three of the prongs contained in FRE 702.

13.2.2.4 Whom Must the Expert Convince? The next phrase in FRE 702 indicates whom the expert, through testimony, is expected to assist: it is the "fact finder". Because the Federal Rules of Evidence, and therefore FRE 702 as well, apply whether the expert testifies at a pretrial hearing or at the trial itself, the expert must understand that at a pretrial admissibility hearing based on a *Daubert* challenge, the judge also acts as the fact finder. The expert testimony at such a hearing is provided solely to assist the judge in determining whether the *Daubert* challenge will be sustained or rejected.

The expert testimony given at trial, by contrast, is initially directed to the judge for the determination of whether the witness qualifies as an expert and, once found to be qualified, then to the jury, if any, for the purpose of presenting the results, conclusions, and expert opinions obtained during the examination process. In a nonjury (bench) trial, the judge will also act as the fact finder.

13.2.2.5 Testifying about Qualifications. The next phrase in FRE 702 states, "a witness qualified as an expert by knowledge, skill, experience, training, or education, may testify thereto in the form of an opinion or otherwise". This phrase describes how courts are to determine whether one is an expert as proffered. The expert needs to be prepared to identify specific information for each of the five criteria listed in the rule: knowledge, skill, experience, training, and education. A well-prepared expert should have the pertinent details for these criteria set out in a curriculum vitae.

The direct testimony on the qualifications typically includes a recital of the person's education (formal and otherwise); specialized training received, including detailed information of the nature, length, and detail of that training; the professional certifications obtained; continuing education pursued; membership and activities in professional societies; awards received; written materials prepared and courses taught; and previous expert testimony offered.

Persons seeking to qualify as expert witnesses need to continually update their curriculum vitae so that lawyers seeking to present their testimony will have an accurate copy available for the court. A well-written, professional curriculum vitae goes a long way to shorten what can otherwise be a lengthy qualification process and possibly avert some cross-examination questions by opposing counsel regarding the expert's qualifications. An impressive curriculum vitae may actually result in the defense offering to stipulate to the expert's qualifications. Under this scenario, the opposing counsel makes a conscious strategic decision to stipulate so that the judge and jury will not be overly influenced by impressive credentials. There are other reasons the defense may stipulate to the expert's qualification (e.g., a simple desire to save time; no intent to aggressively contest the expert's testimony in an effort to downplay its significance; or, when the fingerprint identification is uncontested, as in a self-defense or insanity defense case).

13.2.2.6 Is Expert Opinion Testimony Warranted? The ultimate question on whether expert testimony is warranted at all in a particular case requires the judge to determine, from a common sense perspective, whether an untrained lay person (judge or juror) presented with factual evidence can determine what happened alone, without an expert's assistance. If so, then expert opinion testimony is not warranted. But if the expert's opinion would be helpful to the fact finder in understanding the significance of factual data, then the expert witness is essential and opinion evidence is admissible.

13.2.2.7 Further Requirements of Revised FRE 702. Once the judge determines that an expert is qualified to give opinion evidence under FRE 702, then the expert can so testify. In April 2000 (effective December 2000), the Federal Rules of Evidence were amended to include three further requirements which must also be met. They are "(1) the testimony (must be) based upon sufficient facts or data, (2) the testimony is the product of reliable principles and methods, and (3) the witness has applied the principles and methods reliably to the facts of the case". These three requirements were added by the FRE committee to conform opinion testimony to the mandates of the *Daubert* and *Kumho Tire* decisions. The revision makes it easier to present effective scientific and technical expert testimony whenever such evidence is warranted and also provides a basis for excluding opinion testimony that cannot be said to be based on a reliable methodology.

The first one of these three requirements necessitates that the expert's testimony rest on a sufficient basis that supports a reliable conclusion. Under ideal conditions, known facts or data would present themselves with clear-cut answers and would be totally based upon objective measurements. The reality is that this rarely occurs. In fact, it is in the nature of science that some premises remain in a gray area where a degree of subjectivity is unavoidable. How many data and facts are needed to allow the judge to find a "sufficient" basis for the opinion? That question is still being debated among legal scholars.

What does the forensic science of friction ridge impression examinations offer to the court on that same issue of sufficiency? It has been established by sound and repeated studies that friction ridge examination evidence permits the uncontroverted association of a particular individual with a particular scene or object. If the scene or object is part of a crime, the individualization evidence would certainly offer a logical connection to a case, permitting a jury to draw conclusions as to guilt or innocence of the individualized person.

The second requirement asks whether the testimony will be the product of reliable principles and methods. Here, the expert must not only be able to state the principles and the methods used but be familiar with any research or testing that has demonstrated the reliability. In this regard, friction ridge examination follows an established SWGFAST-approved methodology designed to lead to reliable and verifiable conclusions if the prescribed methodology is followed by a competent examiner.

The third requirement mandates that the witness has applied the principles and methods reliably to the facts of the case. Here the court must determine whether everything the witness testified to previously in connection with the first and second requirements was adhered to in the particular case. It would be a blunder of monumental proportions for an expert to lay out the details of the specific process in satisfying the first and second requirements and then completely abandon that process for the case at hand.

It must be recognized, however, that occasionally exceptions to the use of recommended processes are warranted, indeed required, by the particular circumstances of a case. Methodologies and examination protocols are designed to deal with the normal course of an investigation to the extent that a "normal" course can be anticipated. The nature of criminal activity occasionally does not always follow anticipated paths. Deviating from recommended "standard" processes requires a lot of thought and experience on the part of an examiner, but the justification for the deviation must always be clearly documented in the examiner's notes.

13.2.3 Federal Rules of Evidence — Rule 703

FRE 703, the basis of opinion testimony by experts, states:

> The facts or data in the particular case upon which an expert bases an opinion or inference may be those perceived by or made known to the expert at or before the hearing. If of a type reasonably relied upon by the experts in the particular field in forming opinions or inference upon the subject, the facts or data need not be admissible in evidence in order for the opinion or inference to be admitted. Facts or data that are otherwise inadmissible shall not be disclosed to the jury by the proponent of the opinion or inference unless the court determines that their probative value in assisting the jury to evaluate the expert's opinion substantially outweighs their prejudicial effect.

This rule describes the different types of testimony experts can offer.

13.2.3.1 Testimony about First-Hand Knowledge; The Hypothetical Question. An expert, like any ordinary fact witness, may testify to observations the expert made in examining evidence, the methods used and factual data found, and then express an opinion derived from such first-hand knowledge possessed by the expert. That is one of the traditional forms of expert testimony. But in addition, the first sentence of FRE 703 also permits an expert to offer opinions on facts of which the expert may not have known prior to coming to court, but of which the expert was apprised at the hearing or trial. That is what is known as the typical "hypothetical question" wherein an expert is asked to assume a series of facts stated by the direct examiner (or cross-examiner) and, after these facts have been stated, the expert is asked whether he or she has an opinion based on these facts. These two forms of expert evidence have long been sanctioned by the common law of evidence.

13.2.3.2 Testimony Based on Reports or Examinations Made by Others. The second sentence of Rule 703 represents a change from what previously was the law. It is a change that even today is not followed in all jurisdictions. Normally, if an expert has arrived at an opinion based on facts that the expert was told by someone else, the basis for that opinion is "hearsay", and, at one time, such an opinion was inadmissible in most state and federal jurisdictions.

When the Federal Rules of Evidence were written, the drafters decided to do away with this long-standing prohibition and to permit opinion testimony based on hearsay, provided the hearsay is of the kind that experts in the particular field rely on to make ordinary professional decisions in their careers. Under this portion of the rule, for instance, doctors are now permitted to testify to X-ray reports received from an X-ray technician or information contained in nurses' reports without first having to call the X-ray technician or nurse to court. In or out of hospitals, doctors do rely on such reports to make life and death decisions, and the drafters of the FRE decided to focus on the reliability of such evidence as *determined by the practitioners in the field* rather than as determined simply by technical rules such as the common law prohibition against the use of hearsay evidence. Thus, the FRE significantly broadened the potential scope of expert testimony. FRE 703 now permits professionals to rely upon reports of others without first having to call any of these "others" as witnesses, as long as to do so is a recognized practice in their discipline.

The final sentence of FRE 703 states that the information provided to the expert by third parties who are not in court need not even be shown to be independently admissible in evidence. But the judge decides whether the jury may be informed about that potentially inadmissible evidence. For example, a crime scene investigator develops a latent print at a crime scene, submits a lift or photograph of the latent print to the laboratory, and then advises the expert as to how and what method was used to process the evidence. In such a case, the expert may testify to the development method used by the investigator even though the expert was not present when the latent print was made visible. Such inadmissible hearsay may be presented to the jury if, in the judge's estimation, its probative value in assisting the jury to evaluate the expert's opinion substantially outweighs any prejudicial effect it may have.

13.2.4 Federal Rules of Evidence—Rule 701

FRE 701 on opinion testimony by lay witnesses states:

> If the witness is not testifying as an expert, the witness' testimony in the form of opinions or inferences is limited to those opinions or inferences which are (a) rationally based on the perception of the witness, and (b) helpful to a clear understanding of the witness' testimony or the determination of a fact in issue, and (c) not based on scientific, technical, or specialized knowledge within the scope of Rule 702.

The intent of FRE 701 is to provide a contrast for a better understanding of FRE 702. FRE 701 outlines the conditions under which even a nonexpert may testify to an opinion or draw a conclusion from known facts.

Generally speaking, lay (nonexpert) witnesses may offer opinion testimony in those cases where their opinions are (1) rationally based on their perception and (2) when to do so would be helpful to the jury. Thus, nonexpert witnesses may offer the kind of opinions that ordinary persons would make in their daily lives. Lay witnesses who testify can utter opinions like, "he was drunk", or "he was going way too fast", or "I could hear everything through the wall and they were having an argument".

The law prohibits lay persons, however, from offering opinions on the ultimate issue to be determined. For example, an opinion that "the defendant was grossly negligent" is not considered to be "helpful" to the jurors in forming their own conclusions (rather, it attempts to draw the conclusion for them) and is therefore not permitted. It may be that all persons witnessing the same occurrence would have come to the same conclusion, and therefore the opinion was rationally based on perception. Nevertheless, the type of opinion by a lay witness that goes to the ultimate issue is not permitted under Rule 701. The law is different for expert testimony. Rule 704(a) of the FRE specifically provides that "testimony in the form of an opinion or inference otherwise admissible is not objectionable because it embraces an ultimate issue to be decided by the trier of fact". This provision effectuated a change from the common-law prohibition against "ultimate issue" opinions of all witnesses. That prohibition had already been eroded significantly in many jurisdictions, at least for expert testimony, at the time the FRE were drafted. There is only one exception where FRE 704 on expert testimony retains the prohibition on ultimate issue testimony and that is for behavioral experts testifying to the mental state of an accused in criminal cases. This exception was added as FRE 704(b) in 1984 after a battle of psychiatric experts in the trial of John Hinckley, accused of attempting to assassinate President Reagan, resulted in Hinckley's acquittal.

The last provision of FRE 701, section "c", makes clear that the need to prove the reliability of true expert opinion testimony under *Daubert* and *Kumho Tire* cannot be avoided by seeking to offer the opinion as a lay opinion under FRE 701. Although a person can offer testimony both as an expert and as a lay person in the same case, the 2000 amendment to FRE 701, which added section "c", makes clear that any part of the testimony that is based on "scientific, technical, or other specialized knowledge" will be governed by FRE 702, and not by FRE 701. The admissibility of expert opinion testimony by a friction ridge examiner and about friction ridge examinations will be governed by Rule 702. It cannot qualify as a lay opinion.

13.2.5 The Judge's Instructions to the Jury

During litigation, each side will have an opportunity to request what jury instructions should be sent to the jury. The judge will decide what final instructions will be presented to the jury. These instructions will cover many topics appropriate for the testimony provided and the charges proffered. If expert witness testimony is provided, it is almost certain that the judge will include instructions regarding this type of testimony as well. The following is a typical jury instruction related to expert witness testimony:

> You have heard the testimony of experts in this case. The credibility or worth of the testimony of an expert witness is to be considered by you just as it is your duty to judge the credibility or worth of the testimony of all other witnesses you have heard or evidence you have seen. You are not bound to accept expert testimony as true, and you may weigh and credit testimony of expert witnesses the same as that of other witnesses, and give it the weight to which you think it is entitled. (Adapted from Pattern Jury Instructions approved by several jurisdictions.)

Such an instruction will typically be given to the jury after it has been instructed that it is the sole judge of the credibility of all the evidence it has heard and that it may accept or reject the testimony of any witness, in whole or in part, if the jury finds such evidence (or any part of it) to be unconvincing or not worthy of belief. One or more additional instructions on the duty of the jury in weighing evidence may be given.

It is also permissible for the judge to supplement the standard expert witness jury instruction with special provisions more applicable to a particular case. However, in charging the jury, the judge may not refer to the testimony of any particular witness and may not single out certain testimony or evidence.

Training courses for fingerprint experts should include an awareness of these jury instructions because it may result in altering how the expert articulates certain information during his or her testimony, especially if a defense expert will also be testifying.

13.2.6 The Expert and Potential Impeachment Information

There are three significant cases that mandate what information the prosecution must provide to the defense. Two of these cases apply uniformly across the country as a matter of constitutional law; the third was decided by the 9th Circuit Court of Appeals in an unpublished decision, which is therefore technically not entitled to precedential value. The first two cases are *Brady* v *Maryland*, 373 U.S. 83 (1963) and *Giglio* v *United States*, 405 U.S. 150 (1972). The third is *United States* v *Henthorn*, 930 F.2d 920 (9th Cir. 1991), affirming *United States* v *Henthorn*, 931 F.2d 29 (9th Cir. 1991).

In *Brady* v *Maryland*, the U.S. Supreme Court ruled that anyone accused of a criminal matter has the right to be informed of any potentially exculpatory information within the prosecutor's control that may be favorable to the accused and may be material to either guilt or punishment. Materiality of the evidence means that there is a reasonable probability that had the evidence been disclosed in a proceeding, the result of the proceeding would have been different. If the prosecution is uncertain whether certain materials requested by the defense must be disclosed, it may ask the court to inspect the material in chambers to make that determination.

In effect, if a fingerprint expert knows of any information from an examination of the evidence that could be considered exculpatory to the accused, such information must be provided to the prosecutor and, ultimately, to the court and defense.

In *Giglio* v *United States*, the U.S. Supreme Court ruled that the government is constitutionally required to disclose any evidence favorable to the defense that may impact a defendant's guilt or punishment, including any information that may bear on the credibility of its witnesses, even if the defendant fails to request such information.

In *United States* v *Henthorn*, the Circuit Court of Appeals for the 9th Circuit ruled that the government has a duty to review the personnel files of its testifying officers and to disclose to the defense any information which may be favorable to the defendant that meets appropriate standards of materiality. Obviously, this is information that would go to the qualifications of the experts. Such matters as past errors, required retraining, or any actions that may reflect on the integrity or credibility of the expert are susceptible to this ruling. Although this is not a U.S. Supreme Court rule, it is being followed widely by other jurisdictions.

13.2.7 Federal Rules of Criminal Procedure— Rule 16

The Federal Rules of Criminal Procedure set forth guidelines for a wide range of issues. One of these rules of special interest to fingerprint expert witnesses is Rule 16, Discovery and Inspection, and specifically, Rule 16(a)(1)(F), *Reports of Examinations and Tests*, and (G) *Expert Witnesses*. Unlike the material constitutionally required to be disclosed by the decisions in the preceding section (*Brady* and *Giglio*), these disclosure provisions apply only in federal courts. The various states may or may not have similar discovery provisions in their rules of procedure.

Rule 16(a)(1)(F), *Reports of Examinations and Tests*, states:

> Upon a defendant's request, the government must permit a defendant to inspect and to copy or photograph the results or reports of any physical or mental examination and of any scientific test or experiment if:
>
> (i) the item is within the government's possession, custody or control;
>
> (ii) the attorney for the government knows—or through due diligence could know—that the item exists, and;
>
> (iii) the item is material to preparing the defense or the government intends to use the item in its case-in-chief at trial.

Rule 16(a)(1)(G), *Expert Witnesses*, states:

> At the defendant's request, the government must give to the defendant a written summary of any testimony that the government intends to use under Rules 702, 703, or 705 of the Federal Rules of Evidence during its case-in-chief at trial. If the government requests discovery under subdivision (b)(1)(C)(ii) and the defendant complies, the government must, at the defendant's request, give to the defendant a written summary of testimony that the government intends to use under Rules 702, 703, or 705 of the Federal Rules of Evidence as evidence at trial on the issue of the defendant's mental condition. The summary

provided under this paragraph must describe the witness's opinions, the bases and reasons for those opinions, and the witness's qualifications.

It is apparent from the wording in these two subsections to Rule 16 that fingerprint experts must be prepared to provide copies of their examination documents and to provide a written report setting forth the bases for their conclusions and opinions. Generally, most forensic laboratory reports set forth the conclusions but seldom are the bases for the conclusions included. Therefore, expert witnesses should be aware of Rule 16 and be prepared to respond to discovery requests under Rule 16.

Recently, defense attorneys submitting requests for Rule 16 discovery regarding fingerprint identification and expert testimony have included not only disclosure of the basis for the identification but also information on the scientific bases for the fingerprint discipline. This, of course, goes directly to the *Daubert* issue, which is discussed later in this chapter. The expert will need to be prepared to concisely present the *Daubert*-related information in a succinct report.

Lastly, subsection (G) states the need to provide accurate information on the witness' qualifications. As previously discussed under FRE 702, the fingerprint expert would be well served in maintaining an up-to-date curriculum vitae that could be quickly provided in compliance with a Rule 16 request.

A third subsection of Rule 16 also has direct application to fingerprint expert witnesses. This is Rule 16 (a)(1)(D), *Defendant's Prior Record,* and states:

> Upon a defendant's request, the government must furnish the defendant with a copy of the defendant's prior criminal record that is within the government's possession, custody, or control if the attorney for the government knows—or through due diligence could know—that the record exists.

Because most of the law enforcement agencies in the United Sates rely on fingerprint records to assimilate prior arrest activity, this subsection of the rule is quite important to the booking officer and the fingerprint expert. Often, the arrest record is provided to the defendant and little regard is given to the fact that fingerprints are the basis for this individual's arrest record. However, with the advent of *Daubert* challenges to latent print examinations, it is possible that similar challenges may come to this aspect of the fingerprint discipline as well. It is believed that tenprint fingerprint records will easily withstand such a challenge because these fingerprints are obtained under controlled conditions with the individual arrested being present for each recording or arrest. Recent activities within the fingerprint discipline are being undertaken to further bolster the discipline in these matters. For example, the International Association for Identification has implemented a Tenprint Fingerprint Examiner Certification program for those individuals who would be testifying to such arrest records. This testimony would be based on the defendant's fingerprints being recorded during the booking process after each arrest to demonstrate that the same person was arrested in each instance, regardless of alias names or other false documentation the person may have provided. This certification of tenprint fingerprint examiners will provide the courts with a meaningful measure of competence for the expert's qualifications.

13.2.8 Other Federal Rules of Evidence as They Pertain to Fingerprints and Related Expert Testimony

The conclusions reached by the expert performing a forensic latent print examination ordinarily cannot be stated until the evidence has been admitted. Although the responsibility for presenting the expert's testimony in court lies with the prosecuting attorney to ensure that the foundation of the evidence is properly established, the expert witness, in testifying, must stay within the limits of permissible court testimony.

Forensic laboratories should have standard operating procedures along with a quality assurance program that provides for the integrity of the evidence. Such matters as chain of custody and evidence security from the time it is initially received to the time it leaves the laboratory are crucial for ensuring that evidence will be admitted in court.

FRE 401 demands that the evidence be relevant to the case at hand. Although this may seem obvious, its intent is to preclude the introduction of evidence that serves no benefit in determining the ultimate questions in the case. FRE 401 defines relevant evidence as "evidence having any tendency to make the existence of any fact that is consequence to the determination of the action more probable or less probable than it would be without the evidence".

FRE 403 allows a judge to exclude certain relevant evidence as a matter of judicial discretion. The rule states: "... [R]elevant[ ] evidence may be excluded if its probative value is substantially outweighed by the danger of unfair prejudice, confusion of the issues, or misleading the jury, or by considerations of undue delay, waste of time, or needless presentation of cumulative evidence." And FRE 402 rounds out the matter by simply stating that any irrelevant evidence is inadmissible.

FRE 201 addresses the issue of judicial notice of adjudicative facts. When the court takes judicial notice of a certain fact, the proponent of that fact is excused from proving the fact. Judicial notice of a certain fact adds considerable weight to the evidence because it is typically accompanied by an explanation for the jury that it may take the noted fact as proven and that no further evidence on that point is required. There are, however, limitations on the type of evidence that a judge may judicially note. FRE 201 states:

> A judicially noticed fact must be one not subject to reasonable dispute in that it is either (1) generally known within the territorial jurisdiction of the trial court or (2) capable of accurate and ready determination by resort to sources whose accuracy cannot be reasonably be questioned.

In *United States* v *Mitchell* (discussed more in depth in section 13.3.2.1), the first *Daubert* hearing challenging the science of fingerprints, Judge J. Curtis Joyner took judicial notice that friction ridge skin is unique and permanent, even for small areas. This ruling was stated to be in error by the appellate court. Although the uniqueness of full finger patterns of friction skin may be properly noted judicially and the fact is supported by sound biological evidence—indeed, even the defense ordinarily no longer challenges it—the issue in *Mitchell* was whether small areas of a latent impression were also unique. That fact was found not to be established with certainty because its proof required presentation of conflicting evidence over the better part of a week. Therefore, the uniqueness of incomplete and partially distorted friction ridge impressions is not one that a court could judicially note. Therefore, it is important that the uniqueness of partial latent prints be thoroughly explained by the expert because it is critical in establishing the rationale for stating that conclusions from even partial fingerprints can only have the three possible answers as set forth by the SWGFAST Standards for Conclusion: individualization, exclusion, or inconclusive comparison (SWGFAST, 2004, 358–359).

Article X, Rules 1001 through 1008, of the FRE addresses the contents of writings, recordings, and photographs. These rules set forth the definitions and requirements regarding what constitutes originals or duplicates and the admissibility of each, even if the original is lost or destroyed. A fingerprint expert's case examination documentation is governed by these rules, as well as any photographs of the latent prints, AFIS searches, and known exemplars from an arrest record (see also FRE 902 (4), Self-Authentication, *Certified Copies of Public Records*).

The FRE govern most aspects of presenting evidence and getting it successfully admitted. A fingerprint experts' training program should include a discussion of these rules. This knowledge will certainly assist the examiner in having the evidence and the resulting testimony regarding the evidence admitted.

13.3 Daubert Challenges to "Fingerprinting"

13.3.1 The Legal Origins

13.3.1.1 *Frye v United States*. Early in the past century, a researcher came up with the idea to combine people's instinctive notion about bodily changes that occur when one attempts to deceive with a medical device that was designed to measure blood pressure. The device was a systolic blood pressure cuff; the man was William Marston, who, in 1917, claimed to be able to tell—in an objective fashion and by applying a "scientific" method—whether a person was engaged in verbal deception.

After James Adolphus Frye was charged with murder in the District of Columbia and maintained he was innocent, Marston was asked to examine Frye. After attaching the systolic blood pressure cuff and asking Frye a number of questions, Marston was prepared to testify that Frye spoke truthfully when he denied knowledge of the crime and professed his innocence. The "systolic blood pressure deception test", essentially a rather crude precursor of the modern polygraph, had revealed this fact to the purported expert. But the court would not let Marston testify. On appeal, the issue was whether the trial court had erred in refusing to permit Marston to testify about the test result. The appellate decision became the basis for a most important legal principle that continues to have an impact on expert opinion testimony of types very different from lie detection: it is the case of *Frye* v *United States,* 293 F. 1013 (D.C. Cir. 1923).

The court in *Frye* suggested how courts contemplating whether to admit novel expert testimony ought to proceed:

> Just when a scientific principle or discovery crosses the line between the experimental and demonstrable stages is difficult to define. Somewhere in this twilight zone the evidential force of the principle must be recognized, and while the courts will go a long way in admitting expert testimony deduced from a well-recognized scientific principle or discovery, the thing from which the deduction is made *must be sufficiently established to have gained general acceptance in the particular field in which it belongs.* (Emphasis added.)

The court went on to conclude that the polygraph test had not yet gained such general acceptance in the disciplines of human physiology and psychology; these were the fields wherein the court believed the "lie detector" belonged.

One might wonder what test courts used in deciding whether to admit novel expert testimony prior to *Frye.* The admissibility of scientific evidence in reality depended on whether the person offered as a witness wanting to express opinion testimony was qualified as an expert. If the witness was, then that person was typically competent to render expert opinion testimony. And, prior to the 1923 *Frye* decision, that competence was largely measured by the expert's success in real life. If a person earned a living selling his or her knowledge in the marketplace, then that person would be considered an expert who could testify at trial. Although not very sophisticated, this early principle of "marketplace acceptance" (a concept we might in the post-*Daubert* parlance equate to some early form of peer review) served the law in a more or less acceptable manner for a great number of years.

Initially, the *Frye* rule evoked little interest. Cited only as the rule that held that "lie detector" (polygraph) evidence was inadmissible, the opinion was ignored by most other courts, which is not surprising considering it was only two pages in length and contained no citations of authority or other court precedents supporting the startling new principle that was announced.

When, however, the crime laboratories of the 1960s, fueled by massive federal assistance programs, began to flood the courtrooms with novel types of expert testimony in the post-World War II era, *Frye* was suddenly rediscovered and was applied to a wide variety of different types of expert opinion testimony. *Frye* was, however, applied mainly in criminal cases; at the time of the *Daubert* decision, the *Frye* test had only been discussed in two civil cases: *Christopher* v *Allied-Signal Corp.,* 503 U.S. 912 (1992) and *Mustafa* v *United States,* 479 U.S. 953 (1986). But in criminal cases, it reigned supreme. In short order, the *Frye* test was used to determine the admissibility of opinions derived from voiceprints, neutron activation analysis, gunshot residue tests, bite mark comparisons, questioning with sodium pentothal ("truth serum"), scanning electron microscope analysis, and many other fields.

13.3.1.2 The Adoption of Federal Rule 702. With the approval of the U.S. Supreme Court, Congress passed the FRE in 1975. They became effective July 1, 1975, for all federal courts. The rules thereafter served as a model for law reform and for departing from the fairly rigid common law rules of evidence in a significant number of states as well. FRE 702 deals particularly with expert testimony. It provided, at the time of its passage:

> If scientific, technical, or other specialized knowledge will assist the trier of fact to understand the evidence or to determine a fact in issue, a witness qualified as an expert by knowledge, skill, experience, training, or education, may testify thereto in the form of an opinion or otherwise. (Federal Rule of Evidence 702, as first enacted in 1975.)

This rule of Evidence, when taken in conjunction with other Federal Rules, was sometimes referred to as being based on a liberal "general relevance" standard of admissibility. It treated novel scientific evidence the same as any other evidence: evidence was admissible as relevant, under FRE 401, if it had "any tendency to make the existence of any fact that is of consequence to the determination of the action more probable or less probable than it would be without the evidence" (FRE, 2004, p 3).

Thus, the FRE contained no special rule that, when dealing with "scientific" evidence, novel or otherwise, ensured that science-based testimony is reliable and, therefore, admissible. All evidence was admissible if relevant, provided its use in court was not outweighed by undue prejudice, misleading of the jury, or requiring an undue consumption of time.

The FRE also did not distinguish between the admissibility of expert opinion evidence in criminal as opposed to civil cases. They applied the same standard of admissibility except in a few situations that are specifically earmarked or shaped by constitutional principles.

The next step in legal developments occurred in 1993, when the U.S. Supreme Court handed down a momentous decision that would drastically change the landscape of expert evidence. That decision was *Daubert* v *Merrell Dow Pharmaceuticals, Inc. Daubert* was later followed by another important court case, *Kumho Tire* v *Carmichael*. Both *Daubert* and *Kumho Tire* arose out of civil lawsuits.

[Author's note: As the following discussion of case law appears in a nonlegal document, internal citations for all quotations will not be provided in order to aid readability.]

13.3.1.3 Daubert v Merrell Dow Pharmaceuticals. In *Daubert*, two infants sued the defendant pharmaceutical company, alleging that they suffered limb reduction birth defects as a result of their mothers' ingestion of the drug Bendectin, manufactured by the defendant. The drug was administered to the plaintiff-mothers during their pregnancy in order to combat morning sickness.

The defendant, Merrell Dow Pharmaceuticals, Inc., moved for summary judgment in the trial court, contending that Bendectin does not cause birth defects in humans. In support of their motion, Steven H. Lamm, a physician and epidemiologist with impressive credentials who had served as a birth-defect epidemiology consultant for the National Center for Health Statistics, stated that he had reviewed *all* the relevant literature and that no study found that Bendectin caused human birth defects.

Interestingly, the plaintiffs did not dispute Dr. Lamm's characterization of the medical literature or his conclusion on the lack of a causal connection between the drug and birth defects. However, the plaintiffs responded by offering the testimony of eight equally well-credentialed experts of their own, who had concluded that Bendectin *can* cause birth defects. Their conclusions were based on animal cell studies, live animal studies, and chemical structure analyses. They also based their conclusions on recalculations of data in the studies upon which the defendant's argument rested.

The district court agreed with the defendant and granted the motion for summary judgment. The court concluded that, based on the enormous amount of epidemiological data which had concluded that Bendectin did not cause birth defects, plaintiffs' contrary expert opinion was not admissible to establish causation because the expert's methodology was not "sufficiently established to have general acceptance in the field to which it belongs" (U.S. District Court opinion, reported at 727 F. Supp. 570, 572 (S.D. Cal. 1989)). Furthermore, plaintiffs' experts' recalculations were held to be inadmissible because they had been neither published nor subjected to peer review.

The U.S. Court of Appeals for the Ninth Circuit affirmed the district court's ruling because plaintiffs' evidence was "generated solely for use in litigation" rather than based on published and peer-reviewed scientific knowledge (*Daubert* v *Merrell Dow Pharmaceuticals, Inc.*, 951 F.2d 1128 (9th Cir. 1991)). The U.S. Supreme Court agreed to review this decision because of the "sharp divisions among the courts regarding the proper standard for the admission of expert testimony".

A unanimous court held, simply, that *Frye* did not survive the enactment of the Federal Rules of Evidence and that the admissibility of scientific evidence should be judged according to the FRE evidentiary standard of relevance. The court stated that *Frye's* "rigid" general acceptance standard was in conflict with the "liberal thrust" of the FRE and their "general approach of relaxing the traditional barriers to 'opinion' testimony". The court found that *Frye's* "austere standard" of general acceptance, being "absent from and incompatible with the Federal Rules of Evidence", is no longer to be considered as the guide to admitting testimony based on novel "scientific knowledge".

In interpreting FRE 702, the *Daubert* court stated that if a litigant challenges the admissibility of scientific evidence, it is the function of the trial court to act as a gatekeeper to determine whether the proffered opinion evidence is "relevant" and "reliable".

To guide the district courts, the U.S. Supreme Court articulated several "flexible" factors that they ought to consider in deciding whether a scientific field was sufficiently reliable to warrant admission of opinion evidence based on the discipline.

In 1999, the U.S. Supreme Court applied the *Daubert* requirement of proof of reliability to all forms of expert opinion testimony—whether based on science, applied science, technology, skill, or experience—when it decided *Kumho Tire*.

13.3.1.4 *Kumho Tire Corp.* v *Carmichael*. Plaintiff Carmichael brought a products liability action against a tire manufacturer (Kumho Tire) and a tire distributor (Samyang Tires, Inc.) for injuries he sustained when the right rear tire on his vehicle failed and the vehicle overturned, killing a passenger and injuring others. Plaintiff sought to prove the causal connection between the accident and the defective tire by presenting the testimony of a "tire failure analyst" who wanted to testify that in his opinion a defect in either the tire's manufacture or its design had caused the blowout. He had subjected the tire to a "visual and tactile inspection" to formulate his conclusion. Defendant Kumho Tire moved to exclude the expert's testimony on the ground that the witness' methodology failed to satisfy FRE 702 and the *Daubert* decision. The district court excluded the evidence because it found insufficient indicia of reliability in the expert's methodology. At the same time, the court, as had the trial court in *Daubert*, also granted defendants' motion for summary judgment.

The intermediate appellate court reversed, however, reviewing the question of whether the trial court's decision to apply *Daubert* to this case was appropriate. It did not think it was, and said that the U.S. Supreme Court had intended to apply *Daubert* only to "scientific knowledge" and not to "skill- or experience-based observation".

Whether *Daubert* should be applied to all expert testimony was an issue that had divided trial courts interpreting it and had sparked intense debate on what constituted science and what did not qualify as scientific knowledge. Co-defendant Kumho Tire petitioned for review by the U.S. Supreme Court, which agreed to decide whether *Daubert* applied to experts in the "technical" or "other specialized knowledge" fields as well. FRE 702 includes expert opinions in those areas.

The court held that the *Daubert* requirement of proof of reliability was not limited to scientific knowledge, though that was the way the issue had been presented in *Daubert*. It stated, "Th[e] language [of FRE 702] makes no relevant distinction between 'scientific' knowledge and 'technical' or 'other specialized' knowledge." The court added that *Daubert* and the rules of evidence make clear that all experts may testify to opinions, including those not based on firsthand knowledge or observation.

Thus, without equivocation, the court held that the obligation imposed on trial judges by *Daubert* to act as gatekeepers on the reliability of expert opinion evidence applies equally to all expert opinion testimony, even in areas where the expert opinion was based more on skill and experience, and—this is important—even in cases dealing with fields of expertise that had already been judicially recognized as yielding admissible expert opinion testimony. The court said that to require trial judges to draw a distinction between scientific knowledge and technical or other specialized knowledge would make their job of "gatekeeper" difficult, if not impossible. The court explained:

> There is no clear line that divides the one from the others. Disciplines such as engineering rest upon scientific knowledge. Pure scientific theory itself may depend for its development upon observation and properly engineered machinery. And conceptual efforts to distinguish between the two are unlikely to produce clear legal lines capable of application in particular cases (*Kumho Tire Co.* v *Carmichael*, 526 U.S. at 148, 119 S. Ct. at 1175).

Does this also mean that all of the *Daubert* factors should be applied to technical or experience-based expertise? The court answered that question by saying the factors may be applied to such expert knowledge. That much is obvious from the *Daubert* court's description of the factors of testing, peer review, known error rates, and general acceptance, commanding use of a flexible inquiry. But the court further stressed, "We agree with the Solicitor General that the factors identified in *Daubert* may or may not be pertinent in assessing reliability, depending on the nature of the issue, the expert's particular expertise, and the subject of his testimony." By the same token, the *Daubert* factors may be useful in assessing the reliability of some forms of expertise. Here is a very significant quotation from the *Kumho Tire* opinion for forensic scientists:

> *Daubert* is not to the contrary. It made clear that its list of factors was meant to be helpful, not definitive. Indeed, those factors do not all necessarily apply in every instance in which the reliability of scientific testimony is challenged. It might not be surprising in a particular case, for example, that a claim made by a scientific witness has never been the subject of peer review, for the particular application at issue may never previously have interested any scientist. Nor, on the other hand, does the presence of *Daubert's* general

acceptance factor help show that an expert's testimony is reliable where the discipline itself lacks reliability, as, for example, do theories grounded in any so-called generally accepted principles of astrology or necromancy (*Kumho Tire Co.* v *Carmichael,* 526 U.S. at 151, 119 S. Ct. at 1175).

The court expounded on the latitude that trial courts have in deciding *how* to test an expert's conclusion and to decide whether or when appropriate hearings ought to be conducted to investigate the claims of reliability. The court instructed that a trial judge's inquiry is a flexible one and that the gatekeeping function, of necessity, must be tied to the particular facts of a case. The factors identified in *Daubert* are not supposed to be talismanic, nor do they constitute a definite checklist or a litmus test. Whatever decision a trial court makes on either the admissibility or inadmissibility of proffered opinion evidence, or indeed on whether the evidence is relevant, will be judged by the standard of "abuse of discretion".

In making this point, the court was emphasizing that after *Daubert,* but before the *Kumho Tire* decision was handed down, the U.S. Supreme Court had already applied the abuse-of-discretion standard as the test to use when reviewing the decision of a district court to either admit or deny admission of expert testimony. The case was *General Electric Co.* v *Joiner,* 522 U.S. 136, 118 S.Ct. 512 (1997). (That decision raises the specter that the issue of reliability of a technique might be decided differently in separate district courts, and that, on appeal, both seemingly inconsistent holdings will have to be affirmed if, on the record, the trial court did not abuse its discretion in arriving at its decision.)

What do the decisions in *Daubert* and in *Kumho Tire* mean to forensic scientists beyond the obvious holdings already discussed? There are at least two additional points to be made:

1. It means that the definition of science, the scientific method, and scientific evidence can no longer be used as loosely as experts have been doing. It is no longer sufficient to call yourself a forensic scientist in order to be considered a scientist. It is no longer sufficient to say that something is a subject of forensic science in order for a court to agree that it is dealing with science. Simply saying it does not make it so. The courts may, and many will, require the experts to show that they know what the scientific method consists of and provide the scientific basis for their conclusions. By the same token, each discipline will be judged by its own standards and upon its own experience. The DNA model of expertise, much vaunted for its scientific basis by critics of the forensic sciences, may not be the basis by which other disciplines need or should be judged.

2. It also means that forensic scientists can no longer expect to rely on the fact that courts have long accepted and admitted evidence of their expert conclusions. The court can relitigate the admissibility of a certain type of expert evidence if a litigant can make a credible argument that there has been no previous scientific inquiry of the validity of the assumptions on which a forensic field has long rested. Decades of judicial precedent no longer preclude reviewing whether existing precedent satisfies *Daubert* and *Kumho Tire*. Long-recognized forensic disciplines have been and are being challenged, with more to come.

13.3.1.5 The *Daubert* Factors and Their Relation to the *Frye* Test of "General Acceptance". How *Daubert* "reliability" is to be established still remains an issue of some controversy. The court explained this requirement in these words:

> Ordinarily, a key question to be answered in determining whether a theory or technique is scientific knowledge that will assist the trier of fact will be whether it can be (and has been) tested. Scientific methodology today is what distinguished science from other fields of human inquiry ... [internal citations of the court omitted].

> Another pertinent consideration is whether the theory or technique has been subjected to peer review and publication. Publication (which is but one element of peer review) is not a sine qua non of admissibility; it does not necessarily correlate with reliability ... Some propositions, moreover, are too particular, too new, or of too limited interest to be published. But submission to the scrutiny of the scientific community is a component of "good science," in part because it increases the likelihood that substantive flaws in methodology will be detected. [Internal citations omitted.] The fact of publication (or lack thereof) in a peer reviewed journal thus will be a relevant, though not dispositive, consideration in assessing the scientific validity of a particular technique or methodology on which an opinion is premised.

Additionally, in the case of a particular scientific technique, the court ordinarily should consider the known or potential error,... [internal citations omitted] and the existence and maintenance of standards controlling the technique's operation [internal citations omitted].

Finally, "general acceptance" can yet have a bearing on the inquiry. A "reliability assessment does not require, although it does permit, explicit identification of a relevant scientific community and an express determination of a particular degree of acceptance within that community." (*Daubert* v *Merrell Dow Pharmaceuticals Inc.*, 509 U.S., 509; 593–594)

Looking at the *Daubert* factors more closely, it is evident that one factor in determining whether evidence is "scientific knowledge" is whether a theory or technique can be or has been tested by a scientific body. However, this aspect became less important—perhaps even totally irrelevant—after the decision in *Kumho Tire*, wherein the court applied *Daubert's* required proof of reliability to all expert testimony, including technological as well as skilled and experience-based expert testimony.

After the U.S. Supreme Court decided *Daubert*, Congress enacted an amendment to FRE 702 in 2000 to incorporate the concerns expressed in the *Daubert* case as well as in the *Kumho Tire* case. At the conclusion of the original text of FRE 702 (quoted above in section 13.3.1.2), Congress added the following language (replacing the period after "otherwise" with a comma, and continuing as follows):

if (1) the testimony is based on sufficient facts or data, (2) the testimony is the product of reliable principles and methods, and (3) the witness has applied the principles and methods reliably to the facts of the case. (As amended, April 17, 2000, effective December 1, 2000.)

13.3.1.6 Effect of *Daubert* on Criminal Prosecutions in the Various States. The FRE apply to all proceedings in federal courts. Because the matter of what the rules of evidence mean does not involve federal constitutional rights, the *Daubert* decision was intended to apply only as an interpretive guide to the FRE in federal courts. Nevertheless, the U.S. Supreme Court decisions on expert testimony have had a significant impact on state evidence law as well. Many states have evidence codes or rules of evidence patterned on the FRE. Most—though not all—of these states chose to follow the *Daubert* and *Kumho Tire* interpretations as a way of interpreting their own state-law equivalent of FRE 702.

Some states that followed the *Frye* rule of general acceptance before 1993 disagreed with the new U.S. Supreme Court decisions even though those states did have FRE-based rules of evidence. These states rejected, post-*Daubert*, the latter's more flexible standards and mandated a strict adherence to *Frye* as the standard for admissibility of novel scientific evidence. Indeed, some states that never explicitly followed the *Frye* rule in the past have since been persuaded to adopt it. In many of the states that do not have FRE-based evidence rules and where case law had adopted the *Frye* test for the admissibility of expert evidence prior to 1993, the *Frye* standard remains alive and well as a stand-alone test for admissibility.

Of course, even though *Frye* was nominally discarded in the federal courts, *Frye* survives as one of the four main *Daubert* factors. The only difference in the application of the "old" standard and its modern-day equivalent is that some state and federal courts still tend to analyze the admissibility decision in terms of pre-*Daubert* case law.

The reasons for rejecting the *Daubert* principles and choosing to retain general acceptance as the sole criterion for admissibility may be found in the firm belief that *Daubert's* general relevancy concepts are too flexible, too lenient, or too easy to satisfy—a proposition that has not proven true in the interpretation of the law in some *Daubert* jurisdictions—and that the more conservative approach of general acceptance as the sole standard is better designed to screen out unreliable evidence. Thus, in *State* v *Bible*, 175 Ariz. 549, 589, 858 P.2d 1152, 1181 (1993), the court stated that *Frye* was more likely to avoid placing the difficult task of evaluating the worth of scientific testimony on nonscientist judges or jurors and leaving the decision on the scientific validity of expert opinion testimony upon the shoulders of the expert's peers.

Representative of the states rejecting *Daubert* expressly and choosing to adhere to the *Frye* rule were Arizona, Colorado, Florida, Illinois, Kansas, Missouri, Nebraska, New Hampshire, and Washington. Some other states (e.g., California) retained their *Frye*-like rule without expressly rejecting *Daubert*. Yet others (e.g., Massachusetts) equally retained the venerable *Frye* standard but added a *Daubert*-like inquiry for some cases (as is explained in the discussion of the 2005 *Commonwealth* v *Patterson* decision in section 13.3.2.5).

It is clear that those who expounded in the aftermath of the *Daubert* decision that *Frye* was dead were premature in their assessment. The *Frye* rule, indeed, lives on as an independent principle in some states and as one of the *Daubert* factors in other states and in the federal system.

Daubert, without a doubt, has encouraged a continuation of the trend toward greater judicial scrutiny of scientific evidence. If there was ever a belief that rejection of *Frye* by the U.S. Supreme Court would signify a reduction in the number of pretrial hearings to determine admissibility of novel scientific evidence, that belief has been convincingly shown to be in error. Trial courts hold as many, or more, and as lengthy, or lengthier, hearings on in limine motions challenging admissibility of expert opinions as they did prior to 1993.

That the *Daubert* factors are more lenient and will admit more expert opinion testimony than was the experience under *Frye*—a suggestion the U.S. Supreme Court itself made—has not been shown to be the way the Court's decisions are being interpreted. Even though the Court declared the new standard to be a more flexible and easier-to-meet test than *Frye,* experience has shown so far that trial courts tend to be more rigid in judging the validity of expert opinion testimony in the post-*Daubert* era. Lawyers presenting novel scientific testimony have sought to introduce evidence crossing all the "t"s and dotting all of the "i"s by presenting evidence on all factors of *Daubert*. Opponents of such evidence, likewise, have sought to present testimony to dispute all of the arguments of their adversaries. Courts bound by the new rules are likely to engage in lengthier hearings to determine admissibility and write longer opinions justifying their decisions to admit or deny admission than was the case heretofore.

13.3.2 Daubert Challenges Against "Fingerprints" After 1993

13.3.2.1 Challenges to the Admissibility of Friction Ridge Individualizations. The first challenges to forensic evidence were brought against forensic document examiners (FDEs). A few U.S. District Court decisions wherein the admissibility of expert testimony of handwriting identifications was challenged had resulted in partially prohibiting experts from testifying to the ultimate conclusion that a defendant had written, or did not write, a questioned document in issue. In most cases, though, the admissibility challenges were soundly rejected by trial courts and handwriting identification evidence was found to satisfy *Daubert*. Even when partially successful, judges generally did not exclude the FDE testimony altogether. It is significant that, to date, no federal court of appeals has held that handwriting identification testimony is inadmissible for failure to satisfy the *Daubert* and *Kumho Tire* requirements.

Perhaps emboldened or encouraged by the partial success in a few trial court cases wherein district court judges prohibited forensic document examiners from offering their opinions that a questioned writing was authored by the defendant, academic critics of the forensic sciences in general next turned their attention to fingerprinting. There are four important cases with which all friction ridge impression examiners should be familiar.

13.3.2.2 *United States* v *Mitchell*. The first serious *Daubert* challenge occurred in the 1999 case of *United States* v *Mitchell* (Cr. No. 96–407–1), in which Judge J. Curtis Joyner denied the defense's motion in limine to bar the government's fingerprint experts from testifying. The trial court's decision was not officially reported. Pennsylvania U.S. District Court Judge Joyner had conducted a 5-day *Daubert* hearing in 1999, at the conclusion of which the judge ruled that fingerprint evidence satisfied all *Daubert* factors. He also took judicial notice that "human friction ridges are unique and permanent throughout the area of the friction ridge skin, including small friction ridge areas, … " With the pretrial evidentiary issues settled, Mitchell was thereafter tried and convicted in 2000.

Not surprisingly, he appealed. On April 29, 2004—2 years after the *Llera Plaza* trial court decision by a judge in the same district (discussed below) had taken the fingerprint world by storm—the U.S. Court of Appeals for the Third Circuit, in an opinion written by Circuit Judge Edward R. Becker, decided Mitchell's appeal and upheld the conviction as well as Judge Joyner's conclusion that fingerprinting evidence was admissible. The reviewing court, however, did hold that Judge Joyner improperly took judicial notice of the uniqueness and permanency aspects of fingerprints. The appeals court decision is reported as *United States* v *Mitchell,* 365 F.3d 215 (3rd Cir. 2004), *cert. denied* 125 S. Ct. 446 (2004). It did affirm the trial court's admission of fingerprint evidence on the ground that the discipline satisfied the *Daubert* validity factors.

In its opinion, the court of appeals ignored an issue that had been hotly debated at the *Daubert* hearing—whether fingerprint identification was a science. Recall that the 1999 U.S. Supreme Court decision in *Kumho Tire* had made it unnecessary to draw a distinction between scientific and nonscientific expert testimony, inasmuch as *Kumho Tire* had held that the gatekeeper role of the trial judge in keeping unreliable opinion evidence out of court applied to all expert opinions, whether deemed scientific, technical, or experience-based.

The appeals court in *Mitchell* explored each one of the *Daubert* factors. In doing so, the court's decision, although ultimately favorable to the prosecution, was not overwhelmingly laudatory.

The First Factor — Testability. Testability refers to "whether the premises on which fingerprint identification relies are testable—or, better yet, actually tested". The court concluded that the premises that friction ridge arrangements are unique and permanent, and that a positive identification can be made from fingerprints containing sufficient quantity and quality of detail, were testable and had been tested in several ways. In that regard, the court referred to the FBI's AFIS computer comparison of 50,000 left-sloped patterns against a database of another 50,000 sets of tenprints, a process involving 2.5 billion comparisons. The experiment showed there were no matches of prints coming from different digits. The court referred to several other tests, such as those involving the prints of identical twins, and the fact that an FBI survey showed no state identification bureaus had ever encountered two different persons with the same fingerprint.

The second part of the testability factor involved the fact that making a positive identification depends on "fingerprints containing sufficient quantity and quality of detail". The court was somewhat troubled that the standard of having a point system had been abandoned and that the FBI relied on an "unspecified, subjective, sliding-scale mix of 'quantity and quality of detail'", but because the FBI expert testifying at the hearing had identified 14 points of level 2 detail when matching Mitchell's right thumbprint to the crime scene latent, the court saw the issue in this case as simply whether having 14 points of level 2 detail was enough for a positive identification. Referring again to the AFIS computer check with simulated latents (exhibiting only 1/5 of the size of a rolled fingerprint) and the survey that showed no identification bureau had ever found two matching prints on different digits, the court found this to be "the strongest support for the government on this point". It concluded that the "hypotheses that undergird the discipline of fingerprint identification are testable, if only to a lesser extent actually tested by experience".

The Peer Review Factor. The court did not seem overly impressed by the government's argument that the verification step of ACE-V constitutes effective peer review. Dr. Simon Cole, testifying for the defense, had suggested that fingerprint examiners have developed an "occupational norm of unanimity" that discourages dissent. Although acknowledging that the "cultural mystique" attached to fingerprinting may infect the verification process, the court nevertheless concluded that when looking at the entire picture, "the ACE-V verification step may not be peer review in its best form, but on balance, the peer review factor does favor admission" of friction ridge comparisons and individualizations.

The Error Rate. This is where the experts on both sides had waged the greatest battle at the *Daubert* hearing. The appeals court distinguished between two error rates: false positives and false negatives. The defense included and emphasized errors where examiners had failed to make identifications that could and should have been made. In that regard, the court recognized that a high false negative rate may not be desirable as a matter of law enforcement policy, but said that "in the courtroom, the rate of false negatives is immaterial to the Daubert admissibility of latent fingerprint identification offered to prove positive identification because it is not probative of the reliability of the testimony *for the purpose for which it is offered* (i.e., for its ability to effect a positive identification" (italics in the original).

False positives, on the other hand, would be most troublesome. But the court concluded that, "where what is sought to be proved is essentially a negative (i.e., the absence of false positives) it seems quite appropriate to us to use a burden-shifting framework". Where the government experts testify to being unaware of significant false positive identifications, the burden of producing contrary evidence may reasonably be shifted to the defense. Although the error rate may not have been precisely quantified, the court was persuaded that the methods of estimating it showed it to be very low. (This testimony occurred before the FBI misidentification of Brandon Mayfield in the Madrid, Spain, train bombing terrorist attack (Stacey, 2004, pp 706–718; OIG report, 2006).)

The Maintenance of Standards. The *Mitchell* appeals court found this standard to be "lacking in some measure". The procedural standards of ACE-V were deemed to be "insubstantial in comparison to the elaborate and exhaustively refined standards found in many scientific and technical disciplines" and the court found that this factor did "not favor admitting the (fingerprint) evidence".

As an aside, the question often arises, not surprisingly, whether subjectivity plays a part in the ultimate decision that two impressions were produced by the same skin, and the related question, whether subjectivity negates reliability. In comparing latent impressions of unknown origin with prints of known origin to determine whether a "match" exists, some subjectivity is involved, but the factors that guide the exercise of judgment are clearly spelled out in the detailed observations that are required to be made when going through the first three steps of ACE-V. The view, often advocated by critics, that fingerprinting is unscientific simply because some subjective judgment is involved in declaring a match, had already been rejected by Judge Louis H. Pollak in the *Llera Plaza II* case. He quoted a statement by the United Kingdom's Lord Rooker, who said, "In determining whether or not a latent mark or impression left at a crime scene and a fingerprint have been made by the same person, a fingerprint examiner must apply set criteria in carrying out their comparison. The criteria are objective and can be tested and verified by other experts" (*Llera Plaza II,* 188 F.Supp.2d at 569). And although sometimes critical of fingerprint identification techniques, the second opinion in *Llera Plaza* nevertheless concluded that ACE-V satisfied the *Daubert* and *Kumho* Tire requirements of proof of reliability (*Llera Plaza II,* 188 F. Supp. 2d at 575).

But the rhetorical question remains: Can an opinion obtained without statistical probability studies be said to be scientific? Defense expert Dr. David Stoney joined scientific expert witnesses testifying for the government in *Mitchell* and *Llera Plaza II* in expressing the view that a profession can engage in science despite the absence of statistical support. This is not new to the scientific community, in which the absence of statistical probability studies does not necessarily characterize the process as unreliable or unscientific. Stoney stated that valid science is something that is capable of being proven wrong, and that ACE-V can easily be tested by review of the evidence by other qualified individuals.

The General Acceptance Factor. Little needs to be said on this factor, which the court found to be clearly weighing in favor of admitting the evidence.

To conclude, the *Mitchell* appeals court's decision was that, on the record presented to it, an analysis of the *Daubert* factors showed that "most factors support (or at least do not disfavor) admitting the government's" evidence on friction ridge individualizations. Thus, it held that the district court did not abuse its discretion in admitting it.

This is by no means a strong endorsement, even though it may be seen as such in the practical effect the opinion will likely have. The *Mitchell* decision addressed several other issues:

Individual Error Rates of Examiners. The first and perhaps most important issue deals with the court's recommendation that, in future cases, prosecutors seek to show the individual error rates of expert witness examiners. The National Academy of Sciences has adequately addressed the issue of confusing practitioner error rates and methodological error rates in its discussion of this issue with regard to DNA. As its position is well-stated and is applicable to any of the forensic sciences, no further discussion is required here. What must be understood is the distinction between how the academic scientific community wants to define error rate and what *Daubert* requires may not be one and the same. It has been argued that the U.S. Supreme Court got it wrong and should modify its ruling to ensure the practitioner is included. Others oppose such a change because it would complicate the judge's gatekeeping responsibility even further.

The Critics' Voices. An additional comment by the court suggested there be no limitation placed on the defense's right to present expert testimony. In that regard, the court noted, "Experts with diametrically opposed opinions may nonetheless both have good grounds for their views, and *a district court may not make winners and losers through its choice of which side's experts to admit when all experts are qualified*." (Emphasis added.) But the court went further and said that if there were any question about a proffered expert's competence on a given issue, the court should err on the side of "admitting any evidence having some potential for assisting the trier of fact". A lot of space was devoted in the latter part of the court's opinion to a discussion of the limitations believed to have been imposed on the testimony of some defense experts. No limitations should be imposed, the court said. What saved the case from a reversal on that point was perhaps the failure of the defense to effectively preserve its objections.

Will *Daubert* Hearings Continue? The *Mitchell* court further addressed the question of whether there will be more or fewer *Daubert* hearings in the future. On that issue, the court's opinion was somewhat obscure. First, it said that its *Mitchell* decision did not announce "a categorical rule that latent fingerprint identification evidence is admissible in this Circuit". But then it also said that nothing in the opinion "should be read to require extensive *Daubert* hearings in every case involving latent fingerprint evidence". Further muddling (or perhaps clarifying) what went before, the opinion then stated that "a district court would not abuse its discretion by limiting, in a proper case, the scope of *Daubert* hearings to novel challenges to the admissibility of latent fingerprint identification evidence—or even dispensing with the hearing altogether if no novel challenge was raised". What this probably means is that District Courts of the Third Circuit will now refuse to conduct *Daubert* hearings unless the defense raises arguments not considered in the *Mitchell* litigation.

Judicial Notice of the Reliability of Fingerprint Identification. At the pretrial hearing, District Judge Joyner had taken judicial notice that "human friction ridges are unique . . . including small friction ridge areas . . . ."

What does taking judicial notice really mean? Instead of requiring the parties to present proof of a given fact, a court is permitted to take judicial notice of that fact without requiring proof thereof if the fact is "not subject to reasonable dispute" or "is capable of ready determination" by reference to existing studies or reports. Although there have been reviewing court decisions by state appellate or supreme courts going back 40 or more years taking judicial notice of the uniqueness of fingerprints, the court found these decisions not only not binding on the court, but clearly distinguishable, since the decisions dealt with the uniqueness of complete fingerprints.

Uniqueness of each fingerprint was not the issue here; the issue was uniqueness of small areas of friction skin such as are typically visible in a latent impression. As to that issue, the appellate court felt that the very fact that it took 5 days of testimony to establish the uniqueness of small areas of friction skin showed that the fact was by no means generally known or capable of ready determination. Therefore, Judge Joyner's judicial notice ruling was in error. Because it was not deemed to likely have altered the outcome of the case, it was considered to be harmless error not requiring a reversal.

13.3.2.3 United States v Llera Plaza. The second very significant case that all friction ridge examiners should be cognizant of is the *Llera Plaza* case. Perhaps the case has lost some of its persuasive effect because it was followed in short order by the appeals court decision affirming *Mitchell,* but defense attorneys continue to argue that the criticism leveled toward fingerprinting expertise by Judge Louis H. Pollak in *Llera Plaza* remains valid.

After first ruling, on January 7, 2002, that the government's expert testimony on the ultimate issue of whether there was a match between defendant's known print and a crime scene print would be inadmissible, *(United States* v *Llera Plaza,* 179 F. Supp. 2d 492 (E .D. Pa., 2002) *(Llera Plaza I))* Judge Pollak, of the U.S. District Court for the Eastern District of Pennsylvania, reconsidered and reversed his earlier decision 2 months later in what is now frequently referred to as *Llera Plaza II* (*United States* v *Llera Plaza,* 188 F. Supp. 2d 549 (E.D. Pa., 2002)).

Why did he reverse himself? "In short," he wrote, "I have changed my mind."

When he decided *Llera Plaza* originally, the judge had not held an evidentiary hearing. Both parties had stipulated that the judge could consider the record generated in the *Mitchell* case as well as some written submissions of the attorneys. In his first order, the judge took judicial notice of the uniqueness and permanency of fingerprints and accepted "the theoretical basis of fingerprint identification— namely, that a showing that a latent print replicates (is a 'match' of) a rolled print constitutes a showing that the latent and rolled prints are fingerprints of the same person". However, Judge Pollak also held, in his *Llera Plaza I* order, that the ACE-V method generally used to arrive at match or nonmatch conclusions did not meet the first three *Daubert* factors, and only met the general acceptance factor in the technical as opposed to scientific community of fingerprint examiners. He therefore would allow fingerprint experts for both prosecution and defense to testify to all of the examinations they had performed in an individual case, but would preclude them from testifying that the latent and inked prints were, or were not, from the same person.

The government moved not only for reconsideration of the judge's January 7, 2002, order, but also petitioned for leave to enlarge the record through the presentation of additional evidence. The district judge granted the motion and hearings were held on February 25–27, 2002. Both sides presented additional expert testimony, after which the judge made his now famous statement, "I have changed my mind."

Judge Pollak admitted that the rehearing offered new information or information he had not "previously digested". It appears he was particularly impressed by the FBI expert, Stephen Meagher; and defense expert, Allan Bayle, formerly with New Scotland Yard and now a fingerprint consultant. Meagher, whose testimony in the *Mitchell* case the judge had already read, now became not merely a name in a transcript but "a real person". Allan Bayle, while seeking to aid the defense's arguments by pointing to shortcomings in the FBI's annual proficiency testing method, ended up confirming that the FBI's fingerprint methodology was "essentially indistinguishable" from Scotland Yard's ACE-V methodology. Bayle, to whom the judge deferentially referred as "this formidably knowledgeable and experienced veteran of the Yard", testified that he believed in the reliability of the ACE-V methodology "without reservation". Clearly, the defense's "formidably knowledgeable" Allan Bayle in *Llera Plaza II* ended up aiding the prosecution's case.

Despite Judge Pollak's continuing reservations on the "science" controversy as it pertains to fingerprint methodology when tested against the *Daubert* standards, he decided that by applying the legal mandates expressed in the *Daubert* and *Kumho Tire* cases, (1) judicial notice would be taken of the permanence and individuality of friction skin (fingerprint) patterns, and (2) experts in the field would be permitted to express their opinions on a match of two impressions. This occurred after he heard or read the explanations of law enforcement-trained examiners and university-based scientists in genetics, histology, and fetal development regarding the biological and physiological factors that result in ultimate pattern uniqueness during the prenatal development of friction skin.

If the contention remains that there are shaky parts in the friction ridge examination methodology, the argument does not support exclusion or limitation of testimony, but falls squarely within the U.S. Supreme Court's *Daubert* admonition, "Vigorous cross-examination, presentation of contrary evidence, and careful instruction on the burden of proof are the traditional and appropriate means of attacking shaky but admissible evidence." (*Daubert* v *Merrell Dow Pharmaceuticals, Inc.*, 509 U.S. at 596)

An interesting footnote to Judge Pollak's March 2002 *Llera Plaza II* decision is that in considering the *Daubert* factor of "publication and peer review", none of the scientific books and other publications by scientists were quoted or relied on. Judge Pollak stated that the "writings to date" do not satisfy *Daubert's* publication prong because the voluminous fingerprint literature was not peer reviewed. This no doubt came as a tremendous surprise to those highly credentialed and respected scientists who published studies and to the editors of the refereed journals in which many of these publications occurred.

13.3.2.4 *United States* v *Havvard*. The third case of note in the admissibility battles is *United States* v *Havvard*, 117 F. Supp. 2d 848 (D.C. Ind. 2000), holding that fingerprint identification meets all *Daubert* and *Kumho Tire* requirements. That decision was affirmed in *United States* v *Havvard*, 260 F.3d 597 (7th Cir. 2001). Because the decision is "older" than the previous two cases, and the opinion is readily available on the Internet, it will not be discussed here. Suffice it to say that this was the first federal circuit court of appeals case after *Daubert* that gave an unqualified seal of approval to friction ridge impression evidence.

13.3.2.5 *Commonwealth* v *Patterson*. *Commonwealth* v *Patterson*, 445 Mass. 626 (2005), was decided by the Massachusetts Supreme Judicial Court on December 18, 2005. Like the first *Llera Plaza* opinion of Judge Pollak, the *Patterson* case caused significant concern throughout the community of friction ridge evidence examiners. *Patterson* differs from *Llera Plaza* in at least four significant aspects: (1) *Patterson* is a decision by a state's highest appellate tribunal, and therefore is a binding precedent only on Massachusetts courts; (2) the decision was unanimous and therefore not likely to be altered unless significant progress in scientific research on the issues involved can be demonstrated to the court in another case on the same issues; (3) Massachusetts is a *Frye* jurisdiction but, in deciding the issue before it, the high court applied the *Daubert* factors as well as the general acceptance test; (4) *Patterson* affected only one specialized application of friction ridge examination methodology, that is, simultaneous latent impressions, and gave unqualified approval to normal individualization evidence of latent impressions.

Although critical of one specialized aspect of friction ridge examinations, the court found much of which it approved. Fingerprint individualizations, as well as the ACE-V method, were given a broad seal of approval as meeting both the *Frye* test and the *Daubert* factors. Furthermore, the state high court recognized SWGFAST as a guideline-setting authority in the field of friction ridge examinations. What did not pass muster was the admissibility of what are known as identifications based on "simultaneous prints" when none of the individual impressions contain enough information to justify individualization independently.

Factually, the case is unremarkable. *Patterson* was identified as the maker of four latent impressions on a car that were said to have been simultaneously impressed. Although none of the latent prints contained sufficient detail for individualization on its own, the Boston Police Department's latent print examiner testified that collectively, in his opinion, they could be identified as having been made by the defendant. *Patterson* had been convicted in a first trial, but the conviction was reversed on grounds unrelated to the fingerprint evidence and a retrial was ordered.

Before the retrial could occur, the defense moved to bar the admission of fingerprint evidence in general and simultaneous prints evidence in particular. A hearing was held in 2005, as a result of which the trial court denied the defense motions in all regards. On review to the Supreme Judicial Court of Massachusetts, that tribunal affirmed two parts of the trial judge's order and reversed one part.

Fingerprint identification and ACE-V methodology were held to have satisfied the general acceptance test of the *Frye* decision as well as the reliability assessment dictated by *Daubert,* and therefore those parts of the trial judge's order were affirmed. The high court held, however, that the state had not fulfilled its burden of showing that the process of individualizing latent prints on less than the normal quantum of needed data, solely because they had been said to have been impressed simultaneously, was generally accepted in the profession; nor had the state shown that the process was otherwise validated because no studies dealing with simultaneous impressions had been shown to exist.

Why did the court, while expressing the determination to continue to adhere to *Frye*, consider whether individualizations based on simultaneous prints satisfied the *Daubert* factors? It held that if a technique cannot meet the *Frye* standard for lack of proven general acceptance, a court can still consider whether the expert's findings ought to be admitted, and such admission depends on whether the technique can satisfy a more lenient assessment of reliability—in other words, a *Daubert*-type of inquiry. When it did engage in such a *Daubert* analysis, the court found simultaneous print individualizations wanting.

The court also decided that the verification part of ACE-V, although a generally accepted methodology under *Frye*, nevertheless could not satisfy the *Daubert* factor of peer review because the verifiers know that an identification has already been effected and also know the name of the party who has been identified. The court said, "We share the (trial) judge's consternation with the current verification process."

One important aspect of the decision rejects a mantra upon which critics have relied in the past. Critics of forensic identification evidence have asserted repeatedly that general acceptance must be conferred by a community of scientists, not by users of the technique. That assertion was rejected. The Massachusetts high court held that the community of professionals who judge the reliability and general acceptance of a technique need not contain either academics or research scientists. As long as the community is sufficiently broad so that critics or dissenters within the group have an opportunity to be heard and their arguments considered, the community's approval will suffice to confer general acceptance. The court added, "A technical community, or a community of experts who have some other specialized knowledge, can qualify as a relevant *Daubert* community in the same way as a scientific community can." The fingerprint community was found to meet that requirement.

13.3.2.6 Afterthoughts in the Wake of the Challenges.
Although there are ways in which some aspects of friction ridge impression comparisons can be legitimately challenged, as has been seen in *Commonwealth* v *Patterson*, challenges after 2005, if any, will probably be focused closely upon specific applications and narrow issues. Broad-brush generalizations and condemnations of everything connected with fingerprint identification are perhaps the clearest examples of unscientific analyses that are unlikely to merit court approval.

13.4 Historical Account of Fingerprints, Palmprints, and Footprints in U.S. Courts

The following brief synopsis of early friction ridge impression evidence decisions is presented to provide an historical account of some of the early United States court cases. Most of these cases are from state trials, because fingerprints were utilized generally by state law enforcement agencies prior to their wide utilization by federal law enforcement. Although fingerprints were first utilized by the Federal Bureau of Investigation in 1924 for establishing prior arrest records, it was not until 1933 that fingerprints were used by the FBI as a forensic tool in support of criminal investigations. This portion of the chapter seeks to recognize, as well as possible, a few of the earliest occasions in which specific aspects of friction ridge impression evidence were first approved by the courts.

13.4.1 The First Appellate Decision Admitting Fingerprint Evidence in American Courts

People v Jennings, 252 Ill. 534, 96 N.E. 1077 (1911)

The defendant Thomas Jennings was arrested for murder when four impressions of his left-hand fingers were discovered impressed in fresh paint at the rear of the victim's home near the window through which entry had been gained. The freshly painted railing had been removed by the Chicago Police Department. Jennings was identified using fingerprints on file at the Chicago Police Department, recorded when he had been arrested and returned to the penitentiary for violation of his parole. After his arrest, he was fingerprinted again and, along with other evidence, enlarged fingerprint exhibits were used as evidence at his trial. Four expert witnesses testified that, in their opinion, the impressions on the railing were made by Jennings. After conviction, Jennings appealed, arguing basically that the field of fingerprinting was too novel to support a conviction.

The Illinois Supreme Court, in an exhaustive opinion, rejected defendant's contentions related to fingerprinting and affirmed the conviction, holding that persons experienced in the matter of fingerprint identification may testify to their opinion on whether fingerprints found at the scene of a crime correspond with those of the accused. Justice Orrin N. Carter's opinion also stated:

> We are disposed to hold from the evidence . . . and from the writings we have referred to on this subject, that there is a scientific basis for the system of finger-print identification, and that the courts are justified in admitting this class of evidence; that this method of identification is in such general and common use that the courts can not refuse to take judicial notice of it. . . .

> From the evidence in this record we are disposed to hold that the classification of finger-print impressions is a science requiring study. . . . [T]he evidence in question does not come within the common experience of all men of common education in the ordinary walks of life, and therefore the court and jury were properly aided by witnesses of peculiar and special experience on this subject.

13.4.2 Admissibility of Palmprints as Proof of Identity

State v Kuhl, 42 Nev. 195, 175 P. 190 (1918)

A United States mail stage driver was killed in Elko County, Nevada. A key piece of evidence against Defendant Kuhl was an envelope, secured from one of the rifled mail sacks, on which there was a bloody impression of the palm of a human hand. After Kuhl and another were arrested, experts determined that the palmprint was made by Kuhl. He was convicted of murder in the first degree and appealed. His argument, like that of Jennings in the preceding case, contended that it was improper to use the palmprint evidence and also for expert witnesses to use a "projectoscope" and enlarged photographic images to illustrate their testimony.

The Nevada Supreme Court recognized that the papillary ridges which form the basis of individualization in fingerprint impression extend over the entire palm of the hand and, indeed, over the soles of the feet. The original research done on the individuality of friction skin was not confined to an examination of the finger skin, but also included the skin on the palmar surfaces of the hands and the plantar surfaces of the feet. In rejecting defendant's arguments and affirming Kuhl's conviction, the Nevada Supreme Court, speaking through Justice Patrick McCarran, stated:

> We have gone at length into the subject of palm print and finger print identification, largely for the purpose of evolving the indisputable conclusion that there is but one physiological basis underlying this method of identification; that the phenomenon by which identity is established exists, not only on the bulbs of the finger tips, but is continuous and coexisting on all parts and in all sections and subdivisions of the palmar surface of the human hand.

13.4.3 Admissibility of Footprints as Proof of Identity

Commonwealth v Bartolini, 299 Mass. 503, 13 N.E.2d 382, cert. denied 304 U.S. 562 (1938)

Bartolini had been identified as the maker of a bare sole print found on the linoleum floor of the bathroom where a murder was committed. The courtroom battles about the admissibility of this type of evidence were fierce. Several pioneers in friction ridge impression evidence were called as expert witnesses to buttress the testimony of the Massachusetts State Police expert who, although qualified as a fingerprint expert, was not found to have sufficient experience with footprints.

Bert Wentworth, co-author of the influential and scholarly book *Personal Identification,* and Fredrick Kuhne of New York, who had served as an expert in cases involving the footprints of babies in hospitals, testified that the friction skin on the soles of the feet was as unique as that on the fingers and palms. After hearing Wentworth and Kuhne's testimony, Bartolini was convicted. The conviction was affirmed in a relatively brief opinion. The Massachusetts Supreme Judicial Court stated, in part:

> There was no error in permitting the expert Wentworth to testify that footprints of a naked foot on the linoleum of the bathroom at the house of the deceased were made by the same person who had made prints at the police station identified as those of the defendant. There was ample evidence of special study and knowledge by this witness of the subject of footprints as well as of finger prints. . . . There was also ample evidence that footprints, like finger prints, remain constant throughout life and furnish an adequate and reliable means of identification.

13.4.4 Admissibility of Photographs of Latent Impressions

State v Connors, 87 N.J.L. 419, 94 Atl. 812 (1915)

It was permissible to show, by photographs, the fingerprints found upon the columns or balcony posts of a house without the columns being produced in court. See also the case of *State* v *Kuhl.*

13.4.5 Fingerprinting Not a Violation of Constitutional Rights

In a number of early cases, courts held that requiring a lawfully arrested defendant to submit to fingerprinting did not violate the defendant's constitutional rights. Perhaps one of the earliest ones was *State* v *Cerciello,* 86 N.J.L. 309, 90 Atl. 1112 (1914), a case involving bloody fingerprints found on a hatchet at the scene of a murder. In affirming the conviction, the court held that the defendant's rights had not been violated. The most influential relatively early decision on that issue, however, was *United States* v *Kelly,* 55 F.2d 67 (2d Cir. 1932).

After being arrested upon the misdemeanor charge of having sold gin to federal prohibition agents, Kelly was fingerprinted. A U.S. District Court judge held, however, that the taking of fingerprints, in the absence of a statute, violated defendant's constitutional rights and ordered that Kelly's fingerprints be returned to him. The government appealed this order and, in an exhaustive opinion, the Second Circuit Court of Appeals, speaking through influential Judge Augustus N. Hand, reversed the district court, deciding that the taking of fingerprints upon a lawful arrest, even in the absence of a statute so authorizing, does not violate the arrestee's constitutional rights. Judge Hand said:

> We find no ground in reason or authority for interfering with a method of identifying persons charged with crime which has now become widely known and frequently practiced both in jurisdictions where there are statutory provisions regulating it and where it has no sanction other than the common law.

> [Kelly] argues that many of the statutes and the decisions in common law states have allowed fingerprinting only in cases of felonies. But, as a means of identification it is just as useful and important where the offense is a misdemeanor, and we can see no valid basis for a differentiation. In neither case does the interference with the person seem sufficient to warrant a court in holding finger printing unjustifiable. It can really be objected to only because it may furnish strong evidence of a man's guilt. It is no more humiliating than other means of identification that have been universally held to infringe neither constitutional

nor common law rights. Finger printing is used in numerous branches of business and of civil service, and is not of itself a badge of crime. As a physical invasion it amounts to almost nothing, and as a humiliation it can never amount to as much as that caused by the publicity attending a sensational indictment to which innocent men may have to submit.

13.4.6 Fingerprint Evidence Alone is Sufficient to Support a Conviction

Stacy v State, 49 Okl. Crim. 154, 292 P. 885 (1930)

Defendant was convicted principally on his identification as the person who left his latent prints on the door of a vault that was breached. He argued that a conviction based on evidence of fingerprints found in the place where the crime was committed, and not corroborated by other facts or circumstances, was insufficient to support a conviction. The court disagreed and affirmed. After going through a detailed account of the historical studies on fingerprints and their use as evidence of identity, the court stated:

> From an examination of the authorities cited and others, it appears that an allusion to finger print impressions for the purposes of identification is referred to in writings as early as 600 A.D., and they are traced back to a period some 100 years before Christ. Finger prints were first used as a manual seal to give authenticity to documents. They are found on Assyrian clay tablets of a very early date in the British Museum, and they were also used in the same way by the early Egyptians. From the literature on the subject and from the reported cases, we learn that finger prints have long been recognized as the strongest kind of circumstantial evidence and the surest form of identification. . . .

> We have no doubt but that the finding of the finger prints of the defendant on the door of the vault, with the further proof that defendant did not have access to and had not been at the place burglarized so that the prints could be accounted for on any hypothesis of his innocence, is a circumstance irresistibly pointing to his guilt. . . .

13.4.7 Fingerprints to Identify Individual as a Habitual Criminal

State v Smith, 128 Or. 515, 273 P. 323 (1929)

A person who had been previously convicted of a burglary and similar offenses between 1906 and 1920 was charged with the crime of receiving stolen property—a misdemeanor when committed by a first offender—and was sentenced to life imprisonment as a fourth felony offender under the Habitual Criminal Act. The Supreme Court of Oregon, interpreting an Oregon Habitual Criminal Act statute patterned on the one upheld by New York's highest court in *People* v *Gowasky*, 244 N.Y. 451, 155 N.E. 737, held that it was appropriate to use fingerprints for the purpose of identifying him as the perpetrator of the earlier felonies.

As early as 1917, the New York court, in *People* v *Shallow*, 100 Misc. 447, 165 N.Y. Supp. 915 (1917), held that the use of fingerprints to establish that a defendant had been previously convicted and was therefore eligible for increased punishment violates neither the Fifth Amendment's privilege against compelled self-incrimination nor its state constitutional equivalent. The case was noted in the *Columbia Law Review* and the *Yale Law Review*. The court stated, in part:

> By the requirement that the defendant's finger prints be taken there is no danger that the defendant will be required to give false testimony. The witness does not testify. The physical facts speak for themselves; no fears, no hopes, no will of the prisoner to falsify or to exaggerate could produce or create a resemblance of her finger prints or change them in one line, and therefore there is no danger of error being committed or untruth told.

13.5 Conclusion

Friction ridge impression examinations, whether tenprint to tenprint comparisons or latent print to tenprint comparisons, have been utilized in support of legal proceedings within the United States as well as worldwide since the early 1900s. Latent print evidence, known exemplars of fingerprints and palmprints, and the expert must each individually and collectively pass muster under the scrutiny of the legal requirements in order to be meaningful and useful in assisting the court in determining guilt or innocence. Just as science progresses and changes occur over time, so has the legal system.

13.6 Reviewers

The reviewers critiquing this chapter were Donna Brandelli, William F. Leo, James L. May III, and Lisa J. Steele.

13.7 References

Federal Rules of Criminal Procedure. The Committee on the Judiciary, House of Representatives; U.S. Government Printing Office: Washington, DC, 2004.

Federal Rules of Evidence. The Committee on the Judiciary, House of Representatives; U.S. Government Printing Office: Washington, DC, 2004.

Office of the Inspector General. *A Review of the FBI's Handling of the Brandon Mayfield Case—Unclassified Executive Summary.* U.S. Department of Justice: Washington, DC, March 2006.

Stacey, R. Report on the Erroneous Fingerprint Individualization in the Madrid Train Bombing Case. *J. Forensic Ident.* 2004, *54* (6), 706–718.

SWGFAST—Standards for Conclusions. *J. Forensic Ident.* 2004, *54* (3), 358–359.

SWGFAST. Press Kit; May 14, 2004, www.swgfast.org.

Court Citations

Brady v *Maryland*, 373 U.S. 83 (1963).

Commonwealth v *Bartolini*, 299 Mass. 503, 13 N.E.2d 382, *cert. denied* 304 U.S. 562 (1938).

Commonwealth v *Patterson*, 445 Mass. 626 (2005).

Daubert v *Merrell Dow Pharmaceuticals, Inc.*, 509 U.S. 579, 113 S. Ct. 2786 (1993).

Daubert v *Merrell Dow Pharmaceuticals, Inc.*, 951 F.2d 1128 (9th Cir. 1991).

Frye v *United States*, 293 F. 1013 (D.C. Cir. 1923).

General Electric Co. v *Joiner*, 522 U.S. 136, 118 S. Ct. 512 (1997).

Giglio v *United States*, 405 U.S. 150 (1972).

Kumho Tire Co. v *Carmichael*, 526 U.S. 137, 119 S. Ct. 1167 (1999).

People v *Gowasky*, 244 N.Y. 451, 155 N.E. 737 (1927).

People v *Jennings*, 252 Ill. 534, 96 N.E. 1077 (1911).

People v *Shallow*, 100 Misc. 447, 165 N.Y. Supp. 915 (1917).

Stacy v *State*, 49 Okl. Crim. 154, 292 P. 885 (1930).

State v *Bible*, 175 Ariz. 549, 589, 858 P.2d 1152, 1181 (1993).

State v *Cerciello*, 86 N.J.L. 309, 90 Atl. 1112 (1914).

State v *Connors*, 87 N.J.L. 419, 94 Atl. 812 (1915).

State v *Kuhl*, 42 Nev. 195, 175 P. 190 (1918).

State v *Smith*, 128 Or. 515, 273 P. 323 (1929).

United States v *Havvard*, 260 F.3d 597 (7th Cir. 2001).

United States v *Havvard*, 117 F. Supp. 2d 848 (D.C. Ind. 2000).

United States v *Henthorn*, 930 F.2d 920 (9th Cir. 1991), affirming *United States* v *Henthorn*, 931 F.2d 29 (9th Cir. 1991).

United States v *Kelly*, 55 F.2d 67 (2d Cir. 1932).

United States v *Llera Plaza*, 479 F. Supp. 2d 492 (E.D. Pa., 2002) *(Llera Plaza I)*.

United States v *Llera Plaza*, 188 F. Supp. 2d 549 (E.D. Pa., 2002) *(Llera Plaza II)*.

United States v *Mitchell*, Cr. No. 96–407–1.

United States v *Mitchell*, 365 F.3d 215 (3rd Cir. 2004), *cert. denied* S. Ct. 446 (2004).

CHAPTER 14

SCIENTIFIC RESEARCH SUPPORTING THE FOUNDATIONS OF FRICTION RIDGE EXAMINATIONS

Glenn Langenburg

CONTENTS

- 3   14.1 Introduction
- 3   14.2 The Nature of Scientific Inquiry
- 7   14.3 Scientific Research Related to Friction Ridge Examination
- 26 14.4 Future Directions for Research Related to Friction Ridge Examination
- 27 14.5 Conclusions
- 27 14.6 Reviewers
- 27 14.7 References

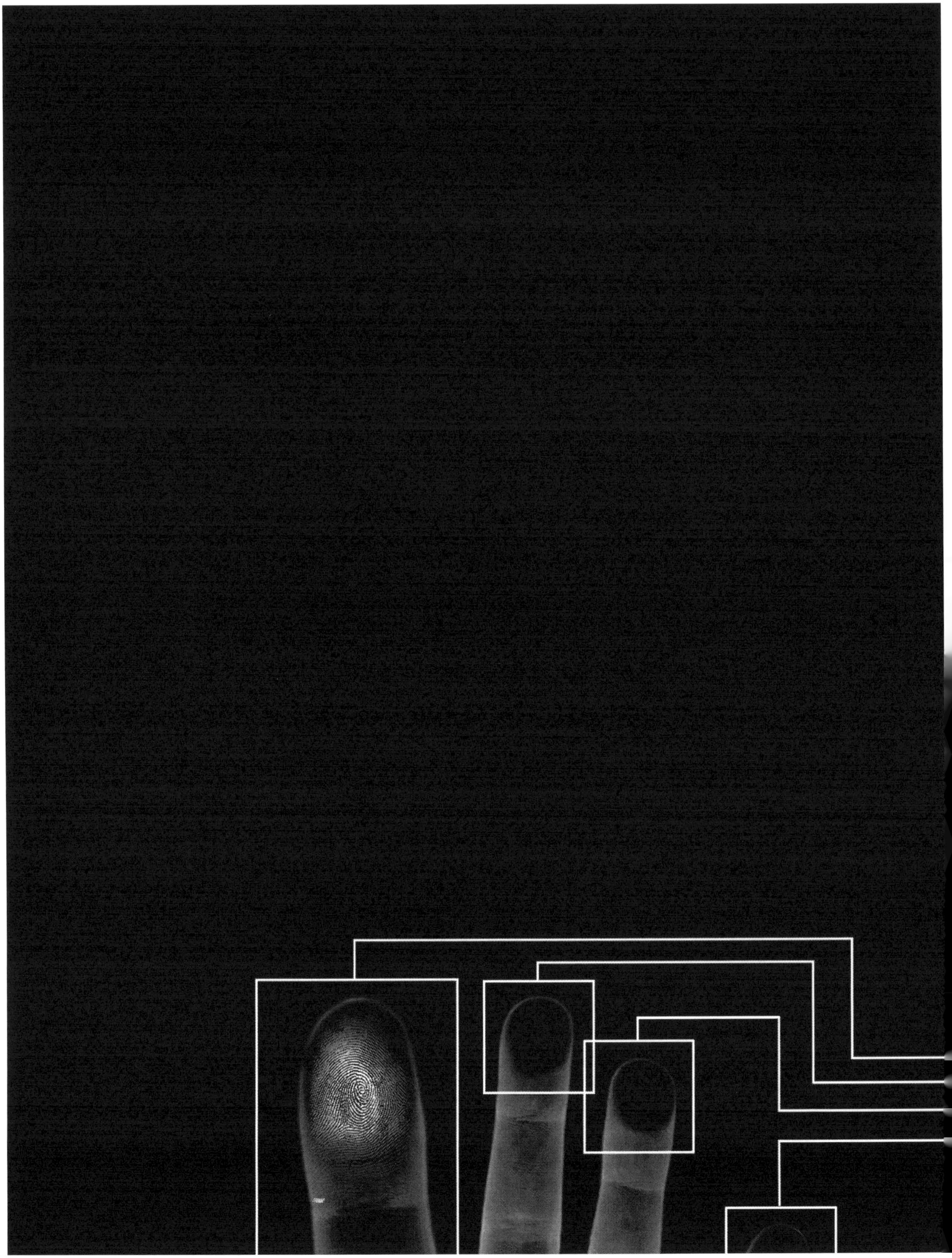

CHAPTER 14

SCIENTIFIC RESEARCH SUPPORTING THE FOUNDATIONS OF FRICTION RIDGE EXAMINATIONS

Glenn Langenburg

14.1 Introduction

When some people think of research, what comes to mind are images of individuals in white lab coats, looking up intermittently to take data measurements and jot down notes. This is a very limited and narrow view of research. Investigative reporters, attorneys, police detectives, engineers, authors, actors, and, of course, scientists, all perform research. The scientist, however, performs scientific research. Simply defined, research is an inquiry into any subject or phenomenon. Scientific research, then, can be defined as a scientific inquiry into a subject or phenomenon.

What makes an inquiry "scientific"? What is science? What is scientific method? What are the rules for a scientific inquiry? The answers to these questions are not simple, and are the subject of an entire realm of philosophy of science. This chapter will review some of these topics, relating the issue to friction ridge skin science. The reader, however, is encouraged to read more regarding the philosophy of science to better understand the complexity of science and scientific inquiry.

14.2 The Nature of Scientific Inquiry

14.2.1 Science and Falsifiability

The word *science* is derived from the Latin *scientia* (meaning knowledge), which is itself derived from the Latin verb *scire* (to know). Science can be defined as a body of knowledge obtained by systematic observation or experimentation. This definition is very broad, and, under such a permissive definition, many fields of study may be defined as science. Scientific creationism, theological science, Freudian psychoanalysis, and homeopathic medicine could arguably be classified as sciences.

Sir Karl Popper (1902–1994) recognized the difficulty of defining science. Popper, perhaps one of the most respected and widely known philosophers of science, separated science from nonscience with one simple principle:

falsifiability. Separation, or demarcation, could be done if a theory or law could possibly be falsified or proven wrong (Popper, 1959, 1972). A theory or law would fail this litmus test if there was no test or experiment that could be performed to prove the theory or law incorrect. Popper believed that a theory or law can never be proven conclusively, no matter the extent of testing, data, or experimentation. However, testing that provides results which contradict a theory or law can conclusively refute the theory or law, or in some instances, give cause to alter the theory or law. Thus, a scientific law or theory is conclusively falsifiable although it is not conclusively verifiable (Carroll, 2003).

Although the Popperian view of science is a widely held view amongst scientists, it is important to note that the U.S. Supreme Court has also taken this view of science (*Daubert*, 1993, p 593). Justice Blackmun, writing for the majority, cited Popper, specifically noting that a scientific explanation or theory must be capable of empirical testing. The issue of falsification was also raised during the *Daubert* hearing for the admissibility of latent print evidence during *U.S. v Mitchell* (July 13, 1999). (For an explanation of *Daubert* hearings, see Chapter 13.)

14.2.2 Scientific Laws and Theories

There is a grand misconception, even within the scientific community, that scientists first make observations; then they postulate a hypothesis; after rigorous testing, the hypothesis is accepted, thus becoming a theory; then the theory, after enjoying many years of success, without any instances of being refuted, is accepted as a scientific law. This hierarchical structure is a myth (McComas, 1996). Schoolhouse Rock (Frishberg and Yohe, 1975) described such a hierarchy for bills on their journey to becoming laws. Such is not the case in science.

Scientific laws and theories, though related, represent different knowledge within science. McComas stated, "Laws are generalizations, principles or patterns in nature and theories are the explanations of those generalizations".

Scientific laws describe general principles, patterns, and phenomena in the universe. Scientific theories explain why these general principles, patterns, and phenomena occur. The verbs associated with laws and theories speak to the nature of these concepts: scientific laws are discovered; scientific theories are invented (McComas, 1996).

Exactly what defines a law and exactly what defines a theory is contested within the philosophy of science. In fact, some philosophers of science (Van Fraassen, 1989, pp 180–181) believe that no laws exist at all. However, the majority of modern philosophers of science believe that laws exist and there are two popular competing definitions: *systems* and *universals* (Thornton, 2005).

The systems definition of a law defines a law within a deductive system. Axioms are stated that allow deductive conclusions. The strength of the law is within the truth of the generalized statement and its simplicity. As an example, if "all human friction ridge skin is unique", and I am a human, then one can deduce from the law (if true) that my friction ridge skin is unique. Instances of nonunique friction ridge skin would obviously show the law to be false.

The universals definition of a law defines the law as a relationship or "contingent necessitation" between universals (universals being just about anything). The wording of such a law would be similar to:

- Humans exist.
- Unique friction ridge skin exists.
- The law is the relationship of these two entities: Humans possess unique friction ridge skin.

In either case, laws can be described by the following features (Hempel and Oppenheim, 1948; Zynda, 1994):

- Laws are universal.
- Laws have unlimited scope.
- Laws contain no designation of individual, particular objects.
- Laws contain only "purely qualitative" predicates.

Theories, on the other hand, are explanations for laws. For example, Sir Isaac Newton discovered the "Law of Gravity". This law is universal, unlimited, not just applicable to a unique object, and is descriptive and predictive. However, this law does not explain how and why gravity works. Scientists of Newton's era proposed waves of gravity emitted from objects, attracting each other, operating similarly to magnetism. The attractive forces of gravity comprised the Theory of Gravity. Later, Albert Einstein found instances where the theory did not hold up (e.g., light bending toward massive objects in space). According to the accepted theory of the time, Einstein's observations were not possible. Einstein proposed a new and revolutionary theory of gravity to explain this phenomenon. Einstein's new theory was called the "General Theory of Relativity" and described curvatures in the space–time continuum. These curvatures were due to massive objects exerting their force of gravity on the space–time continuum, very similar to bowling balls placed on an outstretched blanket. Einstein's proposed theory was not initially accepted, but after years of tests and experiments, his theory gained acceptance.

This is the true nature of science. Laws are discovered. Theories are invented to explain them. The laws and theories are tested by experiments, observations, and hypothesis testing. Hypotheses are woven together into the theories as the theories are modified. Theories are never proven, only continually tested and updated. Theories can be accepted for hundreds of years, but with the advent of newer technology, theories are subjected to new tests and rigors, and eventually outdated or incomplete theories give way, absorbed into new, mature theories. The science of friction ridge skin has experienced exactly such trials.

14.2.3 Laws and Theories in Friction Ridge Examination

If we accept the definition that a scientific law is a generalized description of patterns and phenomena in nature and a scientific theory is the explanation for that law, then what theories and laws exist within the discipline of friction ridge science?

The two most basic laws are:

1) Human friction ridge skin is unique.

> Each individual possesses a unique arrangement of friction ridge skin. Specifically, the ridge arrangements, the robust arrangements of the minutiae within the ridge patterns, and the shapes and structures of the ridges all combine to form a unique arrangement of friction ridge skin in the hands and feet of each individual.

2) Human friction ridge skin is persistent (permanent) throughout the individual's lifetime.

> Specifically, what is meant by persistence is that the sequence of the ridges and the arrangement of the robust minutiae do not change throughout a person's lifetime. This is not to say that the friction ridge skin does not change over time. It does. Friction ridge skin expands as people grow from childhood to adulthood. Skin cells constantly slough off. The substructure of the skin changes over time and ridge heights decrease (Chacko and Vaidya, 1968). The number of visible incipient ridges increases as we age (Stücker et al., 2001). Hairline creases and wrinkles proliferate as we age. All these factors describe a dynamic and changing friction ridge skin. Yet the arrangement of the minutiae and the ridge sequences is very robust and reproducible. There is evidence to support that third-level details (e.g., ridge shapes and pore locations) are persistent; this is explored later in the chapter (see section 14.3.2.2).

The next question of interest is, Are these scientific laws? According to Popper, to satisfy the criteria for scientific laws, these laws must be falsifiable. Clearly, both laws are easily falsifiable. One must simply find instances where different individuals have indistinguishable friction ridge skin or instances where the arrangement of the ridges in friction ridge skin is observed to naturally change over time (excluding injury or trauma, of course). However, in the history of this discipline, no such instances have been demonstrated.

Suppose one individual, in the entire world, actually did have a fingerprint that matched someone else's fingerprint. Obviously, the forensic community would be shocked, and the verity of the law would be questioned. But in a purely Popperian view (Thornton, 2005):

> No observation is free from the possibility of error—consequently we may question whether our experimental result was what it appeared to be. Thus, while advocating falsifiability as the criterion of demarcation for science, Popper explicitly allows for the fact that in practice a single conflicting or counter-instance is never sufficient methodologically to falsify a theory [or law], and that scientific theories [or laws] are often retained even though much of the available evidence conflicts with them, or is anomalous with respect to them.

Thus, Popper advocated constant testing to refute a theory or law. A single instance of falsifiability should spawn additional testing.

Fundamental theories exist that explain the two laws of uniqueness and persistency. Uniqueness is explained by biological variations (genetic influences and random localized stresses) within the developing fetus. Persistence is maintained by the substructural formations of the developing skin (hemidesmosomes, papillae, and basal layer).

These are theories that explain the laws. These theories have empirical evidence and testing that support, but do not conclusively prove, them. Additional information may be learned that will cause these theories to be adjusted and incorporate the new data. Thus, science is evolving and dynamic.

14.2.4 Hypothesis Testing

Theories and laws are commonly challenged through hypothesis testing. The results of testing a hypothesis can support or refute a theory or law. In some instances, the results will call for modifications to be made to a law or theory, which in turn leads to further hypotheses to test under the new or modified law.

Although there are no rigorous formulas or recipes for testing hypotheses and designing experiments (nor should there be), a generic model for hypothesis testing can be described. The steps of this model are often referred to as "scientific method". Huber and Headrick (1999) noted that the term scientific method is a misnomer. They stated that scientific method is derived from epistemology (the study of knowledge and justified belief, according to the *Stanford Encyclopedia of Philosophy*). Francis Bacon defined a basic approach to scientific method encapsulated in four steps: (1) observe, (2) measure, (3) explain, and (4) verify (Huber and Headrick, 1999). This description in modern times has been modified into a hypothesis testing model. The basic steps of the hypothesis testing model have been described as:[1]

- Observation.
- Hypothesis formulation.
- Experimentation.
- Data analysis and conclusion.
- Reproducibility.
- Communication of results.

The researcher must first make a specific observation or note a general problem or query. Then a hypothesis is formulated (often referred to as the "null hypothesis"). The hypothesis is testable and falsifiable. A counter-hypothesis is also formulated. A suitable experiment is designed to test the specific hypothesis. Data from the experiment are collected. These data may be qualitative or quantitative. The data are evaluated, often statistically (though that is not a requirement), and conclusions are drawn whether to accept the hypothesis or reject the hypothesis and accept the null hypothesis. The results of the experiment should be reproducible by another scientist following the methodology. Finally, the results should be communicated to others. This is important not only for sharing the knowledge but also for peer review and critical analysis.

14.2.5 Comparison Methodology and Theory

As an extension of the law that friction ridge skin is unique, if during the deposition of a latent print, the details of the friction ridge skin are sufficiently recorded on a surface via residues on the friction ridge skin, then theoretically *the latent print image can be individualized to the source friction ridge skin*.

This is what Hempel and Oppenheim (1948) refer to as a derived theory (as opposed to a fundamental theory). The derived theory allows application of the principle to specific objects or individuals that would be prohibited by the universality and generality requirements of a law or fundamental theory. However, the theory that latent prints can be attributed to a unique source of friction ridge skin raises some questions that are difficult to answer.

Even if the friction ridge skin is unique down to the cells and ridge units, this issue is secondary to whether a latent print (which will not contain all of the information in the source skin) can be correctly attributed to its source. How much information must be transferred for the examiner to reliably individualize the latent print? What happens to the reliability of the details when subjected to distortions? What tolerances are acceptable regarding distortions and the flexibility of skin?

Ultimately, the latent print will be compared to a source (via known standard reproductions) by an expert. The comparison methodology generally accepted in the United States is the ACE-V methodology. This is an acronym for analysis, comparison, evaluation, and verification. The stages of ACE-V methodology are defined as: *Analysis*—Assessment of the quantity and quality of ridge detail present in an impression; *Comparison*—A side-by-side comparison of the two

---

[1] This basic model can be found in most elementary collegiate science texts in various forms.

impressions; *Evaluation*—The decision process to declare an individualization, exclusion, or inconclusive opinion; *Verification*—Verification of the result by another competent examiner. The ACE process was initially described by Huber as a logical, methodological process for the comparison of handwriting evidence (Huber, 1959). (For more about ACE-V, see Chapter 9.)

It has been argued elsewhere that ACE-V "methodology" is not in any real sense a methodology and is more akin to a "protocol" (Champod et al., 2004). A methodology would typically encompass very explicit steps, instructions, criteria, and a transparent decision model. This has not been accomplished. The ACE-V protocol, however, serves as an appropriate model and descriptor for performing any sort of forensic comparative examination, whereby evidence from an unknown source is compared against appropriate known exemplars to reach an opinion regarding the source of the evidence. As such a protocol, it offers good suggestions for general forensic examinations such as (1) analysis of the unknown should be done separately, prior to comparison to the known exemplar, and (2) there must be verification of the conclusion and peer review of the reasoning used to reach the proffered conclusion.

Wertheim has suggested that ACE-V is analogous to the scientific method (Wertheim, 2000, pp 1–8). Huber and Headrick made a similar analogy for the ACE process with respect to handwriting comparisons (Huber and Headrick, 1999, pp 351–355). The analysis is the assessment (observation) that a latent print has detail sufficient for a comparison. A hypothesis is formed: the latent print originated from Individual A; a null hypothesis is formed: the latent print did not originate from Individual A. The images are compared and agreement is found or not found (experimentation). Based on the degree of agreement (data), one concludes that there is sufficient evidence during the evaluation stage to individualize or exclude (support or reject the hypothesis as a conclusion). The process is then verified by another expert during verification (reproducibility).

As Hughes (1998, pp 611–615) has noted, the practice of friction ridge examination is an applied science. The discipline borrows from other sciences to support and justify the practice of comparing friction ridge images by a specific comparison methodology.

14.3 Scientific Research Related to Friction Ridge Examination

14.3.1 Friction Ridge Skin Is Unique

In order to prove the axiom of unique friction ridge skin to be true, every area of friction ridge skin on the planet (and all the skin of past and future generations) would need to be examined. Obviously, this will never be possible. Therefore, to support this premise, the discipline looks to three areas of support:

- Empirical observations and evidence.

- The theory of the formation of friction ridge skin (i.e., the biological formation).

- Fingerprint individuality models based on probability and statistics.

14.3.1.1 Observations. The empirical evidence, for many years, was generally viewed by the discipline as the *pièce de résistance* of evidence for the claim that friction ridge skin is unique. An expert would anticipate under vigorous cross-examination during trials to be asked, "Well, how do you *know* that no two fingerprints are alike?" The typical answer of course was, "Because in all the history of fingerprints, all the billions of comparisons worldwide, no two fingerprints have ever been found to be identical, from different sources, and this includes identical twins."

Although this fact is important and should not be dismissed, it does not satisfy the argument and does not prove that one person's particular print does not have a matching mate somewhere out there on the planet. All that can be inferred from this fact is that, presently, no two people have been found to have matching fingerprints. Taking it a step further, it does not satisfy that one particular latent print, with just enough distortion and low clarity, might not be mistaken to be from a different source, given that the false source was very similar in appearance to the true source of skin. Latent print examiners should be cautious about resting merely on empirical evidence to support the uniqueness of friction ridge skin. Furthermore, the number of actual comparisons that have been performed, when compared to the total number of possible comparisons available (i.e., every human's friction ridge skin against every other human's friction ridge skin), is only the smallest fraction (cf. by inference, "The Snowflake Paradigm" by Thornton, 1986). Therefore, given what would undoubtedly be an exceptionally small probability (i.e., matching fingerprints between two different people), an impossibly large number of comparisons would need to be done to even have a realistic chance of finding such a match in the population. So even if matching fingerprints were to exist in the population, the chance of discovering them is simply too remote.

The literature lacks research that was specifically conducted to prove that no two areas of friction ridge skin are alike. The absence of such a study stems from (1) as discussed previously, its impossibility, and (2) the profession's consistent reliance on its collective experience and case studies to demonstrate the point. Additionally, it could be argued that, until *U.S. v Mitchell* (1999), the premises and validity of friction ridge skin examinations had not been seriously challenged or scrutinized; therefore, the impetus to scientifically test the law, under the rigors of present-day science, has not existed.

Still, although there is not (and cannot be) any definitive way to prove that all friction ridge skin is unique, there exists empirical evidence that supports the premise. Evidence from "look-alikes" (i.e., close nonmatches—friction ridge skin impressions from two different sources that are very similar in appearance) (IEEGFI-II, 2004, p 13) has been helpful. Evidence from look-alikes can be found in monozygotic twin research and two Automated Fingerprint Identification System (AFIS) studies.

Studies of Monozygotic Twins. If one wanted to find areas of matching friction ridge skin from two different individuals, it would seem that the population of monozygotic twins would be a good place to start the search. Galton (2005, pp 185–187, originally published in 1892) first explored this avenue. He found similarities in patterns, but the minutiae were different. Similarly, other researchers, exploring the hereditary aspects of fingerprints, have examined the prints of monozygotic twins. The works of Wilder, Grüneberg, Bonnevie, and Newman are summarized by Cummins and Midlo (1943, pp 210–245). These researchers all investigated the similarities of fingerprints between monozygotic twins. Their findings mirrored the conclusions of Galton.

Okajima (1967, pp 660–673) found a higher correlation for the number of minutiae present between the fingerprints of identical twins than the number of minutiae present between the fingerprints of fraternal twins. Lin and colleagues (1982, pp 290–304) further investigated this relationship. They examined the correlations for fingerprint pattern, ridge count, and minutiae positioning for 196 pairs of twins (including both identical and fraternal twins). They found that the correlations followed the trend (in decreasing order of correlation): identical twins, fraternal twins, related siblings, and lastly, unrelated individuals. Their work echoed that of previous researchers noted by Cummins and Midlo (1943, pp 235–245). Lin and colleagues (1982) concluded that "although fingerprints [of identical twins] may have a high degree of similarity . . . variations in minutiae distribution still permit their differentiation" (Lin et al., 1982, p 304).

In more recent times, German (*U.S.* v *Mitchell,* July 8, 1999, pp 2–56), in preparation for a *Daubert* hearing, performed similar analyses as Lin and colleagues (1982) with a database of fingerprints of 500 pairs of twins (including both identical and fraternal twins). Again, similarities in patterns, ridge count, and minutiae locations were noted between identical twins, but the prints were still differentiable. German further noted that even in the smallest areas of agreement (clusters of two to three minutiae located in similar positions), he could differentiate the prints based on third-level detail (i.e., the shapes of the ridges and pore locations). However, it should be noted that the work of German was not published. Therefore, it was not peer reviewed and can only be found in the testimony during the *Daubert* hearing in the *Mitchell* case. Moreover, unlike Lin and colleagues (1982), the German study was not conducted with well-defined hypotheses to be tested, the methods to test the hypotheses were not clear prior to the commencement of the work, and it is not clear what metrics were used to determine the strength of the similarities and dissimilarities when comparing mated monozygotic twin prints.

Srihari and colleagues also conducted a large study of twins' fingerprints (Srihari et al., 2008). They used 298 sets of twins and 3 sets of triplets. The researchers used a minutiae-based automatic fingerprint identification algorithm to compute comparison scores. The researchers compared each identical twin to his or her mated identical twin. They also compared scores between twins' fingerprints and unrelated twins' fingerprints, fraternal twins, and non-twins. Comparing the distributions of scores produced, the researchers found that twin pairs have more similarities in level 1 detail and level 2 detail than the general population, but are still discriminable.

All of the previous studies with twins dealt exclusively with known exemplars of their friction ridge skin. What is lacking from the literature is whether an examiner can correctly attribute a latent impression to the correct friction ridge skin source when identical twins have deposited latent prints. The only data of this nature can be found in the 1995 Collaborative Testing Services (CTS) latent print examiner proficiency test (CTS, 1995; Grieve, 1996, pp 521–528). This particular CTS proficiency test included a bloody impression from an individual whose fingerprint exemplars were not provided for the proficiency test. Instead, the fingerprint exemplars from the donor's identical twin, who did not create the bloody impression, were provided. Approximately one in five participants in this proficiency test erroneously individualized the impression to the incorrect source.

Empirical Data. It is unknown exactly which individual or culture first recognized the individuality of fingerprints. From the ancient Middle East to the ancient Chinese, there is evidence in these cultures of an awareness of the uniqueness of fingerprints. (For a timeline of fingerprint science, see Chapter 1.) It was not until 1788 that Dr. J. C. A. Mayer recorded:

> Although the arrangement of skin ridges is never duplicated in two persons, nevertheless the similarities are closer among some individuals. In others the differences are marked, yet in spite of their peculiarities of arrangement all have a certain likeness. (Cummins and Midlo, 1943, p 13)

Mayer is considered the first individual to record the assertion that friction ridge skin is unique.

Many more early pioneers investigating this phenomenon followed, including Sir William Herschel and Dr. Henry Faulds. However, neither Herschel nor Faulds published hard data in support of their theories. In his 1880 letter to *Nature* (Faulds, 1880, p 605), Faulds reported several conclusions, including "absolute identity" of criminals from crime scene latent impressions. However, Faulds never provided the data for his basis, stating only that he examined a "large number of nature-prints" taken from individuals in Japan. His later writings (Faulds, 1911) refer to his examination of "many thousands of living fingers".

In 1970, the International Association for Identification (IAI) organized a committee known as the Standardization Committee. The primary task of the committee was "to determine the minimum number of minutiae of friction ridge characteristics which must be present in two impressions in order to establish positive identification" (McCann, 1971, p 10). For 3 years, the committee addressed this issue and in 1973, the Standardization Committee reached a consensus: "No valid basis exists at this time for requiring that a pre-determined minimum number of friction ridge characteristics must be present in two impressions in order to establish positive identification. The foregoing reference to friction ridge characteristics applies equally to fingerprints, palm prints, toe prints and sole prints of the human body" (McCann, 1973, p 13). This conclusion was arrived at through interviews with professionals in the field, a review of the literature, surveys sent to various international identification bureaus, and the generally accepted view of the profession. It is important to note that during the interviews and surveys, no agency reported any knowledge of an instance where two individuals were found to have matching fingerprints or any other matching areas of friction ridge skin (Moenssens, 2006).

As for concrete empirical studies, two are notable. Fingerprint expert Stephen Meagher (*U.S.* v *Mitchell,* July 8, 1999, pp 56–229; July 9, 1999, pp 2–31), in preparation for a *Daubert* hearing, conducted a survey. He sent images of two latent prints (the images that had been identified to the defendant in this case) to all 50 state laboratories.[2] All agencies were asked to search the two latent prints in their local AFIS databases. Only one agency reported identifications: Pennsylvania, the state in which the defendant had been arrested. Eaton (2005, 2006) reported similar findings in an unpublished pilot study. A single common loop latent print with 12 minutiae, and a second image of the same print, cropped to show 8 minutiae, were sent to 50 agencies (in 9 countries). These agencies searched the images in their AFIS databases. The only agency to report an individualization was the Western Identification Network, which was the only agency that maintained a copy of the civilian tenprint card for the donor of the latent print in this experiment.

Although neither of these results offer substantial proof that all friction ridge skin is unique, it is important to note that, after comparing these latent prints to hundreds of millions of fingerprints combined in the AFIS databases, no

---

[2] It should be noted however (and this concern was raised during the *Mitchell* testimony) that the surveys did not always reach the intended participants. In some states, the surveys were sent to the Criminal Justice Information Services Division instead of the latent print unit. Therefore, the distribution of the surveys may not have been properly controlled.

CHAPTER 14 | Scientific Research Supporting the Foundations of Friction Ridge Examinations

agency reported a match to anyone other than the correct known source. In effect, Meagher and Eaton were not able to falsify the individuality of fingerprints in these noteworthy, albeit limited, instances.

14.3.1.2 Biological Basis. On the basis of a holistic and qualitative understanding of the morphogenetic processes of friction ridge skin formation, latent print examiners have predominantly supported the statement: Nature never repeats itself (McRoberts, 1996; Thornton, 1986). This position has been further supported by the views of numerous biologists, zoologists, and anatomists who have explored the proffered model for friction ridge skin formation (Wilder and Wentworth, 1918, 1932; Cummins and Midlo, 1943; Hale, 1952; Okajima, 1967; Misumi and Akiyoshi, 1984; Montagna and Parakkal, 1974, Montagna et al., 1992; Babler, 1978, 1990, 1991).

Early authors generally referred to the variability of minutiae alone, and thus a probabilistic approach to fingerprint individuality, as evidence for the uniqueness of friction ridge skin (Galton, 2005, pp 100–113; Wilder and Wentworth, 1932, pp 309–328). Cummins (2000, pp 79–90) and Hale (1952, pp 147–173) recognized that the variability in minutiae formations and appearance were attributable to random mechanical stresses during friction ridge formation. The patterns of friction ridge skin and the arrangement of the minutiae, in conjunction with variability in the edge formations (Chatterjee, 1962), pore locations (Locard, 1912; Faulds, 1912, pp 29–39), and ridge widths and heights (Cummins et al., 1941; Ashbaugh, 1999, pp 61–65), provide a seemingly infinite palette of variation, even in the smallest regions. Montagna and colleagues have generally noted that skin (friction ridge and nonfriction ridge skin) differs from individual to individual and is not repeated elsewhere in regions on each individual (Montagna and Parakkal, 1974; Montagna et al., 1992). Montagna and colleagues noted in their observations and study of friction ridge skin and nonfriction ridge skin:

> The palmar and plantar surfaces are filigreed by continuous and discontinuous alternating ridges and sulci [furrows]; the details of these markings and their configurations are collectively known as dermatoglyphics. Each area has unique regional and individual structural variations not matched elsewhere in the same or in any other individual. (Montagna et al., 1992, p 8)

The biological model for the morphogenesis of friction ridge skin supports the perspective for the uniqueness of friction ridge skin. Although not necessarily providing concrete evidence to test the uniqueness of friction ridge skin, the theory does explain why the law holds true.

The biological basis for flexion crease formation has been studied by several researchers (Kimura and Kitigawa, 1986, 1988; Popich and Smith, 1970). With respect to the study of palmar features, empirical frequencies have been reported by Tietze and Witthuhn (2001). They reported frequencies of creases, ridge flow, patterns, and other distinct formations from 35,000 pairs of palmprints. Although these observations do not show "uniqueness" of palmar features, these data are helpful for assessing the rarity of these features.

14.3.1.3 Probability Models for Fingerprint Individuality. Though many early pioneers recorded their empirical observations, it was Sir Francis Galton who developed the first probability model for individuality, resulting from his systematic analysis and study of fingerprints. From Galton's model in 1892 to the present, there have been approximately two dozen or so models, each improving or refining aspects of previous models.

This section will summarize the significant research and models available. The summaries given are very basic and brief. Excellent summaries, discussions, and critiques of these models, including the assumptions, limitations, and strengths of each, have been provided elsewhere (see Stoney and Thornton, 1986a, pp 1187–1213; Stoney, 2001, pp 327–387; Pankanti et al., 2001, pp 805–812).

The Galton Model (1892) (Galton, 2005, pp 100–113). Although Galton devised the first probability model for fingerprint individuality, it was very crude. Using enlargements of fingerprints, Galton dropped square pieces of paper of varying size randomly over the enlargements. He then attempted to predict whether the pieces of paper covered minutiae. Galton built his model on his ability to predict the occurrence of minutiae, dependent on the configuration of the surrounding ridges. He did not base his model on the actual frequencies and distributions of minutiae. Furthermore, he used unrealistic factors to estimate probability of differing pattern types and the number of ridges in a particular region of the print. From these calculations, he arrived at the probability of finding any given arrangement of minutiae in a fingerprint to be 1.45×10^{-11} (i.e., 1 in 68 billion).

The Henry Model (1900) (Henry, 1900, pp 54–58). The second model, proposed by Sir Edward Henry, was a drastic deviation from Galton's approach. Henry proposed that each minutia was an independent, identically distributed event (each occurrence of minutia has the same probability and is not dependent or influenced by any other minutiae). The probability of a minutiae event was 1/4 (.25). The probability of finding 12 matching minutiae was then $(1/4)^{12} = 6 \times 10^{-8}$ (i.e., approximately 1 in 17 million). To account for pattern type, according to Henry's model, pattern type was deemed equivalent to two more minutiae (multiplying the previous results for minutiae by 1/16). Thus, if given a whorl print with 12 minutiae, the probability of finding a whorl print with 12 matching minutiae is $(1/4)^{14}$ or 4×10^{-9} (i.e., approximately 1 in 270 million).

The Balthazard Model (1911) (Balthazard, 1911, pp 1862–1864). Using Henry's approach, Dr. Victor Balthazard (a French medical examiner) also used the probability of a minutia event equal to 1/4, but while Henry's was arbitrary, Balthazard based his use of 1/4 on whether a bifurcation or ridge ending pointed to the left or to the right. He proposed that each of these four possibilities (bifurcation left or right, ridge ending left or right) is equally likely to occur, and thus he arrived at a probability of 1/4 for a minutia event. His model did not include a factor for pattern type. He then reasoned that, in order for his model to satisfy the expectation of only one person on the planet to have a matching configuration to the print, 17 minutiae in agreement would need to be found. By his model, finding 17 matching minutiae had a probability of $(1/4)^{17} = 6 \times 10^{-11}$ (i.e., 1 in 17 billion). He also conceded that if one was certain the donor was restricted to a certain geographical region, then a positive identity could be established with a lower number of minutiae (e.g., 10 to 12 minutiae). In effect, Balthazard proposed the first "minimum point" threshold.

The Locard Model (1914) (Locard, 1914, pp 526–548; Champod, 1995, pp 136–163). The Locard model is not a statistical model, but rather a pragmatic opinion derived from the statistical models of Dr. Edmond Locard's era. Locard established his tripartite rule:

1) If more than 12 concurring minutiae are present and the fingerprint is very clear, then the certainty of identity is beyond debate.

2) If 8 to 12 concurring minutiae are found, then identification is marginal and certainty of identity is dependent on:

   a. the quality (clarity) of the fingerprint,

   b. the rarity of the minutiae type,

   c. the presence of a core and delta in a clear area of the print,

   d. the presence of pores, and

   e. the perfect agreement of the width of the ridges and furrows, the direction of the ridge flow, and the angular value of the bifurcation.

3) If a limited number of characteristic features are present, the fingerprint cannot provide certainty for an identification, but only a presumption proportional to the number of points available and their clarity.

In instances of parts 1 and 2 of the rule, positive identification can be established following discussion of the case by at least two competent and experienced examiners. Locard arrived at these conclusions based on his own experience and observations and the works of Galton, Balthazard, and Ramos.[3] Part 3 of the rule, as noted by Champod (1995, pp 136–150), is highly suggestive of a probabilistic approach to fingerprint evidence and conclusions.

The Bose Model (1917) (Roxburgh, 1933, pp 189–214). Rai Sahib Hem Chandra Bose used the Henry model and also used a probability of 1/4 for a minutia event; however, he clearly did so on a poor assumption. He chose 1/4 as a probability on the basis of his contention that there are four types of minutiae events, all equally likely to occur: a dot, bifurcation, ending ridge, or continuous ridge. Clearly, there are many more continuous ridge events than minutiae and certainly more ridge endings and bifurcations than dots distributed in a typical fingerprint.

The Wilder and Wentworth Model (1918) (Wilder and Wentworth, 1918, pp 319–322). Dr. Harris Wilder and Bert Wentworth used the Henry model as well, but instead of an assumed probability of minutia occurrence of 1/4, they used 1/50. They gave only this reason as justification:

> We have no definite data for knowing the percentage of occurrence of [minutiae in a specific

---

[3] Galdino Ramos. *De Identificacao*, Rio de Janeiro, 1906. Locard (1914) referenced Ramos' work, stating that Ramos calculated that it would take 4,660,337 centuries before two people were born with the same fingerprints. Locard, however, sharply disagreed with Ramos' calculations, stating that they were in error because Ramos used an incorrect number of minutiae in the fingerprint as his basis for calculations. Locard did not state how Ramos computed his values, and thus it cannot be known whether Ramos overestimated or underestimated in his calculations.

pattern]. . . . As a matter of fact it is absurd to use anywhere near as small a ratio as 4 to 1, for the percentage of occurrence of any one of these details; it would be rather 1 in 50, or 1 in 100 . . . (Wilder and Wentworth, 1918, p 321).

The Galton model only recognized and used approximately 35 minutiae on the "bulb" of the finger (i.e., in the central portion of the tip of the finger) (Galton, 2005, pp 97–98). Wilder and Wentworth (as did Balthazard) recognized that there are "60 to 100 separate details" in a full fingerprint (Wilder and Wentworth, 1932, p 319).

The Pearson Model (1930) (Pearson, 1930, p 182). Karl Pearson, an eminent mathematician and statistician of the late 19th century (famous for his many contributions to the field of statistics, including the well-known chi-square test), did not create a fingerprint model per se. Rather, in writing the biography of his good friend and colleague Sir Francis Galton, Pearson critiqued Galton's model. Pearson suggested that a more appropriate estimate of the probability of a minutiae event was 1/36, rather than 1/2 as Galton had used.

The Roxburgh Model (1933) (Roxburgh, 1933, pp 189–214). T. J. Y. Roxburgh's model incorporated several innovative concepts. First, it included a factor for the number of intervening ridges from a minutia to the origin, using a polar coordinate system. All previous (and subsequent) models used rectangular areas or Cartesian coordinate systems. Second, Roxburgh included a clarity factor, recognizing that clarity can be low due to smearing or smudging and sometimes the type of minutiae present in a print may be ambiguous. The factor, termed "Q" for quality, allowed for the adjustment of probabilities based on the quality of a minutia. The Roxburgh model also incorporated factors for pattern type and minutiae type (the latter similar to the Balthazard model).

Roxburgh also provided a table of probabilities for matching crime scene latent prints as a measure of the probability of finding that arrangement of minutiae. The table listed probabilities for 1 through 35 matching minutiae for 4 classes of clarity: "ideal", "good", "poor", and "worst". On the basis of these calculations, he provided a second table (Table 14–1) for the minimum number of minutiae needed to declare a positive identification between a crime scene latent print[4] and a known exemplar. Roxburgh included a factor for error, with upper and lower limits of margin of error of 1/500,000 (if the finger designation is unknown) and 1/50,000, respectively. Roxburgh wrote:

Taking the value of 1/50,000 as the margin of safety, we see then that with a good average print, 8 to 9 points are sufficient for safety; for a poor average print, 9 to 10 points are required; and for a poor print 11 points; and for a very poor print, not showing the form and centre, 15 or 16 points. For a very good print (approaching an ideal print), 7 to 8 points would suffice. (Roxburgh, 1933, p 212)

Roxburgh essentially calculated minimum thresholds based on a quantitative–qualitative examination.

The Cummins and Midlo Model (1943) (Cummins and Midlo, 1943, pp 147–155). The model used by Dr. Harold Cummins and Dr. Charles Midlo is identical to the Wilder and Wentworth model, with the exception of a factor for pattern type. They reasoned that the probability of obtaining the most common fingerprint pattern (an ulnar loop) with similar ridge counts (based on 11 ridges) was 1/31. Thus, as an upper bound, this factor is multiplied with the probability of a minutiae arrangement.

The Amy Model (1946–1948) (Amy, 1946a, pp 80–87; 1946b, 188–195; 1948, pp 96–101). Lucien Amy developed a model that incorporated two essential factors of individuality: the number and position of minutiae and the type of minutiae. Amy first derived data for the type of minutiae from observing frequencies of occurrence in 100 fingerprints. All previous models either arbitrarily assigned frequencies or assumed equal frequencies. Amy used the Balthazard criteria of bifurcation to the left or right and ridge ending to the left or right, but found that these minutiae types were not uniformly distributed. From these distributions, Amy calculated a factor for minutiae type (including orientation).

Amy then calculated the total number of possible minutiae arrangements, given a number of minutiae. He did so using a binomial distribution. This sort of probability distribution and modeling would be akin to calculating how many different ways you can arrange a certain number of cars in a parking lot with a fixed number of spaces, where each car would be parked in a space, but not all spaces filled, and finally, the lot itself having a fixed, given size.

---

[4] Technically, the table was useful for any two images based on the quality of the images, i.e., comparing an "ideal" inked print against a smudged "worst case" inked print.

Table 14–1

Roxburgh's calculation for the minimum number of minutiae needed to declare a positive match, with a margin of error of 1 in 50,000.[1]

Population or Number in Class[2]	Character of Print				
	(i) Ideal	(ii) Good Average	(iii) Poor Average	(iv) Poor	(v) Worst Case
10^1	2	3	3	3	8
10^2	3	3	4	4	9
10^3	4	4	5	6	10
10^4	4/5	5	6	7	11
10^5	5	6	6/7	8	12
10^6	6	7	7/8	9	13
10^7	7	8	8	10	14
10^8	7	8	9	11	15/16
10^9	8	9	10	12	16/17
1.6×10^9 (world)	8	9	10/11	12/13	17
1.6×10^{10} (finger unknown)	9	10	11	13	18

Notes

(1) Table 14–1 shows the number of points that are required for safety for five types of prints. The first four columns are based on decreasing levels of quality; the fifth column was obtained by using the lowest quality print and taking a margin of error of 1/50,000.

(2) The figures are given in each case for the designation of the finger being known. If unknown, the class is multiplied by 10, and the number of points required is as for the next class below in the table.

(Adapted from Roxburgh, 1933.)

To calculate the probability of duplicating a given minutiae arrangement, Amy multiplied these two factors (minutiae type and minutiae arrangements) together and added a correction factor for clusters of minutiae.

Amy also calculated, based on his model, the chance of a false match. Amy showed that as the number of comparisons for a particular arrangement increased, so did the probability of finding a match and so did the chance of a false match. The chance of finding similar configurations in a billion people is much higher than when comparing against one or two individuals. Amy's observations follow directly from the concept that even the rarest of events have expectations of occurrence when the number of trials is very large. This is a critical concept, especially when the potential effects of large AFIS databases are considered, and the possible correlation to recent events (e.g., the Brandon Mayfield incident—section 14.3.3.4) must be considered (Stacey, 2004, pp 706–718).

Amy suggested that if a minutiae configuration is compared against one or two suspects and a match is declared, this is stronger evidence than if a minutiae configuration is compared against one billion individuals. Thus the strength of the match is decreased for a large number of comparisons and the likelihood of a false match is increased, or the criteria for a match must become more stringent when comparing against a large population to achieve the same level of reliability. However, Amy's position is that the truth of the conclusion depends both on the strength of the evidence (the match) and the size of the relevant population.

With respect to a similar debate regarding DNA evidence and DNA database searches, Donnelly and Friedman treated the strength of the evidence (the rarity of a profile) and the strength of the identification decision (the chance the profile originated from the defendant) separately (Donnelly and Friedman, 1999, pp 1–9). According to them, a DNA match either comes from a single suspect provided by police investigation (what they referred to as a "confirmation" case) or the match comes from a large database search (what they referred to as a "trawl" case). In either case, the rarity of the profile does not decrease.[5] However, the chance the profile originated from the defendant (and thus the strength of the prosecutor's case) would depend on whether the suspect was selected from a trawl case or confirmation case. From a statistical approach, the prior probabilities for the prosecutor's hypothesis (guilt) are drastically different in a confirmation case versus the trawl case. In the confirmation case, the police presumably had prior information through investigation to arrive at a particular suspect. The DNA match now adds significant weight to the case. In the "trawl" case, absent any other evidence to tie the suspect to the scene, the prosecutor's case is much weaker given only the DNA match produced from a large database, where there is a greater potential for a false match. The parallels to friction ridge examinations and AFIS databases are important to note, especially as the profession explores a probabilistic approach to friction ridge examinations.

The Trauring Model (1963) (Trauring, 1963, pp 938–940). The model by Mitchell Trauring was not a model for calculating fingerprint individuality per se, but rather for estimating the probability of a false match to an *individual* if searched in a proposed theoretical automated fingerprint identification system. The Trauring model is very similar in assumptions and calculations to the Balthazard model and was derived from the Galton model. However, instead of using the probability of 1/2 (0.50) for a minutia event, Trauring calculated the probability of a minutia event to be 0.1944. This value was based on his observations of minutiae density and his estimate of finding "test" minutiae in a quadrilateral region bounded by a set of "reference" minutiae.

The Kingston Model (1964) (Kingston, 1964; Stoney and Thornton, 1986a, pp 1204–1209). The model by Charles R. Kingston is similar in approach and complexity to the Amy model. Kingston calculated three critical probabilities for assessing fingerprint individuality: (1) observed number of minutiae for a region of a given size, (2) observed arrangements for the minutiae, and (3) observed minutiae type.

Kingston's first factor, probability of observed number of minutiae, was calculated from observations of minutiae density from 100 fingerprints. Kingston found this distribution followed a statistical model known as a Poisson distribution. (Amy had used a binomial distribution, but under these conditions, the binomial distribution is approximately a Poisson distribution.) Thus for a fingerprint area of a specific size, Kingston could calculate the probability of finding *x* number of minutiae in this space.

Also similar to Amy and to the previous analogy of cars in a parking lot, Kingston calculated the number of positions and arrangements for a given number of minutiae. The analogy of the parking lot is even more apropos to Kingston's model, as Kingston's model was based on the assignment of the first minutia into a position, then the second minutia would occupy another position, and so forth. This is similar to cars queued up to park where, after the first car has parked, the second car must find another spot, and so forth.

Kingston's final factor, the minutia type, was based on observed frequencies for almost 2,500 minutiae. Unlike the previous models, which assumed and estimated various distributions, or relied solely upon simple bifurcations and ridge endings, Kingston calculated relative frequencies for ridge endings, bifurcation, dots, enclosures, bridges, triradii, and "other" minutiae.

The Gupta Model (1968) (Gupta, 1968, pp 130–134; Stoney and Thornton, 1986a, p 1191). The model by S. R. Gupta is the last of the simple models based on the Henry model. Gupta made observations of minutiae position frequencies from 1,000 fingerprints. Unlike his predecessors, he was not examining the frequency (rarity) of a particular type of minutiae; rather, he examined how often a particular type of minutiae appeared in a specific position. Referring back to the parking lot analogy, it is akin to observing how often a Ford parks in a particular parking spot (versus a Chrysler, General Motors, or Toyota vehicle). He estimated that bifurcations and ridge endings generally appeared in a particular position with a frequency of 1/10, and less common features (e.g., dots, spurs) with a frequency of 1/100.

---

[5] Some sources believe the rarity of the profile would not change at all under these two scenarios. Donnelly and Friedman (1999) argued that the rarity of the profile actually would change and have more weight after a database search, because a large portion of the population has been effectively excluded as a potential donor, thus empirically demonstrating the rarity of the DNA profile. Literally, the denominator to calculate the rarity of a profile would change after a large database search, because it would be known how many individuals did not have the profile. Significant debate surrounds this issue. The debate illustrates a classic difference between the frequentist and Bayesian approaches.

Gupta also included a factor for pattern type and ridge count for the pattern.

The Osterburg Model (1977–1980) (Osterburg et al., 1977, pp 772–778; Sclove, 1979, pp 588–595; 1980, 675–695). The Osterburg model was proposed by Osterburg, Parthasarathy, Raghavan, and Sclove in 1977. The model was modified by additional work by Sclove in 1979 and 1980. The basic Osterburg method was to divide a fingerprint into square cells, with each cell possessing an area of 1 sq mm. Osterburg observed the relative frequencies of 13 different ridge events in all of these cells. These events included no event (an empty cell), ending ridge, bifurcation, island, dot, and so forth. He calculated the rarity of these events. Notably, he only used 39 fingerprints to do so.

He then reasoned that the rarity of a fingerprint arrangement would be the product of all the individual minutiae frequencies and empty cells. Given a partial 72 sq mm fingerprint, if one has 12 ridge endings (each occupying 1 cell) and 60 empty cells, the probability of this event is $(0.766)^{60} (0.0832)^{12} = 1.25 \times 10^{-20}$, where 0.766 and 0.0832 are Osterburg's observed frequencies of an empty cell and a ridge ending, respectively.

Finally, Osterburg corrected for the number of possible positions this grouping of minutiae can take. This factor was dependent on the size of this partial fingerprint physically fitting into all the fully rolled fingerprint blocks on a tenprint card. Again referring back to the parking lot analogy, it is similar to taking a row of cars and empty spaces from a lot and seeing how many ways you can physically fit that chunk into the entire parking lot. This approach is somewhat similar to Amy's.

One of the largest problems with the Osterburg model is the assumption that each cell event is independent. For example, if a cell contains a minutia, it is unlikely that the surrounding eight cells will also contain minutiae. Minutiae generally do not all group together. Sclove recognized that the presence or absence of minutiae in a group of cells will influence the presence or absence of minutiae in neighboring cells. Sclove modified Osterburg's event frequencies to reflect this dependency.

The Stoney and Thornton Model (1985–1989). Chronologically to this point, knowledge of fingerprint individuality models in the fingerprint community was scarce. Stoney and Thornton, in part to satisfy a portion of Stoney's thesis requirement, critically reviewed all the previously mentioned models, noting each model's flaws and strengths (Stoney and Thornton, 1986a, pp 1187–1216). On the basis of their review, Stoney and Thornton then proposed a set of criteria that the ideal model would possess for calculating the individuality of a print, as well as determining the probabilistic strength of a match. Stoney and Thornton identified that the ideal model must include the following features:

1) *Ridge structure and description of minutiae locations*
   Ridge counts must be considered for measuring distances between features. For features on the same ridge, linear distances should be used, provided there are acceptable tolerances for distortion. (Though this author would suggest, when clarity is sufficiently high, one could count the intervening ridge units, which would not be subject to linear distance distortion.)

2) *Description of minutia distribution*
   Minutiae are not uniformly distributed across a fingerprint and can vary in density (as noted by Kingston) and conditional relationship (as noted by Sclove). An accurate distribution of minutiae for a specific region must be a property of the ideal model.

3) *Orientation of minutiae*
   With the exception of the dot or very short ridge, minutiae possess an orientation along the ridge flow that must be considered.

4) *Variation in minutiae types*
   Relative frequencies for minutiae must be considered and the ideal model should have consideration for the absence of minutiae (similar to the Osterburg/Sclove model).

5) *Variation among prints from the same source*
   The ideal model should account for the flexibility of skin where some features (e.g., ridge flow and linear distances) would not be as robust as other features (e.g., minutiae location on a ridge and ridge counts between minutiae). Poor clarity, distortion, and variability within the source must all be considered.

6) *Number of orientations and comparisons*
   The number of ways to orient a fingerprint fragment can vary. For example, a delta could logically be oriented in three different ways. Also, on an individual with a loop pattern on each finger and toe, and several deltas in the palms and on the soles of the feet, a single delta formation could be compared nearly 60 different ways to one individual alone. The more orientations a print can assume will result in more comparisons that are possible. As Amy

observed, the more comparisons that are performed, the more opportunities that occur for a false match.

The model proposed by Stoney and Thornton was a study of minutiae pairs, within the ridge structure of the print. They performed statistical analyses on 2645 minutiae pairs from 412 fingerprints (all male distal tips of thumbs) (Stoney and Thornton, 1987, pp 1182–1203) and attempted to meet all of the ideal conditions that they had proposed. They were able to meet most of their conditions and developed a model for describing minutiae (Stoney and Thornton, 1986b, pp 1217–1234).

In the Stoney and Thornton model, each pair of minutiae is described by the minutiae events (i.e., type of minutiae, orientation, intervening ridge count, and linear distance) and spatial position of the pair within the entire fingerprint pattern. The combination of all the minutiae pairs is a measure of individuality for that print. Thus Stoney and Thornton described a model that incorporated many of the essential components for determining the individuality of friction ridge arrangements.

Champod and Margot Model (1995–1996) (Champod and Margot, 1996a, 1996b; Stoney, 2001, pp 373–378). Until this point, all previous calculations and minutiae observations had been done by hand and involved small databases of fingerprints (Stoney and Thornton's model thus far used the largest database of 412 prints, albeit thumbtips). The Champod and Margot model was the first to utilize a computerized algorithm to process the fingerprint images. They used a database of 977 fingerprints composed of ulnar loops from the middle and index fingers and whorls from the middle finger.

Champod and Margot, similar to Stoney and Thornton, first performed a systematic statistical description of the minutiae in the fingerprints. They calculated the minutiae density and distribution of minutiae for various regions in the print, the frequencies of the minutiae types, the orientation of the minutiae, and lengths of compound minutiae (e.g., short ridges, enclosures).

Using their data, they then calculated probabilities for specific minutiae configurations and combinations. These probabilities indicate the probability of reoccurrence for a specific minutiae configuration and thus can be expressed as a measure of the strength of the match.

The Meagher, Budowle, and Ziesig Model (1999) (*U.S. v Mitchell*, July 8, 1999, pp 157–198; July 9, 1999, pp 29–139). This model, often referred to as the "50K versus 50K study", was an experiment conducted by the FBI in conjunction with Lockheed Martin, Inc., in response to the first *Daubert* challenge in *U.S. v Byron Mitchell*. This study has not been published, but descriptions of the study and data are found within the documents and testimony provided by Stephen Meagher, Bruce Budowle, and Donald Ziesig in *Mitchell*.

The primary experiment conducted by Meagher and colleagues utilized AFIS computer algorithms to compare each of 50,000 fingerprint images (all left loops from white males) against itself[6] and then the remaining 49,999 images in the database. The result of each comparison produced a score proportional to the degree of correlation between the two images. It is critical to note that all previous models possess calculations of individuality based on predicted minutiae arrangements; however, the scores in this model are a function of the AFIS algorithms and matcher logic.

Presumably, the highest score would result when an image is compared against itself. All of the other 49,999 comparison scores were then normalized (to fit a standard normal curve) to the highest score. The top 500 scores for each print were then examined. From these data, Meagher et al. concluded that, on the basis of the highest normalized score (averaged from all 50,000 trials), the probability of two identical, fully rolled fingerprints is less than 1×10^{-97}.

Meagher and colleagues conducted a second experiment, identical to the first, with the exception that in these trials, "simulated" latent prints were used. These simulated latent prints were cropped images of the original, showing only the central 21.7% area of the original image. The value of 21.7% was used because it constituted the average area of a latent print from a survey, conducted by this group, of 300 actual latent prints.

Each simulated latent print was searched against its parent image and the other 49,999 other images. The scores were calculated, ordered, and the top 500 scores examined.

---

[6] It is important to note that the image is compared against itself. Therefore, the model does not account for intraclass variability, that is, multiple representations of the *same fingerprint* showing variations in minutiae positioning due to distortion and stretching of the skin. This is not to say, for example, two inked prints from the same finger; rather, the image is literally compared against itself. One would obviously expect that the highest match score produced will be from the comparison of the image to itself. This was the case in all 50,000 trials. This important distinction is also a key point of criticism and is considered a fundamental flaw in the model by some reviewers (Stoney, 2001, pp 380–383; Wayman, 2000).

The scores were stratified for minutiae counts in the simulated latent prints; the counts of minutiae in these simulated prints ranged from 4 to 18 minutiae. Meagher and colleagues calculated probabilities of a false match in this second experiment ranged from 1×10^{-27} (for 4 minutiae) to 1×10^{-97} (for 18 minutiae).

The Pankanti, Prabhakar, and Jain Model (2001)
(Pankanti et al., 2001, pp 805–812). The model proposed by Pankanti, Prabhakar, and Jain is more of an assessment for probabilities of false match rates in an AFIS model than an assessment for the individuality of a fingerprint. The model essentially calculates the number of possible arrangements of ridge endings and bifurcations, as seen from the view of an AFIS. However, an important new inclusion is the introduction of intraclass variation for a specific print (i.e., how much variance can be observed for a single fingerprint when several standards are taken from the same fingerprint).

Pankanti and colleagues determined the tolerance for minutiae from a database of 450 mated pairs. These images were pairs of the same fingerprint taken at least one week apart. For each minutia, the corresponding minutia was located in the mate. The spatial differences were calculated for all the corresponding minutiae in the pairs and, on the basis of the best fit of their data, they calculated the theoretical tolerance for locating minutiae. It is important to note that their calculated metric for tolerance is a spatial one (with linear [x,y] and angular [θ] components), not a ridge-based one (as previously noted by Stoney as a critical component). Thus in this model, the computer would accept "matching" minutiae if they possessed a similar location in space (x,y, θ) even if the ridge counts differed significantly from a fixed point.

Using an electronic capture device, Pankanti and colleagues collected a total of 4 images from each of 4 fingers from 167 individuals, for a total of 668 fingerprint images, each in quadruplicate. They repeated this process for a second capture device. They created two databases, one for each of the two capture devices. Given that each fingerprint in the database had four images of the same finger, captured separately, Pankanti and colleagues measured the differences in the minutiae locations for each image to determine the acceptable tolerance based on natural variations for that finger.

On the basis of these calculations, Pankanti and colleagues derived an expression to calculate the probability of a matching fingerprint pattern, given the specific size of a print and the number of minutiae available to match. They calculated that to match 36 minutiae out of an arrangement of 36 minutiae (similar to Galton's proposed 35 minutiae in an average print and including only ridge endings and bifurcations) the probability was 5.47×10^{-59}. To match any 12 of these minutiae, given the same parameters, the probability was 6.10×10^{-8}. (This, of course, implies that 24 of these minutiae do not match, and this would be unacceptable as a model for comparative analysis.) The group calculated the probability for matching all 12 minutiae, given only a 12 minutiae arrangement. This probability was 1.22×10^{-20}.

The group also calculated, using similar parameters and some basic assumptions, a table that was based on many of the previous models for the probability of matching 36 minutiae (considered by this model a full fingerprint) and 12 minutiae (12 on the basis of the "12-point rule", which some have attributed to Locard's tripartite rule). Amy's, Kingston's, and Champod's models were not included because these models were more complex than the other models and included variables not considered by this group (e.g., Kingston's inclusion of minutiae type).

The author of this chapter chose to perform calculations for eight minutiae, given his personal experiences. The author has witnessed examiners in the United States effecting individualizations with eight minutiae and little to no third-level detail. In effect, individualizations have been declared solely on an arrangement of eight minutiae, with minimal, if any, consideration for the frequency of the minutiae type, locale in the print (i.e., delta versus periphery), or complexity of the arrangement. The author calculated as a lower bound, on the basis of the equations provided by Pankanti and colleagues, probabilities for matching eight common minutiae from these models. Pankanti and colleagues' calculations, the author's additional calculations for eight minutiae using the Pankanti parameters, and select values for the remaining models not included by Pankanti and colleagues (i.e., Champod, Amy, Meagher, and Kingston) can all be found in Table 14–2 and the accompanying footnotes.

Summary of Probability Models. There are two very important comments that must be made when one examines the previous proposed probability models for individuality. The first comment is that no matter which model is chosen (and among all the experts who have visited this topic, it is quite clear), one can fairly quickly reach staggeringly small probabilities that two individuals will share an arrangement of minutiae. All of these models demonstrate

Table 14–2

Pankati and colleagues' calculations (with chapter author's additions).

Author and Year	Probability of Matching a Specific Configuration of: 36 Minutiae	12 Minutiae	8 Minutiae
Galton (1892)	1.45×10^{-11}	9.54×10^{-7}	6.06×10^{-6}
Henry (1900)	1.32×10^{-23}	3.72×10^{-9}	9.54×10^{-7}
Balthazard (1911)	2.12×10^{-22}	5.96×10^{-8}	1.53×10^{-5}
Bose (1917)	2.12×10^{-22}	5.96×10^{-8}	1.53×10^{-5}
Wilder and Wentworth (1918)	6.87×10^{-62}	4.10×10^{-21}	2.56×10^{-14}
Pearson (1930)	1.09×10^{-41}	8.65×10^{-17}	1.22×10^{-12}
Roxburgh (1933)	3.75×10^{-47}	3.35×10^{-18}	2.24×10^{-14}
Cummins and Midlo (1943)	2.22×10^{-63}	1.32×10^{-22}	8.26×10^{-16}
Trauring (1963)	2.47×10^{-26}	2.91×10^{-9}	2.04×10^{-6}
Gupta (1968)	1.00×10^{-38}	1.00×10^{-14}	1.00×10^{-10}
Osterburg et al. (1977–1980)	1.33×10^{-27}	3.05×10^{-15}	3.50×10^{-13}
Stoney and Thornton (1985–1989)	1.20×10^{-80}	3.50×10^{-26}	7.50×10^{-17}
Pankanti et al. (2001)[a]	5.47×10^{-59}	1.22×10^{-20}	1.56×10^{-14}
Amy (1946–1948)[b]	$<<6.2 \times 10^{-18}$	3.4×10^{-14}	1.8×10^{-8}
Kingston (1964)[c]	3.90×10^{-97}	3.74×10^{-32}	1.97×10^{-20}
Champod (1995–1996)	Two configurations:	Configuration #1: five ridge endings and two bifurcations = a probability of 2.5×10^{-5} Configuration #2: three ridge endings, one enclosure, one spur, and one opposed bifurcation = a probability of 7.0×10^{-10}	
Meagher et al. (1999)	4 minutiae = 1×10^{-27} 18 or more minutiae = 1×10^{-97} fully rolled print = 1×10^{-97}		

Notes

Using data and equations provided by Pankanti et al. (2001, pp 805–812) and based on the previously listed models, additional calculations have been made to include all the models listed in this chapter and the probabilities for arrangements of eight minutiae. With the exception of Champod, these calculations were based on ridge ending and bifurcation arrangements only and do not include rarer ridge events. In addition, with the exception of Roxburgh's "Quality Factor", none of the models account for clarity or the presence of third-level detail.

[a] Eight-minutiae probability calculated using the parameters (M, m, n, q) equal to (57, 8, 8, 8). The value for M was arrived at by an estimate of A based on an exponential fit to the data, which included all tolerance adjustments, provided in the Pankanti calculations (Pankanti et al., 2001, pp 805–812).

[b] Based on specific arrangements of empty ridges, groupings of bifurcations and ridge endings, and whether they were oriented to the left or right. The specific arrangements for each case are described by Amy (1946b, p 194). Amy's calculations only went as high as 15 minutiae, thus the value provided for 36 minutiae would be significantly smaller than the 6.2×10^{-18} as listed in Table 14–2.

[c] The author could not obtain Kingston's Poisson estimator for the expected number of minutiae/area, as these were empirically derived from Kingston's samples. Therefore, the values given in Table 14–2 correspond to the assumption that the number of minutiae observed in a region was equal to the expected number of minutiae for that region. The calculations are also based on assuming exactly half of the minutiae are bifurcations and half are ridge endings and using values for M (area) similar to those in Pankanti et al. (2001, pp 805–812).

that fingerprint minutiae are highly discriminating features, and, generally, the more minutiae that are shared between impressions, the less likely it becomes to randomly observe these features elsewhere in the population. Although AFIS technology and access to larger databases of images make this possibility more likely, it is still a rare event. Exactly "how rare" is what must be fleshed out. The technology and databases currently exist to adequately estimate these events.

The second comment is that these models have not been validated. The staggeringly low probabilities proposed by the models have not been tested in real-world, large databases. These probabilities may be accurate or they may grossly underestimate or overestimate the truth. It is simply an unknown at this time. The models have value and are important to the development of the discipline, of course. But the fundamental steps of testing, validation, and then refinement, followed by further testing and validation—the very fabric of scientific testing that was outlined at the beginning of this chapter—is missing. Stoney has aptly noted (Stoney, 2001, p 383):[7]

> From a statistical viewpoint, the scientific foundation for fingerprint individuality is incredibly weak. Beginning with Galton and extending through Meagher et al., there have been a dozen or so statistical models proposed. These vary considerably in their complexity, but in general there has been much speculation and little data. Champod's work is perhaps the exception, bringing forth the first realistic means to predict frequencies of occurrence of specific combinations of ridge minutiae. None of the models has been subjected to testing, which is of course the basic element of the scientific approach. As our computer capabilities increase, we can expect that there will be the means to properly model and test hypotheses regarding the variability in fingerprints.

It is imperative that the field of fingerprint identification meets this challenge. Although the theory of biological formation certainly supports the notion of friction ridge skin individuality, it must be supported by further empirical testing. Statistical modeling is a crucial component to achieving this goal, and more research and study in this arena is needed.

---

[7] Pankanti et al. (2001) was published contemporaneously with Stoney's comment, and, therefore, exclusion of Pankanti et al. (2001) was not an oversight or error by Stoney.

All of the previous models dealt exclusively with minutiae configurations. With respect to sweat pore location, significant advances have occurred since Locard's time. Ashbaugh rekindled interest in pores with case examples of sweat pore use for individualization purposes (Ashbaugh, 1983, 1999). Ashbaugh described two methods for comparing pore location (Ashbaugh, 1999, pp 155–157). Significant contributions to sweat pore modeling have been advanced by Roddy and Stosz (Stosz and Alyea, 1994; Roddy and Stosz, 1997, 1999). Most recently, Parsons and colleagues reported further enhancements to pore modeling (Parsons et al., 2008). They concluded that sweat pore analysis can be automated and provide a quantitative measure of the strength of the evidence.

14.3.2 Persistence

14.3.2.1 Persistence of First- and Second-Level Detail.
Although Herschel and Faulds were two of the most prominent early pioneers investigating the persistency of friction ridge skin, it was Galton who provided the first actual data and study. Herschel and Faulds claimed to have examined hundreds, perhaps thousands, of prints to reach this conclusion. Herschel had been employing fingerprints for identifications for approximately 20 years and he had noticed no apparent changes in the ridge formations.

Using a collection of inked prints provided by Herschel, Galton, on the other hand, conducted a very thorough investigation into every single minutiae present in the finger (and in some instances palmar) impressions from 15 individuals (Galton, 2005, pp 89–99). The longest interval between subjects was 31 years; the shortest interval was 9 years. Interestingly, Galton noted a single instance where a discrepancy existed (Galton, 2005, p 97). In this instance an inked impression taken from a young boy (age 2 1/2) was compared against an impression from the same finger when the boy was 15. In the earlier print, a bifurcation is visible that is not present in that region (that is, the ridge is continuous) in the later impression (Figure 14–1). Galton compared, in total, approximately 700 minutiae between these time intervals. He found only the one instance of a discrepancy. Misumi and Akiyoshi postulated that changes in the dermal substructure may have caused the anomaly observed by Galton (Misumi and Akiyoshi, 1984, p 53). They observed several changes with age in the dermal substructure (e.g., papillae proliferation and changes in adhesive forces between the epidermis and dermis) that may affect the appearance of the epidermal ridges and furrows.

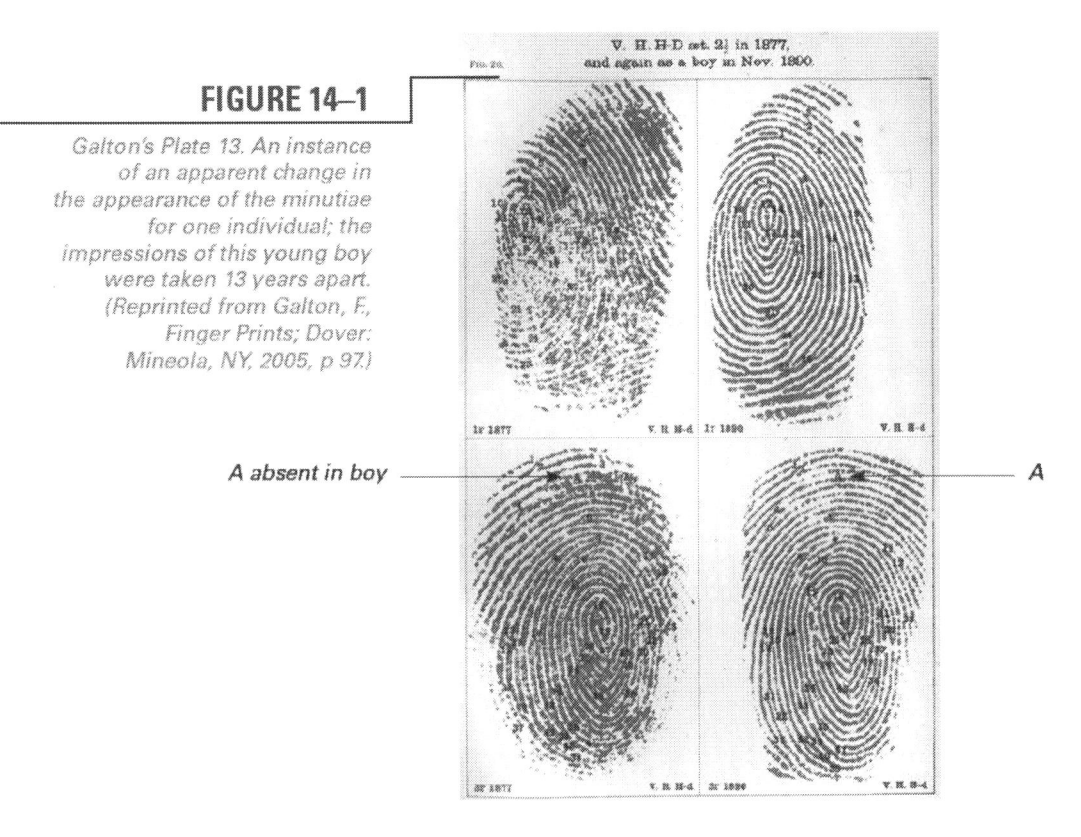

FIGURE 14–1

Galton's Plate 13. An instance of an apparent change in the appearance of the minutiae for one individual; the impressions of this young boy were taken 13 years apart. (Reprinted from Galton, F., Finger Prints; Dover: Mineola, NY, 2005, p 97.)

A absent in boy —————————— A

Wilder and Wentworth (1932, pp 126–131) performed a similar study on the minutiae of one subject, taking prints in approximately 2-year intervals from a young girl starting at 4 years and 11 months old until she was 14 years and 6 months old. Amongst these six time periods of collection, no change was observed in the minutiae of the subject. However, Wilder and Wentworth did note a proliferation of visible incipient ridges as the subject aged. This phenomenon has been observed and explored elsewhere (Stücker et al., 2001, 857–861).

Other instances where impressions have been examined for persistence after extended intervals have been noted in the literature. Herschel made successive impressions of his own fingerprints, starting at age 26, and throughout his life until age 83 (57 years in total) (Cummins and Midlo, 1943, p 40). No changes in minutiae were observed. Welcker (Cummins and Midlo, 1943, pp 40–41) made impressions of his fingers and palms at age 34 and then again later at age 75 (a 41-year interval). Another case is reported by Jennings (Cummins and Midlo, 1943, p 41) of palmprint impressions compared 50 years apart (taken at age 27 and then again at age 77). Finally, Galton continued to investigate the persistency of skin, increasing the number of individuals he compared to 25, with the longest time span being 37 years between prints (Wilder and Wentworth, 1932, p 128). With the exception of Galton's single instance, no other investigator reported any changes in minutiae.

14.3.2.2 Persistence of Third-Level Detail and Creases.
With respect to pores, Locard (1913, pp 530–535) noted that the relative positions of the pores remain unchanged throughout life. Meagher, in a *Daubert* hearing, provided images of a latent print and an inked print, said to be from the same donor with an interval of 10 years (Figure 14–2). The images of the prints contained only two minutiae, but an extraordinary amount of clarity, clearly showing edges and pores. The third-level detail remained unchanged in that 10-year span.

However, the example provided by Meagher is anecdotal. The current literature lacks a comprehensive study demonstrating the persistence of third-level detail. More specifically, what is missing for latent print examiners is a comprehensive study, over a long period of time, demonstrating the persistence of third-level detail in impressions captured from the friction ridge skin.

Persistency of palmar flexion creases was observed by Herschel (Ashbaugh, 1999, p 190). Ashbaugh compared

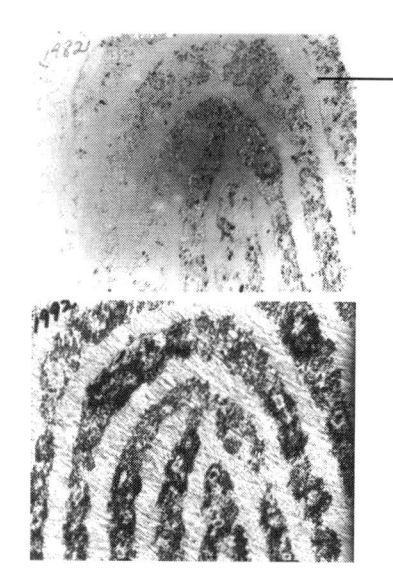

FIGURE 14–2

Exhibits 5-14 and 5-15 from U.S. v Mitchell, Daubert Hearing, July 8, 1999, testimony of Stephen Meagher. The image on the top is a perspiration print left on glass in 1982. The image on the bottom is an inked impression on paper from the same donor taken in 1992.

50 sets of palmprints taken from subjects at two different times, ranging from intervals of 1 to 60 months (Ashbaugh, 1999, p 189). Ashbaugh found that the flexion creases were in agreement, but noted some variation in appearance or prominence due to age, flexibility of skin, or other typical factors. Similarly, Evin and Luff (Ashbaugh, 1999, pp 193–194; Luff, 1993, p 3) reported persistency of palmar flexion creases after performing 600 comparisons (from roughly 100 individuals) with significant times between sample collection.

14.3.2.3 Theory Supporting Persistency of Friction Ridge Skin. The biological mechanisms for maintaining friction ridge skin persistency lie directly in the regenerating layer of skin found at the interface of the dermis and epidermis. This layer is known as the basal layer or stratum basale (germinativum). The persistency of the friction ridge skin is maintained by the basal layer and the connective relationship of these cells through desmosomes and hemidesmosomes. Wertheim and Maceo have reviewed and presented supporting pertinent medical research in this area (Wertheim and Maceo, 2002, pp 35–85; see Chapters 2 and 3).

14.3.3 Comparison Methodology

14.3.3.1 Overview of Comparison Methodologies. With respect to a *Daubert* challenge, at issue for admissibility of the evidence is whether the scientific principles or methodology upon which the conclusions are based are reliable. The previous sections have demonstrated core research supporting the basic principles of friction ridge skin science (i.e., uniqueness and persistence). The second half of this equation is the comparison methodology employed to compare two images, usually a latent print and a known exemplar.

It must first be noted that although ACE-V methodology is the generally accepted methodology in the United States (SWGFAST, 2002, p 2), Canada, Australia, and New Zealand, ACE-V methodology is not the *only* methodology available. For example, many European countries subscribe to the "Method for Fingerprint Identification" as described by the Interpol European Expert Group on Fingerprint Identification (IEEGFI) (IEEGFI-II, 2004). Although this methodology is very similar in most aspects to ACE-V methodology, it has some notable differences.[8] Additionally, probabilistic methodologies have been suggested by some authors (Locard, Stoney, Evett and Williams, Champod), but presently, this approach has been generally rejected as a viable methodology worldwide by examiners and professional bodies representing examiners (SWGFAST, 2002, p 4;

---

[8] For example, although creases, scars, and incipient ridges are completely acceptable features alone on which to make an individualization under the philosophy of ridgeology as applied during ACE-V, these features are not allowed as the sole basis for individualization under the IEEGFI methodology. These features may be used to add more weight to minutiae, depending on their relationship, but minutiae must be present. Additionally, under the IEEGFI-II, minutiae are subjectively weighted by the examiners on the basis of their frequency, location, and adjacent ridge features, and in this role, third-level detail and accidental features may be used to enhance the weight of minutiae. The IEEGFI method is quite innovative and thorough in its instructions for weighting minutiae. A weighting scheme based on the specificity of the features present is not explicit in the ACE-V methodology, though in fairness, may be applied by some examiners, knowingly or subconsciously, during the evaluation stage of ACE-V.

CHAPTER 14 Scientific Research Supporting the Foundations of Friction Ridge Examinations

IEEGFI-II, 2004; Ashbaugh, 1999, p 147;[9] IAI, 1979, p 1). In fact, the penalty for using a probabilistic approach is so harsh that an expert found to give opinions of "probable, possible, or likely individualization" can be decertified and denied continued membership in the IAI (IAI, 1979, p 1). Academically speaking and from a perspective of evolving paradigm shifts in forensic science, exploring the viability of probabilistic evidence may have its benefits. Such efforts should not be summarily dismissed by the profession, because these methods may produce tools to aid or enhance current practices.

14.3.3.2 Research Pertaining to Fingerprint Comparison Methodology. Presently, there are few studies in the literature directly pertaining to the testing and validation of fingerprint comparison methodology. In fact, such works cannot be found prior to the 1993 *Daubert* decision.

Osterburg (1964). Osterburg conducted the first published survey of latent print examiner practices (Osterburg, 1964, pp 413–427). He sent surveys to 180 agencies throughout all 50 states. He received responses from 82 (46%). The surveys asked experts to subjectively rank the relative frequency of 10 types of minutiae characteristics (ending ridges, trifurcations, spurs, islands, etc.) based solely on the expert's training, experience, and personal recollection. Osterburg tabulated the ranked features. He also conducted a literature search to determine the minimum number of minutiae (points) needed to effect a positive identification (individualization). At the time, he found that individuals and agencies used between 6 and 18 minutiae to reach an individualization; the mean response was 12. He found that when experts were willing to reach an opinion below 12 minutiae, it was because they had "unusual characteristics". His study was an attempt to determine what an expert meant by "unusual". Years later, Osterburg and colleagues (1977) empirically measured the frequency of these features. The empirical counts of these features were very similar to the experts' intuitive assessment of rarity.

Evett and Williams (1996). The first actual study of fingerprint comparison methodology was performed by Evett and Williams (1996, pp 49–73). Their research, though conducted in 1988–1989, was not published until 1996, although it was presented at an international symposium in Ne'urim, Israel (Grieve, 1995, p 579). Their work predated the widespread knowledge, articulation, and general acceptance of ACE-V methodology among examiners. Evett and Williams investigated the basis for the 16-point threshold in place at the time in England and Wales. In their study, 10 sets of comparisons were provided to and returned by 130 experts from various bureaus in England and Wales. In addition, the researchers visited bureaus in the United States, Canada, Holland, France, and Germany. They provided experts in these countries with sets of comparisons as well, but did not include these results. They only reported the United Kingdom data, while giving the international results general commentary. The results of the United Kingdom data showed a surprisingly high level of variation among experts (Figure 14–3), not only in the reported number of corresponding minutiae that the expert saw, but also in whether the experts found sufficient agreement to determine an individualization. It is interesting to note that no expert reported an erroneous individualization. However, in one trial with two impressions that did originate from the same source, 8% of the United Kingdom experts erroneously excluded the images from having originated from the same source. Evett and Williams also found no statistical evidence that the number of individualizations reported by the United Kingdom experts was related to the years of experience of the examiner.

As a result of their research, the authors, while recommending standardization for training, certification testing, regular proficiency testing, regular audits of case files, and external blind proficiency testing, unequivocally stated that there is no need for a national predetermined numerical point standard if it can be demonstrated that each expert is operating above a minimum level of competence.

> Guidelines for individualization may be desirable, but these should be general recommendations and the expert should be allowed the freedom to exercise his/her own professional skills. In these circumstances, a rigid numerical point count is not only unnecessary, it is irrelevant. (Evett and Williams, 1996, p 72).

14.3.3.3 Error Rate Studies. With respect to the methodology, another testable *Daubert* factor is the known or potential rate of error (*Daubert*, 1993). In estimating latent print examiner error rates, some critics (Cole, 2005, pp 985–1078; Saks and Koehler, 2005, pp 892–895) have

---

[9] Ashbaugh notably does not specifically state that probability conclusions should not be produced. He merely states that "extensive study is necessary before this type of probability opinion can be expressed with some degree of confidence and consistency within the friction ridge identification science" (Ashbaugh, 1999, p 147).

14–22

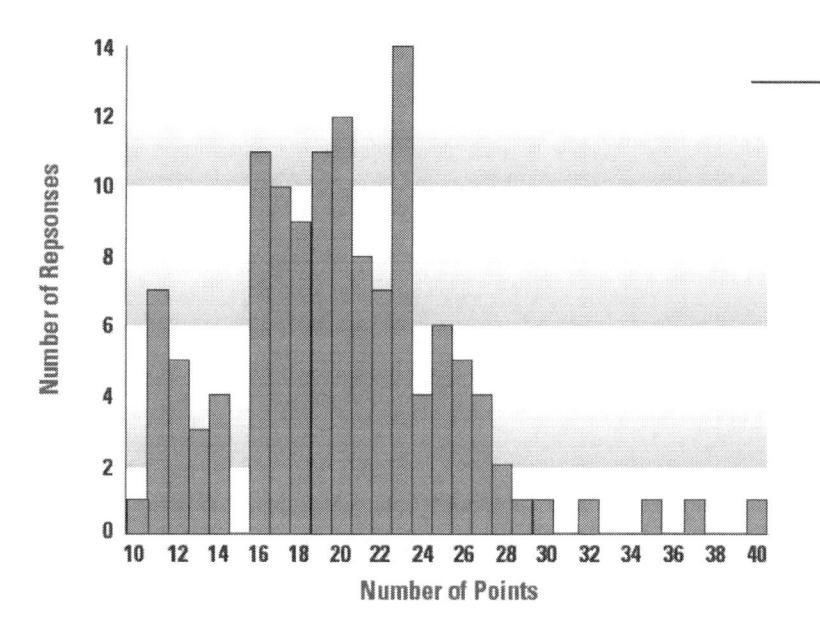

FIGURE 14–3

One graph (re-created) from the Evett and Williams (1996) study, depicting comparison of images marked "B". In reporting the number of minutiae found in agreement between the latent print and the known exemplar, respondents showed great variability. Most notable was the absence of any respondents reporting "15", which was one shy of the 16-point threshold to declare a positive match (for court) in the United Kingdom.

looked to performances of standardized latent print examiner proficiency tests administered through the external testing agency Collaborative Testing Services. Saks and Cole have also looked to anecdotal occurrences in case studies as indicators of a larger-than-reported error rate (Cole, 2005, pp 996–1034; Saks, 2005). Understandably, in the absence of any data produced from within the profession, they had little else to examine.

In an attempt to address the error rate issue, and thus provide the profession, the courts, and critics a better estimate of error than those previously available, Langenburg, Wertheim, and Moenssens conducted a two-stage error rate study (Langenburg et al., 2006, pp 55–92). During the first stage of the study, the researchers evaluated the comparison results of participants in a training course in which the participants compared friction ridge skin impressions (latent prints versus known exemplars). In the approximately 6000 comparisons performed by nearly 100 experts (as defined by the study, these experts possessed over one year of experience in comparing latent prints), the researchers found a total of 61 errors made at the highest level of confidence: 2 erroneous individualizations and 59 clerical errors. Although 59 errors were deemed clerical errors, 2 of these clerical errors wrongly associated the incorrect individual with the evidence; the other 57 were to the correct individual but listed the wrong finger or palm. Criteria were provided in the study for the determination of a clerical error versus an erroneous individualization. In the second stage of this study, 16 experts were asked to independently verify the results of a previous examiner. Each participant was provided with a packet that contained 10 comparisons and the stated results of a previous examiner. Eight of the individualizations for the verifier were accurate. Two of the results were errors and included one of the two erroneous individualizations from the previous stage. The other error would have been a clerical error or a second erroneous individualization, depending on which pack the participant randomly received. The verifier was not alerted that errors would be present in the verification packet. No expert verified any of the errors presented to them in this study. The study listed numerous limitations, most notably the absence of nonmatches (thus false negatives were not studied) and the fact that the experiments were not conducted under "casework" conditions.

Finally, it is important to note the empirical observations of forensic practitioners worldwide. Although these data cannot be readily seen in the literature, one must take into account the collective experiences of the tens of thousands of latent print examiners from around the globe during the last 100 years who have witnessed repeated success, application, and accuracy of the methodology during the training of new examiners, administration of internal competency tests, and other training tools (where the answers are known beforehand by the test administrator). Were the comparison methodology not very accurate, it would be commonplace to see errors frequently during the testing and measuring of examiner competency. This simply is not the case and has not been the author's experience in speaking with trainers here in the U.S. and abroad.

Although these empirical observations should not be dismissed, there are counterarguments to the weight of their support. The pros and cons of using proficiency testing data have been explored elsewhere (Saks and Koehler, 2005, pp 892–895; Langenburg et al., 2006; Cole, 2006b, pp 39–105; Gutowski, 2006). It has been argued that without the ground truth established for the comparison, anything else does not constitute a fair assessment of reliability (Cole, 2006a, pp 109–135). And even with the ground truth established in training exercises, without a standardized and validated model for comparison, the meaning of such results is questionable. For example, let us assume 10 experts all correctly individualize 10 latent prints to the correct 10 sources, for a grand total of 100 correct results and 0 errors. Presumably, these individualizations would exclude all other sources on the planet. The counterargument is that although these 100 conclusions were correct with respect to the ground truth, the relevant question becomes, Were there sufficiently discriminating features in agreement, and no observed differences, to *actually* exclude the world's population as the source of the latent prints? In other words, agreement among examiners is not necessarily de facto proof to support the strength of the evidence and the conclusion thus rendered.

14.3.3.4 Studies of Bias During Comparisons. A rising concern in the literature (Saks et al., 2003, pp 77–90; Steele, 2004, pp 213–240; Haber and Haber, 2004, pp 339–360), and in light of the Mayfield case (Stacey, 2004, pp 706–718), is the issue of whether biases affect the judgments and conclusions of forensic experts and specifically the judgments of the more subjective forensic comparative disciplines (i.e., handwriting, fingerprints, firearms examinations). Although there are many types of bias (e.g., culture, confirmation), some researchers are currently studying contextual information bias with respect to fingerprint examination.

The first study produced by Dror, Péron, Hind, and Charlton (2005, pp 799–809) found strong evidence that contextual information influenced the decision-making processes of nonexperts who participated in the study. Twenty-seven nonexperts (college student volunteers) were provided pairs of images (a latent print and a known exemplar) and asked whether the pair was a match. In addition to the images, the participants were exposed to varying levels of stimuli and contextual information. Dror and colleagues (2005) found that contextual information biased judgments when the matches were more ambiguous (i.e., had a lower quantity and quality of ridge detail or were look-alikes).

They found that when the images were disparate in appearance and clear in detail, contextual information did not influence the participants. The group postulated that either fingerprint experts may be more resistant to these influences because of training and expertise or fingerprint experts may actually be more susceptible to these influences because of overconfidence and rationalization of differences.

A second study by Dror, Charton, and Péron (2006, pp 74–78) involved testing contextual information bias on five experts. For the study, the researchers selected five experts who were aware of the FBI's erroneous individualization in the Madrid Train Bombing case, but had not seen the actual images from the case. The experts were told that these images were from the Madrid Train Bombing case and had been incorrectly individualized by the FBI to Brandon Mayfield (Stacey, 2004, pp 706–718). The experts were asked whether they thought it was a valid match or was erroneous. However, the experts were not provided with images from the Mayfield case; rather, they were each provided with a pair of prints which that expert had personally individualized in casework 5 years prior to the study. Thus each expert was re-examining his own evidence. When provided with these images under the false contextual information, three of the five experts reversed their original opinions and stated the pair was not a match (exclusion), one expert changed his original opinion of a positive match to "inconclusive", and the final expert did not change his opinion but maintained a positive match, in spite of the strong contextual information. A number of concerns regarding the limitations of the study have been raised and discussed online (www.clpex.com), but the study suggests that experts are not immune to contextual information bias.

In the most recent study, Dror and colleagues (2006, pp 74–78) utilized a similar study design to the Madrid Train Bombing context-bias experiment. Six experts were presented their own previous work, but under less extreme circumstances of context bias than the previous study by Dror and colleagues (2005). Eight comparisons, on which the expert had previously provided conclusions several years prior to the study, were presented to each expert. Thus, there were 48 trials for the 6 experts. Twenty-four trials had no context bias and were control trials, 12 trials represented "easy" comparisons under routine bias, and 12 trials represented "difficult" comparisons under routine bias (see Table 14–3). Routine bias was represented by context bias that might be experienced by an expert in daily routine

Table 14–3

Results from Dror and colleagues' experiment.

	1	2	3	4	5	6	7	8
Past Decision	individualization	individualization	individualization	individualization	exclusion	exclusion	exclusion	exclusion
Level of Difficulty	difficult	difficult	not difficult	not difficult	difficult	difficult	not difficult	not difficult
Contextual Information	none	suggest exclusion	none	suggest exclusion	none	suggest individualization	none	suggest individualization
Expert A	consistent	consistent	consistent	consistent	consistent	consistent	consistent	consistent
Expert B	change to exclusion	consistent	consistent	consistent	consistent	consistent	consistent	consistent
Expert C	consistent	change to exclusion	consistent	consistent	consistent	consistent	consistent	consistent
Expert D	consistent	change to exclusion	consistent	change to exclusion	change to individualization	consistent	consistent	consistent
Expert E	consistent	change to cannot decide	consistent	consistent	consistent	consistent	consistent	consistent
Expert F	consistent	consistent	consistent	consistent	consistent	consistent	consistent	consistent

Note

Six experts were presented with eight comparisons on which they had previously rendered opinions. During the re-presentation, the comparisons were presented with context bias one might encounter in daily casework (knowledge of suspect confession, suspect criminal history, etc.).

(Reprinted from Dror et al., 2006, p 610.)

---

casework (a police officer's assertion of the suspect's guilt, knowledge of a confession, etc.). In the 48 trials, 6 trials resulted in responses that were not consistent with the original result provided by the expert. It is further interesting to note, of the six inconsistent results, two were in control trials (i.e., no context bias was provided). Dror and colleagues suggested two possible explanations for these inconsistencies in the control trials. The first possibility is that the experiment may not have been without bias even in the control conditions or, at a minimum, the conditions during the re-evaluation were not identical to the conditions under which the original decision was made. The second possibility is that there is less-than-ideal and less-than-expected reproducibility of expert results, even "within sample". In other words, the decision of an expert, when presented with the same evidence in multiple trials over time, may not be reproducible, and the expert is producing conflicting, inconsistent results. Dror and colleagues suggested further study of this phenomenon. With respect to the remaining four out of six trials of inconsistent responses, Dror and colleagues attributed these inconsistencies to the context bias in the trials, noting that three out of four inconsistencies reflected the bias prompt. However, as with the previous Madrid context-bias experiment, little to no information was provided about the experts or the presentation of the images to the experts, nor are the images available for review.

In contrast to the effect Dror and colleagues observed with respect to the *evaluation* of a latent print and an exemplar (i.e., the decision resulting in an individualization, exclusion, or inconclusive opinion), Schiffer and Champod (2007) reported no effect due to context bias in the *analysis* phase. Schiffer and Champod provided forensic science students at the University of Lausanne, Switzerland, with images of latent prints prior to the students' formal instruction series. Two experiments were conducted. The first experiment provided 39 students with 12 images of latent prints. The students were asked to annotate the minutiae in the images using a standard guideline. Upon completion of an intensive fingerprint instruction course, 29 of these students were provided with the same images to annotate again. Schiffer and Champod found a statistically significant increase in the number of minutiae reported and a decrease in the variation among student responses. Additionally, the number of reported instances declaring the print "exploitable" (i.e., "of value") and "identifiable" significantly increased after the training period. In the second study, 11 images of latent prints were provided to 2 groups of students (48 total students) after the fingerprint instruction course. The images were presented to the students under various context bias circumstances: no bias, presence of a matching exemplar, low-profile property crime case, high-profile terrorist case, and so forth. Students were asked to annotate the images and report the value of each print. Schiffer and Champod reported no difference for any of the factors examined between the two groups. They argued that not all stages of the ACE-V process are similarly vulnerable to bias, and their results supported the robustness of the analysis phase.

14.4 Future Directions for Research Related to Friction Ridge Examination

14.4.1 United States Government-Sponsored Research Available for Accepted Grant Applicants

Although some professional bodies (e.g., the Robert L. Johnson Foundation, created by the IAI) offer small stipends for research, these funds are generally not sufficient to conduct a large-scale study (e.g., a validation study) or a complicated study (e.g., the development of a quantitative model for measuring distortion), which would undoubtedly involve multiple experts and statisticians, a large computerized database, and software and hardware appropriate to the tests. Government agencies or academic institutions must properly fund this research. One agency which has supported open proposals for large-scale friction ridge research is the National Institute of Justice (NIJ). NIJ issued solicitations for Research and Development on Impression Evidence in 2009 and for Research and Development on Pattern and Impression Evidence in 2010. Both solicitations yielded a number of responsive friction ridge analysis project proposals, and multiple grant awards were made for both years (information is available at www.ojp.usdoj.gov/nij/awards/welcome.htm).

14.4.2 Recommended Topics for Research

The Scientific Working Group for Friction Ridge Analysis, Study, and Technology (SWGFAST) has posted on its Web site (www.swgfast.org) a list of recommended areas for study and research.

Another source for recommended research was provided by Budowle, Buscaglia, and Perlman (2006). Some of their notable "high-priority" recommendations include:

- Develop guidelines for describing the quality of ridge features in an image.

- Develop guidelines for sufficiency in declaring a positive match.

- Determine the minimum number of features (if any) that are needed pragmatically for an examiner to declare a positive match in casework.

- Rigorous testing (validation) of the ACE-V methodology as applied by experts.

- Testing for persistence of third-level features.

Many of their suggestions should be strongly considered by serious researchers, because the results of the work could be extremely beneficial and enlightening to the friction ridge identification discipline.

Another major area that needs to be addressed is an objective understanding of distortion and the development of an acceptable metric for tolerance. It was clear from statements made by the investigating bodies in the Brandon Mayfield case (Office of the Inspector General, 2006, pp 6–10) that the examiners had discounted dissimilarities between the latent print and Mayfield's exemplar. However, *a posteriori*, it was determined that the dissimilarities were outside of acceptable tolerance and an exclusion should have been the correct conclusion. Determining acceptable ranges of tolerances, or determining an appropriate weighting scheme for a feature based on the feature's departure from "normality" due to distortion, would be critical updates to any comparison methodology.

Finally, as previously discussed and highlighted by Stoney (see page 14–15), the development of a more complete probability model for fingerprint individuality is needed. The development of this model must be followed up by empirical testing of the model with real-world samples and large databases.

14.5 Conclusions

In a post-*Daubert* environment, there is a need for additional research in the field of friction ridge science. Certainly, any science wishes to expand the depth and breadth of knowledge of the discipline. We in the fingerprint expert community must attempt to challenge and study further the laws and theories that comprise our discipline. Specifically, we must focus our efforts to reevaluate the basic tenets of individualizing friction ridges using modern and enhanced technologies that were not available in Galton's day. There are many unanswered or partially answered questions regarding the individuality of friction ridge skin and the forensic comparison of friction ridge impressions. Although significant advances have been made, many of them in just the last two decades, this is really only the tip of the iceberg. With the advent of newer, more powerful technologies, software, and computer algorithms, we have opportunities to explore our vast fingerprint databases and quickly growing palmprint databases. We need to assess and quantify the full extent of variation of friction ridge features, starting with perhaps the most basic (patterns and minutiae—if one can truly call this "basic") and then attempt to assess and quantify other features such as creases, scars, edge shapes, and so forth.

It should be clear that there are aspects of this discipline that have been well-established and well-studied (particularly the biological theory of friction ridge formation and persistency). However, it should also be clear that there are areas of study that are woefully lacking (e.g., distortion, tolerance).

The absence of available published research into some aspects of the discipline speaks volumes about what our mission should be.

14.6 Reviewers

The reviewers critiquing this chapter were Leonard G. Butt, Christophe Champod, Deborah Friedman, Robert J. Garrett, Andre A. Moenssens, Michael Perkins, Jon T. Stimac, Michele Triplett, John R. Vanderkolk, and James L. Wayman.

14.7 References

Amy, L. Valeur de la preuve en dactyloscopie. *Journal de la Société de Statistique de Paris* 1946a, *88*, 80–87.

Amy, L. Valeur de la preuve en dactyloscopie II. *Journal de la Société de Statistique de Paris* 1946b, *88*, 188–195.

Amy, L. Recherches sur l'identification des traces papillaires. *Société de Médecine Légale* 1948, *28* (2), 96–101.

Ashbaugh, D. R. Poroscopy. *Royal Canadian Mounted Police Gazette* 1983, *45*, 12–17.

Ashbaugh, D. R. *Quantitative–Qualitative Friction Ridge Analysis: An Introduction to Basic and Advanced Ridgeology;* CRC Press: Boca Raton, FL, 1999.

Babler, W. J. Prenatal Selection and Dermatoglyphic Patterns. *Am. J. Phys. Anthropol.* 1978, *48* (1), 21–28.

Babler, W. J. Prenatal Communalities in Epidermal Ridge Development. In *Trends in Dermatoglyphic Research;* Durham, N., Plato, C., Eds.; Kluwer Academic Press: Dordrecht, Netherlands, 1990; pp 54–68.

Babler, W. J. Embryologic Development of Epidermal Ridges and Their Configurations. In *Dermatoglyphics: Science in Transition;* Plato, C., Garruto, R., Shaumann, B., Eds.; March of Dimes: New York, 1991; pp 95–112.

Balthazard, V. De l'identification par les empreintes digitales. *Comptes Rendus, des Academies des Sciences* 1911, *152*, 1862–1864.

Budowle, B.; Buscaglia, J.; Perlman, R. Review of the Scientific Basis for Friction Ridge Comparisons as a Means of Identification: Committee Findings and Recommendations. *Forensic Sci. Communic.* 2006, *8* (1).

Carroll, J. W. Laws of Nature; 2003; plato.stanford.edu/archives/fall2003/entries/laws-of-nature/ (accessed June 30, 2009).

Chacko, L. W.; Vaidya, M. C. The Dermal Papillae and Ridge Patterns in Human Volar Skin. *ACTA Anatomica (Basel)* 1968, *70* (1), 99–108.

Champod, C. Edmond Locard—Numerical Standards and "Probable" Identifications. *J. Forensic Ident.* 1995, *45* (2), 136–163.

Champod, C.; Margot, P. Analysis of Minutiae Occurrences on Fingerprints—The Search for Non-Combined Minutiae. In *Proceedings of the 14th Meeting of the International Association of Forensic Sciences,* Tokyo, Japan, 1996a.

Champod, C.; Margot, P. Computer Assisted Analysis of Minutiae Occurrences on Fingerprints. In *Proceedings of the International Symposium on Fingerprint Detection and Identification.* Almog, J., Springer, E., Eds.; Israel National Police: Jerusalem, 1996b; pp 305–318.

Champod, C.; Lennard, C.; Margot, P.; Stoilovic, M. *Fingerprints and Other Ridge Skin Impressions;* CRC Press: Boca Raton, FL, 2004.

Chatterjee, S. K. Edgeoscopy. *Finger Print Ident. Mag.* 1962, *44* (3).

Cole, S. A. More than Zero: Accounting for Error in Latent Print Identification. *J. Crim. L. and Criminol.* 2005, *95* (3), 985–1078.

Cole, S. A. Is Fingerprint Identification Valid? Rhetorics of Reliability in Fingerprint Proponents' Discourse. *Law and Policy* 2006a, *28* (1), 109–135.

Cole, S. A. The Prevalence and Potential Causes of Wrongful Conviction by Fingerprint Evidence. *Golden Gate Univ. L. Rev.* 2006b, *37* (1), 39–105.

Collaborative Testing Services. *Latent Print Examination Report # 9508;* Collaborative Testing Services, Inc.: Herndon, VA, 1996.

Cummins, H. Dermatoglyphics: Significant Patternings of the Body Surface. *Yale J. Bio. Med.* 2000, *73* (1–6), 79–90.

Cummins, H.; Midlo, C. *Finger Prints, Palms and Soles: An Introduction to Dermatoglyphics;* Dover: New York, 1943.

Cummins, H.; Waits, W. J.; McQuitty, J. T. The Breadth of Epidermal Ridges on the Fingertips and Palms: A Study of Variation. *Am. J. Anat.* 1941, *68,* 127–150.

Daubert v Merrell Dow Pharmaceuticals, Inc. 509 U.S. 579, 1993.

Donnelly, P.; Friedman, R. DNA Database Searches and the Legal Consumption of Scientific Evidence. *Mich. L. Rev.* 1999, *97* (4), 931–984.

Dror, I. E.; Péron, A. E.; Hind, S.; Charlton, D. When Emotions Get the Better of Us: The Effect of Contextual Top-Down Processing on Matching Fingerprints. *Appl. Cognitive Psych.* 2005, *19* (6), 799–809.

Dror, I. E.; Charlton, D.; Péron, A. E. Contextual Information Renders Experts Vulnerable to Making Erroneous Identifications. *Forensic Sci. Int.* 2006, *156* (1), 74–78.

Eaton, J. Fingerprints are Still Unique: A Pilot AFIS Study. Presented at the International Association for Identification Conference, Dallas, TX, August 11, 2005.

Eaton, J. King County Sheriff's Office. Seattle, WA: Personal communication, 2006.

Evett, I.; Williams, R. L. A Review of the Sixteen Points Fingerprint Standard in England and Wales. *J. Forensic Ident.* 1996, *46* (1), 49–73.

Faulds, H. On the Skin—Furrows of the Hand. *Nature* 1880, *22,* 605.

Faulds, H. Finger Prints: A Chapter in the History of Their Use for Personal Identification. *Sci. Am. Suppl.* 1911, *1872,* 326–327.

Faulds, H. *Dactylography or the Study of Finger-Prints;* Milner and Company: Halifax, 1912.

Frishberg, D.; Yohe, T. I'm Just a Bill (Song lyrics); Schoolhouse Rock, American Broadcasting Company: 1975.

Galton, F. *Finger Prints;* Dover: Mineola, NY, 2005.

Grieve, D. L. Symposium Report Israel National Police: International Symposium on Fingerprint Detection and Identification. *J. Forensic Ident.* 1995, *45* (5), 578–584.

Grieve, D. L. Possession of Truth. *J. Forensic Ident.* 1996, *46* (5), 521–528.

Gupta, S. R. Statistical Survey of Ridge Characteristics. *Int. Crim. Police Rev.* 1968, *218* (130), 130–134.

Gutowski, S. Error Rates in Fingerprint Examination: The View in 2006. *Forensic Bulletin* 2006, Autumn, 18–19.

Haber, R.; Haber, L. Error Rates for Human Latent Fingerprint Examiners. In *Automatic Fingerprint Recognition Systems;* Ratha, N., Bolle, R., Eds.; Springer Verlag: New York, 2004; pp 339–360.

Hale, A. Morphogenesis of Volar Skin in the Human Fetus. *Am. J. Anat.* 1952, *91* (1), 147–173.

Hempel, C.; Oppenheim, P. Studies in the Logic of Explanation. *Philos.Sci.* 1948, *15* (2), 135–175.

Henry, E. R. *Classification and Uses of Fingerprints*; 1st ed.; Routledge & Sons: London, 1900.

Huber, R. A. Expert Witness. *Crim. L. Quarterly* 1959, *2*, 276–295.

Huber, R. A.; Headrick, A. M. *Handwriting Identification: Facts and Fundamentals*; CRC Press: Boca Raton, FL, 1999.

Hughes, G. Losing Sight of the Shore. *J. Forensic Ident.* 1998, *48* (5), 611–615.

IAI-Resolution VII. *Identification News* 1979, *29* (8), 1.

IEEGFI-II. *Method for Fingerprint Identification*; Interpol European Expert Group on Fingerprint Identification II: Lyon, France, 2004.

Kimura, S; Kitagawa, T. Embryological Development of Human Palmar, Plantar, and Digital Flexion Creases. *Anatom. Record* 1986, *216* (2), 191–197.

Kimura, S; Kitagawa, T. Embryological Development and Prevalence of Thumb Flexion Creases. *Anatom. Record* 1988, *222* (1), 83–89.

Kingston, C. R. Probabilistic Analysis of Partial Fingerprint Patterns, Ph.D. Thesis, University of California, 1964.

Langenburg, G.; Wertheim, K.; Moenssens, A. A. A Report of Latent Print Examiner Accuracy During Comparison Training Exercises. *J. Forensic Ident.* 2006, *56* (1), 55–92.

Lin, C. H.; Liu, J. H.; Osterburg, J. W.; Nicol, J. D. Fingerprint Comparison I: Similarity in Fingerprints. *J. Forensic Sci.* 1982, *27* (2), 290–304.

Locard, E. Les Pores et l'identification des Criminels. *Biologica* 1912, *2* (24), 357–365.

Locard, E. La poroscopie. *Archives d'anthropologie criminelle, de médicine légale et de psychologie normale et pathologique* 1913, *28*, 528–546.

Locard, E. La preuve judiciaire par les empreintes digitales. *Archives d'anthropologie criminelle, de médicine légale et de psychologie normale et pathologique* 1914, *29* (145), 321–348.

Luff, K. Letter to Fingerprint Society. *Fingerprint Whorld* 1993, *19* (71), 3.

McCann, P. Interim Report of the Standardization Committee of the International Association for Identification. *Ident. News* 1971, *21* (10), 10–13.

McCann, P. Report of the Standardization Committee of the International Association for Identification. *Identification News* 1973, *23* (8), 13–14.

McComas, W. Ten Myths of Science: Reexamining What We Think We Know. ... *School Sci. Math.* 1996, *96*, 10.

McRoberts, A. Nature Never Repeats Itself. *The Print* 1996, *12* (5), 1–3.

Misumi, Y.; Akiyoshi, T. Scanning Electron Microscopic Structure of the Finger Print as Related to the Dermal Surface. *Anatom. Record* 1984, *208* (1), 49–55.

Moenssens, Andre A. Columbia City, IN. Personal communication, 2006.

Montagna, W.; Parakkal, P. *The Structure and Function of Skin,* 3rd ed.; Academic Press: New York, 1974.

Montagna, W.; Kligman, A.; Carlisle, K. *Atlas of Normal Human Skin;* Springer-Verlag: New York, 1992.

Office of the Inspector General. *A Review of the FBI's Handling of the Brandon Mayfield Case—Unclassified Executive Summary.* U.S. Department of Justice: Washington, D.C., March 2006.

Okajima, M. Frequency of Epidermal-Ridge Minutiae in the Calcar Area of Japanese Twins. *Am. J. Hum. Genet.* 1967, *19* (5), 660–673.

Osterburg, J. W. An Inquiry into the Nature of Proof: The Identity of Fingerprints. *J. Forensic Sci.* 1964, *9* (4), 413–427.

Osterburg, J. W.; Parthasarathy, T.; Raghaven, T. E. S.; Sclove, S. L. Development of a Mathematical Formula for the Calculation of Fingerprint Probabilities Based on Individual Characteristics. *J. Am. Stat. Associ.* 1977, *72* (360), 772–778.

Pankanti, S.; Prabhakar, S.; Jain, A. On the Individuality of Fingerprints. In *Proceedings of Hawaii International Conference on System Sciences (IEEE)*, Maui, HI, December 2001; pp 805–812.

Parsons, N. R.; Smith, J. Q.; Thönnes, E.; Wang, L.; Wilson, R. G. Rotationally Invariant Statistics for Examining the Evidence from the Pores in Fingerprints. *Law, Probabil. and Risk* 2008, *7* (1), 1–14.

Pearson, K. Person Identification. In The *Life, Letters, and Labours of Francis Galton,* vol. IIIA; Cambridge University Press: Cambridge, England, 1930; p 182.

Popich, G; Smith, D. The Genesis and Significance of Digital and Palmar Hand Creases: Preliminary Report. *J. Pediatr.* 1970, *77* (6), 1017–1023.

Popper, K. The *Logic of Scientific Discovery;* Hutchinson Education: London, 1959.

Popper, K. *Conjectures and Refutations: The Growth of Scientific Knowledge;* Routledge & Kegan Paul: London, 1972.

Roddy, A. R.; Stosz, J. D. Fingerprint Features—Statistical Analysis and System Performance Estimates. *Proceedings of the IEEE,* 1997, *85* (9), 1389–1421.

Roddy, A. R.; Stosz, J. D. Fingerprint Feature Processing Techniques and Poroscopy. In *Intelligent Biometric Techniques in Fingerprint and Face Recognition*. Jain, L. C., Halici, U., Hayashi, I., Lee, S. B., Tsutsui, S., Eds.; CRC Press: Boca Raton, FL, 1999, pp 37–105.

Roxburgh, T. On the Evidential Value of Finger Prints. *Sankhya: Indian J. Stat*. 1933, *1* (50), 189–214.

Saks, M. Legal Consideration of Fingerprints. Presented at the 1st International Web Conference on Human Identification E-Symposium, April 14, 2005.

Saks, M.; Koehler, J. The Coming Paradigm Shift in Forensic Identification Science. *Science* 2005, *309* (5736), 892–895.

Saks, M.; Risinger, D. M.; Rosenthal, R.; Thompson, W. C. Context Effects in Forensic Science: A Review and Application of the Science of Science to Crime Laboratory Practice in the United States. *Sci. and Justice* 2003, *43* (2), 77–90.

Schiffer, B.; Champod, C. The Potential (Negative) Influence of Observational Biases at the Analysis Stage of Fingermark Individualisation. *Forensic Sci. Int.,* 2007, *167* (2–3), 116–120.

Sclove, S. L. The Occurrence of Fingerprint Characteristics as a Two-Dimensional Process. *J. Am. Stati. Associ*. 1979, *74* (367), 588–595.

Sclove, S. L. The Occurrence of Fingerprint Characteristics as a Two-Dimensional Poisson Process. *Communic. in Stati. Theoret. Meth*. 1980, *A9* (7), 675–695.

Srihari, S. N.; Srinivasan, H.; Fang, G. Discriminability of Fingerprints of Twins. *J. Forensic Ident*. 2008, *58* (1), 109–127.

Stacey, R. Report on the Erroneous Fingerprint Individualization in the Madrid Train Bombing Case. *Journal of Forensic Identification* 2004, *54* (6), 706–718.

Steele, L. The Defense Challenge to Fingerprints. *Crim. L. Bull*. 2004, *40* (3), 213–240.

Stoney, D. A. Measurement of Fingerprint Individuality. In *Advances in Fingerprint Technology;* Lee, H. C., Gaensslen, R. E., Eds.; CRC Press: New York, 2001; pp 327–387.

Stoney, D. A.; Thornton, J. I. A Critical Analysis of Quantitative Fingerprint Individuality Models. *J. Forensic Sci*. 1986a, *31* (4), 1187–1216.

Stoney, D. A.; Thornton, J. I. A Method for the Description of Minutia Pairs in Epidermal Ridge Patterns. *J. Forensic Sci*. 1986b, *31* (4), 1217–1234.

Stoney, D. A.; Thornton, J. I. A Systematic Study of Epidermal Ridge Minutiae. *J. Forensic Sci*. 1987, *32* (5), 1182–1203.

Stosz, J. D.; Alyea, L. A. Automated System for Fingerprint Authentication Using Pores and Ridge Structure. In *Proceedings of SPIE, Automatic Systems for the Identification and Inspection of Humans;* Mammone, R. J., Murley, J. D., Eds.; 1994, Vol. 2277; pp 210–223.

Stücker, M.; Geil, M.; Kyeck, S.; Hoffman, K.; Rochling, A.; Memmel, U.; Altmeyer, P. Interpapillary Lines—The Variable Part of the Human Fingerprint. *J. Forensic Sci*. 2001, *46* (4), 857–861.

SWGFAST. Friction Ridge Examination Methodology for Latent Print Examiners, version 1.01; 2002; www.swgfast.org.

Thornton, J. I. The Snowflake Paradigm. *J. Forensic Sci.* 1986, *31* (2), 399–401.

Thornton, S. Karl Popper. *The Stanford Encyclopedia of Philosophy;* 2005; plato.stanford.edu/archives/sum2005/entries/popper (accessed June 30, 2009).

Tietze, S. Witthuhn, K. *Papillarleistenstruktur der menschlichen Handinnenfläche.* Luchterhand: Berlin, Germany, 2001.

Trauring, M. Automatic Comparison of Finger-Ridge Patterns. *Nature* 1963, *197,* 938–940.

U.S. v Mitchell. CA-No. 96-407, *Daubert* hearing transcript, July 7–9, 12–13, 1999.

Van Fraassen, B. *Law and Symmetry;* Clarendon Press: Oxford, 1989.

Wayman, J. L. *When Bad Science Leads to Good Law: The Disturbing Irony of the Daubert Hearing in the Case of U.S. v. Byron C. Mitchell;* Biometrics Publications: San Jose State University, San Jose, CA, 2000.

Wertheim, K.; Maceo, A. The Critical Stage of Friction Ridge Pattern Formation. *J. Forensic Ident.* 2002, *52* (1), 35–85.

Wertheim, P. A. Scientific Comparison and Identification of Fingerprint Evidence. *The Print* 2000, *16* (5).

Wilder, H. H.; Wentworth, B. *Personal Identification;* The Gorham Press: Boston, 1918.

Wilder, H. H.; Wentworth, B. *Personal Identification;* 2nd ed.; T. G. Cooke: Chicago, 1932.

Zynda, L. Lyle Zynda's Lectures on the Philosophy of Science;1994; www.soc.iastate.edu/sapp/phil_sci_lecture00.html (accessed June 30, 2009).

15.8 Additional Information

Champod, C. *Reconnaissance automatique et analyse statistique des minuties sur les empreintes digitales.* Ph.D., Thesis, Universite de Lausanne, Institut de Police Scientifique et de Criminologie, 1996a.

Epstein, R. Fingerprints Meet *Daubert:* The Myth of Fingerprint "Science" Revealed. *S. Cali. L. Rev.* 2002, *75,* 605–658.

Holt, S. B. *The Genetics of Dermal Ridges;* Charles C Thomas: Springfield, IL, 1968.

Loesch, D. *Quantitative Dermatoglyphics: Classification, Genetics, and Pathology;* Oxford University Press: New York, 1983.

National Institute of Justice. *Forensic Friction Ridge (Fingerprint) Examination Validation Studies;* National Institute of Justice, U.S. Department of Justice; U.S. Government Printing Office: Washington, DC, 2000.

Okajima, M. Frequency of Forks in Epidermal-Ridge Minutiae in the Finger Print. *Am. J. Phys. Anthropol.* 1970, *32* (1), 41–48.

Okajima, M. Epidermal-Ridge Minutiae in the Hallucal Area. *Mitteilungen der Anthropologischen Gesellschaft in Wien* 1977, *34,* 285–290.

Okajima, M. Quantitative and Genetic Features of Epidermal Ridge Minutiae on the Palm of Twins. *Hum. Heredity* 1984, *34* (5), 285–290.

Ökrös, S. T*he Heredity of Papillary Patterns;* Publishing House of Hungarian Academy of Sciences: Budapest, 1965.

Roberts, D. F. Dermatoglyphics and Human Genetics. In D*ermatoglyphics—Fifty Years Later;* Wertelecki, W., Plato, C., Paul, N. W., Eds.; Alan R. Liss Inc.: New York, 1979; pp 475–494.

Samuels, J. Letter regarding "Forensic Friction Ridge (Fingerprint) Examination Validation Studies". National Institute of Justice. U.S. Department of Justice: Washington, DC, June 20, 2000.

CHAPTER 15

SPECIAL ABILITIES AND VULNERABILITIES IN FORENSIC EXPERTISE

**THOMAS A. BUSEY
AND ITIEL E. DROR**

CONTENTS

3 15.1 The Relevance of the Human Mind

4 15.2 Cognitive Psychology

16 15.3 Cognitive and Psychological Elements in Fingerprint Identification

20 15.4 Summary and Conclusions

20 15.5 References

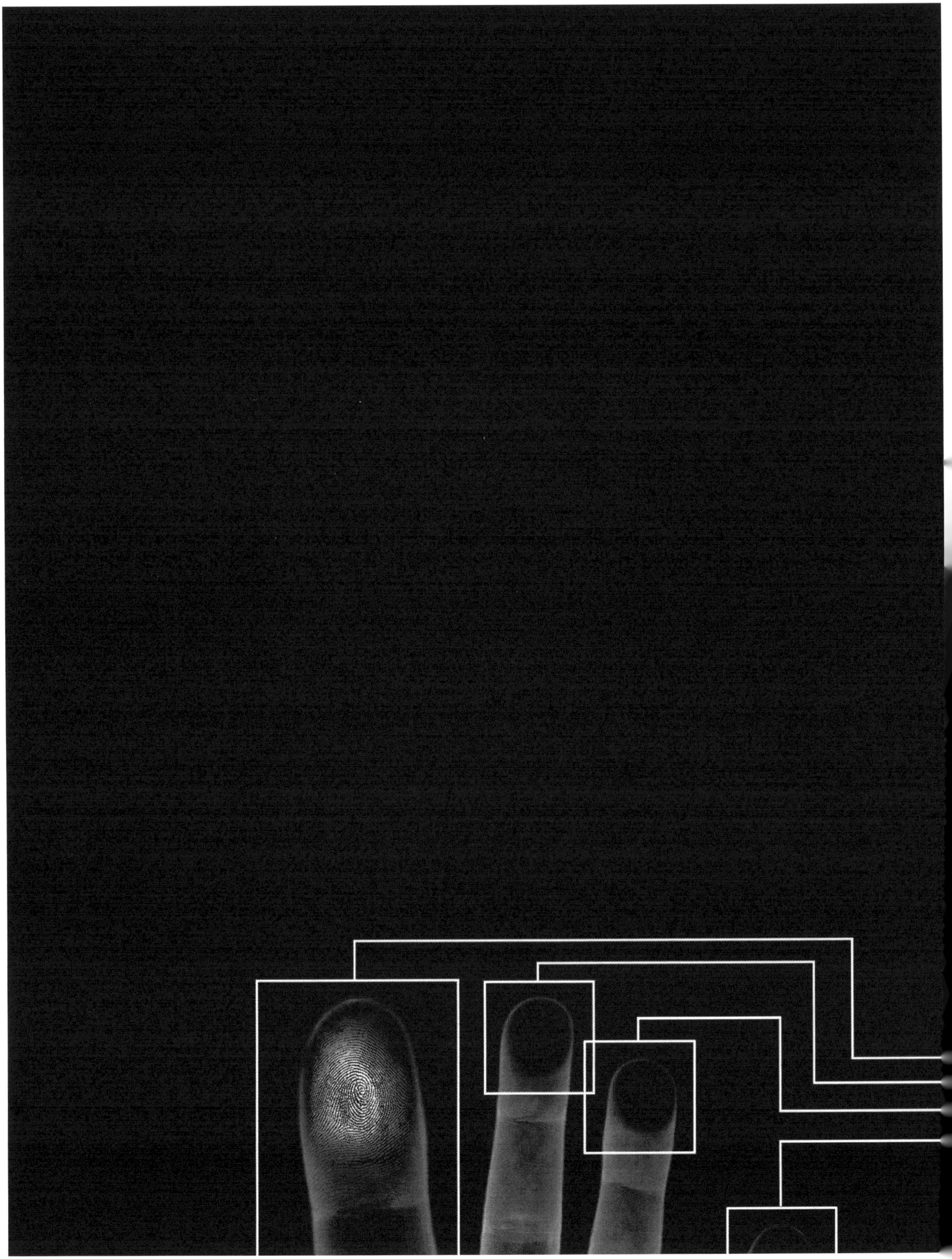

CHAPTER 15

SPECIAL ABILITIES AND VULNERABILITIES IN FORENSIC EXPERTISE

THOMAS A. BUSEY
AND ITIEL E. DROR[*]

15.1 The Relevance of the Human Mind

Latent print examinations are complex perceptual and cognitive tasks. Examiners rely on their visual systems to find similarities in pairs of prints. They then must compare the degree of perceived similarity against that found in previous examinations, and ultimately must decide whether the commonalities found between prints (as well as regions of unexplainable disagreement) merit the conclusion that the prints either did or did not come from the same source (or are inconclusive). This process involves perception, similarity judgments, memory, and decision-making. These abilities vary among people and can be improved with training and experience. They are also subject to potential biases and external influences. This chapter will illustrate, based on knowledge from the visual and cognitive sciences, how an understanding of the human mind is relevant and critical to the fingerprint domain. Such an understanding clearly shows the unique cognitive processes and special abilities of experts, along with their vulnerabilities. This chapter begins with a quick overview of foundational findings in cognitive science and then discusses how these research areas have been extended to latent print examiners. Where possible, links are drawn between basic science findings and the relevant domains of training, selection, and procedures of latent print examinations.

In expert domains, as well as in everyday life, humans process information. Information is perceived, encoded, represented, transformed, stored, retrieved, compared to other information, and evaluated, to name just a few processes. However, the human mind is not a camera and we do not passively process information. It is naïve to think that humans construct and experience reality passively and perceive the environment as "it really is". *Perception is*

---

[*] This chapter was originally two separate chapters, one by Dr. Busey and one by Dr. Dror. The two chapters have been consolidated into this single chapter. The authors would like to thank the reviewers for their comments, and NIJ for supporting this project and their efforts in maintaining its integrity.

far from perfection (Dror, 2005a; see also Humphreys, Riddoch, and Price, 1997; Snyder, Tanke, and Bersheid, 1977). People engage in a variety of active processes that organize and impose structure on information as it comes in from the external world. Information is then further interpreted and processed in ways that highly depend on the human mind and cognition, and less on the environment and the actual content of the information itself. As we dynamically process information, we affect what we see, how we interpret and evaluate it, and our decision-making processes. Thus, to understand expert performance, especially in a highly specialized domain such as human identification, one needs to examine the roles of the human mind and cognition (Dror, in press; Dror and Fraser-Mackenzie, 2008).

Human cognition has been neglected by the fingerprint community, both by the forensic experts themselves as well as by those who design and develop related technology. This chapter is a step toward addressing this oversight; fingerprint identification will be presented within its appropriate context—that of human cognition. The reader will first be introduced to principles that underlie much of cognition and perception, which serve to illustrate human information processing. These principles are illustrated with examples of psychological phenomena that have been chosen for their direct relevance to the latent print examination process. The chapter then turns to a discussion of the development of expertise and how the tools of cognitive neuroscience can be used to describe differences between experts and novices. Finally, important vulnerabilities in the development of expertise are discussed. Throughout this chapter, the authors will argue that it is incumbent upon practicing examiners to treat their professional practice as a scientific endeavor in which they continue to question all aspects of their examinations, gather data on the effectiveness and accuracy of their decisions, and refine training and best practices procedures to avoid cognitive contamination and optimize their decision-making.

15.2 Cognitive Psychology

The human mind is a complex machine. It is incredible in its range and scope, and it is dynamic, flexible, and adaptive. Although complex and intriguing, the essence of the human mind is nevertheless an information-processing machine. As information comes in through our sensory systems, it is processed. This processing may include transformations, comparisons and consolidation with information already stored in the system, evaluations, making decisions, and so forth.

Humans are fortunate to have such a strong computing mechanism as our brain at our disposal because the comparison of two different fingerprints requires a number of cognitive and perceptual capacities that hardware-based computers have yet to equal. Factors such as attention, motivation, perceptual processing, and decision-making all must be brought to bear on the task. In the section below, we briefly cover some of the basic findings in cognitive psychology in order to lay the groundwork for the application of these findings to latent print examinations. It should be noted that a rather large gulf still exists between these basic findings and specific questions related to the forensic sciences. As a result, these topics may seem somewhat abstract but, where possible, links to specific training prescriptions and suggestions for changes in procedures will be made where the science can make a strong case for them.

15.2.1 Studying Human Information Processing

Science without data is not science. Although theorizing and arguments have a role, scientists rely primarily on a dispassionate and agenda-free evaluation of data collected in experiments that are designed to find the truth. Data underlie theory rather than vice versa. Data can come directly from behavioral experiments, in which subjects perform tasks similar to latent print examinations, or data can be gathered indirectly by the use of eyetracking, electrophysiological recordings, computer modeling, or brain imaging.

These data require models for interpretation, which can take the form of verbal descriptions, mathematical formulas, or computer programs, and the field of cognitive psychology has been developed to apply models to such psychological data. An example perhaps familiar to many readers is that of AFIS, which can serve as a model of the fingerprint matching process. This model does not capture the full performance of human experts. Selecting one model out of a set of candidate models or explanations is accomplished on the basis of the level of consistency with the data gathered in experiments. It does not matter whether the data come from behavioral or cognitive neuroscience experiments because the ultimate goal is to use converging methods to place constraints on what the most viable model might be.

In recent years, cognitive psychology has evolved into cognitive neuroscience. In cognitive neuroscience, the study of human information processing has been further advanced by relating it to the human brain (Kosslyn and Koenig, 1992). Examination and studies of the human brain are used to constrain and guide information-processing theories. Although the mind is as distinct from the brain as software is from hardware, the brain provides many important insights into the nature and characteristics of the mind. In cognitive neuroscience, the underlying hardware mechanisms are regarded as being relevant for understanding the higher level mental processes, but that is as far as the interest goes. Thus, in cognitive neuroscience, the neuroscience is a tool for cognitive study rather than a goal itself. The development of cognitive neuroscience came about from novel ways of conceptualizing the brain as an information-processing system. This was achieved, in part, through advanced technologies that allowed new ways to view and study the brain and its operations (CT and MRI, and in particular the functional images PET and fMRI). Such technologies have already been applied to the study of fingerprint expert performance (Busey and Vanderkolk, 2005), as discussed below.

15.2.2 Principles and Key Issues in Understanding Human Cognition

Three issues are especially critical for understanding human cognition: (1) the brain is a limited resource with limited processing capacity, (2) it processes information in an active and dynamic fashion, and (3) performance is dependent on, and limited by, mental representations and *how* information is stored (as much as what information is actually stored). These issues will be explained and illustrated.

The brain is a finite machine and thus its capacity to process information is limited. Information processing has evolved to working within (and overcoming) the confines of this resource. For example, because humans have limited resources, we cannot process all incoming information and thus focus our attention on a subset of the input we perceive and disregard the rest (Sperling, 1960). Our limited resources have, in fact, given rise to much of human intelligence. For instance, because we can only attend to a subset of the information, we need to prioritize which information is the most important to be processed. Thus, we developed sophisticated mechanisms (i.e., intelligence) so as to overcome the limitations in our information-processing capacity and best utilize available resources.

Other ways we deal with our limited resources include data compression. In addition to selective attention, we have developed ways to reduce cognitive load by compressing information to more computationally efficient bits of information (Dror, Schmitz-Williams, and Smith, 2005).

The way information is organized and represented has profound effects on how we process it, what we can do with it, and what information is available. For example, how we represent numbers is not a technical and trivial matter; whether we use "3" or "III" has far-reaching implications on the mathematical operations we can (or cannot) perform. Indeed, Marr (1982, p 21) claims, "This is a key reason why the Roman culture failed to develop mathematics in the way the earlier Arabic cultures had."

The representation of information is also determined by the way people internally encode it. For example, people will find it easy to name the months of the year by their chronological order but impossible to name them by alphabetical order (try it!). In many cases, the same information can be represented in a variety of ways and the specific way that it is represented will later determine how the information can be used and manipulated. The way the mind will mentally manipulate images is highly dependent on how the images are initially represented and encoded (e.g., holistic vs. piecemeal) (Smith and Dror, 2001), and this depends on a variety of factors, including the available cognitive resources (Dror, Schmitz-Williams, and Smith, 2005). These issues are especially acute in experts and affect expert performance in a variety of domains, such as military, medical, policing, financial, and forensics (Dror, in press).

Mental and cognitive representations are essential to the latent print comparison process because individual bits or features of one print must be held in memory long enough to compare against a second image. This process would be impossible without mental representations, and one element of expertise may be an improvement in the ability to hold more information in memory for longer periods of time (Busey and Vanderkolk, 2005).

Before illustrating how these principles and key issues manifest themselves in perceptual, cognitive, and psychological phenomena, it is important to make a distinction between bottom-up and top-down processes (e.g., Humphreys et al., 1997). The bottom-up processes are data driven. The incoming information from the external environment guides the processing mechanisms and the content of information. These types of processes are passive and are dependent on the input itself. Top-down processes are those that depend on the processor (humans in this case) and less on what is processed. In these processes, the state of mind and the information already contained in the system drives the processes. The top-down processes do not depend on the input itself as much as on what is already in the mind of the person processing the information. Every cognitive process, such as learning, thinking, identifying, comparing, matching, decision-making, problem-solving, and all other processes contain at least some elements of top-down processing.

It is not a matter of choice or even conscious processing; the information already contained in the brain, one's state of mind, and many other factors are deeply intertwined in how information is perceived, interpreted, and processed. The dynamic nature of cognition and how the mind works is a clear characteristic of intelligent systems. In fact, as individuals get more experienced and become real experts, the top-down processes play a greater role in how they process information (Dror, in press).

At the psychological level, as attention is turned to the nature and architecture of the human mind, one can observe how the mind has a major role in determining if and how humans understand and interpret information. An intuitive illustration would be when you (or your partner) are pregnant and you start to notice many pregnant women. This is not because there are more pregnant women, but rather your own mental circumstances affect whether and what you see. It is beyond the scope of this paper to give a detailed account of how the mind works and its implications. However, there are many such influences, for example, self-fulfilling prophecies, that illustrate how the mind and psychological elements (such as what we want and wish for) affect what we actually see and are able to do. If we are thirsty, we are more likely to perceive images as containing characteristics of water; our state of thirst modulates our perception (Changizi and Hall, 2001). Our emotional state and mood are further examples of effects of the mind on how we interpret information (Byrne and Eysenck, 1993; Halberstadt et al., 1995; Niedenthal et al., 2000).

Other elements relate to decision-making. As people weigh alternative choices, they consider the evidence for choosing each one. Sequentially moving toward different decision options, one accumulates evidence toward a decision threshold (Dror, Busemeyer, and Basola, 1999).

These decision thresholds and evaluating information in support of decision choices are dependent on psychological elements. Furthermore, one needs to distinguish when information is sought in order to make a decision, and when information is sought out selectively to support an already chosen (or preferred) choice alternative. When information is collected, examined, and interpreted to generate and consider different alternative choices, then information and data are driving the decision-making process; this is a bottom-up progression. However, before information is even collected and processed, people usually already have a preference. This top-down component is often unconscious. Even during the decision-making process itself, even if the decision-maker comes initially with no preconceived decisions or notions, as decisions are considered and made, information is gathered and processed for the purposes of examining, confirming, and validating these decisions. These processes are highly dependent on psychological elements and processes rather than purely on the relevant information. Thus, our mind and mental states play active roles in whether and how we acquire, process, and interpret information as well as in our decision-making (Dror, 2008).

15.2.3 Visual Expertise and Latent Print Examinations

The preceding section illustrates how seemingly simple tasks such as recognition and comparison can be influenced by many different factors. This section discusses results from vision experiments that attempt to explain how practice and experience can improve performance on visual tasks. The discussion is limited somewhat by the fact that relatively little data have been collected on latent print examiners, but fortunately the vision community has adopted a stimulus called a *sine-wave grating* that, with its patterns of light and dark bars, is actually fairly similar to a small patch of a latent print. The following sections summarize the data from different experiments that illustrate how practice can improve performance and offer specific models that explain these improvements. One caveat must be made up-front: the perceptual learning experiments discussed very often have a scale of training on the order of days and weeks, rather than the years that experts often acquire. Thus, smaller differences would be expected between the trained and the untrained subjects in these experiments than when latent print examiners are tested.

15.2.3.1 Overview and studies of perceptual learning.

Perceptual learning is the process by which the sensory system selectively modifies its behavior to important environmental input. The challenge faced by the brain is that, although it needs to change its connectivity and strengthen its neural synapses in order to learn new information, it must also protect itself from unwanted modification that would degrade existing knowledge (Fusi et al., 2005; Kepecs et al., 2002). At the same time, the visual system must select which is the relevant information to be learned. (Using technology and science-based training, the visual system can learn this more efficiently and effectively. See Dror, Stevenage, and Ashworth, 2008.) Humans are consciously aware of only a small part of the visual world, and the bulk of visual processing and visual learning takes place without conscious awareness (Turk-Browne et al., 2005). Somehow, the processes and functionality that make up the visual system, with contributions from higher level conscious processes, must extract the regularities from a set of images or scenes and alter their connectivity to highlight these regularities. The key to this process is the detection of *structure* in a set of images or objects. Without the ability to detect regular structure that brings objects together, the visual system would be forced to adjust its processing anew in response to the latest image received.

Fingerprints, including latent prints, contain regular features that provide structure to guide the learning process. This structure includes the regularity of ridge widths and the existence of eight broad classes of fingerprints as well as smaller features such as minutiae and individual ridge units. The human visual system is well-designed to exploit this regularity. What follows is a discussion of the changes that can occur in the visual system, how these changes are affected by attention and feedback, and how environmental conditions such as the presence of "noise" in latent prints alters the learning process.

Once visual input enters the visual processing stream, it must be interpreted. For the identification sciences, including latent print comparison, the examiner must consider two prints or images and determine whether they come from the same source. This is essentially a similarity computation, since the two versions will never be exact copies. A great deal of work in cognitive science has focused on how humans determine similarity between two objects, and how expertise affects this computation (Dror, in press). This literature can be applied to understanding how latent print examiners consider similarity in the context of a latent print identification, that is, the nature of the features that are used in latent print examinations, how they are processed, and how experience changes how these features are perceived by experts. In order to determine whether two source images such as two fingerprints match, an examiner must first perceive features from one source image and compare them with a second image. Determining the nature of these visual features and the relation between them—and how these features are compared across different instances of an object to enable identification or categorization—is a central goal of the vision sciences. For stimuli such as faces, we suspect that the features are likely to be elements such as the eyes, nose, and mouth. Yet, even with faces, there is much debate in the literature about the exact feature set of faces: these could include eyes and mouths, or even parts of these, or possibly their relation to each other (Zhang and Cottrell, 2004). Less is known about fingerprints, although the features likely include the shape and flow of the ridges, macro-features of core and delta, minutiae and ridge path, ridge edges, and pore shapes and positions. The next section addresses the nature of the development of expertise and looks at studies that help delineate what constitutes a feature from a human perceptual and cognitive perspective.

15.2.3.2 Creation of new feature detectors.

One of the reasons that the feature set is so hard to pin down is that the human visual system is extremely flexible, in that it can adapt its responses to novel stimuli and learn new features. When applied to multiple dimensions, this process is called *unitization*. The neural basis of this kind of perceptual learning was extensively studied by Leventhal and Hirsch (1977), who reared kittens in deprived visual environments and recorded their responses to different patterns. Kittens reared in environments that contained only vertical lines had cells in the visual system that produced only weak responses to horizontal lines. Thus the visual system develops much of its sensitivity to features through experience. These changes in neural processing due to experience can also support new abilities. Unitization creates perceptual units that combine object components that frequently co-occur, such that components that were once perceived separately become psychologically fused together (Schyns and Rodet, 1997). Both Goldstone (2000) and Shiffrin (Shiffrin and Lightfoot, 1997) have addressed the role of unitization in the development of expertise, as discussed below.

Many of the processes of individualizing a print involve comparison of individual features. Unitization may improve the way that candidate features (such as minutiae or

CHAPTER 15 | Special Abilities and Vulnerabilities in Forensic Expertise

ridge features) are extracted from "noisy" stimuli. Latent fingerprints are often corrupted by visual noise when the development medium sticks to the recording surface due to substrates other than the oil left by skin. Experts likely learn to overcome this noise; as one expert put it, their job is to "see through the noise". (This also seems to be an important ability of military fighter pilots; see Dror, Kosslyn, and Waag, 1993, Experiment 5, illustrated in Figure 15–1).

Several possible mechanisms might enable such learning, such as internal noise reduction and improved strategies on the part of observers, and a later section discusses how techniques developed to study visual processing allow tests of these mechanisms. There are specific demonstrations of unitization in the literature. Goldstone (2000) gave participants extended practice in learning to place a complex collection of doodles into Catagory 1, and all of the "near misses" to this pattern belonged in Category 2, as shown in Figure 15–2.

This task encourages unitization. All of the pieces of the Category 1 pattern must be attended to in order to accurately categorize it because each piece is also present in several Category 2 patterns. After 20 hours of practice with these stimuli, participants eventually were able to categorize the Category 1 doodle very accurately and more quickly than would be predicted if they were explicitly combining separate pieces of information from the doodle together. Consistent with other work on perceptual unitization (Gauthier et al., 1998; Shiffrin and Lightfoot, 1997), the theory here is that one way of creating new perceptual building blocks is to create something like a photographic mental image for highly familiar, complex configurations. Following this analogy, just as a camera store does not

FIGURE 15–1

"Seeing through noise" in Dror et al., (1993), Experiment 5, examining the abilities of novices and expert fighter pilots to determine if the 'X' probe is on or off the shaded area with and without visual noise.

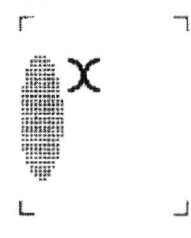

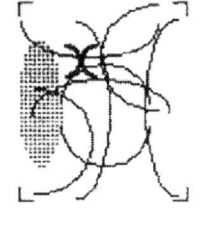

Easy   Difficult

FIGURE 15–2

Doodles in two categories. The letters indicate which segment in the Category 2 items is different from the doodle in Category 1.

Category 1   Category 2

ABCDE

ABCDZ
ABCYE
ABXDE
AWCDE
VBCDE

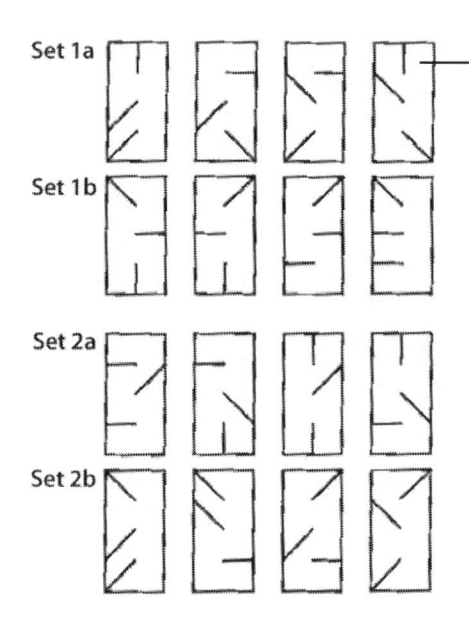

FIGURE 15–3

Stimuli used by Shiffrin and Lightfoot (1997). Over time, observers began to treat the individual line segments as unitary features.

charge more money for developing photographs of crowds than pictures of a single person, once a complex mental image has been formed, it does not require any more effort to process the unit than the components from which it was built. A more complete definition of such a "gestalt" can be found in O'Toole et al. (2001). Blaha and Townsend (2006) have shown that changes in capacity can occur when unitization has taken place. However, the mental representation of the information is critical, and this is highly dependent on the way the objects are presented during learning (e.g., their orientation) and their relative similarity (see Ashworth and Dror, 2000).

Czerwinski et al. (1992) have proposed a process of perceptual unitization in which conjunctions of stimulus features are "chunked" together so that they are perceived as a single unit (see also Newell and Rosenbloom, 1981). Figure 15–3 illustrates this type of stimuli.

Shiffrin and Lightfoot (1997) argued that separated line segments can become unitized following prolonged practice with the materials. Their evidence came from subjects' performance in a feature search task where observers had to scan a visual display of eight items looking for a particular target item. The target item could be either quite similar to the other items (called distracters) or relatively dissimilar. When participants learned a difficult search task in which three line segments were needed to distinguish the target from distracters, impressive and prolonged decreases in reaction time were observed over 20 hour-long sessions.

These prolonged decreases were not observed for a simple search task requiring attention to only one component. In addition, when participants were switched from a difficult task to a simple feature search task, there was initially little improvement in performance, suggesting that participants were still processing the stimuli at the level of the unitized chunk that they formed during the conjunctive training component. The authors concluded that training with difficult stimuli that requires attention to several features at once leads to unitization of the set of diagnostic line segments, resulting in fewer required comparisons. Similar conclusions were drawn by Ahissar and Hochstein (1997) in their work on the "Eureka effect", in which learned stimuli appear to be recognized effortlessly and in an all-or-none fashion.

Although this work has yet to be extended to latent prints, unitization in the context of fingerprints may come about through the analysis of constraints that occur in the development of the friction ridges. For example, ridges have a very even spacing, and features such as ridge endings are associated with nearby ridges shifting inward to preserve this spacing. Fingerprint experts have found that they can use these features in their identifications.

What would it mean for fingerprint experts to develop newly differentiated features? This would change the field's *perceptual vocabulary*. A perceptual vocabulary is the set of functional features that are used for describing objects. A functional feature is defined as any object property that can

FIGURE 15–4

Stimuli used by Busey and Vanderkolk (2005) to address configural processing in latent print examiners.

Clear Fragments

Partially Masked Fragments

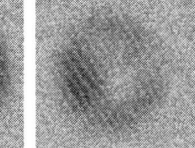

Fragments Presented in Noise

Partially Masked Fragments Presented in Noise

be selectively attended to and is relevant to the task. This implies that the visual system treats it as a unique part of an object. For example, feature X can be used to describe an object if there is evidence that X can be considered in isolation from other aspects of the object. Tying the uniqueness of a feature to selective attention conforms to many empirical techniques for investigating features. Garner (1976) considers two features or dimensions to be separable if categorizations on the basis of one of the features are not slowed by irrelevant variation on the other. Treisman (e.g., Treisman and Gelade, 1980) argues that features are registered separately on different feature maps, giving rise to efficient and parallel searches for individual features and the automatic splitting apart of different features that occupy the same object. Within fingerprints, there are several highly correlated features that are candidates for unitization. As noted, the width between the ridges is very regular, which may provide constraints on how information in degraded areas is interpreted if clear detail is present in adjacent areas. Likewise, y-branching, cores, and deltas are all stereotypical features in prints that are composed of smaller features that have the potential to be joined into a new feature in an hierarchical manner through unitization.

One implication of these studies for training of latent print examiners is that we find fairly consistent and long-lasting effects of perceptual learning after relatively brief training (weeks to months). These studies have not identified how long these changes persist, however.

15.2.3.3 Configural processing of images. Work by Busey and Vanderkolk (2005) looked at configural processing as one technique by which fingerprint examiners could improve the quality of information coming from fingerprint impressions, especially when the prints are corrupted by visual noise. Configural processing is related to unitization in that it allows for the combination of individual features into a larger representation that codes relational information and possibly treats the entire image as a unitary image rather than a collection of features. Because relatively few studies have addressed the expertise exhibited by latent print examiners, these experiments are described in detail below. Busey and Vanderkolk (2005) tested 11 experts and 11 novices with 144 experimental trials. In each trial they presented a fingerprint briefly for one second and then, after a short delay, they presented two prints: one that was a rotated version of the same print, and one that was chosen by human experts to be a very similar print but from a different source. Figure 15–4 shows examples of the test stimuli, and Figure 15–5 shows the technique by which partially masked fingerprints are created.

The researchers modified the two test prints to be either whole or partial prints embedded in visual noise and asked the subjects to identify which print they had seen before. They used the accuracy in the partial print condition along with a mathematical model known as *probability summation* to make a prediction for performance in the whole image condition. They found that experts exceeded this prediction, which is consistent with configural processing.

They followed this finding with an electroencephalogram (EEG) experiment that found similar evidence for configural processing in fingerprint experts (but not novices). Upright faces produce a different brain response than inverted faces when the two EEG waveforms are compared; this has been attributed to configural processing that occurs only for upright faces. In their experiment, they found that experts showed differences for faces as well as fingerprints when both stimuli were inverted. Novices showed

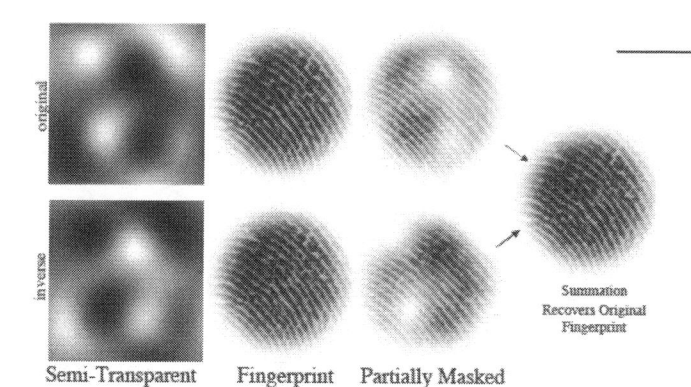

FIGURE 15–5

Method of creating partial masks to test configural processing.

Semi-Transparent Masks | Fingerprint | Partially Masked Fingerprints | Summation Recovers Original Fingerprint

differences only for faces. Thus, the signature of configural processing evidence in the EEG waveform for faces generalizes to fingerprints in latent print examiners. Due to the complex nature of EEG data and analyses, the reader is referred to the primary article (Busey and Vanderkolk, 2005) for more information. These two experiments demonstrate that experts use configural processing to improve their perception of individual features by using evidence from nearby features.

15.2.3.4 Statistical learning of visual input without attention or awareness. What brain processes might support the creation of new features through unitization and holistic representations through configural processing? The basis for this learning is rooted in the notion of *co-occurrences*, which are statistical descriptions of the fact that, in images and objects, two features tend to occur simultaneously. For example, it is the rare face that has only one eye, and this fact does not escape the visual system, which will begin to build up a representation such that when one eye is present, it more readily codes the presence of the other eye. Eventually, cells may emerge in the visual processing stream that code only the conjunction of the two eyes. Evidence with novel stimuli for this process at the single neuron level comes from Baker et al. (2002).

Recent work by Turk-Browne et al. (2005) suggests that this statistical learning (i.e., learning that two features or parts are related to each other in that they tend to co-occur) can occur automatically. Attention is required to select the relevant population of stimuli or features, but learning takes place automatically after that.

This work is an extension of prior studies by Fiser and Aslin (2001), who tested a proposal originally put forth by Barlow (1990), which posited that the visual system initiates learning by detecting "suspicious coincidences" of feature or elements. They presented observers with sets of well-defined simple shapes and varied the likelihood that one feature would appear with another. They gave the observers no instructions about what to do, and no feedback that might identify the nature of the relations among the objects. Despite this, observers spontaneously learned a variety of relations, including which features were presented most often, where they tended to occur on the display, the positions of pairs (regardless of position), and finally which shapes occurred together (regardless of position). These results are important because models of object recognition (presumably including fingerprints) require that the visual system learn these types of relations among features. Similar arguments have been made by Anderson and Schooler (1991), who argued that the structure of human memory may have been influenced by the structure present in the environment.

The fact that learning is relatively automatic and unconscious suggests that the mere act of looking at fingerprints will allow the visual system to extract the statistical regularities that are contained in prints. AFIS operators, for instance, might not perform the actual identifications in large labs but are good candidates for latent print work because of their incidental exposure to fingerprints.

15.2.3.5 How noise and feedback affect learning. Experts who work with visually noisy images (e.g., radiologists, fighter pilots, satellite image analysts, radar operators, and latent print examiners) must learn which aspects of their images are meaningful and which are visual noise. The issue is one of learning to separate the image information from the noise of the images. Dosher and Lu (2005) addressed the question of whether it is better to train using noisy images or clear images. Perhaps surprisingly, participants who trained with clear images were able to generalize this knowledge to noisy images, whereas participants who trained with noisy images were only expert with noisy images and acted like novices with clear images. They attributed this to the existence of two independent processes: external noise filtering and improved amplification or enhancement of weak stimuli. Both of these processes will lead to better performance, but external noise filtering only works when there is noise to filter. Thus, training with clear items allows both processes to develop.

When experts learn in noisy images, they can perform what is called "signal enhancement", which is the process by which the neural detectors in the visual system match their profiles to fit the to-be-perceived features. This could include the process of learning what to look for in an image, which has been demonstrated in the "Eureka phenomenon" (Ahissar and Hochstein, 1997) and more recently has received support from Gold et al. (1999) and Lu and Dosher (2004).

A very faint fingerprint image is limited not by visual noise but by the examiner's ability to discern the structure in the print. One implication of this is that novices (including latent print trainees) should receive much of their training using relatively clear prints shown at different levels of brightness so they can learn both the features they need to attend to and how to improve the amplification of very faint images. This perceptual learning should then generalize to noisy images, which can be introduced later in training.

The notion that expertise relies on conscious and intentional processes as well as unconscious and incidental processes has been addressed by Maddox and Ing (2005). They suggest that the role of the conscious system is to develop and test hypotheses related to a particular task. In their studies, the task was to categorize an object into one of several categories. The unconscious system performs primarily as an information integration process similar to the statistical learning described earlier. When a task involves a simple rule (i.e., red objects belong in one category and blue objects in another), the hypothesis testing system is primarily involved. Not only does feedback improve performance in this task, but delaying the feedback for 5 seconds has no deleterious effects. However, for tasks that involve combinations of dimensions (i.e., Category 1 is small red objects and large green objects, and Category 2 is large red objects and small green objects), delaying the feedback by 5 seconds hurts performance. This suggests that immediate feedback can aid the learning process, at least when the features or dimensions that are necessary for a task are easy to express verbally. However, feedback need not be required, and reliable perceptual learning can be obtained in the absence of feedback (Fahle and Edelman, 1993; Wenger and Rasche, 2006). For fingerprint examinations, when examiners rely on print information that is not easy to verbalize (such as the amount of curvature along a ridge path), they should refine their learning by training on stimulus sets for which the ground truth is known and can be immediately verified.

15.2.3.6 Computing similarity between features. Any comparison between a latent print and a candidate known print will involve some computation of similarity because the latent print is never an exact copy of the inked print. This comparison may be performed on the basis of individual features or the general direction of the first-level general ridge flow, or class characteristics (often used to quickly eliminate a known print from consideration). In some sense, the entire latent-to-inked print comparison can be viewed as a similarity computation with a decision stage at the back end. Within the domain of facial recognition, Steyvers and Busey (2001) have looked at models of the similarity computation process and how similarity ratings can be used to construct dimensional representations that provide input to process-based memory models (Busey, 1998; Busey and Tunnicliff, 1999). This work has built upon prior work from the perceptual learning and categorization literature, done in part by Goldstone (1996, 1999, 2000). This prior experience highlights two areas that are readily generalized to fingerprints. These relate to how experts create psychological dimensions of stimuli (described in detail below) and how they integrate and differentiate these dimensions, depending on the nature of the task.

A *feature* is a unitary stimulus element, and a *dimension* is a set of ordered values. Dimensions for shape could include length, width, curvature, or size. To a novice observer, the many dimensions that make up a complex stimulus may be fused together, whereas an expert may separate out these dimensions through a process called *differentiation*. In the present context, latent prints correspond to one set of dimensions, and the noise that accompanies the prints corresponds to a second set. Experts may learn to separate the two sets of dimensions through dimensional differentiation, although this has not been extended empirically. Goldstone and Steyvers (2001) looked at how training affects dimension differentiation and found that, although experts learn to differentiate dimensions from each other (akin to perceiving the height of an object without being affected by its width), they can sometimes have difficulty switching their attention to previously ignored dimensions. In the process of learning to differentiate dimensions and, in the process, learning to ignore the irrelevant dimensions, experts perform poorly if meaningful variation is introduced into the previously irrelevant dimensions. Thus, fingerprint experts may have difficulty when asked to make judgments that depend in part on differences that exist in the noise dimensions, which presumably they have learned to ignore.

Burns and Shepp (1988) measured the similarity relations between color chips. They found that although novice observers tended to treat the dimensions of hue, saturation, and brightness as integral, experts were more likely to differentiate these dimensions. Goldstone (1996) extended this work to show that people who learn a categorization become sensitized to the relevant dimensions. The categorization work described above suggests that experts learn to separate out the relevant dimensions, which helps them more accurately gauge the similarity of two objects.

This dimensional approach has proven useful in the domain of face recognition, which reveals not only the nature of the dimensions of faces but also provides a psychological space that can be used to make predictions for memory experiments. A *psychological space* is an abstract representation that places more similar faces close together (Valentine, 1991). Busey (1998) gathered a large set of similarity ratings between all possible pairs of 104 faces. These ratings were analyzed using a multidimensional scaling (MDS) analysis package, which attempts to reduce the dimensionality of the data to relevant psychological dimensions that describe how humans compute similarity. The resulting psychological space not only proved interpretable but was then used to make predictions for memory experiments (Busey and Tunnicliff, 1999). Later work by Steyvers and Busey (2001) demonstrated the matches and mismatches between a physical representation computed from images and psychological spaces computed from similarity ratings. In part, the differences come from the fact that some features are more diagnostic than others; experts may use this diagnosticity to adjust their psychological space of fingerprints accordingly. The different processes used by experts result in enhanced performance but also, paradoxically, have degradation as a result of cognitive tradeoffs (Dror, 2009a).

This work suggests that one element of training involves the discovery of relevant psychological dimensions that differentiate fingerprints. These dimensions are not yet known but could be something like general ridge flow, overall fingerprint type, density of minutiae in particular regions, and even idiosyncratic features such as particular constellations of ridges.

15.2.3.7 Similarity vs. categorical decision-making. The previous section describes how the psychological work on similarity computation applies to latent print examinations. There may appear to be a gulf between similarity judgments, which one may think of as a continuous measure, and the type of decision arrived at by latent print examiners. The language may be different in various jurisdictions, but typically examiners testify that two prints either came from the same source or did not come from the same source. They may or may not attach some kind of confidence rating to this conclusion. This might suggest that the similarity literature may have little to do with latent print examinations. However, the authors of this chapter would argue that the decision arrived at by the examiner is, in fact, an implicit similarity judgment. No two prints are ever identical; therefore, the task always requires some element of comparison and similarity computation. Examiners then translate this to a categorical judgment, presumably using some rule such as: "These two prints are more similar to each other than any other close non-match that I have observed" or "The two prints are sufficiently similar that I can conclude that they come from the same source" (see Dror, 2009a, for a discussion of sufficient similarity).

One may want to draw a distinction between the actual underlying cognitive processes involved in fingerprinting, the terminology and language used to express a conclusion, and how this is explained in court. Here, the focus is on the cognitive processes, which result from comparing the similarity of two images. The way fingerprint examiners explain their conclusions, and the way they express their decisions, may vary from one place to another and may change over time; however, the cognitive processes that are the focus of this chapter remain the same.

FIGURE 15–6

Both blackened areas are identical in shape.

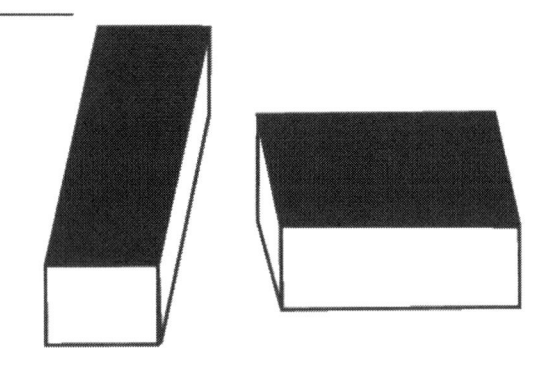

15.2.3.8 Interim summary. This chapter thus far has summarized the findings from the perceptual learning literature as explored by cognitive scientists. What emerges from this summary is a view that the human visual system is remarkably good at extracting the structure that exists in a class of stimuli. This learning process occurs with very little conscious direction beyond the initial selection of relevant features. All that is required is a constant set of example stimuli that provide the kinds of statistical regularities among features or parts that are extracted by the visual processing mechanisms, as well as some selection of what are the relevant features required for the task. This is not to imply that this is an easy process; in fact, the field should argue for more hours of training to provide the large number of examples that are required to identify weak statistical relations. Such complex learning can be enhanced by developing scientific-based training and utilizing technology (see Dror, Stevenage, and Ashworth, 2008).

Experts often ask the question, how much matching information is enough? The perceptual learning literature does not provide a direct answer, but the tools from cognitive science illustrate how different factors trade off. In the next section, a computation modeling approach is used to address the relation between quantity and quality. Image quality could be measured in several ways but, in general, it represents the degree of visible print information relative to the amount of noise caused by dust or other artifacts created when the print was lifted. Image quantity represents the surface area of usable print information, which could be measured in units of ridge widths or square centimeters. Although image quantity and quality can be seen as going together, in principle it is possible to separate the two factors.

15.2.4 Weaknesses and Vulnerabilities in Perceptual, Cognitive, and Psychological Phenomena

Although the active and dynamic nature of cognition is the basis of intelligence and expertise, it also introduces a multitude of elements that make humans vulnerable to distorting information and thus making errors (Dror, in press). As many of these processes are unconscious (e.g., Greenwald, 1992), they are especially problematic and dangerous. This section elaborates and illustrates how human information processing can distort information in a variety of ways. The next section shows how these phenomena relate to fingerprint identification.

Our perceptual information processing can also distort our perception of images. Although the two black shapes above, in Figure 15–6, are identical, they are perceived as being totally different (Shepard, 1981). The active and dynamic nature of the perceptual system not only has the potential to distort the incoming data, as already illustrated, but it can also add information and make us perceive things that are not actually there. For example, in Figure 15–7, one perceives imaginary subjective contours making a white square on top of the black square (Kanizsa, 1976). Furthermore, this imaginary white square incorrectly seems to be of a different shade than its surroundings (compare the shade in points A and B, which are in fact identical).

These examples demonstrate that even the lower level sensory mechanisms are not passive or isolated from a variety of factors that can affect and distort what is perceived. Thus, much of what is perceived, even at the lower level mechanisms, is dependent on the perceiver rather than reflecting an "objective reality". The attention

Special Abilities and Vulnerabilities in Forensic Expertise | **CHAPTER 15**

FIGURE 15–7

Example of subjective contours and illusionary differences in shading (point A and B).

FIGURE 15–8

The same central image can get different interpretation based on visual or mental context.

mechanisms at the perceptual level, as well as at higher levels of information processing (discussed earlier in section 2.2), select only a subset of the information available for further processing. In this way, people actually do not process much of what they see. De facto, they disregard and miss possibly critical information in an image.

Because of these as well as other cognitive mechanisms, the same visual image can, in fact, get different interpretations depending on the context in which it is presented. The middle pattern in Figure 15–8 can either be interpreted as the letter "B" or as the number "13"; either can be induced by providing different contextual information ("13" with the vertical contextual information or "B" with the horizontal contextual information).

Because our minds and psychological state play a central role in how people process information, here too they are subject to vulnerabilities. In fact, the mind can "play many tricks" and cause a wide range of phenomena. The common saying that "love is blind" is a reflection of this effect.

Most people have experienced that when they expect and hope to see something, then they see it even when it is not there (and, similarly, when they are afraid of something, they see it even where it is not). In these situations, the context is not provided by the environment but rather by one's "state of mind" or mental context.

At a more scientific level, this can be demonstrated by showing that interpretation of the central image in Figure 8 as either a "13" or a "B" can be affected by one's state of mind. Rather than manipulating the external context of "A, B, C" vs. "12, 13, 14", the psychological state of mind, in terms of motivation, can be manipulated. If the central image is presented in a context that motivates people to see a number, then they will see it as "13", in contrast to seeing the same image as "B" when they are motivated to see it as a letter (Balcetis and Dunning, 2006). For example, one can be highly affected by states of wishful thinking, cognitive dissonance, escalation of commitment, or confirmation bias. In these cases, the collection and interpretation of

FIGURE 15–9

Both horizontal lines are of equal length

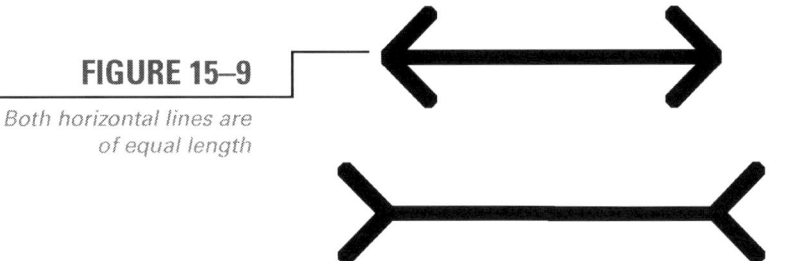

information are driven to justify and verify a decision that has already taken place or to confirm a pre-existing preference or bias.

Again, even if the decision-maker comes initially with no preconceived decisions or biases, as decisions are considered and made, information is gathered and processed for the purposes of confirming and validating these decisions. As already illustrated, these processes are highly dependent on psychological elements and processes rather than purely on the relevant information. Thus, one's mind and mental states can distort and interfere with whether and how information is collected, processed, and interpreted (e.g., Baumeister and Newman, 1994; Kunda, 1990). These effects happen most often without any awareness (e.g., Greenwald, 1992).

15.3 Cognitive and Psychological Elements in Fingerprint Identification

It is clear that fingerprint identification cannot be performed in isolation from human cognition. A whole range of perceptual, cognitive, and psychological elements play an integral role in all the stages of the identification process: from finding and collecting prints, perceiving them, and their analysis, comparison, and evaluation, to reaching judgments, making decisions, and verification. In the sections below, psychological and cognitive phenomena are tied together and related to the world of fingerprint identification, and research that directly examines the fingerprint domain is then presented. Finally, some practical implications and applications of these elements are discussed. Finding ways to move forward and enhance fingerprint identification can only be achieved once we are willing to accept that these influences exist.

15.3.1 Relevance of Cognitive Phenomena to Fingerprint Identification

It is obvious that fingerprint experts, like experts in other domains and nonexperts in everyday life, are susceptible to perceptual, cognitive, and psychological phenomena. However, not all psychological and cognitive phenomena are directly related to fingerprint identification. It is important to consider which ones are relevant, and how. For example, if fingerprint identification requires comparing the length of ridges, then the Müller-Lyer illusion (1889) may be very relevant. In Figure 15–9, the top horizontal line is perceived as shorter than the bottom horizontal line, although the two lines are in fact identical in length (Restle and Decker, 1977).

This is a demonstration of some potential psychological and cognitive phenomena that may be directly related to fingerprint identification. This and other phenomena have been researched within the general scope of psychological investigations. Other scientific investigations have been conducted to directly address fingerprint identification.

15.3.2 Cognitive Research on Fingerprint Expertise and Identification

A number of research studies have examined the possible influence of context on decisions about whether fingerprints match or not (see, for example, Langenburg et al., 2009; Schiffer and Champod, 2007; Dror, Péron, Hind, and Charlton, 2005; Dror and Charlton, 2006; Dror, Charlton, and Péron, 2006). In one study (Dror, Péron, Hind, and Charlton, 2005), pairs of fingerprints were presented to nonexperts. Some pairs of prints were clearly a match, some were clearly not a match, and others were ambiguous. Then, prior to the participants examining the fingerprints, contextual information about the crime at issue (including photos from the crime scene) was presented. Half of the time, the context was neutral. Participants had to judge whether there was sufficient information to make

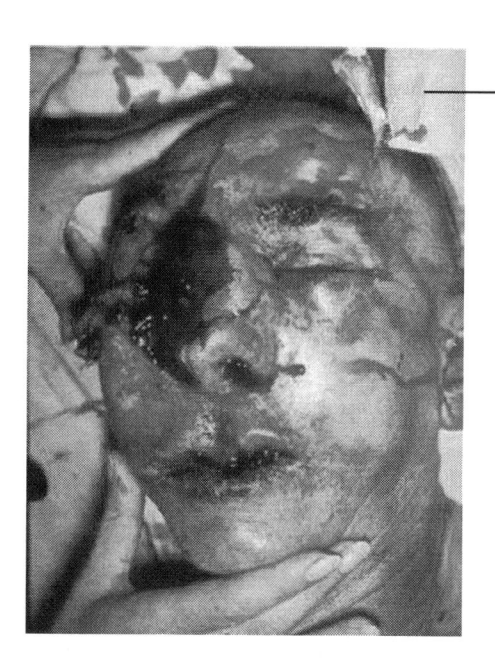

FIGURE 15-10

An image used in the Dror et al. (2005) study.

a sound judgment and, if so, whether the prints matched. However, the other half of the prints were presented within a highly emotional condition, with photos that were scientifically proven to provoke emotional reactions (Lang et al., 1995), such as the photograph in Figure 15-10.

The results of the study showed that emotional context and mood affected how fingerprints were matched. However, the effect of emotional context was dependent on the difficulty of making the match. The emotional manipulation only affected matching decisions when the pairs of fingerprints were ambiguous and there was not enough data to make a clear and simple identification or exclusion decision. (For details, see Dror, Péron, Hind, and Charlton, 2005.)

The 2005 study was conducted on nonexperts. However, emotional experiences do seem to play a role in the work of fingerprint examiners (Charlton et al., in press). Even studies with real experts do not capture the reality in the workplace because the research is laboratory based. In fact, even in the normal working environment, experts behave differently if they know they are being observed, taking part in research, or being tested. As an analogy, if one wants to test and examine how people drive, then examining their driving during an official driving test, or even when they know they are being watched (or within the range of a speed camera), will hardly reflect how they actually drive every day in practice on the road (see Dror and Rosenthal, 2008; Dror, 2009b).

To collect ecologically valid and robust data, Dror and Charlton (2006) and Dror, Charlton, and Péron (2006) employed covert data collected from fingerprint experts during their routine work. A within-subject experimental design was used in which the same experts made judgements on identical pairs of fingerprints, but in different contexts. This is a very robust and powerful experimental paradigm, as participants act as their own controls. This not only provides more meaningful and interpretable data, but each data point carries more statistical power. Furthermore, this allows the researcher to isolate, focus on, and examine the contextual influences themselves rather than revealing possible individual differences between experts. Accordingly, pairs of fingerprints were collected (from archives) that the same experts being examined had examined and judged approximately 5 years earlier as a clear and definite match or exclusion. These previous identifications/exclusions were taken from real criminal investigations.

In these studies, the very same pairs of fingerprints were re-presented to the same experts, only now they were presented within an extraneous context that might bias them to evaluate the prints differently. A control condition included pairs of prints that were presented without manipulating the context. In these two studies, a total of 53 pairs of prints were presented to 11 experienced latent fingerprint experts (none of whom participated in both studies).

In a combined meta-analysis of these two experiments (Dror and Rosenthal, 2008), the reliability and biasability of the fingerprint experts was analyzed and determined. Eight out of the 11 experts made some inconsistent decisions that conflicted with their previous decisions on the same pair of fingerprints. These conflicting decisions mainly occurred in the more difficult prints and with prints that were originally judged as identifications. However, some inconsistent decisions also occurred with relatively easy prints and with prints that were originally judged as exclusions. Furthermore, some inconsistent decisions were observed in the control condition, in which the prints were presented without any contextual manipulation. (For full details and discussion of these results, see the studies; full citations are listed in the References.)

A number of new studies have followed up on this work (e.g., Langenburg et al., 2009; Hall and Player, 2008; Schiffer and Champod, 2007). Although there is some divergence on the interpretations of the different studies (see Dror, 2009b), all consistently and clearly show that biasing effects exist, although they do not necessarily change decision outcomes and their effects vary depending on circumstances. As stated in Langenburg et al. (2009), "There is strong evidence that some fingerprint specialists *can* be biased by contextual information. The decision made by a specialist is not necessarily based solely on the ridge detail when comparing images. More importantly, the bias effect was most often observed during complex comparison trials" (page 577; italics in the original). These studies illustrate some of the potential interferences of psychological and cognitive elements in fingerprint identification. These issues can be further exacerbated by technology (see Dror and Mnookin, 2010) and working procedures, as specified in section 15.3.3.

The changes in the low-level perceptual mechanisms, identified using brain recordings as described in section 15.2.3.3, illustrate that training affects the nature of the information processing mechanisms. As the quality of the information acquired by the visual system improves, the structure of the decision process also changes. For example, as an examiner begins to acquire more experience with harder images, he or she may feel more comfortable "calling" more difficult prints. This entails a change in the implicit decision criteria such that less evidence, if it is of higher quality, might be sufficient to make a determination. Models of decision-making, such as signal detection theory, actually support such a shift in the decision criteria to balance the tradeoffs between correct identifications, correct exclusions, misses, and erroneous identifications. The preceding section,

however, does reinforce the conclusion that as an examiner shifts his or her decision criteria with changes in experience, care must be taken to avoid shifting them too much. Central to any shift in criteria must be a set of procedures to obtain accurate feedback from know fingerprints, either in the form of formal proficiency testing or informal practice working with a community of examiners.

15.3.3 Applications and Implications of Cognitive Research and Phenomena to Fingerprint Analysis and Comparisons

It is clear by now that cognition plays a critical role in fingerprint identification. Nevertheless, there has been relatively little attention to the cognitive and psychological perspectives, and only a small number of studies that are specifically directed at the fingerprint domain have been conducted to explore this or related issues (e.g., Busey and Vanderkolk, 2005; Schiffer and Champod, 2007; Wertheim et al., 2006; Haber and Haber, 2004; Dror, Schmitz-Williams, and Smith, 2005; Dror and Charlton, 2006; Dror, Charlton, and Péron, 2006; Dror, Stevenage, and Ashworth, 2008; Langenburg et al., 2009). The need for systematic research into the cognitive and psychological issues cannot be overstated.

15.3.3.1 Selection and Screening. Although many experts were biasable and unreliable in their judgments (Dror and Rosenthal, 2008), some experts seem to have been relatively immune to many cognitive and psychological influences. Why were those experts not as susceptible as the others? What was it about those experts that made them so consistent, reliable, and unbiasable? More systematic research needs to be done before it can be determined if it had to do with their personalities, cognitive style, training, working culture, or other factors. However, what is clear is that, whatever it is, it is something good that should be sought in every fingerprint expert.

But what are those things that make up a fingerprint expert? What are the cognitive skills and aptitudes that are needed for conducting fingerprint identification? As a first step to further professionalize and enhance fingerprint identification, the field must screen and select the correct people to become experts in this domain. In order to do this, the field first needs to understand the skills and cognitive styles that underpin the ability to conduct fingerprint identification. However, in contrast to other domains of expertise (e.g., Air Force pilots; see Dror, Kosslyn, and

Waag, 1993), there has been no research to this effect in the fingerprint domain; thus, there is a lack of standardized and scientifically based testing of screening applicants.

Only with systematic research into the skills and aptitudes needed for fingerprint identification can the field construct a cognitive profile of fingerprint experts. Then those abilities that are relatively hard-wired and do not change with training will be used for initial selection and screening (e.g., Dror, 2004). There is a need to establish a standardized test for recruitment screening of fingerprint examiners that is based on research and understanding. Proper screening and selection is critical for finding the best candidates for this profession. Investment in initially selecting the right people for the profession is not only very cost-effective but will also avoid problems in the long run.

15.3.3.2 Training. Training—whether it is the initial training involved in becoming an expert, or continuing professional development over the years via workshops and other training opportunities—is a critical aspect in fingerprint expertise. Training in all its forms needs to address the psychological and cognitive influences that may affect the workings of fingerprint experts. Such training can help minimize the elements that can lead to misjudgments and to error. However, such training is practically nonexistent.

This essential training would involve theoretical discussion and hands-on exercises on how to avoid error due to psychological and cognitive factors. To elucidate such training programs would require a whole book in its own right, but generally such training would need to intertwine knowledge of cognition, expert performance, and fingerprint identification. Along with training, continuous blind testing of expert performance is an important aspect that is not currently implemented in most places. Testing experts in nonblind conditions, when they know they are being tested, only examines their theoretical ability to match fingerprints. Just as driving tests do not reflect how people actually drive on the road, non-blind testing of experts does not reflect their practical performance in casework.

Choosing the right people to become fingerprint experts, training them properly, and continuously testing their performance will address many of the issues raised in this chapter, but only at a personal and individual level. Tackling the complexity of cognitive and psychological influences requires addressing these issues both at the individual expert level and at the organizational administrative level (Dror, 2009a).

15.3.3.3 Procedures. Correct working procedures are essential for minimizing psychological and cognitive interferences in making fingerprint matching decisions. Such procedures have to be pragmatic and adapted to the specific realities in which they are implemented. The procedures must consider the cognitive and psychological influences from the initial evaluation of the latent print to the final verification.

In the initial evaluation, for example, there is the issue of whether this should be done in isolation from seeing any potential tenprints (Dror, 2009a). Examining and evaluating the latent print by itself allows judgments to be independent; when such examinations are done with the accompanying tenprint, there are a number of potential problematic issues. The tenprint provides a context and a motivation that can change the way the latent print is examined and evaluated: It can affect the selective allocation of attention, change thresholds and standards for assessing information, cause the perception of characteristics that are not there and/or the dismissal of characteristics that are there, and many other unconscious cognitive and psychological phenomena that have been elaborated upon throughout this chapter.

However, the examination of a latent print against a suspect tenprint may also allow examiners to notice certain bits of information by directing their attention to those areas that do require special attention and further processing (Dror, 2009a). Thus, there is no simple solution and the problems are complex. A possible solution may entail an initial examination and analysis of the latent print in isolation but also allow for retroactive changes after comparison to the tenprints. There is a danger here, too, as this can bring about acceptance of low-quality latent prints that do not contain sufficient information as well as all the other cognitive and psychological issues discussed already. A way to move forward may be an initial examination of a latent print in isolation, and an analysis of it that comprises distinguishing characteristics that are strong and cannot be changed, with weaker characteristics considered when later examining the tenprints (see details at Dror, 2009a). This is only an illustration of the procedural changes that might address cognitive and psychological influences.

These types of issues continue throughout the entire procedure of fingerprint identification (and exclusion), all the way to the final verification procedures. Many existing verifications are perhaps no more than a rubber stamp. The very fact that identifications will be verified (sometimes by more than one verifier) introduces a whole range of issues, from diffusion of responsibility (Darley and Latané, 1968) to conformity, attention, self-fulfilling prophecies, and wishful thinking. Quality assurance would require that look-alike exclusions would be put together along with the real casework verifications, to keep the verifiers alert and to guarantee quality assurance. These issues and development of science-based procedures require further research.

15.3.3.4 Technology. The introduction and development of technologies has had a profound impact on fingerprint identification. These technologies offer great capabilities and opportunities and, with efforts in biometric identification, the field can expect new technologies to continue and emerge in the future. Many times, the overestimation and promise of technology, and the underestimation of the human mind and human experts, lead to a false expectation that machines and technology will take over human performance (Dascal and Dror, 2005). As powerful as these technologies are and will be in the foreseeable future, they will not replace latent print examiners. The important thing is to take advantage of these new technologies and harness them to enhance fingerprint identification. To achieve this, technologies need to be integrated properly with the human experts. This means designing and integrating the technology to work with experts and to complement their work (Dror, 2005b, 2006; Dror and Mnookin, 2010).

Although these technologies will not replace human experts, they will have a great impact on fingerprint identification (Davis and Hufnagel, 2007). In terms of some of the cognitive and psychological issues discussed in this chapter, some issues will be eliminated with the technological developments but other problems will not be affected. In fact, some issues will be exacerbated and new problems may even be created (Dror and Mnookin, 2010). For example, the Automated Fingerprint Identification System (AFIS) gives rise to giant databases that contain larger and larger numbers of fingerprints. With such large databases, the relative similarity of fingerprints found by pure coincidence will increase. With increased similarity and look-alike prints, the difficulty in matching will increase. With greater difficulty in the bottom-up matching of prints, greater opportunity and vulnerability is created for the top-down contextual and motivational components to distort and interfere with the matching process (see Dror et al., 2005; Dror and Mnookin, 2010).

Technological developments in the fingerprint domain are not limited to AFIS. For example, technology offers "image enhancements" (such as color and 3-D transformations). Such enhancements can offer clarity and improved accuracy, but at the same time they present great opportunities to strengthen and enable cognitive and psychological distortions. As before, there are no simple solutions, and the issues and problems are complex. Technology is an important ally to fingerprint experts but must be designed, developed, used, and integrated in a way that enhances fingerprint identification (Dror, 2005b; Dror and Mnookin, 2010).

15.4 Summary and Conclusions

The dynamic and active nature of human information processing enables us to become experts but also makes us distort incoming data and make erroneous decisions. These vulnerabilities are not limited to fingerprint experts and apply equally to other domains. However, the importance of fingerprint evidence being reliable and unbiasable requires that these potential weaknesses be addressed. To achieve this, systematic research must be conducted to examine the cognitive and psychological elements involved in fingerprint identification.

15.5 References

Ahissar, M.; Hochstein, S. Task Difficulty and the Specificity of Perceptual Learning. *Nature* 1997, *387*, 401–406.

Anderson, J. R.; Schooler, L. J. Reflections of the Environment in Memory. *Psychol. Sci.* 1991, *2*, 396–408.

Ashworth, A. R. S.; Dror, I. E. Object Identification as a Function of Discriminability and Learning Presentations: The Effect of Stimulus Similarity and Canonical Frame Alignment on Aircraft Identification. *J. Exp. Psychol.: Applied* 2000, *6* (2), 148–157.

Baker, C.; Behrmann, M.; Olson, C.R. Impact of Learning on Representation of Parts and Wholes in Monkey Inferotemporal Cortex. *Nature Neurosci.* 2002, *5*, 1210–1216.

Balcetis, E.; Dunning, D. See What You Want to See: Motivational Influences on Visual Perception. *J. Pers. and Soc. Psychol.* 2006, *91*, 612–625.

Barlow, H. Conditions for Versatile Learning, Helmholtz's Unconscious Inference, and Task of Perception. *Vision Res.* 1990, *30,* 1561–1571.

Baumeister, R. F.; Newman, L. S. Self-Regulation of Cognitive Inference and Decision Processes. *Pers. Soc. Psychol. Bull.* 1994, *20,* 3–19.

Blaha, L. M.; Townsend, J. T. Parts to Wholes: Configural Learning Fundamentally Changes the Visual Information Processing System [Abstract]. *J. Vision* 2006, *6* (6), 675a.

Burns, B.; Shepp, B. E. Dimensional Interactions and the Structure of Psychological Space: The Representation of Hue, Saturation and Brightness. *Percept. Psychophys.* 1988, *43,* 494–507.

Busey, T. Physical and Psychological Representations of Faces: Evidence From Morphing. *Psychol. Sci.* 1998, *9,* 476–482.

Busey, T. A.; Tunnicliff, J. Accounts of Blending, Typicality and Distinctiveness in Face Recognition. *J. Exp. Psychol.: Learning, Memory, and Cognition* 1999, *25,* 1210–1235.

Busey, T. A.; Vanderkolk, J. R. Behavioral and Electrophysiological Evidence for Configural Processing in Fingerprint Experts. *Vision Res.* 2005, *45,* 431–448.

Byrne, A.; Eysenck, M. W. Individual Differences in Positive and Negative Interpretive Biases. *Pers. and Indiv. Diff.* 1993, *14,* 849–851.

Charlton, D.; Fraser-Mackenzie, P.; Dror, I. E. Emotional Experiences and Motivating Factors Associated With Fingerprint Analysis. *J. Forensic Sci.*, in press, 55 (3).

Changizi, M. A.; Hall, W. G. Thirst Modulates a Perception. *Percept.* 2001, *30,* 1489–1497.

Czerwinski, M.; Lightfoot, N.; Shiffrin, R. M. Automatization and Training in Visual Search. *Am. J. Psychol.* 1992, *105* (22), 271–315.

Darley, J. M.; Latané, B. Bystander Intervention in Emergency: Diffusion of Responsibilities. *J. Pers. Soc. Psychol.* 1968, *10,* 202–214.

Dascal, M.; Dror, I. E. The Impact of Cognitive Technologies: Towards a Pragmatic Approach. *Pragmatics and Cognition* 2005, *13* (3), 451–457.

Davis, C. J.; Hufnagel, E. M. Through the Eyes of Experts: A Sociocognitive Perspective on the Automation of Fingerprint Work. *MIS Quarterly* 2007, *31* (4), 681–703.

Dosher, B.; Lu, Z.-L. Perceptual Learning in Clear Displays Optimizes Perceptual Expertise: Learning the Limiting Process. *PNAS* 2005, *102* (14), 5286–5290.

Dror, I. E. The Effects of Screening, Training, and Experience of Air Force Fighter Pilots: The Plasticity of the Ability to Extrapolate and Track Multiple Objects in Motion. *North Am. J. Psychol.* 2004, *6* (2), 239–252.

Dror, I. E. Perception Is Far From Perfection: The Role of the Brain and Mind in Constructing Realities. *Brain Behav. Sci.* 2005a, *28* (6), 763.

Dror, I. E. Technology and Human Expertise: Some Do's and Don'ts. *Biometric Tech. Today* 2005b, *13* (9), 7–9.

Dror, I. E. Cognitive Science Serving Security: Assuring Useable and Efficient Biometric and Technological Solutions. *Aviation Secur. Int.* 2006, *12* (3), 21–28.

Dror, I. E. Biased Brains. *Police Rev.* 2008, *116,* 20–23.

Dror, I. E. How Can Francis Bacon Help Forensic Science? The Four Idols of Human Biases. *Jurimetrics* 2009a, *50,* 93–110.

Dror, I. E. On Proper Research and Understanding of the Interplay Between Bias and Decision Outcomes. *Forensic Sci. Int.* 2009b, *191,* 17–18.

Dror, I. E. Paradoxical Functional Degradation in Human Expertise. In *The Paradoxical Brain;* Kapur, N., Pascual-Leone, A., Ramachandran, V. S., Eds.; Cambridge University Press: Cambridge, U.K., in press.

Dror, I. E.; Busemeyer, J. R.; Basola, B. Decision Making Under Time Pressure: An Independent Test of Sequential Sampling Models. *Memory and Cognition* 1999, *27* (4), 713–725.

Dror, I. E.; Charlton, D. Why Experts Make Errors. *J. Forensic Ident.* 2006, *56* (4), 600–616.

Dror, I. E.; Charlton, D.; Péron, A. E. Contextual Information Renders Experts Vulnerable to Making Erroneous Identifications. *Forensic Sci. Int.* 2006, *156* (1), 74–78.

Dror, I. E.; Fraser-Mackenzie, P. Cognitive Biases in Human Perception, Judgment, and Decision Making: Bridging Theory and the Real World. In *Criminal Investigative Failures;* Rossmo, K., Ed.; Taylor and Francis Publishing, 2008; pp 53–67.

Dror, I. E.; Kosslyn, S. M.; Waag, W. Visual-Spatial Abilities of Pilots. *J. Appl. Psychol.* 1993, *78* (5), 763–773.

Dror, I. E.; Mnookin, J. L. The Use of Technology in Human Expert Domains: Challenges and Risks Arising From the Use of Automated Fingerprint Identification Systems in Forensics. *Law Probabil. Risk* 2010, *9* (1), 47–67.

Dror, I. E.; Péron, A.; Hind, S.; Charlton, D. When Emotions Get the Better of Us: The Effect of Contextual Top-Down Processing on Matching Fingerprints. *Appl. Cognitive Psychol.* 2005, *19* (6), 799–809.

Dror, I. E.; Rosenthal, R. Meta-Analytically Quantifying the Reliability and Biasability of Fingerprint Experts' Decision Making. *J. Forensic Sci.* 2008, *53* (4), 900–903.

Dror, I. E.; Schmitz-Williams, I. C.; Smith, W. Older Adults Use Mental Representations That Reduce Cognitive Load: Mental Rotation Utilises Holistic Representations and Processing. *Exp. Aging Res.* 2005, *31* (4), 409–420.

Dror, I. E.; Stevenage, S.; Ashworth, A. Helping the Cognitive System Learn: Exaggerating Distinctiveness and Uniqueness. *Appl. Cognitive Psychol.* 2008, *22* (4), 573–585.

Fahle, M.; Edelman, S. Long-Term Learning in Vernier Acuity: Effects of Stimulus Orientation, Range and of Feedback. *Vision Res.* 1993, *33*, 397–412.

Fiser, J.; Aslin, R. N. Unsupervised Statistical Learning of Higher-Order Spatial Structures from Visual Scenes. *Psychol. Sci.* 2001, *12* (6), 499–504.

Fusi, S.; Drew, P.; Abbott, L. Cascade Models of Synaptically Stored Memories. *Neuron* 2005, *45*, 599–611.

Garner, W. R. Interaction of Stimulus Dimensions in Concept and Choice Processes. *Cognitive Psychol.* 1976, *8*, 98–123.

Gauthier, I.; Williams, P.; Tarr, M.; Tanaka, J. Training 'Greeble' Experts: A Framework for Studying Expert Object Recognition Processes. *Vision Res.* 1998, *38*, 2401–2428.

Gold, J.; Bennett, P. J.; Sekuler, A. B. Signal but Not Noise Changes With Perceptual Learning. *Nature* 1999, *402*.

Goldstone, R. L. Isolated and Interrelated Concepts. *Memory and Cognition* 1996, *24*, 608–628.

Goldstone, R. L. Similarity. In *MIT Encyclopedia of the Cognitive Sciences;* Wilson, R. A., Keil, F. C., Eds.; MIT Press: Cambridge, MA, 1999; pp 763–765.

Goldstone, R. L. Unitization During Category Learning. *J. Exp. Psychol.: General* 2000, *123*, 178–200.

Goldstone, R. L.; Steyvers, M. The Sensitization and Differentiation of Dimensions During Category Learning. *J. Exp. Psychol.: General* 2001, *130*, 116–139.

Greenwald, A. G. New Look 3: Unconscious Cognition Reclaimed. *Am. Psychol.* 1992, *47*, 766–779.

Haber, L.; Haber, N. H. Error Rates for Human Latent Fingerprint Examiners. In *Advances in Automatic Fingerprint Recognition;* Ratha, N., Bolle, R., Eds.; Springer-Verlag: New York, 2004; pp 337–358.

Halberstadt, J. B.; Niedenthal, P. M.; Kushner, J. Resolution of Lexical Ambiguity by Emotional State. *Psychol. Sci.* 1995, *6*, 278–282.

Hall, L. J.; Player, E. Will the Instruction of an Emotional Context Affect Fingerprint Analysis and Decision Making? *Forensic Sci. Int.* 2008, *181*, 36–39.

Humphreys, G. W.; Riddoch, M. J.; Price, C. J. Top-Down Processes in Object Identification: Evidence From Experimental Psychology, Neuropsychology, and Functional Anatomy. *Philos. Trans. Royal Soc. London* 1997, *352*, 1275–1282.

Kanizsa, G. Subjective Contours. *Sci. Am.* 1976, *234*, 48–52.

Kepecs, A.; Wang, X.; Lisman, J. Bursting Neurons Signal Input Slope. *J. Neurosci.* 2002, *22*, 9053–9062.

Kosslyn, S. M.; Koenig, O. *Wet Mind;* Free Press: New York, 1992.

Kunda, Z. The Case for Motivated Reasoning. *Psychol. Bull.* 1990, *108*, 480–498.

Lang, P. J.; Bradley, M. M.; Cuthbert, B. N. *International Affective Picture System (IAPS): Technical Manual and*

Affective Ratings. University of Florida, The Center for Research in Psychophysiology: Gainesville, FL, 1995.

Langenburg, G.; Champod, C.; Wertheim, P. Testing for Potential Contextual Bias Effects During the Verification Stage of the ACE-V Methodology When Conducting Fingerprint Comparisons. *J. Forensic Sci.* 2009, *54* (3), 571–582.

Leventhal, A. G.; Hirsch, H. V. Effects of Early Experience Upon Orientation Sensitivity and Binocularity of Neurons in Visual Cortex of Cats. *Proc. Natl. Acad. Sci. U.S.A.* 1977, *74*, 1272–1276.

Lu, Z.-L.; Dosher, B. A. Perceptual Learning Retunes the Perceptual Template in Foveal Orientation Identification. *J. Vision* 2004, *4*, 44–56.

Maddox, T.; Ing, D. Delayed Feedback Disrupts the Procedural-Learning System but Not the Hypothesis-Testing System in Perceptual Category Learning. *J. Exp. Psychol.: Learning, Memory, and Cognition* 2005, *31* (1), 100–107.

Marr, D. *Vision.* Freeman Press: San Francisco, 1982.

Müller-Lyer, F. C. *Arch. Anat. Physiol. (Physiol. Abt.)* 2, 1889, 263–270.

Newell, A.; Rosenbloom, P. Mechanisms of Skill Acquisition and the Law of Practice. In *Learning and Cognition;* Anderson, J. R., Ed.; Erlbaum: Hillsdale, NJ, 1981.

Niedenthal, P. M.; Halberstadt, J. B.; Margolin, J.; Innes-Ker, A. H. Emotional State and the Detection of Change in Facial Expression of Emotion. *Eur. J. Soc. Psychol.* 2000, *30*, 211–222.

O'Toole, A. J.; Wenger, M. J.; Townsend, J. T. Quantitative Models of Perceiving and Remembering Faces: Precedent and Possibilities. In *Computational, Geometric and Process Issues in Facial Cognition: Progress and Challenges;* Wenger, M. J., Townsend, J. T., Eds.; Erlbaum: Hillsdale, NJ, 2001; p 50.

Restle, F.; Decker, J. Size of the Mueller-Lyer Illusion as a Function of Its Dimensions: Theory and Data. *Percept. Psychophys.* 1977, 21, 489–503.

Schiffer, B.; Champod, C. The Potential (Negative) Influence of Observational Biases at the Analysis Stage of Fingermark Individualisation. *Forensic Sci. Int.* 2007, *167,* 116–120.

Schyns, P. G.; Rodet, L. Categorization Creates Functional Features. *J. Exp. Psychol.: Learning, Memory, and Cognition* 1997, *23*, 681–696.

Shepard, R. N. Psychophysical Complementarity. In *Perceptual Organization;* Kubovy, M., Pomerantz, J. R., Eds.; Erlbaum: Hillsdale, NJ, 1981; pp 279–341.

Shiffrin, R. M.; Lightfoot, N. Perceptual Learning of Alphanumeric like Characters. In *The Psychology of Learning and Motivation;* Goldstone, R. L., Schyns, P. G., Medin, D. L., Eds.; Academic Press: San Diego, 1997; Vol. 36, pp 45–82.

Smith W.; Dror, I. E. The Role of Meaning and Familiarity in Mental Transformations. *Psychonomic Bull. Rev.* 2001, *8*, 732–741.

Snyder, M.; Tanke, E. D.; Bersheid, E. Social Perception and Interpersonal Behavior: On the Self-Fulfilling Nature of Social Stereotypes. *J. Pers. Soc. Psychol.* 1977, *35*, 656–666.

Sperling, G. The Information Available in Brief Visual Presentations. *Psychol. Monogr.* 1960, *74*, 1–29.

Steyvers, M.; Busey, T. Predicting Similarity Ratings to Faces Using Physical Descriptions. In *Computational, Geometric, and Process Perspectives on Facial Cognition;* Wenger, M. J., Townsend, J. T., Eds.; Erlbaum: Hillsdale, NJ, 2001.

Treisman, A.; Gelade, G. A Feature-Integration Theory of Attention. *Cognitive Psychol.* 1980, *12*, 97–136.

Turk-Browne, N.; Jungé, J.; Scholl, B. The Automaticity of Visual Statistical Learning. *J. Exp. Psychol.: General* 2005, *134* (4), 552–564.

Valentine, T. A Unified Account of the Effects of Distinctiveness, Inversion, and Race in Face Recognition. *J. Exp. Psychol.* 1991, *43A*, 161–204.

Wenger, M. J.; Rasche, C. Perceptual Learning in Contrast Detection: Presence and Costs of Shifts in Response Criteria. *Psychonomic Bull. Rev.* 2006, *13* (4), 656–661.

Wertheim, K.; Langenburg, G.; Moenssens, A. A Report of Latent Print Examiner Accuracy During Comparison Training Exercises. *J. Forensic Ident.* 2006, *56* (1), 55–93.

Zhang, L.; Cottrell, G. W. When Holistic Processing Is Not Enough: Local Features Save the Day. In *Proceedings of the 26th Annual Cognitive Science Conference,* Chicago, IL, 2004.

APPENDIX A: AUTHOR AND REVIEWER BIOGRAPHIES

Jeffery G. Barnes

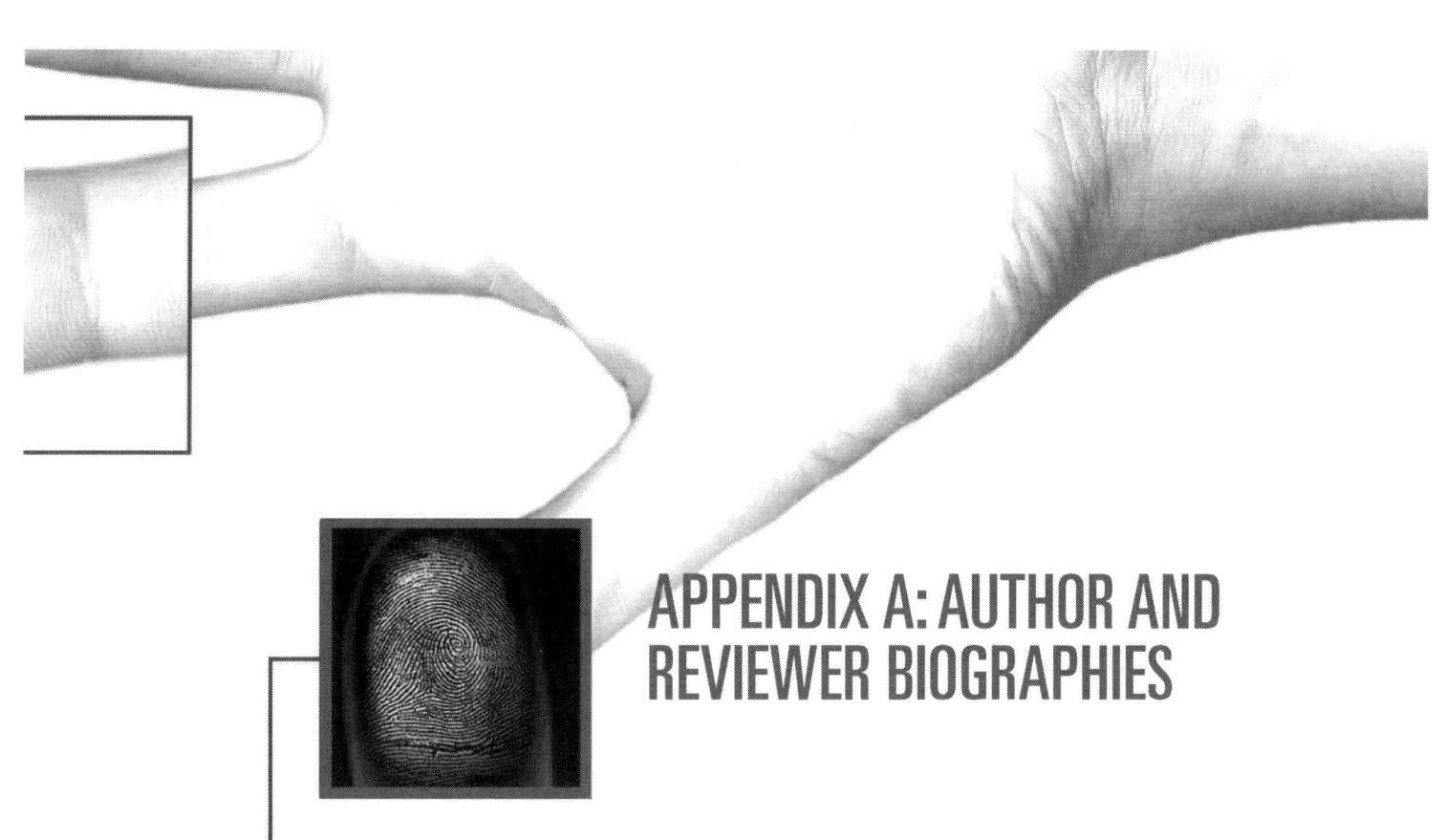

Jeffery G. Barnes double majored at Virginia Wesleyan College, earning a bachelor of arts degree in chemistry and philosophy. He completed graduate school at Virginia Polytechnic Institute and State University, receiving a master of science degree in chemistry. He worked for approximately five years with the City of Virginia Beach Police Department as a forensics services technician, where he earned several awards for his outstanding work. He has been with the Federal Bureau of Investigation (FBI) for almost six years and has earned four on-the-spot awards for excellent performance of duties. As a physical scientist forensic examiner with the latent print operations unit of the FBI Laboratory, he teaches and continues to research the history of the fingerprint science.

Author of Chapter 1 – History. Chapters reviewed: 2, Anatomy and Physiology of Adult Friction Ridge Skin; 3, Embryology, Physiology, and Morphology

Debbie Benningfield

Debbie Benningfield is retired from the latent print laboratory section of the Houston Police Department, where she served for nearly 31 years. Her assignments included tenprint work, automated fingerprint identification systems manager, and deputy administrator. Currently, she is an instructor for Ron Smith and Associates, Inc. She is a certified latent print examiner. In 2003, she was appointed a member of the Scientific Working Group on Friction Ridge Analysis, Study, and Technology and in 2004, she was appointed to the International Association for Identification (IAI) Latent Print Certification Board. In January 2006, the Governor of Texas appointed her as the presiding officer over the newly created Texas Forensic Science Commission. In June 2006, Ms. Benningfield was elected president of the Texas Division of the IAI.

Chapters reviewed: 1, History; 9, Examination Process

APPENDIX A | Author and Reviewer Biographies

Herman Bergman

Herman Bergman started his career in 1995 at the tenprint section of the Dutch Criminal Intelligence Service (CRI). He received in-house education and training in fingerprint history, biology, classification, and automated fingerprint identification systems. He moved to the latent fingerprint section in 1999 and received additional training in development techniques, palmprint comparison, methodology, and AFIS processing. He was certified as a latent print examiner at the Crime Control and Investigation Training Institute in the Netherlands. He is a member of the Ridgeology Working Group (the group's purpose is to assess the desirability of adopting a non-numeric system in the Netherlands), and he has participated in developing a curriculum for latent print examiners seeking certification at the Police Academy. He was also a visiting instructor in the certification program at the Crime Control and Investigation Training Institute. He is a member of the International Association for Identification and the Scientific Working Group on Friction Ridge Analysis, Study, and Technology.

Chapters reviewed: 4, Recording Living and Postmortem Friction Ridge Exemplars; 8, The Preservation of Friction Ridge Information; 9, Examination Process

Steve Bleay

Steve Bleay obtained a bachelor of science degree in materials science from the University of Bath in 1988 and remained at the University of Bath carrying out postgraduate research in electron microscopy of composite materials until 1993. He was awarded a doctor of philosophy degree in 1991. He joined the Defence Research Agency (later QinetiQ) in 1993 and spent 10 years developing stealth materials and carrying out research into the production of novel fibre systems. He joined the Home Office Scientific Development Branch in May 2003 and has been working on novel vacuum metal deposition techniques, recovery of fingerprints from arson scenes, development and production of the IRIS workstation, and digital imaging.

Contributing Author of Chapter 7 – Latent Print Development

Patti Blume

Patti Blume has more than 28 years of experience working for the Orange County (California) Sheriff's Department. Currently, she is a senior forensic specialist assigned to the automated fingerprint identification system (AFIS) unit as the system administrator. Previously, she worked in the Sheriff's Identification Bureau and was assigned to special projects while performing crime scene investigations, impression evidence examinations, latent print comparisons, and evidence processing. Her special projects have included being a project coordinator for accreditation by the American Society of Crime Laboratory Directors/Laboratory Accreditation Board, and she is currently coordinating accreditation for her agency's AFIS system. She has been a regular instructor for the California Department of Justice/California Criminalistics Training Institute, teaching latent print comparisons and latent print techniques. Currently, she is on the editorial board of the *Journal of Forensic Identification* and has participated on the FBI Permanency Project on the persistency of ridge detail. She has an associate of science degree in evidence technology and a bachelor of science degree in public administration, and belongs to various forensic professional organizations.

Chapters reviewed: 2, Anatomy and Physiology of Adult Friction Ridge Skin; 3, Embryology, Physiology, and Morphology; 4, Recording Living and Postmortem Friction Ridge Exemplars; 6, Automated Fingerprint Identification Systems (AFIS); 9, Examination Process; 12, Quality Assurance

Donna Brandelli

Donna Brandelli has a bachelor of science degree in criminal justice from California State University and a master of science degree in forensic science from National University. She is completing her doctor of philosophy degree in human behavior with a focus on criminal justice through Capella University. She is a recipient of the William C. Battles Achievement Award in Criminal Justice and past president of the local division of the Alpha Phi Sigma Criminal Justice Honor Society. She is a member of the American Academy of Forensic Sciences, the Academy of Criminal Justice Sciences, and the International Association for Identification, and is on the editorial board of the *Journal of Forensic Identification*. She has testified as an expert witness in the areas of fingerprint comparison, chemical processing, and crime scene investigation. She created and presented a training class on crime scene preservation geared to first responders, which has been presented to municipal, county, and federal agencies across the country. She is a research partner with the FBI regarding the permanence of friction ridge skin. As an adjunct faculty member, she has taught Introduction to Forensic Science, Introduction to Criminology, and Introduction to Policing and Contemporary Issues in Law Enforcement at the University of Phoenix and American InterContinental University.

Chapter reviewed: 13, Fingerprints and the Law

Mary Ann Brandon

Criminalist Mary Ann Brandon, certified latent print examiner, has been involved in friction ridge science with the Portland (Oregon) Police Bureau for more than 29 years. With two other examiners, she researched and published *"Cloned" Primates and the Possibility of Identical Fingerprints*. Sponsored by the Portland Police Bureau and the International Association for Identification, she initiated the TwinPrint Study in 2000. She taught Forensic Science and Criminal Investigation at Portland Community College for eight years and recently obtained her certification as a medicolegal death investigator in Oregon. She has served on the Scientific Working Group on Friction Ridge Analysis, Study, and Technology for 10 years.

Chapters reviewed: 2, Anatomy and Physiology of Adult Friction Ridge Skin; 3, Embryology, Physiology, and Morphology

Thomas Busey

Thomas Busey received his bachelor of arts degree from Cornell University in 1988 and his doctor of philosophy degree in cognitive psychology from the University of Washington in 1994. He has been on the faculty at Indiana University in the Department of Psychological and Brain Sciences since 1994. He is currently funded by the National Institute of Justice to identify the nature of human expertise in latent print examiners with the goal of improving the understanding of the quantitative analyses of fingerprints.

Coauthor of Chapter 15 – Special Abilities and Vulnerabilities in Forensic Expertise

Leonard G. Butt

Leonard G. Butt is currently employed with the Maryland State Police, Forensic Sciences Division as a forensic scientist. Previously, he worked as a fingerprint specialist for the Drug Enforcement Administration. He is retired from the Baltimore County, Maryland Police Department. His assignments there included crime scene technician, latent print examiner, identification unit supervisor, and interim crime laboratory director. He served on the Printrak AFIS Users' Group Executive Committee and represented the International Association for Identification in the Federal Bureau of Investigation's IAFIS Working Group. Mr. Butt is a certified latent print examiner and a graduate of the FBI National Academy. He is the current chairman of the Scientific Working Group on Friction Ridge Analysis, Study, and Technology.

Chapters reviewed: 9, Examination Process; 10, Documentation of Friction Ridge Impressions: From the Scene to the Conclusion; 14, Scientific Research in the Forensic Discipline of Friction Ridge Individualization

Mike Campbell

Captain of Police Mike Campbell (retired) is a 28 year veteran of the City of Milwaukee Police Department, and served as the commanding officer of its identification division. Upon retirement, he took a position as a training coordinator with Ron Smith and Associates, Inc., a forensic training and consulting company based in Collinsville, Mississippi. He had more than 20 years of experience as a crime scene and fingerprint identification specialist with the department. He was responsible for the day-to-day operation of the crime scene response unit; all evidence photography and digital imaging systems; and the procurement and operation of the department-wide booking, AFIS, and criminal history systems. He has taught more than 250 courses and lectured numerous times on these matters to several thousand students in 25 states and Canada during the last 15 years. He is a member of the Scientific Working Group on Friction Ridge Analysis, Study, and Technology and serves on the International Association of Chiefs of Police Forensic Committee and on the Board of Directors for the International Association for Identification (IAI). Mr. Campbell is a past president of the Wisconsin Law Enforcement Executive Development Association and the Wisconsin Division of the IAI. He also holds active memberships in the Canadian Identification Society and the Midwest Association of Forensic Scientists.

Chapters reviewed: 1, History; 4, Recording Living and Postmortem Friction Ridge Exemplars; 5, Systems of Friction Ridge Classification; 9, Examination Process

Antonio A. Cantu

Antonio Cantu's interests include the chemistry of documents and the chemistry of fingerprints. He received his doctor of philosophy degree in chemical physics from the University of Texas in Austin, Texas. He began his government career in 1972 with what is now the National Institute of Justice. A year later he joined the Bureau of Alcohol, Tobacco, and Firearms. He then joined the Federal Bureau of Investigation in 1983. In 1985, Dr. Cantu joined the U.S. Secret Service and devoted his first eight years to the area of technical security. For the next three years, he developed scientific methods for determining the source of counterfeit currency. After that, he was with the Forensic Services Division, becoming the Chief Scientist. He retired from the U.S. Secret Service in April 2007. He has published many articles, mostly regarding ink analysis and latent print chemical development. In 1980, he received the Forensic Scientist of the Year Award from the Mid-Atlantic Association of Forensic Scientists and in 2002, he received the highly coveted Paul L. Kirk Award from the American Academy of Forensic Sciences.

Contributing Author of Chapter 7 – Latent Print Development

Christophe Champod

Christophe Champod received his master of science degree and doctor of philosophy degree (summa cum laude) in forensic science from the University of Lausanne in 1990 and 1995, respectively. He remained in academia until holding the position of assistant professor in forensic science. From 1999 to 2003, he led the Interpretation Research Group of the Forensic Science Service (United Kingdom), before taking a professorship position at the School of Criminal Sciences (ESC)/Institute of Forensic Science (IPS) of the University of Lausanne. Mr. Champod co-authored the book *Fingerprints and Other Ridge Skin Impressions* (CRC Press, 2004). He is in charge of education and research on identification methods (detection and identification). He is a member of the International Association for Identification and of the Scientific Working Group on Friction Ridge Analysis, Study, and Technology. His research is devoted to the statistical evaluation of forensic identification techniques. The value of fingerprint evidence is at the core of his interests.

Chapters reviewed: 1, History; 6, Automated Fingerprint Identification Systems (AFIS); 7, Latent Print Development; 14, Scientific Research in the Forensic Discipline of Friction Ridge Individualization

Sue Manci Coppejans

Sue Manci Coppejans has worked in the forensic science field with the Alabama Department of Forensic Sciences since June 1992. She is a certified latent fingerprint examiner. She has a bachelor of science degree from the University of South Alabama. She served on the International Association for Identification Latent Fingerprint Certification Board from 1999 to 2003. She has served as a member of the Scientific Working Group on Friction Ridge Analysis, Study, and Technology for the past four years. She has taught numerous classes and given presentations on the topic of fingerprints at international and local meetings.

Chapters reviewed: 4, Recording Living and Postmortem Friction Ridge Exemplars; 7, Latent Print Development

Christine L. Craig

Christine Craig is a crime scene analyst and a footwear and tire track examiner at the Seminole County Sheriff's Office in Sanford, Florida. She is a member of the International Association for Identification and is a certified footwear examiner and certified crime scene analyst. She is also a regional team leader for the fingerprinting section of the Florida Emergency Mortuary Operations Response System.

Ms. Craig has a master of science degree in biology from Virginia Commonwealth University and is currently obtaining a doctor of philosophy degree in ecology at the University of Florida.

Chapters reviewed: 1, History; 7, Latent Print Development

Brent T. Cutro, Sr.

Brent Cutro, currently employed by the Illinois State Police Forensic Sciences Command, began his career in forensic sciences in 1981 after receiving a bachelor of science degree in biology from George Williams College. He has held various positions relating to the science of latent print examination. Some of these positions include latent print section quality assurance coordinator, latent print section advisory committee member, research advisory committee member, and section supervisor. Additionally, he served on Illinois' first AFIS committee in its inaugural year. He is a member of the International Association for Identification and the Midwestern Association of Forensic Scientists, and is a Fellow of the Fingerprint Society. He has been involved with various research projects, most notably including one entitled "A Water Soluble Non-Carcinogenic Fluorescent Pigment as an Alternative to Rhodamine 6G," which was presented at the FBI International Forensic Symposium on Latent Prints held in Quantico, Virginia. In addition to his duties as a latent print examiner for the Illinois State Police, Mr. Cutro has taught many latent print courses, workshops, and classes. He continues to lecture for several colleges and universities and is currently an instructor with North East Multi-Regional Training, Inc., an Illinois law enforcement training organization.

Author of Chapter 4 – Recording Living and Postmortem Friction Ridge Exemplars. Chapters reviewed: 2, Anatomy and Physiology of Adult Friction Ridge Skin; 3, Embryology, Physiology, and Morphology; 9, Examination Process; 10, Documentation of Friction Ridge Impressions: From the Scene to the Conclusion

Itiel E. Dror

Dr. Itiel Dror has expertise and a proven track record in conducting scientific research as well as in improving human performance in applied expert domains. He has a Ph.D. from Harvard University in Psychology and Cognitive Science, and he has published over 75 scientific articles. Dr. Dror has provided training workshops and consultancy to medical doctors, surgeons, frontline police, military fighter pilots, financial executives, forensic examiners, and experts in other domains, all aimed at enhancing decisionmaking and performance. Dr. Dror has worked with a variety of governmental bodies (such as the U.S. Air Force, the U.K. Army and MoD, the U.K. Passport and Identity Services, and Police Forces in the United States, United Kingdom, the Netherlands and Israel). His work focuses on perception, judgement, and decisionmaking, and how expertise, training, and technology can improve performance at the workplace. Dr. Dror divides his time between academia, at University College London (UCL), and applied research and consultancy, at Cognitive Consultants International (CCI). More information is available at: www.cci-hq.com.

Coauthor of Chapter 15 – Special Abilities and Vulnerabilities in Forensic Expertise

Jeri Eaton

Jeri Eaton worked for the King County Sheriff's Department for 20 years and was the supervisor of the latent fingerprint unit. Prior to King County, she worked for the Iowa Division of Criminal Investigation as a latent examiner, crime scene investigator, and forensic photographer. She chairs the Pacific Northwest Region Latent Print Certification Board and is a member of the International Association for Identification (IAI) Crime Scene Certification Board as well as a member of the IAI AFIS Committee. For the past seven years, she has been a member of the Scientific Working Group for Friction Ridge Analysis, Study, and Technology. Ms. Eaton is a past president of the Pacific Northwest Division of the International Association for Identification. She is a certified latent print examiner and certified senior crime scene analyst. She has made presentations and published articles for the IAI and recently conducted a worldwide study on the uniqueness of latent fingerprints for which publication is pending.

Chapter reviewed: 6, Automated Fingerprint Identification Systems (AFIS); 8, The Preservation of Friction Ridge Information

Wayne Eaton

Wayne Eaton is the forensic operations manager for the King County Sheriff's Office Regional AFIS System. Prior to

APPENDIX A | Author and Reviewer Biographies

King County, he managed automated fingerprint identification system (AFIS) and livescan implementation projects for several state and local law enforcement agencies, including integration with other criminal justice systems. He worked with international standards organizations and international focus groups to facilitate AFIS interoperability. Mr. Eaton was manager of systems engineering for 10 years for Sagem Morpho, an AFIS vendor. Before that he worked as a forensic scientist for the Iowa Division of Criminal Investigation Crime Laboratory. He holds a bachelor of science degree in chemistry from Central University of Iowa and a master of business administration degree from City University.

Chapter reviewed: 6, Automated Fingerprint Identification Systems (AFIS)

Michael K. French

Michael K. French is a certified latent print examiner with 13 years of experience in law enforcement and private consultation. He has extensive experience in the development, imaging, examination, and electronic searching of fingerprint evidence, as well as expertise in writing laboratory development, hygiene, and safety guidelines. As a consultant, he specializes in reviewing lab procedures, auditing fingerprint-related casework, and training students in forensic evidence techniques. He worked for the King County Sheriff's Office from 1994 to 2006, where he was a lead examiner during the Green River Homicide Investigation. He has a bachelor of arts degree in public safety from Central Washington University.

Coauthor of Chapter 7 – Latent Print Development

Deborah Friedman

Deborah Friedman holds a master of science degree in forensic chemistry and a masters in business administration. She has more than 25 years of working experience in a crime laboratory. This experience encompasses the forensic science disciplines of trace evidence, biology, latent prints, controlled substances, and crime scene investigations. During the last seven years, she has been employed as the quality manager for the Broward Sheriff's Office Regional Crime Laboratory. Deborah Friedman is one of the founding members and current president of the Association of Forensic Quality Assurance Managers.

Chapters reviewed: 1, History; 12, Quality Assurance; 14, Fingerprints and the Law

Robert J. Garrett

Robert J. Garrett spent more than 30 years in law enforcement. He attended Rutgers University and is a graduate of the New Jersey State Police Academy. Before retiring, he was the supervisor of the crime scene unit of the Middlesex County Prosecutor's Office in New Jersey. Mr. Garrett has authored many articles relating to crime scene subjects and has testified as an expert on a variety of forensic disciplines. He has been a lecturer at state, regional, and international conferences and serves on the editorial board of the *Journal of Forensic Identification*. He served on the Board of Directors of the International Association for Identification and is currently its second vice president, and chairs the association's professional review board. He is certified by the IAI as a senior crime scene analyst and latent print examiner. He is a Fellow of the Fingerprint Society of Great Britain.

Chapters reviewed: 4, Recording Living and Postmortem Friction Ridge Exemplars; 6, Automated Fingerprint Identification Systems (AFIS); 7, Latent Print Development; 8, The Preservation of Friction Ridge Information; 9, Examination Process; 10, Documentation of Friction Ridge Impressions: From the Scene to the Conclusion; 11, Equipment; 14, Scientific Research in the Forensic Discipline of Friction Ridge Individualization

M. Leanne Gray

M. Leanne Gray earned her bachelor of science degree at Northeast Missouri State University. She is a forensic scientist in the United States specializing in latent fingerprint and footwear examination at a state crime laboratory system. She has worked thousands of cases during the past 20 years and has acted as a quality assurance coordinator for both the latent fingerprint and footwear sections. In addition, she has been a training coordinator and was responsible for developing and implementing a comprehensive training program in the area of latent fingerprint examination. She also provides training and consultation via her private business, Gray's Forensic Fingerprint Training & Consultation, which is based in Oregon, Wisconsin. She is a certified latent print examiner.

Author of Chapter 12 – Quality Assurance. Chapter reviewed: 9, Examination Process

Lynne D. Herold

Lynne Herold received her bachelor of science degree from Kent State University in 1974 and her doctor of philosophy degree in biology sciences from the University of Southern California in 1984. She taught Histology at the University of Southern California while completing her doctorate degree and has worked as an adjunct faculty member for the Union Institute and University. She began her career in criminalistics in 1984 with the Los Angeles County Coroner's office. In 1989, she transferred to the Los Angeles Sheriff's Department Scientific Services Bureau, where she is currently employed as a senior criminalist. Her biological studies and specific interest in the microscopic identification of botanical and animal tissues and their structure has been instrumental in providing a foundation for her testimony in many cases in the United States and internationally. She has presented papers and made poster presentations at numerous symposiums and professional seminars conducted by the Federal Bureau of Investigation, the California Association of Criminalists, and the American Academy of Forensic Sciences.

Chapters reviewed: 2, Anatomy and Physiology of Adult Friction Ridge Skin; 3, Embryology, Physiology, and Morphology

Peter T. Higgins

Peter T. Higgins earned a master of science degree in mathematics and computer science from Stevens Institute of Technology in Hoboken, New Jersey. He began his professional career as a mathematician with the U.S. Central Intelligence Agency. He served in various capacities at that agency, to include establishing the Chief Information Technology office and managing research in biometrics. He then joined the Federal Bureau of Investigation in 1992, where he was responsible for the development of the integrated automatic fingerprint identification system (IAFIS). He became the deputy assistant director and was in charge of engineering in the FBI Criminal Justice Information Services Division. He retired from the FBI in 1995 and has been involved with fingerprint agencies in several countries, providing consulting services. He chaired the IAI AFIS committee for five years. He has published in biometrics and AFIS technology. He has lectured at the university level on AFIS and biometric technology.

Contributing Author of Chapter 6 – Automated Fingerprint Identification Systems (AFIS)

Laura A. Hutchins

Laura A. Hutchins has over nine years of experience as a latent fingerprint examiner and is currently employed at the United States Secret Service. Ms. Hutchins received her training at the Federal Bureau of Investigation's (FBI) Laboratory Latent Print Unit. In addition to her FBI latent print certification, she is certified by the International Association for Identification (IAI). Ms. Hutchins is extremely active in the field of friction ridge identification. She has been a member of the Scientific Working Group on Friction Ridge Analysis, Study, and Technology (SWGFAST) since 2005 and is a current board member of and Web editor for the IAI. Additionally, she is a technical reviewer for the *Journal of Forensic Identification* and is the editor for the Chesapeake Bay Division of the IAI. Ms. Hutchins is a member of an Intra-agency working group established by the National Science and Technology Council. Additionally, she has experience business process mapping crime laboratories in order to streamline and implement process improvement. Ms. Hutchins received a Bachelor of Arts degree in anthropology from Marquette University and a Master of Science degree in biological anthropology from the University of Wisconsin.

Author of Chapters: 5, Systems of Friction Ridge Classification; 8, The Preservation of Friction Ridge Information. Chapters reviewed: 1, History; 4, Recording Living and Postmortem Friction Ridge Exemplars; 6, Automated Fingerprint Identification Systems (AFIS); 9, Examination Process

Charles P. Illsley

Charles P. Illsley is a certified latent print examiner with 30 years of experience in various types of forensics examinations. He has testified as an expert witness in laser and forensic light technology, fingerprint identification, and clandestine drug lab manufacture in California, Idaho, Utah, and New York. He retired after 25 years of service with two Utah police departments. Now Mr. Illsley is a part-time forensic consultant for the Utah Attorney General's Office and also consults with various law enforcement agencies on cold case forensics examinations. Mr. Illsley is a life active member of the International Association for Identification. He served on the International Association of Identification Board of Directors and as president in 1998. He is a published author and lectures throughout the United States and Canada on various forensic and expert witness issues. He currently serves on the editorial board of the *Journal of Forensic Identification*. He is also a past president of the Utah Division of the IAI and now serves as chairperson for the Utah Latent Print Certification Committee. Mr. Illsley was a member of SWGFAST from 1996 to 2005 and wrote the cooperative grant proposal that funded the publication and distribution of this sourcebook.

Author of Sourcebook cooperative grant proposal.

Vici Kay Inlow

Vici Kay Inlow is the identification branch chief for the United States Secret Service, Washington, D.C. Prior to working with the Secret Service, she was the senior forensic specialist with the Orange County Sheriff Coroner in Santa Ana, California. She has been involved in the various aspects of forensic identification, crime scene investigation, and research for more than 30 years. Ms. Inlow has taught crime scene investigation, latent impression processing techniques, and friction ridge comparison at various colleges and professional conferences.

Contributing Author of Chapter 7 – Latent Print Development

Ginger A. Kobliska

Ginger A. Kobliska holds a master of science degree in forensic science and is a latent print and footwear examiner for the Indiana State Police at the Indianapolis Regional Laboratory. She is an active member of the American Academy of Forensic Sciences, the International Association for Identification, and the Midwestern Association of Forensic Scientists. She has been a board member of the Indiana Division of the International Association of Identification for several years and has served as its secretary treasurer. In addition, she organizes forensic team building exercises and is a contractor for Ron Smith and Associates, Inc.

Chapter reviewed: 1, History

Peter D. Komarinski

Peter D. Komarinski is a biometric consultant with more than 20 years of experience with automated fingerprint identification systems (AFIS). He is retired from the New York State Division of Criminal Justice Services where he was an AFIS manager. His responsibilities included testing system enhancements and the particular application of latent print identification to AFIS. He is the author of *Automated Fingerprint Identification Systems* (Elsevier Press) and is chair of the IAI AFIS Committee. He has written, lectured, and testified as an expert regarding AFIS.

Chapter reviewed: 6, Automated Fingerprint Identification Systems (AFIS)

Glenn Langenburg

Glenn Langenburg is currently employed by the Minnesota Bureau of Criminal Apprehension as a certified latent print examiner and crime scene investigator. He earned a bachelor of science degree in forensic science from Michigan State University in 1993 and a master of science degree in analytical chemistry in 1999 from the University of Minnesota. He is a doctor of philosophy candidate in the forensic science program at the University of Lausanne, Switzerland. His thesis research centers on the application of the ACE V methodology for fingerprint comparisons. Mr. Langenburg is an adjunct faculty member at Metropolitan State University in St. Paul, Minnesota. He teaches an introductory forensic science course. He has lectured nationally and internationally at forensic science conferences in the United States, Canada, and Europe on topics including Daubert issues, research, and fingerprint methodology. He also teaches several fingerprint comparison workshops. He has the privilege of serving the fingerprint community as a member of the Scientific Working Group for Friction Ridge Analysis, Study, and Technology.

Author of Chapter 14 – Scientific Research in the Forensic Discipline of Friction Ridge Individualization

Deborah Leben

Deborah Leben has been employed with the U.S. Secret Service (USSS) as a fingerprint specialist for 17 years. During this time, she has conducted research, along with other laboratory scientists, relating to the development of latent prints. Other duties include managing information technology projects within the Department of Homeland Security and the USSS. She has a master of science degree in forensic science, a master of science degree in technology management, is a project management professional through the Project Management Institute, and is a certified latent print examiner. She is currently president of the Chesapeake Bay Division of the International Association for Identification (IAI), a member of the editorial board of the *Journal of Forensic Identification,* and a member of the board of directors for the IAI.

Chapter reviewed: 7, Latent Print Development

William F. Leo

William Leo has been a fingerprint examiner for 35 years, and is the lead instructor in the Los Angeles Sheriff Department's Latent Print Examiner Training Program. He has a Bachelor of Science degree in Criminal Justice and a Master of Science degree in Criminology from Indiana State University. He has lectured extensively and has provided expert witness testimony on the scientific and legal foundation of friction ridge identification. He has served as an Adjunct Professor of Administration of Justice at three Southern California Colleges. He has authored numerous papers and the textbook, *Fingerprint Identification*. He is a Past-President of the Southern California Association of Fingerprint Officers.

Chapters reviewed: 1, History; 13, Fingerprints and the Law

Bridget Lewis

Bridget Lewis received an associate of arts degree from the Des Moines Area Community College. She started her career in law enforcement in 1979 as a police cadet with the City of Des Moines, Iowa Police Department. In 1985, she transferred to the identification section and became responsible for the investigation of crime scenes. Since 1996, she has been employed at the Iowa Division of Criminal Investigation as a criminalist in the identification section of the criminalistics laboratory. There she conducts analyses and comparisons on fingerprint, footwear, and tire impression evidence. Ms. Lewis is a certified latent print examiner. She is currently on the board of directors for the International Association for Identification and is also a member of the Scientific Working Group for Friction Ridge Analysis, Study, and Technology.

Chapters reviewed: 1, History; 4, Recording Living and Postmortem Friction Ridge Exemplars; 7, Latent Print Development; 11, Equipment

Alice Maceo

Alice Maceo is currently the forensic laboratory manager for the latent print detail of the Las Vegas Metropolitan Police Department. She has worked in the latent print discipline since 1997 and achieved latent print certification by the International Association for Identification (IAI) in 2001. She is an active speaker at forensic conferences in the United States, Canada, and Europe. She has published articles in the *Journal of Forensic Identification and Fingerprint Whorld*. Since 2001, she has had the honor of participating in the Scientific Working Group on Friction Ridge Analysis, Study, and Technology. In 2004, she earned distinguished member status with the IAI. She has a bachelor of science degree in biology from the University of Alaska.

Author of Chapters: 2 – Anatomy and Physiology of Adult Friction Ridge Skin; 10 – Documentation of Friction Ridge Impressions: From the Scene to the Conclusion. Chapters reviewed: 8, The Preservation of Friction Ridge Information; 9, Examination Process; 12, Quality Assurance

James L. May III

James L. May III has been working in law enforcement since 1993. During his career he has focused on a variety of forensic disciplines, most notably crime scene investigations and infant death investigations. In January 2004, he was recruited by the Centers for Disease Control to assist in co-authoring the book *Sudden, Unexplained Infant Death Investigation*. Mr. May currently works for Tooele City Police Department as a Detective/Forensic Investigator. Over the length of his career, Mr. May has been an instructor for numerous agencies nationwide. He also serves on the editorial board of the *Journal of Forensic Identification*.

Chapter reviewed: 13, Fingerprints and the Law

R. Michael McCabe

R. Michael McCabe retired as a computer scientist from NIST and is currently a senior consultant for Identification Technology Partners. He is a graduate of John Carroll University and American University. Having worked closely with the FBI on fingerprint and other AFIS related projects, he was responsible for the development of the ANSI/NIST-ITL 2007 fingerprint standard in addition to several ANSI and ISO fingerprint standards.

Contributing Author of Chapter 6 – Automated Fingerprint Identification Systems (AFIS)

Stephen B. Meagher

Fingerprint Specialist Stephen B. Meagher is a 35-year veteran of the Federal Bureau of Investigation (FBI) and has been actively involved in the forensic latent print discipline for 29 years. He has conducted forensic examinations in hundreds of criminal cases and has testified as an expert throughout the United States and in Canada. He has held several management positions, including FBI chief for a latent print unit. He is currently managing a program related to legal aspects of the latent print discipline as well as coordinating and conducting research regarding latent print identification. Mr. Meagher planned, coordinated, and led a team of experts in response to the first legal Daubert challenge to the fingerprint science. He has since testified in 19 Daubert hearings in federal and state courts. He has been an instructor or lecturer on every aspect of the forensic latent print discipline to fingerprint experts, the general scientific community, researchers, attorneys, judges, developers, and manufacturers of fingerprint related technology. He has been actively involved in establishing fingerprint standards through the efforts of the National Institute of Standards and Technology. He is a member of the International Association for Identification Board of Directors; vice chair of the Scientific Working Group for Friction Ridge Analysis, Study, and Technology; and vice chair of the Interpol Fingerprint Monitoring Expert Group.

Coauthor of Chapter 13 Fingerprints and the Law

Andre A. Moenssens

Andre A. Moenssens is a forensic consultant and retired professor with emeritus status from two universities. He began his training in fingerprints in Belgium in 1950. He earned a Juris Doctor degree with honors in 1966 and a Master of Laws degree from Northwestern University in 1967. He has qualified as an expert in state and federal courts, and has consulted widely in the U.S. and abroad. Author of several texts on fingerprinting and on scientific evidence, he is also an Editor-in-Chief of the Wiley Encyclopedia of Forensic Science's print version and online update service. He is a member of the International Association for Identification, a Distinguished Fellow of the American Academy of Forensic Science, and member of other professional societies.

Coauthor of Chapter 13 – Fingerprints and the Law. Chapters reviewed: 2, Anatomy and Physiology of Adult Friction Ridge Skin; 14, Scientific Research in the Forensic Discipline of Friction Ridge Individualization

Kenneth Moses

Kenneth Moses has over 40 years of experience in the forensic sciences. A graduate of the University of California at Berkeley, Mr. Moses established the Crime Scene Investigations Unit of the San Francisco Police Department in 1983 and was instrumental in promoting automated fingerprint systems throughout the United States. He served as a member of SWGFAST and as chairman of the AFIS Committee for the IAI, where he vigorously encouraged live scan and digital palmprint technologies.

Author of Chapter 6 – Automated Fingerprint Identification Systems (AFIS)

Julieanne Perez Avila

Julieanne Perez Avila is currently employed at the Wisconsin State Crime Laboratory in Milwaukee as a forensic scientist/latent print examiner. She earned her Bachelor of Arts degree in criminal justice from the University of Wisconsin in 1990 and a Master of Science degree in forensic science from the University of New Haven in 1992. She is a member of the American Academy of Forensic Science, the Midwestern Association of Forensic Scientists, the International Association for Identification, and the Wisconsin Association for Identification.

Author of Chapter 11 – Equipment

Michael Perkins

Michael Perkins is a Crime Scene Analyst Supervisor with the Las Vegas Metropolitan Police Department. He is a distinguished member of the International Association for Identification; serves on the editorial board of the *Journal of Forensic Identification;* and is certified as a latent print examiner, senior crime scene analyst, bloodstain pattern examiner, and forensic photographer.

Chapters reviewed: 5, Systems of Friction Ridge Classification; 10, Documentation of Friction Ridge Impressions: From the Scene to the Conclusion; 11, Equipment; 14, Scientific Research in the Forensic Discipline of Friction Ridge Individualization

Salil Prabhakar

Salil Prabhakar is a leading expert in biometrics and large scale identity systems. He is the chief scientist and director of R&D at DigitalPersona Inc., California. He recently designed the biometric system for the Unique Identification Authority of India as a volunteer. Salil is a co-author of more than 40 technical publications and holds two patents. He co-authored the *Handbook of Fingerprint Recognition* (Springer 2003, 2009), which received the Professional/Scholarly Publishing Division award from the Association of American Publishers. He has co-chaired several Institute of Electrical and Electronics Engineers (IEEE), International Association of Pattern Recognition, and SPIE conferences; has been associate editor for four international journals including IEEE *Transactions on Pattern Analysis and Machine Intelligence;* and is a senior member of IEEE and VP Finance for IEEE Biometrics Council. He received his B. Tech. degree from the Institute of Technology, Banaras Hindu University, Varanasi, India in 1996 and his Ph.D. degree from Michigan State University in 2001, both in Computer Science and Engineering.

Contributing Author of Chapter 6 – Automated Fingerprint Identification Systems (AFIS)

Robert Ramotowski

Robert Ramotowski is employed as a research chemist with the United States Secret Service Forensic Services Division. He has been employed with the U.S. Secret Service in this capacity since 1994. His position involves coordinating research activities within the division in the areas of fingerprint visualization, document examination, ink chemistry, and optical and chemical tagging and tracking technologies. He received a bachelor of science degree in chemistry in 1993 and a master of science degree in chemistry in 1997 from George Washington University.

Contributing Author of Chapter 7 – Latent Print Development

Charles Richardson

Charles "Chuck" Richardson has been employed in the science of fingerprints since 1963. He was a senior fingerprint specialist with the FBI for 18 years, a fingerprint specialist with the United States Secret Service for 10 years, and a senior fingerprint specialist and program manager with the Drug Enforcement Administration for 11 years. He is a certified latent print examiner. Mr. Richardson has been an instructor in all phases of the science of fingerprints at both the FBI and the Department of Justice Academies. He has assisted in the training of FBI and Drug Enforcement Agency (DEA) fingerprint specialists; DEA forensic chemists; and FBI, DEA, and United States Air Force, Office of Special Investigations, special agents. He has also assisted in the training of Assistant United States Attorneys at the Department of Justice's Judge Advocate General's School. In addition, he has conducted 40 hour courses for local police agencies in advanced latent fingerprints and courtroom testimony throughout the country. He currently serves as an instructor for IAI-sponsored training classes. Mr. Richardson is a former member of the Board of Directors of the IAI and a former member of the IAI's Latent Print Certification Board. He has testified in excess of 100 times in federal, state, and military courts in 30 states and Puerto Rico. He is currently a member of the Scientific Working Group on Friction Ridge Analysis, Study, and Technology.

Chapters reviewed: 1, History; 5, Systems of Friction Ridge Classification; 9, Examination Process

Vaughn Sears

In 1981, Vaughn Sears obtained a bachelor of science degree in biochemistry from the University of Sussex. In June 1981, he joined the United Kingdom's Home Office to work in the Fingerprint Development Group. Since then he has carried out research and development on almost all of the

Home Office-recommended fingerprint development processes. He was responsible for the HFE-based ninhydrin and DFO formulations and the blood enhancement dyes acid black 1, acid violet 17, and acid yellow 7. He also carried out many studies of the image capture of fingerprints, including equipment and capture media. He has published more than a dozen scientific papers on fingerprint topics and is the publication manager for both *The Home Office Manual of Fingerprint Development Techniques* and *The Fingerprint Development Handbook*. He is a member of the Royal Society of Chemistry and in 2005, the Royal Photographic Society awarded him the position of an Accredited Imaging Scientist and Associate of the Society.

Contributing Author of Chapter 7 – Latent Print Development

Kenneth O. Smith, Jr.

Kenneth O. Smith, Jr., has been a latent print analyst since 1965. He retired in 2006 as the assistant laboratory director of the United States Postal Inspection Service. He is currently a self-employed forensic latent print examiner. His past credentials include: member of the Scientific Working Group on Friction Ridge Analysis, Study, and Technology; International Association for Identification (IAI) Board of Directors; IAI Representative for Latent Print Proficiency Testing; Chair and Secretary of the IAI Latent Print Certification Board; Virginia Scientific Advisory Committee; and the International Review Committee of the FBI Madrid Bombing case.

Chapters reviewed: 8, The Preservation of Friction Ridge Information; 12, Quality Assurance

Michelle L. Snyder

Michelle L. Snyder is employed as a forensic scientist at the Ohio Bureau of Criminal Identification and Investigation. She has a Bachelor of Science degree in Pre-Medical Biology and a Bachelor of Arts degree in Sociology from Indiana University of Pennsylvania, as well as a Master of Science Degree in Forensic Science from Marshall University. Ms. Snyder serves as the forensic science coordinator for the latent print section to ensure section compliance with ASCLD-LAB accreditation guidelines. She is a member of the International Association for Identification (IAI) and the Chesapeake Bay Division of the IAI.

Chapters reviewed: 1, History; 2, Anatomy and Physiology of Adult Friction Ridge Skin; 3, Embryology, Physiology, and Morphology; 4, Recording Living and Postmortem Friction Ridge Exemplars

Lisa J. Steele

Lisa J. Steele practices law in Bolton, Massachusetts. She is a graduate of Mount Holyoke College and Western New England College School of Law. Ms. Steele has been representing indigent defendants in criminal appeals in Massachusetts and Connecticut since 1995. She was the author of the amicus brief (for the NACDL, Massachusetts Association of Criminal Defense Lawyers, and The Committee for Public Counsel Services) in *Commonwealth* v *Patterson,* a Massachusetts Supreme Court case regarding fingerprint evidence. She is the author of several law review articles about criminal law and science, including *The Defense Challenge to Fingerprints,* 40:3 Crim. L. Bultn. 213 (2004).

Chapter reviewed: 14, Fingerprints and the Law

Jon T. Stimac

Jon T. Stimac has supplemented early research on the solvent HFE-7100 and introduced to the forensic community the use of Un-du as an alternative adhesive separator. For the development of latent print impressions on thermal and carbonless papers, he introduced a specialized ninhydrin formulation and the use of 1,2-indanedione. He has published several technical articles covering these and other topics in international forensic identification journals. Mr. Stimac is a member of SWGFAST and is also active in several regional and international forensic identification organizations.

Chapters reviewed: 7, Latent Print Development; 9, Examination Process; 14, Scientific Research in the Forensic Discipline of Friction Ridge Individualization

B. Scott Swann

B. Scott Swann is with the Federal Bureau of Investigation's (FBI) Criminal Justice Information Services (CJIS) Division. During his 15 year tenure, he has served as an engineer to ensure the integrity of FBI IAFIS repositories, supported multiple technology refreshment implementations, and served as the Unit Chief responsible for directing, coordinating, and administering related biometrics technologies and services. Currently, Mr. Swann is the Science and Technology Lead for Identity Intelligence as part of a joint duty assignment with the Office of the Director of National Intelligence. Mr. Swann is a certified project management professional through the Project Management Institute and holds a master of science degree in software engineering from West Virginia University.

Contributing Author of Chapter 6 – Automated Fingerprint Identification Systems

Lyla A. Thompson

Lyla A. Thompson is the Section Supervisor in the latent print section of the Johnson County, Kansas Criminalistics Laboratory. She has more than 35 years of experience as a latent print examiner employed in Johnson County, Kansas, and with the Independence, Missouri Police Department. She is a member of the Scientific Working Group on Friction Ridge Analysis, Study and Technology. She is a certified latent print examiner currently serving as chair of the International Association for Identification Latent Print Certification Board.

Chapters reviewed: 4, Recording Living and Postmortem Friction Ridge Exemplars; 5, Systems of Friction Ridge Classification; 12, Quality Assurance

Michele Triplett

Michele Triplett is a certified latent print examiner with the King County Sheriff's Office in Seattle, Washington. She holds a bachelor of science degree in mathematics and statistics from Washington State University and has been employed in the friction ridge identification discipline for more than 13 years. She currently serves on the editorial board of the *Journal of Forensic Identification* and is a member of the International Association for Identification General Forensics Subcommittee.

Chapter reviewed: 14, Scientific Research in the Forensic Discipline of Friction Ridge Individualization

John R. Vanderkolk

John R. Vanderkolk, Indiana State Police, has a B.A. in Forensic Studies and Psychology from Indiana University and is the manager of the Indiana State Police Fort Wayne Regional Laboratory. He is a member of the Scientific Working Group on Friction Ridge Analysis, Study, and Technology; the Expert Working Group on Human Factors in Latent Print Analysis; and the editorial board for the *Journal of Forensic Identification*. He is a distinguished member of the International Association for Identification and serves as the chair for its Forensic Identification Standards committee. Mr. Vanderkolk consulted with the Office of the Inspector General in reference to the erroneous fingerprint identification in the Brandon Mayfield case. He also authored the textbook *Forensic Comparative Science – Qualitative Quantitative Source Determination of Unique Impressions, Images, and Objects* (Elsevier/Academic Press 2009).

Author of Chapter 9 – Examination Process. Chapters reviewed: 1, History; 2, Anatomy and Physiology of Adult Friction Ridge Skin; 3, Embryology, Physiology, and Morphology; 14, Scientific Research in the Forensic Discipline of Friction Ridge Individualization

Melissa Wakefield

Melissa Wakefield holds a bachelor of applied science (forensic investigation) from the Canberra Institute of Technology and has studied chemistry with the Australian National University. During these studies, she undertook an independent and ongoing research project to investigate a novel method for developing latent fingerprints on thermal paper. Ms. Wakefield is currently completing a research honours program with the University of Canberra's National Centre for Forensic Studies, with the support of the Australian Federal Police, while teaching fingerprint development techniques and forensic analytical chemistry for CIT's Centre for Forensic Science.

Contributing Author of Chapter 7 – Latent Print Development

James L. Wayman

James L. Wayman received a Ph.D. in engineering in 1980 from the University of California, Santa Barbara. He joined San Jose State University in 1995 to direct the Biometric Identification Research Program, serving as director of the U.S. National Biometric Test Center at San Jose State from 1997 to 2000. He is co-editor of *Biometric Systems* (Springer, London, 2005). He is a Fellow of the British Institution of Engineering and Technology; a Principal UK Expert to ISO/IEC JTC1 SC37 standards committee on biometrics; editor of ISO/IEC 19794-13, "Voice Data Format"; and former editor of ISO/IEC 19794-3, "Finger Pattern Spectral Data Format". He was a member of the U.S. National Academies of Science committees "Whither Biometrics", "Authentication Technologies and Their Implications for Privacy", and "Panel on Information Technology". Mr. Wayman has served as a paid biometrics advisor to nine national governments.

Chapter reviewed: 15, Scientific Research in the Forensic Discipline of Friction Ridge Individualization

Michael J. Wenger

Michael J. Wenger has a doctor of philosophy degree in experimental psychology from Binghamton University and postdoctoral training from Indiana University in mathematical psychology. Mr. Wenger's research focuses on the dynamic interactions of perceptual and memory processes, facial perception and memory, perceptual and cognitive expertise, and latency accuracy relations in perception and cognition. Central to each of these research endeavors is a commitment to developing and testing formal (mathematical and computational) models of the hypotheses and phenomena under consideration, with an emphasis on the tools of computational neuroscience.

Chapter reviewed: Visual Expertise and Latent Print Examinations [Replaced in this volume with Chapter 15 – Special Abilities and Vulnerabilities in Forensic Expertise]

Kasey Wertheim

Kasey Wertheim established his forensic career as a Forensic Scientist for the Mississippi Crime Laboratory, and launched his technical career with a small forensic technology company, LumenIQ, as their director of forensic services. In 2004, he established the Department of Defense Biometric Examination Services Team and formed his own consulting company, and has worked on fingerprint- and technology-related problems for federal clients. Mr. Wertheim has lectured, conducted workshops, published papers, and participated in research projects in the latent print discipline. He earned Distinguished Member status with the International Association for Identification (IAI), served as the chair of the Latent Print Subcommittee of the IAI for two years, was a certified crime scene analyst for five years, serves on the editorial board of the *Journal of Forensic Identification,* and is a certified latent print examiner.

Author of Chapter 3 – Embryology, Physiology, and Morphology. Chapters reviewed: 2, Anatomy and Physiology of Adult Friction Ridge Skin; 6, Automated Fingerprint Identification Systems (AFIS); 8, The Preservation of Friction Ridge Information; 9, Examination Process

Juliet H. Wood

Juliet H. Wood is the Automated Fingerprint Identification System Program Manager at the U.S. Army Criminal Investigation Laboratory and a certified latent print examiner. She served as editor of the Georgia State Division of the International Association for Identification from 2002 to 2006 and is currently on the editorial board of the *Journal of Forensic Identification*. She has a Master of Forensic Science from George Washington University and a Bachelor of Science in Engineering from Columbia University.

Chapters reviewed: 1, History; 4, Recording Living and Postmortem Friction Ridge Exemplars; 7, Latent Print Development; 8, The Preservation of Friction Ridge Information; 11, Equipment; 12, Quality Assurance

Brian Yamashita

Brian Yamashita received a Bachelor of Science (honors) degree in Chemistry from the University of Manitoba and a Ph.D. in Physical Chemistry from the University of Western Ontario in London, Ontario. He joined the Royal Canadian Mounted Police (RCMP) in 1989, where he currently does research and development work in forensic science with an emphasis on forensic identification. He is on the editorial boards of the *Journal of Forensic Identification* and the *RCMP Gazette,* and is the editor of the *Canadian Society of Forensic Science Journal.* He is a member of both SWGSTAIN and SWGTREAD.

Coauthor of Chapter 7 – Latent Print Development

Rodolfo R. Zamora

Mr. Zamora works with the Chandler Police Department, an Internationally Accredited Lab (ISO). He has over 30 years experience doing crime scene work, evidence processing, latent print analysis, and restoring mummified friction skin. He has been involved in teaching around the state of Arizona in these same areas. He is a past president of the Arizona Identification Council (IAI), and past member of the Scientific Working Group on Friction Ridge Analysis, Study, and Technology. He has testified in juvenile, superior, federal, and Iraqi Courts.

Chapters reviewed: 4, Recording Living and Postmortem Friction Ridge Exemplars; 7, Latent Print Development; 9, Examination Process

APPENDIX B: THE ORIGIN OF THE SCIENTIFIC WORKING GROUP ON FRICTION RIDGE ANALYSIS, STUDY AND TECHNOLOGY (SWGFAST)

With the development of the field of DNA analysis, the Federal Bureau of Investigation (FBI) implemented a technical working group to develop best-practice guidelines for the community. Having witnessed the success of the program, in 1992 they explored the concept of promoting the development of additional Technical Working Groups (TWGs) in support of other forensic disciplines. Three members of the latent print community were introduced to this initiative when they attended a meeting with Kenneth Nimmich at the FBI Academy in Quantico, Virginia. They heard about the program that provided for a structured means to develop consensus standards to preserve and improve the quality of service within the DNA discipline. Following this informal presentation, they were asked whether there would be any value in establishing a similar working group to address the latent print discipline. Stephen Meagher from the FBI Laboratory, Curtis Shane of the Naval Investigative Services, and Leonard Butt with the Baltimore County, Maryland, Police Department were all in agreement that they would support such a program. The meeting ended, and time passed.

On June 10, 1995, a group of 15 distinguished individuals came together at the first meeting of what became known as the Technical Working Group on the Forensic Aspects of Friction Ridge Analysis. The following people represented this founding body: David Ashbaugh (Royal Canadian Mounted Police); Margaret Black (Orange County Sheriff's Office, California); Diane Bowman (Oakland Police Department, California); Robin Bratton (Michigan State Police); James Johnson (United States Secret Service); John Nielson (Wisconsin Department of Justice); Curtis Shane (Naval Investigative Services); James Springs (South Carolina Law Enforcement Division); and, from the FBI, Danny Greathouse, John Massey, Stephen Meagher, Eugene Mulholland, Kenneth Nimmich, James Ridgely, and Claude Sparks.

The discussions that took place over the next 11 days served to lay the foundation for what this technical working group would attempt to accomplish. Amazingly, the thought was that this would be a short-term project. Expectations were that it would terminate upon the completion of the issuance of a set of guidelines to satisfy their self-imposed goal.

From the minutes of that first meeting:

> The basic proposed purpose of the group is:
>
> Create guidelines for latent print practitioner knowledge, analytical methodology, and ability to perform friction ridge examinations. To establish and promulgate methods for research and validation of innovative techniques. That the guidelines be recognized by forensic administrators and the judicial arena as the standard for acceptable practices of friction ridge examinations.

By definition, technical working groups are formed to address specific tasks. When the tasks are completed, the group is disbanded. The FBI determined that the established TWGs were to become long-term functioning bodies and they were reestablished as scientific working groups. To reflect this, the name Scientific Working Group on Friction Ridge Analysis, Study and Technology (SWGFAST) was officially adopted in 1998.

Over the years, the primary topics that have been the subject of consideration by the group have not changed very much. These include minimum qualifications and training, certification, proficiency testing, quality assurance, integrity, advancement of the technology, and adoption of guidelines. When appropriate, as events have occurred over the years that had the potential to impact the practicing community at large, attempts have been made to address them individually. There has never been a want of topics to be considered by SWGFAST.

As the role of SWGFAST evolved, its objectives became more refined and are more accurately reflected by the following:

- To establish standards and guidelines for the development and enhancement of friction ridge examiners' knowledge, skills, and abilities.

- To discuss and share friction ridge examination methods and protocols.

- To encourage and evaluate research and innovative technology related to friction ridge examination.

- To establish and disseminate standards and guidelines for quality assurance and quality control.

- To cooperate with other national and international organizations in developing standards.

- To disseminate SWGFAST studies, standards, guidelines, and findings.

SWGFAST's policy is to publish all guidelines and standards for comment from the community prior to being accepted as final documents. By design, this process is meant to ensure that the final work actually represents and satisfies the needs of practitioners as well as the science community and provides a vision that extends beyond that of just the SWGFAST membership.

After being discussed a minimum of three times over the years, in 2007 the decision was made to expand the role of SWGFAST beyond that of the latent print discipline. This was accomplished through the establishment of a standing committee of representatives from the tenprint community. Although it was recognized that each discipline has its own specific responsibilities, the underlying principles and interest are the same. Furthermore, tasks performed by latent print examiners are dependent on the services performed within the tenprint community. Experiences gained as a result of this expansion have revealed that the true differences between the disciplines are really quite minimal.

Evolution in the SWGFAST program is further demonstrated by the diversity represented among its members. SWGFAST has up to 40 Parent Body members and up to 10 members on the Tenprint Committee. Initially, the membership represented managers and practitioners from the latent print community. As consideration was given to new members, it was recognized that there would be significant value in providing a broader representation of backgrounds and interests. Currently, members come from diversified backgrounds and include latent print examiners, tenprint examiners, defense experts, researchers, academics, and managers. This group's diversity provides an objective, yet varied, perspective on all matters of interest to the group. The demographics represented by such a group serve to assure the inclusion of many justified, yet oftentimes opposing, perspectives that are to be discussed during the normal deliberations. This equates to a process that is better able to serve the community by injecting an internal measure of balance and objectivity when considering work on a particular task.

The Origin of the Scientific Working Group on Friction Ridge Analysis, Study and Technology (SWGFAST) — APPENDIX B

SWGFAST maintains a continued commitment to the overall needs of the friction ridge science community. As part of that commitment, the group makes recommendations that extend beyond the practicing community in order to support the discipline. A primary example of that can be found in this *Fingerprint Sourcebook*.

As with the SWGFAST documents, there will be a continuing need to update the materials contained in the *Fingerprint Sourcebook*. Provisions for such updating bring additional merit to the work as being a living document conceptualized to provide ongoing and current support for the profession.

Lenny Butt, Chairman
Scientific Working Group on Friction Ridge Analysis, Study and Technology

APPENDIX C: MEMBERS OF SWGFAST

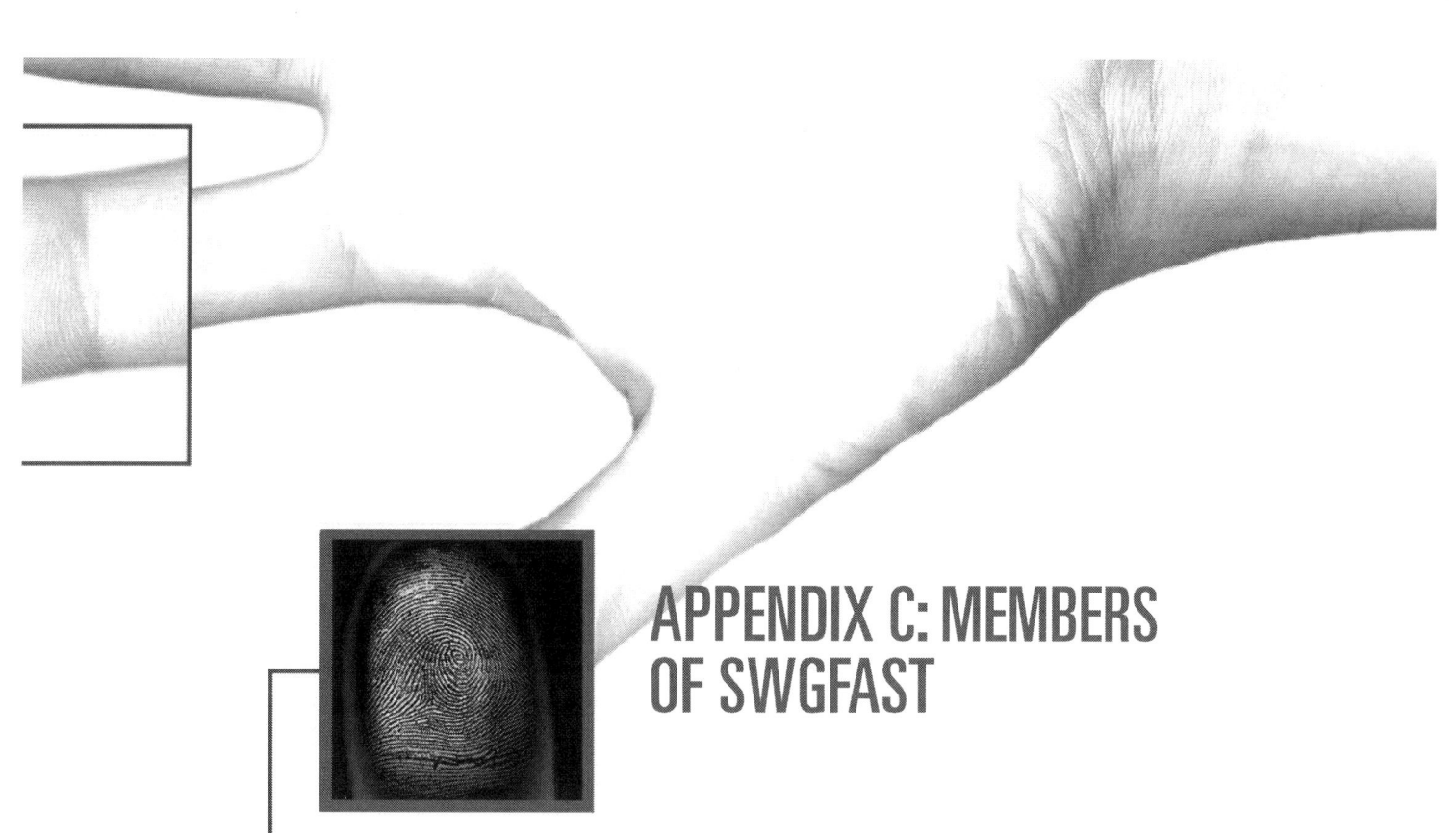

PARENT BODY

NAME	AGENCY	DATES
ARMSTONG, Benjamin	Plano Police, Texas	1996 to 1998
ASHBAUGH, David	Royal Canadian Mounted Police	1995; 2001 to 2005
BELL, Jackie	Federal Bureau of Investigation	1997 to 2002
BENNINGFIELD, Debbie	Houston Police, Texas	2004 to present
BERGMAN, Herman	Oakland Police, California	2006 to present
BLACK John	Private Examiner	2007 to present
BLACK, Maggie	Orange County Sheriff, California	1995 to present
BLUME, Patti	Orange County Sheriff, California	1996
BOWMAN, Diane	Oakland Police, California	1995
BRANDON, Mary	Portland Police, Oregon	1996 to 2007
BRATTON, Robin	Michigan State Police	1995 to 2002
BUTT, Lenny	Maryland State Police	2002 to present
CAMPBELL, Mike	Milwaukee Police, Wisconsin	2003 to 2007
CARTER, Danny	Texas Dept. of Public Safety	1996 to 1998
CHAMPOD, Christophe	University of Lausanne, Switzerland	2005 to present
CLARK, John	Western Identification Network	1999 to present
COPPEJANS, Mary Sue	Alabama Department of Science	2003 to 2008
CURRIE, Ian	Royal Canadian Mounted Police	2007 to 2011

APPENDIX C | Members of SWGFAST

NAME	AGENCY	DATES
EATON, Geraldine	King County Sheriff, Washington	1998 to 2009
FISCHER, Deborah	Florida Dept. of Law Enforcement	1999 to 2002
FITZPATRICK, Frank	Orange County Sheriff, California	1997 to present
FUTRELL, Ivan	Federal Bureau of Investigation	1996
GARRETT, Robert	Private Examiner	2008 to present
GERMAN, Edward	United States Army Crime Lab	1996 to present
GETTEMY, James	Florida Dept. of Law Enforcement	1998 to 2008
GISHE, Melissa	Federal Bureau of Investigation	2007 to present
GREATHOUSE, Danny	Federal Bureau of Investigation	1995
GRIEVE, David	Illinois State Police	1996 to 2008
GRIMM, Michael	Virginia Div. Forensic Science	1998 to 2005
HANKERSON, Larry	Alcohol, Tobacco, Firearms, GA	1999 to 2004
HASTY, Danny	Washington County Sheriff, FL	1996 to 2008
HECKER, Scott	Federal Bureau of Investigation	2008 to present
HICKLIN, Austin	NOBLIS	2009 to present
HOLLARS, Mitch	Federal Bureau of Investigation	2003 to present
HUTCHINS, Laura	United States Secret Service	2006 to present
ILLSLEY, Charles	West Valley Police, Utah	1996 to 2005
INLOW, Vici	United States Secret Service	1998 to 2006
JOHNSON, James	United States Secret Service	1995 to 2007
KILGORE, John	Iowa Crime Lab	1996 to 1997
LANGENBURG, Glenn	MN Bureau of Criminal Invest.	2004 to present
LEWIS, Bridget	Iowa Crime Lab	2002 to present
MACEO, Alice	Las Vegas Metro Police, Nevada	2001 to present
MARTIN, Kenneth	Massachusetts State Police	2000 to 2002
MASSEY, John	Federal Bureau of Investigation	1995 to 1999
MASTERS, Nancy	California Department of Justice	1996
MCFARLANE, Walter	Alaska Crime Lab	1996 to 2001
MCROBERTS, Alan	Private Examiner	1996 to present
MEAGHER, Steven	Federal Bureau of Investigation	1995 to 2007
MICHAUD, Gregoire	Michigan State Police	2006 to 2009
MOENSSENS, Andre	University of Missouri	2005 to present
MOSES, Ken	San Francisco Police, California	1996 to 1997
MULHOLLAND, Eugene	Federal Bureau of Investigation	1995
NEUMANN, Cedric	Pennsylvania State University	2008 to present

NAME	AGENCY	DATES
NEUNER, John	North Carolina State Crime Lab	1995
NIELSON, John	Wisconsin Department of Justice	1995 to 1996
NIMMICH, Ken	Federal Bureau of Investigation	1995 to 1996
PARKER, Charles	Corpus Christi Police, Texas	1996 to 2002
PASE, Barbara	Federal Bureau of Investigation	1996 to 2002
REES, Alison	Alcohol, Tobacco, Firearms, MD	2008 to present
RICHARDSON, Charles	Drug Enforcement Agency, VA	1996 to present
RIDGELY, JAMES	Federal Bureau of Investigation	1995
ROBERTS, Maria Antonia	Federal Bureau of Investigation	2008 to present
ROONEY, Larry	Suffolk County Police, New York	1996 to 1997
SAUNDERS, John	Federal Bureau of Investigation	1996
SCHENCK, Rodney	United States Army Crime Lab	2008 to present
SCHWARZ, Matt	Private Examiner	2011 to present
SHANE, Curtis	Federal LE Training Center, GA	1995 to 1996
SIBERT, Robert	Federal Bureau of Investigation	2000 to 2001
SIMONS, Allyson	Federal Bureau of Investigation	1996 to 2000
SOLTIS, Greg	Federal Bureau of Investigation	2004 to present
SPADAFORA, Anthony	Wisconsin Department of Justice	11996 to 2000
SPARKS, Claude	Federal Bureau of Investigation	1995
SPECKELS, Carl	Phoenix Police, Arizona	2008 to present
SPRINGS, James	South Carolina Law Enforcement	1995 to 1997
STIMAC, Jon	Oregon State Police	2000 to present
STONEY, David	Private Examiner	2011 to present
THOMPSON, Lyla	Johnson County Sheriff, Kansas	1998 to present
TRIPLETT, Michele	King County Sheriff, Washington	2007 to present
TROZZI, Tim	Federal Bureau of Investigation	1996 to 1999
VANDERKOLK, John	Indiana State Police	1996 to present
WALLACE, James	Las Vegas Metro Police, Nevada	2007 to 2009
WEIR, Maria	Los Angeles Sheriff's Department, CA	2010 to present
WERTHEIM, Kasey	Mississippi Crime Laboratory	2003 to present
WERTHEIM, Pat	United States Army Crime Lab	1996 to present
WIENERS, Mike	Federal Bureau of Investigation	1996 to 2004
WILLIS, Bill	FL Department of Public Safety	1996 to 2005
ZABINSKI, Mark	Rhode Island State Crime Lab	2000 to 2009
ZAMORA, Rodolfo	Mesa Police, Arizona	1999 to 2008
ZERCIE, Kenneth	Connecticut State Police	1996 to 2005

APPENDIX C | Members of SWGFAST

STANDING TENPRINT COMMITTEE

NAME	AGENCY	DATES
BLUE, Kenneth	TN Bureau of Investigation	2008 to 2011
BOURQUE, Camille	Los Angeles Police Dept., CA	2008 to present
BURKE, Kevin	Andover Police Department, MA	2008 to present
COTTON, David	FBI - CJIS Division	2008 to present
CRAIG, Jamie	DHS Fingerprint Center, CA	2011 to present
GORDEN, Michael	FBI - CJIS Division	2008 to present
MAYNARD, Mona Lisa	Ohio Bureau of Crim. Ident.	2008 to 2009
MEANS, Joseph	SC Law Enforcement	2008 to present
MILLER, Judith	TX Dept. of Public Safety	2008 to present
SMITH, Charles	FBI - CJIS Division	2010 to present
WHITNEY, Candy	FBI - CJIS Division	2008 to 2010
YADA, Kimberly	Portland Police, OR	2008 to present

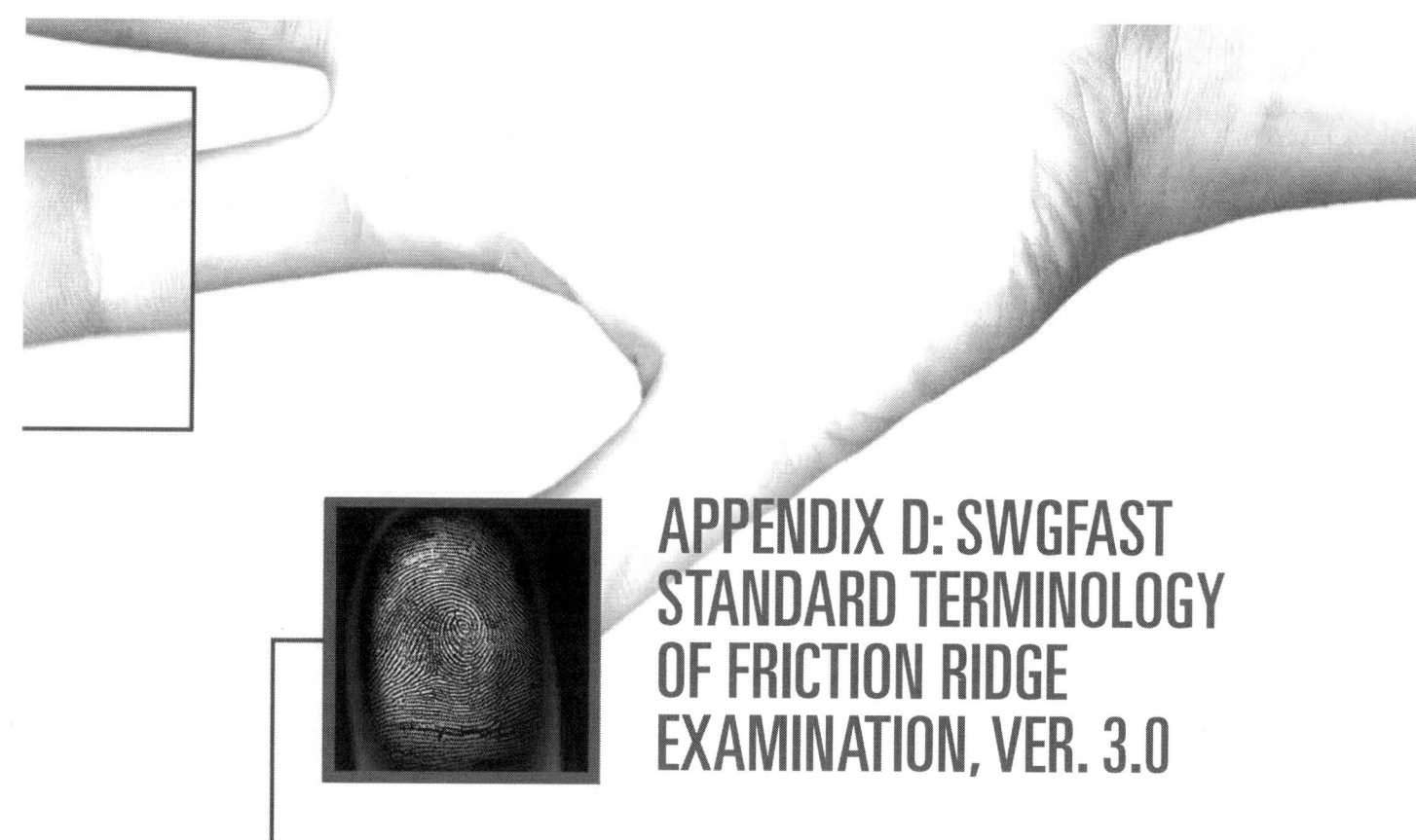

APPENDIX D: SWGFAST STANDARD TERMINOLOGY OF FRICTION RIDGE EXAMINATION, VER. 3.0

Preamble This document provides standard definitions for relevant terminology used in the friction ridge discipline. Common definitions found in other reference sources may not be included.

ACE-V. The acronym for a scientific method; Analysis, Comparison, Evaluation, and Verification (see individual terms).

AFIS. The acronym for Automated Fingerprint Identification System, a generic term for a fingerprint matching, storage, and retrieval system.

Analysis. The first step of the ACE-V method. The assessment of an impression to determine suitability for comparison.

APIS. The acronym for Automated Palmprint Identification System, a generic term for a palmprint (or complete friction ridge exemplar) matching, storage, and retrieval system.

Arch – plain. A pattern type in which the friction ridges enter on one side of the impression and flow, or tend to flow, out the other side with a rise or wave in the center.

Arch - tented. A pattern type that possesses either an angle, an upthrust, or two of the three basic characteristics of the loop.

Artifact. 1. Any distortion or alteration not in the original friction ridge impression, produced by an external agent or action.

2. Any information not present in the original object or image, inadvertently introduced by image capture, processing, compressions, transmission, display, or printing.

Bias. See cognitive bias, confirmation bias, and contextual bias.

Bifurcation. The point at which one friction ridge divides into two friction ridges.

Blind verification. The independent examination of one or more friction ridge impressions at any stage of the ACE process by another competent examiner who is provided with no, or limited, contextual information, and has no expectation or knowledge of the determinations or conclusions of the original examiner.

Bridge. A connecting friction ridge between, and generally at right angles to, parallel running friction ridges.

Characteristics. Distinctive details of the friction ridges, including Level 1, 2, and 3 details (also known as features).

Cognitive bias. The effect of perceptual or mental processes on the reliability and validity of one's observations and conclusions.

Comparison. The second step of the ACE-V method. The observation of two or more impressions to determine the existence of discrepancies, dissimilarities, or similarities.

Competency. Possessing and demonstrating the requisite knowledge, skills, and abilities to successfully perform a specific task.

Complete friction ridge exemplars. A systematic recording of all friction ridge detail appearing on the palmar sides of the hands. This includes the extreme sides of the palms, joints, tips, and sides of the fingers (also known as major case prints).

Complex examinations. The encountering of uncommon circumstances during an examination (e.g., the existence of high distortion, low quality or quantity, the possibility of simultaneity, or conflicts among examiners).

Conclusion. Determination made during the evaluation stage of ACE-V, including individualization, inconclusive, exclusion.

Confirmation bias. The tendency to search for data or interpret information in a manner that supports one's preconceptions.

Conflict. A difference of determinations or conclusions that becomes apparent during, or at the end of, an examination.

Consultation. A significant interaction between examiners regarding one or more impressions in question.

Contextual bias. The effect of information or outside influences on the evaluation and interpretation of data.

Core. 1. The approximate center of a fingerprint pattern.

2. A specific formation within a fingerprint pattern, defined by classification systems such as Henry.

Delta. The point on a friction ridge at or nearest to the point of divergence of two type lines, and located at or directly in front of the point of divergence. Also known as a tri-radius.

Deviation. 1. A change in friction ridge path.

2. An alteration or departure from a documented policy or standard procedure.

Discrepancy. The presence of friction ridge detail in one impression that does not exist in the corresponding area of another impression (compare with dissimilarity).

Dissimilarity. A difference in appearance between two friction ridge impressions (compare with discrepancy).

Dissociated ridges. 1. Disrupted, rather than continuous, friction ridges.

2. An area of friction ridge units that did not form into friction ridges, generally due to a genetic abnormality.

Distortion. Variances in the reproduction of friction skin caused by factors such as pressure, movement, force, and contact surface.

Dot. An isolated friction ridge unit whose length approximates its width in size.

Edgeoscopy. 1. Study of the morphological characteristics of friction ridges.

2. Contour or shape of the edges of friction ridges.

Elimination prints. Exemplars of friction ridge skin detail of persons known to have had legitimate access to an object or location.

Enclosure. A single friction ridge that bifurcates and rejoins after a short course and continues as a single friction ridge.

Ending ridge. A single friction ridge that terminates within the friction ridge structure.

Erroneous exclusion. The incorrect determination that two areas of friction ridge impressions did not originate from the same source.

Erroneous individualization. The incorrect determination that two areas of friction ridge impressions originated from the same source.

Evaluation. The third step of the ACE-V method wherein an examiner assesses the value of the details observed during the analysis and the comparison steps and reaches a conclusion.

Exclusion. The determination by an examiner that there is sufficient quality and quantity of detail in disagreement to conclude that two areas of friction ridge impressions did not originate from the same source.

Exemplars. The prints of an individual, associated with a known or claimed identity, and deliberately recorded electronically, by ink, or by another medium (also known as known prints).

Features. Distinctive details of the friction ridges, including Level 1, 2, and 3 details (also known as characteristics).

Fingerprint. An impression of the friction ridges of all or any part of the finger.

Focal points. 1. In classification, the core(s) and the delta(s) of a fingerprint.

2. Another term for target group.

Friction ridge. A raised portion of the epidermis on the palmar or plantar skin, consisting of one or more connected ridge units.

Friction ridge detail (morphology). An area comprised of the combination of ridge flow, ridge characteristics, and ridge structure.

Friction ridge examiner. A person who analyzes, compares, evaluates, and verifies friction ridge impressions.

Friction ridge unit. A single section of ridge containing one pore.

Furrows. Valleys or depressions between friction ridges.

Galton details. Term referring to friction ridge characteristics (also known as minutiae) attributed to the research of English fingerprint pioneer, Sir Francis Galton.

Henry Classification. An alpha-numeric system of fingerprint classification named after Sir Edward Richard Henry used for filing, searching, and retrieving tenprint records.

IAFIS. The acronym for Integrated Automated Fingerprint Identification System, the FBI's national AFIS.

Identification. 1. See individualization.

2. In some forensic disciplines, this term denotes the similarity of class characteristics.

Impression. Friction ridge detail deposited on a surface.

Incipient ridge. A friction ridge not fully developed that may appear shorter and thinner than fully developed friction ridges.

Inconclusive. The determination by an examiner that there is neither sufficient agreement to individualize, nor sufficient disagreement to exclude.

Individualization. The determination by an examiner that there is sufficient quality and quantity of detail in agreement to conclude that two friction ridge impressions originated from the same source.

Joint (of the finger). The hinged area that separates segments of the finger.
Page 7 of 11

Known prints (finger, palm, foot). The prints of an individual, associated with a known or claimed identity, and deliberately recorded electronically, by ink, or by another medium (also known as exemplars).

Latent print. 1. Transferred impression of friction ridge detail not readily visible.

2. Generic term used for unintentionally deposited friction ridge detail.

Level 1 detail. Friction ridge flow, pattern type, and general morphological information.

Level 2 detail. Individual friction ridge paths and associated events, including minutiae.

Level 3 detail. Friction ridge dimensional attributes, such as width, edge shapes, and pores.

Lift. An adhesive or other medium used to transfer a friction ridge impression from a substrate.

Loop. A pattern type in which one or more friction ridges enter upon one side, recurve, touch or pass an imaginary line between delta and core and flow out, or tend to flow out, on the same side the friction ridges entered. Types include left slant loops, in which the pattern flows to the left in the impression; right slant loops, in which the pattern flows to the right in the impression; radial loops, in which the pattern flows in the direction of the radius bone of the forearm (toward the thumb); and ulnar loops, in which the pattern flows in the direction of the ulna bone of the forearm (toward the little finger).

Major case print. A systematic recording of the friction ridge detail appearing on the palmar sides of the hands. This includes the extreme sides of the palms, joints, tips, and sides of the fingers (also known as complete friction ridge exemplars).

Mark. Term commonly used in the United Kingdom and some Commonwealth countries to designate a latent print.

Matrix. The substance that is deposited or removed by the friction ridge skin when making an impression.

Minutiae. Events along a ridge path, including bifurcations, ending ridges, and dots (also known as Galton details).

Missed individualization. The failure to make an individualization when in fact both friction ridge impressions are from the same source.

NGI. The acronym for Next Generation Identification, the updated version of IAFIS.

Original image. Primary image; with respect to digital images, an accurate replica (bit-for-bit value) of the primary image.

Palmprint. An impression of the friction ridges of all or any part of the palmar surface of the hand.

Pattern classification. Sub-division of pattern type, defined by classification systems such as Henry or National Crime Information Center (NCIC) classifications.

Pattern type. Fundamental pattern of the ridge flow: arch, loop, whorl. Arches are subdivided into plain and tented arches; loops are subdivided into radial and ulnar loops; whorls are subdivided into plain whorls, double loops, pocket loops, and accidental whorls.

Phalanx/Phalange. 1. A bone of the finger or toe.

2. Sometimes used to refer to a segment of a finger.

Poroscopy. A study of the size, shape, and arrangement of pores.

Primary image. The first recording of an image onto media.

Proficiency. The ongoing demonstration of competency.

Quality. The clarity of information contained within a friction ridge impression.

Quantity. The amount of information contained within a friction ridge impression.

Ridge flow. 1. The direction of one or more friction ridges.

2. A component of Level 1 detail.

Ridge path. 1. The course of a single friction ridge.

2. A component of Level 2 detail.

Ridge unit. See friction ridge unit.

Segment (of the finger). The proximal, medial, or distal section of the finger.

Short ridge. A single friction ridge beginning, traveling a short distance, and then ending.

Simultaneous impression. Two or more friction ridge impressions from the same hand or foot deposited concurrently.

Source. An area of friction ridge skin from an individual from which an impression originated.

Spur. A bifurcation with one short friction ridge branching off a longer friction ridge.

Stand-alone. A segment of a simultaneous impression that has sufficient information to arrive at a conclusion of individualization independent of other impressions within the aggregate.

Substrate. The surface upon which a friction ridge impression is deposited.

Sufficiency. The product of the quality and quantity of the objective data under observation (e.g., friction ridge, crease, and scar features).

Sufficient. The determination that there is sufficiency in a comparison to reach a conclusion at the evaluation stage.

Suitable. The determination that there is sufficiency in an impression to be of value for further analysis or comparison.

Target group. A distinctive group of ridge features (and their relationships) that can be recognized.

Technical review. Review of notes, documents, and other data that forms the basis for a scientific conclusion (see ASCLDLAB 2008 Manual).

Tenprint. 1. A generic reference to examinations performed on intentionally recorded friction ridge impressions.

2. A controlled recording of an individual's available fingers using ink, electronic imaging, or other medium.

Tolerance. The amount of variation in appearance of friction ridge features to be allowed during a comparison, should a corresponding print be made available.

Trifurcation. The point at which one friction ridge divides into three friction ridges.

Type lines. The two innermost friction ridges associated with a delta that parallel, diverge, and surround or tend to surround the pattern area.

Verification. The independent application of the ACE process as utilized by a subsequent examiner to either support or refute the conclusions of the original examiner; this may be conducted as blind verification. Verification may be followed by some level of review as specified by agency policy.

Whorl - accidental. 1. A pattern type consisting of the combination of two different types of patterns (excluding the plain arch) with two or more deltas.

2. A pattern type that possesses some of the requirements for two or more different types of patterns.

3. A pattern type that conforms to none of the definitions of a pattern.

Whorl - central pocket loop. A pattern type that has two deltas and at least one friction ridge that makes, or tends to make, one complete circuit, which may be spiral, oval, circular, or any variant of a circle. An imaginary line drawn between the two deltas must not touch or cross any recurving friction ridges within the inner pattern area.

Whorl - double loop. A pattern type that consists of two separate loop formations with two separate and distinct sets of shoulders and two deltas.

Whorl - plain. A fingerprint pattern type that consists of one or more friction ridges that make, or tends to make, a complete circuit, with two deltas, between which, when an imaginary line is drawn, at least one recurving friction ridge within the inner pattern area is cut or touched.

About the National Institute of Justice

The National Institute of Justice — the research, development and evaluation agency of the Department of Justice — is dedicated to improving our knowledge and understanding of crime and justice issues through science. NIJ provides objective and independent knowledge and tools to reduce crime and promote justice, particularly at the state and local levels.

NIJ's pursuit of this mission is guided by the following principles:

- Research can make a difference in individual lives, in the safety of communities and in creating a more effective and fair justice system.

- Government-funded research must adhere to processes of fair and open competition guided by rigorous peer review.

- NIJ's research agenda must respond to the real world needs of victims, communities and criminal justice professionals.

- NIJ must encourage and support innovative and rigorous research methods that can provide answers to basic research questions as well as practical, applied solutions to crime.

- Partnerships with other agencies and organizations, public and private, are essential to NIJ's success.

The National Institute of Justice is a component of the Office of Justice Programs, which also includes the Bureau of Assistance; the Bureau of Justice Statistics; the Community Capacity Development Office; the Office for Victims of Crime; the Office of Juvenile Justice and Delinquency Prevention; and the Office of Sex Offender Sentencing, Monitoring, Apprehending, Registering, and Tracking (SMART).

Our principal authorities are derived from:

- The Omnibus Crime Control and Safe Streets Act of 1968, amended (see 42 USC §§ 3721-3723)
- Title II of the Homeland Security Act of 2002
- Justice For All Act, 2004

To find out more about the National Institute of Justice, please visit:

www.nij.gov

or contact:

National Criminal Justice
Reference Service
P.O. Box 6000
Rockville, MD 20849-6000
800-851-3420
www.ncjrs.gov

Made in the USA
San Bernardino, CA
10 June 2016